Zach—
I hope you will
soon be a CAIA
member.
Keith Black

CAIA
Level II

Founded in 1807, John Wiley & Sons is the oldest independent publishing company in the United States. With offices in North America, Europe, Australia, and Asia, Wiley is globally committed to developing and marketing print and electronic products and services for our customers' professional and personal knowledge and understanding.

The Wiley Finance series contains books written specifically for finance and investment professionals as well as sophisticated individual investors and their financial advisors. Book topics range from portfolio management to e-commerce, risk management, financial engineering, valuation and financial instrument analysis, as well as much more.

For a list of available titles, visit our Web site at www.WileyFinance.com.

CAIA Level II

Advanced Core Topics in Alternative Investments

Second Edition

KEITH H. BLACK
DONALD R. CHAMBERS
HOSSEIN KAZEMI
MARK J.P. ANSON
GALEN BURGHARDT
FRANCOIS-SERGE LHABITANT
JIM LIEW
SUSAN LIEW
GEORGE A. MARTIN
PIERRE-YVES MATHONET
DAVID F. McCARTHY
THOMAS MEYER
EDWARD SZADO
BRIAN WALLS

WILEY

John Wiley & Sons, Inc.

ISBN 978-1-118-36975-3 (cloth)
ISBN 978-1-118-44727-7 (ebk)
ISBN 978-1-118-44728-4 (ebk)
ISBN 978-1-118-44729-1 (ebk)

Printed in the United States of America

10 9 8 7 6 5 4 3 2 1

Contents

PART TWO

Private Equity

Since its inception in 2002, the Chartered Alternative Investment Analyst (CAIA) Association has incorporated state-of-the-art reading materials into its curriculum. This latest curriculum reading represents a milestone in our efforts to continuously improve and update our curriculum. To ensure that the material best reflects current practices in the area of alternative investments, the CAIA Association invited a group of leading industry professionals to contribute to the production of the series, covering core areas of alternative investments: private equity, real assets, commodities, hedge funds, and managed futures. Similar to other books published by the CAIA Association, this book is grounded in the CAIA program's Core Knowledge Outline.

In publishing the books in this series, we are guided by the Association's mission to provide its members with a comprehensive knowledge of alternative investments, to advocate high standards of professional conduct, and to establish the Chartered Alternative Investment Analyst Charter as the educational gold standard for the alternative investment industry.

TEN YEARS OF CAIA AND ALTERNATIVE INVESTMENTS

The quality, rigor, and relevance of this series derive from the ideals on which the CAIA Association is based. After its founding in 2002, the first Level I examination was offered in February 2003, with the first Level II examination taking place in October 2003. I was privileged to be among the first class of 43 candidates who passed the Level I and Level II exams, met the other requirements of membership, and were invited to join the CAIA Association. Many of these founding members were instrumental in establishing the CAIA Charter as the global mark of excellence in alternative investment education. After just 10 years, we now have more than 5,700 members in 75 countries. Those who become members of the CAIA Association have the opportunity to network with other CAIA members, including attending events sponsored by CAIA's 15 chapters, located in financial centers worldwide.

The growth of CAIA, from 43 members to more than 5,700 members in 10 years, closely parallels the growth of the alternative investments industry. Preqin estimates that private equity assets in December 2002 were $767 billion, while closed-end private real estate assets under management (AUM) totaled just $81 billion. At the same time, Hedge Fund Research estimates that the hedge fund industry managed $625.5 billion. By 2011, assets across all alternative investment types had exploded, with hedge funds managing over $2,000 billion, private equity controlling nearly $3,000 billion, and private real estate investing over $500 billion. (See Exhibits P.1 and P.2). In 2003, infrastructure and commodity assets likely totaled less than $20 billion. While these asset classes were nascent in 2003, Preqin now estimates

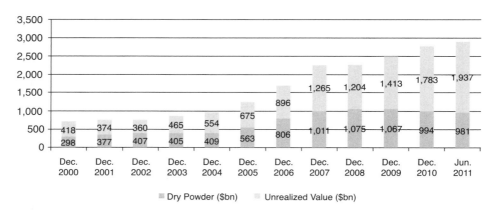

EXHIBIT P.1   Growth of Private Equity Assets under Management (AUM) (in billions of dollars)
Source: Preqin Ltd.

infrastructure assets at $174 billion, while Barclays estimates commodity assets at over $420 billion. In the past 10 years, entire asset classes have been created, with the first commodity exchange-traded fund being offered in November 2004; currently, commodity exchange-traded products hold over $200 billion in assets. Dry powder is the amount of assets controlled by, or committed to, closed-end funds that has not yet been invested by the fund manager. Larger amounts of dry powder indicate the amount of cash available to invest in the underlying assets, which leads some market participants to predict higher deal volume and asset valuation in the coming quarters.

THE HISTORY OF CAIA

The CAIA Association was introduced to the investment community in 2002 by Florence Lombard, then Chief Executive Director of the Alternative Investment Management Association (AIMA), and Dr. Thomas Schneeweis, Director of the Center

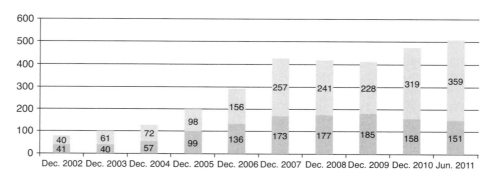

EXHIBIT P.2   Growth of Closed-End Private Real Estate Assets under Management (AUM) (in billions of dollars)
Source: Preqin Ltd.

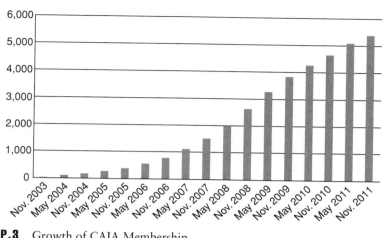

EXHIBIT P.3   Growth of CAIA Membership
Source: CAIA Association.

for International Securities and Derivatives Markets (CISDM). Ten years ago, together with a core group of academic and industry experts determined to fill an unmet need for a standard of education in this bourgeoning sector, they launched the CAIA Charter.

Like the sector of the industry it covers, the CAIA Association has grown rapidly. In 2008, the New York Society of Security Analysts recognized CAIA as the fastest-growing financial credential, and in the past three years alone, membership has more than doubled to more than 5,700. Fostered by a dedicated chapter relations team, the number of CAIA chapters has tripled to 15 from the first five chapters established in 2005; CAIA chapters now provide a platform for educational, career, and networking activities for thousands of alternative investments professionals in the world's major financial centers. CAIA now has six offices globally.

As the Association has grown, its program has evolved and advanced. In 2009, CAIA introduced the first editions of the most complete, authoritative desktop reference volumes on alternative investments ever created: *CAIA Level I: An Introduction to Core Topics in Alternative Investments* and *CAIA Level II: Advanced Core Topics in Alternative Investments*, written and edited exclusively by leading practitioners and academics. Now, in 2012, CAIA Association has published second editions of these volumes to keep pace with the latest strategies and information. Along with *CAIA Level II: Core and Integrated Topics* (which is revised annually to contain the most advanced material) and the *Standards of Practice Handbook* published by CFA Institute, these volumes round out a complete education in alternative investments for any finance professional.

CAIA has also continually provided ongoing educational resources to serve its growing member and candidate base. The suite of offerings includes the *Journal of Alternative Investments*, the official publication of the CAIA Association, and *Alternative Investment Analyst Review*, a digital research digest designed to make keeping abreast of the latest research easier. It also includes the member Self-Evaluation Tool and Member Library, designed to work together to help members stay current on the latest knowledge in alternative investments; multimedia content; educational and conference discounts; and more.

The Association formalized its commitment to advancing the alternative investment industry now and in the future by establishing the CAIA Foundation in 2011. The Foundation partners with sponsors to fund research and scholarships, raising the standard of knowledge and the talent pool in the alternative investment industry for the ultimate benefit of the investor.

BENEFITS OF THE CAIA PROGRAM

CAIA has become the leading-edge alternative investment credential and the unchallenged leading provider of education in alternative investments. Although the establishment of the CAIA Association was largely due to the efforts of professionals in the hedge fund and managed futures space, these founders correctly identified a void in the wider understanding of alternative investments as a whole. From the beginning, the CAIA curriculum has also covered private equity, commodities, and real assets, always with an eye toward shifts in the industry. Today, several hundred CAIA members identify their main area of expertise as real estate or private equity; several hundred more are from family offices, pension funds, endowments, and sovereign wealth funds that allocate across multiple classes within the alternative investment industry. Investment professionals in any asset class, such as real estate professionals, can benefit from a broad-based education in alternative investments, as it is important to see the big picture of institutional portfolios. An understanding of the investment goals and practices of institutional investors, including pensions, sovereign wealth funds, endowments, and foundations, is important for both institutional investors and managers of alternative investment products.

To accomplish this comprehensively, we have fully developed curriculum subcommittees that represent each area of coverage within the curriculum. All of these alternative investment areas share many distinct features, such as the relative freedom on the part of investment managers to act in the best interests of their investors, alignment of interests between investors and management, relative illiquidity of positions for some investment products, and deviations from some of the underpinning assumptions of modern portfolio theory. These characteristics necessitate conceptual and actual modifications to the standard investment performance analysis and decision-making paradigms.

Readers will find the publications in our series beneficial, whether from the standpoint of allocating to new asset classes and strategies in order to gain broader diversification or from the standpoint of a specialist needing to better understand the competing options available to sophisticated investors globally. In either case, readers will be better equipped to serve their clients' needs. The series has been designed to make studying more efficient relative to our past curriculum. Importantly, it is more relevant, having been written under the direction of the CAIA Association with the input and efforts of many practicing and eminent alternative investment professionals, as reflected in each publication's acknowledgments section.

STUDYING FOR THE CAIA EXAMS

"Foundations of the CAIA Curriculum" is an assessment tool for determining a candidate's readiness to enter the CAIA program. These foundational materials cover the quantitative analytics commonly associated with traditional assets, as well as a blend of practical and theoretical knowledge relating to both traditional and alternative investments.

The first book in our series, *CAIA Level I: An Introduction to Core Topics in Alternative Investments*, is a twice-revised edition of Mark Anson's *Handbook of Alternative Assets*. The CAIA Level I required readings are contained in this one text, supplemented only by the CFA Institute's *Standards of Practice Handbook*. Readers should be aware, however, that the Foundations program is important and that Level I candidates are assumed to have mastered all of the content in the Foundations guide in advance of taking the Level I exam.

The second book in our series, *CAIA Level II: Advanced Core Topics in Alternative Investments*, also represents a significant advancement in the coverage of our curriculum. The tools candidates develop in Level I of the CAIA program are applied in the Level II curriculum, which both integrates alternative investments into investor portfolios and presents risk management across asset classes. We believe this new model of curriculum development accurately reflects the skill set required of industry practitioners.

The third volume in this series is titled *CAIA Level II: Core and Integrated Topics*. It is updated annually and designed to address topics that cut across all areas of alternative investments, such as asset allocation and risk-management techniques, as well as new developments in the alternative investment research space and in the industry itself. This book is more frequently revised, which allows the Level II curriculum to rapidly adapt to new research trends in alternative investments as covered in academic and practitioner journals.

Finally, we will continue to update both the *CAIA Level I Study Guide* and the *CAIA Level II Study Guide* every six months (each exam cycle). These guides, available for free download at http://caia.org, outline all of the readings and corresponding learning objectives (LOs) that candidates are responsible for meeting. They also contain important information for candidates regarding the use of LOs, testing policies, topic weightings, where to find and report errata, and much more. The entire exam process is outlined in the *CAIA Candidate Handbook* and is available at http://caia.org/caia-program/exams/candidate-handbook.

I believe you will find this series to be the most comprehensive, rigorous, and globally relevant source of educational material available within the field of alternative investments.

It is my sincere wish that this volume contributes to the continuing growth of the alternative investments industry and, in particular, to the career growth of CAIA members and CAIA candidates.

KEITH H. BLACK, PhD, CFA, CAIA
Associate Director of Curriculum
CAIA Association
September 2012

Acknowledgments

We would like to thank the many individuals who played important roles in producing this book. Each section of this volume was developed by a set of main authors; however, several others were instrumental in bringing this project to its completion. Hossein Kazemi; Nelson Lacey; Donald R. Chambers, CAIA; and Kristaps Licis contributed greatly by providing and revising content in all sections, assisting with the development of the initial section outlines, which are based on the CAIA Core Knowledge Outline (CKO), and reviewing several section drafts. The following people were instrumental in bringing this project to its completion: Aaron Cunningham, CAIA; Brad Case, CAIA; Eliot Geller, CAIA; Hilary Till; James Bachman, CAIA; James Burron, CAIA; Jason Campbell, CAIA; Klaus Springer, CAIA; Robert Murphy, CAIA; Sam Gallo, CAIA; Sue Bannon, CAIA; Robert O'Donnell, CAIA; Jean Michaud; Christine Gaelzer; Thomas Schneeweis; and Timothy Peterson, CAIA.

Keith Black, CAIA, is the author of the first section on asset allocation and portfolio management. The main authors of the private equity section are Pierre-Yves Mathonet and Thomas Meyer. The main author of the real estate section is Donald R. Chambers, CAIA, with contributions from Mark Anson, CAIA. Chapters on timberland, farmland, and intellectual property were contributed by George Martin. The main author of the commodities section is Ed Szado, while chapters were also contributed by Moazzam Khoja, Zeno Adams, Roland Fuss, and Dieter Kaiser. Chapters on hedge funds and managed futures were authored by Hossein Kazemi, David McCarthy, Jim Liew, Susan Liew, and Keith Black, CAIA.

Finally, the second edition contains substantial content from the first edition of the book. Additional authors from the first edition include Urbi Garay, Ernest Jaffarian, Melissa Donohue, Richard Spurgin, Francois Lhabitant, and Simon Stevenson.

Importantly, we owe great thanks to Florence Lombard, Chief Executive Officer of the CAIA Association, and our committee members:

Curriculum Advisory Council

Mark Baumgartner

Jaeson Dubrovay, CAIA

David McCarthy

Armand van Houten, CAIA

Garry Crowder

James Tomeo

Daniel Celeghin

Angelo A. Calvello

Hedge Funds and Fund of Hedge Funds Committee
Solomon Tadesse
Jaeson Dubrovay, CAIA
Daniel Celeghin
Mark Hutchinson
Mark Wiltshire, CAIA

Real Assets Committee
Stephane Amara, CAIA
George A. Martin
Andreas Calianos
Tom Johnson, CAIA
Asif Hussain, CAIA

Commodities and CTAs Committee
Hamlin Lovell, CAIA
David McCarthy
Hilary Till
Joelle Miffre
Richard Spurgin

Private Equity Committee
Pierre-Yves Mathonet
Thomas Meyer
James Bachman, CAIA
Erik Benrud, CAIA
Gitanjali M. Swamy

Due Diligence and Regulation Committee
Jaeson Dubrovay, CAIA
Armand van Houten, CAIA
Tom Kehoe, CAIA
Hamlin Lovell, CAIA
Christopher Schelling, CAIA
Mark Wiltshire, CAIA

Asset Allocation, Risk Management, and Wealth Management Committee
Solomon Tadesse
Joelle Miffre
James T. Gillies, CAIA
Pierre Laroche

Structured Products Committee

Jon Rotolo

Samson Koo

CAIA Curriculum Group

Hossein Kazemi, PhD, CFA, Program Director

Donald Chambers, PhD, CAIA, Associate Director and Level I Manager

Keith Black, PhD, CFA, CAIA, Associate Director and Level II Manager

Jeanne Miller, Project Manager

Andrew Tetreault, Curriculum Assistant

Samantha Dodge, Editorial Consultant

Jamie Thaman, Editorial Consultant

About the Authors

Keith H. Black, PhD, CFA, CAIA, has over 20 years of financial market experience, serving approximately half of that time as an academic and half as a trader and consultant to institutional investors. He currently serves as Associate Director of Curriculum for the CAIA Association. During his most recent role at Ennis Knupp + Associates, he advised foundations, endowments, and pension funds on their asset allocation and manager selection strategies in hedge funds, commodities, and managed futures. Prior experience includes commodities derivatives trading at First Chicago Capital Markets, stock options research and Chicago Board Options Exchange (CBOE) market making for Hull Trading Company, and building quantitative stock selection models for mutual funds and hedge funds for Chicago Investment Analytics. Dr. Black previously served as an assistant professor and senior lecturer at the Illinois Institute of Technology's Stuart School of Business, where he taught courses in both traditional and alternative investments.

He contributes regularly to the *CFA Digest*, and has published in the *Journal of Global Financial Markets*, the *Journal of Trading*, the *Journal of Financial Compliance and Regulation*, the *Journal of Investing*, the *Journal of Environmental Investing*, and *Derivatives Use Trading and Regulation*. He is the author of the book *Managing a Hedge Fund*. Dr. Black was named to *Institutional Investor* magazine's list of "Rising Stars of Hedge Funds" in 2010.

Dr. Black earned a BA from Whittier College, an MBA from Carnegie Mellon University, and a PhD from the Illinois Institute of Technology. He has earned the Chartered Financial Analyst (CFA) designation and was a member of the inaugural class of the Chartered Alternative Investment Analyst (CAIA) candidates.

Donald R. Chambers, PhD, CAIA, is Associate Director of the Level 1 Curriculum at CAIA and is the Walter E. Hanson KPMG Professor of Finance at Lafayette College in Easton, Pennsylvania. He has published 50 articles and numerous books on investments, corporate finance, and risk management. He received a PhD in finance from the University of North Carolina at Chapel Hill and a BS in accounting from SUNY–Binghamton.

Dr. Chambers previously served at the University of Baltimore, Rochester Institute of Technology, Pennsylvania State University, and University of North Carolina at Chapel Hill. He served at Karpus Investment Management as Director of Alternative Investments. Dr. Chambers earned the CAIA designation in September 2003 as a member of the first group of candidates to complete the requirements.

Hossein Kazemi, PhD, CFA, is the Program Director for the CAIA Association. He oversees the development, execution, and analysis of the CAIA program's curriculum and examinations. Dr. Kazemi is one of co-founders of the CAIA Association. In addition, he has worked with universities and industry organizations to introduce them to the CAIA program. Dr. Kazemi is a professor of finance at the Isenberg School of Management at the University of Massachusetts, Amherst. Dr. Kazemi is currently an Associate Director of the Center for International Securities and Derivatives Markets, a nonprofit organization devoted to research in the area of alternative investments, a co-founder of the CAIA Association, and home to CISDM Hedge Fund/CTA Database. He was involved in the development of first investable hedge fund indices as well. He is an associate editor of the *Journal of Alternative Investments*. His research has been in the areas of valuations of equity and fixed-income securities, asset allocation for traditional and alternative asset classes, and evaluation and replication of active management investment products. He has a PhD in finance from the University of Michigan.

Mark J.P. Anson, PhD, CAIA, is a Managing Partner at Oak Hill Investment Management, LP. Dr. Anson previously served as President and Executive Director of Investment Services at Nuveen Investments, Chief Executive Officer at Hermes Pension Management Limited, and Chief Investment Officer at California Public Employees' Retirement System. He has published over 100 research articles in professional journals, has won two "Best Paper" awards, is the author of six financial textbooks, and sits on the editorial boards of several financial journals.

Galen Burghardt, PhD, is Senior Director of Research for Newedge USA, LLC, a joint venture between Calyon and Societe Generale. He is the lead author of *The Treasury Bond Basis* and *The Eurodollar Futures and Options Handbook*, which are standard texts for users of financial futures. His latest book, written with Brian Walls, is *Managed Futures for Institutional Investors: Analysis and Portfolio Construction* (Bloomberg/Wiley, 2011). He was an adjunct professor of finance in the University of Chicago's Graduate School of Business (now the Booth School). He was the head of financial research for the Chicago Mercantile Exchange, and gained access to the world of futures through his work in the Capital Markets Section of the Federal Reserve Board. His PhD in economics is from the University of Washington in Seattle.

Francois-Serge Lhabitant, PhD, is currently the CEO and CIO of Kedge Capital, where he runs more than $6.5 billion invested in hedge fund strategies. He was formerly a member of senior management at Union Bancaire Privée, where he was in charge of quantitative risk management and subsequently of quantitative analysis for alternative portfolios. Prior to this, Dr. Lhabitant was a Director at UBS/Global Asset Management, in charge of building quantitative models for portfolio management and hedge funds. On the academic side, he is currently a professor of finance at the EDHEC Business School (France) and a visiting professor at the Hong Kong University of Science and Technology.

Jim Liew, PhD, is the CEO of JKL Capital Management, LLC. He is also an adjunct professor of finance at New York University Stern School of Business, where he teaches the course Hedge Fund Strategies. Dr. Liew also taught the course Statistical Arbitrage at Columbia, Baruch, and Johns Hopkins. Previously, he worked at a large macro quant fund and at an ultrahigh-frequency statistical arbitrage fund, where he built, backtested, and implemented systematic investment strategies.

Dr. Liew has extensive business experience within the fund-of-funds industry, which includes starting a successful hedge-fund-of-funds business that eventually spun out of the Carlyle Group, managing the World Bank's pension fund direct investments into hedge funds, and sourcing hedge funds and creating institutional investment products at a well-known managed account platform. He has published numerous articles on hedge fund investing and quantitative investment strategies. Dr. Liew currently consults and advises hedge funds, individuals, and institutions on alternative investment opportunities.

Dr. Liew obtained his PhD in finance from Columbia Business School. He currently serves on the Editorial Advisory Board of the *Journal of Portfolio Management*.

Susan Liew, JD, served as the Chief Compliance Officer at Calypso Capital Management, LLC. Mrs. Liew is admitted to practice in New York.

George A. Martin is an associate director at the Center for International Securities and Derivatives Markets (CISDM) at the University of Massachusetts at Amherst. He is also a member of the Real Assets Curriculum Subcommittee of Chartered Alternative Investment Analyst (CAIA) Association and an editorial board member of the *Journal of Alternative Investments*. As part of his research endeavors, he has published a large number of papers on alternative assets, including hedge funds, commodities and real assets, and is a frequent speaker on such subjects. He is also commercially active, as a principal at Alternative Investment Analytics, LLC, and as Senior Advisor to Wood Creek Capital Management, an asset management firm that specializes in real assets. Previously, he was a research fellow at the Brookings Institution. He has BA and MA degrees from Johns Hopkins University.

Pierre-Yves Mathonet is head of the private equity risk management division of the European Investment Fund. He is a permanent member of the private equity subcommittee of the Chartered Alternative Investment Analyst Program and of the Risk Measurement Guidelines working group of the European Private Equity and Venture Capital Association (EVCA). He is also co-directing the Certificate in Institutional Private Equity Investing (CIPEI) course held by the Oxford Said Business School's Private Equity Institute. Before that, he worked as an investment banker in the technology groups of Donaldson, Lufkin & Jenrette and Credit Suisse First Boston and, previously, for the audit and consulting departments of PricewaterhouseCoopers.

Pierre-Yves co-authored several books, including *Beyond the J-Curve* and *J-Curve Exposure*. He holds a master of science cum laude in finance from London Business School and a master of science magna cum laude in management from Solvay Business School in Brussels. He is also a Certified European Financial Analyst cum laude.

David F. McCarthy, PhD, is the Principal of D.F. McCarthy LLC, a consulting and advisory firm. In 2002, he co-founded Martello Investment Management, LP, a specialist fund of funds and advisory firm concentrating on absolute return hedge fund strategies, including global macro and commodity trading adviser (CTA) strategies. From 1994 to 2000, Dr. McCarthy was an investment manager for Global Asset Management (GAM), where he managed GAM's trading funds of funds. He has been an investment officer with the Atlantic Philanthropies, a partner in Rayner and Stonington, a deputy manager of the International Financial Advisory Service of Brown Brothers Harriman & Co., and a consultant with McKinsey & Co. Dr. McCarthy is a faculty member of Fordham University in New York and University College Cork in Ireland. He is a contributor to the Greenwich Roundtable "Best Practices in Hedge Fund Investing" series, and is the author of a number of academic articles on managed futures. He holds a PhD from University College Dublin, an MBA from Stanford University, and a BA from the University of New Hampshire.

Thomas Meyer is a co-founder of LDS Partners, an advisory firm providing solutions for liquidity, portfolio, and risk management for institutional investors in private equity funds. After 12 years in the German Air Force, Thomas worked for the German insurance group Allianz AG in corporate finance and as the regional chief financial officer of Allianz Asia Pacific in Singapore. He was responsible for the creation of the risk management function at the European Investment Fund. He is a Shimomura Fellow of the Development Bank of Japan and was a visiting researcher at Hitotsubashi University in Tokyo and a director of the European Private Equity and Venture Capital Association. Dr. Meyer is co-directing the Certificate in Institutional Private Equity Investing (CIPEI) course held by the Oxford Said Business School's Private Equity Institute. He is a member of the private equity subcommittee of the Chartered Alternative Investment Analyst Program and co-authored a series of books (e.g., *Beyond the J-Curve* and *J-Curve Exposure*).

Edward Szado, PhD, CFA, is the Director of Research of the Institute for Global Asset and Risk Management (INGARM) and a research associate at the Center for International Securities and Derivatives Markets (CISDM). He has a PhD (ABD) in finance at the Isenberg School of Management, University of Massachusetts, Amherst. He is at present a coeditor of the *Alternative Investment Analyst Review* and an assistant editor of the *Journal of Alternative Investments*. He has taught corporate finance, bank management, and risk management at the Isenberg School of Management, University of Massachusetts, Amherst, and the Graduate School of Management, Boston University. He is a former options trader, and his experience includes product development in the areas of volatility-based investments and structured investment products. He is also a Chartered Financial Analyst and has consulted for the Options Industry Council, the Chicago Board Options Exchange, the Chartered Alternative Investment Analyst Association, and the Commodity Futures Trading Commission. His publications include articles in the *Journal of Alternative Investments*, the *Journal of Trading*, the *Journal of Investing*, *Alternative Investment Analyst Review*, *Alternative Investment Quarterly*, *Journal of Investment Consulting*, and the *Investments and Wealth Monitor*.

Brian Walls is the Global Head of Research at Newedge Alternative Investment Solutions, the foremost provider of brokerage services to the managed futures industry. He has worked in the financial services industry for 30 years in the various capacities of trading, operations, management, and research. He was a pioneer of capital introduction services and is a sought after and trusted adviser to many commodity trading advisers, global macro managers, fund of funds, and institutional investors. He is the chairman of the Newedge Index Committee. Brian is the co-author, with Galen Burghardt, of *Managed Futures for Institutional Investors: Analysis and Portfolio Construction*, published by John Wiley & Sons in April 2011.

CAIA
Level II

CHAPTER 1

Introduction

This second edition of *CAIA Level II: Advanced Core Topics in Alternative Investments* represents a substantial revision of the first edition. The topics covered are as dynamic as the alternative investments industry itself, as every textbook underlying the CAIA program adapts to growth in the industry and emerging asset types. Although the private equity and hedge fund parts closely follow those of the previous edition, material on managed futures, commodities, and real estate has been substantially revised. Across most topic areas, coverage on due diligence, liquidity risk, and operational due diligence has been enhanced. The importance of currency markets in global investing is directly addressed in a commodity context as well as within the framework of global macro hedge funds.

1.1 OUTLINE OF THIS BOOK

The book is divided into five parts. The first part discusses endowments, foundations, and pension plans as examples of institutional investors. The final four parts each discuss a sector of alternative investment strategies: private equity, real assets, commodities, and hedge funds and managed futures.

Part One of the book discusses asset allocation and portfolio management from the point of view of institutional investors. Completely new to the second edition are Chapters 2, 3, and 4, which outline the investment challenges and practices of endowments, foundations, and pension plans, which have become some of the world's largest investors in alternative assets. These chapters explore the motivation for those investors to grow their asset allocation to alternative investments. They face special risks and considerations when investing in alternative assets and integrating those assets into their business operations. These include spending rates, inflation, liquidity, rebalancing, tail risk, funding status, and surplus risk. The endowment model as represented by the investment strategy of Yale University's endowment is examined in Chapter 2, while liability-driven investing is a highlight of Chapter 4.

Part Two, which comprises Chapters 5 to 14, discusses the private equity market. Building on the material from *CAIA Level I: An Introduction to Core Topics in Alternative Investments*, it covers advanced topics in private equity investments and describes various routes into those investments. It explains manager selection and monitoring processes; reviews benchmarking in the private equity world, valuation methods, and management of liquidity; explains substrategies of private equity, including buyouts, venture capital, and mezzanine financing. The roles of the general partner and limited partners are outlined, as are the risks that arise in these relationships. This part explores private equity portfolio design through direct investments in funds, co-investments, funds of funds, and secondary investments. The important role of the vintage year is discussed in terms of both liquidity management and diversification.

Part Three presents real assets, including real estate, farmland, timber, and intellectual property investments. Real assets are considered desirable assets because of their potential to provide a hedge against inflation risk. Three chapters in this section, Chapter 16: Unsmoothing of Appraisal-Based Returns, Chapter 21: Farmland and Timber Investments, and Chapter 22: Investing in Intellectual Property, are new to this edition. The Level I book discussed real estate investments in terms of the underlying equity or debt structure. This book divides real estate into publicly traded and private partnership investments, as well as risk characterizations including investments in core, value-added, and opportunistic properties. Various forms of real estate investment and valuation methodologies are discussed, as is the due diligence of real estate investments and the risk-return characteristics of major real estate indices. Of special interest is Chapter 16, which contains all-new material on the unsmoothing of real estate returns. Illiquid assets tend to have return processes that are too smooth, which leads to biases in their risk estimation. Because appraisal-based returns, whether in real estate or in private equity, are not what they seem, investors need to make quantitative adjustments to smoothed returns to calculate more accurate risk exposures before adding these investments to their portfolios. Reflecting the market's dramatic growth in real asset investments, Chapters 21 and 22 have been added to discuss investments in farmland, timber, and intellectual property.

Part Four discusses commodities with a focus on commodity investments through futures and swaps markets. The role of hedgers and speculators is explored, along with how each might impact the term structure of futures prices. The readings provide advanced analysis of commodity markets and explain the role of commodities in asset allocation. This part describes various methods for generating commodity alpha and beta through spot and futures transactions and discusses major commodity indices and their risk-return profiles. The role of fundamental demand and supply factors is explored, as well as the financial market drivers of commodity returns, including linkages to currency markets, interest rates, inflation, and the business cycle. Risk management of commodity strategies is also included, with studies in liquidity risk and event risk management.

The final section, Part Five, discusses hedge funds and managed futures. The first four chapters, 29 to 32, cover managed futures strategies. The structure of the managed futures industry and its regulatory framework are presented, and each managed futures strategy and its risk-return profile are explained. The role of managed futures in diversified portfolios is examined, and performance evaluation and manager selection processes are explained. The distinctions between single-manager and multimanager funds, separate accounts, and platform investments are discussed, which can have important implications for performance, fees, and legal risks. In light of the collapse of MF Global, the importance of collateral segregation is emphasized. Risk measurement and control are presented, and the importance of margin-to-equity ratios is discussed.

Finally, Chapters 33 to 40 discuss investments in hedge funds. New to this edition is Chapter 33, which explores the theory and practice of hedge fund replication and factor modeling. Chapters 34 to 37 discuss specific hedge fund strategies, including convertible arbitrage, global macro, and long/short equity. Foreign currency strategies are examined and their benchmarks are evaluated. The risk-return characteristics of funds of funds and investable hedge fund indices are explained and compared. Due diligence processes for various hedge fund strategies and the role of operational risk are explained. Hedge fund replication products are presented, and various methodologies used in the creation of these products are evaluated. A detailed examination of the global macro strategy is also presented, with examination of the potential role of this strategy in the presence of increased uncertainty in the global markets. Portfolio construction of funds of funds is studied along with the benefits and costs of investing in multimanager products.

1.2 STUDYING FOR THE CAIA LEVEL II EXAMINATION

The reading materials for the CAIA Level II examination include the CFA Institute's *Standards of Practice Handbook*, this volume: *CAIA Level II: Advanced Core Topics in Alternative Investments*, and *CAIA Level II: Core and Integrated Topics*. The syllabus for the exam, which outlines all of the readings and corresponding learning objectives (LOs) that candidates are responsible for meeting, is contained in the *CAIA Level II Study Guide*, which is available for free download at http://caia.org. This document also contains important information for candidates regarding the use of LOs, testing policies, topic weightings, where to find and report errata, and much more. The entire exam process is outlined in the *CAIA Candidate Handbook* and is available at http://caia.org/caia-program/exams/candidate-handbook.

Asset Allocation and Portfolio Management

The Endowment Model

Investors allocating assets to alternative investments need a framework on which to build their portfolios. What should the size of the allocation to traditional investments be, relative to alternative investments? Within alternative investments, how should the portfolio be diversified across asset classes, styles, and managers? For many, the answers come from a study of the investment practices of the managers of the largest endowment and foundation portfolios.

2.1 DEFINING ENDOWMENTS AND FOUNDATIONS

Endowments refer to the permanent pools of capital owned by institutions such as colleges, universities, hospitals, museums, and religious institutions. When well-funded and well-managed, the endowment can provide a permanent annual income to the organization, while maintaining the real value of the assets in perpetuity. The idea of perpetuity is not a theoretical concept. The two largest U.S. university endowments are owned by Harvard University and Yale University, which were founded in the years 1636 and 1701, respectively. Universities that are over 310 years old with assets of over $16 billion each can operate under the assumption that their assets will exist in perpetuity. The assets held by the endowment can generate income that offsets the impact of economic fluctuations over the course of the business cycle.

Most endowments are run by a single organization, but may be funded by thousands of donors. In the United States, each organization is typically organized as a tax-free charity, in which individuals receive a tax deduction for making charitable donations. The investment income of the organization may also be tax-exempt. Donations to the organization can be made in many forms, including cash, real estate, or equity securities, as well as art and other collectibles. Noncash donations are frequently sold and the proceeds reinvested according to the strategic asset allocation of the endowment manager. The endowment fund of a single university may be comprised of thousands of smaller gifts, many of which are segregated to fund specific scholarships, professorships, or the maintenance of specific buildings or academic programs. These restricted gifts may require that the university maintain the **corpus**, the nominal value of the initial gift, while spending the income generated by the gift to benefit the stated purpose.

Exhibit 2.1 shows the significant asset size of the U.S. and Canadian college and university endowment community. As of June 2011, the National Association of

EXHIBIT 2.1   Assets of the Largest North American University Endowments

	Assets ($ Billion) as of June 2008	Assets ($ Billion) as of June 2011	Year Founded
Harvard University	$ 36.6	$ 31.7	1636
Yale University	$ 22.9	$ 19.4	1701
Princeton University	$ 16.3	$ 17.1	1746
University of Texas System	$ 16.1	$ 17.1	1883–1895
Stanford University	$ 17.2	$ 16.5	1891
Massachusetts Institute of Technology	$ 10.1	$ 9.7	1861
Total assets of the six largest endowments	$119.2	$111.5	
Total assets of U.S. and Canadian endowments	$412.8	$408.1	
Number of endowments > $1 billion AUM	77	75	

Source: 2011 NACUBO-Commonfund Study of Endowments.

College and University Business Officers (NACUBO) reported that endowment assets totaled $408.1 billion, with $111.6 billion held by the universities with the six largest endowment funds. The total value of endowments likely exceeded $408.1 billion at June 2011, as this figure includes only assets of the 839 endowments that responded to the survey. Should nonsurveyed colleges and universities also have endowments, then the total assets exceed the amount reported in Exhibit 2.1.

The wealth of college and university endowments is highly concentrated at a small number of institutions. At June 2011, 75 of the 839 colleges and universities reporting to the NACUBO survey had assets exceeding $1 billion. These largest endowments controlled over 70% of the total endowment and foundation assets under management (AUM) held by U.S. and Canadian colleges and universities.

Foundations located in the United States have even greater assets than college and university endowments. At the end of 2009, The Foundation Center estimated that U.S. foundations controlled over $590 billion in assets, the vast majority of which were held by independent, individual, and family foundations.

There are a number of different structures for foundations (see Exhibits 2.2 and 2.3). Some are similar to endowments, while others differ notably. **Operating**

EXHIBIT 2.2   Assets, Gifts, and Giving at U.S. Foundations ($ Billion)

	2009 Total Assets	2009 Total Gifts Paid	2009 Total Gifts Received
Independent foundations	$483.0	$32.8	$27.0
Corporate foundations	$ 19.3	$ 4.7	$ 4.0
Community foundations	$ 49.5	$ 4.2	$ 4.8
Operating foundations	$ 38.4	$ 4.2	$ 5.0
All foundations	$590.2	$45.8	$40.9

Source: The Foundation Center, 2011.

EXHIBIT 2.3 Assets of the Largest U.S. Foundations

	Assets ($ Billion) 2009
Bill & Melinda Gates Foundation	$ 33.9
Ford Foundation	$ 10.7
J. Paul Getty Trust	$ 9.3
Robert Wood Johnson Foundation	$ 8.5
William and Flora Hewlett Foundation	$ 6.9
W.K. Kellogg Foundation	$ 7.2
Total assets of the six largest foundations	$ 76.5
Total assets of U.S. foundations	$590.2
Number of foundations > $1.5 billion AUM	44

Source: The Foundation Center, 2011.

foundations have the greatest similarity to endowments, as the income generated by the endowment is used to fund the operations of the charitable organization. Some of the largest operating foundations are sponsored by global pharmaceutical companies with the goal of distributing medicine to patients who cannot afford to purchase these life-saving remedies.

Community foundations are based in a specific geographical area, concentrating the charitable giving of the region's residents. The gifts and investment returns received by the community foundation are distributed in the form of grants to other charities in the community. In contrast to endowments and operating foundations, community foundations do not operate their own programs, but donate funds to other organizations in their community. For example, The Foundation Center estimates that 28% of the grants made by community foundations in 2009 were awarded to educational charities, 36% to health and human services, 12% to arts and cultural programs, with the remaining 25% granted to charities with various other purposes. A single community foundation may partially fund the operations of dozens of charities within a specific region, typically making grants to organizations with a variety of purposes.

Corporate foundations are sponsored by corporations, with gifts provided by the corporation and its employees. Like community foundations, corporate foundations frequently concentrate their financial donations to charities located in the communities where the firm has the greatest number of employees or customers.

Unlike endowments, many foundations find it difficult to survive in perpetuity. In fact, some foundations are designed to last only for a designated period of time. The ability of endowments, community foundations, and operating foundations to solicit gifts greatly increases the probability of the organization's assets lasting into perpetuity.

Most **independent foundations** are funded by an individual or a family. The foundation may be founded by a single gift, often by the senior executive of a large corporation who donates wealth in the form of stock. Donating stock to any charity may provide significant tax benefits. The charitable donation may be tax deductible at the current market value, while capital gains on the appreciated stock position are eliminated by the donation. When tax law allows for this structure, the donors reduce their tax burden in two ways: first from the forgiven capital gains taxes on the stock's appreciation and second from the tax deduction on the current market value of the charitable donation.

Independent foundations may present an exceptional challenge for a portfolio manager. First, the wealth of the foundation is often concentrated in a single stock, which increases the idiosyncratic risk of the portfolio. Maintaining this undiversified portfolio can lead to spectacular wealth or gut-wrenching drawdowns, so foundations may wish to reduce the size of the single stock position either rapidly or on a specific schedule. Second, independent foundations typically do not receive gifts from external donors. Once the foundation has been established by the individual or the family donation, many independent foundations do not receive subsequent gifts.

2.2 INTERGENERATIONAL EQUITY, INFLATION, AND SPENDING CHALLENGES

James Tobin stated that the key task in managing an endowment is to preserve equity among generations. The investment goal of an endowment manager should be to maintain **intergenerational equity**, balancing the need for spending on the current generation of beneficiaries with the goal of maintaining a perpetual pool of assets that can fund the operations of the organization to benefit future generations. Stated quantitatively, intergenerational equity may be expressed by a 50% probability of maintaining the real, or inflation-adjusted, value of the endowment in perpetuity. When the probability of the endowment surviving perpetually is low, such as 25%, the current generation has an advantage due to the high spending rate of the endowment. Conversely, a high probability of perpetuity, such as 75%, gives an advantage to future generations, as the endowment would likely survive indefinitely even if the current rate of spending were increased.

The challenge of the endowment manager is to maintain the long-term, inflation-adjusted value of the endowment's corpus or principal value. The value of the endowment is constantly changing: growing with gifts, falling with spending to fund the organization's mission, and changing with the net returns to the investment portfolio. External forces can also impact the assets and spending of an institution, as gifts, research grants, and governmental funding may change substantially from one year to the next.

$$\text{Change in endowment or foundation value} = \text{Income from gifts}$$
$$- \text{Spending} + \text{Net investment returns}$$

In fiscal year 2011, NACUBO estimated that the average endowment spent 4.6% of assets. Larger endowments with assets above $500 million spent 5.2%, while smaller endowments with assets below $50 million had spending rates below 4.0%. Although endowment spending funded 10.5% of the budget of the average university, 37% to 55% of the budgets of Harvard, Yale, and Princeton universities were recently funded by endowment spending. In contrast to endowments, which typically have flexibility in their **spending rate** (which is the fraction of asset value spent each year), U.S. law requires that foundations spend a minimum of 5% per year on operating expenses and charitable activities. Should charitable contributions received by endowments and foundations decline during times of weak investment returns or rising inflation, the real value of an endowment can fall substantially in a short period of time. Given that foundations have a minimum spending requirement of 5%, while endowments have flexibility in their spending rate, it is easier for endowments to operate in perpetuity than for foundations to do so. This is because endowments can reduce spending rates below 5% of the endowment value during times of crisis.

For an endowment or a foundation to last in perpetuity and provide grants of growing value to its beneficiaries, the returns to its portfolio must exceed the rate of inflation by a wide margin. Exhibit 2.4 shows that the Consumer Price Index (CPI) measure of inflation rose by an annual average of 2.9% in the 10 years ending June 2011. In August 2011, the CPI was weighted 36% on housing prices, 13% on medical and educational expenditures, 23% on commodities, and 28% on other goods and services. During the same time period, the Higher Education Price Index (HEPI), a measure of price inflation most relevant to U.S. colleges and universities, rose by an annual average of 3.3%. Salaries of faculty and administrators comprise 45% of HEPI, clerical and service employee salaries are a 27% weight, and fringe benefits are 13% of the calculation; services, supplies, and utilities are approximately 15% of college and university expenditures. The rate of inflation as measured by HEPI is typically higher than that measured by the CPI.

EXHIBIT 2.4 Returns of North American University Endowments

Index	Ending June 2011			
	1 year	3 years	5 years	10 years
60% MSCI World Equity Index, 40% Barclays Global Aggregate Bond Index	22.3%	3.2%	5.0%	7.4%
60% Russell 3000 Equity Index, 40% Barclays U.S. Aggregate Bond Index	20.5%	5.9%	5.6%	5.9%
40% Russell 3000, 20% MSCI World Equity Index, 40% Barclays Global Aggregate Bond Index	23.0%	4.8%	5.5%	7.1%
MSCI World Index Free U.S. Currency	30.5%	0.5%	2.4%	4.8%
Russell 3000 Index	32.4%	4.2%	3.6%	4.0%
Barclays Capital Global Aggregate	10.5%	6.4%	8.2%	10.4%
Barclays Capital U.S. Aggregate	3.9%	6.9%	7.4%	7.5%
Endowments over $1 billion	20.1%	2.4%	5.4%	6.9%
Total endowment	19.2%	3.1%	4.7%	5.6%
Consumer Price Index	1.4%	2.0%	2.8%	2.9%
Higher Education Price Index	2.3%	1.8%	2.7%	3.3%

Source: Bloomberg, 2011 NACUBO-Commonfund Study of Endowments.

In order to maintain the real value of assets into perpetuity, as well as to meet a payout ratio of 5%, a foundation that does not have any gift income has an aggressive **return target**: the rate of inflation plus 5%, or even higher when the foundation's spending rate exceeds 5%. When measured relative to CPI inflation over the prior 10 years, this return target is 7.9%, a rate substantially higher than stock and bond returns over the same time period. Return targets are even higher when the institution faces a higher inflation rate such as HEPI, but lower when there is a substantial and regular flow of donations to the organization. For institutions without substantial gifts, endowment values likely declined in real terms over the past decade due to investment returns that fell short of the targeted return of inflation plus 5%.

David Swensen, the Chief Investment Officer of Yale University and author of *Pioneering Portfolio Management* (2009), challenges endowment managers to resist the temptation to increase spending rates after periods of extremely high returns. He argues that limiting spending will allow the endowment to better survive cyclical drawdowns and better compound wealth in perpetuity.

2.3   THE ENDOWMENT MODEL

Aggressive return targets, as well as the perpetual life of many endowments and foundations, have led to an equally aggressive asset allocation. This asset allocation, which typically includes substantial allocations to alternative investments, has been called the **endowment model**.

Universities with large endowments have been early adopters of alternative investments, and are well known as sophisticated investors across all areas of alternative investments. The financial success of these investors has been much discussed, and has even spawned a subset of investors who seek to earn higher returns by following similar investment strategies. Many credit the endowment model, or at least the most articulate description of the endowment model, to David Swensen. Most of the U.S. colleges and universities with endowment assets in excess of $1 billion tend to invest large portions of their endowment portfolios in alternative investments, following the example of Yale University.

The six largest endowment funds, as shown in Exhibit 2.1, suffered substantial drawdowns and liquidity issues in 2008 and 2009, as assets declined from $119.2 billion in June 2008 to $95.0 billion in June 2010. After a $31.8 billion (−26.7%) loss in value in the year ending June 2009, including spending and gifts, the endowment model attracted some criticism. However, Exhibit 2.4 shows that in the 10 years ending June 2011, endowments with assets exceeding $1 billion earned returns of 6.9%, far surpassing the returns to domestic equity markets or a 60% domestic equity/40% domestic fixed income allocation that is the traditional benchmark for institutional investors. Ten-year annualized returns of 6.9% refute the idea of a lost decade, rendering the three-year drawdown of an annualized −3.5% from 2008 to 2010 relatively benign, at least when viewed in hindsight.

According to the 2011 NACUBO-Commonfund Study of Endowments, the world's largest college endowments continue to increase their allocation to alternative investments. Year after year, allocations to domestic equities decline while allocations to alternative investments and international equities increase. At June

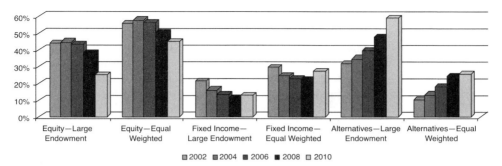

EXHIBIT 2.5   Asset Allocation of Large versus Average College and University Endowments
Source: NACUBO, 2010.

30, 2011, the latest time period available, these endowments held 12% in U.S. equity, 16% in international equities, 12% in fixed income and cash, and 60% in alternative investments. As shown in Exhibits 2.5 and 2.6, alternative asset allocations have exploded since 2002: hedge fund allocations grew from 17.8% to 22.8%, private equity and venture capital allocations increased from 8.2% to 19.2%, and natural resources experienced dramatic increases from 1.7% to 8.4% of endowment portfolio holdings. These highly successful investors now allocate more to international equities than to U.S. equities, more to hedge funds than to fixed income, and more to private equity and venture capital than to domestic public equities. The largest endowments have increased their allocation to alternative investments from 32.5% in 2002 to 60.0% in 2011.

Swensen believes strongly in an equity orientation, seeking to participate in the ownership of both public and private equity securities and real assets. The role of fixed income is to provide liquidity and a tail hedge that serves to reduce potential losses in the portfolio. Yale University chooses not to invest in either investment-grade or high-yield bonds due to the inherent principal-agent conflict. As Swensen explains the conflict, corporate management explicitly works for stockholders and may choose to make decisions that benefit stockholders, even when those decisions are to the detriment of bondholders. Given this conflict and the fact that the total

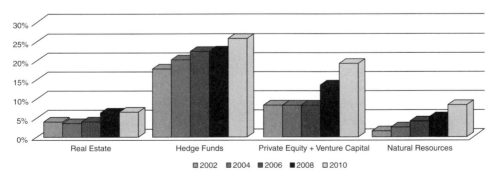

EXHIBIT 2.6   Exposure to Alternative Investments within Large Endowment Funds
Source: NACUBO, 2010.

returns to corporate bonds are less than 1% above government bonds on a long-term, net of defaults basis, the incremental return to corporate bonds may not warrant inclusion in the endowment portfolio. While sovereign bonds provide liquidity and a tail hedge in a time of crisis, corporate bonds can experience a reduction in liquidity and disastrous loss of value during extreme market events, producing the opposite effect that fixed income should have on a portfolio. Similarly, foreign bonds are not held in the Yale University portfolio because, while the return may be similar to that of domestic sovereign bonds, the addition of currency risk and unknown performance during times of financial crisis is not consistent with Swensen's goals for the fixed-income portfolio.

Not all endowments have a similar affinity toward alternative investments. Exhibit 2.5 shows the asset allocation of the equally weighted endowment, which averages asset allocation across all 839 endowments surveyed by NACUBO, ranging from those with assets below $25 million to those over $1 billion. While the average endowment has a smaller allocation to alternatives than the largest endowments, the equal-weighted average allocation to alternative investments more than doubled (from 11.8% to 27.0%) between 2002 and 2011. In fact, the allocation to alternative investments at college and university endowments increases monotonically with asset size: Endowments between $25 million and $50 million have a larger allocation than those below $25 million, while those with $100 million to $500 million in assets have larger allocations than endowments with assets between $50 million and $100 million. Returns over the past 10 years reflect the same patterns: The largest endowments have both the highest returns as well as the largest allocation to alternative assets.

2.4   WHY MIGHT LARGE ENDOWMENTS OUTPERFORM?

Investors worldwide, from pensions, endowments, and foundations to individual investors and sovereign wealth funds, have become attracted to the endowment model, seeking to emulate the returns earned by the largest endowments over the past 20 years. However, evidence shows that not all aggressive allocations toward alternative investments necessarily earn similar returns. This may be due to key advantages particular to large endowments. The literature discusses at least five such advantages that may explain the excellent returns earned by large endowments in recent years:

1. An aggressive asset allocation
2. Effective investment manager research
3. First-mover advantage
4. Access to a network of talented alumni
5. Acceptance of liquidity risk

Investors lacking these advantages may find it difficult to earn top returns, even when following the endowment model.

2.4.1 An Aggressive Asset Allocation

In the world of traditional investments, a number of studies, including Ibbotson and Kaplan (2000), Brinson, Hood, and Beebower (1986), and Brinson, Singer, and Beebower (1991), showed that the strategic asset allocation of pension plans accounted for between 91.5% and 93.6% of the variance in fund returns. The remaining portion of the variance in fund returns, just 6.4% to 8.5%, can be explained by security selection and market timing. (Note that it was the variance in returns that was measured, rather than the amount of returns.)

Return attribution = Contributions from strategic asset allocation
+ Security selection + Market timing/tactical allocation

The returns from **strategic asset allocation** are measured by multiplying the targeted long-term asset allocation weights by the benchmark returns to each asset class. **Security selection** is defined as the return within asset classes relative to a benchmark, such as the return to the domestic fixed-income portfolio when compared to the domestic fixed-income benchmark. **Market timing** is measured as the return earned from the variation of asset class weights versus the policy or target asset class weights. Value is added from market timing, or **tactical asset allocation**, when the returns to overweighted asset classes outperform the returns to underweighted asset classes. For example, when the actual equity allocation is 42% and the target equity allocation is 40%, the return to market timing is positive when the equity index outperforms the returns of the other asset classes in the portfolio.

Swensen (2009) explains the role of tactical asset allocation and rebalancing. Investors are encouraged to be contrarian and consider valuation when making allocations. Rather than considering what peers were doing, Swensen entered alternative asset classes earlier and more aggressively than other institutional investors. In contrast to the common practice of increasing allocations to asset classes after a period of outperformance, Swensen sought to aggressively **rebalance** back to the strategic asset allocation weights by selling outperforming asset classes and buying underperforming ones. This can be psychologically difficult, as it requires buying equities during a crash and selling certain assets when other investors are clamoring to increase their allocations to those assets. Market timing between risky and less risky asset classes, such as equities versus cash, can be dangerous due to the large difference in expected returns. While generally eschewing market timing, Swensen suggests tilting the portfolio toward undervalued assets and away from overvalued assets between asset classes with similar long-term return expectations, such as between real estate and natural resources. Rebalancing can add significant value, so Swensen sought to aggressively rebalance in real time. In a volatile year, such as 2003, Yale's rebalancing activity added as much as 1.6% to annual returns.

Brown, Garlappi, and Tiu (2010) analyzed the returns to endowment funds over the period 1984 to 2005, and found a much different story than seen in prior literature regarding return attribution in pension plans. This study showed that just 74.2% of the returns could be explained by the endowment's strategic asset allocation. With market timing explaining 14.6% of returns and security selection explaining 8.4%, endowment funds showed a much larger contribution to returns from dynamic asset allocation and manager selection.

While it can be easy to replicate the asset allocation of endowment funds, investors seeking to emulate the success of the endowment model will find it much more difficult to profit from market timing and security selection. One reason may be that, while pension plans are seen to focus largely on passive allocations within each asset class, endowment funds place a much greater emphasis on manager selection. Brown, Garlappi, and Tiu also found that the return from policy allocation is quite similar across endowments. The contribution from asset allocation explained just 15.3% of the return differences across endowments, while selection explained 72.8% and timing contributed to just 2.5% of return differences. The endowment model, then, does not seem to be an asset allocation story, but rather a story of superior manager selection.

2.4.2 Effective Investment Manager Research

From a risk-budgeting perspective, many endowment managers prefer to spend the majority of their active risk budget in alternatives. On average, these large investors now allocate to eight managers within traditional asset classes and over 11 in alternative asset classes. Endowments have exploited both their networks of successful alumni and their first-mover advantage in allocating to the best-performing managers, many of whom have now closed their funds to new investors. While common wisdom assumes that the sole secret to endowment success is the large allocation to alternative investments, the top endowments enhance performance further by allocating to managers who outperform. In fact, the largest endowments have historically outperformed in nearly every asset class, both traditional and alternative. Those investors seeking to replicate the success of endowments should be cautioned that although this outperformance within asset classes can add up to 2% per year to performance, it is unlikely to be replicated by an alternatives-heavy allocation if investors lack the talented staff and valuable network of invested managers that many endowments have cultivated.

Consider the important implications of Exhibit 2.7, which contrasts the returns within asset classes between the largest and relatively small college endowments. The return difference at the portfolio level of 3.7% over the five-year period from 2003 to 2007, 14.2% versus 10.5%, is not surprising, as it was previously known that the larger endowments had a greater allocation to alternative investments. However, Exhibit 2.7 shows a tremendous influence of superior manager selection or greater risk tolerance at the top endowment funds. Of the four traditional asset classes and six alternative asset classes, the larger endowments outperformed the smaller endowments in nine out of 10 asset classes. Even in the asset classes considered most efficiently priced, such as publicly traded equity and fixed income, large endowments outperformed smaller endowments. When moving to the alternative investment arena, the margin of outperformance widened. The manager selection within private equity and natural resources strategies added tremendous value, where large endowments compounded returns of 17.2% and 25.4% whereas smaller endowments earned just 7.9% and 18.6% within the same asset classes during the same time period.

Swensen (2009) demonstrates the importance of manager selection within the alternative investment universe. In liquid, efficient markets, the dispersion of returns across asset managers is relatively small. For example, in U.S. fixed income over the 10-year period ending in 2005, there was just a 0.5% difference in returns between

EXHIBIT 2.7   Large Endowments Outperform in Most Asset Classes, 2003–2007

	Endowments > $1 billion	Endowments $50 million to $100 million
Total return	14.2%	10.5%
Equity U.S.	12.4%	12.0%
Equity non-U.S.	20.2%	17.9%
Fixed income U.S.	5.6%	5.4%
Fixed income non-U.S.	10.6%	6.8%
Public real estate	20.5%	16.1%
Private real estate	15.5%	11.0%
Hedge funds	11.6%	8.8%
Private equity	17.2%	7.9%
Venture capital	3.1%	4.2%
Natural resources	25.4%	18.6%
Standard deviation of annual returns	6.4%	3.7%

Source: 2008 NACUBO-Commonfund Study of Endowments.

managers at the first and third quartiles of returns. Equity markets have return dispersion across managers of between 1.9% and 4.8%. Pension plans often invest in passive index funds rather than active managers in traditional asset classes. However, index funds are generally unavailable in most alternative investment asset classes.

In contrast, the value added by active managers in alternative investments can be quite substantial. In inefficient markets, managers have a greater opportunity to profit from skill, information, and access to deal flow. Within the hedge fund arena, which Swensen terms absolute return, the spread between first-quartile and third-quartile managers averages 7.1%. The difference is even larger in asset classes with less liquid investments and longer fund lives. In real estate, top managers outperform below-average managers by 9.2% per year, while the difference is 13.7% in leveraged buyouts and 43.2% in venture capital. In many cases, especially in private equity, investments are not attractive when investing in the median manager. In order for a private equity investment to outperform public equity on a risk-adjusted basis and adequately compensate for the liquidity risk in these investments, investors need to allocate to managers who deliver returns far above the median manager in each asset class.

2.4.3 First-Mover Advantage

It appears that the largest endowments have significant skill in selecting the top-performing managers within each asset class. Lerner, Schoar, and Wang (2008) explain that this ability to select top managers may be related to the **first-mover advantage:** large endowments invested in many alternative asset classes years earlier than pension funds and smaller endowments. For example, Takahashi and Alexander (2002) explain that Yale University made its first investments in natural resources in 1950, leveraged buyouts in 1973, venture capital in 1976, and real estate in 1978. In contrast, Lerner, Schoar, and Wang explain that corporate pensions started investing in venture capital only in the 1980s, while public pension plans did not make their first venture capital investments until the 1990s.

Many of the funds of managers who have earned top-quartile performance in these asset classes have been closed to new investors for many years. Newer investors seeking access to top managers in alternative investment asset classes, especially in venture capital, are destined to underperform when the top managers allow commitments only from those investors who participated in their earlier funds.

Lerner, Schoar, and Wongsunwai (2007) show that endowments earn higher average returns in private equity, likely due to the greater sophistication of their fund-selection process. Endowment funds have higher returns than other investors when making allocations to first-time private equity fund managers. Once an endowment fund has become a limited partner in a private equity fund, it seems to be more efficient at processing the information provided by each general partner. The follow-on funds that endowments select for future investment outperform funds to which endowments decline to make future commitments.

Mladina and Coyle (2010) identify Yale University's investments in private equity as the driving factor in the endowment's exceptional performance. It can be difficult to emulate Yale's outperformance in private equity and venture capital investments, as its venture capital portfolio has earned average annual returns of 31.4% since inception through fiscal year 2007. In fact, this study suggests that, without the private equity and venture capital investments, the returns to the Yale endowment would be close to that of the proxy portfolio.

2.4.4 Access to a Network of Talented Alumni

Perhaps the first-mover advantage and manager-selection skill of top endowments can be attributed to the superior **network effect**. An institution has a positive network effect when it has built relationships with successful people and businesses that may be difficult for others to emulate. Alumni of the universities in Exhibit 2.1 are noted for being among the most successful U.S. college graduates, in both an academic and a business sense. As measured by scores on the SAT® exam,[1] Harvard, Yale, Stanford, Princeton, and the Massachusetts Institute of Technology routinely select from the top 1% to 5% of students. In 2003, the median SAT score for all college-bound students, including both the verbal and mathematics scores, was approximately 1,000. Top universities attract students with average scores exceeding 1,400. Graduates of these schools also tend to have the highest initial and midcareer salaries.

A study by Li, Zhang, and Zhao (2011) correlated manager-specific characteristics to the returns of the hedge funds they managed. In contrast to the median SAT score of all college-bound students of 1,000, Li, Zhang, and Zhao found that the middle 50% of hedge fund managers attended colleges and universities with average SAT scores between 1,199 and 1,421, demonstrating that the majority of hedge fund managers attended the most competitive colleges and universities. Within this group of studied hedge fund managers, the research showed that hedge fund managers who attended undergraduate colleges with higher SAT scores have higher returns

---

[1] SAT is a registered trademark of the College Board.

and lower risk than the median hedge fund manager. On average, fund managers who attended universities with higher average SAT scores earned higher performance. For example, a 200-point difference in SAT scores, such as that between 1,280 and 1,480, was correlated with higher annual returns of 0.73%. Not only did managers who attended top universities have higher returns, but they did so at lower risk and earned greater inflows during their tenures as fund managers. The authors suggest that talented managers are attracted to hedge funds due to the incentive fee structure, which rewards performance over asset gathering. In contrast to their studies on hedge fund managers, Li, Zhang, and Zhao found that SAT scores did not seem to affect the asset gathering or excess returns earned by mutual fund managers, as these managers are compensated for gathering assets, not for earning excess returns.

Many alumni of top universities wish to continue an association with their alma mater, the university from which they received their undergraduate degree. The ability of top endowment funds to outperform can be perpetuated by this important network of relationships, to the extent that these talented professionals choose to work for the university's endowment fund or guarantee the endowment access to invest in funds they manage.

2.4.5 Acceptance of Liquidity Risk

Endowments have a perpetual holding period. With low spending rates and limited liabilities, endowments have a much greater tolerance for risks, including liquidity risk. When viewed in light of the age of leading universities, which now surpasses 300 years, the 10-year lockup period of private equity vehicles appears relatively short-term. As the longest-term investors, charged with protecting the real value of endowment principal for future generations of students, universities are seeking to earn **liquidity premiums** by investing in privately held vehicles, with the idea that their perpetual nature allows them to easily handle this liquidity risk. Anson (2010) estimates the liquidity premium for private equity at 2% and direct real estate at 2.7%, while other studies estimate liquidity premiums as high as 10%.

Swensen (2009) explains that less liquid investments tend to have greater degrees of inefficient pricing. On average, investors overvalue liquid assets, which leaves undervalued and less liquid assets for investors with long-term investment horizons. Investors making commitments to long-term assets, such as private equity and private real estate, know that these investments are typically held for 10 years or longer and so require a significant due-diligence process before making such a long-term commitment. Investors in more liquid asset classes may not take their investments as seriously, knowing that the investment may be exited after a short-term holding period. Investments that appear to be liquid in normal markets may have constrained liquidity during times of crisis, which is the time when liquidity is most valued.

2.5 CONCLUSION

It is important for investors and analysts to understand the endowment model, which seeks a high allocation to alternative investments in order to meet aggressive targets requiring long-term returns that exceed the rate of inflation by at least the amount of required spending. Portfolio managers and asset allocators seeking to emulate the returns of the most successful endowments must realize that simply mimicking the asset allocations of top endowments will not guarantee similar returns, as endowments have historically added significant value through manager selection and market timing. The special risks of investing according to the endowment model are covered in the next chapter.

CHAPTER 3

Risk Management for Endowment and Foundation Portfolios

When applied by the largest investors, the endowment model has created impressive returns over the past 20 years. However, this style of portfolio management comes with a special set of risks. First, portfolio managers need to be concerned about the interactions among spending rates, inflation, and the long-term asset value of the endowment. Second, a portfolio with as much as 60% invested in alternative assets raises concerns of liquidity risk and the ability to rebalance the portfolio when necessary. Finally, portfolios with high allocations to assets with equity-like characteristics and low allocations to fixed income require the portfolio manager to consider how to protect the portfolio from **tail risk,** which is a large drawdown in portfolio value during times of increased systemic risk.

3.1   SPENDING RATES AND INFLATION

There is an important tension between the spending rate of the endowment, the risk of the endowment portfolio, and the goal of allowing the endowment to serve as a permanent source of capital for the university. When the endowment fund generates high returns with a low spending rate, the size of the endowment fund increases. This may lead to concerns about intergenerational equity, as the spending on current beneficiaries could likely be increased without compromising the probability of the endowment continuing into perpetuity. Conversely, a conservative asset allocation with a high spending rate may favor the current generation, yet imperil the real value of the endowment in the long run.

Kochard and Rittereiser (2008) present a history of endowment spending models. From the founding of the Harvard University endowment in 1649 until the 1950s, endowments were typically managed conservatively, with a focus on earning income from a fixed income–dominated portfolio. It was clear what the spending rate should be, as the entire portfolio yield was typically paid out to support the programs of the university. When bonds matured at face value, the notional value of the corpus was maintained. This sounds relatively straightforward, as the current beneficiaries received a strong income and the requirement of maintaining the nominal value of gifts made to the foundation was easily achieved. Unfortunately, this conservative asset allocation earned little in the way of real returns, and the focus on minimizing drawdowns led to a low total return and stagnation of the nominal value of endowments.

Between the 1950s and 1970s, this conservatism began to fade. Rather than spending the income generated on the portfolio, endowment managers came to embrace the concept of total return. Consider a fixed-income portfolio with a 5% current yield, which allowed a 5% spending rate. Though the yield was high, the nominal return to the portfolio, net of spending, was zero. In this scenario, the spending needs were easily met, yet the value of the endowment declined in real terms, as the goal of maintaining the real, or inflation-adjusted, value of the corpus was not achieved. A **total return** investor, who considers both income and capital appreciation as components of return and invests to maximize the portfolio's risk-adjusted return, may realize that a 5% current yield is not needed in order for the endowment to have a spending rate of 5%. Moving from a portfolio dominated by fixed income to one with a healthy mix of equity investments may reduce the yield to 3%, while increasing total returns to 7.5%. With a total return of 7.5%, including income and capital appreciation, the endowment can afford a spending rate of 5% while maintaining the real value of the portfolio, as the 2.5% return in excess of the spending rate can be used to offset the impact of inflation. In order to generate 5% spending, the entire income of 3% is spent, and 2% of the portfolio is sold each year to meet the spending rate.

The investing behavior of endowment managers started to change between 1969 and 1972. The 1969 publication, *Managing Educational Endowments*, suggested that endowment portfolios had previously invested with overly conservative as-set allocations. Endowment managers were chastised for building underperforming portfolios that were underweighted in equities, not celebrated for serving the university by reducing the risk of loss. The publication proposed that trustees may have imperiled the university by forgoing higher returns that could have increased both the income and the corpus of the endowment. The 1972 Uniform Management of Institutional Funds Act subsequently allowed endowment managers to consider total return when setting the spending rate. This Act also allowed the use of external in-vestment managers and encouraged trustees to balance the long-term and short-term needs of the university.

It was during the bull market in public and private equities, from 1982 to 2000, that endowment managers dramatically increased their equity exposures. This pro-duced extremely strong returns that boosted the values of endowments by large multiples, net of spending. The post-2000 drawdown in equity markets led endow-ments to have an even stronger focus on alternative investments, moving to increase exposure to hedge funds and other assets with lower correlations to equities while reducing exposure to publicly traded equities.

Once the asset allocation is determined, a spending rule must also be estab-lished. The earliest endowments spent income only, which tilted the portfolio toward income-producing securities. Later, endowments moved toward spending at a fixed percentage of the current value of the endowment, such as 4%. This fixed spending rate, however, created volatility in the amount of income available to the university. In a year when the return and gifts received by the endowment generated a 20% increase in endowment value, the income to be spent also increased by 20%. Con-versely, during a 20% drawdown, the spending rate of the university was slashed by a significant amount. A sticky spending rate, such as $3 million per year, provides certainty of income to the university, but can create concerns of intergenerational equity after a large gain or loss in the value of the endowment.

Recognizing that volatility in the income provided to university operations was unwelcome, more flexible spending rules were developed. Spending 4% of the average value of the endowment over the trailing three to five years creates a smoothing process that dampens the impact of the volatility of portfolio returns on the income provided to the university.

David Swensen developed a spending rule for Yale University: Each year, the endowment could spend at a rate equal to 80% of the prior year's dollar spending plus 20% of the endowment's long-term spending rate (4.5%). This formula incorporates the prior 10 years of endowment value into the spending rate calculation, providing a stronger smoothing effect than a simple moving average rule.

Swensen (2009) expresses concern about the impact of inflation, market volatility, and high spending rates. The majority of endowments, 70%, use spending rates of between 4% and 6%, with 5% being a popular spending rate. Yale has set its long-term spending rate at 4.5%, as simulations show that, based on a five-year average of endowment values, a 5% spending rule has a 50% probability of losing half of the endowment's real value at some point over the course of a generation. Using a longer averaging period and a lower spending rate reduces the probability of this disastrous decline in the real value of the endowment portfolio.

Inflation has a particularly strong impact on the long-term, real value of university endowments. Ideally, endowments should seek to maintain the real value of the corpus, rather than the legal requirement of the notional value. When maintaining the real value of the corpus, long-term spending rates can keep up with inflation. When maintaining the nominal value of the corpus, long-term spending has an ever-declining value in real terms.

The focus on inflation risk has led many endowments to increase allocations to real assets in recent years, as the largest endowments increased their average allocations to real estate and natural resources from 6% to 16.8% between 2002 and 2011. Interestingly, while endowments invested a greater portion in real estate than in natural resources in 2002 (4.3% vs. 1.7%), they are currently investing a larger amount in natural resources than in real estate (9.0% vs. 7.8%). **Real asset** investments include inflation-linked bonds, both public and private real estate investments, commodity futures programs, as well as both direct and private equity fund investments in mining, oil and gas, timber, farmland, and infrastructure. Ideally, the real-assets portfolio would earn long-term returns similar to equity markets, with yields similar to fixed income, while experiencing low volatility and low correlation to the fixed income and publicly traded equity assets in the portfolio as well as higher returns during times of rising inflation.

A report from Bernstein (2010) calculated the betas of several asset classes to inflation. Just a few assets demonstrated a positive **inflation beta**, where the assets act as an effective inflation hedge. The majority of assets have a risk to rising inflation; that is, they have a negative inflation beta. According to Bernstein, commodity futures offered the greatest inflation beta at 6.5, while farmland had a beta of 1.7. In the fixed income sector, 10-year Treasury Inflation-Protected Securities (TIPS) had a beta of 0.8, while three-month Treasury bills had a beta of 0.3. Equities and long-term nominal bonds had a strong negative reaction to inflation, with the S&P 500 exhibiting an inflation beta of –2.4 and 20-year U.S. Treasury bonds suffering returns at −3.1 times the rate of inflation. Within equities, smaller-capitalization stocks had an even greater risk to rising inflation. Companies with lower capital expenditures and fewer physical assets also had a stronger negative response to rising inflation.

3.2 LIQUIDITY ISSUES

In the aftermath of the 2008 financial crisis, many pension funds and endowments have begun to reevaluate their asset allocation policies and, in the process, they are paying increased attention to their risk and liquidity management practices. **Liquidity** represents the ability of an entity to fund future investment opportunities and to meet obligations as they come due without incurring unacceptable losses. These obligations include the annual spending rate as well as the capital calls from private equity and real estate limited partnerships. If there are mismatches between the maturity of an entity's assets and its liabilities, the entity is exposed to **illiquidity risk**.

While liquidity is certainly a risk for endowments, these funds have long lives and can afford to take a fair amount of illiquidity risk. Recent studies (Aragon 2004; Los and Khandani 2009; Sadkay 2009) have shown that the illiquidity premium is generally positive and significant, ranging from 2.74% to 9.91% for some investment strategies. The size of this premium varies through time, with studies suggesting that illiquidity premiums declined in the years leading to the financial crisis. Therefore, similar to management of other risks, a portfolio manager has to consider carefully the trade-off between the illiquidity risk and the illiquidity premium in determining the size of the illiquid assets in the overall portfolio. These studies also show that, everything else being the same, funds with long lockup periods generally provide a higher rate of return to investors. A long lockup period is a vital tool employed by managers to reduce the cost of liquidity risk. During the recent financial crisis, funds with long lockup periods were not under pressure to sell their assets at distressed prices. It is important to note that, if the underlying assets of a fund are less liquid than the liquidity provisions it offers to its investors, then the cost of liquidity risk would increase for all investors, even if only a small fraction of the fund's investors decide to redeem their shares during periods of financial distress. The fact that some pension funds and endowments have decided to reduce their allocations to illiquid assets may signal that the illiquidity premium will be higher in the future. Pension funds and endowments cannot afford to ignore such an important source of return if they are to meet the needs of their beneficiaries.

Effective liquidity risk management helps ensure the ability of a pension fund or an endowment to meet its cash flow obligations, which may not be completely predictable as they are affected by external market conditions. Due to lack of effective liquidity risk management, many funds experienced severe liquidity squeezes during the latest financial crisis. This forced some to sell a portion of their illiquid assets at deep discounts in secondary markets, to delay the funding of important projects, and, in certain cases, to borrow funds in the debt market during a period of extreme market stress. These experiences have led some to question the validity of the so-called Yale model of pension and endowment management and, in particular, to discourage pension funds and endowments from allocating a meaningful portion of their portfolios to alternative assets.

Chacko et al. (2011) explain that illiquidity risk rises during a crisis, as declining liquidity and rising volatility increase bid-ask spreads and reduce trading volumes. The book notes that alternative investments have a very high liquidity risk, with private equity, venture capital, real estate, hedge funds, and infrastructure exhibiting liquidity betas in excess of 1.0. While these investments tend to have higher returns over long periods of time, the underperformance during times of crisis can be substantial due to the large exposure to liquidity risk. Chacko et al. also discuss **liquidity-driven investing**, suggesting that the liquidity of investments should be related to the time horizon of the investor. Tier 1 assets are invested in short-term fixed income; tier 2 assets are invested in risky, liquid assets such as stocks; and tier 3 assets are both risky and illiquid, such as private equity and hedge funds. The endowment should estimate the spending and capital calls for the next 10 years, and invest those assets exclusively in tier 1 and tier 2 assets, which can be liquidated quickly at relatively low cost. Tier 3 assets are designed as long-term investments. As such, the size of this allocation should be designed to prevent the need to liquidate these assets in the secondary market before maturity.

One measure of illiquidity risk is the sum of the endowment's allocation to private equity and real estate partnerships combined with the potential capital calls from commitments to funds of more recent vintage. Bary (2009) reports, "At Harvard, investment commitments totaled $11 billion on June 30, 2008; at Yale, $8.7 billion, and Princeton, $6.1 billion. These commitments are especially large relative to shrunken endowments. Harvard's endowment could end this month in the $25 billion range; Yale's is about $17 billion, and Princeton's, $11 billion, after investment declines, yearly contributions to university budgets and new gifts from alumni and others."

Takahashi and Alexander (2002) from the Yale University endowment office discuss the importance of understanding the capital call and distribution schedule of private equity and real estate investments. In these private investment vehicles, investors commit capital to a new fund, and that capital is contributed to the fund on an unknown schedule. A typical private equity or real estate fund will call committed capital over a three-year period, focus on investments for the next few years, and then distribute the proceeds from exited investments in years 7 to 12 of the partnership's life. Once an alternative investment program has matured, it may be possible for distributions from prior investments to fully fund capital commitments from new partnerships.

However, when starting a new program, it can be challenging to accurately target the allocation of contributed capital to these long-term partnerships. One rule of thumb is to commit to 50% of the long-term exposure, such as a $10 million commitment once every three years to reach a long-term allocation of $20 million. Takahashi and Alexander offer specific estimates for the speed at which committed capital is drawn down for a variety of different fund types. Real estate funds may draw down uncalled capital at the fastest rate, with an estimate of 40% of uncalled capital to be drawn each year. Venture capital is slower, with 25% the first year, 33.3% the second year, and 50% of the remaining capital called in each subsequent year. Leveraged buyout funds may require a 25% contribution in the first year, while 50% of remaining capital might be called in each subsequent year. Notice that not all committed capital is eventually called, so some investors may implement an **overcommitment strategy**, offering capital commitments in excess of the targeted investment amount.

During the 2008 crisis, it became very difficult for managers to exit investments, as private equity funds couldn't float initial public offerings and real estate funds couldn't sell properties. As a result, distributions were much slower than expected. When distributions slowed and capital calls continued, some endowments and foundations found it challenging to meet their commitments. The price of a missed capital call can be steep, up to as much as a forfeiture of the prior contributed capital, and perhaps a ban from participating in future funds offered by the general partner.

One feature of the endowment model is the minimal holdings of fixed income and cash. For example, going into 2008, Yale's target for fixed income was 4%, with leverage creating an effective cash position of −4%. Princeton University had a combined weight of 4%, while Harvard University held approximately 8%. Although income from dividends, bond interest, and distributions from private funds added to the available cash, in many cases the income, fixed income, and cash holdings were not sufficient to meet the current year's need for cash. With a 5% spending rate, it became necessary for these endowment funds to borrow cash or sell assets at fire-sale prices in order to guarantee the university sufficient income to fund its operations. To the extent that the endowment also had capital calls for private equity and real estate funds, the need for immediate cash was even greater. In some cases, universities cut spending, including halting building programs and even eliminating some faculty and staff positions, while raising tuition at higher rates than in prior years.

When cash is scarce, it can be difficult to have such large allocations to illiquid alternative investments and such small allocations to cash and fixed income. Sheikh and Sun (2012) explain that the cash and fixed-income holdings of an endowment should be at least 6% to 14% of assets to avoid liquidity crises in 95% of market conditions. To completely eliminate liquidity risk, cash and fixed-income holdings may need to be as high as 35%, far above the allocations that most endowments are comfortable making, given their high expected return targets. By drawing down this cash cushion, the endowment can continue to fund spending to support the university budget, while avoiding a liquidity crisis causing the distressed sale of assets at the low point in the market or an emergency increase in the debt burden. Greater cash holdings are necessary for universities with larger outstanding commitments to private equity and real estate funds, greater leverage, higher spending rates, more frequent rebalancing, or larger allocations to less liquid assets.

To avoid liquidity crises, Siegel (2008) suggests laddering allocations to private equity and real estate funds, ideally at a schedule in which distributions from maturing funds are sufficient to fund capital calls of partnerships of more recent vintages. When adding real estate and private equity partnerships to the portfolio, investors are encouraged to spread the new commitments over multiple years rather than making a large initial commitment in a single vintage year. In addition to spreading capital commitments over time, Siegel suggests that liquidity can be improved by growing the gift income of the endowment, borrowing, or reducing the allocation to less liquid alternative investments. Private equity and real estate partnerships are less liquid investments, while commodity futures funds and hedge funds with lockups of one year or less are more liquid alternative investments.

Leverage can also create liquidity issues. Short-term leverage, such as that provided by prime brokers to hedge funds, may not be sustainable or affordable during times of crisis. When credit lines are reduced or not renewed, investors may have to repay loans on short notice, which can require the sale of investments at very low prices. Many fixed-income arbitrage and convertible-bond arbitrage funds suffered significant losses during the most recent crisis, as a reduction in leverage from eight times to four times required the immediate sale of half of the portfolio. When the market knows that these sales are coming, and a number of hedge funds are simultaneously forced to sell due to credit line reductions as well as investor redemptions, illiquidity risk is extreme as buyers of these fixed-income assets wait to purchase until the prices of the convertible and mortgage-backed bonds have fallen precipitously. Endowments and foundations that invest in leveraged hedge funds must be prepared for the potentially large drawdowns in these strategies, as well as the potential for the erection of gates that prevent investors from redeeming their assets from hedge funds during times of market crisis.

The liquidity crisis of 2008 brought criticism to the endowment model. Williamson (2011) quotes Daniel Wallick, principal of Vanguard's Investment Strategy Group, as saying that the endowment world's pre-2008 blind emulation of the Yale approach has passed. Endowments and foundations today need to focus on having greater access to liquidity in their funds, which may lead to declines in the commitments toward future private equity and real estate funds and to increases in the cash and fixed-income allocations. Within alternatives, the focus has turned toward more liquid holdings, such as equity hedge funds and commodity futures investments. Between June 2008 and June 2010, Commonfund notes that cash allocations increased by 4%, while U.S. equity allocations fell by 8% and international equity allocations declined by 2%. Alternative investments, especially those with greater liquidity and lower volatility, increased allocations by 6%.

Not everyone, though, thinks that the endowment model has passed its prime. Keating (2011) believes that, after some tweaks in liquidity, conviction in the endowment model has actually strengthened. He notes that the Harvard University endowment has changed its cash target from −5% to +2%, while reducing its uncalled capital commitments to real estate and private equity partnerships by over $4 billion in the past two years. Similarly, Yale University increased its cash holdings to 4%, while putting external lines of credit into place. Keating (2010) states that the liquidity crisis was not caused by an overallocation to alternative investments, but by an underallocation to fixed-income and cash investments.

There are important lessons to be learned from the experiences of pension funds and endowments during the recent financial crisis. Plan sponsors, portfolio managers, and asset allocators could use the framework set forth by the Bank for International Settlements to create a robust process to estimate their liquidity needs and establish a clear liquidity risk tolerance that reflects the needs of their current and future beneficiaries. They should establish sound processes for identifying, measuring, monitoring, and controlling liquidity risk. This process should include estimates of future cash flows arising from both assets and liabilities. A sound and robust risk management process should allow pension funds and endowments to take full advantage of the available investment opportunities, including earning premiums for bearing illiquidity risk at levels that their institutions can tolerate.

3.3 REBALANCING AND TACTICAL ASSET ALLOCATION

Among large endowments, the growth rate of allocations to alternative investments may be approaching the largest possible level. Other institutional investors continue to increase allocations to alternative investments in hopes of catching up with the top universities, in terms of both returns and the size of the assets allocated to alternative investments. In addition to a large allocation to alternative investments, emulating the largest endowments also requires aggressive rebalancing, careful sourcing of top-performing managers, and the embrace of liquidity risk. This is easier said than done, however, as inevitable market crises will test the patience and liquidity structures of investors with large holdings in alternative investments.

Another reason to maintain liquidity in an endowment or foundation portfolio is to facilitate rebalancing activity. Swensen believes strongly in keeping portfolio weights close to the long-term strategic weights, a practice that requires regular rebalancing. Without rebalancing, the asset allocation of the portfolio will drift, with the asset classes earning the highest return rising in weight relative to the rest of the portfolio. Assuming that the highest-performing asset class is also more volatile and increasingly overvalued, the risk of the portfolio rises significantly when rebalancing activity is delayed. Market price action makes it relatively easy to rebalance publicly traded securities, as the investor is buying as prices fall and selling as prices rise. Investors who rebalance are providing liquidity to the market, and liquidity providers often get paid for providing that service to other investors. This is the time when value is created, as many times purchases during a time of price weakness can create significant value. It can take courage, though, to buy an underweighted asset class when prices are falling and most other investors are selling. To the extent that bonds increase in value as a flight-to-quality asset when equities decline, investors may need to move quickly to rebalance before returns start to move in the opposite direction.

Rebalancing, however, can be regularly undertaken only in liquid asset classes. Within alternatives, hedge funds may have quarterly redemption windows and lockup periods of one to three years. Private equity and real estate funds must typically be held until assets are fully distributed, a process that can take 10 to 12 years. Funding capital calls to private equity and real estate funds can change the asset mix, as traditional investments are typically sold to fund the increasing allocation to the less liquid alternative investments. To the extent that alternative investments have net asset values that are smoothed or reported with a time lag, publicly traded investments will decline in allocation rapidly during times of crisis. It is important to understand the role of pricing in these less liquid asset classes, as the net asset value adjusts slowly to changes in public market valuation. Investors may react by rebalancing only within the liquid alternatives and traditional assets, while slowly changing allocations to less liquid alternative investments by modifying the size of future commitments.

There are a number of approaches to rebalancing, such as those discussed by Kochard and Rittereiser. Some investors will rebalance on a calendar basis, for example, only after discussions at a quarterly meeting of the investment committee. Other investors will tie the rebalancing activity to the actual asset allocation when compared to the long-term policy asset allocation. While some investors have exact targets for the domestic equity allocation, such as 30%, others might have ranges of 25% to 30%. Those with an exact target may establish a rebalancing deviation, such as a decision to rebalance when the equity allocation has strayed 2% from its target weight. Investors with asset allocation ranges may wait to rebalance until the allocation has moved outside of the range. When range-based investors rebalance, they must also decide whether to rebalance to the closest edge of the range or to the center of the range.

For liquid investments, rebalancing can be accomplished through the use of securities or derivatives. Investors seeking to rebalance during late 2008 or early 2009 needed to sell fixed income and buy equity securities in order to restore the liquid portion of the portfolio back to the strategic asset allocation weights. While the crisis led to both declines in equity prices and increases in yields on risky fixed-income securities, the drawdown in the equity portfolio was much larger. As spreads on investment-grade and high-yield corporate bonds widened significantly, sovereign bond yields declined due to the flight-to-quality response. Even though investors desired to rebalance, many managers of fixed-income funds, especially in convertible bonds or mortgage-backed securities, had restricted liquidity by suspending redemptions or implementing gates. Experienced investors noticed a tremendous opportunity to rebalance using the derivatives markets. When the S&P 500 index traded above 1,400 in May 2008, the 10-year Treasury yielded 3.8%. At the market low in March 2009, Treasury notes had rallied to a yield of 2.8%, while the S&P 500 traded below 700. There was quite a window for rebalancing, as the S&P 500 was valued at below 900 from the end of November 2008 to the end of April 2009. Investors who sold 10-year Treasury note futures and bought futures on the S&P 500 at any time during late 2008 or early 2009 had a tremendous profit from the rebalancing trade. This was because by the end of 2009 Treasury yields had returned to 3.8% while the S&P 500 had moved above 1,100, producing a profit of at least 24% on the equity trade alone. Investors who kept their fixed-income funds intact while hedging the change in Treasury yields multiplied their profits as yield spreads declined from record levels in the spring to more normal levels by year-end.

Those schooled in options theory may notice that rebalancing activity is simply a short strangle trade, where both out-of-the-money calls and puts are sold. If the investor is committed to reducing the equity allocation after prices have risen 10%, it can make sense to sell index call options 10% above the market. This brings discipline to the rebalancing process and allows the fund to earn income through the sale of options premium. This income can be either spent by the sponsor of the endowment or foundation fund or used to reduce the risk of the investment portfolio. Similarly, committing to buy equities after a 10% decline could be implemented through the sale of equity index put options with a strike price 10% below the current market level. While this approach can earn significant options premium and bring discipline to the rebalancing process, it is not without risk. The greatest risk is when the market makes a move larger than 10% in either direction. The sale of options guarantees rebalancing will occur at the level of the strike price, while those without options hedges may be able to rebalance after the market has moved by 20% to 30%. Of course, there can be significant fear or euphoria after such a move, and some managers may hesitate to rebalance due to the foibles understood by students of behavioral finance.

Some endowments may employ internal tactical asset allocation (TAA) models or external asset managers offering TAA strategies. As opposed to strategic asset allocation, which regularly rebalances back to the long-term target weights, tactical asset allocation intentionally deviates from target weights in an attempt to earn excess returns or reduce portfolio risk. TAA models take a shorter-term view on asset classes, overweighting undervalued assets and underweighting overvalued assets. While the risk and return estimates underlying the strategic asset allocation are typically calculated for a 10- to 20-year period, the risk and return estimates used by tactical asset allocation are typically much shorter, often between one quarter and one year. Tactical models are most useful when markets are far from equilibrium, such as when stocks are expensive at 40 times earnings or high-yield bond spreads are cheap at 8% over sovereign debt. TAA models can employ valuation data, fundamental and macroeconomic data, price momentum data, or any combination of the three.

A number of alternative investment styles employ TAA analysis. Managed futures funds focus on price momentum, while global macro funds more commonly analyze governmental actions to predict moves in fixed-income and currency markets. TAA funds may employ both methodologies, but are different from managed futures and macro funds. First, managed futures and macro funds take both long and short positions and often employ leverage; TAA funds are typically long-only, unlevered funds. Second, TAA funds may reallocate assets across a small number of macro markets, whereas managed futures and global macro funds may have a much larger universe of potential investments.

Because TAA strategies can be difficult to employ successfully, many investors will place limits on the size of tactical positions. For example, when stocks are overvalued, the equity allocation may be 10% below the long-term target weight. If the fund were allowed to swing between 100% equity and 100% fixed-income allocations, substantial opportunity costs could be incurred. In this case, a TAA portfolio may have been fully invested in fixed income when equity prices moved 25% higher, between the end of February and May 2009. Due to the similarity in long-term return estimates, it is less risky to tactically allocate between assets of similar risk and return (hedge funds versus commodities versus stocks) than between assets of different risk and return (equity versus cash), which carry a much higher opportunity cost.

3.4 TAIL RISK

In the Foreword to Swensen (2009), Charles Ellis commented that Yale was good at playing defense, because the endowment was built to withstand the inevitable storms that face capital markets. This resiliency was recently put to a severe test, as the Yale endowment lost 25% of its value in the year ending June 2009. This has been termed a tail event, where the returns were at the extreme left tail of the endowment's return distribution.

Bhansali (2008, 2010, 2011) has repeatedly encouraged investors to manage the risk of catastrophic loss of portfolio value, termed tail risk. When portfolios preserve value during bear markets, the long-term value of the endowment fund can be increased. The key to minimizing drawdowns is to build some protection into the portfolio by making an allocation to assets that will maintain value or even rise in value during times of crisis.

The most straightforward hedge is an increased weight on cash and risk-free debt in the portfolio. A rising allocation to cash, however, will reduce the expected return of the portfolio and potentially lead to lower long-term wealth. The most aggressive endowment and foundation investors have clearly not used cash and fixed income as a tail hedge, as the allocation to this defensive asset class is typically quite low.

In times of market stress, correlations between many types of assets tend to rise. This increases portfolio volatility above that assumed in the mean-variance optimization that may have been used to determine the initial asset allocation. Page, Simonia, and He (2011) state that private equity, real estate, and hedge funds earn a liquidity premium, but sell put options on liquidity risk. When equity markets decline in a crisis, these alternative investments also experience losses. Investors may wish to estimate the equity betas of their portfolios during periods of both normal and extreme market moves. Once the equity exposure of the portfolio, including other assets that behave like equity during a time of crisis, is determined, the hedging process can begin. Page, Simonia, and He estimate that the typical endowment portfolio may derive over 70% of its risk from equity markets. With an allocation of 31% equity, 17% fixed income and cash, and 52% in alternative investments, the risk can be parsed two ways. First, the risk can be decomposed into 81% equity and 19% corporate spreads, currency, commodity, and other. When including liquidity risk, this risk decomposition changes to 61% equity, 25% liquidity, and 14% corporate spreads, currency, commodity, and other.

A second method to reduce tail risk is to employ options hedges on the equity-linked portion of the portfolio. The simple purchase of equity put options can be quite expensive. Equity put options provide the purest hedge against tail risk, offering the potential to provide a greater than 500% return during times of increasing systemic risk. For example, an investor who spends 5% of portfolio value each year on equity put options may expect those options to be worth 25% of the portfolio value at the bottom of the bear market. This approach, though, may simply be smoothing returns: transferring the losses on options in good years to profits on options in years of declining equity markets.

The cost of **equity options hedges** can be reduced through the use of collars or put spreads. In a collar, a call option is sold above the market. While this limits the potential return from the equity-linked portion of the portfolio, the premium earned from the sale of the call option can offset the cost of the put options. In a put spread, the investor purchases one put option, at perhaps 10% out-of-the-money, while selling a second put option, at perhaps 25% out-of-the-money. This strategy can insure losses on the equity portfolio of up to 15%, but after the market has fallen 25%, the investor participates fully in market declines. The cost of a put spread may be 30% to 70% less than the cost of a long put option, depending on the implied volatility, strike price, and maturity of each option.

Bhansali (2008, 2010, 2011) advocates an opportunistic approach to hedging, which leans heavily on the idea that correlations between risky assets rise in a crisis. While equity options are a pure hedge against the dominant risk in most investor portfolios, they are often the most expensive. During extreme market events, markets with cheaper hedging vehicles may have moves as large as equity markets. Bhansali proposes building portfolios of put option hedges from the currency, commodity, and credit markets and call options on volatility indices, buying hedges when they are cheap and selling hedges when they are expensive. To take advantage of the flight-to-quality nature of market crises, call options on high-quality bonds may also be employed.

To the extent that this basket hedging approach is exchange traded, the hedges will be liquid even during a crisis. Investors can sell their hedges immediately after a large market decline, gaining access to cash at a time when asset markets are experiencing declining liquidity and new borrowings may be expensive or infeasible. This defensive strategy may allow investors to play offense by buying assets from other investors who are in need of cash. During 2008 and 2009, investors with cash were able to buy shares of hedge fund, private equity, and real estate partnerships at a discount in the secondary market from investors who were unable to raise the cash to fund their spending rates or capital calls.

Investors need to be careful, though, when hedges are purchased in the over-the-counter market. Trades in the over-the-counter market incur counterparty risk, which can be at its highest point during times of market crisis.

Within each asset class, investors can structure allocations to reduce exposure to extreme market events. Just as Swensen does at Yale, the fixed-income portfolio can focus on high-quality bonds that will grow in value during a crisis, while avoiding corporate bonds, where yield spreads widen quickly during a market stress event. In hedge funds, it may be wise to reduce allocations to arbitrage strategies, such as convertible arbitrage or mortgage-backed securities arbitrage, which rely on tightening spreads, the availability of leverage, and liquid markets to earn their returns. Some hedge fund strategies have historically risen in value during times of market crisis. Macro, managed futures, and some volatility arbitrage funds are designed to have their largest returns during times of extreme market moves, so some investors specifically allocate assets to these strategies to reduce the tail risk of their portfolios. While these strategies are not as certain to perform as a put options strategy during times of market stress, the expected cost of these strategies is lower, as the long-term return to these hedge fund strategies far exceeds the negative expected return of programs that regularly purchase equity put options.

3.5 CONCLUSION

Worldwide, investors of all types have become enamored of the endowment model of asset allocation, which is typified by large allocations to alternative investments and small allocations to fixed income and cash. While this strategy has posted substantial returns over the past 20 years, investors cannot blindly increase allocations to alternative investments and hope to generate large returns. Those wishing to replicate the results of the most successful endowment and foundation investors need to consider the risks to inflation, liquidity, and extreme market events, while adding value through rebalancing and the successful selection of active managers. A focus on alternative investments also requires a greater degree of investment manager due diligence, evaluating both investment and operational risks.

CHAPTER 4

Pension Fund Portfolio Management

Pension plans (also known as pension schemes or superannuation plans) manage assets that are used to provide workers with a flow of income during their retirement years. Because pension plans may control the largest pool of capital in the world, asset managers need to be aware of the goals and challenges of managing these plans. In a study of 13 developed countries, private and public pension plan assets totaled over $26 trillion, averaging 76% of gross domestic product (GDP) (Towers Watson 2011). It is estimated that 58% of the world's workers are covered by some form of pension plan (Whitehouse 2007). The world's top 15 pension plans controlled over $4,360 billion in assets in 2011 (see Exhibit 4.1).

In most of the developed world (North America, Europe, Japan, and Australia), life expectancy exceeds 80 years. Workers may start a career around age 20, work for approximately 40 years, and retire from work between ages 60 and 67. Workers need to save during their careers in order to maintain an adequate standard of living during retirement. It can be difficult for an individual worker to adequately plan for retirement, as investment returns and one's life expectancy are unknown. Depending on their chosen career and income, workers may lack either the ability to save or the investment knowledge to appropriately invest their assets.

There are a number of reasons why pension plans can be attractive, both for employers and for employees. Companies offering pension plans may be able to attract and retain higher-quality employees, while employees may seek out companies offering strong pension benefits. Employees value the income promised by a pension plan, which may be used as a substitute for their personal savings. In many countries, retirement plan assets grow on a tax-deferred basis. Employees' and employers' contributions to retirement plans are not taxed in the year that the contributions are made. The gains on the investment portfolio are not taxed in the year they are earned, but taxes are paid by employees when the assets are withdrawn during retirement. Ideally, the employee will pay a lower tax rate during retirement than during the working years, which further increases the tax benefit of pension plan investments.

In contrast to what occurs when employees individually save for retirement, pension funds have several advantages. First, the pension fund can hire internal staff and external managers who are highly trained in finance to watch the investment portfolio on a daily basis. Economies of scale are also earned by large pension plans, as larger investment sizes can reduce investment fees and afford a larger staff.

Pension plans can also make long-term investments, with a time horizon that may be as long as the lifetime of the youngest employee. Asset allocation decisions are made with the average employee in mind. When individual investors make

EXHIBIT 4.1   The World's Largest Pension Plan Sponsors, 2011

Fund	Country	Assets ($ Million)
Government Pension Investment Fund	Japan	$1,432,122
Government Pension Fund	Norway	$ 550,858
Stichting Pensioenfonds ABP	Netherlands	$ 318,807
National Pension Service	Korea	$ 289,418
Federal Retirement Thrift Investment Board	U.S.	$ 264,013
California Public Employees' Retirement System	U.S.	$ 214,387
Pension Fund Association for Local Government Officials[a]	Japan	$ 189,633
Canada Pension Plan[b]	Canada	$ 149,142
Employees Provident Fund	Malaysia	$ 145,570
Central Provident Fund	Singapore	$ 144,844
California State Teachers Retirement System	U.S.	$ 138,888
New York State Common Retirement Fund	U.S.	$ 133,023
Stichting Pensioenfonds Zorg en Welijn PFZW	Netherlands	$ 133,002
National Social Security Fund	China	$ 129,789
Government Employees Pension Fund (GEPF)[a,b]	South Africa	$ 128,232

[a]Estimate.
[b]As of March 31, 2011.
Source: Pensions & Investments.

retirement investments, asset allocation becomes inherently more conservative over time, as the employee's lifetime is uncertain and the ability to fund investment losses during retirement is limited. **Mortality risk,** the age at which someone dies, is highly uncertain for an individual investor, but can be quite predictable when averaged over a large number of employees and retirees covered by a pension plan. Longer lifetimes require larger retirement assets. For an individual investor, spending rates may be conservative, again because the life span is uncertain. However, for a pension plan with known benefits, the asset allocation and benefit levels may not be significantly impacted by the death of a single beneficiary. **Longevity risk,** the risk that an individual will live longer than anticipated, affects different investors in different ways. For life insurance companies, the risk is that their beneficiaries die at a younger age than predicted, as the life insurance benefit will be paid at an earlier date and a higher present value. For individuals and pension plans, the risk is that lifetimes will be longer than anticipated, as retirement spending or retirement benefits will last for a longer time period, requiring a larger number of monthly benefit payments or months of retirement spending.

There are three basic types of pension plans: defined benefit, governmental social security plans, and defined contribution. Each plan varies in the asset management risks and rewards, and whether the employer, the employee, or taxpayers have the ultimate risk for the performance of the investment portfolio.

4.1   DEFINED BENEFIT PLANS

Defined benefit (DB) plans provide a guaranteed income to retirees, but can be risky for employers. In a **defined benefit plan,** the employer takes all of the investment risk while offering a guaranteed, formulaic benefit to retirees.

For example, consider an employer that offers a retirement benefit of 1.5% of salary for each year the employee worked before retirement. If the salary to which the benefits apply is $50,000 and the employee has worked for 40 years, the retiree will be paid retirement benefits in the amount of $30,000 per year (1.5% × 40 years × $50,000) for the rest of the retiree's life. This provides the worker with a **retirement income-replacement ratio** of 60%, which is the pension benefit as a portion of final salary.

DB plans are not **portable**, meaning that benefits earned at one employer do not continue to accrue at another employer. In many cases, workers who die before retirement age receive no benefits from a DB plan and their heirs receive no lump sum or recurring benefit payments. DB plans reward workers who spend their entire career with a single employer. Contrast an employee who worked for 40 years at one firm to another employee who worked 20 years at each of two employers. Each employer provides a benefit of 1.5% of the average of the final five years of salary multiplied by the number of years of service. The worker started with an income of $15,787 in 1971, and retired in 2011 with an income of $50,000 after receiving annual salary increases of 3% over 40 years. If the worker served her entire career with one employer, the annual benefit would be $28,302 (1.5% × 40 years × the final five-year salary average of $47,171). The benefits would be quite different had she worked for two employers. The retiree worked at the first employer from 1971 to 1991, with an average annual salary in the final five years of $26,117. The annual benefits of $7,835 (1.5% × 20 years × $26,117) are determined in 1991, but not paid until retirement in 2011. The second employer pays annual benefits in the amount of $14,151 (1.5% × 20 years × $47,171). Compared to the annual benefit of $28,302 after working the entire career for a single employer, the employee splitting careers between two firms earns an annual pension of only $21,986 ($7,835 plus $14,151), which is $6,316 per year less than if she had worked for a single firm.

A lack of portability may be an even greater issue for an employee who works a large number of jobs in a career, as many firms have vesting periods of five to 10 years. An employee must work for the entire **vesting period** in order to earn any retirement benefits. In a worst-case scenario, consider an employee who worked for 45 years, serving nine years at each of five employers. If each employer required a minimum of 10 years of service to qualify for a DB pension, the employee would have earned no retirement benefits, even after working for 45 years at firms offering DB plans.

4.1.1 Defining Liabilities: Accumulated Benefit Obligation and Projected Benefit Obligation

It can be challenging to model the liability of an employer's DB plan. Defining the liability is important, as employers need to reserve assets each year to plan for future benefit payments. A number of assumptions need to be made to calculate the amount owed in retiree benefits. These assumptions include:

- The amount of employee turnover and the years of service at the date of separation
- Average wages at retirement, which requires the current wage, estimated retirement age, and annual wage inflation from today until retirement

- The assumed age of worker death, as the number of years of benefits to be paid is the difference between the age at retirement and the age at death
- The number of current employees, hiring plans, and the anticipated age of all employees

The **accumulated benefit obligation (ABO)** is the present value of the amount of benefits currently accumulated by workers and retirees. This number may be very small for a young firm with young workers, such as a four-year-old technology start-up filled with young college graduates. In this scenario, current workers have had only four years to accrue benefits and the firm may not anticipate retirements for another 40 years. Their ABO is relatively easy to calculate, as the number of workers, their tenure, and average salary are all known. Of course, future wage growth and the average employee life span need to be assumed.

The **projected benefit obligation (PBO)** is the present value of the amount of benefits assumed to be paid to all future retirees of the firm. This number is much more challenging to calculate, as the number of workers at the firm in the future, employee turnover levels, and years of service are unknowns. As long as the firm has current employees, the PBO is always greater than or equal to the ABO. When the firm and its employees are young, the ABO may be much smaller than the PBO. For example, the PBO may assume 40 years of service, while employees at the young firm have accrued only four years of service. In a mature firm with a large number of retirees and an older workforce, the ABO will be of a similar magnitude to the PBO. The difference between the ABO and the PBO is primarily based on the current versus future salaries and years of service of current employees.

4.1.2 Funded Status and Surplus Risk

The **funded status** of a pension plan is the amount of the plan's current assets compared to its PBO. The funded status may be expressed in terms of currency, such as €2 billion underfunded, or in percentage terms, such as 70% funded (or 30% underfunded) if a plan's assets are 70% of the PBO. Plans should strive to be close to 100% funded. Overfunded plans, such as those with assets of 120% of PBO, may attract attention from employees who would like to earn larger benefits, or from corporate merger partners who may wish to disband the pension and keep the surplus value. Underfunded plans, such as those where assets are 70% of the PBO, may require larger employer contributions and attract regulatory scrutiny.

The funded status of pension plans can vary sharply over time, as shown in Exhibit 4.2. The assets of the plan grow with employer contributions, decline with retiree benefit payments, and change daily with returns to the investment portfolio. The PBO also changes over time, as the present value factor is based on corporate bond yields. As corporate bond yields rise, the PBO declines. Conversely, declines in corporate bond yields lead to an increasing PBO.

The Citigroup Pension Liability Index tracks corporate bond yields that can be used to discount future values of the PBO. At December 31, 2009, the discount rate was 5.98%, while the duration of PBO benefits was estimated at 16.2 years. By year-end 2011, the discount rate had fallen to 4.40%. The pension plan's PBO can be compared to a short position in corporate bonds, which will change in value by the approximate amount of $-1 \times$ change in yields $\times$ duration. Over this two-year

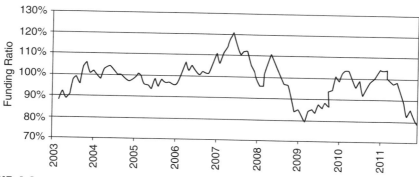

EXHIBIT 4.2 Estimated Funding Ratio of UK Pension Schemes
Source: The Purple Book (2011).

period, the 1.58% decline in corporate bond yields has led to an increase of 25.6% (−1 × 1.58% × 16.2) in the present value of the PBO, assuming that duration and future benefit assumptions remain unchanged.

The **surplus** of a pension plan is the amount of assets in excess of the PBO. The **surplus risk** of a pension plan is the tracking error of the assets relative to the present value of the liabilities. Consider the example in Exhibit 4.3, where assets are invested 60% in the S&P 500 and 40% in the Barclays Aggregate Bond Index. The liabilities are assumed to have a duration of 16.2 years and a discount rate tracked by the Citigroup Pension Liability Index. From 1997 to 2011, the volatility of the asset portfolio was 11.9%, while the volatility of liabilities based only on the change in corporate bond yields was 9.9%. Because assets and liabilities had a correlation of −0.26 over this time period, the surplus risk was even higher, as the volatility of the annual difference between asset and liability returns was 17.4%.

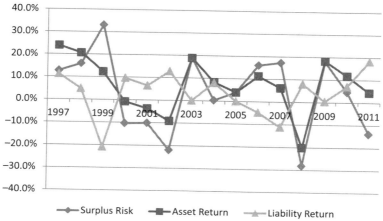

EXHIBIT 4.3 The Volatility of Pension Assets and Liabilities Creates Surplus Risk
Source: Authors' calculations based on returns to the S&P 500, Barclays Aggregate Bond Index, and the Citigroup Pension Liability Index.

4.1.3   Why Defined Benefit Plans Are Withering

Each pension plan has a **required return assumption** that is used to calculate the employer's annual contribution. As shown in Exhibit 4.4, all of the 126 U.S. public pension plans surveyed by the National Association of State Retirement Administrators (NASRA) and the National Council on Teacher Retirement (NCTR) used return assumptions between 7% and 8.5% in 2010, with over 44% using an estimate of 8%. Should long-term investment returns fall below this assumed return, either the plan will become underfunded or additional employer contributions will be required. The required return is also a key driver of asset allocation, as investment policy is set in an attempt to earn the required return. That is, plans with higher required return assumptions may pursue a more aggressive asset allocation in order to earn the investment profits needed to justify both the current level of benefits promised as well as the employer contributions.

Plan sponsors, whether in the public or private sector, are increasingly becoming concerned about the affordability of DB plans. While corporate plan sponsors use a corporate bond yield as the discount rate, public plans use the required return assumption as the discount rate. The calculations underlying Exhibit 4.3 show an average annual return on assets of 6.4% from 1997 to 2011, while the present value of liabilities increased by an annual average of 2.8% during a time of declining interest rates. This means that, over a 15-year period, asset returns exceeded liability returns by only 3.6% per year for corporate plans. When the public plan sponsor is making contributions based on an 8% required return, actual returns of 6.4% per year will lead to declining funded ratios over time.

Regulatory changes, at least in the United States, are also making corporate DB plans less attractive. The Pension Protection Act of 2006 requires that corporate employers disclose the plan's funded status to plan participants. The Act also requires employer contributions to be commensurate with the funding status, with underfunded plans requiring greater contributions and overfunded plans requiring

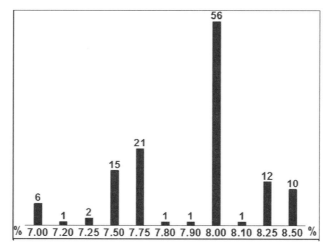

EXHIBIT 4.4   Distribution of Investment Return Assumptions, Fiscal Year (FY) 2010
Source: Public Fund Survey of the NASRA and the NCTR.

lower contributions. Underfunded plans must increase required contributions by an amount that projects the plan to be fully funded within seven years.

Investors are also concerned about the risk of investing in the equity securities of companies with underfunded pensions. The funded status of U.S. pension plans is now required to be disclosed on corporate balance sheets. Merton (2006) states that companies with large pension deficits may trade at lower multiples of earnings and book value, exhibit higher betas, and may experience higher stock price volatility. The higher beta caused by pension risks can increase the firm's weighted average cost of capital by up to 2.7%, which makes it more difficult to find profitable operating investments.

Employees are also concerned about DB plans. The declining number of DB plans offered by companies and their lack of portability make such plans less relevant today. Employees are working at a greater number of firms during their careers than did previous generations. The U.S. Bureau of Labor Statistics (BLS 2010) estimates that Americans born between 1957 and 1964 held an average of 11 jobs before the age of 44, and only 12% of this population held four or fewer jobs during the first half of their career. It is therefore difficult for the majority of younger workers to accrue meaningful retirement income under a DB system.

As a result, as shown in Exhibit 4.5, DB plans are declining as a share of assets among U.S. pension plans.

Should a plan sponsor no longer wish to offer a DB plan to its employees, it has the option to freeze or terminate the plan. As a less drastic measure, the employer may move to a two-tier structure, offering newly hired employees a less generous pension benefit than previously hired employees. A **frozen pension plan** is one where employees scheduled to receive DB pension benefits will no longer continue to accrue additional years of service in the plan. An employee with 20 years of service when the plan is frozen might retire five years later with 25 years of service but the benefits would be tied to only 20 years of service. A **terminated pension plan** is no longer operated by the employer. Once a plan has been terminated, all assets will leave the control of the employer and either be paid out in lump sums to employees or be used to purchase annuities that will pay future benefits to retirees. Freezing or terminating pension plans is extremely popular in the United Kingdom, where *The Purple Book* (2011) estimates that only 16% of UK plans are open to new participants and allow current participants to continue to accrue benefits. Olsen (2012) states that "46% of U.S. corporate DB plans are active and open to new hires, while 24% are closed, 24% are frozen and 1% are being terminated."

EXHIBIT 4.5   Defined Benefit Assets of the Top 1,000 U.S. Pension Plans Are Losing Share over Time

	2002	2004	2006	2008	2010
Total plan assets ($ million)	4,329,015	5,351,019	6,487,729	6,395,807	6,561,617
Total DB assets	3,243,189	3,969,566	4,776,551	4,618,163	4,651,389
Total non-DB assets	1,085,826	1,381,453	1,711,178	1,777,644	1,910,229
% non-DB assets	25.1%	25.8%	26.4%	27.8%	29.1%

Source: Author's calculations, *Pensions & Investments.*

4.1.4 Asset Allocation and Liability-Driven Investing

Pension plan sponsors have conflicting goals when designing the asset allocation of the plan. The first goal is to earn a high return on pension assets, which will be used to reduce the employer's long-term contributions required to fund employee benefits. The second goal is to minimize the degree of underfunding or the amount of surplus risk incurred in the plan.

As can be seen in Exhibit 4.6, a survey of 1,000 U.S. DB pension plans shows that allocations to equity investments have fallen from 2002 to 2010, while alternative investments have risen from 11% to 19% of DB plan assets. Consistent with the data on endowments and foundations from Chapter 2, pension plans with larger amounts of assets have larger allocations to alternative investments. Preqin (2011) reports that public pensions comprise 29% of private equity assets, while 13% comes from private pensions and an additional 21% is invested by endowments and foundations. Similarly, nearly half of global investment in infrastructure comes from these investors, including 20% from public pensions, 16% from private pensions, 8% from superannuation plans, and 8% from endowments and foundations.

As assets of U.S. DB plans have risen from $3,243 billion in 2002 to $4,651 billion in 2010, the dollar amount invested in alternative assets has exploded. While survey data can be incomplete, the authors' analysis of data provided by *Pensions & Investments* (*P&I*) shows that U.S. DB plans had over $225 billion invested in alternatives in 2002 and over $612 billion in 2010. In 2002, the *P&I* survey had limited categories for alternative investments, with allocations dominated by $105 billion in real estate and $73 billion in private equity. By 2010, the number of alternative investment categories tracked by the survey had more than doubled. While real estate ($192 billion) and private equity ($293 billion) remained the largest allocations, hedge funds and funds of funds had risen to $120 billion. Furthermore, real assets, including timber, commodities, oil and gas, and infrastructure, had attracted over $40 billion in pension investments, despite not being included in the 2004 survey.

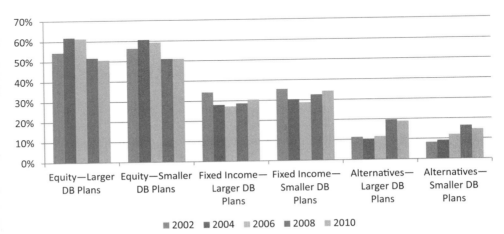

EXHIBIT 4.6 Asset Allocation of Larger DB Plans ($10 Billion or Greater AUM) and Smaller DB Plans (Under $10 Billion AUM)
Source: Authors' calculations, *Pensions & Investments.*

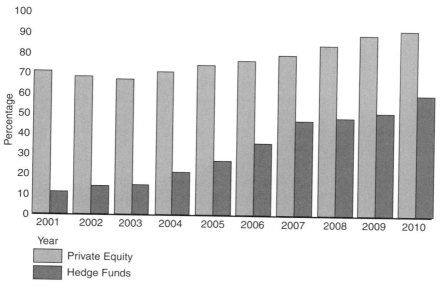

EXHIBIT 4.7 Share of Large U.S. DB Plans ($1 Billion or more AUM) Investing in Hedge Funds and Private Equity from 2001 to 2010
Source: GAO (2012), GAO analysis of *Pensions & Investments* annual survey data, 2001–2010.

The U.S. Government Accountability Office (GAO 2012) discusses the trends of U.S. pension plan investments in private equity and hedge funds. As shown in Exhibit 4.7, while the majority of large U.S. DB plans have invested in private equity for over a decade, hedge fund investments are relatively new, with half of plans making their first investment in hedge funds in the past 10 years. Plans invested in private equity averaged a 9% allocation, while those invested in hedge funds had allocations larger than 5% of assets. As with endowments and foundations, larger plans were more likely to invest in alternative assets than smaller and midsize plans.

While investing in equity and alternative investments may earn higher long-term returns, these risky assets are subject to substantial short-term volatility, whether measured against a benchmark of zero, the plan's required return, or the change in the present value of the plan's liabilities. Companies wishing to reduce surplus risk may have a very large fixed-income allocation. While this reduces surplus risk, the large fixed-income allocation reduces the likely return on assets, which increases the plan sponsor's long-term contributions.

Liability-driven investing (LDI) seeks to reduce surplus volatility by building a portfolio of assets that produces returns that are highly correlated with the change in the plan's liabilities. The simplest way to immunize pension liabilities is to invest in a corporate bond portfolio with a duration matching that of the liabilities. Other ways to reduce surplus risk include derivatives overlays, such as a swap receiving long-duration bond returns or a swaption that increases in value as interest rates decline. (See Exhibit 4.8.)

Meder and Staub (2007) discuss the asset allocation necessary to hedge the ABO and PBO exposures. The ABO does not count future benefit accruals; it simply

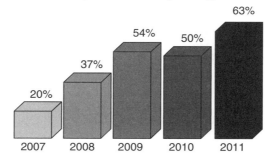

EXHIBIT 4.8   Poll Results of Pension Management Research Panel Liability-Driven
Investing Survey
Source: "5th Annual Liability-Driven Investing (LDI) Poll: More Plan Sponsors Using LDI
Than in Years Past," SEI Institutional Solutions, December 2011.

has exposure to declining nominal bond rates, which increases the present value
of benefit payments. The PBO is more complicated, as future wage inflation may
be correlated to both equities and inflation rates. One suggested asset allocation is
85% nominal bonds, 5% real bonds, and 10% equities. Employers with younger
workers would have a higher allocation to equities. Plans may offer retirees a **cost
of living adjustment (COLA)**, which increases the benefits paid to employees along
with the rate of inflation. For example, consider a retiree earning a pension of $2,000
per month. After five years of 4% inflation rates and a 75% COLA (75% of 4%),
the retiree's pension will have risen by 3% per year to $2,318 per month. Plans
offering benefits with large percentage COLA adjustments would need to have large
allocations to inflation-protected bonds, in order to reduce surplus risk. **Inflation-
protected bonds** earn a nominal coupon, while the principal value rises with the rate
of inflation. Due to the superior hedging capabilities of real bonds, their total return
tends to be very low. In 2012, the real return of 15-year U.S. Treasury Inflation-
Protected Securities (TIPS) was negative.

Investors, then, may wish to protect their portfolios against inflation without
earning the low real returns offered by inflation-protected bonds. A growing number
of investors are turning to real assets to gain inflation protection while attempting to earn higher returns than offered by inflation-protected bonds, such as TIPS.
In addition to the automatic inflation protection offered by TIPS, Martin (2010)
demonstrates that a number of real assets can serve as long-horizon inflation hedges,
including commodities, timber, and farmland. While equities are not a good hedge
against long-horizon inflation, it is uncertain whether infrastructure, real estate, or
intellectual property investments are good hedges against inflation. Specific investment characteristics, such as fixed-rate debt and revenues tied to inflation, improve
the ability of infrastructure or real estate to serve as an inflation hedge. Assets with
fixed-rate leases and variable-rate debt may actually be hurt by inflation, even though
they are real assets, such as real estate or infrastructure.

4.2 GOVERNMENTAL SOCIAL SECURITY PLANS

Government social security plans may provide retirement income to all previously employed citizens of a specific country, regardless of whether the worker was employed in the public sector or in the private sector. The main requirement for earning benefits from these systems is that retirees must have worked for a minimum amount of time, such as 10 years over the course of a career, and paid contributions into the system. Social security benefits are typically portable, meaning that employees continue to accrue service credits whenever they are paying contributions into the system, regardless of the number of employers in a career. Some employees, especially of governmental entities, do not receive these benefits, as neither employees nor their employers paid the required contribution. Whitehouse (2007) estimates that the average retirement benefit in 24 high-income Organization for Economic Cooperation and Development (OECD) countries is 31% of average earnings.

DB plans often have benefits explicitly tied to employee income, without a cap on the amount of benefits that may be earned. Social security plans are quite different, in that there are caps on earnings, which means that retirees with lower career-average incomes may earn a higher retirement income-replacement ratio than higher-income retirees. U.S. workers retiring in 2012 at the age of 66 were eligible for a maximum monthly retirement benefit of $2,513. This maximum benefit is paid to higher-income workers, such as those with incomes over $110,100 in 2012. The Investment Company Institute (ICI 2011) quotes U.S. Congressional Budget Office (CBO) estimates of a retirement income-replacement ratio of 71% for the lowest quintile of U.S. workers, which declines to just 31% for the highest quintile of workers. Social security systems may also provide income security to the dependents of workers, paying benefits to the spouse or children of workers who die or become disabled during their working years.

4.3 DEFINED CONTRIBUTION PLANS

During times of low investment returns and rising amounts of regulatory pressure, many employers no longer choose to offer DB plans. Employers that do not offer DB plans will not see surplus risk on their balance sheets, and the contributions to employee retirement plans will be less variable. These employers will not see pension costs rise during times of low investment returns; however, they will also not earn the upside during times of high investment returns. Towers Watson (2011) estimates that global pension assets in 2010 were 56% defined benefit (DB) plans and 44% defined contribution (DC) plans. The mix between DB and DC plans varies widely by country, with 81% of Australian assets invested in DC plans, whereas 98% of Japanese assets are in DB plans. Using ICI (2011) estimates, U.S. DB plan assets of $8,300 billion are now smaller than the combined $4,500 billion in DC assets and $4,700 billion in individual retirement accounts.

The most common alternative retirement plan offered by employers is a **defined contribution plan,** where the employer makes a stated contribution to each covered employee on a regular basis. In a DC plan, there is no surplus risk for the employer, as assets always match liabilities. A common structure for a DC plan is one in which an employer offers each employee an annual amount of 3% of salary, with perhaps a **matching contribution** of 50% of the amount contributed by the employee. For example, an employee will contribute 6% of salary to the DC plan, while the employer will contribute 3% plus a matching contribution of 3% (50% of 6%). This employee would place 12% of salary into a retirement account.

In contrast to DB plans, DC plans are portable, meaning that the employer contributions become the asset of the employee once the vesting period is completed. This portability is better for employees who work multiple jobs in a career, and for employees who work for firms that may not have the financial strength to pay long-term pension benefits in the amount promised. When leaving an employer, the employee is able to roll over the balance in the DC plan into the plan offered by the next employer or into an individual retirement account. Given that DC plans are personal accounts, the employee contribution, investment gains, and vested portion of employer contributions can be given to the employee's heirs should the employee die before retirement.

In a DB plan, the longevity risk is incurred by the employer. The employee is guaranteed the monthly benefit for life, whether that life is longer or shorter than anticipated. This means that employees cannot outlive their assets. In a DC plan, however, there is no guarantee as to the amount of assets accumulated or the amount of monthly income in retirement, meaning that longevity risks directly impact the employee. Employees with low contributions, low investment returns, or long lives may have a significant probability of "living too long," meaning that their assets may be exhausted or their spending rate curtailed in their final years of life. Employees need to plan for at least 20 years of retirement income, as Maginn et al. (2007) estimate that, in the United States, a 65-year-old couple has a 78% chance that at least one of them will live beyond age 85.

The employer makes the asset allocation decisions in a DB plan, but asset allocation decisions in DC plans are made by the employees, typically using the fund choices provided by the employer. The employer may offer a range of investment choices, such as up to 20 mutual funds. However, it is the employee's decision as to how much to contribute to the retirement account, as well as how to allocate the assets across the allowed investment choices. Leaving the decision making to employees, most of whom are not trained in making investment decisions, can lead to a wide variety of employee outcomes. Some employees may retire without any retirement assets, either because they did not choose to participate in the plan or because they were allowed to invest all of their assets in their employer's stock, which ended up worthless at the end of a bankruptcy proceeding. Some employers may offer the option of a brokerage window, which allows employees to invest in a broader variety of mutual funds, or even individual stocks. While employees with a high degree of financial sophistication can benefit from a brokerage window, the sheer number of options or the ability to concentrate risk in more narrow investments can cause excessive risk for some plan participants.

On the other hand, a diligent saver with good investment returns can potentially earn a larger retirement benefit in a DC plan than in a DB plan. In the earlier example, the employee started with a salary of $15,787 and worked for 40 years, before retiring at a final salary of $50,000 with a single-employer DB pension plan income of $28,302. The same employee, when covered by a DC plan, could have invested 6% of her salary and earned employer contributions in a similar amount. Assuming salary raises of 3% per year, investment returns of 8% per year, and annual contributions in the amount of 12% of salary, the employee would have accumulated over $699,000 at retirement. This amount includes employee and employer contributions of approximately $71,400 each over the course of the career, and over $550,000 in investment earnings. With a spending rate of just 4.05%, the employee would earn the same amount as the DB pension plan income of $28,302. If the DC account earned annual returns of at least 4.05% during retirement, the nominal value of the retirement account would either be stable or rising for the rest of the employee's life. The principal balance, at the date of death, would be passed on to the retiree's heirs. In contrast, most DB plans do not offer value to the family of the retiree, unless there is a promise to pay some portion of the pension income for the rest of the spouse's life. For a diligent saver who was blessed with high investment returns over the course of a career, the DC plan is far superior to a DB plan, in terms of both portability and the ability to pass significant assets along to heirs. Unfortunately, many DC plan participants either save too little or invest too conservatively, and end up faced with the prospect of earning far fewer benefits from the DC plan than if the employee had worked for a single employer offering a DB plan. When plan participants have the ability to withdraw from or borrow against the assets in the DC plan before retirement, it becomes even more difficult to accumulate the assets necessary to ensure a strong income during retirement.

Given that employees are making their own investment decisions, many employers offer simple fund choices for DC plan participants. In some cases, employees are allowed only the choice to allocate assets across domestic stocks, domestic bonds, cash, and global stocks. Other plans will allow participants to invest in equity securities of the employer, as well as over 20 funds in a variety of geographies or asset classes.

Employees do not generally allocate DC plan assets in the same careful way that professional managers allocate DB plan assets. Employees often invest in just a single fund, resulting in a 100% equity or 100% cash allocation, or they diversify contributions equally across all investment choices. Employees also do not rebalance frequently or change allocations when their investment needs become more conservative as retirement approaches. This lack of rebalancing results in a **drifting asset allocation**, where the highest-returning asset classes grow as a share of the portfolio. For example, an employee may have decided at age 30 to direct 70% of contributions to an equity fund and 30% to a fixed-income fund, given his investment needs at the time. If stock returns were substantially higher than bond returns over the next 20 years, the now 50-year-old employee may find himself with an 85% equity, 15% fixed income portfolio at a time when a 60% equity, 40% bond mix is more appropriate for his circumstances.

Due to a lack of investor sophistication as well as regulatory restrictions, most DC plan participants do not have the ability to directly invest in alternative investments. When alternative investment choices are offered in DC plans, they typically focus on commodities or real estate. It is quite rare for individual employees to be able to invest in private equity or hedge funds through DC plans.

After the Pension Protection Act of 2006, many employers made changes to their DC plans' designs in order to alleviate a number of problems with DC plan investments. In the past, employers may not have mandated DC plan participation, and when they did, all employee contributions were placed in cash, unless otherwise directed by the employee. Recently, employers have been automatically enrolling new employees in DC plans, setting the employee contribution at 1% to 3% of salary, and automatically increasing annual contributions by one-third of the employee's salary increase. For example, an employee contributing 2% of salary would have a contribution rate of 4% after earning 3% salary increases for two years. Finally, the default investment option may now be a target-date fund, rather than cash.

A **target-date fund** allows employees to choose a single investment option for the course of their career, without worrying about rebalancing or changing investment needs. A young employee hired in 2012 might invest in a target-date fund, anticipating a retirement in the year 2050, while an employee approaching retirement may be invested in a fund targeting a retirement date of 2020. The 2050 target-date fund assumes that a young employee with an average risk tolerance may be invested 85% in equity and 15% in fixed income. This asset allocation would be regularly rebalanced by the fund manager, becoming more conservative over time. Ultimately, the 2050 fund (in 2040) would resemble the 2020 fund (today), with an asset allocation of 50% equity and 50% fixed income, matching the investment needs of an individual approaching retirement. Target-date funds are often managed as a fund of funds structure, with a mutual fund company allocating assets to between three and 20 mutual funds managed by the mutual fund firm. In this structure, funds with private equity, hedge funds, commodity, or real estate investments may be included in the target-date products at allocations between 5% and 20%. Jewell (2011) quotes a Morningstar survey estimating that target-date funds now hold over $340 billion. ICI (2011) estimates that 10% of DC plan assets in 2011 were invested in target-date funds, while Casey Quirk estimates that nearly half of all U.S. DC assets will be held in target-date funds by 2020 (Steyer 2011).

Private Equity

CHAPTER 5

Private Equity Market Landscape

The growing interest in private equity (PE) investing has arisen in part as a result of its potential to earn superior long-term returns when compared to those of public equities and in part due to the diversification benefits it provides. Investments in PE funds offer access to privately held companies not available in the traditional investor landscape and to the expertise of intermediaries (the PE managers) in creating value by proactively influencing the management and operations of these companies.

Institutional investors typically focus on the organized PE market, where professional management is provided by intermediaries. There is also an informal PE market, which is composed of angel capital and is, not without justification, often referred to as family, friends, and fools. Companies can also receive funding from the founder's savings and efforts, commonly known as blood or sweat equity. The number of investments made in the informal PE market is probably several times larger than the number in the organized PE market; however, it is difficult for institutional investors to gain the information and access necessary to invest in this informal market effectively.

5.1 MAIN STRATEGIES

Private equity funds refer to a multitude of investment strategies with varying risk-return profiles (see Chapter 10) and liquidity profiles (see Chapter 14). The three primary, and most important, types of strategies are venture capital, buyout, and mezzanine. These strategies form the bulk of a typical institutional investor's private equity portfolio.

Venture capital (VC) relates to equity co-invested with entrepreneurs to fund their young and potentially fast-growing companies and is often active in technology sectors such as telecommunications, life sciences, and clean technology. Venture capital has two subcategories, depending on the stage of development of the funded company:

1. **Early stage.**[1] This stage is split into seed and start-up stages. The seed stage takes place before a company is set up and any new product is sold. The financing provided is used to fund research, to assess an initial concept, and to develop a new product. Once successful, further financing is provided during the start-up stage to establish the company and begin to market its new product.

---

[1] The term *later stage* refers to expansion, replacement, and buyout stages of investment.

2. **Expansion stage.** A company in this stage (also called development capital stage), which may or may not have reached profitability, has already established the technology and market for its new product. The financing provided is used to allow greater or more rapid growth by increasing production capacity, developing markets or products, or providing additional working capital.

VC investments are not comparable with traditional financial assets, such as public equity or bonds, and have characteristics that make it difficult to apply traditional portfolio management techniques. These investments are still generally in the cash-burning stage and may be several years away from profitability.

Buyout[2] relates to capital provided as a mix of debt and equity to acquire from current shareholders an established business, business unit, or company (generally privately held or a spin-off from a large private or public company). *Buyout* is a generic term that comprises a change of ownership with the support of private equity investors. A management buyout (MBO) occurs when the current management acquires the company, whereas a management buy-in (MBI) takes place when new managers come from outside the company. When a public company is bought entirely and delisted from the stock exchange, the transaction is referred to as public-to-private (P2P). In buyout funds, portfolio companies are established, have tangible assets, and are normally beyond the cash-burning stage, which allows the use of debt to finance part of the transaction. In these cases, buyouts are referred to as leveraged buyouts (LBOs).

Mezzanine relates to capital provided through the issuance of subordinated debt, with warrants or conversion rights to finance the expansion or transition capital for established companies (usually privately held, below investment grade, or both). Mezzanine financing is halfway between equity and secured debt. While mezzanine financing gives a more predictable cash flow profile, it is unlikely to provide capital returns comparable to other private equity financing forms.

Beyond these three strategies, other specific strategies exist:

- **Rescue (or turnaround).** Under this strategy, capital is provided to help established companies recover profitability after experiencing trading, financial, operational, or other difficulties.
- **Replacement capital (also called secondary purchase).** This strategy relates to capital provided to acquire existing shares in a company from another PE investment organization.

5.2 MAIN DIFFERENCES BETWEEN VENTURE CAPITAL AND BUYOUT

VC and buyout transactions differ in several significant aspects, notably their business model, their deal structuring, the role of the PE manager, and valuation. These and other differences are summarized in Exhibit 5.1 and discussed in the following sections.

---

[2] Some in the investment industry use the term *private equity* to refer only to buyout investing, while others, as is done in this book, refer to both venture capital and buyout investing as private equity.

EXHIBIT 5.1 Buyout–Venture Capital Comparison

	Buyout	**Venture Capital**
Sector	Established industry sectors	Focus on cutting-edge technology or rapidly growing sectors
Stage	Stable growth and mature stages	Seed, start-up, and expansion stages
Approach	Financial engineering, corporate restructuring	Industry know-how, product development and commercialization
Uncertainties	Risk is measurable	Risk is difficult to measure (uncertainty)
Source of returns	Leverage, company building, multiple arbitrage	Company (and market) building, finding follow-on investors
Selection	Intensive financial due diligence	Limited financial due diligence but extensive sector/product due diligence
Valuation constraints	Cash flow projections overlooked by credit lenders	None; often no non-VC third party oversight
Business model	High percentage of success with limited number of write-offs	A few winners with many write-offs
Financing	Club deals and large investment	Limited syndication; several investment rounds
Monitoring	Cash flow management	Growth management
Success factor	Backing experienced managers	Backing entrepreneurs

The classic argument presented for diversifying among private equity classes, and especially between buyout and VC strategies, is that they often exhibit negative correlations and differ in terms of growth and value investing. To begin with, buyout transactions are largely debt-financed and tend to perform well during depressed public equity market periods, when debt is cheap. However, if depressed equity prices are accompanied by a widening of credit spreads (e.g., during the financial crisis of 2008–2009), then leveraged buyout transactions may not be feasible. Second, VC relies on the stock market as the most profitable exit route, and therefore, when close to exit, often shows strong correlation with small-cap indices. Consequently, VC would be expected to do better during equity bull markets when initial public offering (IPO) activity is more robust. Historically, buyouts have provided more stable returns with an orientation toward minimizing risk, whereas VC has occasionally produced higher rates of return in certain markets but brings the possibility of higher losses. Thus, investors seeking long-term stable returns would be inclined to overweight buyout, while those seeking higher returns would do so through increased exposure to VC.

5.2.1 Business Model

Attractive VC investment opportunities can be difficult to assess and are usually concentrated in a few high-technology sectors, which often results in a relatively high number of small investments. Returns stem from taking large risks to develop new businesses, and concentrating efforts and capital through several incremental funding rounds. The goal is to build companies that can be sold or taken public with a high multiple of invested capital. These few big wins need to compensate for many failures. VC-funded companies can be seen as works in progress, with intermediate stages of completion. These stages of completion are often distinguished by milestones, such as rounds of financing (rounds A, B, C.) or, in the case of biotech companies, perhaps phases of clinical trials (phases I, II, III). In this respect, they are development projects that cannot be prematurely exited without risking the loss of most, if not all, of one's invested capital. Thus, VC transactions should be viewed as long-term investments.

Large capital requirements and lower risk levels result in most buyout managers making a smaller number of investments compared to venture capitalists. A multitude of approaches can be combined in a transaction, such as divestment of unrelated businesses, vertical or horizontal integration through acquisition, financial engineering, and company turnaround. Buyout managers need to give extensive strategic- and business-planning advice, and they tend to focus on consistent rather than outsized returns. Because they target established enterprises, buyout firms experience fewer outright failures but have more limited upside potential.

5.2.2 Deal Structuring

VC transactions do not typically involve debt, but venture capitalists gain control of a company over time through a series of equity investments. Returns stem from building companies and from managing growth. Valuation is complicated by the lack of appropriate comparisons, which explains why venture capitalists carry out more extensive sector/product due diligence and more limited financial due diligence compared to buyout managers. They typically provide not only financing for building businesses but also industry know-how, relevant contacts, and management expertise. The investments can be relatively small and are overwhelmingly equity or quasi-equity financed, with little or no leverage.[3] Successful exit strategies require VC managers to secure follow-on financing.

Buyout transactions, on the other hand, typically use both equity and debt financing to acquire companies. Assets of the acquired company are used as collateral for the debt, and the cash flow of the company is used to pay off the debt. Buyout managers conduct intensive financial due diligence and occasionally rely on sophisticated financial engineering. **Financial engineering** refers to the process of creating an optimal capital structure for a company. In private equity, the capital structure is often made up of different types of financial instruments, such as multiple layers of debt, mezzanine, and equity, each carrying a different risk-reward profile. The ability to analyze a company's balance sheet and extract operational efficiencies, as opposed to the implementation of financial legerdemain, is the primary driver of a successful transaction. Generally, there are few limitations to investment size, given

---

[3] One could argue that there is implicit leverage through the intensive use of optionlike mechanisms and due to the fact that there is constrained financing: Start-ups are never fully financed, and seldom do funds have the financial resources to fund all their investments.

the high number of both privately held and publicly traded stable-growth and mature companies that can be targeted.

5.2.3 Role of the PE Manager

Depending on the strategy, the role of the PE manager can differ dramatically. Venture capitalists look to launch new or emerging companies, whereas buyout managers focus on leveraging an established company's assets. Venture capitalists back entrepreneurs, whereas buyout managers deal with experienced managers. Venture capitalists often play an active role in the companies in which they invest, by either sitting on the board of directors or becoming involved in the day-to-day management of the company.

In buyout transactions, a greater proportion of time and manpower is spent analyzing specific investments and adjusting the business model. Buyout managers look to leverage their expertise to turn around underperforming businesses, to improve profitable businesses, or to optimize the companies' balance sheet and the financing. They typically engage in hiring new management teams or retooling strategies. In an operating company, it is easier to give guidance to a seasoned management team, whereas in early-stage investments, one often needs to build and coach the management team from the ground up.

5.2.4 Valuation

The valuation of a VC investment can pose significant problems, given the often limited operating history of the investment, and is compounded in cases in which the company has yet to generate a profit. Traditional valuation methods, such as discounted cash flow methodologies, can be applied to VC investments only by making numerous assumptions, often using unreliable information. The valuation of a VC investment is mainly based on the analysis of intangibles, such as patents or the founder's entrepreneurial skills, competence, and experience, as well as on the assessment of the expected market size for the portfolio company's products or the presumed exit value relative to existing comparable public companies. Thus, VC valuation is usually based not on cash flow or earnings but on multiples where comparable companies exist; where they do not, valuation becomes even more difficult to quantify.

There are relatively few investors and little or no consensus on valuation. A lack of third-party oversight, such as by debt providers, can make venture capital prone to losses from overvaluation. In addition, because the value placed on a young company cannot be verified except through future rounds of investment, it may take years to uncover overinflated and unsustainable valuations.

In buyout investments, valuation risk is more limited. To begin with, the valuation of portfolio companies is more straightforward, enabling one to choose from a rich toolbox of accepted instruments for quantitative analysis, such as discounted cash flows or multiples. The leverage required for transactions leads to scrutiny from a syndicate of commercial lenders and often due diligence by underwriters of a high-yield bond offering. The influence of these credit providers eliminates some of the potential risks inherent in the leverage. There will be restrictions on the amount of leverage they provide, which implicitly sets an upper boundary on the total valuation for the targeted business.

5.3 PRIVATE EQUITY FUNDS AS INTERMEDIARIES

There are different routes for investing in private equity (see Exhibit 5.2). Few institutions have the experience, the incentive structures, and the access that would allow them to invest directly in nonpublic companies, so most investors seek intermediation through the **limited partnership structure**. For institutions, the most relevant approaches to investing in private equity are through fund-of-funds specialists as intermediaries or through similarly structured, dedicated in-house private equity investment programs that invest directly in funds. Other routes are via publicly quoted private equity vehicles or through a dedicated account managed by a private equity specialist.

Reading Exhibit 5.2 from left to right, the various programs are defined as follows:

- In a fund-of-funds structure, the PE fund investment program buys units of a PE fund general partner, which in turn purchases units of a PE fund, which further invests in a portfolio company.
- A PE fund is more direct in that the investment is into a PE fund and then into a portfolio company.
- A PE fund with **co-investment** adds a co-investment leg wherein the PE fund investment program has an additional investment in a certain portfolio company, typically at preferential management and performance fee terms.
- **Going direct** eschews PE funds altogether, as the PE fund investment program makes direct investments into a portfolio company, similar to a co-investment but without the input of a PE fund manager.

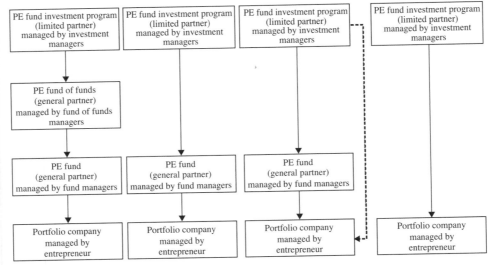

EXHIBIT 5.2   Private Equity Funds Investment Program

The organized private equity market is dominated by funds, generally structured as limited partnerships, which serve as principal financial intermediaries. Fund management companies, also referred to as private equity firms, set up these funds. Private equity funds are unregistered investment vehicles in which investors, or **limited partners (LPs)**, pool money to invest in privately held companies. Investment professionals, such as venture capitalists or buyout managers, known as **general partners (GPs)** or fund managers, manage these funds. Tax, legal, and regulatory requirements drive the structuring of these investment vehicles with the goal of increasing transparency (investors are treated as investing directly in the underlying portfolio companies), reducing taxation, and **limiting liability** (investors' liabilities are limited to the capital committed to the fund). From a strictly legal standpoint, limited partnership shares are illiquid; in practice, however, **secondary transactions** occasionally take place, in which investors sell their shares before the termination of the fund. Private equity funds principally serve the following functions:

- Pooling of investors' capital for investing in private companies
- Screening, evaluating, and selecting potential companies with expected high-return opportunities
- Financing companies to develop new products and technologies, to foster their growth and development, to make acquisitions, or to allow for a buyout or a buy-in by experienced managers
- Controlling, coaching, and monitoring portfolio companies
- Sourcing exit opportunities for portfolio companies

This is a classic principal-agent (LP-GP) relationship, which, because information in PE markets is incomplete and highly asymmetric, requires some specific agreements to cover the resulting problems of moral hazard and conflict of interest. While the specific terms and conditions plus investor rights and obligations are defined in nonstandard partnership agreements, the limited partnership structure—or comparable structures used in the various jurisdictions—has evolved over the last decades to include the following standards (see Chapter 6 for more details on fund structures):

- The fund usually has a **contractually limited life** of seven to 10 years, often with a provision for an extension of two to three years. The fund manager's objective is to realize, or exit, all investments before or at the liquidation of the fund.
- As with wine, the fund will have a **vintage year**, that is, the year in which the first capital is drawn down from investors to be invested in a company.
- Investors, mainly pension funds, endowments, private equity funds of funds, public institutions, banks, insurance companies, or high-net-worth individuals or family offices, are the limited partners and commit a certain amount of money to the fund.
- **Commitments** (capital pledges by investors in private equity funds) are drawn down as needed, or just in time, to make investments or to pay costs, expenses, or management fees. Because private equity funds do not typically retain large pools of uninvested capital, their general partners make **capital calls** (or **drawdowns**) once they have identified a company in which to invest. Therefore, the main part of the drawdown gets invested immediately.

- A significant portion, though not typically all, of the committed capital is drawn down during the **investment period**, typically the first three to five years, during which new opportunities are identified. After that, during the divestment period, only the existing portfolio companies with the highest potential are further supported, with some follow-on funding provided to extract the maximum value through exits. The manager's efforts during this time are concentrated on realizing or selling the investments.
- When **realizations** (sales of portfolio companies) are made, or when interest payments, dividends, or recapitalizations are received, they are distributed to investors as soon as feasible. Funds may have a reinvestment provision, wherein the proceeds of realizations within the investment period or a similar time frame may be reinvested in new opportunities and not distributed to investors. Under this scenario, the fund is self-liquidating as the underlying investments are realized. However, these returns will come mostly in the second half of the fund's lifetime. **Distributions** to investors can also take the form of securities of a portfolio company, known as in-kind distributions, provided that these securities are publicly tradable or distributed when the fund gets liquidated. Legal documentation may also allow for some reinvestment of realizations, normally subject to a cap amount.
- **Management fees** depend on the size of the fund, generally ranging from 2.5% of committed capital for small funds to 1.5% for larger funds. The fees are often based on the amount of committed capital during the investment period and on the value of the portfolio thereafter. There are considerable differences from one fund to the next regarding directorship fees or transaction costs. These can have an impact on the returns and often account for material differences between gross and net returns.

  The main upside incentive for general partners comes in the form of **carried interest,** typically 20% of the profits realized by the fund. Carried interest is usually subject to a **hurdle rate,** or **preferred return,** so that it begins to accrue only once investors have received their capital back and a minimum pre-agreed-on rate of return. Once the preferred return has been attained, GPs typically receive 100% of returns to a point at which they would have received the carried interest on the entire amount. This is called a catch-up and is synonymous with the soft hurdle concept used by hedge funds.
- There is a private equity **fund-raising cycle** that begins anew each time the general partners need to raise capital for another fund. Typically, limited partnership agreements do not allow follow-on funds by the same manager before the end of the initial fund's investment period or until a large part of the initial fund has been invested.

5.4 PRIVATE EQUITY FUNDS OF FUNDS AS INTERMEDIARIES

Many institutions outsource their private equity fund investment program either through a dedicated account or by pooling assets with other investors. Private equity funds of funds are probably the most common type of institutional investment program. The authorizing entity for a private equity fund investment program is the principal who provides the resources, while the manager of the program is the principal's agent and conducts the investments in private equity funds as a limited partner.

Funds of funds, which are generally organized by specialist asset managers, banks, or insurance groups, are vehicles that pool capital from a group of investors to invest in a diversified portfolio of funds. Some funds of funds specialize in certain private equity sectors or geographies, while others follow a more generalist approach. Funds of funds manage the following, often complementary, activities:

- Primary investments in newly formed limited partnerships. Because of the blind-pool nature of such investments, the assessment of the fund management team's skills is key (see Chapter 9).
- Selective, direct co-investments alongside the primary investments. This activity requires direct investment experience and skills.
- Secondary investments in existing funds or portfolios of direct investments. This is generally a niche activity for most funds of funds; however, in recent years, secondary specialists have emerged, such as Coller Capital, Greenpark Capital, and Lexington Partners. This activity requires both co-investment skills for the assessment of the companies already in the portfolio and primary investment skills for the blind-pool part of the transaction.

While investment in a particular private equity fund can have a blind-pool nature, a fund of funds can have established relationships with fund managers via existing investments. Therefore, its future portfolio is somewhat predictable and is not necessarily a **blind-pool investment**. A newly created portfolio is likely to be largely composed of follow-on funds raised by these known managers. In fact, funds of funds are marketed on either a partially blind or a fully informed basis. For a partially blind pool, some of the intended partnership groups are identified, while for a fully informed pool, virtually all of the intended partnerships have been identified.

5.4.1 Private Equity Funds-of-Funds Costs

Funds of funds are often seen as less efficient because of the additional layer of management fees. This double layer of fees is perceived to be one of the main disadvantages of this structure. Funds of funds would have to outperform direct fund investment to compensate for this additional layer of fees.[4] However, given the resources required to manage a portfolio of private equity funds internally, investing through a fund-of-funds structure might well prove more cost-efficient in the end.

An additional cost of outsourcing to a fund of funds is the carried interest. Whether an in-house program can work without investment performance–related

---

[4] Jo (2002) analyzed 48 U.S.-based funds of funds launched between 1992 and 1999 (13 asset managers, 15 banks, and 20 independent funds). For asset managers, there was an average management fee of 0.85% and an average carried interest of 3.8% (only 5 of the 13 asset managers charged a carried interest). For investment and commercial banks, management fees were in the range 0.88% to 1.25%; 12 of the 15 banks charged a carried interest, with the average being 6.6% and the typical carried interest being just 5%. At the end of the 1990s, annual management fees were in the region of 0.8% and carried interest was at 10%; five years later, the difficult market environment brought those down to 0.7% and 5%, respectively.

incentives is debatable. According to Otterlei and Barrington (2003), the annual costs of an in-house team can be significant compared to that of a typical fund of funds. Even with a 5% carried interest charged by the fund-of-funds manager, these authors find that the fees have an insignificant impact on the net returns of the investor. However, information is an asset in the often opaque environment of private equity. Taking the fund-of-funds route versus that of direct investor can lead to a loss of information and control, essentially a cost in itself.

Because private equity programs follow a learning curve, inexperienced institutions may initially have little option other than to go through a fund-of-funds vehicle. Ultimately, they can become limited partners in funds and, with increasing sophistication, build their own portfolio of companies, either through co-investing or by independently sourcing deals. In conclusion, funds of funds are often used as a first step into private equity and may well be worth the additional layer of fees in exchange for avoiding expensive learning-curve mistakes and providing access to a broader selection of funds.

5.5 PRIVATE EQUITY FUNDS OF FUNDS VALUE-ADDED

Investing in funds of funds can allow investors access to the private equity market in a quick and diversified manner. Before making such an allocation, there are several factors that investors need to consider.

5.5.1 Diversification and Intermediation

Funds of funds can add value in several respects and are seen as safe havens for private equity investors. Especially in the case of new technologies, new teams, or emerging markets, a fund of funds allows for reasonable downside protection through diversification. Not surprisingly, various studies have shown that because of their diversification, funds of funds perform similarly to individual funds but with less pronounced extremes (see Weidig and Mathonet 2004; Mathonet and Meyer 2007). In the absence of funds of funds, smaller institutions may have difficulty achieving meaningful levels of diversification. Even for larger institutions, investments in private equity funds and especially VC funds may be too cost-intensive when the size of such investments is small compared to the administrative expenses. A fund of funds can mediate these potential size issues either by scaling up through pooling of commitments of smaller investors and providing each of them with sufficient diversification, or by scaling down through sharing administrative expenses and making such investments less cost-intensive by allowing larger commitment to the fund of funds.

5.5.2 Resources and Information

Funds of funds can provide the necessary resources and address the information gap for inexperienced private equity investors through their expertise in due diligence, monitoring, and restructuring. Investing in private equity funds requires a wide-reaching network of contacts in order to gain access to high-quality funds, trained investment judgment, and the ability to assemble balanced portfolios. Liquidity management can also be quite challenging. It demands a full-time team with insight and an industry network; adequate resources; access to research databases and models; and skills and experience in due diligence, negotiation, and contract structuring. Depending on the overall market situation, access to quality funds can be highly competitive, and being a newcomer to the market can pose a significant barrier. Funds of funds are continuously involved in the private equity space, speak the language, and understand the trade-offs in the industry.

5.5.3 Selection Skills and Expertise

Investors expect funds-of-funds managers to be able to invest in top-performing funds, either by having access to successful invitation-only funds or by identifying the future stars among the young and lesser-known funds. Funds-of-funds managers may also play the role of educator in explaining to comparatively unsophisticated investors that a particular fund, despite suffering horrible losses in the early years, is still viable and merely reflecting the early stages of its J-curve (see section 5.7). While funds of funds are more willing to give the fund managers sufficient latitude to focus on their portfolio companies, they are often better skilled and experienced in restructuring failing funds, if that is ultimately required. In turn, fund managers often welcome funds-of-funds investors as a more stable and experienced source of cheap pooled capital.

5.5.4 Incentives, Oversight, and Agreements

For institutional investors, direct investment is problematic because such institutions often cannot offer their employees adequate performance-related pay. For typical conservative and seniority-based institutions like banks, pension funds, or insurance companies, a theoretically unlimited carried interest does not always fit well into the compensation scheme. While institutional investors do not lack staff with the intellectual caliber to evaluate investment proposals and to structure transactions, generating profitable exits in private equity programs requires very hard work over protracted time periods. Moreover, the lack of incentive (or the conflict of interest) to take risk and to find value may affect investment decisions. Furthermore, there is a significant learning curve, and without performance-related pay, employees may jump ship as soon as they are competent in the area and understand their opportunities better. Finally, for larger institutions, intermediation through funds of funds allows them to focus on their core businesses. This advantage tends to outweigh most cost considerations.

5.6 THE RELATIONSHIP LIFE CYCLE BETWEEN LIMITED AND GENERAL PARTNERS

There is a symbiotic relationship between limited partners and general partners. A limited partner's investment strategy is built around a small number of relationships with general partners who focus on specific segments, such as stages or sectors, of the market. This specialized focus can often limit the scalability of a particular fund, especially in the case of VC, in which limited partners may find it difficult to identify and access additional fund managers of comparable quality.

General partners, for their part, want financially strong, dependable, knowledgeable, and long-term limited partners. Limited partners should have industry expertise and familiarity with the nuts and bolts (particularly valuations and benchmarking) of the private equity business. Adverse selection exists in the private equity market. Poor-quality general partners, be they lacking experience or falling into decline, will court inexperienced limited partners. Because of poor results, both will sooner or later exit the market.

To maintain continuous investment in new portfolio companies, general partners need to raise new funds as soon as the capital from their latest active fund is fully invested (or reserved for follow-on investments), about every three to five years. Therefore, relationships between limited and general partners follow a life cycle and are forged through various rounds of investment, eventually resulting in a virtuous circle of growing experience and fund size.

Investors, as well as fund managers, depend on forging these long-term relationships. Anecdotal evidence suggests that experienced market players profit over protracted time periods from these relationships. Initial criteria are very stringent, and fund managers usually cannot get rich through their first funds. However, a favorable track record is an asset in itself. For more reputable funds, fund-raising is less costly. To minimize their expenses, fund managers generally turn first to those who invested in their previous partnership, provided that the fund's performance was satisfactory.

While it is easy to see how fund managers benefit from a loyal and reliable investor community, these long-term relationships can also be advantageous for limited partners for several reasons:

- In the opaque private equity market, the search for and due diligence of funds is a costly exercise, and limited partners often prefer familiar fund managers to unproven investment proposals.
- Such long-term relationships may provide access to a quality deal flow of co-investment opportunities in portfolio companies within an established framework.
- It is especially desirable for an investor to hold on to good fund managers, as the best teams will have an established investor base, which may eliminate the need to seek out new funding sources to the detriment of adding value to the portfolio companies when making new investments or exits.
- There is likely to be better planning, as limited partners make clear their intentions to participate in follow-on funds. As limited partners form a network, even if they do not have the means to continue, they often refer other investors to a good team. Predictable closings put money to work more efficiently.

The life cycle of the fund manager–investor relationship (see Exhibit 5.3) can be divided into three phases: (1) entry and establish; (2) build and harvest (or grow and compete); and (3) decline (lost competition), exit (gave up or made it), or transition to new managers (spinouts). The main differences between these phases are summarized in Exhibit 5.4.

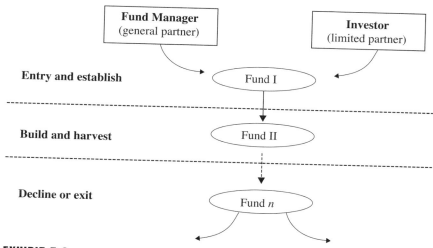

EXHIBIT 5.3   Fund Manager–Investor Relationship Life Cycle

During the entry and establish phase, substantial entry barriers into the private equity market exist for both general and limited partners. Lacking a verifiable track record, new teams find it difficult to raise their first fund. Furthermore, analysis of historical benchmark data supports the hypothesis that new teams suffer from higher mortality than do established or institutional-quality fund managers. First-time funds note the importance of differentiation or innovation as it applies to fund-raising and thus often pursue specialized investment strategies.

New limited partners also face entry barriers, suffering the initial informational disadvantages that make it extremely difficult to identify or gain access to the best managers, particularly when their funds are oversubscribed. For limited partners,

EXHIBIT 5.4   Fund Manager–Investor Relationship Life-Cycle Model

Fund Characteristic	Entry and Establish	Build and Harvest	Decline or Exit
Investment strategy	Differentiation	Star brand	Unexciting
Fund-raising	Difficult fund-raising	Loyal limited partner base	Limited partners leave and are replaced by other types of investors (secondary plays, new entrants in market)
Performance	Unknown: either top or out	Likely top performer	Not top but consistent performer
Size	Fund is too small	Fund size is right	Fund size too large/too many funds
Economies of scale	Fund is too small to get rich	Best alignment of interests	Senior managers made it
Management team	Management team forming	Management team performing	Succession issues, spinouts

it takes the disciplined execution of a long-term investment strategy to build up a portfolio of funds that gives attractive and sustainable returns.

Since investors are mainly interested in the cash returned, the fund manager–investor relationship tends to be relatively stable throughout the build and harvest phase. Lerner and Schoar (2004) present evidence on the high degree of continuity in the investors of successive funds and the ability of sophisticated investors to anticipate funds that will have poor subsequent performance.

It is an oversimplification to assume that investors invest only in top performers and that below-average funds are unable to continue. As in most relationships, there is a certain degree of tolerance for mistakes and failures, at least over a period of time. It is clear that there are limits to disappointing results, but all things being equal, investors will tend to go with fund managers they already know or who have been referred to them through their network even if the fund's performance at times has been subpar.

Eventually, the relationship ends in the decline or exit phase. Not surprisingly, the terms *marriage* and *divorce* are often used in the context of relationships between fund managers and their investors. A gradual decline may occur either as a result of past successes, which potentially decrease the financial motivation of senior fund managers, or due to an improperly planned succession, which leads to the departure of middle management. In addition, the limited partners may eventually end the relationship if they lose confidence or trust in the team—for example, if the team becomes arrogant or fails to deliver. Some limited partners do not invest in follow-on funds and may be replaced by less deep-pocketed or experienced investors, or by secondary investors who choose to invest as a one-off financial play.

5.7 THE J-CURVE

One of the first private equity fund concepts that investors will encounter is the (in)famous **J-curve**, also referred to as the hockey stick (see Exhibit 5.5). The

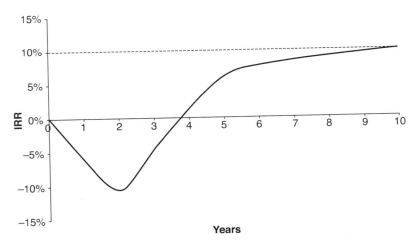

EXHIBIT 5.5 Fund Standard J-Curve

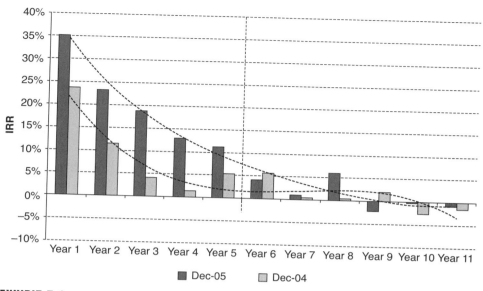

EXHIBIT 5.6 Old versus New J-Curve. Gap between the European Investment Fund (EIF) portfolio's final IRR projections and interim IRRs as of December 2005 versus December 2004

Source: Mathonet and Monjanel (2006) and European Investment Fund.

European Private Equity and Venture Capital Association (EVCA) defines the J-curve as the "curve generated by plotting the returns generated by a private equity fund against time (from inception to termination)." The classic fund performance J-curve is caused mainly by the fact that valuation policies followed by the industry combined with the uncertainty inherent in private equity investments prevent the revaluing of promising investments upward until quite late in a fund's lifetime, while fees, costs, and expenses are immediately deducted. As a result, private equity funds tend to demonstrate an apparent decline in value during the early years of existence, the so-called valley of tears, before beginning to show the hoped-for positive returns in the later years of the fund's life. After about five years, the interim internal rate of return (IIRR) will give a reasonable indication of the definitive IRR.[5] This period is generally shorter for buyout funds than it is for early-stage and expansion funds.

Some time ago, it was postulated that the 2005 introduction of the International Private Equity and Venture Capital Valuation Guidelines (IPEV Valuation Guidelines)[6] would drive the J-curve to extinction, as a truly fair value for funds would eliminate the conservative bias caused by early expensing of costs and deferred

---

[5] The traditional internal rate of return (IRR) is the implied discount rate that makes the net present value of all cash flows zero. The interim IRR is the IRR of unliquidated funds, as it considers for its computation the fund net asset value (NAV) as a last distribution. Therefore, interim IRRs are estimates rather than realized rates of returns. Chapter 6 presents the formal definition and an example of the calculation of this important concept.

[6] Available at www.privateequityvaluation.com (accessed October 2007).

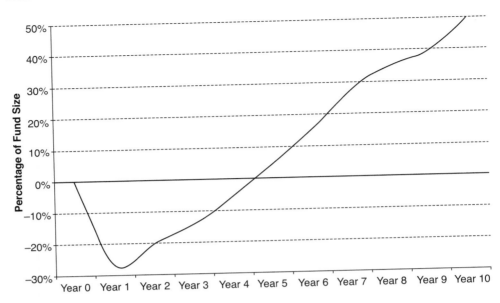

EXHIBIT 5.7   Cash Flow J-Curve

recognition of increases in the values of promising investments.[7] Instead, Mathonet and Monjanel (2006) found that the gap between the final IRR (or the expected IRR) and the IIRR narrowed in years 1 through 5, after which the IIRR became, on average, a reasonably reliable estimator of the final performance (see Exhibit 5.6).

But other J-curves can also be observed in private equity funds: the **cash flow J-curve** and the **net asset value (NAV) J-curve**. The net asset value (NAV) of a fund is calculated by adding the value of all of the investments held in the fund and dividing by the number of outstanding shares of the fund. The NAV J-curve is a representation of the evolution of the NAV versus the net paid in (NPI), which first decreases during the early years of the fund's existence and then improves in its later years. The cash flow J-curve is a representation of the evolution of the net accumulated cash flows from the limited partners to the fund, which are first increasingly negative during the early years of existence before making a U-turn and becoming positive in the later years of the fund's life. This is explained by the fact that in standard private equity fund structures, commitments are drawn down as needed, or just in time, and when realizations are made after having successfully developed these newly founded companies, they are distributed as soon as practical (see Exhibit 5.7).

5.8 CONCLUSION

This chapter has provided an overview of the private equity industry. Venture capital funds are high-risk, high-return investments in small growth companies. General

---

[7] See Meyer and Mathonet (2005).

partners of VC funds focus on the entrepreneur's business model and are often involved in the firm's board of directors and strategic planning process.

Buyouts are lower-return, lower-risk investments focused on more mature companies. GPs investing in buyouts may seek to modify the firm's capital structure and implement operational improvements.

Funds of funds diversify over a number of private equity partnerships. Although going this route adds a second layer of fees, funds of funds may be the best way for new and small investors to access the private equity market.

General partners have a life cycle moving through three stages: (1) entry and establish, (2) build and harvest, and (3) decline or exit. There can be high barriers to entry for new managers, but once established, GPs may be able to build long-term relationships with LPs who may invest in funds across several vintage years.

CHAPTER 6

Private Equity Fund Structure[*]

Regulatory changes in the United States in the late 1970s permitted greater private equity (PE) investment by pension funds, but it was mainly the intermediation through limited partnerships that fostered the widespread adoption of private equity in institutional portfolios. According to Prowse (1998), the growth of private equity shows how organizational innovation, assisted by regulatory and tax changes, can create new possibilities and ignite activity in a particular market. The limited partnership as the dominant structure in private equity investment results from the extreme information asymmetries and incentive problems that arise in the private equity market. While the limited partnership structure does not exist in all jurisdictions, most local legislation allows for this well-established form to be used. This explains why in PE funds managers are commonly called general partners (GPs) and investors are called limited partners (LPs). These terms are used interchangeably in the PE chapters of this book.

For the private equity fund, the **limited partnership agreement** (LPA) defines its legal framework and its terms and conditions. The LPA has two main categories of clauses: (1) investor protection clauses and (2) economic terms clauses. Investor protection clauses cover investment strategy, including possible investment restrictions, key-person provisions, termination and divorce, the investment committee, the LP advisory committee, exclusivity, and conflicts. Economic terms clauses include management fees and expenses, the GP's contribution, and the distribution waterfall. The **distribution waterfall** defines how returns are split between the LP and GP and how fees are calculated. LPAs are continuously evolving, given the increasing sophistication of fund managers and investors, new regulations, and changing economic environments. In essence, the LPA lays out conditions aimed at aligning the interests of fund managers with their investors, and discouraging the GP from cheating (**moral hazard**), lying (**adverse selection**), or engaging in opportunism (**holdup problem**) in whatever form. In economics, the holdup problem is a situation in which two parties (in the case of private equity, a GP and an LP) refrain from cooperating due to concerns that they might give the other party increased bargaining power and thereby reduce their own profits. Incentives are designed so that the fund manager's focus is on maximizing terminal wealth and performance, and ensuring that contractual loopholes are not exploited (e.g., by producing overly optimistic interim results).

---

[*] This chapter was not written by lawyers. It contains information of a general nature and is meant only to illustrate principles.

One private equity management company can act as a group, managing several such partnerships in parallel. Typically, LPAs do not allow follow-on funds with the same strategy (or significant overlap) by the same manager before the end of the investment period or before a high percentage (usually more than 70%) of the active fund has been invested.

For the general partner, an operating agreement sets the division and vesting of carried interest among individual fund managers. The management company enters into agreements with all employees and with the general partners. For the management company, an additional operating agreement may be required to define the division of management fees and the licensing of name and trademark.

The main documents of the fund offering are the private placement memorandum, which describes the general investment proposal; the subscription agreement, which contains the contractual capital commitment and securities law exemptions; and the LPA.

Exhibit 6.1 presents a summary of the typical private equity limited partnership structure, in which the relationships among the management company, the general partner, the limited partners, and the fund are outlined. Needless to say, intensive communication between general and limited partners at all stages of the investment process is the most effective nonstructural method for creating alignment and avoiding surprises. However, to retain their limited partner status and legal protections, LPs need to ensure that their involvement is not construed as control of the fund.

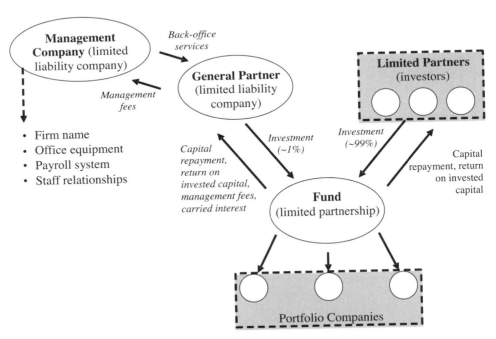

EXHIBIT 6.1 Limited Partnership Structure

6.1 KEY FEATURES

In its current form, the limited partnership is viewed as a good fit for the existing market environment, yet the environment is continuously evolving. However, given the success of the current limited partnership structure, it is more likely we will see adjustments to the LPA terms and conditions rather than broad structural changes. To some degree, an increasing standardization can be observed—as illustrated by the issuance of the Private Equity Principles of the Institutional Limited Partners Association (ILPA).[1] But evolution still exists, notably due to the highly fragmented private equity market, competition, and variations in local regulations, which can precipitate different fund terms and conditions in the LPA. As the industry develops, fund sizes may diverge and specialist players may emerge, rendering standard terms inappropriate for ensuring the alignment of interests in all situations. Deviations from the mainstream or even newly evolving best practices arise out of the need for new fund managers to differentiate themselves. In addition, new terms and conditions can result from changes to the regulatory and economic environments.

It is through the proper alignment of the economic interests of investors and managers—not just through the LPA covenants, the advisory boards, or the committees composed of limited partners—that one can eliminate many of the problems associated with the principal-agent relationship, especially in those scenarios that cannot be foreseen. To be successful, the structure must address management fees, performance-related incentives, hurdle rates, and, most importantly, commitments to the fund by the general partners of significant portions of their wealth alongside that of the limited partners. Additional clauses may be required to cover reinvestments and clawbacks, as well as noneconomic terms such as key-person provisions, joint and several liability, and disclosure obligations. Together, these clauses provide limited partners with moderate but sufficient control over the management of the fund. These key LPA features are described in the following sections.

6.1.1 Corporate Governance in Private Equity Funds

The law and the LPA define and restrict the degree of control limited partners have over the activities of the general partners. Such controls relate, for example, to waiving or accepting investment restrictions, extending the investment period or fund duration, handling key-person-related issues, or participating in an LP advisory committee (LPAC). The LPAC's responsibilities are defined in the LPA and normally relate to dealing with conflicts of interest, reviewing valuation methodologies, and any other consents predefined in the LPA. The limited partners can make decisions with either a simple majority (e.g., the decision to extend the investment period or the fund's duration) or a **qualified majority** (e.g., the decision to remove the general partner without cause). A qualified majority is generally more than 75% of the limited partners as opposed to the 50% required for a simple majority.

---

[1] These principles were developed to encourage discussion between LPs and GPs regarding fund partnerships. They focus on alignment of interest, governance, and transparency.

Occasionally, limited partners may be offered positions on the investment committee. However, it is not clear whether limited partners should actually take on this role. In limited partnership structures, an overactive limited partner could become reclassified as a general partner, thereby losing his or her limited liability. Generally, international industry professionals recognize that fund managers should make investment and divestment decisions without the direct involvement of investors, so as not to dilute the responsibility of the manager, create potential conflicts of interest with nonparticipating investors, or expose limited partners to the risk of losing their limited liability. Also, investors do not normally have the legal rights or the required skills and experience to make such decisions.

Another important element of corporate governance is reporting to limited partners. Various private equity associations or industry boards, including the European Private Equity and Venture Capital Association (EVCA), the Institutional Limited Partners Association (ILPA), the International Private Equity and Venture Capital Valuation Board (IPEV Valuation Board),[2] and the Private Equity Industry Guidelines Group (PEIGG),[3] have released guidelines for valuation and reporting. The obligation to disclose in compliance with these guidelines is increasingly being made part of contractual agreements. While some general partners reduce the level of detail provided to the bare minimum and share it with all limited partners, others share different levels of detail depending on the specific type of investor.[4]

6.1.2 Investment Objectives, Fund Size, and Fund Term

In LPAs, the description of investment objectives should be specific but not too narrow. Lerner (2000) argues that private equity funds are blind pools for a reason. Investors should not attempt to put overly restrictive limits on a fund manager's flexibility, which could block the fund manager's ability to profit from unanticipated opportunities. Further, with uncertain investments, severe information asymmetry, and difficulties in monitoring and enforcing restrictions, fund managers may simply find ways around narrow restrictions.

The fund size, in terms of capital committed by the limited partners, needs to be in line with these investment objectives. However, various factors, such as the required management resources or number of potential opportunities, implicitly set a minimum or maximum size of the fund.

Fund lives or terms are typically seven to 10 years, with possible extensions of up to three years. This represents a trade-off among a better internal rate of return (IRR), sufficient time to invest and divest, and the degree of illiquidity still acceptable for the investors. Normally, the extension of a fund's life is approved annually by a simple majority of LPs or members of the LPAC, one year at a time versus two or more at once, during which time management fees are either reduced or eliminated altogether to stimulate quick exits.

---

[2] See www.privateequityvaluation.com (accessed October 2007).

[3] See www.peigg.org/valuations.html (accessed July 2007).

[4] Associated with the Freedom of Information Act debate in the United States on transparency for public-institution limited partners, this approach is seen as a way out of the dilemma. It even goes so far as to oblige such limited partners to destroy the material provided by the fund manager as soon as it is practical for them to do so.

Normally, proceeds are distributed to investors as soon as feasible after the realization of or distribution of a fund's assets, but in some cases, limited partners grant fund managers the discretion to reinvest some of the proceeds that are realized during the investment period.

6.1.3 Management Fees and Expenses

In private equity, compensation is overwhelmingly performance driven, and there is a consensus that general partners should not be able to make significant profits on management fees alone. Management fees provide a base compensation so that the fund manager can support the ongoing activities of funds. These fees need to be based on reasonable operating expenses and salaries, and be set at a level that is modest enough to ensure that the fund manager is primarily motivated by the carried interest, but sufficient to avoid the manager's departure to greener fields. During the investment period, fees are on a commitment basis rather than only being levied against capital that has been invested. If fees were based only on invested capital, the management might have an incentive during the investment period to pursue volume instead of quality. Also, the fees on committed but uninvested funds can be viewed as paying for the staffing required for due diligence during the investment period. At the end of the investment period or with the raising of subsequent funds, fees ramp down and are levied only against capital still under management. Fees are adjusted according to the proportion of the portfolio that has been divested.

When management fees are low, the fund manager may be looking for other compensation, such as that earned by sitting on the boards of directors of portfolio companies, providing advisory or management services, or advising on or structuring transactions. To counter these incentives for distraction from investment management or the double payment of the fund management services, LPAs mandate that these fees be fully or partially set off against the management fees (i.e., fees-offset clause).

6.1.4 Carried Interest

Carried interest, or carry, is the share in the fund's profits received by the fund manager. Carried interest should be directed predominantly to the professional staff responsible for the success of the fund, and vest in parallel with the expected value-creation time line. It remains largely uncontested over time that the fund manager's main incentive is performance based through the realization of carried interest. Carried interest is calculated on either a **fund-as-a-whole** or a **deal-by-deal** basis. In both cases, the carried interest is normally payable if the IRR of a fund exceeds the hurdle rate or preferred return (see section 6.1.5). In the majority of cases, previous losses and overall portfolio performance are also taken into account. It is generally accepted that a carried interest of 20% aligns manager and investor interests appropriately. Typically, limited partners favor the fund-as-a-whole over the deal-by-deal methodology for carried interest calculations, as it further aligns manager and investor interests.

In order to compare these two methods for calculating carried interest, we may consider the simplified scenario shown in Exhibit 6.2, in which limited partners contribute in the first year €100 million to fund investments A and B, at €50 million each, with an 80/20 carry split.

EXHIBIT 6.2   Illustration of Deal-by-Deal Carried Interest

Year 1, Deal-by-Deal

| | Limited Partners | | General Partner | Total |
	Investment A	Investment B		
Original contributions	−€50 million	−€50 million		−€100 million
Acquisition of investments A and B Closing balance	−€50 million	−€50 million		−€100 million

Year 2, Deal-by-Deal

| | Limited Partners | | General Partner | Total |
	Investment A	Investment B		
Opening balance	−€50 million	−€50 million	€0 million	−€100 million
Sale of investment A for €90 million Return of capital	€50 million			€50 million
80/20 split of residual amount	€32 million		€8 million	€40 million
Closing balance	€32 million	−€50 million	€8 million	−€10 million

Year 3, Deal-by-Deal

| | Limited Partners | | General Partner | Total |
	Investment A	Investment B		
Opening balance	€32 million	−€50 million	€8 million	−€10 million
Total write-off of investment B Return of capital		€0 million		€0 million
80/20 split of residual amount				
Closing balance	€32 million	−€50 million	€8 million	−€10 million
Subtotal	−€18 million		€8 million	−€10 million

Investment A is sold in the second year for €90 million. The profits of €40 million for this investment are distributed to limited and general partners in line with the agreed-on 80/20 split. In the third year, investment B fails and is written off entirely.

The fund as a whole has a loss of €10 million and gives no right to carried interest for the general partner, while under the deal-by-deal approach, the general partner would receive €8 million of carried interest and the limited partners would have a loss of €18 million.

6.1.5 Preferred Return or Hurdle Rate

The preferred return, often called the hurdle rate, has become a standard limited partnership term. The rationale for its introduction was to ensure that general partners are compensated only for outperformance (see Maxwell 2003). Therefore, limited partners have first priority to receive all distributions up to their commitment (or capital invested), plus the preferred return, before the general partner gets access to carried interest. In theory, then, the preferred return is an annual compound interest rate on the invested capital that is set well above the currently prevailing risk-free rate of return, but at or below the historical performance of public equity.

If the hurdle rate is set too low, it becomes meaningless as an incentive and just creates administrative problems. Though high hurdle rates aim to give an incentive for fund managers to outperform, they can also have the opposite effect. Managers of funds with overly high hurdle rates (or of struggling funds) can be demotivated if it becomes unlikely that they will receive carried interest. High hurdle rates may also lead to excessive risk taking.

There are also some conceptual issues with preferred returns. General partners are faced with the dilemma of whether to realize an investment over a short period of time to optimize the IRR or to hold on to it and try to optimize the multiple. For example, is it better to generate a 50% IRR for a period of three months, which yields a $1.11\times$ multiple on capital invested, or only a 10% IRR for a period of three years, leading to a $1.33\times$ multiple? The standard preferred return, being based on the IRR, gives incentive to the former. An alternative is to base the preferred return on the multiple.

Incentive fees are used to reward managers when the fund does well, but the absence of these fees alone does not provide sufficient punishment for when the manager underperforms. With this kind of structure, the more risk a manager takes, the greater the upside potential, with little immediate downside impact from losses. This is why the general partner's capital contribution is so important.

6.1.6 General Partner's Contribution

Excessive risk taking can be reduced or eliminated if managers have a significant portion of their personal wealth in the fund. The manager in this case, being directly exposed to fund losses, no longer has the incentive to take excessive risks, to work on non-fund-related activities, or to abandon ship once the prospects for generating carry and launching a follow-on fund become highly unlikely.

Typically, investors in private equity funds see 1% of the fund's committed capital as a standard and acceptable contribution for general partners to make. This contribution, also known as hurt money, should be contributed in cash rather than through the waiver of management fees (or as surplus from the management company's budget). However, in the case of wealthy managers, 1% may sometimes be too low.[5] To better understand this relationship, it makes sense to look at the

---

[5] See Meek (2004): "Those that offer to put up the standard one per cent of the fund just because that is the standard, for example, are unlikely to convince investors that they truly believe in the investments they make. . . . Adveq's André Jaeggi agreed. 'The appropriate level of contribution depends on the fund manager's circumstances. If Kleiner Perkins partners agreed to put in ten per cent of the fund, that's a very significant amount, but it might not hurt the partners as much as a one per cent contribution made by newer players. . . . The general partner has to be at risk.' Or, in the words of another investor: 'I'm not interested in what the percentage is. I'm interested in how much it hurts the manager to lose the contribution.'"

general and limited partners' relative exposure. Typically, the general partner's contribution to the fund is a significant share of his or her personal wealth, whereas the limited partners' investment, although in absolute terms far higher, represents an immaterial share of the institution's overall assets. It is a challenge to determine the appropriate contribution level for the general partner that provides a reasonable incentive but is not excessively onerous. An analysis of profits earned from past investments, salaries, budget surpluses, and so forth may provide useful information for determining a contribution level that is appropriate for a particular general partner.

6.1.7 Key-Person Provision

While traditional management firms depend on key personnel, the key-person provision is more common and pertinent to private equity, where the judgment and trust of key persons is critical. Depending on the size, experience, and depth of the team, the inability of one or several of the key persons to carry out their duties could have a substantial adverse effect on the partnership.

If one or several of the named key persons depart the team, stop committing sufficient time to the management of the fund, or sell their interests in the management company, the **key-person provision** allows limited partners to suspend investment/divestment activities until a replacement or replacements are found. The limited partners can even terminate the fund if they so choose. Key-person clauses may also be put in place in anticipation of the retirement of senior fund managers.

6.1.8 Termination and Divorce

LPAs may foresee a for-cause removal of the general partner and include a **bad-leaver clause**. If exercised, normally following a simple majority vote of the LPs, investments are suspended until a new fund manager is elected or, in the extreme, the fund is liquidated. In practical terms, conditions leading to a for-cause removal are difficult to define and determine. In private equity, very little can be legally enforced; issues are highly subjective, and taking matters to court carries high legal risk for an investor, as it is very difficult and lengthy to prove wrongdoing.

The **good-leaver** termination clause enables investors to cease funding the partnership with a vote requiring a **qualified majority**, generally more than 75% of the limited partners. This without-cause clause provides a clear framework for shutting down a partnership that is not working, or when confidence is lost. The good-leaver clause sometimes provides for compensation amounting to six months to one year of management fees; the bad-leaver clause provides no such compensation. Normally, the bad-leaver clause foresees no entitlement to carried interest. This contrasts with the good-leaver clause but includes a vesting schedule, so that part of the carry remains available to incentivize the new team being hired.

In deciding whether to exercise one of these clauses, reputation considerations play a key role, as the market consists of a small number of players who repeatedly interact with one another. General partners who are removed with or without cause may subsequently be unable to raise funds or participate in investment syndicates

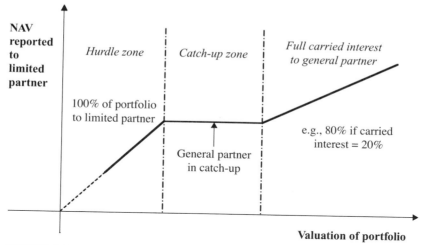

EXHIBIT 6.3   Impact of Catch-Up on NAV Attributed to Limited Partner

with other partnerships. To avoid such disastrous outcomes, general partners tend to agree on a fund restructuring to prevent a forced removal.

6.1.9   Distribution Waterfall

Exits realized by the fund are distributed according to a distribution waterfall. As per the EVCA glossary, exit is the "[l]iquidation of holdings by a private equity fund. Among the various methods of exiting an investment are: trade sale; sale by public offering (including IPO); write-offs; repayment of preference shares/loans; sale to another venture capitalist; sale to a financial institution." Normally, the limited partners are first returned all the capital invested plus fees and expenses (i.e., all drawn capital), or sometimes the total commitment (both drawn and undrawn capital). They then receive the **preferred return** on the investment (i.e., the hurdle zone), normally compounded per annum. (See Exhibit 6.3.) This is followed by the **catch-up period**, during which the general partner receives all or the major share of the distributions. The catch-up period ends when the agreed-upon **carried-interest split**, or stated share of the fund's profits to be received by the general partner and the limited partners, is reached. Thereafter, distributions are shared between fund managers and investors in the proportion agreed to in the legal documentation, normally 20% for the general partners and 80% for the limited partners. This mechanism is also not standardized (e.g., whether an interest rate such as a hurdle rate is compounded on a quarterly or on an annual basis). Sometimes there is a full catch-up, while other agreements may foresee only a partial catch-up or no catch-up at all. With a 100% catch-up, the limited partners are effectively excluded from all new distributions until the general partner has fully recovered his or her agreed-upon share of the profit.

To put it in more mathematical terms, the function that maps the gross NAV onto the net NAV is not information preserving. In situations in which there is

EXHIBIT 6.4   Example of Waterfall Using a Hurdle Rate

	Limited Partners	General Partner	Total
Original contributions	−€100 million		−€100 million
Sale of investment for €200 million			
Return of capital	€100 million		€100 million
Preferred return for limited partners	€8 million		€8 million
Catch-up for general partner		€ 2 million	€2 million
80/20 split of residual amount	€72 million	€18 million	€90 million
Closing balance	€80 million	€20 million	€100 million

a 100% catch-up, several different gross NAV values, representing the underlying portfolio's value, will be mapped to the same net NAV due to the fund's limited partners.

As a simplified example of the basic waterfall, we assume a €100 million contribution by the limited partners in the first year to fund an investment, an 8% hurdle rate, a 100% catch-up, an 80/20 carry split, and the sale of the investment by the fund in the second year for €200 million. In this case, the sales proceeds are distributed as shown in Exhibit 6.4.

Note that simply splitting the profit of €100 million (the difference of €200 million in sales proceeds minus the €100 million purchase price) on an 80/20 basis would have given the same result. The reason for this is that the fund's return is above the catch-up zone, and therefore the hurdle is extinguished and does not make any difference.

The simplest and, from the viewpoint of the limited partner, most desirable solution is that general partners do not take carried interest until all invested, or sometimes even all committed, capital has been repaid to investors. In this scenario, however, the several years it could take for the fund's team to see any gains could lead to demotivation. An accepted compromise is that general partners take lower percentages of early distributions until contributed capital is returned, either distributing the excess to limited partners directly or putting it into an escrow account. Investors often require that fund managers escrow 20% to 30% of their carried interest proceeds as a buffer against potential clawback liability.

A **clawback** is a liability triggered when, at the end of a fund's life, the limited partners have received less than the sum of contributed capital and a certain amount of the fund's profits. Clawback is relevant in such situations as when early investments do well and repay more than the invested capital plus the preferred return, but later investments fail. A clawback ensures that the managers will not receive a greater share of the fund's distributions than they are entitled to. Responsibility for payment of the clawback rests with the persons or entity that received the carried interest distributions. In such a case, the general partner is required to return some proceeds to make the investor whole.[6]

---

[6] Associated with this is joint and several liability: If a manager leaves the fund, and the fund ends up with a liability, this clause makes the remaining team members responsible for the departed person's share of the liability.

But clawback can also exist for limited partners. In this case, it is triggered when, at the end of a fund's life, the general partners have received less than their share of the fund's profits. Such clawback is relevant in situations in which a portion of the committed capital has not been drawn, and limited partners have received full repayment of their commitment plus hurdle before the general partner has access to his or her carry.

6.2 CONFLICTS OF INTEREST

Consulting activities, previous funds, new fundraising activities, chairmanships, or personal participation in individual portfolio companies provide fertile breeding ground for conflicts of interest. Walter (2003) differentiates between two types of conflicts of interest. Type 1 conflicts of interest, "between a firm's own economic interests and the interests of its own clients, usually reflected in the extraction of rents or mispriced transfer of risk," are usually addressed or mitigated through an alignment of interests. Type 2 conflicts of interest, "between a firm's clients, or between types of clients, which place the firm in a position of favoring one at the expense of another," are more problematic, as fund managers may have multiple relationships with various clients.

Conflicts of interest need to be minimized to focus the fund manager's attention on the fund. Even if such outside activities are not directed against the limited partners, investors want to ensure that the management team is completely dedicated and that the day-to-day management of the fund is not left to less experienced team members. There are also inherent conflict-of-interest issues in so-called captive, or sponsored, funds linked to a single institution, such as a bank or a financial consulting group. Here the independence of the management team is a prerequisite for securing investment commitments.

In conducting due diligence, the objectivity and expertise of a partnership's management need to be scrutinized. Even if the current fund is structured to align interests and to avoid conflicts with previous or parallel funds, if market conditions are changing or more interesting opportunities emerge, the manager may get distracted.

While investors attempt to reduce such potential for conflicts by crafting appropriate LPAs, the interests of fund managers may diverge from those of limited partners, even with the most carefully considered deal structures. Consequently, continuous monitoring[7] is needed to identify the emergence of diverging interests in time to prevent problems.

6.3 FINDING THE BALANCE

The LPA sets the economic incentives and penalties that make the agent (i.e., the fund manager) perform in line with the interests of the principals (i.e., the investors). Fund managers as individuals should do well if the funds they manage perform well, and much less well when the funds underperform. They must establish a favorable track record to raise new partnerships.

With poor performance, they will be put out of business. There is a series of trade-offs, and it becomes clear that, for a limited partner, a perfect fund structure

---

[7] See Chapter 14 for a more detailed discussion on monitoring.

EXHIBIT 6.5   Net Return to Limited Partners as a Function of Management Fees and
Carried Interest—Net IRR (assuming 3× gross multiple; 100% invested)

		Carried Interest		
		20.0%	25.0%	30.0%
Management fee	2.0%	21.5%	20.8%	20.0%
	2.5%	20.4%	19.6%	18.7%

Note: These calculations are based on the break-even analysis described in Mathonet and
Meyer (2007), which is based on the Yale model (see Takahashi and Alexander [2002]).
Standard-fund cash flow patterns as well as terms have been used. The gross IRR is the
measure of the total performance of a fund's investments (both realized and unrealized), and
the net IRR is the same measure but considers the cost of the fund structure (mainly the effect
of carried interest and management fees).
Source: Flag Venture Management (2003).

does not exist. Sophisticated investors recognize the importance of ensuring that
fund managers receive the correct incentives to outperform. They are not looking for
cheap private equity. Instead, they are looking for an appropriate and fair balance—
a legitimate alignment of interests achieved through terms that are suitable to fund
type, size, and investment style.

The alignment of interests also requires compromises between the parties, as
general and limited partners are in a kind of prisoners' dilemma. Even if limited
partners could somehow negotiate highly favorable terms in a difficult fund-raising
environment, those terms would not guarantee the fund manager's continued attention to the fund for its lifetime. For example, if economic conditions change, fund
managers have a strong incentive to quickly raise another fund with more favorable
conditions, potentially from another group of investors, and may no longer focus
their attention on the original fund. On the other hand, if general partners can base
management fees on contractual conditions, they are often quite accommodating, in
order to maintain their relationship with their investors for follow-on funds.

The magnitude of any fee changes also has to be taken into account. Flag Venture
Management (2003) refers to an analysis showing that a 50-basis-point reduction
in management fees can boost net returns to limited partners by 100 basis points
or more (see Exhibit 6.5). Surprisingly, this exceeds the impact investors would
realize from a reduction in the carried interest from 25% to 20%. We can conclude
that achieving the appropriate fee structure is challenging and requires a continuous
balancing process that takes into account the level of capital commitments to a fund,
the value of the fund's assets, and the carried interest, as well as other fund terms
and conditions.

CHAPTER 7

The Investment Process

In general, the investment process consists of a number of steps that result in an initial investment strategy and portfolio allocation. There are challenges at all steps of the private equity (PE) investment process, and no process is ideal or optimal in all cases. The most appropriate investment process for a given manager depends on that manager's objectives and tolerance for risk. This means that trade-offs are inevitable. The idiosyncrasies of private equity (its long-term nature, its illiquidity, and the peculiarity of its risks) mean that a balance must be found between the various components of the process, illustrated in Exhibit 7.1.

7.1 PROCESS DESCRIPTION

The main decisions to address in the investment process include strategic asset allocation, fund selection, level of diversification, and liquidity management. The challenge of managing an investment program requires an appropriate balance between an efficient selection that drives return and an effective allocation of capital and investment that drives exposure. Being highly selective and investing only a restricted share of the total amount earmarked for private equity in a few top-quality funds would maximize the expected returns but ignore the impact of undrawn commitments. Being highly diversified smooths the cash flows and allows for a nearly full investment of the capital allocated to private equity, thereby lowering risk and enhancing total return but at the expense of potentially eliminating extreme positive returns.

For private equity, the three key performance drivers are portfolio design (see Chapter 8), management of liquidity (see Chapter 14), and fund manager selection (see Chapter 9).

Because of the idiosyncrasies of private equity, it can be difficult to quantify the risks involved. Due to the opaque nature of the industry, not all outcomes are known, information is difficult to assemble, and the quality of data is generally very poor. This is most notable in the case of technology-focused venture capital (VC) funds, which face rapid industry advances, newly evolving business models, short boom-to-bust periods, and long investment periods, making it very difficult, if not impossible, to systematically collect data with any statistical merit.

That said, there is a significant number of assessable or even measurable factors in private equity, more than are typically perceived, that can be used in place of

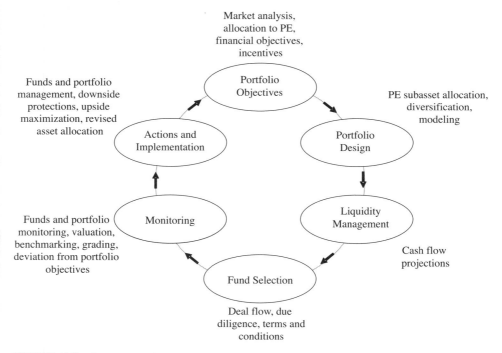

Market analysis, allocation to PE, financial objectives, incentives

Portfolio Objectives

Funds and portfolio management, downside protections, upside maximization, revised asset allocation

Actions and Implementation

PE subasset allocation, diversification, modeling

Portfolio Design

Liquidity Management

Monitoring

Cash flow projections

Funds and portfolio monitoring, valuation, benchmarking, grading, deviation from portfolio objectives

Fund Selection

Deal flow, due diligence, terms and conditions

EXHIBIT 7.1 Investment Process

quantitative risk measures. A clearer differentiation between risk and uncertainty[1] can be a useful tool for the management of a private equity investment program. Although a precise quantification is nearly impossible, except in very specific situations, experts can associate experiences and opinions on various dimensions with categories for return expectations. They can also put lessons learned into a new or changed context and extrapolate from their experience. For these categories, an approximate quantification can be estimated and used to manage the uncertainty-return trade-off. For example, experts might grade funds (see Chapter 9) subjectively with regard to risk and return, and then use the grades to select an appropriate aggregate risk level.

7.1.1 Portfolio Objectives

The starting point of any investment process is the definition of the portfolio objectives. These objectives should be set, or at least agreed on, by the investor (or

---

[1] Economists typically differentiate between risk and uncertainty. Risk exists when a probability based on experience can be attached to an event, whereas uncertainty exists when there is no objective way to determine the probability. In efficient markets, there is little differentiation between risk and uncertainty, as uncertainty is practically the same for all participants. In private markets, however, investors are exposed to different degrees of uncertainty.

authorizing entity). Identifying trends in the market and the amount of capital that can be profitably invested is crucial for establishing the investment strategy and setting targets. Construction of the portfolio requires the identification of attractive sectors and investment strategies. It is important that investment program managers receive the proper incentives to align their interests with those of the authorizing entity. The result of this analysis is a formalization of portfolio objectives that should ideally include the level of allocation to private equity; the targeted private equity markets; the financial objectives (e.g., desired risk-return profile) and nonfinancial objectives (e.g., for a public institution, support to emerging managers); and the high-level strategy to achieve them (e.g., core-satellite, diversification, or co-investments; see Chapter 8).

Modern portfolio theory (MPT) provides the theoretical basis for investors' acceptance of alternative assets. According to this theory, adding noncorrelated assets to a portfolio can improve the portfolio's risk and return characteristics. The common argument is that by adding private equity to a portfolio of publicly quoted stocks and bonds, one can move the portfolio closer to the efficient frontier, which improves the risk-return trade-off.[2] Using this approach, practitioners rely on adjusted historical risk, return, and correlation figures as reasonable approximations of the future when incorporating private equity investments into their portfolio models.[3]

According to Steers (2002), it is almost impossible to use standard risk-return optimization models to determine the appropriate allocation to private equity, because it is difficult to estimate the correct risk premium and correlation with other asset classes. Additionally, the standard internal rate of return (IRR) performance measure used for private equity funds is time weighted and capital weighted, whereas for public market assets it is traditionally time weighted (for more on IRR in private equity investments, see Chapter 10). This means that an analysis of the correlations between private equity and other asset classes is not possible without making significant adjustments, such as computing private equity returns under an assumption that intervening cash flows are invested in public market indices. The challenges to using modern portfolio theory for PE assets are numerous, and are further explained under the portfolio design section.

Public and private equity returns may be more closely correlated than is commonly believed. The biases and the infrequent revaluations common to private equity result in an artificial dampening of both volatility and correlation analysis relative to public equities. Indeed, the uncertainty and imprecision of valuation of private equity (see Chapter 12) masks the natural correlation between public and private equity, and blurs the inherent risks. According to the *Economist* (2004), "to say that private equity is less volatile and thus less risky is a bit like saying that the weather does not change much when you stay inside and rarely look out of the window." Barber and Zage (2002) argue that there are more similarities between public and private equities than there are differences, and certainly more similarities than many private equity practitioners acknowledge. "[Regardless of]

---

[2] See, for example, Fort Washington Capital Partners (2004).
[3] See Simons (2000), Artus and Teïletche (2004), and Kaserer and Diller (2004).

whether buyouts or VC, poor private equity practice is likely to produce higher correlations with the public markets, since it involves 'surfing the wave' rather than creating value." The idea is that high-quality private equity investing practices may achieve alpha (i.e., not correlated with market performance), while poor practices may have high systematic risk because returns are dominated by public equity market trends.

At the end of the day, private companies operate in the same economic environment as public companies. They face the same trading conditions, interest rates, and regulatory regimes. Furthermore, exiting PE portfolio companies are generally dependent on public markets to provide valuation reference points and needed liquidity through sales of shares to other companies (strategic buyers) or initial public offerings (IPOs). Therefore, at least some degree of correlation between public and private equity returns is to be expected.

Therefore, some institutions apply a **naïve allocation** by committing equal amounts to different funds and capping their private equity exposure at around 5% to 10%, although some foundations have as much as 30% allocated to private equity. This naïve allocation can be estimated based on the analysis of the following basic dimensions:

- If the allocation is not large enough, the returns will not allow for the establishment of a dedicated team, which is a required condition if one expects to achieve above-average performance. Conversely, if the allocation is too large, it may not be possible to find sufficient investment opportunities, or it may drive performance down if lower-quality funds need to be selected.
- If the allocation is not large enough versus the overall portfolio, it will have an insignificant impact on the overall portfolio performance. If the allocation is too large compared to the overall portfolio, the investor risks being underdiversified and overexposed to risk specific to private equity, such as illiquidity.
- The benefit of adding private equity has to be analyzed in the context of the existing portfolio. The goal is to determine the various risk dimensions that investors would like to diversify (e.g., industry sector, country, or company size) and to assess the impact of the private equity allocation on these dimensions within the overall existing portfolio. For example, a high-tech early-stage allocation will have a more important diversification impact on a portfolio invested mostly in the old economy.
- The institution's liquidity needs should also be part of the analysis. The constraint essentially depends on the institution's regular liquidity needs to support its ongoing business. An investor with high regular liquidity needs and no excess capital is in no position to launch a private equity program. The lower the ongoing liquidity needs and the higher the excess capital, the more funds the investor can allocate to private equity. In general, the more mature a private equity program, the more liquidity it is likely to be generating, again increasing the funds available for allocation to private equity.
- Finally, if in doubt, it is always worth tracking other institutions' allocations as a gauge for how attractive they perceive private equity to be compared to other asset classes.

7.1.2 Portfolio Design

The objective of the preceding analysis is to determine the appropriate allocations to the various private equity market segments[4] and to estimate the optimal level of diversification. Some practitioners believe that asset and subasset allocations are key investment policy decisions and that private equity portfolios should be managed more like public equity portfolios, drawing on many of the same tools and accepted principles while adjusting for market specificities. The MPT suggests that underdiversified portfolios have a higher risk without adequate compensation in expected returns. However, as explained previously, there are challenges in applying the MPT to private equity.

The MPT employs rigorous mathematical techniques for designing portfolios. For the model to work, one must be able to quantify each asset's expected return and risk as well as the correlations of the return of each asset relative to the return of all other assets in the portfolio. While public market managers have reliable statistical data to support their analysis, private equity and, in particular, VC managers lack such data. Indeed, the analysis of private equity returns, volatility, and correlations is limited by the relatively short time series of publicly available data. Those data are not fully representative of the market and are often biased by the survivorship issue.[5]

Most of all, data do not fully capture the uncertainty inherent in innovation-driven asset classes such as VC, since relevant past data would rarely be available on investments that emphasize new concepts. Moreover, the MPT assumes a normal return distribution, which clearly does not hold for private equity. In fact, the distribution of private equity returns departs significantly from the normal distribution. Empirical results on private equity indicate large standard deviations of period returns, as well as significant skewness and excess kurtosis.[6] As a result, it is questionable whether private equity can be integrated into the MPT framework or what modifications would make it permissible to do so.

A more detailed description of the portfolio design is provided in Chapter 8.

7.1.3 Liquidity Management

Liquidity management is one of the key performance drivers in private equity. (See Chapter 14 for a description of the various approaches used by practitioners.) It can be a difficult task to put money efficiently to work while maintaining a balance in the portfolio composition and preserving the quality of the individual fund investments.

Just looking at the capital invested in portfolio companies does not give the full picture of a fund's performance. Investors are rightly concerned with the total return

---

[4] The classification of the various private equity market segments should be driven by their different risk profiles (see Chapter 10). The classical ones are identified by their stage focus (venture capital vs. buyout) and geography (United States, European Union, and Asia), but more refined classifications are also used, including the less developed but often important for portfolio design emerging niche markets.

[5] Survivorship bias is the tendency for failed companies to be eliminated from performance studies after the companies have ceased operations.

[6] See Mathonet and Meyer (2007).

on all resources dedicated to private equity, which should include undrawn capital (or at least the additional liquidities needed for the program). If a large part of the capital remains uninvested or parked in low-returning assets such as Treasury bills, the resulting drag on total return can be significant. To keep a program permanently and fully invested in portfolio companies, the so-called overcommitment strategy may need to be employed, whereby more commitments are signed than can be met with existing capital resources (see Chapter 14).

Funds of funds may certainly lose investors if they fail to deliver sufficiently attractive returns, but they can also go bust, and some have already experienced significant problems in this area because they have not mastered the management of liquidity required to run such overcommitment strategies (see section on over-commitment in Chapter 14). There is anecdotal evidence that funds of funds have been struggling with this issue, and that overcommitment strategies have not worked out.[7] The high degree of uncertainty regarding the timing of cash flows renders fund investing and liquidity management exceptionally challenging.

7.1.4 Fund Selection

Gaining access to top-quartile performers is critical to the fund selection process. In recent decades, top-quartile PE funds have achieved returns that were significantly higher than those of average funds (see Exhibit 8.1 in the next chapter). This fund-selection skill is often considered the core competence of private equity specialists and is seen as a key performance driver for generating attractive returns for a port-folio of funds, which helps explain why private equity investing is predominantly characterized as an alpha-seeking exercise. A more detailed description of the fund manager selection process is provided in Chapter 9.

7.1.5 Monitoring

Limited partners should monitor the composition of their portfolios, identify trends within the private equity markets, and evaluate the economic environment on an ongoing basis. For a limited partner, monitoring should include the specific fund investments as well as the overall composition of the relationships managed. Only through ongoing monitoring can a limited partner make informed, proactive port-folio decisions.

Analyzing concentration across all partnerships in the portfolio (e.g., by indus-try, stage, geography, vintage years, and cross-holdings between funds) can provide valuable insights. Stress tests can provide early-warning signals and increase the transparency of the portfolio. Tracking overall commitment level, contributions and distributions, return on investment to date, or expected final return on investment is also important for portfolio management. Identifying overexposures may lead to a review or an adjustment of investment objectives and, where severe imbalances exist, may require active management to mitigate such overexposures.

---

[7] See Mathonet and Meyer (2007), Chapter 4, for a detailed description and analysis of a real-life example.

At the individual fund level, compliance with contractual terms and investment style needs to be tracked. Fund monitoring is based on regular meetings with all parties involved and should include the following:

- Tracking planned versus implemented strategy
- Reviewing the fund's financial investment, valuation, and divestment information
- Analyzing the impact of relevant market trends
- Assessing the risk of both individual investments and the overall portfolio
- Measuring/benchmarking performance (see Chapter 10)
- Verifying legal and tax compliance

Monitoring may also be relevant for liquidity planning (see Chapter 14). A more detailed description of the monitoring process is provided in Chapter 11.

7.1.6 Actions and Implementation

The last step in the investment process is the implementation of portfolio management decisions. These decisions can be taken at three levels: individual fund, portfolio composition, and portfolio objective, which in turn can affect the rest of the investment process.

Active management is constrained because private equity assets are long-term and illiquid, and offer only limited (in quality and over time) opportunities to increase investment or to sell. Co-investing, secondary and primary transactions, securitization, and restructuring of funds are the common means of actively managing the portfolio. The main purpose of fund restructuring is to stop value destruction rather than to create new opportunities. In practice, these tools can be applied only sparingly, as rebalancing the portfolio through buy and sell transactions can be very expensive and opportunities relatively scarce.

7.2 RISK MANAGEMENT

The approach to risk management for a portfolio of private equity funds rests on the pillars of measurement, control, and mitigation.

7.2.1 Risk-Measurement Framework

When discussing the risk and return expectations of any investment, the starting point is a proper valuation of the asset. There is a difference between an accounting-rules-based valuation approach and a market-based concept of the economic or financial value of a fund. Modeling the economic reality as closely as possible is key to efficient management. Typically, fund values are estimated by first valuing every portfolio company individually, then aggregating these valuations to a portfolio value, and finally calculating the investor's respective share in the fund. In Chapter 12, we explain why this approach often does not reflect the economic reality.

In line with financial theories and secondary market practices, private equity funds should be valued through a discounted cash flow approach. Such an approach provides risk managers with future expected cash flow (see Chapter 14) and discount-rate estimates (see Chapter 13).

7.2.2 Risk Control

There is no definitive risk-adjusted pricing available for primary private equity fund investing. An efficient risk-adjusted price setting (comparable to high-yield bonds, for which, at least in theory, the greater the risk, the higher the interest rate)[8] does not exist. All primary positions are bought at par (i.e., without premium or discount), and there is no predefined coupon payment but only a predefined cost structure and uncertain performance. While fund structure and management fees may vary among individual funds, the variations are insufficient to represent differences in risk and are not intended to do so. For such a blind-pool investment, the uncertainty does not allow a full risk adjustment in the pricing of the fund. Rather, this is accomplished more through an industry-wide adjustment of terms driven by currently prevailing market conditions than through a differentiated pricing mechanism.

The lack of data, the blind-pool nature of the investments, and the fact that virtually all investments are highly risky all make differentiation and quantification of risks in private equity difficult. The private equity fund market is unable to differentiate precisely between the amount of risk found in different industries or geographical sectors, and can offer only broad comparisons to main risk profiles such as buyout versus VC funds. Within the institutional private equity asset class, traditional quantitative measures like beta cannot distinguish reliably between differences in risk, and therefore investors must defer to their own judgment.

Within the private equity universe, we can mostly use nonquantitative approaches to risk control by constraining managers to invest only in assets of equivalent risk. Since risk differentials are challenging to measure, it is neither possible nor meaningful to try to select funds based on risk-control issues so long as the investments are restricted to institutional-quality private equity funds. Therefore, being highly selective is the typical approach to fund selection. How the cutoff is set depends on the accessible universe of funds and portfolio objectives.

7.2.3 Risk Mitigation

In principle, one mitigates risks by choosing to avoid, support, control, or transfer them. Private equity investors hope to minimize risk by rigorously weeding out inferior proposals and by negotiating special contract provisions with the general partners of the funds chosen for investment.

Clearly, risk taking cannot be avoided entirely and should not be, as PE is by nature a high-risk asset class. One reason is that the supply of institutional-quality teams is insufficient to meet industry demand, and the number of top funds with a verifiable track record is lower than the number that eventually perform in the top quartile. In addition, an index-tracking passive-investment approach is not available and may not be possible in such an illiquid market.

---

[8] For secondary transactions, however, premiums or discounts are applied. Here, even for low-quality investments, profits can be made.

Many risks in private equity need to be evaluated, accepted, monitored, and perhaps even controlled. A possible adverse impact can be mitigated through diversification or controlled through monitoring. On a portfolio of funds level, a risk-transfer mechanism, such as an overdraft facility,[9] can be used to manage liquidity risk. Securitization, which is the process of pooling various types of assets that are then sold to investors, is another risk-transfer mechanism. However, this financial engineering technique is generally applicable only on a portfolio of funds level. For the private equity investments themselves, risk transfer is difficult to implement. On the individual portfolio company level, there are occasionally guarantees, such as those provided by the Société Française de Garantie des Financements des PME in France, or the scheme run by the German bank TBG (since abandoned). Generally, risks cannot be quantified to a degree that allows for the application of sophisticated risk-transfer tools used elsewhere in the financial industry. Some degree of risk sharing can be achieved through relationships with co-investing limited partners. With their financial strength, they can step in when other investors are defaulting. Co-investing limited partners can help address operational issues, which may even lead to reduced expenses through sharing of monitoring efforts. These limited partners impose market discipline and can assist in facilitating continuity, as follow-on funds with the same managers can be closed more quickly.

---

[9] A credit facility provided by a lending institution to allow, within certain limits and fee arrangements, withdrawals in excess of deposits.

CHAPTER 8

Private Equity Portfolio Design

The design of a private equity (PE) portfolio can begin once an investor (typically an institutional investor) has decided what portion of his or her total portfolio of assets will be allocated to this alternative asset class and what objectives are set for this allocation. Given the illiquidity of private equity, investors strive to earn returns higher than those of public equity markets. Investors also desire to invest in funds with above-average returns, because an important part of the perceived risk of private equity is that of investing in a fund that underperforms both the private equity and the public equity benchmarks.

8.1 THREE APPROACHES TO PRIVATE EQUITY PORTFOLIO DESIGN

Private equity portfolio design is usually described as either bottom-up or top-down. The **bottom-up approach** is based on fund manager research, in which the emphasis is on screening all investment opportunities in the targeted PE markets and picking the perceived best fund managers. A **top-down approach** analyzes the macroeconomic conditions surrounding the targeted PE markets and then determines the strategic asset allocation (i.e., the combination of industry sectors, countries, fund styles, and so on, that are best for meeting the PE program objectives under the likely scenarios).

While appearing to be in opposition, the bottom-up and top-down approaches are complementary and are typically used in tandem. This method, called the **mixed approach,** either starts with a bottom-up strategy, to which increasing top-down optimization is added, or starts as an iterative short process cycle, in which bottom-up screenings are followed by top-down analysis and then by bottom-up screenings. Finally, investors who claim to have a top-down, a bottom-up, or a mixed approach all stress the importance of taking a proactive approach to fund selection (see Chapter 9). Investors cannot just wait for investment opportunities to arrive but must proactively search for the funds that fit their investment strategy and start making contacts with these funds before they go to the market to raise capital. This requires a constant monitoring of the markets.

8.1.1 Bottom-Up Approach

As private equity is characterized by a high differential between top-quartile and lower-quartile fund performance (see Exhibit 8.1), investing in the asset class requires

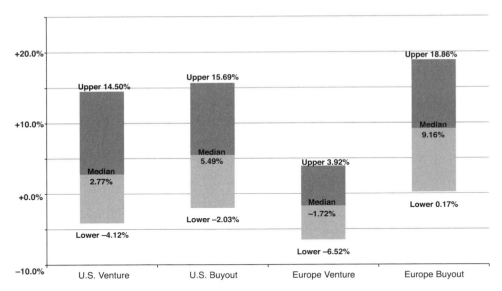

EXHIBIT 8.1 Top-Quartile versus Average Private Equity Performance
Source: Thomson ONE, fund performance (cumulative returns) since inception, all mature funds (older than five years), data as of June 2011.

good manager-selection skills. Therefore, investors generally follow a bottom-up approach, as it is widely believed that the quality of the fund management team is the most essential criterion, much more significant than such factors as sector or geographical diversification. The starting point of a bottom-up approach, also called the screening technique (see Exhibit 8.2), is the identification of suitable investments, or those perceived to be the best. This is followed by intensive analysis and due diligence in order to rank the funds by their attractiveness and identify which managers are the likely top performers. The investor conducts the due diligence necessary to select the manager, then negotiates the structuring of the limited partnership agreements as well as the inclusion of covenants regarding the postcommitment monitoring, leading to the final fund-investment decision.

The bottom-up approach has several compelling features. As it depends solely on ranking, this approach is simple, easy to understand, and robust. It enhances the expected performance by concentrating the portfolio in the highest-alpha funds (i.e., funds with the highest expected performance uncorrelated with the market), while controlling for risk by diversifying across multiple funds.

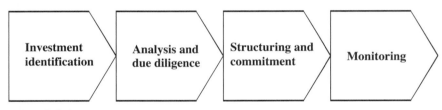

EXHIBIT 8.2 Bottom-Up Approach

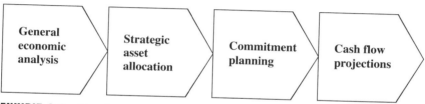

EXHIBIT 8.3 Top-Down Approach

However, the bottom-up approach is not without problems. As it is very opportunistic, it can lead to an unbalanced portfolio (e.g., a portfolio excessively concentrated in a specific sector), carrying considerably more risk than intended, or miss some important macroeconomic changes or opportunities (e.g., aging population or renewable energy).

8.1.2 Top-Down Approach

The top-down approach (see Exhibit 8.3) takes the big picture as its starting point as opposed to individual fund selection. Investors who follow a top-down approach place more emphasis on the management of the strategy, the asset allocation, and the diversification of the portfolio.

The top-down approach is a process that analyzes the macroeconomic conditions surrounding the targeted PE markets and attempts to determine the strategic asset allocation (i.e., the combination of industry sectors, countries, and fund styles that are expected to be the most likely to meet the PE program objectives under the likely scenarios). The main criteria used in the evaluation process are political, economic, and currency risks. Other criteria examined include, for example, the extent to which each particular market has accepted private equity as a form of financing and investment, and the degree to which the environment is conducive to entrepreneurial activity. In this context, the investor takes into account various factors influencing the ability to invest, such as due diligence standards, accounting and tax issues, and the enforceability of legal rights (this last issue is particularly relevant in the case of many emerging markets). Finally, the availability of both attractive investment opportunities and exit opportunities for investments is considered. In the broadest sense, the decision to allocate commitments to vintage years could also be considered part of a top-down approach. After establishing the strategic asset allocation, the investor determines what resources will need to be committed to the fund. This commitment planning depends on the investor's desired exposure level, risk tolerance, and the available resources for investing. The final commitment strategy is determined based on cash flow projections and stress testing, as well as choosing funds that best fit the desired allocation.

There are also investors who aim to imitate the top-down approach adopted with public equity, whereby past performance of the assets in terms of risk, return, and correlation measures is used. These investors ultimately hope to exploit perceived low levels of correlation in different private equity markets. While such an approach certainly has its merits, there are practical problems associated with it, mainly in terms of the limited availability and quality of financial data for private equity. As data become reliable for fully liquidated funds only close to realization, any quantitative approach based on historical data reflects an outdated economic environment and will be even less indicative of the future. Even without being overly rigid or quantitative, a top-down approach can be used to generate alpha (by trying to spot the next big thing in private equity) or provide a sanity check that helps avoid fads. Based on prescreening criteria derived from this high-level allocation, investors can limit the time they spend on analyzing individual investment proposals.

Apart from the questions associated with determining the weight of subportfolios, the major shortcoming of a top-down approach is that in reality, strict allocations are not possible. In practice, it may be difficult to find and have access to a sufficient number of superior managers to fill in each predetermined subclass allocation. Indeed, often only one or two superior managers operate in a particular sector, and they each raise capital only every three to four years. On the other side, some superior managers may operate in a market segment without any allocation, thereby missing some potential high returns. Therefore, in order to adopt a top-down approach, investors cannot just wait for investment opportunities to arise but must proactively search for them so as to have a sufficiently large number of funds available to fill in their desired allocations.

8.1.3 Mixed Approach

As both pure bottom-up and pure top-down approaches are not problem-free, most investors follow a combined, or mixed, approach (see Exhibit 8.4). Even a strong believer in the top-down approach would rarely invest in funds that are not of high quality just to fulfill a target allocation. Likewise, no fund picker would commit all her money to a single sector based solely on the opportunity to invest in outstanding teams. Investors are conscious of the importance of diversification, but instead of diversifying on the basis of the correlation among the different asset classes, they define their target allocation on the basis of the investment strategies of the funds in which they invest.

Shearburn and Griffiths (2002) follow an investment strategy that can be considered representative of many private equity funds of funds (FoFs). They invest exclusively in established private equity markets, such as the United States, the

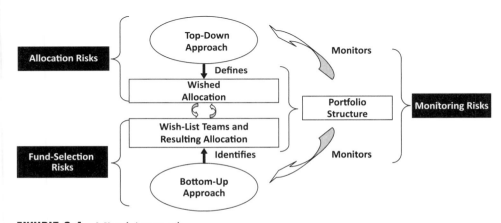

EXHIBIT 8.4   Mixed Approach

United Kingdom, and selected European economies; target the premier league of private equity funds in Europe and the United States; and diversify by stage, focus, geography, and vintage year. The goal is to create a portfolio that is diversified according to specified investment strategies or dimensions. In this portfolio, all the strategies or dimensions have equal weight. More specifically, these authors describe an approach that "consists in creating a portfolio of unique private equity strategies that are diversified from one another over multiple dimensions. These dimensions might include industry focus, investment size, geographic focus and private equity sub-asset class (such as leveraged buyouts, venture capital, growth capital and distressed investments)." They then assemble a portfolio of superior managers capable of generating extraordinary returns, with each manager's strategy being as distinct as possible from all the other strategies in the portfolio. Investors using this approach weight each strategy equally in the portfolio in order to minimize the concentration of funds. This means, for example, investing the same amount in a London-based large buyout private equity manager as in a Silicon Valley–based early-stage venture capitalist. This manager-driven, equally weighted approach to portfolio construction also drives the weighting of private equity subsectors, even in situations in which an investor may have a strong point of view.

Finally, there is an evolution in the adoption of the different approaches. For the early stages of an investment program, one of the main objectives is to put capital quickly to work in the best available teams in order to minimize idle liquidity. Young programs cannot count on an established relationship, so the available universe of investment opportunities is restricted to a limited number of accessible wish-list funds. This makes a top-down approach difficult to implement, as allocation targets would make little sense. Once a sizable portfolio has been built, however, a top-down approach becomes a more appropriate means of identifying concentration (e.g., in sectors or in teams).

8.2 RISK-RETURN MANAGEMENT APPROACHES

The goal of portfolio design is to combine assets that behave in fundamentally different fashions to optimize the risk-return relationship. Because many of the traditional analytical approaches are not fully relevant to private equity, additional techniques are required. For example, by dividing the portfolio into two or more subportfolios, the management of the risk-return relationship can be improved. Similarly, as discussed in section 8.2.2, understanding the benefits and limitations of diversification for portfolios invested in private equity funds can lead to improved risk-return management.

8.2.1 Core-Satellite Approach

The **core-satellite approach** is a way of allocating assets to protect and grow wealth. The portfolio is structured in various subportfolios, which can then be designed using one of the construction techniques (bottom-up, top-down, or mixed). Such an approach is based on behavioral portfolio theory, in which portfolios can be constructed as layered pyramids (see Exhibit 8.5). For example, a well-diversified core, or bottom layer, may provide downside protection for the portfolio (risk aversion),

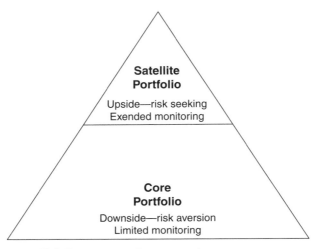

EXHIBIT 8.5   Core-Satellite Pyramid

while a less diversified satellite, or top layer, may look to generate upside gains (risk seeking).[1] This approach aims to increase risk control, reduce costs, and add value.

This may be an effective strategy for institutions that want to diversify their portfolios without giving up the potential for higher returns generated by selected active management strategies. Another advantage is the flexibility to customize a portfolio to meet specific investment objectives and preferences. The core-satellite approach also provides the framework for targeting and controlling those areas in which investors believe they are better able to control risks or are simply willing to take more risks. What constitutes core versus satellite depends on the investor's focus and expertise. Some see venture capital (VC) as satellite, while others view a balanced buyout and VC funds portfolio as core. Another benefit to this approach is that it facilitates spending more time on the satellite portfolio, which is expected to generate excess performance, and less time on the lower-risk core portfolio.

Another option is to structure the portfolio as two subportfolios:[2]

1. The core portfolio typically aims to exploit established relationships, with institutional-quality fund managers raising funds that are expected to generate a predictable base return. If there is no change in the current environment, such mainstream funds are perceived to be the safe bet. A solid core of high-quality relationships allows limited partners to stay in the game long enough to seize the golden opportunities, but exclusive reliance on the core would leave them susceptible to a long-term decline.

---

[1] See Statman (2002): "The desire to avoid poverty gives way to the desire for riches. Some investors fill the uppermost layers with the few stocks of an undiversified portfolio like private individuals buy lottery tickets. Neither lottery buying nor undiversified portfolios are consistent with mean-variance portfolio theory but both are consistent with behavioural portfolio theory."

[2] For more details, see Mathonet and Meyer (2007).

2. The satellite portfolio can be interpreted as a bet on radical changes, and aims to explore new relationships (or opportunities). Typically, allocations to funds in the satellite portfolio are comparatively small and will, for the most part, have only a limited impact on the portfolio; but, once established, they can offer a more predictable base return and form part of the core portfolio. These funds should be seen as real options, having no value if not exercised (i.e., investing larger amounts in successor funds) from time to time.

The balance between core (exploitation) and satellite (exploration) portfolios should be based on the following:

- The *time horizon* for the private equity fund's investment program. The more long-term oriented, the higher the value of the option and therefore the higher the degree of exploration that should be undertaken (i.e., bigger satellite).
- The *resources available*. With a larger reserve buffer, a higher degree of exploration is possible. The initial stages of a private equity fund's investment program are dominated by a primarily exploitation-oriented bottom-up approach to build up slack resources that enable exploration going forward.
- The *anticipated changes* (or *volatility*) of the private equity market environment. The more disruptive an expected market environment is, the more one needs to spread out one's options, whereas in a stable environment, exploration can be reduced to a minimum.

8.2.2 Diversification

Diversification is another area in which limited partners attempt to manage the risk-return relationship in private equity funds. Diversification should be increased as long as the marginal benefit of adding a new asset to a portfolio (i.e., the marginal contribution of the asset toward portfolio risk-return optimization) exceeds the marginal cost (i.e., basically the transaction costs, the time and money spent on researching the asset, and, due to the lower quality of the asset, the marginal negative contribution toward expected portfolio return). Therefore, another key question related to the portfolio design is the optimal number of positions. For private equity funds, it is difficult to determine the optimum diversification level. To answer this, a series of additional questions needs to be addressed:

- What is the investor's ability to identify and, even more importantly, access top teams?
- What trade-off is the investor searching for between risk taking and profit seeking? What is the investor's risk appetite? Arguably, fund-of-funds managers who co-invest their own personal wealth and have the fund of funds' full resources allocated to the asset class are in a different risk position than an institution that allocates an immaterial share of its assets to private equity. Additionally, the risk appetite of both investor groups may differ significantly.
- Does the investor have other noncommercial or strategic objectives, such as promoting technologies or creating employment?

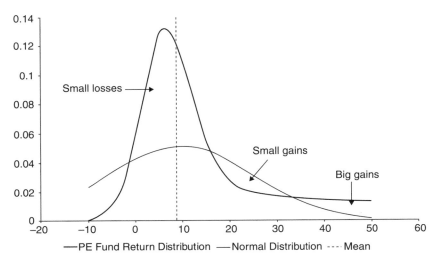

EXHIBIT 8.6 Private Equity Fund Return Distribution versus Normal Distribution

Empirical evidence shows that the distribution of private equity fund returns is quite dissimilar to the normal distribution.[3] It exhibits a relatively high probability of small losses (i.e., positive skewness) and a relatively high probability of extreme outcomes (i.e., excess kurtosis) (see Exhibit 8.6). Diversification has two impacts: It lowers risk as long as asset returns are not perfectly correlated and, due to the law of large numbers, should bring the distribution closer to normal. For private equity funds, and especially VC, the distributions of returns share characteristics with lotteries: A few extraordinary winners will compensate for many small losses. As in a lottery, in which buying all tickets guarantees picking the winner but also ensures that associated costs exceed the total gain, being invested in too many funds ensures that the few top performers cannot adequately compensate the many funds with mediocre or substandard returns. Therefore, in VC as in a lottery, a common strategy is to make few bets under the assumption that selection skills (or luck) will deliver the winners without having to support too many losers.

There is no formulaic answer to the diversification question, but research suggests that for most assets, sufficient diversification is achieved with about 20 positions in whatever one is seeking to diversify.[4] Exhibit 8.7 illustrates the situation for U.S. VC fund portfolios, but the conclusions are similar for buyout funds and in Europe:

- About 80% of the standard deviation is diversified away with a portfolio of 20 to 30 funds.

---

[3] We are more likely to encounter symmetrical return distributions where there is equilibrium between supply and demand and many market participants push prices in one or the other direction. Therefore, it is not surprising that for private equity, return distributions are asymmetric.

[4] See Flag Venture Management (2001), Weidig and Mathonet (2004), and Meyer and Mathonet (2005).

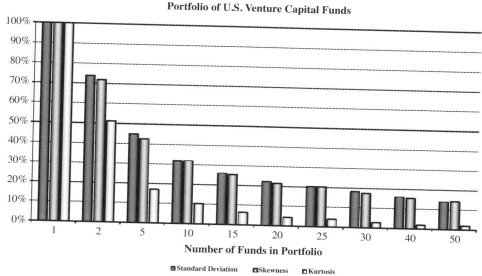

Portfolio of U.S. Venture Capital Funds

Number of Funds in Portfolio

■ Standard Deviation   ■ Skewness   □ Kurtosis

EXHIBIT 8.7   Standard Deviation, Skewness, and Kurtosis of Portfolio of Fund Returns with Increasing Diversification

- Skewness decreases more or less at the same rate as standard deviation.
- More than 80% of the kurtosis is diversified away with a portfolio of five funds.

The simulations performed in Exhibit 8.7 suggest that there is no need to have more than 20 to 30 funds in a portfolio. In fact, when investors are seeking diversification that will not eliminate the desired skewness and kurtosis, it does not make sense to have more than five funds in a portfolio.

Probably the strongest argument against a high level of diversification is the quick fading of the fund quality. There are simply too few excellent fund management teams within a vintage-year peer group. Therefore, overdiversification not only leads to a reduction in positive skewness and kurtosis but also depresses the portfolio's expected return. The fading of quality and the loss of positive skewness and kurtosis are more of an issue for VC than for buyouts. For buyouts, the distribution function looks more symmetrical, and there are usually more high-quality teams. Finally, these notions hold only for the plain-vanilla limited partnership stakes in funds. Options, like co-investment rights, can justify a higher level of diversification.

8.2.3 Naïve Diversification

Due to the poor quality of the available data, Markowitz diversification is difficult to apply to the private equity arena.[5] An alternative is naïve diversification.[6] As mentioned previously, naïve diversification is the optimal strategy when there is

---

[5] For a review of Markowitz's mean-variance theory, see Bodie, Kane, and Marcus (2008).
[6] See King and Young (1994) on an application of naïve diversification to real estate fund portfolios.

no information that allows differentiation among assets. Lhabitant and Learned (2002) further argue that modern portfolio theory is seldom applied to the full degree[7] and that **naïve diversification** (also called 1/N heuristics) in practice usually produces reasonably diversified portfolios that are somewhat surprisingly close to the efficient frontier. However, naïve diversification approaches can be refined. Brands and Gallagher (2003) found that for equity funds of funds, investment strategies that ensure equal representation across investment styles perform better than a naïve sampling approach. See also Shearburn and Griffiths (2002): "Finally, these investors choose a sufficient number of strategies to provide diversification and spread risks. Based on quantitative analysis, Goldman Sachs pursues this approach to portfolio construction, targeting 18–25 different strategies in the broad-based private equity portfolio we manage."

Albeit less rigorous than traditional portfolio models, naïve diversification is valuable to the prudent investor, as it can avoid extreme concentrations by ensuring an even distribution among the following dimensions:[8]

- Number of fund managers and stage focus
- Vintage years and calendar years
- Geography
- Industry sectors

In general, a diversification strategy that doesn't take into account the specificities of this asset class can be quite inefficient. Overdiversification may lead to capping the upside. Furthermore, investing in many teams without managing the diversification of each risk dimension, such as industry sectors and geography, can seriously damage the portfolio. Diversification sets in more slowly when funds are highly correlated. As stated previously, there are also diseconomies of scale. The number of investments, rather than the invested amounts, sets the cost base, such as legal expenses, due diligence, and monitoring effort, of a portfolio of funds. It also becomes increasingly difficult to identify and gain access to suitable funds, as the number of quality opportunities is limited. Consequently, for private equity fund portfolios, diversification may be of reduced use for the management of risk versus return.

---

[7] See Lhabitant and Learned (2002): "Very few investors effectively take correlations (that is, the non-linearity of risk) into account when making complex portfolio decisions. Rather, they prefer to allocate assets using simpler rules, such as dividing allocations evenly among the assets available.... Many respondents even admitted to having no asset-allocation strategy at all!"

[8] Standard & Poor's conducts ratings for structured notes backed by a portfolio of private equity funds. The basis of the rating is the analysis of a portfolio of private equity funds' diversification level in a multidimensional fashion. The following dimensions signal how diversified a portfolio is: number of fund managers or general partners and number of funds or limited partnerships, vintage years and calendar years, type of private equity funds or strategies, industry or sector, geography, and single investment exposure. In the opinion of Standard & Poor's, it's mainly portfolio diversification that provides downside protection to holders of the rated notes (Erturk, Cheung, and Fong, 2001).

8.2.4 Market-Timing and Cost-Averaging Approaches

In order to get a good level of diversification, many investors have adopted what is called a **cost-averaging approach**. This proven method of **vintage-year diversification** consistently invests a fixed amount of money throughout all years and steadily commits to the best funds around, regardless of whether the current environment is seen as good or bad. This disciplined approach helps minimize overexposure to vintage years with high valuations (or an unfavorable exit environment). The cost-averaging principle sets an annual investment target for each private equity fund type, or a more or less constant target throughout funding cycles, thus avoiding any inclination to try to time the cycles.

The **market-timing approach** involves varying investment levels across vintage years in an effort to invest more in years with better prospects and less in years with inferior prospects. When using this approach, it is dangerous to assume that what has worked well in the past will continue to do so; emotional expectations are shaped by one's most recent experience. Also, the private equity market overreacts and experiences disruptions in trends. During market upswings, it is important to go for quality and be more restrictive than other investors; during depressed market conditions, however, it could make sense to be more flexible, as very often the overall vintage-year quality can turn out to be attractive. It is important to stick to the budgeted allocation, as new opportunities to invest in VC or buyout funds tend to coincide with the rise and fall of returns of each strategy (see Exhibit 8.8).[9] Careful investors avoid the temptation to overweight commitments to the hot strategy of the moment; they stick to a long-term plan.

8.3 THE RISK PROFILE OF PRIVATE EQUITY ASSETS

Private equity fund asset subclasses do show quite different risk profiles. Looking at the two main ones—that is, venture capital and buyouts in the United States and Europe—interesting observations can be made (see Exhibits 8.9 through 8.12).[10] The following historical data are obviously not a perfect guide to the future, but they still allow for some general observations:

- Considering only the average multiple, U.S. VC funds have clearly outperformed all other asset subclasses, with returns of 2.4× versus returns around 1.6×.
- The outperformance of U.S. VC funds has been obtained with a much higher risk level, as evidenced by the standard deviation above 3.0× compared to levels below 2.0× for European VC and below 1.0× for European and U.S. buyout

---

[9] See also on this subject Kaplan and Strömberg (2008), who note an inverse correlation between the amount of funds raised in a given vintage year and subsequent returns.

[10] These figures have been produced with the same approach as the one followed by Weidig and Mathonet (2004) but with updated data. Mathonet and Meyer (2007) also used the Thomson Reuters database and dropped all funds raised before 1987 and those younger than five years—that is, funds up to vintage-year 2001. The risk profile was produced based on a Monte Carlo simulation of 10,000 runs with a realistic selection (i.e., each vintage year has the same probability of being drawn), allowing for multiple draws.

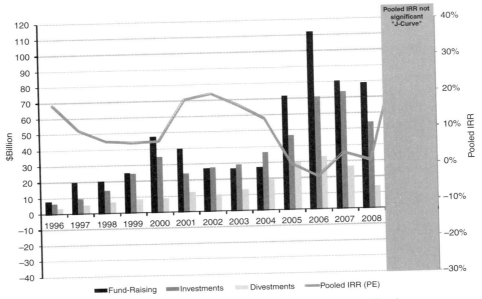

EXHIBIT 8.8   Pooled Internal Rate of Return by Vintage Year versus Yearly
Activity Figures
Source: Thomson ONE and PEREP Analytics.

funds. Other risk measures, such as skewness or kurtosis, further support the
higher risk level of VC funds, both in the United States and in Europe.

- Looking at the return-to-risk ratio,[11] buyout funds in the United States and
Europe appear to offer better risk profiles than do VC funds in those areas.
- The probability of a loss tells us that approximately four out of 10 European
VC funds, three out of 10 U.S. VC funds, and two out of 10 U.S. and European
buyout funds will show a loss. The average loss given a loss is quite similar for
all asset subclasses at around 30%.
- There have been very few total losses in all of the funds included in the Thomson
Reuters database (only a few U.S. VC funds). This comes notably from the fact
that distributions also include equalization fees, which cannot be considered as
either a repayment from the fund or some small distributions or immaterial exits
from some of the investments made. To make all investors equal, the investors
who become limited partners in subsequent closings have to make up their
contributions as if they had invested at the time of the first closing. **Equalization
fees** play this role and are a prefinancing charge, normally based on Treasury
security interest rates and on the fund's cash flows that occurred before the last

---

[11] The return-to-risk ratio we have used is similar to a Sharpe ratio, which is a measure of
risk-adjusted performance of the asset. The ratio is calculated as: $S = \dfrac{\frac{1}{N}\sum\limits_{i=1}^{N}(R_i - 1)}{\sigma}$ where R is the
fund return or multiple, the return on a benchmark is set to 1, $\frac{1}{N}\sum\limits_{i=1}^{N}(R_i - 1)$ is the expected
average excess return, and σ is the standard deviation of the excess return.

Venture Capital Funds

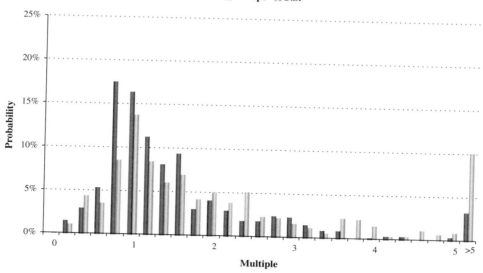

Buyout Funds

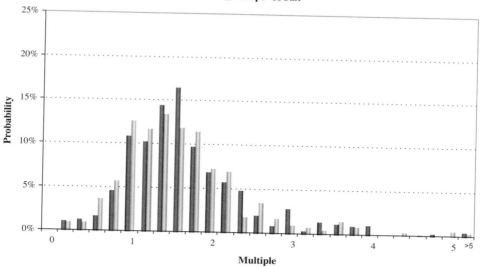

EXHIBIT 8.9 The Risk Profile of Venture Capital and Buyout Funds: Europe versus United States

Source: Mathonet and Meyer (2007), using Thomson Reuters (Thomson ONE), and their own simulations; fund performance since inception, all mature (older than five years) funds, data as of June 2006.

European Venture Capital Investment Vehicles

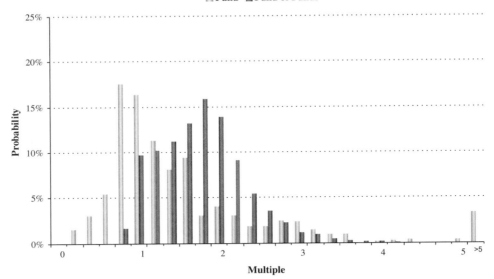

U.S. Venture Capital Investment Vehicles

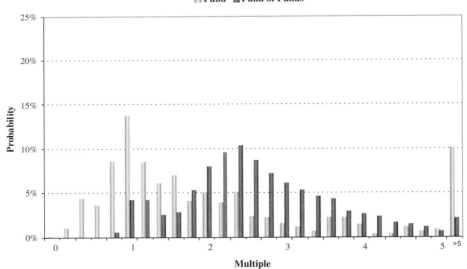

EXHIBIT 8.10   The Risk Profile of Venture Capital Investments: Europe versus
United States
Source: Mathonet and Meyer (2007), using Thomson Reuters (Thomson ONE), and their
own simulations; fund performance since inception, all mature (older than five years) funds,
data as of June 2006.

European Buyout Investment Vehicles

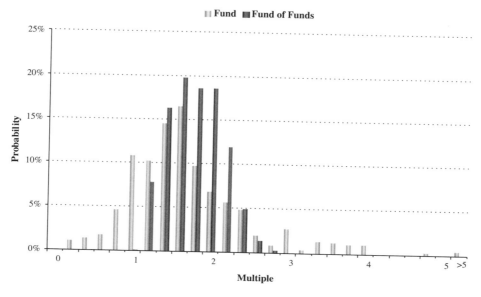

U.S. Buyout Investment Vehicles

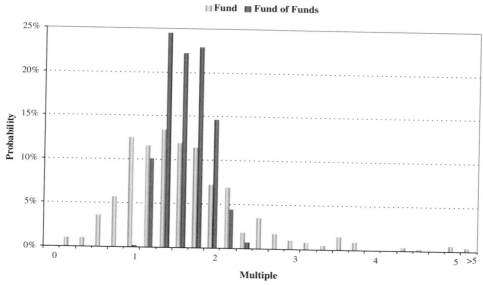

EXHIBIT 8.11 The Risk Profile of Buyout Investments: Europe versus United States
Source: Mathonet and Meyer (2007), using Thomson Reuters (Thomson ONE), and their own simulations; fund performance since inception, all mature (older than five years) funds, data as of June 2006.

EXHIBIT 8.12 The Risk Profile of Venture Capital and Buyout Investments: Europe versus United States

| | Buyout | | | | VC | | | |
| | Europe | | United States | | Europe | | United States | |
	Funds	FoFs	Funds	FoFs	Funds	FoFs	Funds	FoFs
Average multiple	1.6	1.7	1.5	1.5	1.6	1.7	2.4	2.6
Median multiple	1.5	1.7	1.4	1.5	1.1	1.6	1.5	2.4
Standard deviation	0.8	0.3	0.8	0.3	1.9	0.6	3.1	1.0
Skewness	1.4	0.2	1.9	0.2	6.0	0.8	4.0	0.7
Kurtosis	3.4	−0.6	7.3	−0.7	50.1	1.3	21.4	0.8
Probability of a loss	16%	0%	22%	0%	38%	11%	30%	5%
Average loss given a loss	−31%	−3%	−27%	−3%	−32%	−12%	−32%	−11%
Probability of total loss	0%	0%	0%	0%	0%	0%	0%	0%
Expected multiple in bottom decile	0.5	1.2	0.5	1.1	0.4	0.9	0.4	1.0
Expected multiple in top decile	3.4	2.3	3.3	2.0	5.4	2.8	9.5	4.6
Probability of a multiple above 3	6%	0%	5%	0%	8%	2%	22%	30%
Probability of a multiple above 2	22%	19%	21%	5%	20%	24%	37%	72%
Return-to-risk ratio	0.8	2.0	0.7	2.0	0.3	1.2	0.5	1.6
Semideviation below a multiple of 1	0.16	0.00	0.16	0.00	0.24	0.05	0.22	0.03
Sortino ratio	3.8	669.0	3.3	240.2	2.5	14.7	6.6	56.0

Source: Mathonet and Meyer (2007), using Thomson Reuters (Thomson ONE), and their own simulations; fund performance since inception, all mature (older than five years) funds, data as of June 2006.

closing. They are distributed to the earlier investors in the proportions defined by the previous closing before the new investors joined. Therefore, we have also looked at the probability of losing more than 80% of the capital initially invested, which to some degree can be assimilated to a total loss, and have found that for all asset subclasses, about 1% of the funds do lose more than 80% of the capital initially invested.

- Standard deviation is not all bad for this type of asymmetric distribution and cannot alone be a reliable measure of risk. We have, therefore, considered other indicators, such as the expected multiple in bottom and top deciles, the probability of a multiple above a certain threshold, semideviation, and the Sortino ratio.[12] While the standard deviation is much higher for U.S. VC funds, this is not the case when looking at the semideviation below a multiple of 1. The gap between buyout funds and VC funds is much narrower, and the highest figure is now observed for European VC funds.

- Looking at the downside, we do not see large differences between the various asset subclasses. The expected multiples in bottom deciles are similar in U.S. and European VC and buyout funds. The main differences come from the upside. There is a much higher probability to reach a multiple above 3× in U.S. VC funds (22%) than for all other submarkets (below 10%). The expected multiple in top deciles is also much higher in U.S. VC funds (9.5×) than in European VC funds (5.4×) and buyout funds (around 3.4×).

Investors rarely invest in only one private equity fund but instead construct portfolios of such funds. As for portfolios of private equity funds or funds of funds, asset subclasses also show quite different risk profiles. Looking at the main ones (i.e., portfolio of buyouts and venture capital funds in the United States and Europe; see Exhibits 8.10 through 8.12), the following observations can be made:

- As expected, for all submarkets, the average returns remain unchanged between funds and funds of funds (FoFs),[13] and the standard deviation, skewness, and kurtosis all decrease. However, our simulations do not account for program size and diseconomies of scale, which in reality should impact and decrease the average returns. Of course, funds of funds charge an additional layer of fees, which will create a difference in the net returns between funds of funds and portfolios of private equity funds.

- For funds of funds, U.S. VC outperformance has been obtained under a higher risk level, as evidenced by the standard deviation around 1.0× compared to 0.6x for European VC and below 0.5× for European and U.S. buyouts. Other risk

---

[12] Frank Sortino's ratio is a measure of a risk-adjusted return of an investment asset. It is an extension of the Sharpe ratio. While the Sharpe ratio takes into account any volatility in return of an asset, the Sortino ratio differentiates volatility due to up and down movements. The up movements are considered desirable and not accounted for in the volatility. Here, the ratio is calculated as: $S = \dfrac{\frac{1}{N}\sum_{i=1}^{N}(R_i - 1)}{\sigma_d}$

[13] Due to the selection process (realistic selection, multiple draws allowed), the average returns are not exactly the same, though statistically they should be. However, the differences observed are minor.

measures, such as the skewness and the kurtosis, further support the higher risk profile of VC in both the United States and Europe.

■ The return-to-risk and Sortino ratios naturally always improve with diversification, as they simply compare the mean return (stable) to a risk measure (always decreasing). And as for funds based on these ratios, buyouts in the United States and Europe appear to offer better risk profiles than does VC.

■ The probability of a loss tells us that one out of 10 portfolios of European VC funds, less than one out of 10 portfolios of U.S. VC funds, and close to zero out of 10 portfolios of U.S. and European buyout funds will show a loss. The average loss given a loss is around 12% for VC and 3% for buyouts.

■ The probability of total loss is now totally remote for all funds of funds, as the probability of losing more than 40% of the capital invested is also equal to zero for all submarkets.

■ Standard deviation of fund portfolios or funds of funds is a much better indicator of risk, as distributions are much less asymmetric. We have still considered other indicators, such as the expected multiple in bottom and top deciles, the probability of a multiple above a certain threshold, semideviation, and the Sortino ratio. As for funds, looking at the semideviation below a multiple of 1, the gap between buyouts and VC is much narrower and is higher for VC, with the maximum observed for European VC.

■ Looking at the downside, we do not see large differences between the various asset subclasses. The expected multiples in bottom deciles are similar in all submarkets. The average loss given a loss is a bit higher for VC (around 12%) than for buyouts (around 3%). For VC, there is a lower probability to suffer a loss in the United States (5%) than in Europe (11%), and for buyouts in general, the probability is very low (close to 0%). As for funds, the main differences come from the upside. There is a much higher probability (higher than for funds) to reach a multiple above 3 in U.S. VC (30%) than for all other submarkets (below 3%). The expected multiple in top deciles is also much higher in U.S. VC (4.6×) than in the other submarkets (below 3.0×). It is interesting to note that because of higher average returns for U.S. funds, the probability of a U.S. fund of funds reaching a multiple above 3 increases with diversification, whereas for the other submarkets it is the opposite because of lower average returns.

In conclusion, there is some discrepancy between submarkets in the upside combined with relatively similar downsides. Diversification is beneficial to all segments, as it decreases the level of risk taken by investors. However, it also normalizes the risk profile and limits the upside potential. One exception has been portfolios of U.S. VC funds, which show improving profiles thanks to their historically high average returns. Finally, as for funds, knowing that these conclusions depend on (1) the hypothesis that the future will be similar to the past, (2) that our statistical data are representative of the market, and (3) that investors may have different return-risk preferences, these general conclusions also have to be challenged and adapted to each investor's objectives and expectations.

CHAPTER 9

Fund Manager Selection Process

While a wide divergence between top- and bottom-quartile performers (see Exhibit 8.1 in the preceding chapter) may provide an opportunity to perform extremely well by selecting top-performing managers, it also exposes the portfolio to a high degree of underperformance risk. And if an institution is unlucky or unskilled enough to pick a bottom-quartile manager, the returns will likely prove to be very disappointing.

Manager selection and access are seen to be among the keys to sustainable outperformance in private equity (PE), forming a distinct part of the investment process that can be efficiently structured. Manager selection is not mechanical but requires industry experience and resources to conduct both research and due diligence. Unfortunately, this is easier said than done, and the advice to focus on top funds is probably as helpful as the observation that to become rich, one needs to acquire a lot of money. Further, it is more difficult to identify superior managers than it is to weed out obviously inferior managers. The key is to be highly selective and to strike a proper balance between seeking exposure to top funds and diversifying. Thorough consistent, detailed analysis and discipline in the due diligence process are critical.

To make matters worse, few investors, advisers, and consultants have experience and familiarity with the unique aspects of private equity. Because the industry and its practices are continuously evolving, categorizations are fuzzy and there are no clear dos and don'ts. That makes the identification and evaluation of fund managers more important and also more challenging in the private equity universe. Consequently, one needs a different selection process for fund managers in private equity (see Exhibit 9.1) than for fund managers of publicly quoted assets.

9.1 DETERMINATION OF THE WISH LIST OF FUND CHARACTERISTICS

The development of an investment strategy is important to efficiently manage the process, and it forms the starting point of the fund manager selection process. Based on the investment strategy of the investor and the resulting portfolio design, a wish list of fund characteristics needs to be established. The wish list defines the types of proposals that are consistent with the investment strategy of the investor.

Next, an active deal sourcer will identify wish-list funds to be specifically targeted for investment. Investors make a market mapping, in which all management teams are ranked by their perceived attractiveness (see Exhibit 9.2).

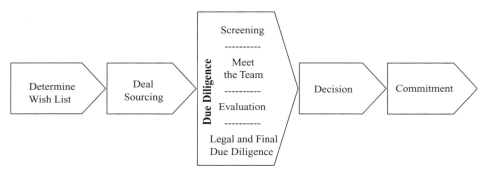

EXHIBIT 9.1   Private Equity Fund Manager Selection Process

Attractive teams are normally those that have been able to generate top performance during several market cycles and are, therefore, the most likely to continue to
do so in the future. One way to classify the manager teams is to rank them based on
this dual-dimension approach: (1) the quality of their track record, from bottom to
top performer, and (2) the duration of their joint experience, from none to several
market cycles. From this, the following classification is suggested:

- A blue-chip team is a team that has been able to generate a top-quartile performance for all of its funds through at least two business cycles (i.e., a sequence of
  more than three funds).
- An established team is a team that has been able to generate a top-quartile
  performance for most of its funds (more than three funds) through at least two
  business cycles.
- An emerging team is a team with limited joint history but with all the characteristics to become an established team.

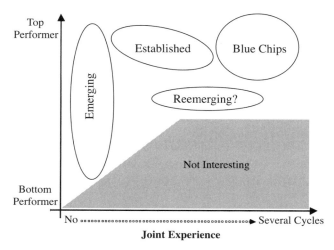

EXHIBIT 9.2   Market Mapping of Fund Performance
through Several Business Cycles

- A reemerging team is a previously blue-chip or established team that has been through a restructuring following recent poor performance or some significant operational issues and has regained the potential to reemerge as an established or blue-chip team.
- Teams not included in the preceding categories are not interesting.

9.2 DEAL SOURCING

Investors in private equity funds need to use their network of industry contacts to identify and establish contact with high-quality fund managers. It is critical to get as many opinions and leads as possible. This can be achieved by having discussions with other investors or entrepreneurs, employing advisers and consultants, and researching the press.

Reactive deal sourcing, in which investors often get showered with investment proposals, is not an efficient way of approaching selection. With this approach, literally hundreds of private placement memoranda need to be checked as to whether they comply with the set wish-list characteristics or investment criteria. First-time teams often have to approach as many investors as possible, but top teams typically get referred to limited partners by word of mouth and, therefore, need to be actively sourced. Developing long-term relationships as well as exploring opportunities that fit the set criteria are critical. For this purpose, teams have to be identified and approached even before they start their fund-raising. This process requires establishing a calendar of when these teams are expected to go to the market to raise capital for their next fund offering.

A historical review of private equity performance reveals two important trends: (1) median (but not average) private equity returns tend to underperform public equity indices, and (2) there is a wider gap between top-quartile and bottom-quartile PE returns than there is for funds of quoted assets. It is generally believed that there is a high degree of repeatability or persistence of top-quartile performance in private equity. This belief is supported by several studies, such as that by Kaplan and Schoar (2005), which concluded that returns persist strongly across subsequent funds of a partnership, particularly for venture capital (VC) funds. Rouvinez (2006) concluded that there is strong evidence of serial persistence of a higher return in private equity.

Kaplan and Schoar (2005) studied the performance of private equity funds between 1980 and 2001 from the Venture Economics database (now Thomson Reuters). They performed a regression analysis on lagged returns using public market equivalent (PME) (defined as return correlation between the return of subsequent funds; see Chapter 10), and found the following for private equity:

- The correlation coefficient is positive and strongly significant. The point estimate is 0.54, which implies that a PE fund with 1% higher performance in the previous fund is associated with a 54-basis-point higher performance in the current fund.
- The coefficients on both the previous fund and the fund before that are positive and significant. The coefficients imply that a 1% increase in past performance is associated with a combined 77-basis-point increase in performance in subsequent funds (the sum of the two coefficients on lagged performance).

Rouvinez (2006) studied the performance of private equity funds with vintage years earlier than 2000, using data from the Venture Economics database as of December 2005. He analyzed the probability of transition from one quartile to another when considering successive funds and found the following:

- As opposed to the world of mutual funds, there is strong evidence for serial persistence of higher returns in private equity.
- There is about a 33% probability that managers with top-quartile funds do remain in the top quartile with their successor fund, with about a 53% probability that they will outperform the market median.
- There is about a 40% probability that managers with lower-quartile funds do not come back to market with future fund offerings.

Under the assumption that past and future performances of a team are correlated, funds raised by teams that have performed well in the past tend to be oversubscribed. If returns have been high, limited partners from prior funds are highly motivated to commit to follow-on funds, and general partners will reward their loyalty with virtually guaranteed access to future funds.

In fact, private equity is a closed community in which past relationships provide access to funds in high demand, while newcomers are often turned away. Frequently, when a team with a strong track record raises a new fund, investors in previous funds quickly commit, often leading to oversubscription. General partners are interested in maintaining the relationship with the existing limited partnership base. Searching for new limited partners is an expensive exercise, and it creates uncertainty regarding the timing of closing and future relationships.[1] Consequently, fund managers tend to avoid this exercise whenever possible. In the extreme, it will not even be known to outside parties that the team may be raising a new fund. Having access to a network of contacts is required to identify top teams and to know about the timing of their fund-raising activities. While top teams give priority allocations to their previous investors, they may also allocate a share of the new fund to investors who could add value, such as deal flow, exit opportunities, and industry expertise. Nonetheless, access is far less a problem for limited partners who are financially strong and have demonstrated that they are long-term players in the market. For newcomers, however, this is a significant barrier to entry. This means that investors building a

---

[1] See also Lerner and Schoar (2004). The authors presented the theory that by choosing the degree of illiquidity of the security, private equity fund managers can influence the type of investor the firm will end up attracting. This allows managers to screen for deep-pocketed investors (i.e., those that have a low likelihood of facing a liquidity shock), as they can reduce the general partner's cost of capital in future fund-raising efforts. Their analysis is based on the assumption of an information asymmetry about the quality of the manager between the existing investors and the market. The general partner faces a problem when he or she has to raise funds for a subsequent fund from outside investors, because the outsiders cannot determine whether the manager is of poor quality or the existing investors were hit by a liquidity shock. Transferability constraints are less prevalent when private equity funds have limited partners that are known to be subject to few liquidity shocks (e.g., endowments, foundations, and other investors with long-term commitments to private equity).

new allocation to private equity may not be able to invest with top-quartile managers, even when they have knowledge of the managers' fund-raising schedules.

9.3 DUE DILIGENCE: IMPORTANCE AND LIMITATIONS

As fund selection is one of the key performance drivers in private equity, due diligence is a requirement for prudent investors as well as the basis for better investment decisions. The due diligence process covers all the activities associated with evaluating an investment proposal and is commonly defined as "the process of investigation and evaluation, performed by investors, into the details of a potential investment, such as an examination of operations and management and the verification of material facts.[2]

9.3.1 Due Diligence as a Requirement for Originators

According to Camp (2002), the concept of due diligence essentially denotes a legal obligation imposed on parties involved with the creation of prospectuses (directors, officers, underwriters, lawyers, accountants, and others) to use due diligence to ensure that they contain no material misstatements or omissions. In the context of private equity funds, the phrase *due diligence* is used slightly differently. Funds are issuing securities privately and are, therefore, not required to provide their investors with the same level of information they would if they were selling the same securities in the public markets. However, in practice, the level of disclosure often ends up being much more important.

9.3.2 Due Diligence as a Basis for Better Investment Decisions

By consistently and methodically performing their due diligence, investors hope to make better investment decisions. Every fund promises a top-quartile performance. According to Kelly (2002), the marketing line most often heard is that one's fund is in "the first quartile of returns." While this may often be genuinely believed, new funds, in particular, are difficult to benchmark. Likewise, every fund-of-funds manager claims to follow a methodical and thorough due diligence procedure. In essence, there are few differences in the processes followed, but investors agree on the desired characteristics: a skilled and experienced management team, a good track record, a sensible and consistent strategy, and an alignment of interests between investors and fund managers.

As information on private equity funds is not publicly available, it is necessary to collect data on the funds considered for investment. The management of this activity is seen as the main source of competitive advantage, even to the extent that other tasks critical to the success of the investment program, such as liquidity management, are overshadowed by this activity.

---

[2] *Source:* InvestorWords.com (2011) at www.investorwords.com/1596/due_diligence.html (accessed September 2011).

9.3.3 Limitations

Due diligence is generally based on cross-referencing and cross-checking, but often the lack of suitable comparables and information makes the analysis highly subjective. The high reliance on qualitative aspects and judgment can become a liability. Without proper incentives, investors have the tendency simply to raise the thresholds higher and higher to avoid personal exposure to criticism. As a result of this conservatism, potentially good investment proposals might be rejected. For example, in many cases, newer partnerships are avoided, not necessarily because the fundamentals are not right or because the investment proposal is not convincing, but simply because not all points of the due diligence can be supported with tangible evidence. An open mind toward new ideas is required, and clear reasons why certain fund characteristics are to be avoided need to be stated.

Once a reputable institution has committed itself to invest in a fund, other investors tend to believe that it has carried out a proper due diligence. However, one should not rely on other investors' findings and judgments. Information provided by other limited partners needs to be taken with a grain of salt, but should also not be ignored. It could well be that investors who have committed to an investment subconsciously try to protect themselves by bringing other institutions to commit; if others make the same mistake, the first investors may be less subject to blame.

9.3.4 Private Equity Fund Due Diligence: A Step-by-Step Process

To reduce uncertainty to a minimum, a study of the entire market would be necessary. To assess the quality and relative performance expectations of funds, a professional manager can analyze hundreds of factors, the majority of them being qualitative rather than quantitative. As this is associated with significant costs, every investor will approach the due diligence process from a cost-benefit perspective. The due diligence process can be structured in the following stages (see Exhibit 9.1 earlier in the chapter): screening, meeting the team, evaluation, and final and legal due diligence.

9.3.4.1 Screening Due diligence requires significant time and effort, and there are many more managers than can be analyzed in detail. Therefore, the first step of the due diligence process consists of a preliminary screening. The objective is to quickly eliminate proposals that do not fit or that are to be avoided based on the criteria and objectives laid out under the portfolio design. This could be because these proposals are in the wrong industry sector, stage, or geographical focus, or do not meet minimum quality requirements. Deals screened out are de facto, meaning they are not worth spending further time and effort on.

Assuming that no elimination criteria are detected, there is a preliminary evaluation of the fund manager's proposed investment strategy, the management team's overall quality, the team's track record, the fund's structure, and the fund's main terms. Appropriate analysis for this phase involves determining whether the fund's strategy is convincing, whether it differentiates itself from other proposals, and, most importantly, whether there is potential for future success.

Proposals should be taken forward only if there is a good fit with the investor's portfolio strategy and if the wish-list criteria are met. This screening process narrows down investment opportunities to a manageable few that merit a more in-depth due diligence.

9.3.4.2 Meeting the Team

Paraphrasing real estate, in which the three key investment success factors are "location, location, location," in private equity they might be "team, team, team."[3] Consequently, the next step in the due diligence process is a meeting with the fund management team in its offices to better understand the personalities, experience, dynamics, and qualifications of the team members. Attributes to examine in this phase include the overall management team's quality and competencies, member synergies, team cohesion, the fairness of the incentives, and the motivation of the team and the individual team members. The organizational structure and the decision-making process also need to be understood. This evaluation is highly subjective and can be performed only by an experienced investment manager.

There should also be a detailed analysis of the team's track record, that of the group and of its individuals. The expected drivers of performance need to be identified, and potential deal breakers need to be identified and clarified. These involve items related to proposed terms and conditions, alignment of interest factors, potential conflicts of interest that the team is unwilling to negotiate, or situations in which a gut instinct tells the investor not to move forward.

Comfort level with the fund manager is also important to ascertain. This is because the limited partner will be monitoring the fund manager for years. Hence, incompatible views can create instability in this relationship. At the other extreme, there is a danger that personal aspects can blur the picture. One should not forget that a limited partner's commitment is quite important to the fund, and through management fees and carried interest, a significant portion of this investment ends up in the team's pockets. Who would not try to show one's best side to potential investors under these circumstances?

9.3.4.3 Evaluation

In the next step, the proposal is evaluated against other opportunities on the limited partner's long list. As no funds are equivalent, this is the critical step. In this phase, it is important to examine the relative performance among fund managers on the long list, as well as each fund's position in the competitive landscape.

In private equity, there exists a high degree of uncertainty, as investment decisions must often be based on incomplete information and data. This implies that the entire due diligence process is of an imprecise nature. Therefore, the assessment of investment proposals not only requires expertise but also involves pattern recognition. Camp (2002) argued in the context of direct investments, but the same argument applies to funds: that perhaps "the most important thing that separates [a] good venture capitalist from the rest of the pack is a dependable gut." Unfortunately, this is the point at which most investors, faced with high uncertainty levels, would tend to throw all analytical rigor overboard and start to rely entirely on their judgment and their gut instinct.

---

[3] It is also often argued, not without justification, that what matters most is the mix of all the key success factors.

Limited partners do not usually attempt to value a private equity investment proposal as they would in the case of traditional asset classes. As primary positions in private equity funds are bought at par, the investment decision is either yes or no, and apart from negotiations around terms and conditions, there is no meaningful pricing mechanism to adjust for perceived risks. As a result, institutions have the tendency to impose an ever-growing list of criteria in the hope that this will help them avoid mistakes. We believe that this is fundamentally wrong and only leads to homogeneity and quasi-standardization in an asset class that requires innovation and evolution. Instead, we propose a structured assessment of the following two main dimensions of a fund's value:

1. The fund's **expected economic value** is mainly dependent on the quality of the proposal. We propose basing the assessment on a grading methodology (see following paragraphs) supported by a qualitative scoring.[4] The purpose of the qualitative scoring is to benchmark the fund against best practices for the private equity market. Dimensions assessed are notably management team skills, management team stability, management team motivation, conflicts of interest, structuring and costs, and validation through other investors.
2. Second, there can be a **real option value** associated with investment in the fund. For example, although investing in a first-time fund is generally perceived to be more risky than investing in an established fund, it normally allows access to the team's subsequent offerings if the fund becomes a top performer and is oversubscribed in subsequent fund-raisings.

Assessing the value of intangibles is difficult, particularly in the case of the real option value. Therefore, this valuation cannot be precise. But given the context of intangibles, a structured process is helpful, and techniques such as qualitative scoring[5] or a grading system can improve the quality of the decision.

Grading private equity funds requires classifying all funds into specific unambiguous classes where all members share similar characteristics. As the private equity industry thinks in terms of top-quartile funds, the quartile statistics form the basis for an intuitively simple grading scale. Due to the scarcity of reliable data on the private equity market, grades finer than these values do not appear to be meaningful. Under the assumption that the fund maintains both its ranking and its current quartile position within its peer group, its return is expected to fall into the respective quartile of the benchmark. That leads to the definition of the expected performance grades that are presented in Exhibit 9.3.

Grades can be assigned based on the evaluation of both quantitative and qualitative criteria. It is a relative ranking within the fund's specific peer group that combines a quantitative scoring, a qualitative scoring, a method to combine the two evaluations, the internal age, and a final review leading to an adjustment of the grade if necessary (see Exhibit 9.4 and Chapter 13 in Meyer and Mathonet, 2005).

---

[4] See, for example, Edvinsson and Malone (1997) or Chapter 15 in Meyer and Mathonet (2005).
[5] See, for example, Edvinsson and Malone (1997) or Chapter 15 in Meyer and Mathonet (2005).

EXHIBIT 9.3 Private Equity Manager Grading System

Grade	Description
P–A	At the time of the grading, the fund's rank falls into the first quartile of the peer group.
P–B	At the time of the grading, the fund's rank falls into the second quartile of the peer group.
P–C	At the time of the grading, the fund's rank falls into the third quartile of the peer group.
P–D	At the time of the grading, the fund's rank falls into the fourth quartile of the peer group.

In essence, this system is based on general considerations and experience rather than on sophisticated mathematical modeling. It cannot be regarded as precise and also clearly relies on the judgment of the evaluators.

The grading is based on the assumption that all investors are treated pari passu (i.e., with the same rights) and relates to the assessment of the fund, not to the structuring of the acquisition or investment into the fund. For example, secondary transactions are often at a steep discount to the net asset value (NAV). This, however, does not affect the fund's grade, as it may be the reflection of other variables. Furthermore, a fund with poor performance becomes a sunk cost once the purchase price has been paid, and it is only the intrinsic quality of the fund that will support the future cash flows. Finally, it has to be kept in mind that a fund with the highest ex ante grade of P–A may also fail, and that funds with the lowest grading of P–D can well turn out to be spectacular winners. Moreover, simply funding all P–A graded funds should not be equated with selectivity: an ex ante P–A grading states that the proposal closely complies with current best-market practices for funds, but it does not address the question of whether there are better funds around or whether future market practices will be best.

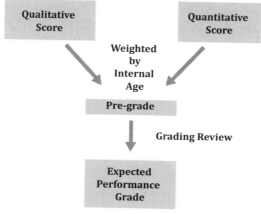

EXHIBIT 9.4 Grading System

9.3.4.4 Final and Legal Due Diligence At the previous stage, an investor may have formed a hypothesis that the proposal fits the desired strategy of his or her private equity investment program and that it is of acceptable quality. This last step of the selection process before decision and commitment is an exhaustive and costly exercise. It comprises the legal due diligence and final in-depth due diligence. Limited partnership agreements often incorporate unique terms or, in the case of funds operating offshore, are structured to comply with their jurisdiction's unique rules. Therefore, such agreements need to be drafted by experts, something that is very expensive to do too early in the process when the final investment decision is still very uncertain. However, any negotiation and changing of terms and conditions is meaningful only before investing, and therefore all sides often have to work under serious time pressure.

The last phase of this final analysis focuses on a more detailed review of the key issues identified previously and also sets the theme for future monitoring activities.

Finally, investors in private equity funds need to use their network of industry contacts to perform independent reference checks. It is advisable to get second opinions from co-investors in the portfolio, entrepreneurs, competitors, or industry advisers. Also, existing investors' commitments should be verified. In addition, contact with the other prospective limited partners may help expedite changes to the fund's terms and conditions.

9.4 DECISION AND COMMITMENT

Due diligence can be seen primarily as information gathering and evaluation and not as a decision-making tool. In practice, the distinction is seldom made; due diligence is used to weed out inferior funds and accept the remaining proposals. The results of the due diligence process should be used only as input for a decision-making process that takes into consideration not only the quality of the investment proposal but also the program's portfolio composition.

Finally, this is not a one-sided decision. Teams may have their own due diligence criteria for selecting potential investors. They should examine whether the investor's commitment is long-term, if the investor understands the business, if the investor has a reputation for being difficult, or if the investor is a **defaulting investor** (one who has previously reneged or is anticipated to renege on capital commitments). In a case in which public institutions seek to become limited partners, their investment restrictions (particularly those related to industry sectors and geography) and their transparency requirements need to be acceptable to the fund managers. In order to protect the private information of the general partner, some private equity fund managers may not allow commitments from investors who are required to publicly disclose information regarding their investment program, such as U.S. pension plans subject to the Freedom of Information Act.

CHAPTER 10

Measuring Performance and Benchmarking in the Private Equity World

Measuring and benchmarking in the private equity (PE) world is as important as for any other asset classes. For individual transactions, it will not only be a key part of the due diligence process through the track record analysis but also be a key performance indicator during the monitoring phase. The same is also true for a portfolio of funds, either for self-assessment or, in the case of funds of funds, for the selection of a manager.

Private equity investments have key characteristics that distinguish this asset class from others. These characteristics explain why private equity performance measures are different from the ones commonly used for other asset classes such as the time-weighted rate of return. This implies that not only benchmarking but also, for example, portfolio construction techniques will be different.

10.1 INDIVIDUAL FUNDS

Both investors and investment managers have an interest in performance measurement. Investors conduct performance measurement for three purposes: (1) to monitor changes in the value of their investments, (2) to evaluate and compare investment managers, and (3) to obtain inputs for asset allocation. Investment managers are also interested in performance measurement, in their case to evaluate and improve their investment process and to market their services to and communicate with current and potential investors.

Due to its unique characteristics, performance measurement in private equity is particularly challenging. These inherent characteristics have also rendered the set of metrics commonly used to measure performance of other investments flawed and unable to present a complete and unambiguous picture of a private equity manager's performance.

10.1.1 Performance Measures

Venture capital (VC) associations and the CFA Institute deem the interim internal rate of return (IIRR),[1] which is a cash-weighted IRR and the since-inception IRR, to

---

[1] Note that as database providers are focusing on net return to the limited partners, it is the fund's net IIRR and not the gross that has to be benchmarked. Also note that the NAV is

be the most appropriate return measure for VC and private equity funds.[2] Implicit in this decision is the recognition that when a management contract calls for a series of investments and divestments to be spread out over time at the discretion of the manager, a rate of return-based performance measurement and evaluation that is time weighted is not appropriate. As the performance measure traditionally used for standard asset classes such as public equity is normally time weighted, this makes direct comparison with private equity more difficult and global portfolio construction, including private equity, more complex.

The **internal rate of return (IRR)** is the implied discount rate that makes the net present value of all cash flows equal to zero. Mathematically, the IRR is found by solving the following equation:

$$\sum_{t=0}^{T} \frac{D_t}{(1 + IRR_T)^t} - \sum_{t=0}^{T} \frac{C_t}{(1 + IRR_T)^t} = 0$$

where D_t is the fund distribution during the period t, C_t is the capital contribution or drawdown during the period t, and IRR_T is the investors' net internal rate of return at maturity T.

The IIRR, which is the IRR of unliquidated funds, is a cash flow–based return measure that considers the residual value or net asset value (NAV) of the partnership's holdings as a final cash inflow. **Interim IRRs (IIRRs)** are only estimates rather than actual realized rates of return. Mathematically, the IIRR is found by solving the following equation:

$$\sum_{t=0}^{T} \frac{D_t}{(1 + IIRR_T)^t} - \sum_{t=0}^{T} \frac{C_t}{(1 + IIRR_T)^t} + \frac{NAV_T}{(1 + IIRR_T)^T} = 0$$

where NAV_T is the latest net asset value of the fund at time T, and $IIRR_T$ is the investors' net interim internal rate of return at time T.

The IRR is often perceived to be the most accurate method for calculating the returns of PE, as this performance measure incorporates the time value of money. But it also assumes that distributions are reinvested at the IRR, which may be unrealistic and, if removed, may have a significant impact on the total return. Further discussion of this appears in Chapter 12, where we assess the components of IIRR. To correct this weakness, the **modified IRR (MIRR)**, which assumes a given reinvestment rate, is therefore preferred by some investors. The modified IRR is the IRR calculated taking

---

sometimes a gross figure (i.e., before deduction of a possible carried interest for the general partner), while the cash flows are net to the limited partners.

[2] See Geltner and Ling (2000): "In 1993, AIMR proposed performance measurement guidelines that recommended a time-weighted approach. After investors and fund managers expressed concerns, a special sub-committee of private equity industry investors and experts appointed by AIMR studied the applicability of time-weighted returns to the private equity industry. They recommended that fund managers and intermediaries present their private equity performance results on the cash-weighted IRR basis." The CFA Institute Global Investment Performance Standards (GIPS) guidelines were updated in http://gipsstandards.org/standards/guidance/develop/pdf/gs_private_equity_clean.pdf. Accessed January 2012.

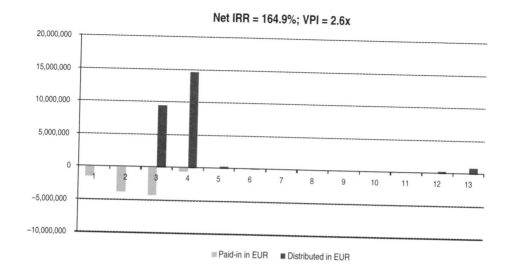

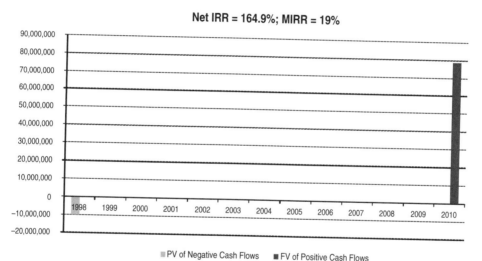

EXHIBIT 10.1 Modified IRR Example

into consideration the investor's cost of capital and reinvestment opportunities (see Exhibit 10.1). Mathematically, it is found by solving the following equation:

$$\left(\sum_{t=0}^{T} D_t \times (1 + RR_T)^{T-t} \bigg/ \sum_{t=0}^{T} \frac{C_t}{(1 + CoC)^t} \right)^{1/T} - 1 = MIIRR_T$$

where RR_T is the expected reinvestment rate for the period until time T, CoC is the investors' cost of capital for the period until time T, and $MIIRR_T$ is the interim modified IRR for the period until time T.

The IRR is not the only performance measure used by the industry. The following represent some of the other commonly used performance measures:

- The **total value to paid-in ratio (TVPI, or total return)** is a measure of the cumulative distribution to investors plus the total value of the unrealized investments relative to the total capital drawn from investors:

$$TVPI_T = \frac{\sum_{t=0}^{T} D_t + NAV_T}{\sum_{t=0}^{T} C_t} = DPI_T + RVPI_T$$

- The **distribution to paid-in ratio (DPI, or realized return)** is a measure of the cumulative distribution to investors relative to the total capital drawn from investors:

$$DPI_T = \frac{\sum_{t=0}^{T} D_t}{\sum_{t=0}^{T} C_t}$$

- The **residual value to paid-in ratio (RVPI, or unrealized return)** is a measure of the total value of the unrealized investments relative to the total capital drawn from investors:

$$RVPI_T = \frac{NAV_T}{\sum_{t=0}^{T} C_t}$$

Note that these ratios are measures of net returns to invested capital and therefore do not take the time value of money into account, as distinct from the IRR. It should also be stressed that the private equity industry does, in effect, attempt to appraise the NAV at the end of each quarter (see Chapter 12). IIRR, TVPI, and RVPI are computed based on these residual values. Their estimations are the most problematic components of return evaluation and are among the main reasons that quantitative benchmarking should be complemented by a qualitative analysis.

10.1.2 Benchmarking Private Equity Funds

Benchmarking aims to evaluate the performance of a specific entity by comparison to a standard or a point of reference. In the case of private equity funds, the analysis is normally performed using the past financial performance of a particular fund manager and, as such, forms part of the due diligence process. However, benchmarking can also cover the current financial performance and is thus also used in the monitoring process. Benchmarking is not the only tool that is used in track record analysis. Many other tools exist, such as the portfolio performance dispersion or the winners' dependence analyses used to assess the level of risk.[3] The most intuitive approach is to compare a private equity fund against a group of funds that have a similar risk profile (i.e., that have the same style or specialization, also called a peer group). Ideally, these funds should represent the closest competitors of the fund to be benchmarked.

In the case of private equity, there exists an ongoing discussion on the validity of benchmarks. According to Geltner and Ling (2000), appraisal-based peer universe benchmarks are, in principle, valid and useful tools for investment performance evaluation purposes. However, Kelly (2002) sees private equity as an "asset class nearly impossible to benchmark." The author raises the issue that there are sometimes too few observations within one vintage year to benchmark. Furthermore, he mentions that general partners are often vague regarding the methodology used for calculating the reported returns, rendering the comparison somewhat questionable. Bailey, Richards, and Tierney (1990) define the so-called **Bailey criteria** as a grouping of characteristics to gauge the appropriateness of investment benchmarks. We now proceed to present these criteria and how they apply to private equity:

- *Unambiguous/knowable. Are the names and weights of assets that comprise the benchmark clearly identifiable?* Private equity benchmarks provide only aggregate data and thus do not give a complete representation of the available asset set.
- *Investable. Is the option being analyzed available by forgoing active management and simply holding the benchmark assets?* It can be in public but not in private equity markets.
- *Measurable. Is it possible to frequently calculate the benchmark performance?* The data provided by private equity funds do not allow one to accurately and frequently measure their risk and return characteristics. Valuation guidelines, such as those put in place by various PE associations, define an appraisal policy to improve the coherence and consistency, making the comparison between funds more meaningful. However, the industry uses several different performance measures, such as IRR or multiples, which can sometimes offer varied pictures.
- *Specified in advance. Is the benchmark constructed and mutually agreed on prior to the manager evaluation?* Private equity is considered to be an absolute-return asset class. Consequently, benchmarks are of less relevance for the evaluation of managers, whose incentives are not normally based on an index.
- *Appropriate. Is the benchmark consistent with the manager's investment style?* As the private equity market is continuously evolving, there is a risk of using an inappropriate evaluation benchmark. If a benchmark does not well represent the style or specialization of the fund (e.g., in the case of emerging markets funds or new technologies not yet represented in the benchmark), comparisons can be problematic.

Private equity benchmarks suffer deficiencies in nearly all of these dimensions. However, most of the time practitioners can live with these shortcomings or see them as inconsequential. Thomson Reuters, Cambridge Associates, and Preqin are

---

[3] For a more detailed description of track record analysis, see Chapter 10 in Mathonet and Meyer (2007).

database providers for private equity investors. These databases contain peer groups that can serve as benchmarks. However, it must be noted that private equity funds provide performance information predominantly on a voluntary basis.[4] For this reason, these databases do not necessarily capture the same data, which can result in reported returns differing by as much as several percentage points for some peer groups.

Another common criticism is **survivorship bias**,[5] which refers to the fact that managers or funds that perform poorly tend to go out of business and therefore drop out of the peer universe. As a result, statistical data will cover only the currently existing funds and present an average historical performance that is likely to be upwardly biased. On the other hand, according to Geltner and Ling (2000), it is not necessary to have a fixed and constant set of funds in the benchmark, and Swensen (2000) argues that survivorship bias may be less of a problem for long-term-oriented illiquid investments, such as private equity, as this population does not change rapidly. Indeed, managers of private equity funds enter and exit the benchmark statistics with considerably less frequency than their counterparts focusing on traditional marketable securities, since the limited partnership structure precludes an easy departure from the industry.

10.1.3 Classical Relative Benchmarks

Many investors attempt to apply traditional public equity methodologies to private equity. In efficient markets, managers can decide to be passive or active, depending on whether or not they structure a portfolio to closely mimic the market (or an index). In less efficient markets, such as those in which private equity operates, managers have to be active, as they cannot track a benchmark given the aforementioned deficiencies.

Following an active investment strategy implies, by definition, that the risk level taken by the manager will be changing. This changing risk can be controlled in one of the following two ways: nonquantitatively, by constraining the manager to invest only in assets having the same risk profile as the benchmark, and quantitatively, by adjusting the manager's ex post returns to reflect the market's price of risk. In theory, risk can be controlled by using risk-adjusted return measures in both the benchmark and the fund.[6] But in private equity, only the nonquantitative approach to controlling for risk can be used.[7]

---

[4] See Shearburn and Griffiths (2002): "Precisely because private equity is private, published data in the field is not particularly reliable."

[5] It is to be noted that though survivorship bias is often raised in the context of private equity, this issue is also relevant for public equity. Databases on private equity must also face the problem that they do not contain the performance data of all active fund managers. This is because some private equity managers may decide not to provide information to databases, as they would prefer to maintain exclusivity. Another problem is that private equity returns are usually not adjusted for the statistical problems caused by the market's inherent illiquidity of private equity investments and the consequent infrequent pricing.

[6] Returns must be adjusted for risk in the way that the capital market prices risk. This is done on the basis of, for example, the Treynor ratio: the portfolio's excess return over risk-free investments divided by its systematic risk as represented by its beta.

[7] As will be described in Chapter 13, it is very difficult to reliably measure the risk level in private equity investments.

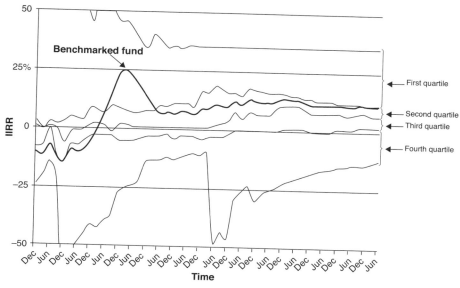

EXHIBIT 10.2 Individual Fund Benchmarking: Quartile Evolution since Inception

It is common practice in private equity to use a vintage, geographic, and stage focus-specific benchmark, often referred to as a peer-group cohort (e.g., 1995 European buyout funds), and to express the result in terms of the quartile it lies in within the benchmark group. The quartile is a relative measure and does not reflect any qualitative assessment. A top performer in a dismal vintage year may barely return the invested funds, whereas in some spectacular vintage years even fourth-quartile funds have returned double-digit returns. Exhibit 10.2 shows one example of individual fund benchmarking. The benchmarked fund starts as a fourth-quartile fund and moves after several quarters into the first-quartile area to peak with a 25% IIRR. Then, it goes down into the second quartile and ends its life at the boundary between the first and second quartiles.

A **top-quartile fund** by definition belongs to the 25% best-performing funds in its peer group at the time of benchmarking, which erroneously leads to the conclusion that only 25% of funds may legitimately be qualified as top quartile. The fact is that many more funds in the market are being labeled top quartile.[8] One reason is that, except for the 25% ratio itself, nothing else in this definition is cast in stone. Whether best performance refers to total value or IIRR, net (IIRR of a portfolio or fund considering the effect of management fees and carried interest) or gross (IIRR of a portfolio or fund without taking into account the effect of management fees and carried interest), realized (based on historical data) or not realized (based on historical or estimated data) is open to interpretation. The composition of the peer group may vary between analyses, resulting in different funds being identified as

---

[8] The "best of category" issue is also observed in other asset classes, in which the choice of benchmarks, performance measure, and so on can be used to try to convince investors that the considered asset belongs to the "best of category."

being in the top quartile. Also, because several return measures exist, each with its own advantages and disadvantages, a fund can wind up in different quartile positions depending on which measure is employed. It is thus a good practice to benchmark the fund using a variety of measures, but also to use judgment.

10.1.4 Other Relative Benchmarks

In some cases, there are simply not enough funds to obtain a meaningful peer-group cohort. As the industry is private, the data providers mostly rely on voluntary participation, which can mean that certain markets are not effectively covered. In these cases, more general or alternative benchmarks must be used.

- **Extended peer group.** When a representative peer-group cohort is too limited, it is simplest to extend the peer universe to the most similar funds. For example, if the number of 2005 European early-stage funds is not sufficient, the universe of all 2005 European VC funds or the universe of the 2004–2006 European early-stage funds could potentially be used as alternatives.[9]
- **Public market equivalent (PME).** The goal of the public market equivalent (PME) methodology is to calculate a private equity equivalent public index return, which provides a basis for comparison. The methodology[10] involves the estimation of a public market equivalent terminal value, which is substituted for the NAV in the IIRR calculation. Each actual cash flow is hypothesized to have been invested in a public index (for cash contributions) or divested from the same public index (for cash withdrawals). The size of the terminal position is the accumulation of this hypothetical program of buying and selling units of the public index using the fund's actual cash flow schedule.[11] Once the final number of units is estimated, it is valued using the index's concurrent value. Then the NAV is replaced by this terminal value (i.e., the number of units times the index value), and the private equity equivalent public index IIRR is calculated. The resulting return is a cash-weighted return indicating hypothetical performance if the investor had invested the actual cash flows in a public index rather than in the private equity (see section 10.1.6).

10.1.5 Absolute Benchmarks

Private equity is often perceived as an absolute-return asset class. Therefore, it is meaningful to use absolute-return targets to evaluate performance. The most straight-forward one is the comparison of the fund performance against the private equity investment program target or required rate of return. Another often-used absolute benchmark is a target expressed as a premium over public equity (e.g., 300 to 500 basis points over public equity). This benchmark is a hybrid, being both a relative

---

[9] The vintage year may be a less important differentiator than type of VC funds, since two consecutive vintage years have about eight common years in their existence.

[10] For a more detailed description, see Cheung et al. (2003).

[11] The fact that the fund's cash flow schedule is used explains why only the terminal value has to be changed for the calculation of the public market equivalent IIRR.

(public index)[12] and an absolute (premium) benchmark. Its use is justified by the fact that the private equity allocation is often obtained at the expense of public equity and thus can be considered a sort of perceived opportunity cost to private equity.

Finally, the performance can be measured against the absolute returns of the historical peer-group cohort for all the vintage years or the mature ones.

10.1.6 Benchmarking Examples

Let us take a look at an example to illustrate the use of the formulas just presented. Suppose that we have the following values for distributions, contributions, and NAVs for two French private equity funds (named PE Fund 1 and PE Fund 2) that belong to the vintage year 2000-stage focus buyout (amounts in euro millions):

	2000	2001	2002	2003	2004	2005	2006
PE Fund 1	−200	−800	200	−2,000	−600	2,000	3,500
PE Fund 2	−1,500	−1,500	−800	−200	500	1,500	5,000

Positive numbers correspond to years in which investors received net distributions, negative numbers correspond to years in which investors made net contributions, and the figures for 2006 correspond to the NAVs of each of the two funds at the end of that year. To benchmark these funds, we need to do the following three steps:

1. Calculate the IIRR, the TVPI, the DPI, and the RVPI for the two funds.
2. Perform a classical benchmark analysis based on the following information collected for 31 European private equity funds categorized as vintage year 2000-stage focus buyout, from inception to December 31, 2006:
   - The maximum return (measured using the IIRR) registered by a private equity fund was 34.80%.
   - The highest quartile of PE funds had a return of 13.20% or more.
   - The median return was 6.50%.
   - The lowest quartile funds had returns of 0% or less.
   - The minimum return was −9.50%.
3. Compare the returns offered by the two private equity funds to those of public securities (as measured by the French stock exchange using the CAC 40 Index as benchmark), calculating the gap between the IIRR of each PE fund and the public market equivalent. *Note:* The value of the CAC 40 Index during the 2000–2006 period was as follows:

	2000	2001	2002	2003	2004	2005	2006
CAC 40	5,926	4,625	3,064	3,558	3,821	4,715	5,542

---

[12] As we explain in Chapter 13, private equity funds are most likely to be correlated, at least to some degree, with public equity. For example, in an article by the Center for International Securities and Derivatives Markets (2006), the correlation between private equity and the S&P 500 was 0.55 (1991–2007).

Solution to 1: Calculate the IIRR, the TVPI, the DPI, and the RVPI for the two funds.

Recall that the interim IRR (IIRR) is defined as the discount rate that makes the present value of the distributions, the contributions, and the NAV equal to zero. Therefore, in the case of PE Fund 1, the IIRR is found by solving the following equation:

$$\frac{-200}{(1 + IIRR)} + \frac{-800}{(1 + IIRR)^2} + \frac{200}{(1 + IIRR)^3} + \frac{-2,000}{(1 + IIRR)^4} + \frac{-600}{(1 + IIRR)^5}$$
$$+ \frac{2,000}{(1 + IIRR)^6} + \frac{3,500}{(1 + IIRR)^7} = 0$$

Solving this equation using a financial calculator or Excel (function IRR or XIRR), we obtain an IIRR = 16.53%. Following the same procedure for PE Fund 2, we find that its IIRR is a lower 12.53%. As can be seen, PE Fund 1 is more profitable than PE Fund 2 by exactly 4%. Notice that we would need to compare these IIRRs to the discount rates or required rates of return applicable to each private equity fund to determine whether these returns were greater than the required minimum returns (further discussion on the discount rates applicable in private equity appears in Chapter 13).

TVPI: In the case of PE Fund 1, the TVPI is:

$$TVPI_T = \frac{(200 + 2,000) + 3,500}{200 + 800 + 2,000 + 600} = 1.58$$

In the case of PE Fund 2, the TVPI is 1.75. Thus, PE Fund 2 has a higher ratio of total distributions and NAV to total contributions between 2000 and 2006 than does PE Fund 1. As mentioned previously, this measure does not take into account the time value of money. Also, note that even though the drawdowns or paid-in had a negative sign in the table (given that they represent a use of cash to private equity funds), we used their values expressed in positive numbers in the denominator of the equation. We followed this convention because it generates a more meaningful sign (i.e., a positive value) for the TVPI index, which is more easily interpreted than benefit-to-cost ratios are usually expressed and interpreted. We followed the same procedure when calculating the total value of drawdowns in the case of the next two indices (DPI and RVPI).

DPI: In the case of PE Fund 1, the DPI is:

$$DPI_T = \frac{200 + 2,000}{200 + 800 + 2,000 + 600} = 0.61$$

In the case of PE Fund 2, the DPI is 0.50. Therefore, PE Fund 1 has a higher ratio of total distributions to total commitments between 2000 and 2006 than does PE Fund 2. As mentioned previously, this measure does not take into account the time value of money.

RVPI: For PE Fund 1, the RVPI is:

$$RVPI_T = \frac{3,500}{(200 + 800 + 2,000 + 600)} = 0.97$$

In the case of PE Fund 2, the formula gives us an RVPI of 1.25. It can be seen that PE Fund 2 has a higher ratio of NAV to total contributions than does PE Fund 1. Again, note that this measure does not consider the time value of money.

Solution to 2: Perform a classical benchmark analysis based on information collected for 31 European private equity funds categorized as vintage year 2000-stage focus buyout, from inception to December 31, 2006.

Based on the information provided, we can construct the following table to help visualize the performance of PE Funds 1 and 2 using a classical benchmark analysis:

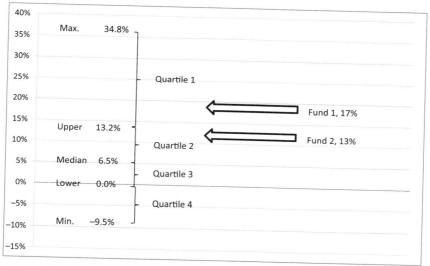

From	To	Sample Size	Max.	Upper	Median	Lower	Min.
Inception	12/31/06	31	34.8%	13.2%	6.5%	0.0%	−9.5%

PE Fund 1   17% in Quartile 1

PE Fund 2   13% in Quartile 2

It can be seen that PE Fund 1 had an excellent return when compared to its peers, as its IIRR was located between the upper and the maximum returns corresponding to the 31 European private equity funds used in the sample. In the case of PE Fund 2, the observed return was less impressive, although its IIRR was still above the median private equity fund return of the sample.

Solution to 3: Compare the returns offered by the two private equity funds to those of public securities (as measured by the French stock exchange using the CAC 40 Index as benchmark), calculating the gap between the IIRR of each PE fund and the public market equivalent.

PE Fund 1

PE Fund

		2000	2001	2002	2003	2004	2005	2006	IIRR
Drawdowns	(1)	−200	−800		−2,000	−600			
Repayments	(2)			200			2,000		
Terminal NAV	(3)							3,500	
Cash flows	(4) = (1) + (2) + (3)	−200	−800	200	−2,000	−600	2,000	3,500	16.5%
Index value	(5)	5,926	4,625	3,064	3,558	3,821	4,715	5,542	−1.1%
Acquired units	(6) = −(1)/(5)	0.03	0.17		0.56	0.16		X	
Sold units	(7) = −(2)/(5)			−0.07			−0.42		
Cumulated units	$(8)_t = (6)_t + (7)_t + (8)_{t-1}$	0.03	0.21	0.14	0.70	0.86	0.44	0.44	

Public Market Equivalent

		2000	2001	2002	2003	2004	2005	2006	IIRR
Investment	(1)	−200	−800		−2,000	−600			
Divestment	(2)			200			2,000	=	
Terminal portfolio value	(9) = (8) × (5)							2,419	
Cash flows	(10) = (1) + (2) + (9)	−200	−800	200	−2,000	−600	2,000	2,419	9.1%
Over (+) or under (−) performance	(4)–(10)								7.4%

PE Fund 2

PE Fund

		2000	2001	2002	2003	2004	2005	2006	IRR
Drawdowns	(1)	−1,500	−1,500	−800	−200				
Repayments	(2)					500	1,500		
Terminal NAV	(3)							5,000	
Cash flows	(4) = (1) + (2) + (3)	−1,500	−1,500	−800	−200	500	1,500	5,000	12.5%
Index value	(5)	5,926	4,625	3,064	3,558	3,821	4,715	5,542	−1.1%
Acquired units	(6) = −(1)/(5)	0.25	−0.32	0.26	0.06			X	
Sold units	(7) = −(2)/(5)					−0.13	−0.32		
Cumulated units	$(8)_t = (6)_t + (7)_t + (8)_{t-1}$	0.25	0.58	0.84	0.89	0.76	0.45	0.45	

Public Market Equivalent

		2000	2001	2002	2003	2004	2005	2006	IRR
Investment	(1)	−1,500	−1,500	−800	−200				
Divestment	(2)					500	1,500	=	
Terminal portfolio value	(9) = (8) × (5)							2,471	
Cash flows	(10) = (1) + (2) + (9)	−1,500	−1,500	−800	−200	500	1,500	2,471	2.5%
Over (+) or under (−) performance	(4)–(10)								10.0%

The IRR of PE Fund 1 is 16.5%. The annual growth in the CAC 40 from 2000 to 2006 is −1.1%. As stated previously, private equity return measures, which are cash flow weighted, cannot be compared directly to publicly quoted asset return measures, which are time weighted. To make this comparison possible, we use the public market equivalent (PME) methodology, which allows the practitioner to convert the time-weighted measures used for publicly quoted assets into a cash-flow-weighted methodology, which can then be used to benchmark a private equity fund. An analyst should also consider the dividends paid by the stocks tracked by the public market index. In order to more accurately compare private equity and public equity, a total return index, which includes dividends, should be used for each.

In our simplified examples (we assumed only one cash flow per year), PE Fund 1 had a series of cash flows between 2000 and 2006 and a terminal interim value (i.e., the NAV of the fund) of €3,500 in 2006, leading to an IRR of 16.5%. During the same period, a public market index (which is representative of the strategy followed by this fund) had a time-weighted return of −1.1% per annum, suggesting a significant underperformance versus the fund. The PME index is obtained by buying index units for each drawdown and selling index units for each distribution for an equal cash flow amount. For example, in 2000, €200 was drawn, which if invested in the public market index would have allowed the purchase of 0.03 index units. In 2002, the fund distributed €200, which if divested from the public market index would have required selling 0.07 index units. At the end of 2006, the terminal value of the PME is obtained by calculating the remaining index units and valuing them at the terminal index value. In our example, we have 0.44 (rounded from 0.4365) remaining index units, which at €5,542 per unit are valued at €2,419. This contrasts with the fund investor, who holds €3,500 at the end of the period. Based on this, we can then calculate an IRR for the PME (note that except for the terminal value, all the cash flows are identical to the ones of the fund), which can then be compared to the IRR of the fund. The IRR for the public market equivalent is 9.1%. We find that the gap, or excess IRR, for the return of PE Fund 1, 16.5%, relative to the PME, is 7.4%. For PE Fund 2, the IRR for the public market equivalent is 2.5%, underperforming the fund's IRR of 12.5% by about 10%.

10.2 PORTFOLIO OF FUNDS

10.2.1 Performance Measures

Because a private equity portfolio is an aggregation of funds, its performance measures are simply the aggregation of the measures used for the individual funds (IIRR, TVPI, DPI, or RVPI), and can be calculated based on one of the following methods:

- *Simple average:* the arithmetic mean of the private equity funds' performance measures:

$$IIRR_{P,T} = \frac{1}{N} \sum_{i=1}^{N} IIRR_{i,T}$$

Here, $IIRR_{P,T}$ is the IIRR of the portfolio P at the end of period T, $IIRR_{i,T}$ is the IIRR of fund i at the end of time period T, and N is the number of funds in the portfolio.

- *Median:* the value appearing halfway in a table ranking the performance of each fund held in the portfolio
- *Commitment weighted:* the **commitment-weighted** average of the funds' performance measures:

$$IIRR_{P,T} = \frac{1}{\sum_{i=1}^{N} CC_i} \sum_{i=1}^{N} CC_i * IIRR_{i,T}$$

Here, CC_i is the commitment made to fund i.

- *Pooled:* portfolio performance obtained by combining all individual funds' cash flows and residual values together, as if they were from one single fund, and solving the equation for $IIRR_{P,T}$:

$$\sum_{t=0}^{T} \sum_{i=1}^{N} \frac{CF_{i,t}}{(1 + IIRR_{P,T})^t} + \sum_{i=1}^{N} \frac{NAV_{i,T}}{(1 + IIRR_{P,T})^T} = 0$$

Here, $CF_{i,t}$ is the net cash flow during period t between the fund i and the investor, T is the number of periods, $NAV_{i,T}$ is the latest NAV of the fund I, $IIRR_{P,T}$ is the IIRR of the portfolio P at the end of time period T, and N is the number of funds in the portfolio.

Arguably, the pooled measure gives the true financial return of the portfolio. However, it may also make sense to use the others, depending on what one wishes to measure. For example, the simple average can be a good indicator of the selection skills, while the commitment-weighted average can be useful in assessing the added value resulting from the decision of what size commitment to make to each specific fund.

Finally, in some cases, the IRR may fail to properly assess long-term performance. This comes from the fact that when IRR is positive, large inflows in the later years will not boost the return, but when IRR is negative, they will in absolute terms. This further explains why it is important to also assess the performance with, for example, the multiple. An alternative for this problem is to use the time-zero IRR, which is a pooled IRR calculated with the assumption that all portfolio investments start on the same date. This is used to prevent the order of investments from affecting the portfolio IRR (see Exhibit 10.3). The IRR methodology can lead to multiple or incorrect answers when cash flows change signs at various times. The problem can be compounded when using the pooled approach, as multiple funds over multiple time periods are more likely to cause misleading IRR calculations.

10.2.2 Benchmarking Private Equity Fund Portfolios

To benchmark a portfolio of private equity funds, the portfolio needs to be compared against another similar portfolio of private equity funds. But there are two problems with this comparison: (1) publicly available database providers report too few funds of funds to make a comparison meaningful, and (2) these funds of funds implement various investment strategies, have different portfolio compositions, and, most of

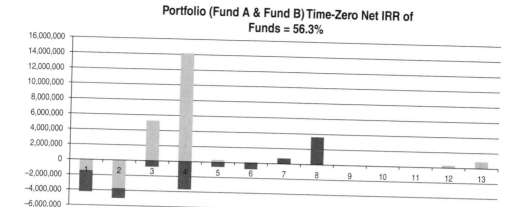

EXHIBIT 10.3 Time-Zero Net IRR—Two-Fund Portfolio Example (Fund A and Fund B)

all, usually have a different vintage-year structure. To circumvent these problems, synthetic portfolios can be generated with the same allocation to the various asset subclasses (e.g., vintage year, stage, and geographies) as the one to be benchmarked. Such benchmarking allows one to evaluate the portfolio manager's selection skills (i.e., how good he or she was at selecting the best fund managers within the defined allocations). If the portfolio is composed of 40% buyouts and 60% VC, the synthetic portfolio would need to have this same 40/60 split.

As the performance of a portfolio is the aggregation of individual funds' performance, the benchmarking of a portfolio is simply the extension of the benchmarking of an individual fund. In doing so, it is important to use the same aggregation method for both the portfolio and the benchmark.

10.2.3 Commitment-Weighted Benchmark

The portfolio benchmark is constructed using the commitment-weighted average of the benchmark for each individual fund comprising the peer group cohorts (e.g., the same vintage, geographic, and stage focus):

$$BM_{P,T} = \left(\frac{1}{\sum\limits_{i=1}^{N} CC_i} \right) \sum_{i=1}^{N} CC_i \times BM_{i,T}$$

where $BM_{P,T}$ is the portfolio benchmark at the end of time period T, CC_i is the commitment to the fund i, N is the number of funds in the portfolio, and $BM_{i,T}$ is the benchmark of fund i at the end of time period T. To compare apples to apples,

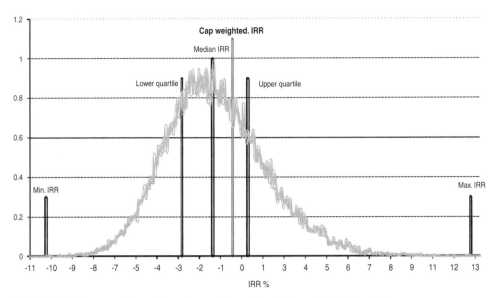

EXHIBIT 10.4   Portfolio of Funds Benchmarking: Monte Carlo Simulation

one must compare the commitment-weighted portfolio performance to that of the commitment-weighted benchmark.

10.2.4   Monte Carlo Simulation

The Monte Carlo simulation[13] is one technique that can be used to generate portfolios similar to the one being benchmarked. This is done by drawing, at each simulation run, the same number of funds as in the portfolio out of all the relevant peer-group cohorts, and then weighting the performances by the commitment size of the funds in the portfolio. For example (ignoring for simplification reasons the vintage year and the geographical risk dimensions), for a portfolio composed of eight early-stage funds and five later-stage funds, the simulation will draw for each run eight funds out of the early-stage peer benchmark group and five out of the later-stage peer benchmark group. After weighting the performance of each fund drawn according to a corresponding commitment size, a portfolio performance is obtained. This is repeated many times so that a distribution can be created, which is then used to benchmark the portfolio. The commitment-weighted IIRR of the portfolio is then compared against this synthetic benchmark (see Exhibit 10.4).

   The results obtained from this approach should be analyzed with care. This is because, by construction (meaning the random picks), it is implicitly assumed that the fund manager knows and has access to the entire population of the peer benchmark groups. Furthermore, it is also implicitly assumed that the manager makes no decision on the allocation among the PE markets or the level of diversification,

---

[13] A description of a Monte Carlo simulation can be found in Weidig and Mathonet (2004).

which in reality is often not the case. These limitations can be resolved by running a simulation better reflecting the flexibility granted to or the constraints imposed on the manager. For example, while a portfolio can be composed of 60% buyout funds and 40% VC funds, the composition of benchmark portfolios might range between 50% and 75% of buyout funds and 25% and 50% of VC funds, if this is what is prescribed in the investment policy imposed on the assessed manager.

CHAPTER 11

Monitoring Private Equity Fund Investments

Investors in private equity (PE) funds may assume that little can be done, besides divesting on the secondary market, to prevent problems once the due diligence process has been completed and the commitment to the fund has been made; however, ongoing monitoring throughout the life of a private equity investment is a necessary control mechanism. In such a long-term business, initial due diligence findings quickly become obsolete, while changes to the economic environment can fundamentally alter the balance between investor and fund manager interests. The information asymmetry and moral hazard–related problems associated with such changes can be lessened through monitoring.

11.1 APPROACH TO MONITORING

Monitoring involves the routine and systematic collection of information. In 1997, Robbie, Wright, and Chiplin noted that private equity limited partners typically engage in few monitoring actions. The authors expected this trend to continue, as a more proactive approach often raises questions about cost-effectiveness.

11.1.1 Monitoring as Part of a Control System

Monitoring involves more than simply the issuance of warnings. Instead, it should be seen as part of a larger control system within the investment process (see Exhibit 11.1). Its role is to observe, verify, and control in an attempt to make the portfolio perform in a desired way.

The monitoring process involves identifying problems and developing a plan to address them. Because of the illiquidity of a private equity fund, the investor's ability to react to infrequently identified problems is somewhat limited. In many situations, a solution will require finding a consensus with the fund manager and the other co-investors, or building alliances with co-investors to exercise pressure and act jointly. This explains why due diligence should focus not only on the fund manager but also on the co-investors.

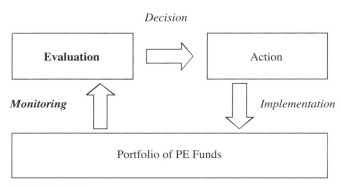

Decision

EXHIBIT 11.1   Control System

11.1.2   The Trade-Offs of Monitoring

In many ways, the limited partnership agreement's terms and conditions reflect a trade-off in various dimensions. It is neither possible nor meaningful to anticipate the expected behavior of the general partner over a time frame of 10 or more years. Market conditions fluctuate, fund management teams evolve, co-investors change, investments do not materialize as planned, and new opportunities arise. In hindsight, limited partners may conclude that certain provisions of the agreement were overly restrictive and worked against their interests, while other issues may not have been addressed in sufficient detail. The monitoring exercised by investors is intended to bridge this gap.

The appropriate approach and level of intensity of monitoring is not inconsequential. Investing in and monitoring private equity investments involve more effort and higher costs relative to an otherwise equivalent publicly traded investment. Such costs need to be weighed against potential benefits. Turning the monitoring findings into management actions, as well as choosing the appropriate time and degree of intervention, poses a dilemma. This is because intensive monitoring and its associated interventions can effectively dilute the fund manager's responsibility and lead to limited partners being reclassified as general partners and, in an extreme case, negate their limited liability status. Private equity, in particular, requires the long-term view, and limited partners should avoid overreacting to bad news, especially during the early years of a fund's lifetime. However, the private equity investor's reaction, when necessary, is typically too little, too late, to prevent further deterioration of the investment.

11.2   THE MONITORING OBJECTIVES

While monitoring is an important instrument for ensuring compliance with the limited partnership's terms and conditions and for gathering information, it is not necessarily linked to the performance of the fund. Monitoring should not be confused with the management of portfolio companies, an activity in which, in accordance with industry practices, limited partners have no involvement. Rather, the limited partner is responsible for managing the portfolio of funds and monitoring fund managers.

Investments are made in the context of a general portfolio strategy. As a result, monitoring must encompass not only individual funds but also the limited partner's overall portfolio composition. Indeed, while a detailed asset allocation process can promote effective diversification and eliminate the problems associated with haphazard fund selection, in the case of private equity it is often problematic to obtain equal weightings across funds and, at the same time, be represented in all key market segments. In addition, significant changes in investment valuations due to market fluctuations and distribution activity may cause the allocation to private equity to rise above or fall below the desired limits. To ensure that the allocation remains within the established ranges, limited partners must consistently monitor and adjust the portfolio structure.

11.2.1 Monitoring to Protect Downside

Limited partners monitor fund managers in order to control risk. In conventional asset classes, reducing risk means moving money into safer investments. But unlike most investors, limited partners cannot easily withdraw their commitments. Through monitoring activities, however, a limited partner may be able to identify severe shortcomings in time to reduce downside risks, either through a restructuring or by selling the position on the secondary market.

11.2.2 Monitoring the Risk of Style Drift

Monitoring is also important for ensuring style discipline. As limited partners are investing in a blind pool, the investment is mainly based on the fund managers' declared investment strategy. Funds will not necessarily adhere to it, nor should they in certain instances. For example, in a difficult market environment, it makes sense to deviate from the declared investment strategy and to look for investments in more promising areas. While style tracking in private equity is not as applicable as it is in the context of the hedge fund industry, limited partners nevertheless need to ensure that fund managers stay within the confines of their core expertise and style. Limited partners should be concerned with any change to a private equity fund strategy. Indeed, style drift may have serious consequences for the risk-return profile of the fund and can create unexpected exposure for limited partners. This reinforces the need to constantly monitor and adjust the portfolio structure.

Style drift describes the tendency of investment managers to deviate over time from their initially stated and agreed-on investment style. In private equity, fund managers explain their investment practices and their strategies during the initial due diligence. Limited partners expect fund managers to be reasonably consistent in following these practices. However, adherence to a stated investment style may not always hold true in the world of private equity funds, where secrecy and flexibility are critical to success. Cumming, Fleming, and Schwienbacher (2004) researched this issue and found that style drift in private equity is more common than was previously perceived.

Changes in style are often observed in geographical focus, between buyout and venture capital (VC) focus or by targeted industries. The skill sets required for fund managers and the investment objectives of buyouts and VC funds differ in important ways. While related, the two fields are sufficiently distinct to make the transfer of skills difficult. Nevertheless, there is anecdotal evidence that VC funds that raised excessive amounts of money were not able to resist the temptation to put the money to work in buyouts, rather than return the unutilized commitments to investors.[1] When deal flow dries up, fund managers often consider other markets. For example, U.S. VC funds may look for investments in Europe, while European VC funds try to gain access to Silicon Valley. Limited partners view this geographic drift with skepticism because, particularly in the case of VC, hands-on involvement of the fund manager is essential. Moreover, with the change in geography, investors may become exposed to foreign-exchange-rate risks they had not accounted for previously. Of course, business is global. Investors may welcome geographical diversification of a fund when the general partner dedicates local resources in each country where investments are made and when the general partner informs the investors in the precommitment stage of the discussion.

In order to alleviate the risk of style drift, the up-front design of the limited partnership agreement is important, as the covenants guide the behavior of the fund manager. Because of the blind-pool nature of private equity fund investing, it is crucial for limited partners to set the risk profile of their investment at the time of commitment. Moreover, given private equity's lack of liquidity, the limited partner cannot easily adjust portfolio holdings or rebalance them if general partners undertake actions that are inconsistent with governing documentation. That said, there are risks associated with adhering too closely to a declared investment strategy, especially when market conditions change significantly, creating new opportunities.

11.2.3 Creating Value through Monitoring

For fund investments, the management of the upside is primarily delegated to the fund managers, assuming that appropriate incentives have been provided. This underscores the importance of selecting the right teams. While the general partner is able to create value at the individual private equity fund level, the limited partner can create significant value through monitoring activities at the portfolio of funds level, as illustrated in the following situations:

- Intensive contact with the fund managers is important when deciding whether to invest in a follow-on fund (i.e., re-ups). It improves the due diligence process and can lead to a quicker finalization of contracts after incorporating improvements based on the previous experience with the fund manager. Moreover, a strong relationship can extend to junior team members ready to spin out and set up their own fund.
- The study undertaken by Lerner, Schoar, and Wongsunwai (2007) suggests that investors in private equity owe their success to superior reinvestment skills. The authors specifically refer to the example of endowment funds. These funds were

---

[1] Likewise in buyouts; see Henderson Global Investors (2002): "The opportunistic buoyancy of sentiment upon which many of today's large private equity funds were raised has contributed to the 'style drift' (e.g., CLECs, PIPEs, IT incubators) and subsequent portfolio problems evident amongst some of the highest profile managers in the asset class."

found to be less likely to reinvest in a partnership, but if they did invest in the follow-on fund, its subsequent performance was significantly better than those of funds they let pass. This finding underscores the importance of monitoring for improved decision making.

- Networking and liaising with other limited partners is an important instrument for gathering intelligence on the overall market and gaining knowledge of other funds,[2] and may help an investor gain access to deals that might otherwise not appear on the institution's radar screen. It can also improve access to secondary opportunities in advance of the less favorable auction process.
- In the context of a co-investment strategy, monitoring is important for screening interesting investment opportunities that may arise.
- Lessons learned from monitoring can also be applied in the future to improve the due diligence process and the selection of future investments.
- Access to information may enable a limited partner to optimize the management of commitments through more precise cash flow forecasting.

11.3 INFORMATION GATHERING IN THE MONITORING PROCESS

The private equity sector is called private for good reason, and **transparency** has its limitations. Transparency is the degree to which investment holdings and strategies are disclosed to investors. The typical monitoring process follows a dual approach (see Exhibit 11.2), separating formal from informal reporting. There is a tendency for larger investors to differentiate between obtaining specific qualitative data by direct interaction with investment managers and obtaining quantitative or standardized data provided by the back office. As the reporting quality and detail vary considerably among different funds, the monitoring needs to focus on filling the gaps present in the reporting. To avoid the risk of reporting overloads, an appropriate balance must be struck between the provision of specific information and the provision of standardized information to the limited partners.

11.3.1 Transparency

Although reporting to investors can often be more transparent for private equity investments than it is for public ones, this transparency is normally kept to a minimum for noninvestors. Indeed, private investments have generally been exempt from registration with such authorities as the Securities and Exchange Commission (SEC) in the United States, the Financial Services Authority (FSA) in the United Kingdom, or L'Autorité des Marchés Financiers (AMF) in France.[3] Thus, the development of valuation and reporting standards in private equity has been driven more by industry

---

[2] Being perceived as a professional and serious investor also increases negotiation power vis-à-vis the fund managers. In a comparatively small industry, a strong network is a credible threat against a team that would otherwise be unwilling to compromise.

[3] This refers only to private equity investments and, in some jurisdictions, to private equity companies. In the case of fund managers, in some jurisdictions (e.g., the United Kingdom, France, and Italy) registration is an obligation.

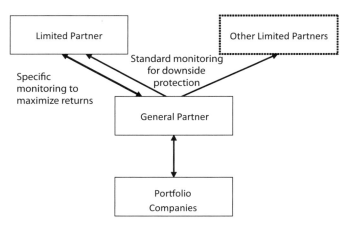

EXHIBIT 11.2 Monitoring Process

players than by regulatory bodies, although this has to some degree changed with a tightening of regulatory regimes for alternative investments worldwide.

Historically, the appearance of private equity as unregulated was the by-product of a careful balancing of specific exemptions from certain aspects of regulation and the sustained efforts of PE and VC associations to maintain high standards of investment conduct by private equity fund managers. In the United States, private equity fund managers, like hedge fund managers, have historically relied on the same exemption from registration under the Investment Advisers Act.

The information required for the management of the portfolio of private equity funds is, in principle, the same as that needed for the investment decision (i.e., the information gathered through the due diligence process). This information is supplied by the fund managers but is also collected from outside sources.[4] While a significant amount of the information should be provided in a low-cost, standardized manner, proprietary information can lead to a competitive advantage.

11.3.2 Standard Monitoring Information

Monitoring is built around the information supplied in fund management reports. Therefore, reliable, appropriate, and timely management of information is crucial. PE associations' reporting and valuation guidelines, such as those issued by the Institutional Limited Partners Association (ILPA), the International Private Equity and Venture Capital (IPEV) Valuation Board, or the European Private Equity and Venture Capital Association (EVCA), define the standard level of information to be provided. Generally, investors in private equity funds complain about inadequate disclosure, inconsistent reporting, and the often significant time lag in receiving this information. Major problems with a portfolio company eventually appear in the reporting. Often the damage has been done by then, and little corrective action

---

[4] Also, the administration of capital calls and distributions by general partners offer opportunities to conduct monitoring by limited partners, as in this context; for example, contractual terms can and should be checked.

remains possible. This raises the question of whether large institutional investors will become more active or proactive in addressing the following issues:

- Incomplete information creates uncertainty and consequently increases risks. Should institutions, possibly together with PE associations, persuade industry players to provide more detail and transparency in reporting?
- Transparency in reporting is tied to the question of valuation and risk. Can investors get a truer and fairer picture of their investments through more detailed and better quality investment reporting?
- There is overall agreement among industry players that formal accounting-related information should be standardized. EVCA reporting guidelines are seen as sufficient in general, but the information reported greatly depends on the general partner's willingness to disclose this information in its reporting framework.
- Increased disclosure appears to be an admirable objective, especially to those accustomed to public markets. However, it needs to be kept in mind that there are practical obstacles to disclosure. The answers to these questions need to be pondered against the background of the private equity market's dynamics and from a cost-benefit viewpoint.
- In private equity, information collection and analysis can be prohibitively expensive, and there are market forces that work against transparency.[5] Any attempt to go against these dynamics would be expensive and time-consuming, and might ultimately be unsuccessful.
- The huge information asymmetry in private equity explains and justifies the need for intermediation. An increased level of detail will not allow a nonexpert to verify a fund manager's reporting and appraisal. Moreover, due to its imprecise character, any qualitative information is, by definition, of low quality. If one does not want to rely on the intermediary's judgment, the only alternative is direct investing, which requires an entirely different approach and skill set.
- As private equity fund investments are buy-and-hold and illiquid, a fund's limited partners are unable to react quickly to new information. Moreover, for such a long-term-oriented investment, short-term developments do not, in most cases, materially affect the fund's valuation.

Based on these points, one could conclude that although a higher degree of transparency would be desirable, the public market cannot be seen as the benchmark. It is mainly the limited partners' monitoring that can overcome the nontransparency and the reporting time lags of this asset class, but only to the extent that the general manager is willing to cooperate toward enhanced disclosure.

11.3.3 Specific Information

General partners are extremely reluctant to disclose all information to investors. Their dilemma is obvious: On the one hand, there is an obligation to disclose information so that investors are able to understand the portfolio's progress; but on the

---

[5] We expect that information targeting downside protection will be more likely to be standardized and shared among all limited partners. Ultimately, to remove the fund manager, a majority vote of the limited partners is required. Therefore, it is in all investors' interests that everybody knows how the portfolio is performing.

other hand, further information, especially at a level of detail that allows an independent risk assessment, may potentially reduce the chance that the limited partners will commit to follow-on funds and increase the chance they will start investing directly. There is also the investment rationale for maintaining a high degree of confidentiality. Indeed, a fund with a niche strategy that consistently yields above-average returns will attract competition. General partners fear that too much information given to the outside helps competitors imitate their strategy, access their deal flow, or jeopardize their negotiating position. Cullen (2004) cites an example in which a limited partner was given financial information regarding a deal that was later shared with a competitor and ultimately caused the fund to lose the deal.

Moreover, if disclosed to a wider audience, information can be highly damaging. It may even have an adverse impact on the trading ability of a portfolio company, as it could result in reduced credit lines or lead the company's potential clients to choose to partner with the competition. Conversely, news of success may breed competitors. In the extreme, the fund manager might even be sued for disclosing harmful information.

Interestingly, however, it is not only the fund managers but also the limited partners who may prefer to limit the degree of transparency. Making star funds public knowledge may attract competitors. Limited partners need to protect their privileged access to follow-on funds or to new teams that set up their own vehicles outside the old fund. As private equity funds are not scalable, limited partners may be concerned about being locked out of follow-on funds because, as suggested by Lerner and Schoar (2004), general partners have a preference for deep-pocketed investors. Better to keep the information quiet than to attract a feeding frenzy of competing investors.

11.4 ACTIONS RESULTING FROM MONITORING

Results of the monitoring and its evaluation can lead to decisions on a series of possible actions. These can range from simply changing the monitoring intensity to intervening at the individual fund or perhaps even portfolio company level. The monitoring intensity should be a function of the total exposure of a private equity fund, its final expected performance, and its operational status (see Exhibit 11.3).

It does not make sense to spend too much time on monitoring funds that are already quite advanced in their life cycle or beyond recovery. It is also not money well spent to focus scarce monitoring resources on teams that are highly professional or on funds over which other experienced limited partners already exercise significant oversight. In these cases, if one is dissatisfied, one would simply not invest in the follow-on fund. Finally, the cost of control must be relative to the size of the asset.

Limited partners want to influence the actions being taken as a result of changed circumstances. This often means taking part in the decision-making process, vetoing decisions,[6] or simply exercising pressure on the fund manager. One of the more

---

[6] An illustrative list of considerations would be the appointment and the remuneration of the managers, the approval of annual reports, the approval of the budget, decisions on unforeseen investments (loans or side funds), issues of new shares, extension of the investment period, and so on.

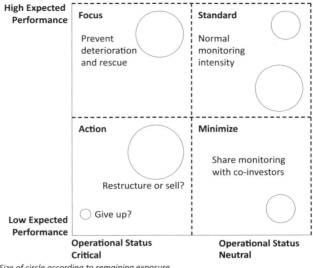

Size of circle according to remaining exposure
(NAV plus undrawn commitments)

EXHIBIT 11.3   Monitoring Intensity Management

obvious and common monitoring actions is the increased use of renegotiation of management fees and fund size toward the end of a fund's life.

Due to the illiquidity of private equity funds, the tool set for the management of the portfolio is comparatively restricted. Active trading of positions through the secondary market to significantly rebalance the portfolio in line with allocation targets is often not feasible. At the fund level, the first approach to adjusting the portfolio structure is the continuous review of the ongoing investment pipeline in primary fund investments. However, this strategy may be restricted by the availability of suitable investment opportunities or by delays in closing the deals. Moreover, when the private equity portfolio is large, the adjustment via primary transactions may be slow and insufficient.

Another approach for investors is to attempt to exit their investments in private equity funds before maturity. There are two main exit routes:

1. **Secondary transactions.** A secondary market for limited partnership shares exists, although it offers limited liquidity and is expected to remain rather inefficient. Often the stake in a private equity fund cannot be sold off without the consent of the general partners and possibly the consent of other limited partners. Secondary transactions take place at a negotiated price, often at a substantial discount to net asset value (NAV).
2. **Securitization.** This involves the transfer of the limited partnership share to a **special purpose vehicle (SPV)** for a collateralized fund obligation.[7] The SPV is a

---

[7] A special purpose vehicle is a special entity, typically located in a tax- and/or legal-efficient offshore location, established by a company to answer a certain financial or legal problem (e.g., to pay lower taxes).

distinct legal entity that issues senior and junior notes and uses the proceeds from the issuance to invest in a private equity fund of funds. (For such securitizations, see Chapter 19 in Mathonet and Meyer [2007].)

However, these transactions require expertise, and opportunities are often scarce. Alternatively, co-investing alongside fund managers is a tool for increasing exposure to certain sectors, but it also requires specific skills. Finally, a further option is to adjust allocations using public small-cap equities as a proxy for private equity investments. This could be a meaningful investment in which a significant pool of undrawn commitments needs to be managed.

Active involvement mainly relates to individual funds and can take the following forms:

- In situations in which a fund management team has clearly demonstrated that it is not up to the job or that it is not cooperating with its limited partners, the simplest and most obvious action of a limited partner is not to commit to the follow-on fund. This is also most feared by the fund managers, as often the loss of a reputable investor sends a clear negative signal to the market. Not only would the team need to go back to the capital market for fund-raising, but it would do so with a tarnished reputation.

- During the lifetime of a fund, agreements are not carved in stone. If it becomes clear that the original investment strategy cannot be successfully implemented and no credible alternative is brought forward, investors can influence the fund manager to reduce management fees or even release limited partners from portions of their commitments. More often than not, general partners give in to reducing fund size. This investor-friendly behavior can build up goodwill and ease the next fund-raising exercise.

- Of course, general partners have the right to refuse such voluntary actions. However, this often results in pressure, activism, and even lawsuits from limited partners who want some or all of their money back. In the extreme, and if there is an agreement among limited partners, the fund management team can be terminated without cause. Even without recourse to such extreme measures, the threat of action or the noise of complaints from investors can be highly damaging to the reputation of a fund manager. This in turn can have serious implications for future fund-raising ambitions.

- Investor default is questionable, as it constitutes a contractual breach, but it may be the instrument of last resort if the fund manager is clearly incompetent.[8] There can be substantial penalties when a limited partner does not pay a requested drawdown. The limited partner will likely forfeit all prior investments in the fund. The investor may also find it difficult to continue investing in private equity, as other fund managers may refuse to accept new commitments from investors who did not fulfill their prior obligations.

---

[8] See Meek (2003): "In one instance the limited partners of a U.S. fund have simply refused to honor any future drawdowns, taking the view that to do so would simply be throwing good money after bad."

CHAPTER 12

Private Equity Fund Valuation

As previously mentioned in the context of monitoring, it is fair to say that there is a trade-off in terms of costs and benefits to private equity fund valuation. This trade-off also exists between the valuation's level of precision (i.e., attempt to minimize errors) and timeliness.

When discerning the value of private equity funds, it is necessary to differentiate among the following concepts:

- A valuation for accounting purposes that primarily aims to ensure the timeliness of the reported value and its compliance with accounting standards such as Financial Accounting Standard (FAS) 157 or International Accounting Standard (IAS) 39 and/or valuation guidelines such as the International Private Equity and Venture Capital Valuation Guidelines (IPEV Valuation Guidelines), developed and launched in 2005[1]
- The economic value of limited partnership shares that can be used for portfolio management purposes
- The price that can be obtained on the secondary market

In this chapter, we describe the three main approaches employed to value private equity funds: the net asset value (NAV) approach, the internal rate of return (IRR) approach, and the economic value approach.

12.1 NET ASSET VALUE (NAV)

Limited partnership shares have traditionally been valued by multiplying the NAV of the fund by the percentage of shares owned in the fund. In private equity, the NAV is often referred to as a fund's residual value, as it represents the value of all investments remaining in the portfolio minus any liabilities net of fees and carried interest as of a specific date. This is a bottom-up technique in which individual companies are

---

[1] Available at www.privateequityvaluation.com (accessed September 2011). Organizations that developed the IPEV Valuation Guidelines include the Association Française des Investisseurs en Capital (AFIC), the British Venture Capital Association (BVCA), and the European Private Equity and Venture Capital Association (EVCA).

valued (normally according to industry valuation guidelines) and then aggregated to compute the private equity fund value.[2]

The goal of private equity investing is to earn attractive long-term returns rather than to try to profit from short-term movements. Private equity is a buy-and-hold investment strategy in which companies are developed over a substantial period of time, and general partners have a fair chance of timing the exit. From the limited partner's viewpoint, valuations will be very different, depending on whether the investment is held until maturity.

When the fund's NAV has been estimated in compliance with accounting standards (such as FAS 157 or IAS 39) or valuation guidelines, it can normally be used for accounting purposes.[3] However, the NAV can produce a result that is often quite distinct from the economic reality of the fund. In order to be truly fair, and assuming efficient markets, such value should equal the present value of the fund's expected cash flows. Even if the fair value of individual companies could be established, their aggregation would often not provide the limited partners with the economic value of a private equity fund for the following reasons:

- *Undrawn commitments.* The expected future cash flows of a private equity fund are generated not only out of the NAV but also out of investments still to be made.[4] During the first years of a fund's life, the main value to be created will depend on the fund manager's future activities. For successful teams, the fair value of the existing portfolio may fall short in expressing the total value to be created. When portfolio companies underperform, writing down the portfolio to its fair value may be insufficient to cover the existing losses as well as the losses to be expected from the future investments.
- *Private equity fund added (or deducted) value.* If one accepts that the management team of a private equity fund adds significant value to the private equity companies, this value-added should be reflected.
- *Future fund expenses.* As these portfolio companies will not be realized now but over the remaining lifetime of the fund, additional management fees, expenses, and eventually catch-up and carried interest will be charged against their fair value and reduce the cash flows to the investors and, therefore, the fund's value.[5]

---

[2] For the sake of completeness, other asset or liability items (e.g., net cash) have to be taken into account to get to the fund's value.

[3] For an illustration of the impact of the introduction of such guidelines or standards, see Exhibit 5.6 in Chapter 5.

[4] This view is also supported and therefore more consistent with the treatment of undrawn commitments under the New Basel Accord. According to the Basel Committee on Banking Supervision (2001), the undrawn commitments to private equity funds also need to be risk-weighted.

[5] Some reporting guidelines, such as the ones published by the EVCA, recommend reporting valuation net of management fees and carried interest. But this netting refers only to past management fees and carried interest plus, eventually, the carried interest implied by the current portfolio.

- *Capital constraints for venture capital funds.* Even if a portfolio company theoretically has a value during the early investment stages, success will depend on the fund's intentions going forward. Most of the time, early-stage portfolio companies are technically insolvent, as financing is typically done through various rounds with ratchet mechanisms and milestones. At any time, the fund might exercise the implicit option to abandon the support for a portfolio company if better projects emerge. Ultimately, valuation is a matter of negotiation, in which much depends on a fund's position in the market. In the extreme, if a fund has no liquidity left, it either is forced to abandon a promising early-stage investment or has to accept a highly unfavorable valuation.

It is important to differentiate between the value of the portfolio companies, as seen from the viewpoint of the general partner, and the value of the fund, comprising not only the portfolio companies but also the undrawn commitments and the quality of the general partner. Under a breakup assumption the NAV might be too high, as the portfolio companies most likely cannot be liquidated at the ascribed valuation, while as an estimate of the fund's terminal wealth it will often be too low.

12.2 INTERNAL RATE OF RETURN (IRR)

The traditional IRR for a project completed at time T can be found by solving the following equation for IRR:

$$\sum_{t=1}^{T} \frac{CF_t}{(1 + IRR)^t} = 0$$

where CF_t is the net cash flow at time t, and T in this case is the lifetime.

In Chapter 10, it was shown that the interim IRR (IIRR) is a rough but widely used estimation of IRR performance and forms the basis of most published performance statistics in private equity prior to the termination of the investment. For active funds, the $IIRR_T$ is computed by taking the NAV as the last cash flow at time T:

$$\sum_{t=1}^{T} \frac{CF_t}{(1 + IIRR_T)^t} + \frac{NAV_T}{(1 + IIRR_T)^T} = 0$$

As explained previously, the IIRR usually follows a J-curve, as it is low or negative in the early years and later converges to the final, and likely much higher, IRR (see Exhibit 5.5 in Chapter 5).

Notice that, in theory, the IIRR equation can be divided into three parts: the past cash flows from the portfolio (up to and including time T), CF_t^{PAST}; the future distributions of the current portfolio, CF_t^{PORT}; and the future drawdowns and distributions from new investments, CF_t^{NEW}, which generally cannot be stopped

EXHIBIT 12.1   IIRR Components Assessment

IRR Component	Assessment
Past cash flows	Quantitative only
Current portfolio (NAV)	Quantitative, but qualitative review recommended
Future cash flows	Qualitative, based on historical data and scenarios

without investors agreeing to cancel part of them, or the investor defaulting or selling the position.

$$\sum_{t=1}^{T} \frac{CF_t^{PAST}}{(1 + IIRR_T)^t} + \sum_{t=T+1}^{\infty} \frac{CF_t^{PORT}}{(1 + IIRR_T)^t} + \sum_{t=T+1}^{\infty} \frac{CF_t^{NEW}}{(1 + IIRR_T)^t} = 0$$

Also, notice that whereas the NAVs approximate the middle expression of the preceding equation, the use of NAVs in IIRR computations neglects the right-hand term (i.e., the future investments' cash flows), even though the weight of these factors changes over time. Therefore, taken at face value, the NAV may lead to short-term thinking in portfolio management. This is because the expected future cash flows of a fund are generated not only out of the existing portfolio companies but also out of the investments to be made, including the undrawn commitments. Therefore, to estimate the expected investment performance for a fund's entire lifetime, all three components of the IIRR need to be assessed (see Exhibit 12.1).

For the current portfolio, limited partners should have a valuation review policy in place, such as the one described in Mathonet and Monjanel (2006). Such a policy should take the quality of the appraising fund managers into consideration. Finally, for the assessment of the fund's future cash flows (as represented by the third part of the equation), a qualitative assessment of the general partner's quality is also required. Though limited partners do not typically participate in the official accounting valuation of a fund, an internal determination of the likely economic value of the fund could be useful for portfolio allocation and manager selection purposes. (See Exhibit 12.2.)

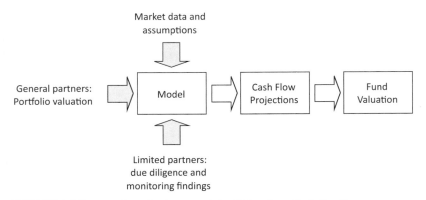

EXHIBIT 12.2   Fund Cash Flows and the Valuation Modeling Process

12.3 ECONOMIC VALUE APPROACH

To work around the shortcomings of NAV, some limited partners use models to determine the economic value of a private equity fund. Examples of the **economic value approach** used in practice to forecast cash flows are based on bottom-up or top-down approaches.

These two economic value approaches seem to come much closer to the economic reality of funds. However, they cannot be used for accounting purposes, as they fail to meet accounting standards.

12.3.1 Bottom-Up Cash Flow Projection

To obtain a more useful valuation, a fund can be modeled from the bottom up by analyzing its main value drivers in detail and aggregating these individual components. Here an investor must first obtain information on the quality of the fund managers, the legal structure of the partnership, and the current portfolio holdings. Next, exit projections for the underlying portfolio companies are determined, including exit multiples and timing, along with future capital calls resulting in company-level cash flow streams. These cash flow streams are then combined and filtered through the partnership structure to arrive at a series of net cash flows, which represent the cash flows the limited partner can expect to receive. These cash flows must then be discounted, typically by the target return or the cost of capital (see Chapter 13), to arrive at a present value for the fund.

However, limited partners may have difficulty determining exit scenarios for individual companies, especially in situations in which even the general partner is unable to provide meaningful exit guidance. Furthermore, even if a limited partner were able to project accurate portfolio company exit values on a consistent basis, institutions with large portfolios would have to conduct extensive due diligence on potentially thousands of companies every quarter, which might not be feasible from a resource perspective. This high workload calls for practical solutions, such as the **modified bottom-up approach** described in detail in Mathonet and Meyer (2007).[6] In this approach, when it is difficult or too costly to determine specific exit scenarios for individual companies, various alternative inputs are used at the fund manager or market level, including fund manager track record data or broad VC secondary market insight. Based on these inputs, global exit scenarios are determined and used for individual companies without specific scenarios, as well as for undrawn capital. Then, as before, these cash flow streams are combined, possibly adjusted depending on the partnership structure, and discounted to yield a present value for the fund.

12.3.2 Top-Down Cash Flow Projection

Meyer and Mathonet (2007) have described in detail another option for valuing a fund, the grading-based economic model (GEM), which could be seen as a **modified**

---

[6] The modified bottom-up approach was developed by Cogent Partners, an international investment bank specializing in transactions of private equity secondary assets, private equity research, and the investment of alternative assets.

comparable approach.[7] The GEM does not rely on the projection of individual portfolio company exit values but rather on a high-level evaluation of the overall private equity fund and on information on the past performance or cash flows of comparable funds. This technique is based on the assumption that the comparable funds' historical performance or cash flows are representative, and that a grading system (see Exhibit 9.3 in Chapter 9) allows for an identification of these comparables. To apply this relative valuation technique, it is necessary to identify the best comparable peer group and obtain its historical cash flows or performance data. The grading system is used to control for any qualitative differences between the funds that might affect the value. After the relative position of a fund within a peer group has been estimated and a grade determined, the expected final IRR of the fund and cash flows are forecast based on the peer group historical cash flows and performance data.

Forecasting cash flows for any alternative asset class is a challenge and requires significant effort and experience. Practitioners typically need to use a number of complementary approaches, such as estimates, projections, and scenarios, which are further described in Chapter 13.

---

[7] See Chapter 16 in Meyer and Mathonet (2007).

Private Equity Fund Discount Rates

D iscount rates are particularly difficult to estimate in the case of private equity (PE), but they are important. As with any financial asset, it is worth investing in a private equity fund only if its expected rate of return is at least equal to the investors' required rate of return or cost of capital. Moreover, when cash flows can be projected, the discount rate allows for estimating the economic value of a fund, as we saw in the previous chapter. Therefore, the question of how to set this rate is of high interest for private equity investors. Finance theory postulates that the risk in an investment should be the risk borne by a well-diversified investor, and that the return to be expected should be commensurate with this risk.

13.1 THE CAPITAL ASSET PRICING MODEL (CAPM)

The capital asset pricing model (CAPM) defines the relationship between risk and return using the following equation:

$$E(R_A) = R_f + \beta_A[E(R_M) - R_f]$$

Here, $E(R_A)$ is the expected return of asset A; R_f is the risk-free rate of return; β_A is the beta, or the systematic risk of asset A; and the term $[E(R_M) - R_f]$ is the market risk premium. If we know an asset's systematic risk, the risk-free rate, and the market risk premium, we can use the CAPM to estimate its expected return.

Even though in theory the CAPM holds whether we are dealing with financial assets or real (physical) assets, it is not clear that it can easily be applied to private equity funds. The CAPM assumes that investors hold well-diversified portfolios. Knowing that the vast majority of private equity fund investors are large and sophisticated institutions, such an assumption appears sensible. The model also assumes that there are no transaction costs, that buyers and sellers are fully informed, that assets are tradable, and that the market is always in equilibrium. Obviously, these assumptions are not necessarily accurate in the context of private equity. However, if the objective is to estimate a fair value as defined in the International Accounting Standards (IAS), it is implied that parties are knowledgeable and willing, and that the transaction is at arm's length. Given this, such assumptions may appear to be more plausible.

Assuming for the moment that the CAPM can be used for private equity funds, it is necessary to get access to the required data. Indeed, accuracy depends not only on the model used but also on the availability and quality of the financial data used in the model. And as we just saw, the CAPM requires three inputs: the risk-free rate, the expected equity risk premium, and the beta.

13.1.1   The Risk-Free Rate and the Equity Risk Premium

The risk-free rate in the CAPM equation is an estimation of the pure time value of money. In the case of the United States, the returns on Treasury securities issued by the federal government, with maturities similar to those of the projects being analyzed, are the preferred estimation for the risk-free rate.

The CAPM does not reflect the total risk (and even less the total uncertainty)[1] that an investment carries, but quantifies the marginal risk that it adds to a diversified portfolio. This is explained by the nature of the total risk, which can be broken down into two components: the investment-specific (or idiosyncratic) risk and the market (or systematic) risk. As the former can be diversified away whereas the latter cannot, diversified investors require an excess return for being exposed to the latter. Such a distinction is important and explains why investors in private equity funds often have a misperception of the risk taken. Indeed, many investors expect a premium as compensation for the fund's total risk, when in fact only its systematic portion should be rewarded. Although this approach is perfectly acceptable when investors are diversified, it is much less so in the context of an investor holding only one position (e.g., the entrepreneur) or a few positions.

Moskowitz and Vissing-Jørgensen (2002) have analyzed the returns to private equity. The analysis they conducted was based on data derived from the U.S. Survey of Consumer Finances and various national income accounts, and predominantly relates to nonintermediated investments in nonpublic companies, as opposed to intermediated investments undertaken by private equity funds. They estimated that the additional premium required to compensate an investor for the risk of holding a single position was at least 10% per year. Using recent initial public offerings (IPOs) of high-tech companies, Kerins, Smith, and Smith (2001) estimated that the required additional premium for entrepreneurs with 25% of their wealth in a single VC project is in the range of 25%. This is a good illustration of the importance of the additional premium required by an investor exposed to total risk, or at least to a significant portion of it, compared to a fully diversified investor exposed only to systematic risk.

In the CAPM, this extra return over the risk-free rate is estimated based on a measure of the relative risk added by an asset to a diversified portfolio (i.e., the beta) and on the risk premium over the risk-free rate expected by a diversified investor holding the market portfolio. This premium is normally estimated by using either

---

[1] Economists typically differentiate between risk and uncertainty. Risk exists when a probability based on past experience can be attached to an event, whereas uncertainty exists when there is no objective way to determine an event's probability. In efficient markets, there is little differentiation between risk and uncertainty, as uncertainty is practically the same for all participants. In private markets, however, investors are exposed to different degrees of uncertainty. Measurement of events and their chances turns uncertainty into risk. For private equity, it is difficult in practice to draw a line separating risk and uncertainty, and most of the time the distinction is not made.

historical data or the level implied by the current market prices. In the United States, the premium estimated with historical data from the period 1926–2007 is about 8.5%. Although this approach is commonly used, there are some limitations to it. First, there can be surprisingly large differences in the estimated premium,[2] notably due to differences in the time period used,[3] in the choice of the risk-free security,[4] and in the use of arithmetic versus geometric averages. Second, the survivorship bias has an impact on market data and results in higher estimates than do the real historical risk premiums. Third, while it is already difficult to estimate a reliable premium based on historical information for mature markets such as the United States, it becomes even more challenging for markets with short and more volatile histories. One solution is to consider the U.S. premium as a basis and to adjust it in order to account for the additional systematic risk of each country.

The alternative to the historical risk premium is to estimate the equity risk premium implied by current market prices. Obviously, the implied equity risk premium changes over time much more than does the long-term historical risk premium. Applied to the U.S. market, the average implied premium is about 4%.[5]

Undoubtedly, the equity risk premium discussion will continue. Some argue that the premium is probably below the 6% annual premium figure estimated in much of the financial literature. Using an expected equity risk premium in the range of 4% to 5% can be considered reasonable.

13.2 PRIVATE EQUITY FUND BETAS

Not being specific to private equity, the risk-free rate and the equity risk premium are not problematic and can be determined with relative ease using publicly available market information. This leaves only the private equity fund beta for us to estimate.

13.2.1 Estimation Based on Quoted Comparable Firms

When an asset is not publicly traded, it is common practice to use the beta of a similar quoted asset as a proxy. As the most liquid stock in the European private equity industry is probably 3i plc, its beta can give an indication. It is a world leader in private equity, and is listed on the London Stock Exchange. Although its focus and portfolio composition have evolved over time, 3i is still potentially a good comparable for a portfolio of European private equity funds. Nevertheless, it is still worth looking at it in more detail.

---

[2] According to Damodaran (2001), investment banks, consultants, and corporations estimate the risk premium in U.S. markets to range from 4% to 12%.

[3] Shorter periods are used to provide an estimate that will better reflect the current risk aversion of the average investor. In doing so, it is assumed that the risk premium is changing over time and that, therefore, using a shorter time period will provide a more accurate estimate.

[4] The risk-free rate to be used to estimate the discount rate should be the government (AAA) zero coupon bond rates with a maturity equal to the private equity fund's duration. Therefore, to be consistent, the same risk-free rate should be used when estimating the equity risk premium.

[5] The difference from the historical premium could be due to the survivorship bias.

EXHIBIT 13.1 3i plc—Historical Beta
Source: Bloomberg.

The evolution of 3i's beta over time, which is presented in Exhibit 13.1, remained relatively stable over two clearly differentiated periods, before and after the peak of the Internet bubble of the late 1990s. Before the bubble, the beta was in the 0.6 to 0.8 region, supporting the hypothesis that an investment in private equity was an effective way to diversify a portfolio. Postbubble, the picture changed, with betas above 1.0 and up to approximately 1.7, supporting the alternative hypothesis that an investment in private equity is correlated with public equity and is somewhat more risky.

However, 3i is not the only quoted private equity asset. For instance, Bauer, Bilo, and Zimmermann (2001) researched other **publicly traded private equity (PTPE)**. They classify PTPE into three groups: listed companies whose core business is private equity (e.g., 3i); quoted investment funds (e.g., Schroder Ventures International Investment Trust); and specially structured investment vehicles (e.g., Castle Private Equity). They identified more than 200 PTPEs and, after liquidity constraints, more than 100 that were considered to be acceptable for their investigations. Over the period of January 1988 to May 2000, the authors calculated the volatilities of the various public equity indices and PTPEs. The PTPE volatilities were similar to those observed in the public markets. In their study, they did not calculate correlations or betas. However, assuming that all PTPE risk is systematic, betas can be easily calculated by comparing volatility levels. Following this procedure and making the assumption that the correlation of a stock (X) with the market (M) is equal to 1, the estimation of the beta can be simplified as follows:

$$\beta = \frac{\text{cov}_{XM}}{\text{var}_M} = \frac{\text{corr}_{XM} \times \text{vol}_X \times \text{vol}_M}{\text{vol}_M^2}$$

$$= \frac{1 \times \text{vol}_X \times \text{vol}_M}{\text{vol}_M^2} = \frac{\text{vol}_X}{\text{vol}_M}$$

EXHIBIT 13.2 PTPE Betas against Major Indices

Index	Volatility (annualized)	Implied PTPE Beta
MSCI	12.35%	1.08
S&P 500	14.47%	0.92
NASDAQ	21.33%	0.63
STOXX	15.37%	0.87
Russell 2000	15.88%	0.84
PTPE (overall, without incubators)	13.37%	1.00

Datasource: Datastream/Bloomberg (1988–5/2000).
Source: Bauer, Bilo, and Zimmermann (2001) and author calculations.

The betas obtained with this approach are in the range of 0.63 to 1.08 (see Exhibit 13.2). For example, the beta of PTPE with respect to the S&P 500 index was 0.92 (i.e., 13.37%/14.47%) between 1988 and 2000. This result suggests that the stocks of publicly traded private equity companies were slightly less risky than those of the market, as measured by the S&P 500 index.

The authors further refined their analysis by splitting the PTPE into the following subclasses: incubators,[6] ventures,[7] private equity funds, buyout houses, and balanced funds. Making the same assumption as before (i.e., that all risk is systematic), betas can be calculated for these subclasses (see Exhibit 13.3). For VC, the betas were in the range of 1.40 to 2.42, with a mean of 1.94.[8]

These results support the hypothesis that VC is more risky and buyout is less risky than public equity. Assuming a market risk premium of 5%, VC would require a risk premium in excess of 400 basis points over public equity. Final conclusions cannot be drawn based on this analysis, as the sample used is limited and most likely not fully representative of the VC market. In addition, there are several important dimensions that have not been taken into account in the study that may be key factors for estimating betas, such as geographical location and industry sector.

Recently, Zimmermann et al. (2004) further researched the risk and return of PTPE. This work, which is the continuation of the work of Bauer, Bilo, and Zimmermann (2001), defines and discusses different indices for PTPE and leads to the creation of new benchmarks for private equity, called the LPX index family. The PTPEs that compose these indices have been selected based on several liquidity criteria. Although the authors have not calculated correlation coefficients, betas can

---

[6] Bauer, Bilo, and Zimmermann (2001) define *incubators* as follows: "they also invest in early stage and growth companies with business activities related mainly to the internet. However, the support of the portfolio companies and the organizational structure deviates from traditional venture capitalists. Incubators focus on providing any necessary resources to shorten the time-to-market of their portfolio companies. Sometimes they form an investment conglomerate to exploit synergies between their portfolio companies."

[7] Bauer, Bilo, and Zimmermann (2001) define *venture* as follows: "they invest directly in early or expansion stage companies which are active in technology- and innovation-driven sectors and have great growth potential."

[8] These results call for a judgment on which of these indices gives the best beta estimate. In short, indices that are market weighted and that include more securities should be favored.

EXHIBIT 13.3 Breakdown of PTPE Betas by Stage

	Ventures	Incubators	Buyouts	PE Funds	Balanced	Overall	Overall (without incubators)
Sample size	39	27	12	28	12	124	97
Volatility (ann.)	29.9%	41.8%	9.4%	13.8%	17.1%	16.9%	14.6%
Betas							
MSCI	2.42	3.39	0.76	1.12	1.39	1.37	1.18
S&P 500	2.07	2.89	0.65	0.96	1.18	1.17	1.01
NASDAQ	1.40	1.96	0.44	0.65	0.80	0.79	0.69
STOXX	1.95	2.72	0.61	0.90	1.11	1.10	0.95
Russell 2000	1.88	2.63	0.59	0.87	1.08	1.07	0.92
Max.	2.42	3.39	0.76	1.12	1.39	1.37	1.18
Min.	1.40	1.96	0.44	0.65	0.80	0.79	0.69
Mean	1.94	2.72	0.61	0.90	1.11	1.10	0.95

Data source: Datastream/Bloomberg (PTPE: 5/1996–2/2001; public indices: 1986–2000).
Sources: Bauer, Bilo, and Zimmermann (2001) and author calculations.

still be calculated by making the same assumption as before (i.e., that all risk is systematic). The betas are in the range of 0.55 to 1.25, depending on the index chosen (see Exhibit 13.4).

13.2.2 Alternatives to the Standard Regression Betas

As previously indicated, the performance of private equity funds cannot be easily compared to that of public equity, mainly due to differences in return measurement practices. As funds have little historical data and almost no comparables that have been listed for any significant period of time, the conventional approaches to estimating risk parameters cannot be easily employed. However, there are some alternatives to simple regression betas. The first is to develop an alternative measure of relative risk to beta. The second is to estimate bottom-up betas, which reflect the businesses a firm is operating in and its current financial leverage. The third approach is to modify and correct the return data to make the estimation of the beta possible.

EXHIBIT 13.4 LPX50

	LPX50 VW	LPX50 EW	MSCI World	NASDAQ
Volatility	18.50	15.04	14.76	27.44
Implied beta versus MSCI World	1.25	1.02	1	N/A
Implied beta versus NASDAQ	0.67	0.55	N/A	1

Base date: December 31, 1993, to July 2, 2004.
Source: Bloomberg.

13.2.2.1 Relative Risk Measures   Relative risk measures require assumptions about the nature of risk. For example, the **relative volatility** measures the volatility of an asset relative to the average volatility across all assets in that market. Relative volatilities are standardized around 1. A relative volatility greater than 1 indicates above-average risk, whereas a relative volatility less than 1 indicates below-average risk. The relative volatility can be used in much the same way as the traditional beta estimate to compute expected returns. The relative volatility measure does not require a correlation measure and hence is less noisy. However, this comes at a cost. The relative volatility measure is based on the assumption that total risk and market risk exposures are perfectly correlated. This is the same approach we used previously to estimate betas.

13.2.2.2 Bottom-Up Beta   Another alternative, the **bottom-up beta** approach, consists of estimating risk parameters using the financial characteristics of the portfolio companies. Such an approach is based on a feature that betas possess: the beta of a combination of two assets is a weighted average of the individual asset betas, with the weights based on market value. Consequently, the beta for a fund is a weighted average of the betas of all of the different businesses the fund has invested in and can be estimated using the following seven steps:

1. Identify the type of businesses (industries) that make up the private equity fund's portfolio.
2. Estimate the unleveraged beta for each type of business.
3. Calculate the leverage for each portfolio company, using market values if available. If not, use the target leverage specified by the management of the company (which is preferred) or industry-typical debt ratios.
4. Estimate the leveraged beta for each portfolio company using the unleveraged beta from step 2 and the leverage from step 3. Note that there is no debt in the VC industry, but the deal structuring often implies leverage.
5. Calculate the unleveraged beta for the fund (i.e., the beta for the fund ignoring the fund's own leverage) by calculating the weighted average of the portfolio companies' leveraged betas, using market values. If the market values are not available, use a reasonable proxy, such as the last reported valuation or the cost.

   The formula to calculate a company's unleveraged beta is:

$$B_U = \frac{B_L}{[1 + (1 - T_C) \times (D/E)]}$$

where B_U is the firm's beta with no leverage, B_L is the firm's beta with leverage, T_C is the corporate tax rate, and D/E is the company's debt-to-equity ratio. For example, let's say B_L is 1.6, T_C is 35%, and the D/E ratio is 1 to 2, or 0.5. Substituting the values into the equation renders:

$$B_U = \frac{1.6}{[1 + (1 - 35\%) \times (1/2)]} = 1.2$$

which is slightly lower than leveraged beta. This is because leverage adds risk.

6. Calculate the fund's leverage, using market values if available. If not, use the target leverage specified by the management (better) or industry-typical debt ratios, which for VC funds is normally zero.
7. Estimate the fund's leveraged beta using the unleveraged beta from step 5 and the fund's leverage from step 6.

This approach provides better beta estimates for funds for three reasons. The first is that although regression betas are noisy and have large standard errors, averaging across regression betas reduces the noise in the estimate. The second reason is that the beta estimates reflect the fund as it exists today, since it is computed based on current weightings of its different businesses. The final reason is that the leveraged beta is computed using the current financial leverage (or even better, the expected or target financial leverage) of the firm, rather than the average leverage over the period of the regression. This approach is generic and can be applied to funds in any market. The dark side of this approach is that it remains difficult to identify quoted companies that are comparable to VC companies and that, as for many private equity funds, future cash flows are generated not only from existing investments but also from investments yet to be made. Such an approach requires an assumption on the nature of these future investments.

Ljungqvist and Richardson (2003) used a bottom-up approach to estimate betas based on a private database of actual cash flows of VC and buyout funds over the prior two decades. This data set consisted of 73 funds raised over the period 1981–1993, composed of 88.2% buyout and 11.8% VC funds. In terms of geography, the breakdown was 91.1% U.S., 7.4% EU, and 1.5% Latin American funds. The authors looked at each fund's investments in detail, assigning industry betas to the portfolio companies in order to estimate the fund's risk. In doing so, they made the simplifying assumption that the leverage of the private company coincided with that of the industry, which allowed them to use the industry-leveraged beta based on one of 48 broad industry groups chosen by Fama and French (1997). Their estimates suggest that buyout funds (nonventure funds) (beta of 1.08) are riskier than the market but less risky than VC funds (beta of 1.12). However, no final conclusion can be drawn, as buyout funds typically use more leverage than the industries they invest in, and VC funds use little or no leverage.

13.2.2.3 Beta Based on Modified and Corrected Data   The absence of a market with continuous trading leads to the use of appraisals as prices. The resulting difficulties of stale pricing or smoothing make the measurement of true volatilities and correlations with other asset classes difficult. In order to measure betas, data need to be corrected and adjusted. Artus and Teïletche (2004) estimated the optimal share of private equity in the portfolio of diversified European portfolios. In doing so, they had to estimate all the required inputs to estimate betas. To obtain a time-weighted return as required for the CAPM, the authors did not use final internal rates of return (IRRs) but "periodical aggregated returns built on the sum of all the funds for a specific period of time (i.e., the sum of the cash flows and NAVs between the starting and the ending dates of the chosen period)." They then used autocorrelation analysis to correct the aggregated quarterly return data generated by the smoothing process. The authors acknowledge that the results obtained did not lead to a fully satisfactory solution (see Exhibit 13.5). The results observed for VC illustrate, as explained previously, the common misperception of the risk taken. Indeed, many

EXHIBIT 13.5 Risk, Performance, Correlation, and Betas of European Private Equity

Returns (%)	Venture Capital	Buyouts	Equities
Average	11.3	9.9	7.7
Std. deviation	34.0	10.0	20.6
Correlation Matrix			
VC	1.00	0.33	0.50
Buyouts	0.33	1.00	0.11
Equities	0.50	0.11	1.00
Beta			
Vs. equities	0.83	0.06	1.00

Sources: Artus and Teïletche (2004) and author calculations.

investors expect a premium as compensation for the total risk (i.e., the volatility or standard deviation), whereas only its systematic portion should be rewarded, as evidenced by the beta. The result observed for buyout with a beta of 0.06 is surprisingly low and does not reflect, in our view, the reality. This most likely can be explained by the valuation smoothing observed in private equity.

Kaserer and Diller (2004) complemented the study of Artus and Teïletche (2004) by focusing on individual cash flows, which are not impacted by the smoothing process and therefore do not require any correction. To obtain a time-weighted return, they constructed a benchmark for returns based on the assumption that distributions are reinvested in either quoted securities or bonds (see Exhibit 13.6).

The results obtained from these two studies, although quite interesting, most probably contained other imperfections through their corrections and adjustments. We do not believe that these results can be used to estimate VC fund discount rates. However, it is worth stressing that when the data are corrected, the betas of VC tend to come closer to 1, further supporting the notion that VC is not much different from public equity.

EXHIBIT 13.6 Risk, Performance, Correlation, and Betas of European Private Equity

Returns (%)	PE (Equity Reinvestment)	PE (Bond Reinvestment)	MSCI Europe
Average	9.8	8.1	11.5
Std. deviation	19.0	9.0	18.1
Correlation Matrix			
PE (equity reinvestment)	1.00	N/A	0.90
PE (bond reinvestment)	N/A	1.00	0.04
MSCI Europe	0.90	0.04	1.00
Beta			
Vs. MSCI Europe	0.94	0.02	

Sources: Kaserer and Diller (2004) and author calculations.

CHAPTER 14

The Management of Liquidity*

Investments in private equity (PE) funds have proved to be risky for a number of reasons, but principally because of the long duration of the exposure and the lack of liquidity. Managing the liquidity of a private equity fund investment program needs to take into account the existing interdependencies among the overall investment strategy, the management of the undrawn capital, and the available resources and aspects of timing. It is a difficult task to put money efficiently to work while maintaining a balance in the portfolio composition and the quality of the individual fund investments. Therefore, modeling the cash flows of such investments is an important part of the management process and potentially allows one to do the following:

- Improve investment returns for the undrawn capital
- Increase the profit generated by the private equity allocation through overcommitment
- Calculate an economic value when a discount rate is available
- Monitor the cash flows and risk-return profiles of a portfolio of private equity funds

Achieving a high total return for the overall investment program is a complex task that requires not only quantitative modeling and financial engineering skills but also a high degree of judgment and management discipline. There is no quick fix for this, and only a disciplined approach can deliver small improvements that eventually add up to a significant impact. As a result, it is likely to take many years before an investment program is able to reach sustainable high total-return levels and a stable long-term allocation.

14.1   PRIVATE EQUITY CASH FLOW SCHEDULES

Though it may sound simple for an investor to make a 5% portfolio allocation to private equity, the mechanics of the asset class render this level of precision impossible. Investors have little control of the timing of their investments and the

---

*The authors are grateful to Juan Delgado-Moreira, PhD, CFA; Hamilton Lane; and Dr. Michael Jean Gschrei of Dr. Gschrei & Associates GmbH for their valuable comments and suggestions. The views expressed in this section are the authors' and are not necessarily shared by the aforementioned contributors.

return of capital from those investments. Access to specific managers and investment styles is not always available, as managers raise new funds periodically, such as every third year, while the market environment may make it easier or more difficult for managers to raise capital for investment in a specific stage, sector, or geography.

A cash flow schedule for a single investment may evolve in the following manner: The general partner embarks on fund-raising conversations in January 2012. The fund solicits preliminary commitments during the entire year, requesting that investors sign commitments by December 31, 2012. The fund starts operating the following year and is labeled a 2013 vintage year with a stated three-year investment period. A given investor signs a $10 million commitment to the fund. The general partner agrees to **draw down capital**, which means to request cash from a limited partner only upon identification of suitable investment opportunities or to cover management fees or expenses. As a result, the manager draws down $2 million in 2013, $3 million in 2014, $2 million in 2015, and up to an additional $3 million before the fund's end of life. The size and the timing of these drawdowns are determined exclusively by the general partner, as long as the amount does not exceed the size of the limited partner's commitment. Available evidence shows that for U.S. and European venture capital (VC) funds, the majority of the capital is called between the first and fifth year of the fund's life. It must be noted that there is a substantial variation in the speed of capital calls over vintage years and geographies.

Exits are even more difficult to predict, as both the timing and the size of the exit are highly uncertain. A VC manager takes an initial stake in the company during the investment period of the fund, perhaps in the third year. Ideally, the fund holds the investment for a five-year period, in which company growth, innovation, operational improvements, and financial engineering add value to the underlying investment. During the later years of the fund, after the investments have matured and gained in value, the fund enters the **harvesting period**, in which the fund seeks to exit its investments. The value of these investments is related to the growth of the company, the value added by the fund manager, and the market environment at the time of the exit period. For example, according to available evidence, VC funds of the 1996 vintage earned extremely large returns due to the robust nature of the 1998–2000 initial public offering (IPO) market for technology stocks. These same empirical results show that exits are quite variable, with the majority of distributions from venture funds occurring after year six.

In order for the investor to maintain an average allocation of 5% to private equity, it will be necessary to estimate the speed and size of drawdowns as well as the size and timing of exits. Given that vintage years and strategies have quite different experiences, investors need to build their private equity allocations over several vintage years and be prepared to have an allocation range, rather than an exact target, for the size of their allocation to private equity.

14.2 SOURCES OF LIQUIDITY

Commitments are generally met through cash inflows, supplemented by assets readily convertible to cash, or through a company's capacity to borrow. To achieve a competitive total return on committed capital, the investor needs to manage the investment of uncalled capital during the drawdown period and the reinvestment of distributed capital. The maturity structure of treasury assets (i.e., investments that will fund PE commitments) and private equity funds should be matched, and there should be well-diversified and stable **sources of funding**, such as the following:

- *Follow-on funding.* In the case in which the limited partner is managing the liquidity, he or she may be able to step in as a provider of follow-on funding, which is especially meaningful, as access to other sources of liquidity may take time.
- *Liquidity lines.* A short- and medium-term borrowing facility could be managed by the limited partner. Cash needs to be available to meet capital calls, but a liquidity line is used should these resources run out. Structuring a sensible liquidity line needs to reflect such factors as the expected amount and timing of cash needs, or the rating of the liquidity provider.
- *Maturing treasury investments.* While it is tempting to maintain undrawn capital in short-term instruments, such a policy is likely to adversely impact the total return. To achieve higher returns, the profiles of the private equity fund cash flows need to be predicted and matched with those of a treasury portfolio composed of assets with the same maturities, but also expected to produce a return above short-term instruments. Because of the uncertain schedule, a maturity structure can only have a limited match.
- *Realizations of other investments.* With such a mismatch, the risk of illiquidity increases. Therefore, cash cannot simply be provided for by maturing treasury assets only but occasionally requires a liquidation or realization of other existing positions. To limit the potential for losses resulting from market fluctuations, strict criteria for the eligibility of investments need to be applied.
- *Sell-off of limited partnership shares.* Private equity funds are illiquid investments, and early redemption is usually not allowed. Limited partners are generally prohibited from transferring, assigning, pledging, or otherwise disposing of their limited partnership interests or withdrawing from the partnership without the prior consent of the general partners, who can grant or withhold consent at their sole discretion. However, there is a growing secondary market where seasoned fund investments may be liquidated. But a realization of limited partnership shares in an attempt to increase liquidity is problematic, as it takes considerable time to identify buyers and negotiate the transaction, which may take place at a premium or a discount to the net asset value (NAV) of the fund.
- *Distributions from private equity funds.* A reinvestment plan should be established that takes into account the uncertainty inherent in the timing and magnitude of distributions from private equity funds. As investments in private equity funds are speculative and require a long-term commitment, there is no certainty regarding timing and amounts of distributions. It is also possible that part of the return is received as a **distribution in kind** in the form of marketable restricted securities. Consequently, reinvestment planning exposes one to considerable liquidity risks.
- *Limited partner default.* If several capital calls cannot be met simultaneously, the last resort is for the investor to default. However, in addition to the damage

to reputation suffered by the defaulting limited partner, there are stiff penalties associated with not meeting a drawdown request. These penalties include the termination of the limited partner's right to participate in the fund's future investments, the loss of entitlement to distributions or income, the mandatory transfer or sale of its partnership interests, the continuing liability for interest in respect of the defaulted amount, the partial or total forfeiture of the partnership interest, and the liability for any other rights and legal remedies the fund managers may have against the defaulting investor. Defaulting limited partners may continue to be liable for losses or expenses incurred by the fund.

14.3   INVESTMENT STRATEGIES FOR UNDRAWN CAPITAL

Program managers should not be given resources that are not needed for investing in private equity funds. If large liquidity buffers are planned, the program's return target requires that undrawn capital be managed to maintain liquidity while reducing the opportunity costs of investments in lower-return assets. We identified the following main strategies for managing undrawn capital in Exhibit 14.1.

To minimize the amount of idle capital in the hands of the fund, drawdowns should ideally be just in time or possibly also subscription based, and an overcommitment strategy should be followed (see section 14.5). In situations in which large positions of undrawn capital cannot be avoided, the return could be increased by maximizing exposure either to long-term bonds—which requires predictability and planning—or to other higher-yielding asset classes. For this purpose, Kogelman (1999) suggested public equity.

The management of undrawn capital should be left to the limited partner, who will determine if flexible follow-on financing can be arranged. In any case, the premium between liquid assets and illiquid private equity funds sets limits to returns on the undrawn capital. Alternatively, capital can be put to work more efficiently by investing in other assets that also fall into the fund's core expertise, such as publicly quoted private equity or other liquid alternative assets.

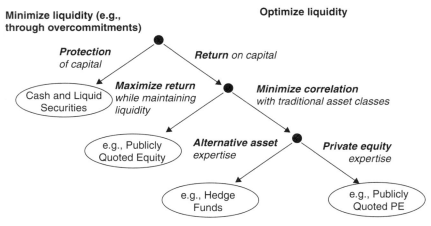

EXHIBIT 14.1   Main Strategies for Managing Undrawn Capital

14.4   CASH FLOW PROJECTIONS

Investments in illiquid assets present particular challenges for portfolio management, as there is a high degree of uncertainty inherent in the timing and amount of cash flows. The main objective of strategic commitment steering is to build up and maintain a balanced and stable portfolio in line with the investment strategy. The portfolio balance depends not only on the level of commitment to fund investments but also on the rate and timing of drawdowns and distributions. Effective management of a private equity program requires a reasonably accurate assessment of the individual fund's future cash flow pattern to enable the steering of commitments and portfolio balance. Maximizing the return on undrawn commitments will often require taking positions in assets with limited liquidity. A profitable realization of such positions may take two to three months or more. This process needs to be started as early as possible. Thus, the establishment of efficient treasury management also relies heavily on projection and planning methodologies.

Projection models have to be simple and sensible on a theoretical basis. They should be able to incorporate and respond to actual cash flow experience and valuations. Such models should also be able to analyze the portfolio impact of varying return scenarios and changing rates of investments and repayments. Projections need to consider existing deals with known characteristics as well as future deals with unknown characteristics or characteristics yet to be chosen (such as commitment levels).

Sophisticated alternative-investment and fund-of-funds managers have developed proprietary approaches[1] that take a series of inputs into consideration:

- *Market and empirical data.* These data come mainly from data services such as Thomson Reuters, but internal data can also form the statistical input for forecasting expected drawdowns and distributions. They are complemented by an assessment of the vintage year quality and the investment and exit environment (empirical data on expected drawdowns and repayments).
- *Expert judgment.* As purely quantitative approaches have their limits, significant judgment is required for estimations and valuations. The main problem is the quality of data in an opaque market. It is only with a high level of expertise that the accurate interpretation of empirical and observed data is possible.
- *Fund data.* These data on actual drawdowns and distributions form the basis for the valuation of individual private equity fund investments (monitoring input on actual drawdowns and distributions). Also, monitoring of the private equity fund portfolio quality is of relevance; for example, although write-offs are not immediately relevant for cash flows, they can reduce further financing needs.
- *Models.* Projections are generated with the help of various models. Generally, the accuracy of predictions is higher for mature programs than it is during the early years.

---

[1] The Partners Group's model (see Wietlisbach [2002]) differentiates between strategic and tactical commitment steering. Its private equity management approach rests on the following four pillars: empirical data, actual data, investment advisory, and quantitative management.

EXHIBIT 14.2 Approaches to Projecting Cash Flows

	Estimates	Forecasts	Scenarios
	Tactical		Strategic
Term	Short-term (~3–6 months)	Medium-term (~1–2 years)	Long-term (over 2 years)
Based on	Current market situation	Specific market environment	Uncertain market environment
Approach	Data gathering and analysis	Quantitative modeling	Planning

Very simplistically, one can differentiate three approaches to carrying out projections:

1. *Estimates* use an assessment of current conditions to identify possible future events. The priority is accuracy, which implies a relatively short time horizon and an intensive data-collection process.
2. *Forecasts* go beyond the short-term horizon, primarily relying on trend-based analysis. Often expert opinion is required for making an assessment concerning the continuity or modification of current trends.
3. *Scenarios* can be thought of as a range of forecasts, but both their construction and their intent are more complex. They aim to describe different environments based on plausible changes in current trends.

There is a significant difference between scenarios and forecasting. Presumably, forecasts are attempts to predict the future, while scenarios aim to enable better decisions about the future. Of course, the distinction is not as clear-cut, as depicted in Exhibit 14.2, and typically projection tools combine elements of all of these approaches.

14.4.1 Estimates

To estimate is to form an opinion based on imperfect data, comparisons, or experience. Because statistics are of lesser value over the short term (or for a single position), in this situation estimation techniques can be more meaningful than are forecasts. Estimates can be applied to new commitments in private equity funds to be signed within the next few months and to liquidity events in the near future within private equity funds already committed, as follows:

- New commitments in private equity funds and their first drawdowns can be derived from deal pipeline analysis with reasonable accuracy for a period of three to six months ahead. Investment managers are typically already in discussions with potential investors. They have a good understanding of the current fund-raising environment, the resulting likelihood of commitments to materialize, and the size of these commitments.
- There is a series of liquidity events that is either known or reasonably likely to happen. Occasionally exits (e.g., in the form of IPOs) are publicly announced, and possible price ranges are discussed.

A regularly updated calendar of such events forms the starting point for estimating short- and medium-term liquidity needs. Such an approach is also appropriate for pricing secondary transactions, but in this case estimates are used until full liquidation of the positions. The use of this technique for long-term purposes tends to be quite time-consuming and information-intensive, leading to significant costs that cannot necessarily be justified for classical portfolio projections, but it may be appropriate in the case of secondary transactions in which higher benefits can be expected.

14.4.2 An Example of Estimation Techniques

Distributions from private equity funds to their investors are obviously more sensitive to short-term information and changes. Estimates can be significantly improved through closer interaction with general partners and by incorporating judgment.

Baring Private Equity Partners (BPEP) has pioneered a cash flow model with the objective of generating the most accurate possible projections of net capital flows from BPEP directly managed funds to investors. In order to measure the uncertainty of exit values and dates, the model has incorporated a probabilistic methodology. BPEP investment managers are routinely asked to provide earlier, median, and latest exit dates, and minimum, median, and maximum exit values, as well as the attached probabilities for each event and the basis for the estimates. Such an estimate will take the following form (see Exhibit 14.3), with:

$$P_{a;\min} + P_{a;\mathrm{med}} + P_{a;\max} = 1 \quad \text{and} \quad P_{t;\min} + P_{t;\mathrm{med}} + P_{t;\max} \leq 1$$

where $P_{a;\min}$, $P_{a;\mathrm{med}}$, and $P_{a;\max}$ are the probabilities of the minimum, median, and maximum cash flow amount occurring, and $P_{t;\min}$, $P_{t;\mathrm{med}}$, and $P_{t;\max}$ are the probabilities of the earlier, median, and latest cash flow date occurring.

The fact that the probabilities for cash flow dates do not necessarily add up to 1 allows for the situation in which the cash flow is not certain to take place at all. BPEP applies this estimation exercise consistently and rigorously using valuations

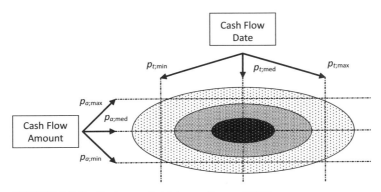

EXHIBIT 14.3 Estimate Grid According to BPEP

arrived at in compliance with industry guidelines. This approach calls for the following comments:

- The accuracy of the model's projections depends on the estimates for price and date of portfolio exits and, therefore, is subject to the uncertainties of market conditions and buyer sentiment.
- Exit values and dates are uncertain and continuous variables. Since they are based on established valuation methods, estimates of exit values are more likely to be accurate than estimates of exit dates.
- Exit dates can be estimated over only a short time frame. Typically, after more than one year, estimates cease to be of relevance, and forecasting techniques become more important.

A limited partner needs to overcome significant barriers to access timely information of sufficient quality that allows a bottom-up analysis and precise projections. For a limited partner, a bottom-up analysis, due to the lack of detailed information, is usually possible only with limitations, and estimates will often lack precision.

Generally, fund managers will feel reluctant to disclose information on likely financing or will exit events before the deals actually close in order to protect their negotiation positions. Consequently, this is not made part of the standard reporting, and only in rare cases, such as with an IPO, are investors informed in advance. However, there are various analytical techniques that can be used to form educated guesses (as was the case in evaluating secondary transactions). The basis for such an estimate could be discussions with the fund's management on possible new investments or planned realizations, or an assessment of the maturity of the fund and the current exit conditions.

The combination of three exit values and three dates gives nine possible outcomes per portfolio company. Just combining 10 companies would give $9^{10} = 3.5$ billion different outcomes. A relatively simple Monte Carlo simulation helps to determine the range for possible outcomes. With a sensitivity analysis (taking into account longer or shorter time periods or lower or higher realization levels), the robustness of results can be checked using the following three methods:

1. The estimates can be interpreted as inputs for a discrete distribution. Volatility, as expressed by the standard deviation of the returns and, therefore, a judgment on risk is implied by the inputs.
2. Another approach would be to take the investment managers' inputs as a continuous distribution. Their average estimate is taken, and a normal distribution is assumed as to both value and timing, with a set standard deviation for both the exit value and the exit timing.
3. A third alternative used by BPEP is a nonnormal probability distribution created ad hoc, following the shape of the curves defined by the three exit values and/or times and the associated probabilities. Here, each deal can have a different curve.

If applied consistently, this too, despite its simplicity, can be highly useful in assessing likely cash flow patterns over a short time frame. A structured analytical process and interview technique, possibly with scoring to link categories to probabilities, can further improve the quality and consistency of estimates and allow for calibration of the model.

When aggregating the estimates into projections, the private equity fund's structure is also relevant. For example, the preferred return (or hurdle rate) can heavily distort the cash flow to the limited partner. With 100% catch-up, once the limited partners have the preferred return, they cease to share further new realizations until the general partner has made a full recovery.

14.4.3 Implementation Issues

For short-term estimates in a bottom-up approach, the private equity funds and their portfolio companies are analyzed in detail. It is obvious that a thorough bottom-up analysis is a resource-intensive exercise; therefore, especially for large portfolios, all companies cannot be continuously reviewed. Also, different general partners will provide information with varying levels of detail and reliability, while some may not even respond to requests. However, in most cases, it is possible to split the portfolio into parts, with higher and lower probabilities of cash flows, and focus attention on the parts of the portfolio with higher activity levels (e.g., mature companies in booming market segments are more likely to exit than recently funded and young companies). Even in more active market situations, many funds can be eliminated from such an exercise right away:

- Funds that are so early in their lives that no positive cash flows can be expected
- Funds in later stages with portfolio companies that are too young to be likely candidates for exits
- Funds in market segments that are comparatively flat

In a real-life situation, such a bottom-up analysis would need to be combined with a macro view that takes into account the different private equity funds' geographical orientations, ages, industries, and stage focuses as a starting point. This narrows the population down to a meaningful list of funds to be analyzed. For the relatively idle part of the portfolio, simplistic techniques like "next quarter's forecast is equal to last quarter's realized cash flow," in combination with medium-term forecasts, can be applied. Even if estimation techniques occasionally lack precision, they are an indispensable tool for anticipating liquidity shortfalls and serve as an early-warning system to supervise limits. For an illiquid asset class such as private equity, it is critical to continuously monitor developments and initiate changes as early as possible.

14.4.4 Forecasts

All forecasts are based on the assumption that the past can be extended into the future and built on statistical extrapolation of variables. Such approaches are mainly quantitative and aim to predict over the medium term. For private equity funds, a forecasting approach needs to factor in, among other items, such criteria as the fund's life-cycle characteristics, age, empirical data for comparable funds, and market data (e.g., stock market indices).

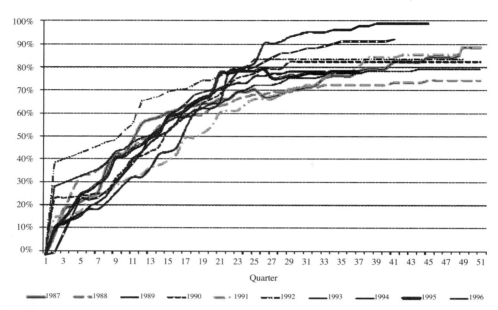

EXHIBIT 14.4   European VC Funds (Vintages 1987 through 1996): Cumulative Paid In
Source: Thomson Reuters.

A private equity fund's life-cycle characteristics are typically modeled through cash flow libraries based on historical fund data. This could be data from one's own investments or provided by data services such as Thomson Reuters. The underlying assumption is that the pattern (timing, amount of cash flows) is the same for each fund or quality of fund, and that scaling can be applied.

This approach is meaningful, especially for drawdowns, as capital calls depend on investments in young companies not ready for exits, and therefore the link to markets is less important. Drawdowns tend to follow a reasonably predictable schedule but show marked differences between investment environments (see Exhibits 14.4 and 14.5).

Although the private equity market is very cyclical, any environment does not necessarily resemble another historical period. For example, in the late 1990s, venture capitalists drew down capital at unprecedented rates with atypical returns. Historical data for any previous period provided a poor template for modeling these vintages. Moreover, there is little historical data available for European funds. For distributions, the pattern appears to be less predictable than for contributions. Differences are even more pronounced for the U.S. market (see Exhibits 14.6 and 14.7). These limitations, the incompleteness of the cash flow library, and the unavailability of data in general pose restrictions to such approaches; therefore, applications should monitor feedback and consult expert opinion as well.

One alternative is to use public market indices as part of an econometric model. Small company equity markets generally serve as the primary exit vehicle for private equity investments either through an IPO or via company valuation in the case of mergers and acquisitions. To be of any predictive value, econometric forecasts need

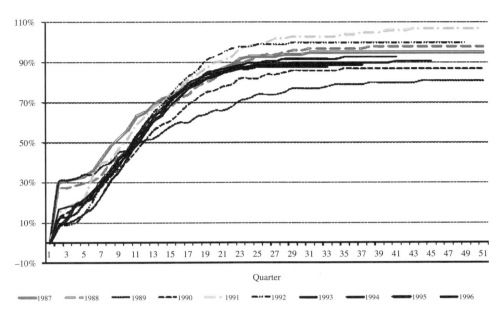

EXHIBIT 14.5 U.S. VC Funds (Vintages 1987 through 1996): Cumulative Paid In
Source: Thomson Reuters.

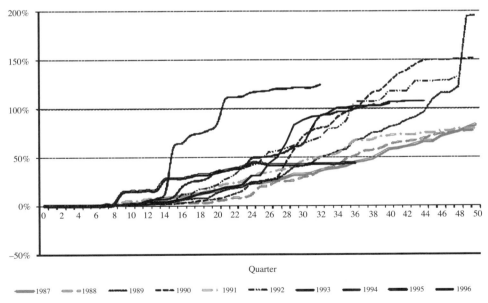

EXHIBIT 14.6 European VC Funds (Vintages 1987 through 1996):
Cumulative Distribution
Source: Thomson Reuters.

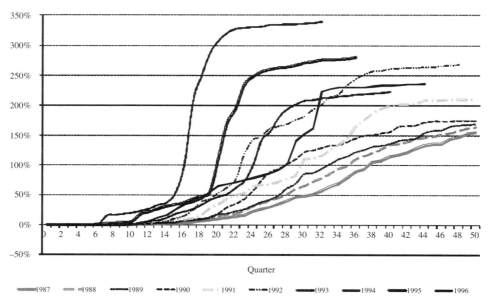

EXHIBIT 14.7   U.S. VC Funds (Vintages 1987 through 1996): Cumulative Distribution
Source: Thomson Reuters.

to consider several explanatory variables and thus carry significant model risk, made worse by the low availability and quality of private equity data.

A continuous review and validation of input parameters and results is critical. Consequently, it is important that all trend-based forecasting approaches be used only with a stern warning and only in conjunction with alternative approaches such as reality checks. For example, results should be consistent with the assumed scenario. Blindly following econometric models representing a specific market environment is an accident waiting to happen.

14.4.5 Scenarios

While forecasting gives the most likely picture of the future against which plans can be judged, long-term projections in particular are fraught with considerable uncertainty, regardless of the kind of forecasting problem. If the environment changes radically, statistical extrapolation techniques fail. As forecasts do not communicate uncertainty (especially in the VC industry, which thrives on innovation), reliable forecasting has its natural limits. The nearer term one looks at, the more predictable the future is. In the very short term, most people are inclined to estimate or forecast, whereas long-term planning relies on scenarios. Scenarios are a set of reasonably plausible but structurally different futures that are a useful tool for setting out a course in the face of significant uncertainty.

Scenarios can be an individual's isolated opinion or can be discussed in groups. This approach is built on the assumption that some people can be more expert than others in predicting what will happen or in excluding what will not happen. This

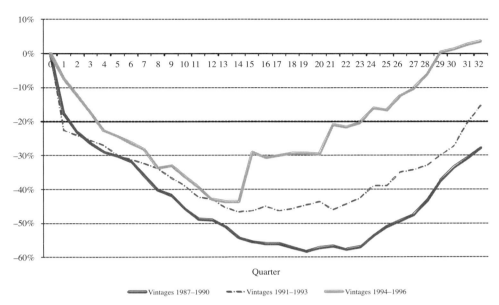

EXHIBIT 14.8   European VC Funds: Cumulative Cash Flow Scenarios
Source: Thomson Reuters.

expertise is based on experience, closeness to markets, and access to privileged information. Another feature of scenarios is that they are abstract, simplified, and do not consider the same level of detail as forecasts. Consequently, their results lack precision and often cannot differentiate among the natures of cash flows. The assumptions underlying the scenarios need to be documented. Also, intervention points need to be defined; for example, under which circumstances should the scenario be seen as invalid and a new round of scenario development be required? Scenario development helps users think through the process, understand the environment better, and enhance the capability to recognize unexpected events.

Partners Group analyzed empirical cash flow patterns of U.S. VC funds during different time periods and found marked differences between averages of the periods 1981–1985, 1986–1990, and 1991–1995.[2] For illustration, three time periods with the scenarios normal (pre-1990), emerging (1991–1993), and post-1993 boom are presented. Exhibit 14.8 suggests that scenarios can be quite different. While differences for the European VC market are not as pronounced as those of the U.S. VC market (see Exhibit 14.9), they can nevertheless be significant and form the basis for a scenario discussion.

A scenario-based tool like the Yale Model (Takahashi and Alexander 2001) could aid the strategic commitment steering for an investment program. This model considers NAVs, commitments, drawdowns, repayments, funds' lifetimes, exit patterns, and growth rates. It does not give variances but only averages. The variety of possible outcomes is not described by volatilities but approximated through the choice of scenarios.

---

[2] See Wietlisbach (2002).

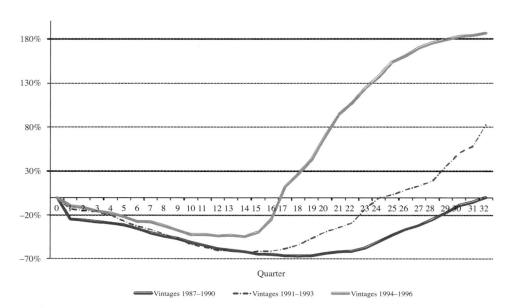

EXHIBIT 14.9   U.S. VC Funds: Cumulative Cash Flow Scenarios
Source: Thomson Reuters.

14.5   OVERCOMMITMENT

As explained in Chapter 5, the cash flow J-curve (see Exhibit 5.7) results from the fact that in standard private equity fund structures, commitments (which are firm) are drawn down as needed or just in time (see Exhibits 14.4 and 14.5). When realizations are made, after having successfully developed these newly founded companies, they are distributed as soon as is practical (see Exhibits 14.6 and 14.7). During the life of a fund, the net cash outflow (as well as the market exposure often measured by the NAV) will not be as high as the initial commitment. The timing and size of cash flows to and from a single private equity fund are not known until they are announced. But for a diversified private equity fund investment program, they follow a predictable pattern that can be estimated, forecasted, or planned.

Ideally, investors should find ways to minimize the opportunity cost of these nonproductive resources allocated to private equity. On one side, the time lag between commitment and actual investment can be reflected in the maturity profile of the treasury investments to give some extra basis points of return. On the other side, limited partners can implement an overcommitment strategy in which more than the available resources are committed in order to achieve the target investment or exposure level.

$$\text{Overcommitment ratio} = \frac{\text{Total commitments}}{\text{Resources available for commitments}}$$

An overcommitment strategy is not simply setting a maximum allocation of commitments per year but needs to be underpinned by a detailed understanding of

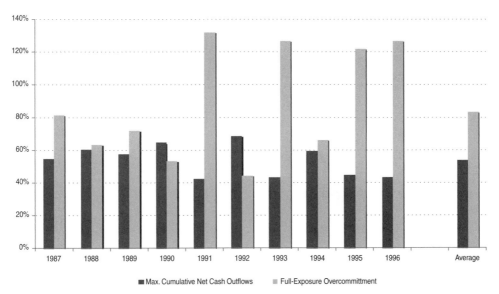

EXHIBIT 14.10   Maximum Net Average Cash Outflow per Vintage Year and Implied
Needed Overcommitment Ratio
Source: Thomson Reuters.

the cash flow profiles of private equity funds. An overcommitment ratio of less than
100% suggests an inefficient use of resources. **Overcommitment ratios** of 125% to
140% have been documented.[3] The overcommitment ratio can be determined on the
basis of empirical data (see Exhibit 14.10). Assuming that, on average, not more than
70% of commitments are actually called, an overcommitment level of around 140%
would be feasible.[4] An investor with an overcommitment ratio of 140% would sign
commitments for private equity investments in the size of 7% of the fund, while
maintaining a strategic asset allocation of just 5% to private equity (7%/5% =
140%). But the reality can be significantly different, and large fluctuations around
averages can be observed, notably during some overheated market conditions (see
Exhibit 14.11).

As stated previously, the implementation of a successful overcommitment and
investment strategy for undrawn capital largely depends on the quality and precision
of cash flow projections. Other sources of liquidity have to be taken into account
as well. The limited partners' overall portfolio composition has an impact on such
projections. In a diversified private equity portfolio, cash flow patterns of various

---

[3] Examples: Schroders Private Equity Fund-of-Funds (listed on the Dublin stock exchange),
130% overcommitment ratio; VCH Best-of-VC, 140% overcommitment ratio. Hewitt Investment Group recommends overcommitment ratios of 125% to 135% (see Schwartzman
[2002]).

[4] See Schaechterle (2000): "Analysis of statistical data from Venture Economics funds that
invest in private equity have a peak level of 65% leaving the remainder of the investors'
committed capital invested in short-term investments. The resulting opportunity costs dilute
the overall performance of an investor's private equity allocation by approximately one-third."

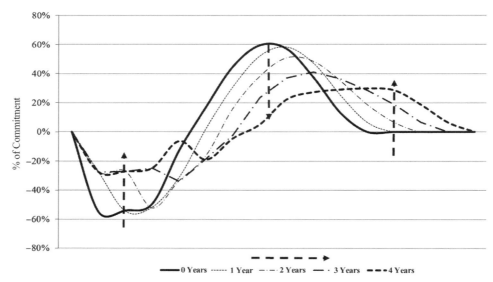

EXHIBIT 14.11 Time Diversification: Cumulative Cash Flows (as Percent of Commitment) over Time for a Portfolio of Two Private Equity Funds with Commitments Made with a 4-, 3-, 2-, 1-, or 0-Year Gap between the Two Funds

fund types can be exploited within a portfolio approach. Buyout and mezzanine funds typically draw down commitments more quickly than do VC funds, which tend to stretch drawdowns in parallel with their stage financing approach. Buyout and mezzanine funds also tend to start distributing more quickly, as they usually have annual income components, such as interest on subordinated debt or dividends on preferred stock. They also invest in established companies requiring fewer years to exit.

To achieve a higher overcommitment level, the limited partner's portfolio needs to be diversified over several vintage years. As distributions begin to come in, they theoretically supplement resources available to be spent on new capital calls. If there is no vintage-year diversification in the extreme, all private equity funds achieve their maximum investment level simultaneously. As Exhibit 14.11 shows, diversification over time is essential for an overcommitment strategy.

As commitments are firm and private equity is a long-term illiquid asset, an overly aggressive overcommitment and treasury strategy may leave limited partners short of liquidity and expose them to the risk of defaulting on a capital call. Consequently, achieving a high level of resources actually invested in private equity is a very challenging task, as it needs to take all these interdependencies into consideration. A real-life case study in Mathonet and Meyer (2007)[5] further highlights the perils of overcommitting and should serve as a warning that just looking at simple ratios is not sufficient for controlling risk.

---

[5] See Mathonet and Meyer (2007), Chapter 4, "Risk Management Lessons from a Listed Private Equity Fund-of-Funds."

14.6 CONCLUSION

To conclude, we would like to make a final observation that, as is often stated in this industry, investing in private equity has a lot in common with winemaking. In talking about wine, some authors argue that only those civilizations that drank wine survived when the overall water quality turned poor, as it did regularly. Similarly, we believe that when traditional asset classes enter turbulent market conditions, investors who have invested in private equity (venture capital in particular) and investors who have used the approaches and tools discussed in this material will be better equipped to navigate through these turbulences.

In private equity, some claim to have found ways to rapidly generate above-market returns, but we remain skeptical. As with making wine, there are series of obstacles to overcome, and if one gives up, the effort may go unrewarded. Inevitably, some vintage years will be disastrous. But a well-stocked wine cellar may help us survive these downturns, and eventually the spectacular vintages may make the effort worthwhile. For these reasons, one cannot switch into and out of winemaking; it is a decision for life (and most likely the lives of one's children). The same applies to private equity: To some extent, it can be seen as a decision for one's professional life, and most likely the life of one's successor.

Three

Real Assets

CHAPTER 15

Real Estate as an Investment

R eal estate has been a very large and important portion of wealth for thousands of years. Even as recently as a century ago, real estate dominated institutional portfolios and was referred to as property. During recent decades, the preeminence of real estate has yielded to the growing importance of intangible assets. Yet real estate remains a valuable part of any well-diversified portfolio.

The transition of real estate from dominating traditional institutional-quality investments to being an alternative investment raises important issues as to how to evaluate real estate on a forward-looking basis. This chapter provides an overview of the attributes, asset allocation, categories, and return drivers of real estate.

15.1 ATTRIBUTES OF REAL ESTATE

Real estate, and any other asset for that matter, should be included in a portfolio until the marginal benefits of additional investment equal the marginal costs of additional investment. An optimized portfolio is achieved when additional investments in each asset and asset class are equally attractive. In other words, exposure to each type of real estate investment, and to real estate overall, should be added until the net benefits have diminished to the point that allocations to other investments are equally attractive.

15.1.1 Five Potential Advantages of Real Estate

What are the aspects of real estate that make it attractive or unattractive relative to other asset classes? There are five common attributes of real estate that can encourage its inclusion in an investment portfolio:

1. Its potential to offer absolute returns
2. Its potential to hedge against unexpected inflation
3. Its potential to provide diversification with stocks and bonds
4. Its potential to provide cash inflows
5. Its potential to provide income tax advantages

These potential advantages, the first three of which are related to portfolio risk, do not necessarily come without costs. In particular, to the extent that markets are competitive and efficient, market prices of real estate will tend to adjust, such that any relative advantages to real estate will be offset by lower expected returns.

This list of potential advantages to real estate investment is not comprehensive. For example, another motivation could be to own all or part of a trophy property that offers name recognition, prestige, and enhanced reputation to the owner. An example would be a large, high-quality office property in a prominent location.

15.1.2 Three Potential Disadvantages of Real Estate

There are also aspects of real estate that can discourage its inclusion in an investment portfolio:

1. Heterogeneity
2. Lumpiness
3. Illiquidity

Real estate is a highly heterogeneous asset. Not only are the physical features of the individual properties unique in terms of location, use, and design, but varying lease structures can lead to large differences in income streams. This heterogeneity is particularly troublesome in the initial and ongoing due diligence processes. Accordingly, due diligence of real estate investments can require specialized analysis and managerial skill.

The second key characteristic of real estate is lumpiness, including the indivisibility of direct ownership. **Lumpiness** describes a situation in which assets cannot be easily and inexpensively bought and sold in sizes or quantities that meet the preferences of the buyers and sellers. Listed equities of large companies are not lumpy, because purchases and sales can easily be made in the desired size by altering the number of shares in the transaction. Direct real estate ownership may be difficult to trade in sizes or quantities desired by a market participant. While growth in real estate investment trusts (REITs, introduced in Level I) and in a number of alternative real estate investment vehicles has led to divisible investment opportunities at an indirect ownership level, investors at a single-property level are still faced with the choice of buying the entire asset or not. The indivisible nature of real estate assets leads to problems with respect to high unit costs (i.e., large investment sizes) and relatively high transaction costs.

The final major disadvantage relates to the liquidity of real estate. As a private, non-exchange-traded asset with a high unit cost, real estate can be highly illiquid, especially when compared to stocks and bonds. An important implication of illiquidity is its effect on reported returns as well as added risk challenges.

All three of these characteristics complicate performance measurement and evaluation. The goal of each investor is to find the level and composition of real estate exposure that optimize the portfolio when considering all benefits and costs.

15.2 ASSET ALLOCATION

The heterogeneity of real estate includes the diversity of its subclasses. This section discusses major methods of categorizing real estate and differentiating among real estate investments. Understanding the substantial differences among categories of real estate investments provides two important outcomes. First, a better understanding of the breadth of real estate investment opportunities helps refine an asset allocator's decision as to how much capital to allocate to real estate. Second, an understanding of the different categories of real estate facilitates the decision of how to allocate funds within the real estate portfolio.

15.2.1 Heterogeneity within Subcategories

Real estate is not only heterogeneous among subcategories, but it can also be highly heterogeneous within its subcategories. Although categorization and subcategorization of real estate may serve a useful role in asset allocation and analysis, care must be taken to avoid development of an oversimplified view of real estate. Although assets within various real estate categories and subcategories typically share general characteristics, there may be instances in which tremendous differences in economic nature exist.

For example, consider two office buildings that are similar in size, construction, and location. The first office building has a 20-year, noncancelable lease with a large and well-capitalized corporation. The lease essentially locks in the rental revenues for the entire property for the next two decades. In this case, the income of the property will be similar to that of a corporate bond, and the value of the property to the investor will tend to fluctuate in response to the same factors that affect the value of a corporate bond issued by the tenant (i.e., riskless interest rate changes, and changes in the credit spread on the debt of the tenant).

The second office building in the example is vacant. Both buildings are located in a geographic area with an economy strongly linked to oil prices. The value of this empty real estate asset will be especially sensitive to the supply of and demand for office space in the local real estate market. Thus, the value of this property will be driven by the forces that affect the region's economy, in this case, oil prices. The vacant property's value may behave more like equity prices in general and oil stock prices in particular. However, if the building begins to attract long-term tenants with long-term, noncancelable leases, the property's fundamental economic nature may transition from being more like an oil stock to being more like a corporate bond.

This example shows that assets within a specific type of real estate (e.g., private commercial real estate) may behave as highly debtlike securities or as highly equitylike securities depending on the characteristics of the individual properties. Furthermore, a particular property may experience dramatic changes in its investment characteristics due to an event such as the signing of a very long-term, noncancelable lease.

15.2.2 Top-Down Asset Allocation

Asset allocation approaches differ by the extent to which the process is focused on top-down allocation versus bottom-up allocation. **Top-down asset allocation** emphasizes allocation based on the analysis of general categories or types of investments. Section 15.3 provides numerous distinctions that can be used to place real estate into different categories. Exhibit 15.1 illustrates the concept of target asset allocation using one set of potential categories and weights. To the extent that the

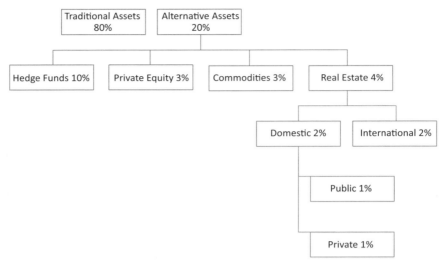

EXHIBIT 15.1 Asset Allocation

allocation illustrated in Exhibit 15.1 is based on general portfolio objectives, the asset allocation process is a top-down asset allocation.

For example, an asset allocator would typically be concerned about the overall return, risk, liquidity, and, perhaps, taxability of the overall portfolio. In the case of liquidity, a top-down asset allocator includes a concern for liquidity in selecting the portfolio weights, along with a preference for a higher return and other perceptions as to how each category serves these overall portfolio objectives. Thus, in considering liquidity, a pure top-down asset allocator would determine the weights for each category based in part on an analysis of the liquidity of each category of real estate and the extent to which illiquidity offers a risk premium. This liquidity concern and other general portfolio objectives may cause the asset allocator to make allocations at each level that ultimately decide that 1% of the total portfolio should be allocated to domestic, publicly traded equity real estate.

It should be noted that further detail regarding asset allocation could be illustrated in Exhibit 15.1. For example, in the category of publicly traded domestic real estate equity, the asset allocator may further divide the category by property type (office, industrial, retail) and by investment management (in-house vs. external, active vs. indexed). Furthermore, other categorizations could be used, along with greater refinement of the level of detail (e.g., international vs. domestic could be broken into finer distinctions).

15.2.3 Bottom-Up Asset Allocation

Bottom-up asset allocation refers to an emphasis on the attractiveness of individual investment opportunities as the primary driving factor of the asset allocation process. The asset allocator may determine that some subcategories of real estate or particular properties offer exceptionally attractive investment opportunities, whereas other categories or properties are unattractive. To the extent that these analyses of individual opportunities or subcategories exert the dominant effect on the ultimate asset allocation, the asset allocation strategy would be a bottom-up strategy.

For example, an asset allocator may have internal staff and established relationships with outside managers that lead the allocator to believe that particular subcategories offer attractive levels of alpha. The asset allocator may favor some categories based on extensive experience and knowledge in those categories, while avoiding categories in which the allocator has limited knowledge and experience. To the extent that individual asset selection exerts a major effect on the ultimate asset allocations among major categories, the process is bottom-up. Most asset allocation methods are a mix of top-down and bottom-up, in that allocations among major categories tend to be driven by general portfolio objectives, while allocations within subcategories are driven by the allocator's perceptions of the opportunities available.

15.3 CATEGORIES OF REAL ESTATE

This section describes the main characteristics of various real estate assets, beginning with four especially common categories that can be used to differentiate real estate:

1. Equity versus debt
2. Domestic versus international
3. Residential versus commercial
4. Private versus public

Each of these categories is briefly discussed in the following four sections, followed by discussions of other methods of categorizing real estate.

15.3.1 Equity versus Debt

The traditional method of distinguishing between equity claims and debt claims is to use the legal distinction between a residual claim and a fixed claim. A **mortgage** is a debt instrument collateralized by real estate, and real estate debt is typically defined as including all mortgages. Note, however, that mortgages with enormous credit risk can behave more like equity, and ownership of properties with very long-term leases can behave like debt.

Unlike debt claims on traditional operating firms, mortgages tend to be more standardized, have more limited recourse, and have asset-related covenants. Therefore, the value of traditional corporate debt often focuses more on the profitability of the operating firm than on the value of the firm's tangible assets. However, the value of mortgages is more closely associated with the value of the real estate than the profitability of the borrower.

15.3.2 Domestic versus International

One of the primary motivations to real estate investing is diversification. International investing (i.e., cross-border investing) in general and international real estate investing in particular are regarded as offering substantially improved diversification. However, the heterogeneity of most real estate and the unique nature of many real estate investments make international real estate investing more problematic than international investing in traditional assets. Other challenges include lack of knowledge regarding or experience with foreign real estate markets, lack of relationships with foreign real estate managers, time and expenses of travel for due diligence, political risk, foreign currency exposures, and taxation differences. For these reasons, a large share of international real estate investing is done by investing in the stock of listed property companies (LPCs), including REITs, in foreign countries. The continuing emergence of derivative products related to real estate investments in particular nations or regions is an important potential opportunity for exploiting the benefits of international diversification without the challenges of direct international investments.

The extent of appropriate international investing depends on the locale of the asset allocator. A U.S. asset allocator or an asset allocator of another country with a very large economy may be able to achieve moderate levels of diversification without foreign real estate investing. However, an asset allocator in a nation with a small economy may experience high levels of idiosyncratic risk in the absence of foreign investments.

15.3.3 Residential versus Commercial

One of the most important drivers of the characteristics of a real estate investment is the nature of the real estate assets underlying the investment. A broad distinction, especially in mortgages, is residential real estate versus commercial real estate.

Housing or residential real estate properties: Residential real estate includes many property types, such as single-family homes, town houses, condominiums, and manufactured housing. The housing or residential real estate sector is traditionally defined as including owner-occupied housing rather than large apartment complexes. Within residential real estate, the institutional investor is primarily concerned with investing in mortgages on housing and residential real estate. Ownership in the mortgages is usually established through pools of mortgages.

Commercial real estate properties: Commercial real estate properties include the following categories, among others: office buildings, retail space, industrial centers, hotels, and apartment buildings. Small properties may be directly and solely owned by a single institutional investor. Alternatively, collections of numerous smaller properties and large commercial properties may be managed by a real estate company through private equity real estate funds that, in turn, are owned by several institutional investors as limited partners. Within commercial real estate, the institutional investor can access opportunities through either debt or equity investments.

For the most part, residential and commercial real estate require very distinct methods of financial analysis. For example, the credit risk of mortgages on residential real estate is typically analyzed with a focus on the creditworthiness of the borrower. Mortgages on commercial real estate tend to focus on the analysis of the net cash flows from the property.

15.3.4 Private versus Public

Exposure to the real estate market, especially the equity side, can be achieved via private and public ownership. **Private real estate equity** investment involves the direct or indirect acquisition and management of actual physical properties that are not traded on an exchange. **Public real estate investment** entails the buying of shares of real estate investment companies and investing in other indirect exchange-traded forms of real estate (including futures and options on real estate indices, and exchange-traded funds based on real estate).

Private real estate is also known as physical, direct, or non-exchange-traded real estate. Private real estate may take the form of equity through direct ownership of the property or debt through mortgage claims on the property. The private real estate market comprises several segments: housing or residential real estate properties, commercial real estate properties, farmland, and timberland. The relative advantages of investing in the private side of real estate equity are that investors or investment managers have the ability to choose specific properties, exert direct control of their investments, and enjoy the potential for tax-timing benefits.

Public real estate is a financial claim in the form of equity, debt, funds, or derivative positions, and may be a claim on either underlying private real estate positions or underlying public real estate positions. Public real estate is also known as securitized, financial, indirect, or exchange-traded real estate. Thus, public real estate intermediates the ownership of private real estate through one or more levels of contracts designed to facilitate real estate ownership, reduce costs, or increase liquidity relative to direct ownership. For example, securitization has substantially increased the liquidity and accessibility of real estate investments.

Real estate investment trusts (REITs) are securitized pools of real estate that are an important form of public real estate, especially in the United States. The relative advantages of investing in public commercial real estate (as opposed to private) include liquidity, greater investor access, relatively low transaction costs, the potential for better corporate governance structures, and the transparency brought by pricing in public capital markets (Idzorek, Barad, and Meier 2007).

One of the most important characteristics of a REIT is that, due to the trust structure, income distributed by a REIT to its shareholders is not taxed at the REIT level but is taxed at the investor level after it flows through the REIT. In order to enjoy this tax status in the United States, REITs are subject to two main restrictions: (1) 75% of the income they receive must be derived from real estate activities, and (2) the REIT is legally obligated to pay out 90% of its taxable income in the form of dividends. Other restrictions relate to the ownership structure of the REIT. As long as a REIT is in compliance with the relevant restrictions, it may deduct dividends from its income when determining its corporate tax liability (i.e., it pays corporate income taxes only on retained taxable income).

REITs can invest both in the private real estate market (equity REITs) and in real estate–based debt (mortgage REITs). Generally, if a REIT has 50% or more of its assets in the private real estate equity market, it is viewed as an equity REIT; if over 50% of its assets are invested in real estate debt, it is viewed as a mortgage REIT. This distinction is important in return analyses. For example, unlike equity REITs, mortgage REITs tend to move in line with bank stocks due to their underlying asset base. Equity REITs dominate the REIT sector, in terms of both number available and market capitalization.

15.3.5 Real Estate Categorization by Market

Institutional investors often categorize private commercial real estate equity investments by the size of the real estate market in which the real estate is located. Real estate assets are said to trade in the **primary real estate market** if the geographic location of the real estate is in a major metropolitan area of the world, with numerous large real estate properties or a healthy growth rate in real estate projects. Primary real estate markets tend to have easily recognizable names. Using the United States for illustration, examples would range from cities such as Orlando, Florida, to metropolitan areas such as Manhattan. Large institutional investors focus on investments in these primary markets. **Secondary real estate markets** include moderately sized communities (in terms of number and size of large real estate projects) such as Knoxville, Tennessee, and Omaha, Nebraska, as well as suburban areas of primary markets. **Tertiary real estate markets** tend to have less recognizable names, smaller populations, or smaller real estate projects.

15.3.6 Risk and Return Classifications

From the perspective of an asset allocator, the most useful categorization approach of real estate should center on the most important characteristics of the portfolio. The primary characteristics of a portfolio are risk and return. Therefore, asset allocators should consider including a categorization approach that focuses on the risk and return profiles of the assets.

Chapter 17 discusses a classification of real estate that includes three types: core, value-added, and opportunistic. These three categories assist the analysis of real estate and asset allocation decisions by grouping together real estate that possesses similar risk and return. Section 15.2.1 demonstrated the heterogeneity of real estate and the potential for the risk and return of an investment in a particular real estate subcategory to be more like the risk and return of investments in a different real estate category. The heterogeneity of real estate within each category may lead an asset allocator to focus on distinguishing investments based on their risk and return, perhaps using a classification system such as the core, value-added, and opportunistic categories discussed in Chapter 17.

15.3.7 The Focus on Private Commercial Real Estate

Most of the focus in Chapters 16 through 20 is on private commercial (i.e., income-producing) real estate rather than on public real estate, residential real estate, or commercial mortgages. There are three reasons for this:

1. Most commercial real estate throughout the world is privately held rather than publicly traded.
2. Most of the equity of residential real estate is held by the occupier of the property rather than by an institutional investor.

3. The pricing of the equity claims to private commercial real estate drives the pricing of the credit risk in the pricing of commercial mortgages. In other words, real estate debt may be viewed through the structural model as being well explained through an understanding of the risks of the equity in the same property.

Thus, in the next five chapters on real estate, the material emphasizes the risk and returns of equity ownership of private commercial properties, whether owned directly or held through limited partnerships.

15.4 RETURN DRIVERS OF REAL ESTATE

Real estate returns are generally perceived as being fundamentally different from the returns of other assets. For example, real estate is generally believed to offer substantial inflation protection and distinct diversification benefits. These distinctions are often justified based on historical tendencies, derived through empirical analysis of past prices and returns.

An understanding of the inflation-protection potential of real estate requires a distinction between **anticipated inflation** and unanticipated inflation. The anticipated, or expected, inflation rate is the expected rate of change in overall price levels. Expectations vary across market participants and are generally unobservable. Accordingly, indications of anticipated inflation are often based on surveys of consensus estimates, inferred from past inflation, or inferred from other market information such as interest rates. For example, in a particular year, economists may forecast that prices will rise, on average, by 3% in the next year.

To the extent that a market is informationally efficient, the level of anticipated inflation should be incorporated in the price and, therefore, the expected rate of return on various assets. For example, the **Fisher effect** states that nominal interest rates will incorporate both real interest rates and a premium for anticipated inflation (while other models include the effect of expected taxation). The net result is that every asset in an informationally efficient market provides identical protection from anticipated inflation, since every asset's price adjusts to compensate the buyer for anticipated inflation. Thus, stable or previously anticipated inflation rates are not a return driver, or determinant, by themselves.

The more challenging issue is that of unanticipated inflation. **Unanticipated inflation** is the realized rate of inflation minus the anticipated inflation. The effect of unanticipated inflation on an investment's realized return is crucial, and the risk of unanticipated inflation is an important consideration in risk analysis. Realized inflation in a particular period exerts its primary effect through its role in modifying future expectations of inflation. Because changes in expected inflation can exert substantial effects on prices, realized inflation can be an important driver of most real estate returns. In other words, deviation in realized inflation rates relative to previously anticipated inflation rates (i.e., unanticipated inflation) can be a very important return driver due to its role in changing anticipations of future inflation rates. Unanticipated inflation is the most important inflation-related risk.

The sensitivity of various real estate investments to unanticipated inflation may be analyzed through empirical analyses of past returns or fundamental analysis of the investment's sources of risk and return. A challenge in empirical analysis of the effects of unanticipated inflation is in developing an objective and accurate estimate of the consensus-expected inflation rate, which cannot be directly observed. An estimate of the anticipated inflation rate is necessary to estimate the unanticipated inflation rate as the difference between the realized and expected inflation rates.

Another challenge is that there are typically different rates of anticipated inflation over different time horizons. Changes in anticipation of inflation over various time horizons could each be expected to exert different effects on various real estate investments. Furthermore, realized rates of inflation may be studied over different time intervals. Thus, the price reaction and inflation protection offered by an investment should be expected to differ based on whether the realized inflation signals a long-term change in expected inflation or a more transient shift in inflation anticipation.

Inflation may have different effects on different types of properties. Inflation may hurt the value of bondlike properties that have long-term leases at fixed rates. Though properties are typically valued on a pretax basis and before financing costs (interest), investors in real estate equity that are leveraged with adjustable-rate mortgages may also suffer from higher financing costs during times of inflation. Inflation, however, can benefit owners of leveraged properties that are financed with fixed-rate debt. Properties with lease structures that may benefit from inflation include those with short-term leases or leases in which payments contractually rise with the rate of inflation.

CHAPTER 16

Unsmoothing of Appraisal-Based Returns

U sing past data to infer the future risks and returns of real estate is an important part of real estate analysis, portfolio allocation, and risk management. The primary purpose of this chapter is to focus on one of the most crucial tasks of empirical analysis of real estate returns: data unsmoothing. The effects of smoothed data are not limited to values based on real estate appraisals. Smoothing can affect additional real estate valuation other than appraisals, as well as other alternative investments, such as hedge funds and private equity funds. Therefore, the unsmoothing procedures discussed in this chapter are central to the analysis of alternative investments.

There are substantial challenges faced by real estate appraisers and other financial professionals who are asked to place values on an asset through time, as economic conditions change. Consider a major market movement in the midst of a more general period of financial stability. For example, suppose that the equity market experiences a general and rapid price rise of 10%. It is possible that the reported prices of other asset classes that tend to be correlated with equity markets may indicate a delayed reaction to that rise and the accompanying changes in economic conditions. To the extent that a price or return series demonstrates a delayed response, due perhaps to the valuation methods used by appraisers or other financial professionals responsible for publishing prices, the resulting price or return series is referred to as a **smoothed** series.

Tradable prices that are smoothed can be arbitraged if transaction costs are relatively small. Nontradable prices, such as appraisals, cannot be arbitraged, and therefore the smoothing may be more pronounced and permanent. Smoothed price and return data interfere with risk management and other financial analysis, and therefore unsmoothing of the data is essential. This chapter discusses **unsmoothing** of a price index or return series—the process of removing the effects of smoothing from a data series. The next section introduces smoothed pricing and the principles of unsmoothing.

16.1 SMOOTHED PRICING

Exhibit 16.1 provides a numerical illustration of the concept of smoothed pricing. Overall equity market returns, shown in column 2, are assumed to experience a 10% surge in prices in the midst of a larger time period of stable values. Three other

EXHIBIT 16.1 Illustration of Price Smoothing

(1) Time Period	(2) Market Returns	(3) Unsmoothed	(4) Lightly Smoothed	(5) Strongly Smoothed
1	0%	0%	0%	0%
2	10%	8%	6%	4%
3	0%	0%	2%	4%
4	0%	0%	0%	0%
Mean	2.5%	2%	2%	2%
Std. dev.	5.0%	4.0%	2.8%	2.3%
Corr. w/mkt.	1.00	1.00	0.94	0.58
Beta	1.00	0.80	0.53	0.27

return series are illustrated in columns 3, 4, and 5, each of which eventually responds with an 8% rise (ignoring compounding for simplicity), consistent with having true underlying (unsmoothed) betas of 0.80. The unsmoothed return series experiences its entire price response (8%) to the market in the same time period as the market. The lightly smoothed return series reflects 75% of its 8% price response in the same period as the market, but reflects another 25% of its price response in the subsequent time period. The strongly smoothed return series experiences half of its price response in the same period as the market, and the other half in the subsequent period.

16.1.1 Price Smoothing and Arbitrage in a Perfect Market

In a perfect market (i.e., one without transaction costs or trading restrictions), arbitrageurs should exploit profit opportunities caused by the consistently delayed price responses contained in smoothed prices. Any asset with consistently delayed price responses will be purchased after general prices rise and short-sold by arbitrageurs after general prices decline. In this way, arbitrageurs will consistently profit from delayed price rises using the long positions, and profit from delayed price declines using the short positions. For example, an arbitrageur could buy the strongly smoothed asset at the end of time period 2 (immediately after the market rises) and expect, on average, to receive an alpha of 4% in time period 3, as the asset's price experiences a delayed response to the large market rise in time period 2. In the case of a large market decline in a perfect market, the arbitrageur can short-sell a smoothed price immediately after a large decline in the prices of similar assets that are not smoothed. Note that the arbitrageur can hedge risk by taking offsetting positions in similar assets that are not smoothed.

Competition both to buy assets with smoothed prices before delayed price increases and to short-sell assets with smoothed prices before delayed price declines will drive away delayed prices in tradable assets by forcing prices to respond more quickly. Eventually, in a perfect market, competition between arbitrageurs will force prices to respond fully and immediately in the absence of transaction costs. For example, in the case of a large rise in unsmoothed prices, arbitrageurs will vie to establish positions earlier and earlier in the anticipation of subsequent price movements.

Arbitrageurs will force previously smoothed prices to respond to price changes as quickly as they are reflected in unsmoothed prices. Thus, in perfect markets, any smoothing of price returns is unsmoothed by the actions of arbitrageurs whenever assets can be traded at the stated prices.

16.1.2 Persistence in Price Smoothing

There are two primary culprits that prevent smoothed return series from being unsmoothed by arbitrageurs. First, the return series may not indicate true trading opportunities. Appraisals, for example, are typically indications of price that do not represent either bids to buy or offers to sell. Appraisals are used to value portfolios for accounting purposes and to construct price indices. In both cases, the appraisals represent estimated values, not market prices.

Second, even if a smoothed return series indicates trading opportunities (i.e., prices at which transactions may be made), the underlying assets may have substantial transaction costs or other barriers to arbitrage. For example, in real estate, the time and transaction costs of buying and selling assets in order to exploit delayed pricing responses may be prohibitively expensive relative to the potential gains from moderate price smoothing. Real estate sales commissions, real estate transfer taxes, legal costs, financing costs, search costs, inspection costs, and so forth provide substantial barriers to arbitrageurs seeking to exploit the lags in price changes caused by price smoothing. Limited partnership holdings in real estate and private equity funds may have a stated life, such as 10 years. During this period, liquidation of fund interests is generally infeasible until the general partner exits the underlying investments.

In addition to transaction costs, other barriers exist to trading assets that exhibit smoothed pricing. For example, international open-end equity mutual funds were notorious for allowing stale prices to cause smoothing in their reported prices (net asset values). Arbitrageurs exploited the smoothed pricing by establishing long positions in international funds when domestic markets rose sharply, and establishing neutral positions in international funds when domestic markets declined (and when foreign markets were already closed). Many mutual fund companies implemented more accurate pricing methods or erected powerful barriers against short-term trading of such funds, such as a 2% redemption fee on positions held for less than 90 days.

Due to the actions of arbitrageurs and other market participants, assets with tradable prices, low transaction costs, and minimal trading barriers do not typically require unsmoothing. The need to unsmooth prices tends to be greater for nontradable prices and assets with high transaction costs or trading barriers.

16.1.3 Problems Resulting from Price Smoothing

The smoothing of the last two return series in Exhibit 16.1 generates lower standard deviations, lower correlations with the market, and much lower reported betas. For example, note that the true beta of 0.80 is indicated in the estimated beta of the unsmoothed return series, but the lightly smoothed return series has a reported beta one-third smaller than the unsmoothed return series, and the strongly smoothed return series has a reported beta two-thirds smaller. Similarly, the standard deviations of the smoothed series are substantially lower, as smoothing causes the largest outliers of the unsmoothed series to be muted. The primary problem resulting from price smoothing is that it causes substantial understatement of both volatility and correlation.

Risk understatement may cause inappropriately high allocations to assets with smoothed prices. Portfolio optimization models will tend to overweight assets with understated risk. Furthermore, underestimated price correlations due to price smoothing may distort the estimation of appropriate hedge ratios and interfere with risk management.

Though risk can be understated through price smoothing, long-term historical mean returns are not substantially affected by the price-smoothing process. Nevertheless, investors selecting investments with high Sharpe ratios will be attracted to asset classes with smoothed prices, as the mean return in the numerator of the Sharpe ratio is typically only slightly affected by smoothing, while the denominator contains artificially low estimates of standard deviation. Smoothing results in artificial increases in the estimated Sharpe ratio and other similar performance measures.

16.2 MODELS OF PRICE AND RETURN SMOOTHING

In order to detect, correct, or exploit smoothing, it is necessary to form a belief with regard to its particular nature. A model is a precise expression of the nature of the smoothing, which can be used to determine a method for estimating the unsmoothed prices or returns. This section discusses the primary approaches to modeling smoothing.

16.2.1 Reported Prices as Lags of True Prices

Define P_t^{reported} as the reported or smoothed price of an asset at time t, and P_t^{true} as the true price. An example of a reported price would be a price index based on appraisal values or a hedge fund's net asset value that is subject to smoothing by a fund manager. The true price of the asset is defined as the best indication of the market price at which the asset would trade with ready buyers and sellers.

For example, consider a real estate index in which at least one of two things happens: (1) the prices contained in the index partially represent lagged market values, or (2) the prices in the index contain the professional judgment of appraisers who based their opinion at least partially on a series of lagged market values. In either case, current reported prices are a function of past true prices. For example, Equation 16.1 contains a very general model of smoothing that expresses the reported price as a moving average of the current true price and past true prices:

$$P_t^{\text{reported}} = \alpha + \beta_0 P_t^{\text{true}} + \beta_1 P_{t-1}^{\text{true}} + \beta_2 P_{t-2}^{\text{true}} + \cdots \quad (16.1)$$

Equation 16.1 allows the reported and smoothed price index at time t (P_t^{reported}) to depend not just on the contemporaneous true price (P_t^{true}) but also on the true prices in previous time periods. The relationships between the current reported price and the true prices are specified using a set of parameters denoted as β_i. A potentially simpler model that has only one parameter specifies an exact relationship between the parameters in Equation 16.1, as shown in Equation 16.2:

$$P_t^{\text{reported}} = \alpha\, P_t^{\text{true}} + \alpha(1 - \alpha) P_{t-1}^{\text{true}} + \alpha(1 - \alpha)^2\, P_{t-2}^{\text{true}} + \cdots \qquad (16.2)$$

where α is a parameter greater than zero and less than or equal to 1 that determines the speed of the decay function. A decay function is simply a numeric construct that puts less weight on older valuations and more weight on more recent valuations. For example, consider the case of $\alpha = 0.50$ in Equation 16.2. In this case, the current reported price depends 50% on the current true price, 25% on the true price of the previous observation date, 12.5% on the true price of the observation date from two periods before, and so on. Put differently, the true price in a particular period is only 50% reflected in the reported price of the same time period, 25% reflected on a one-period-delayed basis, 12.5% reflected on a two-period-delayed basis, and so on. A value of $\alpha = 0.60$ places 60% weight on the current true price, 24% weight on the immediately prior true price, and so on. The weights of the prices in Equation 16.2 sum to 1. A value of $\alpha = 1.00$ indicates that true prices are immediately and fully reflected in reported prices. A value of α approaching zero indicates that the effect of a true price on reported prices occurs on a more delayed basis.

Equation 16.2 can be factored to generate a highly simplified expression for true price as a function of the current reported price and the one-period lagged value of the reported price, as shown in Equation 16.3:

$$P_t^{\text{true}} = (1/\alpha) \times P_t^{\text{reported}} - [(1 - \alpha)/\alpha] \times P_{t-1}^{\text{reported}} \qquad (16.3)$$

The importance of Equation 16.3 is that it expresses the most recent true but unobservable price as a simple equation involving the most recent smoothed index value and the previous smoothed index value, both of which are observable. Equation 16.4 rearranges Equation 16.3 into a potentially more intuitive form:

$$P_t^{\text{true}} = P_{t-1}^{\text{reported}} + \left[(1/\alpha) \times \left(P_t^{\text{reported}} - P_{t-1}^{\text{reported}}\right)\right] \qquad (16.4)$$

Equation 16.4 indicates that the true price differs from the previously reported price by an amount based on the most recent price change in the reported price series. Consider the case of a rising reported value ($P_t^{\text{reported}} > P_{t-1}^{\text{reported}}$), and note that in Equation 16.4, the expression $1/\alpha$ is greater than 1 (assuming that α is between zero and 1). In this case, the true value of the asset is expressed as the previously reported value of the asset ($P_{t-1}^{\text{reported}}$) plus the reported price change increased by a factor of $1/\alpha$. For example, with $\alpha = 0.60$, a \$10 change in the reported price implies a \$16.67 difference between the current true price and the previous reported price. The muted price change of \$10 in the reported (and smoothed) index is consistent with a much larger change in the true underlying price.

The primary importance of Equation 16.4 is that given an estimate of the parameter α, the equation can be used to generate the estimated true prices and their changes (i.e., the unsmoothed prices) from a series of smoothed prices. Fisher (2005) estimates a value of $\alpha = 0.40$ for private unleveraged annual real estate returns in the United States. Inserting $\alpha = 0.40$ into Equation 16.4 indicates that true prices should be estimated based on a price change that is 2.5 times larger than the most recent reported price change.

16.2.2 Modeling Lagged Returns Rather Than Prices

Section 16.2.1 focused on prices. Often the relationship is specified based directly on returns. Generally, there is a small difference between imposing the lagged structure specified by Equation 16.2 on prices and imposing the same structure on returns.[1] But as an approximation, Equation 16.1 can be written in terms of returns, as in Equation 16.5:

$$R_{t,\text{reported}} \approx \beta_0 R_{t,\text{true}} + \beta_1 R_{t-1,\text{true}} + \beta_2 R_{t-2,\text{true}} + \cdots \qquad (16.5)$$

where $R_{t,\text{reported}}$ is the return on the reported price series in period t, and $R_{t,\text{true}}$ is the return on the true but unobservable price series in period t.

16.2.3 Estimating the Parameter for First-Order Autocorrelation

Equation 16.3 indicates that true prices can be determined from reported prices using the parameter α. Accordingly, estimated values of true prices can be determined from reported prices using an estimation of the parameter.

An intuitive interpretation of α is that it is determines the extent to which the reported price (or return) in a particular time period is determined or driven by the value of the true price (or return) in the same time period. The higher the value of α the more the current reported value is driven by current changes in the true value rather than past changes.

Equation 16.6 is formed by multiplying each side of equation 16.4 by α, substituting $\alpha = 1 - \rho$, and rearranging the terms:

$$P_t^{\text{reported}} = (1 - \rho) P_t^{\text{true}} + \rho P_{t-1}^{\text{reported}} \qquad (16.6)$$

---

[1] To demonstrate the details, the following equation is identical to Equation 16.1 except that the relationship is expressed for the reported price of the previous time period ($P_{t-1}^{\text{reported}}$) rather than the current time period (P_t^{reported}):

$$P_{t-1}^{\text{reported}} = \alpha + \beta_0 P_{t-1}^{\text{true}} + \beta_1 P_{t-2}^{\text{true}} + \beta_2 P_{t-3}^{\text{true}} + \cdots$$

Subtracting each side of the equation from the respective sides of Equation 16.1, assuming that the parameters are constants, and rearranging the terms generates this equation:

$$\Delta P_t^{\text{reported}} = \beta_0 \Delta P_t^{\text{true}} + \beta_1 \Delta P_{t-1}^{\text{true}} + \beta_2 \Delta P_{t-2}^{\text{true}} + \cdots$$

where Δ indicates single-period price changes (e.g., $\Delta P_t^{\text{reported}} = P_t^{\text{reported}} - P_{t-1}^{\text{reported}}$). Thus, the modeling of prices is similar to the modeling of price changes. However, returns are not equivalently modeled. For example, in order to convert each price change in the preceding equation into returns, each price change must be divided by its initial price, but the prices differ.

Equation 16.6 can be expressed as an approximation in terms of price changes and returns, as depicted in Equations 16.7 and 16.8:

$$\Delta P_t^{\text{reported}} = (1 - \rho)\,\Delta P_t^{\text{true}} + \rho \Delta P_{t-1}^{\text{reported}} \tag{16.7}$$

$$R_{t,\text{reported}} \approx (1 - \rho)\,R_{t,\text{true}} + \rho\,R_{t-1,\text{reported}} \tag{16.8}$$

where ρ is the first-order autocorrelation coefficient, given the assumption that the reported price series (or return series) is autoregressive of order one (Gallais-Hamonno and Nguyen-Thi-Thanh 2007).[2] The use of ρ in place of α is to place the emphasis on a statistical interpretation of the relationships.

Equation 16.8 expresses **first-order autocorrelation** in the reported return series because the smoothed return in period t (the left-hand side of the equation) is correlated by ρ with the smoothed return in the immediately preceding time period (the last term on the right-hand side). The most current return of the smoothed return series depends partially on the new market information contained in the true return (R_t^{true}) and partially on the smoothed return of the previous time period. The parameter ρ specifies the relative importance of the two explanatory variables, with higher values of ρ indicating greater smoothing.

For example, assume that ρ in Equation 16.8 is equal to 40% and that the true underlying price changes in a particular asset class in the last five time periods were 0%, 0%, 10%, 0%, 0%. Applying Equation 16.8 to obtain a series of smoothed prices would generate the following return series: 0%, 0%, 6%, 2.4%, 0.96%. Note that the smoothed return for time period 4 is 2.4% rather than 4.0%. The reason for this is that in Equation 16.8, ρ is multiplied by the lagged smoothed return (6%), not the lagged true return (10%). Similarly, the impact of the 10% true return on the smoothed returns will continue to be experienced forever, but with a rapidly diminishing effect.

16.2.4 Four Reasons for Smoothed Prices and Delayed Price Changes

There are four primary explanations for first-order autocorrelation in a price index, such as an index of real estate prices. One explanation is that a price index is being based on observed prices of the most recent transactions of each component of the index and that old or stale prices are being used for index components that have not recently traded. Returning to the previous example, $\rho = 40\%$, and a series of true underlying price changes in a particular asset class in the last five time periods is 0%, 0%, 10%, 0%, 0%. In the case of a transaction-based price index, Equation 16.8 and $\rho = 40\%$ would be consistent with the idea that 60% of the most recent underlying asset values were based on a transaction that occurred in the current time period (and reflected the true return of 10% in period 3), while the impact of the 10% true return on the remaining 40% of the underlying asset values will be

---

[2] The fact that ρ is the first-order autocorrelation coefficient can be verified by solving for the correlation coefficient between $R_{t-1,\text{reported}}$ and the right-hand side of Equation 16.8 (the formula for $R_{t,\text{reported}}$). Under the realistic assumption that $R_{t,\text{true}}$ is uncorrelated with the previous reported return, $R_{t-1,\text{reported}}$, the correlation between $R_{t,\text{reported}}$ and $R_{t-1,\text{reported}}$ is easily shown to be ρ.

reflected through time as they transact in subsequent time periods (as reflected in period 4 and period 5 returns of 2.4% and 0.96%).

A professional appraiser may also generate a series of smoothed prices. One reason is that the appraiser observes price changes on a delayed basis and only on those properties that transacted. Another reason is that the appraiser may exhibit the behavioral phenomenon known as anchoring. **Anchoring** is the observed tendency of humans to give disproportionate weight or reliability to previous observations. In the previous example, an appraiser may be reluctant to believe that underlying assets have truly risen by 10%. The appraiser may move his valuations 60% in the direction of 10% during the first period, and then continue to adjust valuations in the subsequent periods.

A third major reason for smoothed pricing is that even current transaction prices in an efficient market may be selected such that they signal lagged price responses. Consider an efficient real estate market with two types of properties of approximately equal total market value. Assume that one of the property types experiences a 5% true price growth, while the other type experiences a 25% true price growth. Based on the assumption of equal weights, the true total real estate price index should indicate a 15% price increase. However, in a rapidly rising market of real estate prices, investors may be systematically biased toward transacting in those property types with characteristics that caused lower price growth (5%). The primary explanation for the tendency of market transactions to be dominated by assets that rise less in price during a bull market may be behavioral, such as the reluctance of buyers to accept the 25% price increase of the other property type. Simply put, more buyers are willing to buy property types with 5% higher prices than are willing to buy property types with 25% higher prices, even when the higher prices of each property type reflect true market values. It should be noted that this is only one of many scenarios that could occur, and some of the scenarios would generate the opposite result.

Continuing the example, if 80% of the properties that transact are of the type that experienced lower price growth (5%), then the average price changes of the observed transactions would be 9%, found as [(80% × 5%) + (20% × 25%)]. The 9% average price index change is 60% of the true price change (15%) for the entire market. Presumably, buyers will increasingly buy the property types that have risen in price by 25% once the new and higher price level becomes familiar. Similarly, price declines will be reported on a smoothed basis if sellers are reluctant to sell the property types that have declined the most.

The final reason of the four primary reasons for smoothed prices is the potential delay between the setting of a price on a real estate transaction and the reporting of the transaction. A real estate price may be negotiated months before the transaction occurs, and the reported price of the transaction may become known to the appraiser or index on a delayed basis as well.

16.3 UNSMOOTHING A PRICE OR RETURN SERIES

The previous section discussed smoothing and provided simple examples of how smoothed prices are formed through delayed responses to true price changes. But the objective in practice is to estimate true returns from smoothed returns. This section discusses unsmoothing: the process of estimating a true but unobservable price or return series from an observable but smoothed price or return series.

16.3.1 Unsmoothing First-Order Autocorrelation Given ρ

Equation 16.8 can be factored by solving for the true return based on the reported or smoothed returns, as shown in Equation 16.9 (and for expositional simplicity, replacing the approximation sign with an equality sign):

$$R_{t,\text{true}} = (R_{t,\text{reported}} - \rho\,R_{t-1,\text{reported}})/(1 - \rho) \qquad (16.9)$$

Returning to the example of the true return series (0%, 0%, 10%, 0%, 0%) used in the previous section to generate the smoothed return series of 0%, 0%, 6%, 2.4%, 0.96%, Equation 16.9 can be used along with $\rho = 0.40$ to back out the true return series from the reported series. Inserting the smoothed return series (0%, 0%, 6%, 2.4%, 0.96%) as the reported returns in Equation 16.9 and continuing to use $\rho = 0.40$, the implied true returns are as follows:

$$R_{3,\text{true}} = (R_{3,\text{reported}} - \rho\,R_{2,\text{reported}})/(1 - \rho) = [6\% - (0.40 \times 0\%)]/(1 - 0.40) = 10\%$$
$$R_{4,\text{true}} = (R_{4,\text{reported}} - \rho\,R_{3,\text{reported}})/(1 - \rho) = [2.4\% - (0.40 \times 6\%)]/(1 - 0.40) = 0\%$$
$$R_{5,\text{true}} = (R_{5,\text{reported}} - \rho\,R_{4,\text{reported}})/(1 - \rho) = [0.96\% - (0.40 \times 2.4\%)]/(1 - 0.40) = 0\%$$

Note that the smoothed return series can be used without error to find the underlying true return series if the process follows a first-order autocorrelation process without an error term and if ρ can be estimated without error. Of course, in practice, the returns do not conform perfectly to the first-order autocorrelation model, and the coefficient ρ must be estimated and is subject to estimation error. Thus, the unsmoothed estimations contain errors. More complex models may be appropriate when the smoothing takes place over more than one time period, such as a fourth-order autocorrelation model, when smoothing of quarterly returns takes place over a one-year period. The following section discusses the three-step process for unsmoothing a reported price or return series to estimate a true price or return series.

16.3.2 The Three Steps of Unsmoothing

Unsmoothing a return series containing autocorrelation involves three steps:

Step 1: The first step is determining or specifying the form of the autocorrelation. As throughout this chapter, first-order autocorrelation is being assumed (as shown in Equation 16.8).

Step 2: The second step is estimating the parameter(s) of the assumed autocorrelation process. In our example of a first-order autocorrelation coefficient, the only parameter is ρ, as indicated in Equations 16.8 and 16.9. The first-order autocorrelation coefficient of a series is found as the correlation coefficient between each observation and the observation from the same series in the previous time period, as depicted in Equation 16.10:

$$\hat{\rho} = \text{corr}\left(R_{t,\text{reported}} - R_{t-1,\text{reported}}\right) \qquad (16.10)$$

Equation 16.11 depicts the formula for a correlation coefficient based on covariance and standard deviations:

$$\rho_{i,j} = \sigma_{i,j}/(\sigma_i\,\sigma_j) \qquad (16.11)$$

where $\rho_{i,j}$ is the correlation coefficient between two variables, $\sigma_{i,j}$ is the co-variance between the two variables, and σ_i and σ_j are the standard deviations of the two variables. The correlation coefficient between each observation and its value in the previous time period can be estimated using sample statistics. Let's return to the example of a smoothed return series of 0%, 0%, 6%, 2.4%, 0.96%. Using Equation 16.11, the estimated correlation coefficient between that series and the one-period lagged return series of 0%, 0%, 0%, 6%, 2.4% is 0.037. Note that the estimated value of ρ (0.037) is far from its assumed and true value (0.40). The explanation for the difference is the small sample size and estimation error.

Step 3: The third step is inserting the estimated correlation coefficient in place of ρ in Equation 16.9 and solving for R_t^{true}, as shown by Gallais-Hamonno and Nguyen-Thi-Thanh (2007). Using Equation 16.9 and the estimated correlation coefficient (0.037) rather than the true correlation coefficient (0.40) generates the series (0%, 0%, 6.2%, 2.3%, 0.9%):

$$R_{2,\text{true}} = (0\% - [(0.037 \times 0\%)]/(1 - 0.037) = 0\%$$
$$R_{3,\text{true}} = (6\% - [(0.037 \times 0\%)]/(1 - 0.037) = 6.2\%$$
$$R_{4,\text{true}} = (2.4\% - [(0.037 \times 6\%)]/(1 - 0.037) = 2.3\%$$
$$R_{5,\text{true}} = (0.96\% - [(0.037 \times 2.4\%)]/(1 - 0.037) = 0.9\%$$

The smoothed return series for time periods 2 through 5 (0%, 6%, 2.4%, 0.96%) is unsmoothed as 0%, 6.2%, 2.3%, 0.90%, slightly closer to the assumed true return series (0%, 10%, 0%, 0%) from which the example was derived. The reason for the very limited success was the poor estimation of ρ (0.037 as an estimation of 0.40). As was demonstrated in section 16.3.1, the use of $\rho = 0.40$ to unsmooth the return series generates the exact true series. The success of the unsmoothing therefore depends on the proper specification of the autocorrelation scheme and especially the accurate estimation of the parameter(s). It would be expected that the estimation of ρ should improve as the sample size is increased and that the poor estimation of ρ in the example was attributable to the use of such a small sample.

16.3.3 Unsmoothing Using Prices Rather Than Returns

As indicated in Equation 16.8, the unsmoothing of returns is an approximation if the true relationship is based on prices. The process illustrated for returns throughout this chapter can easily be performed using price changes and Equation 16.7, even if the data are provided as a series of returns. The six steps to unsmoothing a return index based on a model of smoothed price changes (Equation 16.7) are:

1. Convert the returns to a price index using a cumulative wealth index that includes compounding.
2. Convert the price index to a series of price changes using subtraction.

3. Apply Equation 16.11 to estimate the correlation between the price change series and its lagged value.
4. Apply Equation 16.9, substituting price changes for returns.
5. Use the unsmoothed price changes to form a price index.
6. Convert the unsmoothed price index back into returns.

16.3.4 Unsmoothing Returns with More Than First-Order Autocorrelation

The previous sections discuss first-order autocorrelation, wherein the return of the smoothed series is fully explained by the true return in the same period and the smoothed return from the previous time period. More advanced analyses of return autocorrelation allow for the current true return or price to depend on the previous reported or smoothed returns or prices of two or more previous periods on a more general basis than first-order autocorrelation. For example, let's assume that lagged effects up to k periods generate Equation 16.12:

$$R_t^{\text{reported}} = \alpha + \beta_1 R_{t-1}^{\text{reported}} + \beta_2 R_{t-2}^{\text{reported}} + \cdots + \beta_k R_{t-k}^{\text{reported}} + \varepsilon_t \quad (16.12)$$

Note that the effect of the true return in time period t on R_t^{reported} is assumed to be captured by the intercept and error term, since true returns in period t are assumed to be uncorrelated with previous returns.

The important distinction between Equation 16.12 and first-order autocorrelation (Equation 16.9) is that first-order autocorrelation specifies the exact relationship between the coefficients (i.e., βs) and reduces the coefficients to being specified by one parameter (ρ). Equation 16.12 provides a more general (flexible) specification by allowing the current reported return to depend on returns of various lags without constraining their relationships to each other.

Finally, note the case of $k = 1$ in Equation 16.12, which generates the simple linear regression coefficient between R_t^{reported} and $R_{t-1}^{\text{reported}}$. A useful formula for a simple regression coefficient from regressing variable y_t on variable x_t is that $\beta = \rho_{x,y} \sigma_y / \sigma_x$. Note that in the case of regressing a variable on its lagged value, the true standard deviation of each series is equal, so that $\sigma_x = \sigma_y$ and $\beta = \rho_{x,y}$ (and the estimated standard deviations of the original and lagged series approach each other as the sample size increases). Thus, the true slope coefficient from a linear regression between a variable and its lagged value is equal to the correlation coefficient, which in turn is equal to the first-order autocorrelation coefficient. Therefore, the first-order autocorrelation assumed throughout the examples in this chapter is the case of $k = 1$ in the more general model shown in Equation 16.12.

16.4 AN ILLUSTRATION OF UNSMOOTHING

The purpose of this section is to provide a detailed example of the unsmoothing of an actual return series with first-order autocorrelation. This section follows the three-step procedure discussed in section 16.3.2.

16.4.1 The Smoothed Data and the Market Data

Exhibit 16.2 contains five years of quarterly return data from two popular U.S. real estate indices. The time period of analysis is shortened to 20 quarters in this analysis so that all of the data can be shown in a concise exhibit. Column 3 contains returns based on the National Council of Real Estate Investment Fiduciaries National Property Index (henceforth NCREIF NPI) discussed in detail in Chapter 18. The NCREIF NPI is based on appraised prices of private real estate properties and is therefore likely to contain substantial price smoothing. Column 4 contains returns based on the all-equity REIT index of the FTSE National Association of Real Estate Investment Trusts (NAREIT) U.S. Real Estate Index Series (henceforth REIT index), which is based on closing market prices of publicly traded equity real estate investment trusts (REITs). To the extent that the market for REITs is informationally efficient, the return series should not have autocorrelation. The REIT index serves in the example as a proxy of a true return series, and the NCREIF NPI serves as a proxy of a smoothed return series. Though both series have similar mean returns, the standard deviation of returns based on the NCREIF NPI is substantially lower than that of the REIT index, as shown in Exhibit 16.2. Part of the volatility difference can be explained by the fact that the NCREIF NPI reflects no leverage (i.e., reflects underlying real estate assets without leverage), while the REIT index series reflects the returns of REITs that generally reflect levered real estate positions.

Note the very large negative returns of the REIT index in the fourth quarter of 2008 and the first quarter of 2009. Note further that the appraised series (the NCREIF NPI) shows only relatively modest negative returns in the same two quarters, apparently reflecting the tendency of appraised prices to move in only partial response to true market price changes (although the muted reaction can also be explained at least in part by the lack of leverage in the NCREIF NPI relative to the REIT index).

Note also that the REIT index has very large gains in the next two quarters (the second and third quarters of 2009). However, the NCREIF NPI continues to drift downward throughout 2009, possibly continuing to reflect the previous declines on a lagged basis. Investors generally find it impossible to sell short private real estate at appraisal-based prices in order to take advantage of these smoothed returns, since private funds are typically not available for short selling. During a time of market turmoil, it is also difficult to sell funds of private real estate investments, as many open-end funds either cease redemptions or erect gates. Statistical analysis, detailed in the following sections, can provide objective indications of these tendencies. The subsequent sections assume first-order autocorrelation between returns.

16.4.2 Estimating the First-Order Autocorrelation Coefficient

In Exhibit 16.2, the returns to the NCREIF and NAREIT indices for the first quarter of 2007 are 3.62% and 3.46%, respectively. The same returns, when lagged, are located in the row for the second quarter of 2007. The lagged time series, with 19 quarters of data, has one less observation than the unlagged time series, meaning that their estimated standard deviations will differ, even though they are based mostly on the same data.

EXHIBIT 16.2　Unsmoothing of Quarterly Returns, 2007–2011

Year	Quarter	Returns		Lagged Values		Unsmoothed Values	
		NCREIF	NAREIT	NCREIF	NAREIT	NCREIF	NAREIT
2007	1	3.62%	3.46%				
2007	2	4.59%	−9.04%	3.62%	3.46%	9.37%	−12.19%
2007	3	3.56%	2.59%	4.59%	−9.04%	−1.52%	5.52%
2007	4	3.21%	−12.67%	3.56%	2.59%	1.49%	−16.52%
2008	1	1.60%	1.40%	3.21%	−12.67%	−6.33%	4.95%
2008	2	0.56%	−4.93%	1.60%	1.40%	−4.57%	−6.52%
2008	3	−0.17%	5.55%	0.56%	−4.93%	−3.77%	8.19%
2008	4	−8.29%	−38.80%	−0.17%	5.55%	−48.31%	−49.99%
2009	1	−7.33%	−31.87%	−8.29%	−38.80%	−2.60%	−30.12%
2009	2	−5.20%	28.85%	−7.33%	−31.87%	5.30%	44.16%
2009	3	−3.32%	33.28%	−5.20%	28.85%	5.95%	34.39%
2009	4	−2.11%	9.39%	−3.32%	33.28%	3.85%	3.37%
2010	1	0.76%	10.02%	−2.11%	9.39%	14.90%	10.18%
2010	2	3.31%	−4.06%	0.76%	10.02%	15.88%	−7.60%
2010	3	3.86%	12.83%	3.31%	−4.06%	6.57%	17.08%
2010	4	4.62%	7.43%	3.86%	12.83%	8.37%	6.07%
2011	1	3.36%	7.50%	4.62%	7.43%	−2.85%	7.52%
2011	2	3.94%	2.90%	3.36%	7.50%	6.80%	1.74%
2011	3	3.30%	−15.07%	3.94%	2.90%	0.15%	−19.60%
2011	4	2.96%	15.30%	3.30%	−15.07%	1.28%	22.90%
	Mean	0.84%	1.20%		Mean	0.52%	1.24%
	Std. dev.	4.01%	17.32%		Std. dev.	13.38%	21.81%
				Autocorrelations			
				83.13%	20.14%		

Sources: www.reit.com and www.ncreif.org/property-index-returns.aspx.

The formula for the correlation coefficient of a sample is used to compute the first-order autocorrelation of each series. The appraisal-based NCREIF NPI has an estimated autocorrelation coefficient of 83.1%, whereas the market-price-based REIT index has an estimated autocorrelation coefficient of 20.1%. It should be noted that the sample period covers the highly unusual real estate market collapse that coincided with the financial crisis that began in 2007. Accordingly, the observed correlations may not be representative of more normal economic conditions due to the presence of outliers and their potentially disproportionate influence.

16.4.3　Unsmoothing the Smoothed Return Series Using Rho (ρ)

Columns 7 and 8 of Exhibit 16.2 unsmooth the original return data in the first and second data columns using the estimated autocorrelation coefficients (83.1% and 20.1%, respectively). The unsmoothed returns are computed using Equation 16.9.

For example, the first unsmoothed return for the NCREIF NPI is 9.37%, using Equation 16.9 and unrounded numbers:

$$R_{t,\text{true}} = (R_{t,\text{reported}} - \rho\, R_{t-1,\text{reported}})/(1 - \rho)$$
$$9.37\% = [4.59\% - (0.831 \times 3.62\%)]/(1 - 0.831)$$

Note in the case of the NCREIF NPI that relatively small changes in the returns between two adjacent time periods in the smoothed series often generate large changes in the unsmoothed returns. For example, the −8.29% smoothed return in the fourth quarter of 2008 generates a massive −48.3% decline in the unsmoothed return for the same quarter. However, the −7.33% smoothed return in the next quarter (the first quarter of 2009) generates only a −2.60% decline in the unsmoothed return for the same quarter. The unsmoothing technique captures the likelihood that the second large negative return (−7.33% in the first quarter of 2009) was a lagged reaction to the events of the fourth quarter of 2008 due to smoothing.

16.4.4 Interpreting the Results of Unsmoothing

Exhibit 16.2 lists the standard deviations of both the unsmoothed and smoothed return series. Note that the standard deviation of the smoothed NCREIF NPI (4.01%) increases to 13.38% when the returns are unsmoothed. To the extent that the return series has been properly and accurately unsmoothed to reflect true values, the true volatility of the asset is over three times the volatility perceived based on smoothed values. Note also that the REIT index contains positive autocorrelation and that the estimated standard deviation of the unsmoothed REIT index (21.81%) is modestly higher than the estimated standard deviation of the original REIT index (17.32%). It is possible that the positive autocorrelation of the market prices contained in the REIT index is a spurious outcome of the incredible turmoil of the real estate market during the financial crisis that began in 2007.

The original NCREIF NPI exhibited volatility less than one-quarter that of the original REIT index. The unsmoothed NCREIF NPI exhibited volatility more than one-half that of the unsmoothed REIT index and approximately three-quarters that of the original REIT index. These values appear somewhat in line with the higher risk of the assets underlying the REIT index due to the use of leverage underlying the REIT index's assets. The dramatic increase in estimated risk for the NCREIF NPI that results from unsmoothing the actual data highlights the importance of unsmoothing. Asset allocations based on volatilities of the smoothed data would dramatically overweight assets with smoothed returns in a mean-variance optimization framework. Improved unsmoothing of the return data in Exhibit 16.2 might be attained using autocorrelation techniques more general than the first-order autocorrelation model illustrated.

Smoothed returns generate dangerous perceptions of risk if the returns are not unsmoothed and if the short-term volatility of the returns is used without adjustment to estimate longer-term risk. The estimated quarterly standard deviation of the returns of the NCREIF NPI illustrated in Exhibit 16.2 is approximately 4%. Without taking autocorrelation into account, the estimated annualized standard deviation of the same series would be 8% (found by multiplying the quarterly standard deviation by the square root of the number of quarters in each year). Based on an annualized standard deviation of 8% and an expected return of perhaps 6%, a portfolio allocator might not expect a very large annual loss. However, the correlated string of quarterly losses from the fourth quarter of 2008 to the end of 2009 shows the tremendous longer-term loss potential generated from positive autocorrelation even when short-term volatility appears modest.

Smoothed returns understate not only the volatility but also the correlation of the smoothed returns to the returns of other asset classes. Exhibit 19.4 in Chapter 19 shows the correlation between smoothed and unsmoothed return series for the time period between the third quarter of 1995 and the final quarter of 2011. The stated, appraisal-based NCREIF NPI returns had a correlation of 0.22 to the REIT index and a correlation of 0.20 to the Russell 3000 U.S. stock index. After unsmoothing the NCREIF NPI returns, the correlation between NCREIF and REIT rose to 0.50, while the correlation to the Russell 3000 rose to 0.39. Assets with low volatility and low correlations to other asset classes are highly diversifying and earn large weights in a mean-variance optimization process. Using a simple first-order autocorrelation unsmoothing process finds that the unsmoothed NCREIF returns have three times the volatility and twice the correlation to other asset classes as did the stated, appraisal-based returns. Using unsmoothed returns in the mean-variance process leads to substantially lower weights for private real estate in the optimal portfolio.

Underestimating risk in smoothed returns results in inflated estimates of risk-adjusted returns, including the Sharpe ratio. In fact, overestimation of risk-adjusted performance due to smoothing of returns may explain the so-called real estate risk premium puzzle, which asks why private equity real estate investments seem to offer abnormally high risk-adjusted returns relative to other investments.

The lesson is clear. Autocorrelation of returns can provide deceptive indications of long-term risk relative to short-term risk. Smoothing of returns can dangerously mask true risk. Unsmoothing of returns is a relatively advanced technique that is rarely used by less sophisticated real estate analysts. However, unsmoothing of returns can be an important method of providing estimates that better indicate true risk and facilitate more appropriate decisions regarding asset allocation.

CHAPTER 17

Core, Value-Added, and Opportunistic Real Estate

C hapter 15 provided numerous examples of distinctions that portfolio allocators can make when categorizing real estate. As detailed in that chapter, the primary subgroup on which real estate equity analysis is focused is commercial (income-producing) real estate. This chapter focuses on the analysis of commercial real estate by institutional investors.

Institutional access to private commercial real estate investment is typically through limited partnerships involving one or several properties. An institution purchases all of the limited partnership interests or a portion thereof (along with other institutions) to have exposure to the underlying assets as well as to enjoy the managerial services of the general partner.

Styles are a primary method by which asset allocators can provide organization and structure to their universe of available investments. For example, in public equities, the styles of growth and value are often used to classify equities. By categorizing investments, an asset allocator attempts to construct better portfolios, use more appropriate benchmarks, and perform better return attribution.

The premier approach to organizing investment within the category of private commercial real estate equity is through **styles of real estate investing,** which refers to the categorization of real estate managers or real estate investments based on risk and return expectations. In 2003, the National Council of Real Estate Investment Fiduciaries (NCREIF) defined styles within real estate investment. Specifically, NCREIF identified three styles that relate to the underlying assets of commercial real estate investing: core, value-added, and opportunistic. These styles may be thought of as a way to classify either real estate equity investment or real estate managers.

The primary purpose of using styles of real estate investing is to provide a framework within which an asset allocator can structure top-down investment management decisions. In other words, real estate investment styles assist an asset allocator in organizing and evaluating real estate opportunities. Real estate investment styles also facilitate improved bottom-up investment management to the extent that they allow more appropriate benchmarking and performance attribution. Furthermore, style analysis can allow asset allocators to better understand the strategy being pursued by managers of real estate funds and to monitor style drift.

17.1 DEFINING THE THREE NCREIF REAL ESTATE STYLES

The three NCREIF styles divide real estate opportunities from least risky (core) to most risky (opportunistic), with value-added in the middle. In terms of risk, core properties are most bondlike, and opportunistic properties are most equitylike. Core properties tend to offer reliable cash flows each year from rents and lease payments, while value-added properties offer potential capital appreciation and typically have little or no currently reliable income. Each of the three styles is more fully described in the following paragraphs.

Core real estate includes assets that achieve a relatively high percentage of their return from income and are expected to have low volatility. Core properties are the most liquid, most developed, least leveraged, and most recognizable properties in a real estate portfolio. Though these properties have the greatest amount of liquidity, they are not sold quickly relative to traditional investments. Core properties tend to be held for a long time to take full advantage of the lease and rental cash flows that they provide. The majority of their returns comes from cash flows rather than from value appreciation, and very little leverage is applied. Core properties are somewhat bondlike in the reliability of their income.

Value-added real estate includes assets that exhibit one or more of the following attributes: (1) achieving a substantial portion of their anticipated return from appreciation in value, (2) exhibiting moderate volatility, and (3) not having the reliability of core properties.

Value-added properties begin to stray from the more common and lower-risk real estate investments included in the core real estate style. The value-added real estate style includes hotels, resorts, assisted-care living facilities, low-income housing, outlet malls, hospitals, and the like. These properties tend to require a subspecialty within the real estate market to be managed well and can involve repositioning, renovation, and redevelopment of existing properties.

Relative to core properties, value-added properties are anticipated to produce less income and to rely more on property appreciation to generate total return. However, property appreciation is subject to great uncertainty, and value-added properties as a whole have experienced prolonged periods of poor realized appreciation.

Value-added properties can also include new properties that would otherwise be core properties except that they are not fully leased, such as a new apartment complex or a new shopping center. A value-added property can also be an existing property that needs a new strategy, such as a major renovation, new tenants, or a new marketing campaign. These properties tend to use more leverage and generate a total return from both capital appreciation and income.

Pennsylvania's Public School Employees' Retirement System (PSERS) identifies value-added real estate as follows:

> *Value-added real estate investing typically focuses on both income and growth appreciation potential, where opportunities created by dislocation and inefficiencies between and within segments of the real estate capital markets are capitalized upon to enhance returns. Investments can include high-yield equity and debt investments and undervalued or impaired*

properties in need of repositioning, redevelopment, or leasing. Modest lever-
age is generally applied in value-added portfolios to facilitate the execution
of a variety of value creation strategies. (PSERS 2007)

Opportunistic real estate properties are expected to derive a substantial part
of their return from property appreciation and may exhibit substantial volatility
in value and returns. Simply put, opportunistic real estate returns are more equitylike. The higher volatility of opportunistic properties relative to the other two
styles may be due to a variety of characteristics, such as exposure to development risk, substantial leasing risk, or high leverage, but may also result from a
combination of more moderate risk factors, which in total create a more volatile
risk profile.

Opportunistic real estate moves away from a core/income approach to a capital
appreciation approach. Opportunistic real estate is often accessed through real estate
opportunity funds, sometimes called **private equity real estate funds** (**PERE funds**),
which are simply private equity funds that invest in real estate. Given the traditional
risk-taking nature of private equity funds, PERE funds often focus on real estate with
a high risk and return profile, particularly those properties that require extensive
development or are turnaround opportunities. Nevertheless, a substantial portion of
PERE funds includes value-added and core properties.

The majority of the return from opportunistic properties comes from value
appreciation over a three- to five-year period. Rollover risk is high because total
return is based on value appreciation. **Rollover** in real estate in this context refers
to changes in ownership, whereas rollover in real estate more generally refers to
changes in financing (e.g., converting a construction loan to a permanent mortgage
loan) or changes in the nature of a real estate project that facilitate investment
liquidity and capability to exit (e.g., completion and full leasing of a project). Since
opportunistic properties are held for a shorter term and for their potential to achieve
capital appreciation, the risk of failed or delayed rollover is a substantial component
of the total risk.

The high rollover risk of opportunistic properties is in contrast to the low rollover
risk of core properties. Within the core real estate style, sales of the underlying real
estate are infrequent, and properties are held for a long time to harness their income-
producing attributes. Due to their high focus on value appreciation, opportunistic
real estate managers tend to resemble traders and value enhancers compared to core
managers, who are operators of properties. Therefore, opportunistic managers tend
to pursue some event (typically a rollover) that will result in the real estate being
quickly and dramatically revalued. The capital appreciation of opportunistic real
estate can come from development of raw property, redevelopment of property that
is in disrepair, or acquisition of property that experiences substantial improvement
in prospects through major changes, such as urban renewal.

The investment policy statement of the California Public Employees' Retirement
System (CalPERS) identifies opportunistic real estate as follows:

Opportunistic real estate investing is the financing, acquisition, or invest-
ment in real estate assets, real estate companies, portfolios of real estate
assets, and private and public REITs that do not have access to traditional

public equity or debt financing. Opportunistic real estate investing consists of strategies that seek to exploit market inefficiencies with an emphasis on total return. Opportunistic investments require specialized expertise and the flexibility to respond quickly to market imbalances or changing market conditions. Investments may include non-traditional property types and/or assets that involve development, redevelopment, or leasing risks. Leverage is typically incorporated into this strategy to further enhance total returns. (CalPERS 2006)

Finally, opportunistic real estate investing is often the way institutional investors expand their property holdings outside their domestic country. Often, institutional investors access cross-border property opportunities through a private equity real estate limited partnership. For example, public companies in Germany have been selling their investment holdings of apartment housing to private investors, as these real estate properties represent investments outside the core expertise of the operating companies. The properties were held to house the workers of the operating companies. The workers still reside there, but the properties are now in the hands of professional property managers.

17.2 DIFFERENTIATING STYLES WITH ATTRIBUTES

The three NCREIF styles can be differentiated using eight major real estate attributes or characteristics. These attributes were developed by NCREIF to distinguish the three types of real estate asset styles:

1. Property type (purpose of structure, e.g., general office vs. specialty retail)
2. Life-cycle phase (e.g., new/developing vs. mature/operating)
3. Occupancy (e.g., fully leased vs. vacant)
4. Rollover concentration (tendency of assets to trade frequently)
5. Near-term rollover (likelihood that rollover is imminent)
6. Leverage
7. Market recognition (extent that properties are known to institutions)
8. Investment structure/control (extent of control and type of governance)

The styles and their attributes can be used to organize individual properties. Exhibit 17.1 provides descriptions of the three NCREIF styles using the eight attributes of individual real estate properties.

Real estate style analysis can be applied to real estate managers (i.e., portfolios) in addition to individual properties. Exhibit 17.2 provides summary descriptions of the characteristics of real estate portfolios classified into the three NCREIF styles.

17.3 PURPOSES OF REAL ESTATE STYLE ANALYSIS

Real estate styles are essentially locators. In other words, they are categories designed to help identify the space in which each property resides or a real estate manager

EXHIBIT 17.1 The Underlying Eight Attributes of the Three Real Estate Styles

	Core Attributes	Value-Added Attributes	Opportunistic Attributes
Property type	The major property types only: office, apartments, retail, industrial.	Major property types plus specialty retail, hospitality, senior/ assisted-care housing, storage, low-income housing.	Nontraditional property types, including speculative development for sale or rent, and undeveloped land.
Life-cycle phase	Fully operating.	Operating and leasing.	Development and newly constructed.
Occupancy	High occupancy.	Moderate to well-leased and/or substantially preleased development.	Low economic occupancy.
Rollover concentration	Core assets tend to be held for a long period of time, forming the central component of the real estate portfolio, which is geared toward generating income and not sales appreciation.	Moderate rollover concentration—a higher percentage of the assets are held for a short- to intermediate-term sale and roll over into new assets.	High rollover concentration risk—most of these assets are held for appreciation and resale.
Near-term rollover	Low total near-term rollover.	Moderate total near-term rollover.	High total near-term rollover.
Leverage	Low leverage.	Moderate leverage.	High leverage.
Market recognition	Well-recognized institutional properties and locations.	Institutional and emerging real estate markets.	Secondary and tertiary markets and international real estate.
Investment structure/ control	Investment structures often have substantial direct control.	Investment structures tend to have moderate control but with security or a preferred liquidation position.	Investment structures often have minimal control, usually in a limited partnership vehicle and with unsecured positions.

operates. There are three main reasons for introducing styles into real estate portfolio analysis:

1. *Performance measurement.* Investors continually look for tools that can provide them with a better understanding of an investment's or a sector's objectives and success in accomplishing those objectives. This includes identifying peer groups, return objectives, range of risk taking, return or performance attribution, and peer performance. Simply put, styles may be useful in identifying appropriate benchmarks.

EXHIBIT 17.2   Real Estate Portfolio Style Definitions

Core Portfolio Definition	Value-Added Portfolio Definition	Opportunistic Portfolio Definition
A portfolio that includes a preponderance of core attributes. As a whole, the portfolio will have low lease exposure and low leverage. According to the NCREIF Open-End Diversified Core Equity (ODCE) index for 2011Q4, the average leverage of core funds was 25%. A low percentage of noncore assets is acceptable. Such portfolios should achieve relatively high income returns and exhibit relatively low volatility. The portfolio attributes should reflect the risk and return profile of the National Property Index (NPI).	A portfolio that generally includes a mix of core real estate with other real estate investments that have a less reliable income stream. The portfolio as a whole is likely to have moderate lease exposure and moderate leverage. According to the NCREIF ODCE index for 2011Q4, the average leverage of value-added funds was 55%. Such portfolios should achieve a substantial portion of the return from the appreciation of real estate property values and should exhibit moderate volatility. A risk and return moderately greater than the NPI is expected.	A portfolio predominantly of noncore investments that is expected to derive most of its return from the appreciation of real estate property values and that may exhibit substantial volatility in total return. The increased volatility and appreciation risk may be due to a variety of factors, such as exposure to development risk, substantial leasing risk, high degree of leverage, or a combination of moderate risk factors. A risk and return profile substantially greater than the NPI is expected.

2. *Monitoring style drift.* It is a fact of investing that portfolio managers occasionally drift from their stated risk, return, or other objectives. Classifying different styles of real estate investments allows an investor to assess the association between a portfolio and its underlying investment products as the portfolio changes over time. Identifying the concentration of a portfolio in terms of the styles for each property facilitates a better understanding of the portfolio's risk level at any given point in time. Tracking style drift is another benefit of assessing the style of a portfolio.

3. *Style diversification.* The ability to compare the risk-return profile of a manager relative to its style may allow for a better diversification of the portfolio, since an investor may be able to construct a portfolio that has a more robust risk-return profile if there is a better understanding of each real estate manager's style location. Simply put, style may be useful in understanding and controlling risk.

It should be noted that the preceding real estate styles are primarily applied to private commercial real estate equity, although the concepts can also be applied to publicly traded real estate, such as equity REITs.

17.4 REAL ESTATE STYLE BOXES

The first part of this chapter detailed the use of the NCREIF real estate styles to differentiate real estate properties and portfolios by their risks and returns. Chapter 15 discussed numerous other categorizations, including the division of real estate properties by the size of the market in which the property is located. Properties in primary real estate markets such as London are distinguished from properties in secondary (midsize) and tertiary (small) markets. These categorizations can be used to create and use real estate style boxes. **Real estate style boxes** use two categorizations of real estate to generate a box or matrix that can be used to characterize properties or portfolios.

Exhibit 17.3 illustrates style boxes for traditional investments. In the case of the equity style box on the left, the box has equity style on the horizontal axis (e.g., value vs. growth) and capitalization size on the vertical axis. In traditional bond analysis, duration is usually on the horizontal axis, with credit quality on the vertical axis.

Style boxes are applied to individual assets, managers, or portfolios. For a style box of an individual stock or bond, the box contains an X in the square most descriptive of the asset. Similarly, managers can be identified with an X in a style box to denote their primary focus. The equity style box in Exhibit 17.3 illustrates the use of an X in a single square to denote the primary characteristic of a hypothetical small-cap growth stock. Portfolios and funds are often identified with percentages in each square denoting the percentage of the fund's or portfolio's holdings that are invested in assets of each location. The fixed-income box on the right of Exhibit 17.3 illustrates the use of percentages in each of the nine squares.

Exhibit 17.4 illustrates real estate style boxes. There is no uniform standard for style boxes in the real estate industry. Clearly, for private commercial equity, the styles of NCREIF are prime candidates for the horizontal axis. Primary, secondary, and tertiary real estate markets are potentially useful for the vertical axis. The left side of Exhibit 17.4 illustrates a potential style box and hypothetical allocations. In this illustration, a real estate style box serves as a method of better understanding the top-down allocations of a real estate portfolio. A real estate style box can also

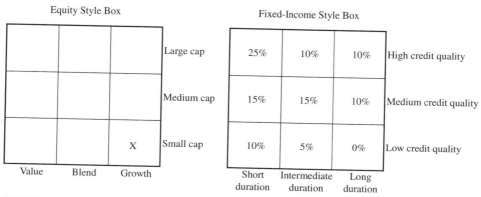

EXHIBIT 17.3 Equity and Fixed-Income Style Boxes

Real Estate Allocation Style Box

50%	15%	5%	Primary
10%	5%	5%	Secondary
5%	5%	0%	Tertiary
Core	Value-added	Opportunistic	

Gross Expected Returns Style Box

E(R) = 7%	E(R) = 7.5%	E(R) = 10%	Primary
E(R) = 7.5%	E(R) = 8%	E(R) = 11%	Secondary
E(R) = 8%	E(R) = 9.5%	E(R) = 12%	Tertiary
Core	Value-added	Opportunistic	

EXHIBIT 17.4   Real Estate Style Boxes

be used to denote the location of a single manager or a single property by placing an X in the relevant square.

Note that the box format can be used to organize views of estimated expected returns, volatilities, alphas, and so forth, including metrics discussed in the remainder of this chapter. The right-hand side of Exhibit 17.4 illustrates the concept of using a real estate style box as a tool to organize estimated real estate metrics by inserting arbitrary estimates of expected gross returns (before fees) into a real estate style box.

17.5 CAP RATES AND EXPECTED RETURNS

A somewhat crude but widespread metric in real estate valuation is the capitalization (cap) rate. The **cap rate** of a real estate investment is the net operating income (NOI) of the investment divided by some measure of the real estate's total value, such as purchase price or appraised value:

$$\text{Cap rate} = \text{NOI/Value} \qquad (17.1)$$

where NOI is usually viewed on an annualized basis and represents the expected, normalized cash flow available to the owner of the real estate, ignoring financing costs. Value in Equation 17.1 is an estimate of the market value of the real estate on an unlevered basis.

For example, if a real estate project has a current market value of $125 million and expected annual cash flows from rent, net of operating expenses, of $10 million, then the cap rate = ($10 million/$125 million) = 8%.

The exact specifications of the NOI for the numerator of the cap rate (recent, current, forecasted) and the value (beginning of period vs. end of period, transaction price vs. appraised price) for the denominator of the cap rate vary between users and purposes. Note that NOI does not reflect financing costs, and therefore the NOI-based approach for estimating value depicted in Equation 17.2 is intended for analysis of unleveraged property values.

Cap rates are often viewed as direct estimates of expected returns. Thus, a property with a cap rate of 9% is expected to generate a return of 9% to the investor on an unleveraged basis. The view of a cap rate as an estimated expected return is at best a crude approximation in that it typically ignores anticipated capital gains or losses as well as anticipated growth or decline in income. Nevertheless, cap rates are a good starting point for an analysis of expected returns.

Cap rates are also viewed as required rates of return and are used to perform risk adjustment in valuation of properties. Thus, an investor may search for a core property that offers a cap rate of at least 7% while demanding a cap rate such as 9% on a value-added property that is perceived as having higher risk.

Cap rates are often used to establish values for particular properties. Equation 17.2 rearranges Equation 17.1 to express property value as depending on NOI and cap rates:

$$Value = NOI/Cap\ rate \qquad (17.2)$$

A prospective buyer or analyst divides the estimated NOI of a property by an industry standard cap rate to obtain an estimate of the property's unleveraged value. For example, an investor considering the purchase of a property that offers $350,000 per year in net operating income may decide that if cap rates on comparable properties are 7%, then the property is worth $5,000,000.

Other metrics that are commonly used to assess real estate investment opportunities mirror the approaches discussed in Chapter 10 on private equity, including the internal rate of return (IRR) approach and the multiple of the cash in (the cash projected to be received from an investment on a project) to the cash out (the investment in the project). Numerous ratios of operating performance, interest coverage, and leverage are also used, most of which are analogous to financial ratios used throughout corporate finance. Cap rates represent a tool that is widely used in real estate but less so in other areas of finance.

NCREIF and other organizations estimate cap rates for various commercial property types in the United States. The overall weighted average of cap rates for core commercial property in the United States has varied between 5% and 10% since the mid-1980s. The higher end of the range was reached in the mid-1990s, whereas the lower end of the range was a result of the onset of the financial crisis that began in 2007. Estimates of recent cap rates on U.S. commercial property (in early 2012) ranged near long-term averages (7% or perhaps slightly higher) for core real estate properties in primary real estate markets.

17.6 DEVELOPING RISK AND RETURN EXPECTATIONS WITH STYLES

There are two major levels at which estimation of risk and return involving real estate should be performed by an asset allocator: (1) at the categories or styles level, and (2) at the individual fund, manager, or property level. The investor will then compare the risk and return of prospective funds, managers, or properties with the risk and return required or anticipated for the associated categories.

In traditional investments such as equities, an analyst's expectations of risk and return may be predominantly driven using measures of risk derived from observation of historical market returns and prices. Thus, measurement of the risk of a particular stock (or a category of stocks, such as midsize domestic equities) may be derived from observation of the volatility and correlation of its past returns. However, much of real estate equity involves private real estate, with little or no direct and consistent observations of market prices.

The unique nature of each real estate property and the general lack of liquidity make the tracking of real estate returns and the formation of risk and return estimates more difficult than for publicly traded asset classes. However, it is important when using styles to have some range of risk and return expectations in order to value properties and to determine how a real estate property or investment manager should be monitored and evaluated. In the context of real estate styles, the challenges of estimating risk and return for the value-added and opportunistic segments of the market are daunting, while the process for core properties is less difficult.

The key to developing risk and return estimates for real estate styles is to begin by estimating the expected risks and returns of the core real estate properties, and then to express the estimates for the value-added and opportunistic segments relative to the core style. Thus, an analyst may use cap rates or historical returns to estimate that the expected return of core real estate properties is, for example, 8%, and then estimate the expected returns of value-added and opportunistic real estate by estimating a premium by which those segments exceed the expected returns of the core segment.

17.6.1 Core Real Estate Expected Return

Development of expected risk and return estimates for core real estate properties can be based primarily on past returns and current metrics, such as cap rates. The NCREIF NPI discussed in Chapter 16 provides an appraisal-based historical database of core property returns. The 25 years (100 quarters) ending on December 30, 2011, had a mean quarterly return of 1.80%.

As detailed in Chapter 16, the NCREIF NPI is generally believed to be a smoothed index due to the use of appraised values. Despite the problems with smoothed data discussed in Chapter 16, data smoothing would typically have only a small effect on long-term historical mean returns. Any effect of smoothing on mean returns emanates only from the extent to which the starting and ending valuations are smoothed. Over a 25-year observation period, even major valuation errors in starting and ending values have minor effects on mean returns. For example, if the pricing error due to smoothing for the initial valuation is 10% higher than the final valuation, a 25-year annual mean return would be biased downward by only $10\%/25 = 0.4\%$ (ignoring compounding).

Note further that consistent pricing errors may have little or no effect on mean returns. If the index consistently overstates (or understates) the values of the underlying properties, then the returns of the index will match the returns of the true market values. For example, if the index values are consistently 10% lower than the true values, the mean of the returns of the index will be the same as the mean returns of the true prices (ignoring income).

As the observation interval is lengthened, the effects of valuation errors, including smoothing, on the estimated mean return of an index are decreased, and the estimated mean return approaches the true mean return. Thus, the 25-year historical annualized mean return for unleveraged core real estate of 7.3% is probably a reasonable estimate of the average returns experienced in the United States by core real estate investors over that period. Of course, the question remains as to whether the mean of past returns is indicative of the expected future returns.

17.6.2   Core Real Estate Risk

The 25 years of quarterly returns of the NCREIF NPI ending on December 30, 2011, had a quarterly standard deviation of 2.4%. Without adjustment for smoothing, the implied annualized volatility is 4.8% (found by multiplying the periodic standard deviation by the square root of the number of the periods in one year—in this case, the square root of 4).

Smoothing of returns interferes far more in risk estimation than in long-term return estimation. The smoothing of returns can severely dampen the observed and estimated volatilities and correlations of returns. Thus, the estimated standard deviation of the quarterly returns of the smoothed series (2.4%) needs to be adjusted for the effects of smoothing on implied annual volatility of true real estate values. The degree of volatility dampening depends on the degree of return smoothing. Equation 17.3 expresses a rough approximation of the volatility of a return series that has been smoothed with first-order autocorrelation, as described in Chapter 16:

$$\text{True volatility} \approx \text{Smoothed volatility}/(1 - \rho) \qquad (17.3)$$

where ρ is the first-order autocorrelation of the smoothed series. It is assumed that the underlying true series has no autocorrelation.

Using an arbitrary estimate of general real estate return autocorrelation (0.60) and applying Equation 17.3 to unsmooth the NCREIF NPI's return volatility increases the quarterly return volatility from 2.4% to 6.0% (found as 2.4%/0.40 = 6.0%), which annualizes to 12.0% volatility. However, the NCREIF NPI appears to have an autocorrelation coefficient higher than 0.6, so the unsmoothed volatility could be much higher. Note also that Equation 17.3 can be factored as: Smoothed volatility $\approx$ True volatility $\times$ $(1 - \rho)$. Thus, a smoothed returns series with first-order autocorrelation of 0.60 could roughly be expected to exhibit only 40% of the volatility of the true returns series.

Estimation of systematic risk using smoothed historical data is even more problematic than the estimation of volatilities. Equation 17.4 denotes the relationship between systematic risk measures based on true returns and smoothed returns:

$$\beta_{\text{true series}} = \beta_{\text{smoothed series}}/(1 - \rho) \qquad (17.4)$$

where $\beta_{\text{true series}}$ is a systematic risk measure based on the true return series underlying the smoothed series and a particular market index, $\beta_{\text{smoothed series}}$ is a systematic risk measure based on a smoothed return series and a particular market index, and ρ is the first-order autocorrelation of the smoothed series.

Thus, if a smoothed return series has a β equal to 0.20, the true but unobservable return series would have β of 0.50 (using an estimated autocorrelation coefficient of 0.60).

The implication in the case of both systematic risk estimation and volatility estimation is that a smoothed return series exhibits dramatically lower risk than is contained in the true return series. Chapter 16 demonstrates an unsmoothing procedure that can be used to estimate the underlying true return series and its risks. However, the accuracy of the unsmoothing procedure depends on the accuracy of the model specifying the smoothing (e.g., first-order autocorrelation) as well as the accuracy of the estimation of the parameters of the model (e.g., the autocorrelation coefficient). Substantial errors in specifying the unsmoothing model and estimating its parameters can generate large errors in the estimation of the risks of the true underlying assets.

17.6.3   Return Estimates for Noncore Assets and the Risk-Premium Approach

While data on core real estate returns are reasonably available and reliable, data on value-added and opportunistic risk and returns are more problematic. Accordingly, the expected risks and returns of value-added and opportunistic real estate are typically estimated and expressed relative to core risk and returns. Risk-premium methodologies can serve as effective tools both in estimating the current expected returns of core properties and in developing expected returns for value-added and opportunistic properties.

As previously discussed, expected returns from real estate are often assumed to be approximately equal to cap rates. Cap rates are often expressed as a cap rate spread. The **cap rate spread** is the excess of the cap rate over the yield of a default-free 10-year bond (such as the 10-year Treasury rate in the United States). A typical cap rate spread for core real estate over the 10-year Treasury rate is 2% to 3%, or 200 to 300 basis points.

Throughout finance, expected investment returns are often modeled using a **risk premium approach**, which expresses a risky asset's return as the sum of a riskless return and a premium for bearing the risk of that asset. The risk premium approach is illustrated in Equation 17.5:

$$E(R_i) = R_f + \text{Risk premium}_i \qquad (17.5)$$

where $E(R_i)$ is the expected return on asset i, R_f is the riskless interest rate, and risk premium$_i$ is the risk premium, or spread, of asset i relative to the riskless rate. Note that risk premium$_i$ is a premium peculiar to asset i; it is not a risk premium such as the premium on the market portfolio that is used to determine cross-sectional expected returns of other assets based on their correlation with the market.

The key contribution of the risk premium approach in Equation 17.5 is its potential to incorporate the current riskless interest rate in forming expectations of future returns for the same asset for different market conditions. Since riskless interest rates vary primarily due to inflation expectations, Equation 17.5 may be viewed as a method of adjusting return expectations for different anticipated inflation levels as well as different interest rate levels. For example, in the late 1970s, U.S. inflation rates reached double-digit levels. It would be unreasonable to believe that investors expected single-digit nominal returns on competitively priced assets when expected inflation reached double-digit levels. The reason is that nominal after-tax interest rates must exceed expected inflation rates for real rates to be positive.

The maturity of the default-free interest rate used in the risk premium approach varies and is generally determined by the investment horizon of the application. Outside of real estate, analysts often use a very short-term rate, such as an overnight rate or a three-month rate, to capture the rate earned in the absence of default risk and interest rate risk. In U.S. real estate, the 10-year Treasury rate is typically used as the default-free interest rate against which to evaluate cap rates and risk premiums. Presumably, the 10-year bond is selected to more closely approximate the longevity of real estate holdings. The decision of which riskless interest-rate maturity to use is a matter of professional judgment.

Riskless U.S. interest rates on 10-year-maturity Treasuries over the same 25-year period used previously to estimate the NCREIF NPI returns averaged approximately 5.7%, and average interest rates on 1-year-maturity Treasuries were approximately 4.3%.

Using Equation 17.5, the 7.4% NCREIF NPI average annualized return and the 1-year and 10-year Treasury averages generate 25-year average risk premiums of 3.1% and 1.7%, respectively. Note, however, that in 2011 and 2012 cap rates on core real estate, perhaps in the area of 7%, exceeded the 10-year Treasury rate (which ranged around 2% to 3%) by 4% to 5%, well out of line with average historical experience for core real estate (2% to 3%). Perhaps these observed cap rate spreads over 10-year Treasuries in 2011 and 2012 can be explained by the extraordinarily low Treasury yields associated with attempts to emerge from the global financial crisis. Alternatively, in view of the extreme volatility in real estate prices since the onset of the global financial crisis that began in 2007, it may be reasonable to argue that the recent estimated risk premiums exceed historical risk premiums to compensate prospective real estate investors for the unusual levels of risk. A final possibility is that the market believed that current estimates of net operating income, capital appreciation, or both were too high.

Development of an estimate of the expected returns of value-added and opportunistic real estate investing may take three primary approaches: (1) the use of observed cap rates for those styles of real estate investment, (2) the use of a risk premium approach (based on the estimation of their risks relative to the risks of core real estate investments), or (3) the use of absolute hurdle rates.

The direct use of observed cap rates in market transactions to estimate expected returns for value-added and especially opportunistic properties may be rather inaccurate because the estimations of net operating income for these styles are much less reliable than are the estimations of NOI for the core style. The use of absolute hurdle rates may be inappropriate due to their failure to consider different interest rates and expected inflation levels. Accordingly, it may be argued that the best estimate of expected returns on noncore properties can be found by adding a risk premium to the expected returns estimated for core properties.

17.6.4 Examples of Return Estimates for Noncore Style Assets

At particular points in time, investors may develop absolute target rates of return for properties with value-added and opportunistic styles rather than relying on observed cap rates or cap rate spreads. This section reviews two examples of the setting of returns by institutions.

PSERS defines its opportunistic return target in absolute terms. It sets a hurdle rate for opportunistic real estate investing at 13% or greater, depending on the level of risk taken. A return below 13% falls into the value-added real estate style.

CalPERS also defines its opportunistic return target in absolute terms. It cites an expected return hurdle rate of 13% or greater. The CalPERS investment policy goes further to note that investment staff may adjust this 13% hurdle rate depending on the characteristics of the individual opportunistic real estate fund or changes in the marketplace, including changes to the inflation rate, capital market risk levels, or levels of available investment opportunities. The CalPERS investment policy for opportunistic real estate (2006) provides additional guidance:

> *Opportunistic investments shall provide superior returns with acceptable risk levels when compared to direct equity U.S. real estate investments. Additionally, rates of return will reflect the unique strategies associated with the investment opportunities and shall include, but are not limited to, such factors as relative stages of development and/or redevelopment, targeted property types, entity or debt vehicles, relative control or liquidity or both that are associated with the investment, and other structuring techniques used to mitigate taxes and currency exposure, if any.* (CalPERS 2006)

The last part of the CalPERS policy statement mentions taxes and currency exposure because many institutional investors look at real estate investing outside of their home country as being opportunistic in nature, since it involves a market in which real estate is valued differently, in which development issues such as planning and zoning can be much more difficult, and in which property management must recognize the peculiar nature of the foreign market. So, for example, when a U.S. institution invests overseas, it loses its U.S. tax-exempt status and must deal with the conversion of the total return back into U.S. dollars. This raises the currency and tax issues mentioned in the CalPERS investment policy. These are additional risk factors for which additional expected returns must compensate.

One of the difficulties of assessing the return expectations for opportunistic real estate is that many of these investments take place through private limited partnerships (i.e., private equity real estate). Because these limited partnerships are private, returns tend to be based on appraised values rather than market values.

CHAPTER 18

Real Estate Indices

Real estate indices are an increasingly important aspect of real estate investment management. The uses of real estate indices include the estimation of risks and returns for assisting the asset allocation decision-making process, as well as the specification of benchmarks for performance attribution. Performance attribution provides valuable information both for bottom-up investment management (e.g., in the selection of properties or managers) and for top-down investment management (in the determination of asset allocations).

In valuation, real estate investors often focus on the most recent sales of similar and nearby properties to form their central gauge of price change. But best practices for institutional investing call for a more structured and less localized view of valuation and performance attribution. This chapter focuses on the challenges and opportunities of real estate indexation.

The two main approaches to indexation are appraisal based and transaction based, each of which has its own potential problems. This chapter compares these approaches and reviews many of the most popular real estate indices, which vary in terms of methodology used (e.g., appraisal-based vs. various types of transaction-based approaches). The prevalence of a variety of indexation methodologies highlights the fact that all methodologies have nontrivial problems and that real estate analysts should be aware of the challenges associated with each methodology.

18.1 THE MECHANICS OF APPRAISAL-BASED INDICES

The National Council of Real Estate Investment Fiduciaries (NCREIF) National Property Index (NPI) is used in this chapter to illustrate appraisal-based indices due to the NPI's size and popularity. NCREIF is a U.S. not-for-profit institutional real estate investment industry association.[1] NCREIF collects data from its members, which include, for the most part, institutional real estate investment managers (mostly pension fund managers). NCREIF maintains a massive data set of real estate income and pricing data, and uses those data to publish the NPI and its subindices as well as several other indices, such as a farmland index and a timberland index.

The NCREIF NPI is based on financial information from member institutional investors with combined assets of approximately $1 trillion. Members are required to

---

[1] Note: Information in this chapter regarding the NCREIF NPI is from the "Users Guide to the NPI," www.ncreif.org/public_files/Users_Guide_to_NPI.pdf, accessed January 2012.

report information on their real estate holdings on a quarterly basis. Most valuations are appraisal based. The reason for the use of appraisals is the illiquid nature of real estate: Properties simply do not turn over frequently enough to compute short-term returns using prices from transactions performed in an arm's-length manner. NCREIF compiles the information on a value-weighted basis to publish the NPI. Accordingly, the NCREIF NPI used in Chapters 16 and 17 is calculated quarterly, which is a relatively infrequent interval compared to the daily calculations of most stock, bond, or even commodity indices.

18.1.1 Formula for Returns Based on Appraisals

The change in value of each property in the NCREIF NPI is calculated every quarter on an "as if" basis: as if the property were purchased at the beginning of the quarter at its appraised value, held for income during that quarter, and sold at the end of the quarter at its end-of-quarter appraised value. If the property was actually acquired or sold during the quarter, the transaction price is used in place of either the beginning or the end value.

The total return on the index is calculated as the sum of an income return and a capital value return. The income portion of the total return of each property is a fraction, with net operating income (NOI) in the numerator and an estimate of the property value in the denominator. The estimate of the property value is based on the beginning-of-period appraised value, with adjustments for any capital improvements, any partial sales, and reinvestment of NOI.

The numerator of the capital value return is the change in the estimated value of the property from the beginning of the quarter to the end of the quarter, adjusted for capital improvements and partial sales such that increases in value due to further investments are not included as profits, and declines in value due to partial sales are not deducted as losses. The denominator of the capital value return is the same as the denominator for the income portion.

The NCREIF NPI is calculated on an unleveraged basis, as if the property being included in the index were purchased with 100% equity and no debt. As a result, the returns are less volatile, and there are no interest charges deducted. The returns to the NPI are calculated on a before-tax basis and therefore do not include income tax expense. The returns are calculated for each individual property and are then value-weighted in the index calculation.

As mentioned, the turnover of most real estate properties is infrequent (every six or seven years, on average), so the NCREIF NPI is based primarily on appraised values rather than market transactions. The members of NCREIF report the value of their properties every quarter.

18.1.2 Appraisal Frequency for the NPI

Appraisals are professional opinions of value and are commonly used to estimate the market value of a real estate property. For institutional investors, appraisals are typically performed once a year on real estate properties. Appraisals are generally based on one of two methods.

The first is the comparable sales method. In this approach, the real estate appraiser looks at sales of similar properties in the same geographic region (if not city) as the property being appraised. These actual sales prices give the appraiser an estimate of the cost (i.e., price) per square foot of similar real estate properties. The appraiser then adjusts this cost per square foot for the unique characteristics of the property being appraised: better parking or access, better location, newer lobby, longer-term tenants, and so on. This process has the advantage of being based on actual sales transactions. However, the accuracy of the process is lower when there is a lack of frequency of property sales, and because every property is unique, it is hard to adjust a square-foot calculation value from one property to form the value of another.

The second method is a discounted cash flow analysis. This has become the more accepted practice by real estate appraisers for commercial properties. In this valuation approach, the appraiser estimates the cash flows from a property and discounts them to form a present value to the property. This approach has the advantage of valuing the unique characteristics of the property being appraised. However, it is subject to forecasting errors of occupancy, lease growth rates, expenses, holding period for the property, terminal value of the property, inflation estimates, and the like.

Although the NCREIF NPI is a quarterly index, NCREIF properties are not formally appraised every quarter. Most properties are formally valued at least once per year, but many are appraised only every two or even three years. Appraisals cost money; therefore, there is a trade-off between the benefits of having frequent property valuations and the costs of those valuations as a drain on portfolio performance. In fact, many institutional real estate investors value their portfolio properties only when they believe there is a substantial change in value based on new leases, changing economic conditions, or the sale of a similar property close to the portfolio property.

Even when properties have been recently appraised, it is possible that the appraisal process will be driven by old information, such as previous transactions on comparable properties, or by delays in the willingness of appraisers to adopt new valuation standards caused by changes in market conditions, such as cap rates. Thus, even recent appraisals can cause smoothing due to delays in fully reflecting changes in true value. Finally, note that the NCREIF NPI is published quarterly and that quarter-end values are published with a time lag. Thus, even ignoring appraisal-based smoothing, a major decline in asset prices that occurs in October would not be reflected in quarterly index figures until the December 31 appraisal, and the December 31 value would not be published until almost one month later. In contrast, market indices, such as real estate indices based on REIT market prices, are continuously updated.

18.1.3 Real Estate Price Discovery

The contrast between appraised real estate values and market prices of real estate is related to price discovery. Geltner, MacGregor, and Schwann (2003) define **price discovery** as "the process by which the opinions of market participants about the value of an asset are combined together into a single statistic, its market price."

Geltner, MacGregor, and Schwann note that there is a lack of good quality information on price due to (1) the unique nature of real estate properties, (2) the relatively long holding periods of most properties, and (3) the possible confidentiality of information on transactions. They note that "appraisers have to make an optimum assessment of value, based on fundamental variables and market information, including transactions and a market-wide appraisal index. However, transaction prices are a noisy signal and it is the appraiser's role to extract the signal from the noise in an efficient manner. This involves a process of optimal combination of past and current information and leads to appraisal smoothing."

They note that a consequence of this process is that price discovery first occurs in one market and then is transmitted to other markets. Unlike major modern markets for financial securities, wherein transaction information is quickly recorded and disseminated electronically worldwide, in real estate markets, information is often recorded and disseminated slowly, with price discovery occurring over periods of months and perhaps years.

18.2 NON-APPRAISAL-BASED INDICES

Alternatives to appraisal-based indices are those based on reported prices of transactions. It should be noted that appraisal-based indices are partially and indirectly based on transactions. Most appraisal-based indices use transaction prices when a property within the index is traded during the reporting period (e.g., calendar quarter). Further, appraisals are usually either partially or fully based on the reported prices of comparable transactions (i.e., the comparable sales approach). This section focuses on indices that are explicitly based on reported prices of real estate transactions.

18.2.1 Transaction-to-Transaction Indices

A **transaction-to-transaction index**, also known as a **repeat-sales index**, is based on the changes in value (returns) of properties with two reported transactions over an observation period, which permits a computation of a return between the two dates of the transactions. The returns for those properties that have turned over twice (or more) are used to infer the price changes for all properties. The process of converting numerous price changes on unique properties over various time intervals into a single index of prices involves a number of econometric techniques, such as regression, which vary in complexity and details. The advantage of using observed transaction prices is that the prices are market based and therefore expected to reflect all information available to the market participants.

The two primary criticisms of repeat-sales indices are (1) that the properties that are most highly represented in the compilation of the index are those properties that transacted most frequently, which may be unrepresentative of all of the properties that underlie the index, and (2) that the properties that turned over may have had major idiosyncratic changes in value, such as through major improvements that were made to facilitate the transaction. Despite these potential problems, as well as other smaller problems associated with this methodology, repeat-sales indices are becoming increasingly popular, perhaps due to the availability of the data. It should also be noted that transaction data reflect delayed information due to the time lag between the negotiation of a transaction price and the actual exchange. Thus, a transaction that is negotiated on January 1, with a price based on information available on January 1, is revealed when the transaction is consummated months later.

18.2.2 Hedonic Price Indices

The concept of a **hedonic price index** applied to real estate transactions involves using observed real estate transactions of some properties to estimate the prices of all properties, including those that did not transact. Hedonic price indices infer the prices of real estate properties that have not recently traded by directly modeling the heterogeneity of real estate properties.

The three steps of forming a hedonic price index using transaction prices are:

1. Model the value of real estate properties as being a function of specified characteristics of the properties.
2. Use a sample of prices observed from recent transactions to fit the parameters of the real estate valuation model.
3. Use the estimated valuation parameters to estimate the values of the properties within the index that did not transact.

As a very simplified example, a model of office properties may be valued using a model with two variables: size (square feet of space) and quality (class A, B, or C).[2] Data on recent office property transactions are recorded with a sale price, size, and quality class for each. The parameters for the size and quality variables are estimated based on an econometric model, with price per square foot as the dependent variable. The estimated parameters from the models are then used to infer the prices of all properties and form an index of overall value.

The primary difference between transaction-based hedonic price indices and repeat-sales indices is that hedonic price indices include all properties that transacted at least once, while repeat-sales indices include only the data from properties that transacted multiple times. A hedonic price index uses observed price levels on some real estate to infer price levels on all real estate. A repeat-sales index uses observed changes in prices on some real estate to infer changes in prices on all real estate. The reliability of both approaches depends on the accuracy of the modeling, including the effects of property differences and timing differences.

18.2.3 Market-Traded Real Estate Vehicles

A final major valuation method for real estate indices is based on tracking the market prices of investment vehicles with underlying real estate assets. The United States and several other countries have publicly traded real estate investment trusts (REITs). REITs typically contain leverage and differ in underlying real estate investments (e.g., mortgage vs. equity, office vs. retail). Nevertheless, many REITs are traded with regular and substantial volume. Thus, indices based on market prices of real

---

[2] Class A office buildings represent the highest-quality real estate in terms of construction and infrastructure, and are located in desirable areas. Class B buildings are generally a little less desirable. Class C buildings are in the lowest classification of office buildings and are older, located in less desirable areas, and in need of renovation. See "A Guide to Office Building Classifications; Class A, Class B, Class C," available at www.squarefeetblog.com/commercial-real-estate-blog/2008/07/06/a-guide-to-office-building-classifications-class-a-class-b-class-c/, accessed January 28, 2012.

estate–related securities are becoming increasingly important in the monitoring of real estate market conditions.

18.2.4 Sample Biases in Transaction-Based Indices

Transaction-based real estate indices suffer from sample selection bias to the extent that the properties that are represented in the index differ from the aggregated mix of all such assets. For example, in transaction-based indices, a bias arises to the extent that properties transacted during a particular period and used to calculate an index may not be representative of the entire universe of properties. A bias toward a particular type of property, location of property, size of property, and so forth, would interfere with the representativeness of the sample. Although the effects of sample selection bias also affect residential property indices, they are likely to be especially severe for commercial properties because the universe of commercial properties is typically small and the number of transactions in any particular time period is even smaller. The effects of randomness on the attributes of a sample tend to be larger when the sample is small.

There is another reason to be concerned about sample selection bias other than the idea that the sample of properties with transactions will deviate from the universe of all properties due to randomness. As Haurin (2005) points out,

> In a normal market, the real values (i.e., deflated values) of some properties will rise while others may decline. If the owners of properties with falling values tend to choose not to sell their properties, while owners of properties with rising values tend to choose to sell (or vice versa), then the sample of transacted properties is clearly not random and is biased towards a particular price outcome. It is also plausible that the choices of whether to sell properties with rising and falling values change over the real estate cycle and thus the nature of the sample selection bias will change over time. This changing bias results in an estimated transaction-based price index that differs from a theoretical price index that would track market values of the stock of all properties. (Haurin 2005)

Thus, there may be systematic reasons to believe that the sample of properties that have transacted will have substantially different characteristics from the universe of properties and that, more importantly, the differences in characteristics will be related to recent price changes. The result is that the sample will reflect price changes unrepresentative of the universe.

18.3 DESCRIPTION OF MAJOR REAL ESTATE INDICES

This section offers a brief description of the main real estate indices available, divided into various categories. As indicated in Exhibit 18.1, most of the major real estate indices in the world are based on market prices of real estate securities. Real estate indices can differ as to whether they are indices of values (prices) or total return (including income). Those indices based on total return can also differ in terms of whether the returns are gross or net of fees.

EXHIBIT 18.1   Summary of Popular Real Estate Indices

Name	Region	Methodology	Type of Property	Source of Values
S&P/ASX 200 A-REIT Index	Australia	Market	Commercial	REIT
Bloomberg Canadian REIT	Canada	Market	Commercial	Closed-end trust
Shanghai Stock Exchange Property Index	China	Market	Commercial	Stock
EURO STOXX Real Estate (Price) EUR	EMU	Market	Commercial	Stock
Bloomberg Europe 500 Real Estate Index	Europe	Market	Commercial	Stock
IPD Germany Annual Property Index	Germany	Repeat sales	Commercial	Private
Hong Kong Hang Seng Properties Index	Hong Kong	Market	Commercial	Stock
Tokyo Stock Exchange REIT Index	Japan	Market	Commercial	REIT
FTSE ST Real Estate Index	Singapore	Market	Commercial	Stock
SWX IAZI Real Estate Performance Index	Switzerland	Hedonic	Commercial	Private
SWX IAZI Private Real Estate Price Index	Switzerland	Hedonic	Residential	Private
FTSE 350 Real Estate Supersector Index	UK	Market	Commercial	Stock
FTSE UK Commercial Property Index	UK	Appraisal	Commercial	Private
IPD UK Annual All Property Index	UK	Appraisal	Commercial	Private
FTSE NAREIT All Equity REITs Index	U.S.	Market	Commercial	REIT
NCREIF National Property Index (NPI)	U.S.	Appraisal	Commercial	Private
NCREIF Transaction Based Index (TBI)	U.S.	Hedonic	Commercial	Private
S&P/Case-Shiller U.S. National Home Price Index	U.S.	Repeat sales	Residential	Private
CoStar Commercial Repeat-Sale Indices	U.S.	Repeat sales	Commercial	Private
Green Street Advisors Commercial Property Price Index	U.S.	Mixed	Commercial	Private[a]

[a]Reflects valuations based on professional analysis of property owned by listed equity REITs.

18.3.1 Housing or Residential Real Estate Properties Indices

Institutional investors have limited investment interest in residential real estate equity other than multifamily properties (i.e., apartment buildings, which are usually classified as commercial). However, residential real estate prices assist in the analysis of residential mortgages and provide economic data useful in general economic and real estate analysis. In addition, derivatives can be used to provide institutional investment in residential real estate equity. Accordingly, residential real estate indices are included in Exhibit 18.1.

A popular but primitive type of index of residential property prices is the reporting of mean or median housing prices over various time periods. The major problem with these indices as an indication of real estate value changes is that they are affected by shifts in the quality and size of the properties that happen to transact within each time period. Further, observed prices may reflect changes in the condition of the properties, especially substantial improvements.

The values of U.S. homes or residential real estate properties are tracked by Standard & Poor's Case-Shiller Home Price Indices, which consist of metropolitan regional indices, composite subindices, and a national index. The indices are constructed using the repeat-sales methodology. The repeat-sales methodology requires observation of the sales prices of specific single-family homes that are sold at least twice within the observation period. The new sale price is combined with the previous sale price to form a sales pair. The price differences in the sales pairs within a particular region are measured and used to infer changes in the levels of the index for that region.

18.3.2 Private Commercial Real Estate Properties Indices

NCREIF publishes a variety of subindices of the NPI (discussed earlier), which are briefly reviewed here. Of the five major categories, commercial office properties is the largest (almost 40%), with about 60% of the index somewhat equally split among apartments, retail, and industrial properties. Hotels make up the smallest weight of the index (about 2%).

1. *Offices:* As an index of core real estate properties, the NCREIF NPI Office Properties Index contains Class A office buildings. Class A office buildings are the top-tier office buildings in major metropolitan centers (primary real estate markets) around the United States, where one would expect to find the headquarters and satellite offices of Fortune 1000 public companies, as well as private companies in the asset-management business, consulting, legal, accounting, engineering, and other professions. Class A office buildings are considered the least risky in the office market, with prime locations, stable tenants, strong property management, and long leases.
2. *Apartments:* Sometimes called multifamily housing, these are complexes of multiple-tenant properties. Located in urban areas or in the suburbs, apartments cater to working professionals who are early in their careers and have not

accumulated enough savings to purchase a first home. Rents and income tend to be high, but this is also a more volatile part of the real estate market.

3. *Retail:* These are the commercial properties in major and regional shopping centers, neighborhood (unanchored) shopping centers, outlet malls, and so on.

4. *Industrial:* These properties include mostly warehouses, along with manufacturing facilities, office parks, and other productive facilities.

5. *Hotels:* These include luxury, budget, and midpriced hotels as well as other leisure properties. Hotels are a relatively new addition to the NCREIF NPI. Hotel properties are often considered value-added style properties rather than core style properties in that, for example, they have the risk of being leased day-to-day.

Collectively, the four larger types of properties (offices, apartments, retail, and industrial) form the core style portion of a real estate portfolio. The real estate properties in the NCREIF NPI are also classified by region. Recently, about two-thirds of the total market value of the NCREIF NPI was roughly equally split between properties in the U.S. West and East regions. The South region contained about two-ninths of the value, with the remaining one-ninth attributable to the Midwest region.

NCREIF has begun producing the **Transactions-Based Index (TBI)**. The TBI is a hedonic index using transaction data from the NCREIF database. The index relies on a hedonic methodology based on analysis of prices per square foot (i.e., property sale price divided by number of square feet in the property).

18.3.3 Farmland and Timberland Indices

The NCREIF Farmland Index (not shown in Exhibit 18.1) is a quarterly appraisal-based index that measures the investment performance of a large pool of individual agricultural properties acquired in the private market solely for investment purposes. Only income-generating agricultural properties are included in the index. According to NCREIF, all properties in the Farmland Index have been acquired, at least in part, on behalf of tax-exempt institutional investors, the great majority being pension funds. As such, returns reflect properties held in a fiduciary environment.

The NCREIF Timberland Index (not shown in Exhibit 18.1) is a quarterly index that measures the investment performance of institutional timberland investments. To qualify for the index, a property must be held in a fiduciary environment and marked to market at least once per year. The lack of quarterly appraisals for many properties in this index makes the annual return series more reflective of changes in the market than the quarterly series.

18.3.4 Public Real Estate Equity Indices

There are numerous indices based on real estate securities. In the United States, the FTSE National Association of Real Estate Investment Trusts (NAREIT) U.S. Real Estate Index Series consists of a family of REIT performance indices that covers the different sectors of the U.S. commercial real estate space. Constituents of the FTSE NAREIT Composite Index are classified as either equity REITs (which own predominantly equity real estate in the form of buildings) or mortgage REITs (which own predominantly real estate debt). Equity REITs can be further subdivided by property sector: industrial/office, retail, residential (apartments and manufactured homes), diversified (specialized), lodging/resorts, health care, self-storage, and timber. The industrial/office and retail sectors are further broken down into three subsectors each.

Other widely used public real estate equity indices (not shown in Exhibit 18.1) are the S&P U.S. REIT Composite Index, the Dow Jones Wilshire Real Estate Investment Trust Index (DJW REIT), the Dow Jones Wilshire Real Estate Securities Index (RESI), and the MSCI U.S. REIT Index.

18.3.5 Real Estate Debt or Mortgage Indices

In the United States, secondary trading of pools of residential mortgages is a large and well-developed market, with substantial and prompt revelation of values. Prices are revealed through the pricing of a number of investment vehicles and indices, including pass-through pools, structured products such as residential mortgage-backed securities (RMBSs), and numerous mortgage-backed security (MBS) indices. Furthermore, the FTSE NAREIT Mortgage REIT Index provides indication of mortgage values through the public valuation of mortgage REITs.

The pricing and performance of private commercial mortgages in the United States can be measured using a wide offering of indices, especially those that track the value of public commercial real estate debt structured as commercial mortgage-backed securities (CMBSs).

CHAPTER 19

Public versus Private Real Estate Risks

A primary challenge of real estate investment management is to assess the relative reliability of the conflicting indications of risk generated by observations of publicly traded real estate investments, such as REITs, and privately held real estate. Privately held real estate is typically highly illiquid, taking months or even years to trade at competitive prices. This illiquidity is driven by the extent to which each property is unique. The high illiquidity of most real estate can raise serious challenges for portfolio management, including cash management, risk measurement, and risk management. Public real estate is highly liquid, with readily observable market prices. But indices of public real estate prices indicate substantially higher volatility and substantially lower diversification benefits than do indices of private real estate.

This chapter focuses on the extent to which analysis of publicly traded real estate may be used to provide information on the risks and returns of private real estate. It begins with an empirical analysis of the differences between the returns of public (market-based) real estate and those of private (appraisal-based) real estate.

19.1 MARKET-BASED VERSUS APPRAISAL-BASED RETURNS

Chapter 16 provided an analysis of the differences between market-based and appraisal-based real estate returns over a five-year period that included the global financial crisis that began in 2007. The analysis of Chapter 16 discussed the delayed reaction of appraisal-based returns relative to market-based returns and illustrated unsmoothing. This section analyzes data on appraisal-based and market-based U.S. real estate returns over a 25-year period.

19.1.1 Histograms of U.S. Real Estate Returns

Exhibit 19.1 is a histogram of the quarterly returns of the NCREIF NPI over the 25-year period from the first quarter of 1987 through the fourth quarter of 2011. The simple average quarterly return of the 100-quarter return distribution is 1.8%, and the quarterly standard deviation is 2.4%. The critical issue is whether the concentration of outcomes near the center in Exhibit 19.1 is an accurate reflection of the stability of real estate values or a result of smoothing due to the appraisal methodology.

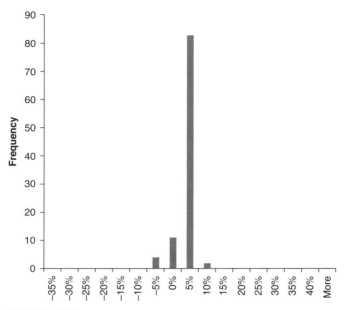

EXHIBIT 19.1   NCREIF NPI

Next, market-based returns are examined as a contrast to appraisal-based returns. Exhibit 19.2 is a histogram of the quarterly returns of the All Equity REITs Index of the FTSE NAREIT U.S. Real Estate Index Series (REIT index) over the same 25-year period from 1987 through 2011. The REIT index has a simple average quarterly return of 2.9% and a quarterly standard deviation of 9.9%. Note that the annualized standard deviation of 9.9% quarterly (assuming no autocorrelation) is

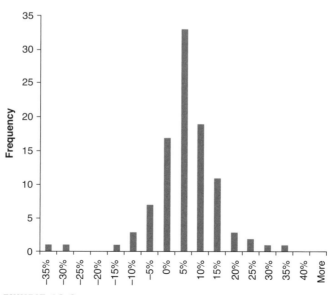

EXHIBIT 19.2   REIT Returns

19.8%, which is in line with the very long-term annualized standard deviation of value-weighted indices of U.S. equity returns.

19.1.2 Relationship of Appraisal-Based and Market-Based Volatilities

The critical issue is whether the much wider dispersion of the market-based returns (Exhibit 19.2) relative to the appraisal-based returns (Exhibit 19.1) is due to one or more of the following four explanations:

1. Lower accuracy of smoothed appraisals relative to market prices
2. Differences in the risks of the underlying assets
3. The use of leverage in most REITs
4. The result of liquidity-induced volatility attributable to liquidity shifts in equity markets

Regarding the lower accuracy of appraisal-based pricing, there is evidence regarding smoothing. Cannon and Cole (2011) compared appraised real estate values from the NCREIF NPI over a 25-year period with transaction prices on the same properties observed within two quarters of the appraisals. They report: "Our findings are sobering. On average, appraisals are more than 12% above or below subsequent sales prices, and this result holds true for both external and internal appraisals." In attributing the price differences, they find that "appraisals appear to lag the true sales prices" and that "under- and overvaluations are highly correlated across properties at the same points in time."

In the first of these explanations, REIT returns are viewed as superior indications of real estate risks and returns when compared to appraisal-based returns, because market-based returns reflect valuations from equity markets with a moderate to high degree of informational market efficiency. To the extent that the market prices of REIT's differ substantially from their true values, it can be argued that market participants would be able to earn superior rates of return by purchasing underpriced REITs or short-selling overpriced REITs. Presumably, competition to trade mispriced REITs will tend to drive REIT prices toward their true values. Appraisals are not generally subject to arbitrage and therefore may be more likely to diverge from the true values of the underlying property.

The second potential explanation of the observed differences between REIT returns and appraisal-based returns is that the two return series are based on substantially different underlying assets. However, most of the equity REITs underlying the REIT index analyzed in Exhibit 19.1 own portfolios of large institutional-quality properties highly similar to the core properties that dominate the NCREIF NPI.

The third possible explanation is that leverage accounts for the higher volatility of the market-based index (the REIT index) relative to the appraisal-based index (the NCREIF NPI). The REIT index returns include the effects of leverage, but the NCREIF NPI is an unlevered index. Although much of the property that underlies the NCREIF NPI is held on a leveraged basis, when its financial performance is reported, it ignores financing costs and uses asset values rather than equity values. In the real estate industry, leverage is a key component of most property purchases. Almost all institutional investors use leverage of perhaps 50% in the purchase of their real estate portfolios, which should result in a doubling of equity volatility relative to asset volatility. Equity REITs use leverage averaging roughly 40%. However, the market-based REIT index returns exhibited four times the volatility of the appraisal-based NCREIF NPI returns. Leverage differentials can probably explain only less than half of the difference in volatility.

The fourth potential explanation is that equity market trading of real estate investments injects volatility into the REIT prices that is attributable to equity market volatility and liquidity rather than to true changes in the values of the underlying real estate properties.

In summary, even adjusted for leverage, appraisal-based returns have dramatically lower volatility than do market-based returns. Chapter 16 provided a brief analysis of the degree of smoothing in the NCREIF NPI. The evidence of smoothing in appraisal-based indices is strong, and therefore the first of the four potential explanations (lower accuracy of smoothed appraisals relative to market prices) may account for all of the leverage-adjusted volatility differences. But the potential remains that the divergence between the NCREIF NPI and the REIT index is attributable at least in part to inefficient pricing of REITs during periods of high equity market volatility. This issue, revisited later in the chapter, is critical in determining whether market prices or appraisals should be used in estimating real estate risks.

19.1.3 The Importance of Accurate Pricing and Risk Estimation

The previous sections illustrated the large volatility differences between appraisal-based and market-based real estate index volatilities and discussed potential explanations. The two valuation approaches offer substantially different indications of the volatilities and correlations of real estate returns. The importance of accurate risk estimation can be viewed at two levels.

On an investor-based level, better portfolio management decisions can be made with better estimates of risk. To the extent that investors are using appraisal-based returns to form estimations of real estate risk, they will require an insufficiently low return on the real estate if the returns understate risk. As a result, the portfolio will be overallocated to real estate, and the portfolio manager will be underestimating the portfolio's level of risk.

From a macroeconomic perspective, accurate pricing of assets requires accurate estimation of risk. If real estate investors as a group underestimate the required return on real estate investment due to underestimation of real estate risk, the asset class will be overpriced, and the level of investment made in real estate will be inefficiently high. In other words, to the extent that real estate risk is underestimated, real estate projects offering relatively low rates of return (i.e., relatively low benefits to society) will be funded even though the risks of those projects, if correctly estimated, would indicate that the projects reduce wealth relative to other investments.

19.2 ARBITRAGE, LIQUIDITY, AND SEGMENTATION

The divergence between the returns of appraisal-based real estate indices and those of market-based real estate indices should not be lightly dismissed as being fully attributable to the smoothing caused by appraisals. Appraisal methodologies use the same information and follow the same decision-making process as the investors who trade private commercial real estate. Especially in times of extreme market stress, investment professionals within the real estate industry are likely to place less reliance on REIT values than on fresh appraisals as indications of the true value of real estate.

This section discusses explanations for the divergence between appraisal-based indices and market-based indices in the context of similar circumstances with other investments. Arbitrage drives similar assets toward similar prices. Real estate professionals should view the tendencies of similar assets to converge and diverge in value in investments other than real estate to develop a clearer understanding of real estate prices.

For example, the availability of securities offering highly liquid exposure to asset classes and asset subclasses within traditional investments plays an important role in traditional portfolio management. Exchange-traded funds (ETFs) are an example of an innovation that has tremendously facilitated risk management for some assets. Do similar tools exist within real estate, or are they emerging? This section begins with a discussion of ETFs in order to introduce related opportunities and challenges in real estate risk management.

19.2.1 Pooling of Securities versus Securitization

An important distinction exists between the pooling of securities and securitization. The **pooling of securities** is any collection of securities in a single entity, such as a mutual fund. **Securitization** is generally defined as the pooling of non–publicly traded assets into publicly traded ownership units (securities). Thus, an ordinary equity mutual fund is generally viewed as a pooling of securities but not as a securitization, because the underlying equities are already publicly traded securities.

Publicly traded real estate products, such as most REITs, are forms of securitization, since they hold underlying assets that are not publicly traded securities. ETFs generally have publicly traded securities as their underlying assets. As indicated in the next few sections, the liquidity of the underlying assets has important implications for the relationship between the pool's value and risk and the value and risk of the underlying securities.

19.2.2 Exchange-Traded Funds and Arbitrage

The emergence of ETFs has substantially improved the ability of traditional equity portfolio managers to control their risk exposures quickly and cost-effectively. What makes ETFs so popular and useful? The answer is not just that the units themselves are tradable. Many types of securities exist, such as closed-end funds, that are themselves liquid and that have publicly traded underlying assets. Nevertheless, many closed-end funds have limited usefulness for hedging and benchmarking. The difference between closed-end funds and ETFs is that the relationship between closed-end funds and their underlying securities is not easily arbitraged.

The key to ETFs is the ability of market participants to arbitrage any difference between the market price of the ETF and the per-share value of its underlying portfolio. Most ETFs are constructed to facilitate arbitrage activities that drive the market prices of the ETF toward the per-share value of the ETF's underlying portfolio, or its net asset value (NAV).

For example, most ETFs allow owners of shares in the ETF to redeem their ETF shares for shares in the portfolio of securities that underlie the ETF. If an ETF trades at a substantial discount to its NAV, an arbitrageur can (1) buy the ETF shares in the market, (2) tender the shares to the corresponding fund in exchange for shares in the ETF's underlying portfolio, and (3) sell the shares received from the tender into the market at a net profit. The extent to which the ETF's market price is below its NAV will determine the profit of this arbitrage transaction before transaction costs. Thus, ETF prices should not stray from underlying NAVs by more than the transaction costs involved (provided the ETF's NAV is based on market prices).

Conversely, most ETF trading is performed with ETFs that allow large investors to tender securities eligible to serve as the assets underlying the ETF to the fund in exchange for new shares in the ETF. If an ETF becomes overpriced relative to its NAV, an arbitrageur can (1) short-sell the ETF in the market, (2) buy eligible and representative shares for the ETF's underlying portfolio, (3) convey the shares to the corresponding fund in exchange for the acquisition of new shares in the ETF, and (4) use the new ETF shares to cover the original short position in the ETF. This arbitrage activity of short-selling ETF shares will drive down the price of the ETF until any excess of the ETF's market price above its NAV is at least as small as the transaction costs involved.

The key benefit of the potential of many ETF prices to be arbitraged when they deviate substantially from their NAVs is that market participants can establish long and short positions in ETFs with confidence that ETF prices will be near their NAVs not only during periods of market calm but also during periods of moderate stress. This liquidity means that the risk of traditional equity portfolios can be continuously and effectively managed using ETFs. In other words, traditional equity portfolio management can rely on efficient pricing of highly liquid products such as ETFs, options, and futures contracts to manage risks. Should real estate investors similarly rely on publicly traded real estate products such as REITs to manage the risks of private real estate equity holdings?

19.2.3   The Hedging of Private Real Estate Values with Public Real Estate Values

Consider an institution wishing to hedge some or all of its position in private real estate equity. The position consists of highly illiquid holdings in limited partnerships corresponding to a variety of U.S.-based private properties. The institution is considering hedging its real estate holdings with an ETF product that correlates with a broadly diversified major index reflecting the overall performance of equity REITs in the United States. The institution considering the hedging notes that the properties underlying the REITs and the properties underlying the institution's private property holdings are highly similar in terms of type, size, and general location. Given the similarity of the underlying real estate and substantial evidence regarding the level of informational efficiency of major financial markets, can an ETF of REITs serve as an effective hedge of true risks?

The evidence in Chapter 16 and in Exhibits 19.1 and 19.2 indicates that publicly traded real estate securities exhibit extremely high volatility, even adjusted for leverage differentials, when compared to appraisals of private real estate. In periods of market stress, the divergence can be startling. For example, Exhibit 16.2 in

Chapter 16 listed the quarterly returns of the NCREIF NPI and the REIT index for the five years ending in December 2011. Note that beginning in the fourth quarter of 2008, the REIT index declined approximately 60% in value within six months. However, in the next nine months, the REIT index roughly doubled. Thus, a $100 position in the index would have declined to $41 and recovered to $78 in just five quarters. During the first six months of the same period, the NCREIF NPI fell only about 15%, then continued falling another 8% in the next six months, rather than rebounding like the REIT index did.

The key question to the institution considering a hedge for its private real estate holdings is this: Did the REIT index's movement correlate highly with true private real estate values? If so, the REIT index will serve as a suitable hedge for its private positions even if appraised prices indicate otherwise. If not, then the REIT index may be adding unnecessary risk.

Clearly in this example the REIT index did not move in tandem with the NCREIF NPI appraisal-based index. To the extent that the underlying properties are similar, one or both of the indices must be in substantial error. There are reasons, detailed in Chapter 18, to believe that appraisal-based valuations contain substantial errors. Thus, a reasonable argument exists that private real estate portfolio managers should rely on the informational efficiency of publicly traded REIT prices and use REITs and REIT ETFs as risk-management tools.

But publicly traded REIT valuations could also be in substantial error, in which case REITs would serve as poor risk-management tools. The reason that REIT prices may substantially diverge from reflecting the true values of their underlying properties is that there is no method of quickly and safely arbitraging perceived differences between REIT valuations and their underlying assets.

19.2.4 Two Views of REITs as Indicators of Private Real Estate Values

The previous example of the performance of the REIT index relative to that of the NCREIF NPI in 2008 and 2009 indicated tremendous divergence in valuation. There are two primary interpretations of this divergence in performance:

1. The REIT index's huge price decline followed by a near 100% price increase accurately represents the true changes in the values of real estate properties adjusted for the effects of leverage.
2. The REIT index's returns and their high volatility emanate from a source of risk uncorrelated with the underlying economic fundamentals of the real estate, such as volatility in the U.S. stock market driven by illiquidity and stress.

In the first explanation, REIT prices are informationally efficient. In the second explanation, REIT prices can diverge enormously from reflecting true real estate values due to market stress. There is substantial disagreement on which of these explanations is more accurate.

If the first explanation is accurate, then relevant REIT index values and the true value of private real estate are highly correlated. Accordingly, market-traded real estate products can be used to hedge the risks of private real estate. If the volatility levels between REITs and an investor's private properties differ due to leverage, the hedge ratio can be adjusted and an effective hedge can be maintained as long as the two real estate values (true private values vs. public prices) are highly correlated.

But if the second explanation is accurate (that REIT-based returns are poorly correlated with true underlying private real estate values), then the hedge will tend to be ineffective, especially in times of equity market turbulence. In times of high-equity market volatility, the hedge may actually add to the total risk of the investor.

The problem with resolving whether publicly traded real estate values are highly correlated with private real estate values is that, unlike with publicly traded securities, values of private property cannot be observed unless they are traded frequently. Empirical efforts to resolve the issue are not definitive. However, Fisher et al. (2003) empirically analyzed publicly traded real estate versus appraised private properties and concluded that "the general pattern of price discovery seems to involve the NAREIT Index typically moving first . . . followed last by the appraisal-based NCREIF Index. The total time lag between NAREIT and NCREIF can be several years, as measured by the timing of the major cycle turning points."

19.2.5 Financial Market Segmentation

In financial markets, **market segmentation** refers to the differences in pricing of similar assets trading in separate markets, attributable to the differences in the markets themselves. The differences in the markets are typically attributed to the differences in the clienteles that participate in the markets. In finance, a **market clientele** is a general type of market participant that dominates a particular market.

For example, two futures contracts may trade in different markets but with the same underlying assets. One of the futures contracts will have a large notional value and be traded on an exchange dominated by institutions and other large investors. The other futures contract will have a much smaller notional value and be traded on an exchange dominated by much smaller investors. Market segmentation in this instance would refer to differences in price, risk, and returns of the two contracts, attributable to the differences in the clienteles of the market. Depending on the circumstances, arbitrageurs may or may not be able to integrate the two markets.

The evidence in this chapter that REIT valuation and private real estate valuation diverge substantially may indicate that the real estate investment market is segmented. Many institutions, such as endowments, may have limited need for liquidity throughout their portfolios and may view their investments with longer-term horizons. These investors may be drawn to private real estate investments under the belief that these investments have relatively low risk given their steady cash flows and relatively low dispersion in values at the longer-term horizon point, at which the investment might be liquidated. Such institutions may view REITs as riskier due to their volatile market prices.

Investors with shorter-term time horizons and a higher need for liquidity may perceive REITs as providing the liquidity they desire with low transaction costs. These shorter-term investors may perceive private real estate as having just as much risk as or higher risk than REITs because of the steep price discounts and high transaction costs that they may be forced to bear in liquidating private real estate during periods of stress.

Within this market segmentation view, both public and private real estate are accurately priced for their respective clienteles. Barriers to arbitrage activity, such as transaction costs and short-selling limitations, allow the valuations to diverge on a short-term basis.

19.2.6 Real Estate Turnover, Dealer Sales, and Agency Costs

It is possible that the legal and managerial structure of REITs may cause REIT market values to diverge from the values of privately owned real estate. For example, Mühlhofer (2008) provides a tax-based rationale for the apparent divergence between U.S. REIT market prices and appraisal-based indications of private real estate prices based on rules regarding dealer sales.

Dealer sales are transactions that are taxed unfavorably in the United States based on indications that the investor is a shorter-term dealer in the assets being sold rather than a long-term investor. The rules regarding dealer sales mean that if a REIT trades a particular percentage of properties within a particular time period and with a particular holding period, any capital gains from the transactions will be fully taxed at the REIT level.

Mühlhofer argues that REIT managers are constrained by the tax rules into suboptimal portfolio management, including reluctance to exploit inefficient private real estate values. Mühlhofer states:

> *This study addresses the short-term disparity between REIT returns and direct property returns, and argues that this phenomenon is due to the trading constraints in the direct property market imposed on REITs (the dealer rule), which render them unable to time markets in order to realize short-term property appreciation profits.... [R]esults suggest that it is fallacious to treat REITs as a direct substitute for property in a multiple asset portfolio, as is often done.* (Mühlhofer 2008)

In 2008, the rules regarding dealer sales were relaxed. An act of Congress revised the taxability of REITs engaged in turnover (sales) of real estate properties. Humphreys (2008) describes the new rules as follows:

> *In general, the [rules]... subject a REIT to a 100% tax on net income derived from the sale or disposition of property that is stock in trade, property includible in inventory, or property held for sale to customers in the ordinary course of a trade or business. Under prior law, a prohibited transaction tax did not apply to a REIT's sale of a real estate asset if certain safe harbor requirements were met, including a four year holding period for the asset.... For sales of applicable items occurring after the enactment date, the minimum holding period under the safe harbor is reduced from four years to two years. Also, a REIT will satisfy the Sales Restriction Test if it sells no more than 10% of the aggregate "fair market value" of all its assets, thus providing a REIT with the option to use fair market valuation over basis valuation under the Sales Restriction Test. In effect, the alternative Sales Restriction Test and reduced holding period under the Act will allow REITs greater flexibility to dispose of property without incurring a prohibited transaction tax.* (Humphreys 2008)

Given the relaxation of the rules regarding dealer sales, the evidence that REIT values and appraisal-based values diverged very substantially through 2008 and 2009 (as discussed earlier) undermines the argument that taxation of REIT turnover causes these valuation differences. However, differences in agency relationships may also cause differences between the values of private and public real estate. For example, REITs have managers with dispersed shareholder bases, while most major real estate partnerships are formed and monitored by relatively small groups of limited partners. The reduced agency costs and higher responsiveness of private real estate managers to institutional investors may lead private real estate managers to pursue lower volatility strategies. Conversely, REIT managers can be highly responsive to shareholders through such incentives as stock options.

19.2.7 Real Estate Price Volatility and Liquidity

Advocates of the informational efficiency of major securities markets, such as the markets in which U.S. REITs trade, argue that market prices of REITs provide better indications of value than do appraised prices of real estate. Within this view, REIT returns reflect true (but leveraged) changes in the economic value of the underlying real estate. In other words, when REIT returns indicated massive and quick declines followed by a partial rebound, the values were accurate indications of the prices at which typical private commercial real estate was being transacted (adjusted for leverage).

Did private commercial real estate properties trade at tremendously reduced values in the spring of 2009, and did those values substantially rebound by September 2009? More generally, do actual private property transactions fluctuate in line with the value changes reflected in public REIT prices?

Practitioners who liquidated U.S. property holdings under duress in late 2008 and early 2009 may have had to suffer the same low prices implied by REIT prices due to the financial and credit crisis of the time. To real estate investors with liquidity problems, the huge decline in real estate prices may have been a valid indication of the prices they would be forced to accept in liquidating existing positions. But to well-capitalized real estate investors, it may be argued that the fire-sale prices were not accurate indications of the true value of their holdings. A foundation of this argument is that during a liquidity crisis, there is a very high likelihood that real estate prices will rebound when the crisis eases. If so, it stands to reason that the value of private real estate holdings of an investor certain to be able to ride out the crisis without liquidating positions might have been better indicated by professional appraisals than by market-based indications of value.

The hypothesis that short-term REIT prices imply erroneous indications of the value of a portfolio of real estate that is well capitalized suggests that publicly traded real estate securities do not offer effective risk-management tools for portfolio management of illiquid assets even when the underlying assets are similar.

In the case of holdings of publicly traded assets, the actions of arbitrageurs help force ETFs and other products, such as derivatives, to maintain pricing relationships that facilitate cost-effective hedging. But alternative investments are often illiquid. Therein lie the challenges of investment management, as well as the potential rewards of alternative investments from the illiquidity premium and complexity premium that may be available.

In the case of private real estate, if short-term REIT prices are at times truly out of line with the value of the underlying well-capitalized office and industrial properties, then arbitrageurs could presumably exploit the divergence by purchasing the underpriced asset and short-selling the overpriced asset. But there are two difficulties with this strategy in the case of REITs and real estate properties. First, the purchase and subsequent sale of private real estate take substantial time, transaction costs, capital, and expertise. Second, the short sale of privately held real estate is virtually impossible, and even the short sale of a REIT may be difficult in times of extreme market stress.

19.2.8 Evidence from Correlations over 25 Years

Exhibit 19.3 plots the 20-quarter rolling correlation between the quarterly returns of the appraisal-based NCREIF NPI and the concurrent quarterly returns from the market-based all-equity subindex of the FTSE NAREIT U.S. Real Estate Index Series. Each point in the exhibit is based on the 20 quarters of returns leading up to the date on the horizontal axis. Casual observation of the diagram indicates virtually no consistently positive or negative correlation between the returns of the two real estate indices over the entire time period. The general range of the correlation is between −0.30 and +0.30.

The rolling correlation does spike up at the end of 2008, when two quarters of simultaneous large negative returns registered as the financial crisis that began in 2007 deepened. These returns were shown in detail in Exhibit 16.2 in Chapter 16. Note, however, that the correlation between the two indices in Exhibit 19.3 plummets back within its historical range starting in 2009, when the indices move in opposite directions. (As shown in Exhibit 16.2 and discussed previously, the REIT index recovered while the NPI continued to drift downward.)

The evidence from Exhibit 19.3 shows that other than during periods of extraordinary market stress, there is no historical basis to indicate that REITs can serve as an effective short- to intermediate-term hedging vehicle for appraised values.

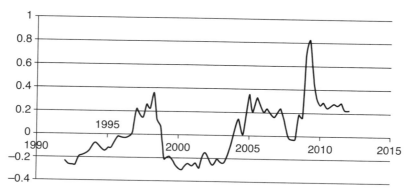

EXHIBIT 19.3 Rolling Correlations between NAREIT and NCREIF NPI Appraisals

EXHIBIT 19.4   Correlations of Returns on U.S. Real Estate and Equity Indices

	NCREIF NPI	REIT Index	Unsmoothed NCREIF NPI	Unsmoothed REIT Index
NCREIF NPI	1.00	0.22	0.53	0.19
REIT Index	0.22	1.00	0.50	0.99
Unsmoothed NCREIF NPI	0.53	0.50	1.00	0.49
Unsmoothed REIT Index	0.19	0.99	0.49	1.00
Russell 3000 Index	0.20	0.62	0.39	0.64
Russell Midcap Index	0.17	0.68	0.43	0.69
Russell Midcap Value Index	0.20	0.80	0.47	0.80
Russell Midcap Growth Index	0.12	0.47	0.32	0.50
Russell 2000 Index	0.15	0.71	0.36	0.72
Russell 2000 Value Index	0.17	0.82	0.39	0.82
Russell 2000 Growth Index	0.12	0.55	0.31	0.58

19.2.9   Real Estate as a Diversifier

Exhibit 19.4 contains summary statistics for U.S. equity market indices (Russell indices), the NCREIF NPI, the REIT index, and unsmoothed versions of the NCREIF NPI and the REIT index. The analysis covers the 16.5-year period from the third quarter of 1995 through the final quarter of 2011. The exact time interval was based on data availability of the Russell indices. The unsmoothed returns for the NCREIF NPI and the REIT index were based on the first-order autocorrelation method detailed in Chapter 16.

First, note from Exhibit 19.4 that the correlation of the NCREIF NPI with the REIT index is only 0.22. In finance, prices of assets tend to exhibit higher correlation when returns are measured in longer intervals of time (monthly and quarterly) rather than shorter intervals of time (minutes and days). The reason is that returns over very short periods of time tend to be dominated more by idiosyncratic returns than by systematic returns. Thus, the result that the quarterly returns of indices with highly similar assets have correlations of only 0.22 raises serious questions about the reliability and accuracy of one or both of the indices. It should be noted that the leverage implicit in the REIT index will cause much higher volatility in that index relative to an unleveraged index (the NCREIF NPI). But leverage should not have a major effect on correlations. For example, consider two portfolios with almost identical underlying assets, except that portfolio L is leveraged 2:1, and portfolio U is unleveraged. If the leverage ratio is continuously maintained, the returns of portfolio L should have two times the volatility of the returns of portfolio U but a correlation coefficient equal to 1.0.

Second, note in Exhibit 19.4 that the correlation of the NCREIF NPI with the most general of the U.S. market indices listed (the Russell 3000) is 0.20, while the correlation of the REIT index with the Russell 3000 Index is 0.62. Also note, however, that the NCREIF NPI does not have a higher correlation with any of the other Russell equity indices, while the REIT index has its greatest correlation (0.82) with the Russell 2000 Value Index, a value-weighted index that roughly omits the largest 1,000 U.S. equities and includes the mid-caps and larger small caps that comprise the next 2,000 largest firms. The Russell 2000 Value Index represents those firms within the Russell 2000 Index that exhibit the equity style of value (having lower price-to-earnings ratios and lower expected growth rates). The high observed correlation is consistent with the view of U.S. REITs as having capitalizations ranging from the larger end of the small caps to the smaller end of the mid-caps. Further, REITs are usually viewed as having the style of value rather than growth, owing to their relatively large earnings and small expected growth rates. The high dividend payout ratios of REITs limit the ability of internally generated capital to fund growth rates. Thus, the REIT index behaves in tandem not simply with the overall stock market but with the sector of the market that is most fundamentally related in terms of size and growth. The NCREIF NPI indicates slightly higher correlations with value stocks than with growth stocks, but does not indicate strong tendencies to correlate with small stocks. A possible interpretation of the correlations is that the REIT index appears to reflect more economically reasonable behavior than does the NCREIF NPI.

The unsmoothed version of the REIT index behaves much like the smoothed version in terms of correlations with Russell indices, and the smoothed and unsmoothed versions have a correlation of 0.99. This is consistent with the low autocorrelation of the REIT index (0.15), which is attributable to its prices being determined in competitive markets. The unsmoothed version of the NCREIF NPI, however, has a correlation of only 0.53 with the original NCREIF NPI, indicating its high autocorrelation (0.85) and the resulting major effect of unsmoothing.

The unsmoothed version of the NCREIF NPI has a substantially higher correlation with the REIT index and with the equity indices, indicating that the unsmoothing process removes lags that prevent a more timely recognition of changes in the values of the underlying assets. However, the REIT index still appears to maintain a substantial edge in the reasonableness of its correlations as being indicative of the accuracy and speed with which it reflects true value changes in its underlying real estate assets.

The REIT correlations in Exhibit 19.4 appear to be intuitively reasonable and consistent. Unfortunately, the high correlations indicate that equity REITs do not offer substantial diversification benefits. The NCREIF correlations in Exhibit 19.4 would appear to indicate substantial diversification benefits if the index were tradable. However, given that the underlying appraised values are not tradable, the results may simply indicate that the appraised values are too smoothed and too lagged to be trusted.

In an analysis of earlier data, Clayton and MacKinnon (2001) find similar results: "The results show that, over the entire 1978–1998 sample period, REIT returns exhibited the greatest sensitivity to bonds and stocks (both small and large cap). After accounting for these public market factors, there was no role for unsecuritized real estate in explaining REIT returns."

The question as to whether real estate serves as an effective diversifier is complex. The answer depends on which, if either, of the real estate indices accurately reflects underlying real estate values: appraisal-based indices or market-based indices. The belief that U.S. commercial real estate equity serves as a powerful diversifier to a portfolio of U.S. equities must be based on two assumptions: (1) that equity REIT prices do not accurately reflect the value of their underlying real estate, and (2) that commercial real estate property values have a low correlation with U.S. equities.

19.3 PUBLIC REAL ESTATE PRODUCTS

Traditionally, REITs have been the most important public real estate investment vehicle. REITs and analogous entities are common in the United States and some other countries, but are not popular in all countries. However, in recent years, a number of alternative public real estate investment vehicles have been launched. These new real estate investments include options and futures on real estate indices, exchange-traded funds based on real estate indices, and closed-end real estate mutual funds.

19.3.1 Options and Futures on Real Estate Indices

Derivative products allow investors to cost-effectively transfer risk exposure related to either the equity or the debt sides of real estate investments without having to actually buy or sell properties. This is accomplished by linking the payoff of the derivative to the performance of a real estate return index, thus allowing investors to obtain exposures without engaging in real estate property transactions or real estate financing.

The CME Group, the combined entity created by the 2007 merger of the Chicago Mercantile Exchange (CME) and the Chicago Board of Trade (CBOT), offers futures contracts based on the S&P/Case-Shiller Home Price Indices for major U.S. cities, as well as a composite index of all the cities.

The emergence of derivatives on housing prices offers three major potential benefits: (1) price revelation, (2) better risk management, and (3) the ability to short-sell residential real estate. Note that, unlike major securities markets for stocks and bonds, the cash market for residential real estate provides virtually no opportunity to establish short positions.

The effectiveness of real estate derivatives to offer effective risk-management tools to home builders, developers, and investors depends on two critical factors: First, the index on which the derivatives are based must accurately represent the changes in the value of the underlying cash market, and second, the derivatives must offer substantial liquidity. Standard & Poor's Case-Shiller Home Price Indices and their futures contracts are detailed here as an example of the type of innovation that may be emerging to bring advanced risk-management tools to all areas of equity real estate investing.

19.3.2 Exchange-Traded Funds Based on Real Estate Indices

As discussed earlier, most ETFs trade on exchanges at approximately the same price as the net asset value (NAV) of their underlying assets due to provisions that allow for the creation and redemption of shares at NAV. ETFs have the advantage of being a relatively low-cost investment vehicle; are tax efficient; and offer stocklike features (such as liquidity, dividends, the possibility to go short or to use with margin, and in some cases the availability of calls and puts).

While the first ETFs were based on only stock and bond indices, ETFs are now also based on assets such as real estate, currencies, and commodities. Exchange-traded funds based on real estate indices track the following:

- Global real estate values (such as through the iShares S&P World Ex-U.S. Property Index Fund, the SPDR DJ Wilshire International Real Estate ETF, the WisdomTree International Real Estate Fund, and the iShares FTSE EPRA/NAREIT Global Real Estate Ex-U.S. Index Fund)
- Global regions (such as through the iShares FTSE EPRA/NAREIT Asia Index Fund, the iShares FTSE EPRA/NAREIT Europe Index Fund, and the iShares FTSE EPRA/NAREIT North America Index Fund)
- Broad U.S. exposures (such as through the First Trust S&P REIT Index Fund, the iShares Cohen & Steers Realty Majors Index Fund, the iShares Dow Jones U.S. Real Estate Index Fund, the iShares FTSE NAREIT Real Estate 50 Index, the streetTRACKS Wilshire REIT ETF, and the Vanguard REIT Vipers ETF)
- U.S. sectors (such as the iShares FTSE NAREIT Residential Index, the iShares FTSE NAREIT Industrial/Office Index, the iShares FTSE NAREIT Retail Index, and the iShares FTSE NAREIT Mortgage REITs Index)

There is even an ETF with leverage (ProShares Ultra Real Estate) and an ETF with a short exposure (ProShares UltraShort Real Estate).[1]

Subject to the possible disconnect between private real estate values and public market prices, ETFs facilitate access to real estate assets for both small and large investors; and similar to options and futures on real estate indices, ETFs based on real estate indices can also be used either to hedge risks or to speculate.

19.3.3 Closed-End Real Estate Mutual Funds

Closed-end real estate mutual funds are exchange-traded mutual funds that have a fixed number of shares outstanding. Closed-end funds issue a fixed number of shares to the general public in an initial public offering, and, in contrast to the case of open-end mutual funds, shares in closed-end funds cannot be obtained from or redeemed by the investment company. Instead, shares in closed-end funds are traded on stock exchanges. Because shareholders cannot create or redeem closed-end fund shares directly with the fund, arbitrageurs cannot continuously keep closed-end fund prices at or near their NAVs. Like other closed-end funds, real estate closed-end funds often trade at premiums or substantial discounts to their NAVs, especially when the NAVs are not based on market values. Real estate closed-end funds usually liquidate their real estate portfolios and return capital to shareholders after an investment term (typically 15 years), the length of which is stated at the funds' inception. Closed-end real estate funds invest in properties, REITs, or both, and experienced substantial growth until the time of the real estate crisis of 2007–2008.

---

[1] All of the fund names and classifications are from Seeking Alpha and were located at http://seekingalpha.com/article/30370-real-estate-reit-etfs on January 22, 2012.

CHAPTER 20

Portfolio Allocation within Real Estate

The top-down decision of how much of a portfolio of traditional and alternative assets should be allocated to real estate is a complex one. Institutional real estate investing is increasingly moving away from allocations being driven by naïve diversification. Naïve diversification refers to simplistic allocations of a portfolio to a variety of investments without careful reasoning. Naïve diversifiers often place a small percentage of their overall portfolio in real estate or other alternative investments in the hope that risk will be diversified and return will be enhanced.

The chief investment officer (CIO) of an institution should avoid an asset allocation process that searches available investments in order to scatter portfolio allocations among diverse opportunities that appear to offer attractive returns. Since virtually all analysts make errors to a degree in predicting future returns, a disorganized search that focuses on locating attractive returns runs the risk of suboptimal diversification among opportunities that overweight assets with benefits that have been overestimated.

Diversification by institutions should be driven by reason and evidence in the pursuit of an optimal portfolio. A starting point for optimal diversification is to begin with a target portfolio equivalent to the market portfolio prescribed by the capital asset pricing model (CAPM), and to adjust from market weights to optimal weights that include the objectives and constraints of the investor.

The general prescription of the CAPM—that each asset class should be represented in proportion to its total market value—is not valid for real estate. In other words, the market weight is generally not an optimal weight for every investor in terms of allocation to real estate. The reason for this is that real estate offers unique advantages (e.g., preferential income tax treatment) and disadvantages (e.g., illiquidity and lumpiness) that should drive the portfolio allocation decision on an investor-by-investor basis.

This chapter summarizes the major issues that should be considered in top-down asset allocation decisions regarding real estate. Chapter 15 summarized five potential advantages and three potential disadvantages to real estate investment. This chapter focuses on indications that may drive optimal allocations to real estate toward being overweighted or underweighted relative to the weights of the market portfolio.

20.1 INCOME TAXATION

An essential element of real estate portfolio allocation, even for tax-free institutions, is income taxation. The essential idea is this: Investors in high income tax brackets should concentrate on (i.e., overweight) real estate investments that offer substantial income taxation advantages, and investors in low or zero income tax brackets should generally avoid (i.e., underweight) investments that offer substantial income tax advantages.

20.1.1 Depreciation Tax Shields

The primary potential tax advantage to real estate is the deductibility of depreciation on buildings for income tax purposes. Thus, a property generating net cash revenues from rent and leases of $5,000,000 per year will generate taxable income of only $3,000,000 per year if the taxpayer is able to claim $2,000,000 per year in depreciation expense.

The tax advantages to the deductibility of depreciation for income tax purposes are detailed in the CAIA Level 1 core curriculum, using the after-tax internal rate of return (IRR). The effect of depreciation was demonstrated using after-tax IRRs and was shown to cause effective income tax rates to differ from stated income tax rates. Specifically, effective tax rates were shown to depend on the extent to which the depreciation allowed for tax purposes exceeded, equaled, or was lower than the actual decline in the value of the real estate. If the depreciation allowed for tax purposes exceeds the actual economic decline in the value of the real estate (which it usually does), then effective tax rates can be substantially lower than stated tax rates.

This analysis of the tax advantages of depreciation focuses on the present value of the depreciation tax shield. The **depreciation tax shield** is the prospective stream of reduced income taxation that a particular investor will experience as a result of being able to deduct depreciation:

$$\text{Depreciation tax shield}_t = \text{Depreciation}_t \times \text{Tax}_t \qquad (20.1)$$

where depreciation$_t$ is the amount of depreciation that the investor can deduct in year t, and tax$_t$ is the investor's marginal tax rate in year t. Thus, depreciation tax shield$_t$ is the amount by which the investor's income taxes in year t are reduced as a result of being able to deduct depreciation at the tax rate, tax$_t$.

The **present value (PV) of the depreciation tax shield** is computed by discounting the stream of cash flows at an appropriate interest rate. Assuming that tax rates are constant and that the investor will be able to enjoy the tax shield with certainty, the cash flows can be discounted at the riskless rate, R_f, as illustrated in Equation 20.2:

$$\text{PV of depreciation tax shield} = \sum_t (\text{Depreciation}_t \times \text{Tax}_t)/(1 + R_f)^t \qquad (20.2)$$

For example, a building offering a $10,000,000 depreciable base to be evenly depreciated over 20 years (using straight-line depreciation) will permit deduction of an annual depreciation of $500,000 per year. At a marginal tax rate of 40%, the annual depreciation tax shield is $200,000 per year. At a discount rate of 5%, the present value of the 20-year tax shield is $2.49 million.

However, the depreciation taken against the building lowers the book value of the building over time. When the real estate is ultimately sold, the taxpayer will typically owe taxes on the profit, including the recaptured depreciation. Thus, the taxable profit on the date of the real estate's sale will be $1 higher for each

$1 of accumulated depreciation, and depreciation does not typically change the total nominal amount of taxes paid if tax rates are steady.

Depreciation reduces the present value of taxes. Assuming that the building in the previous example is sold after 20 years for a value above its original cost, the taxpayer will owe taxes on the recaptured depreciation of $10,000,000. Continuing with a tax rate of 40% and a discount rate of 5%, this tax liability of $4,000,000 in 20 years has a present value of $10,000,000 $\times$ 0.40/(1.05)^{20}, or $1.51 million. Thus, the net gain to the taxpayer from being able to deduct depreciation is $2.49 − $1.51 = $0.98 million.

If the asset being depreciated for tax purposes is holding steady or appreciating in actual market value, then the ability to depreciate the building may be viewed as an interest-free loan from the government to the taxpayer (i.e., the reduced taxes may be viewed as a loan against future taxes). In other words, relative to not having the real estate and paying full income taxes on all revenues at the stated tax rates, the real estate investor may be viewed as using depreciation as a shield to postpone taxes and increase the discounted value of all its future cash flows.

20.1.2 Deferral of Taxation of Gains

Real estate can offer taxable investors the advantage of deferred taxation of investment gains until the assets are liquidated. As in the case of common stocks, gains are typically taxed on the sale of the investment rather than being marked to market. Some investments, such as a series of short-term bond investments that are rolled over annually, cause annual taxation of gains.

Annual taxation of gains causes after-tax growth equal to the product of the pretax rate of gain (r) and 1 minus the marginal tax rate (1 − Tax):

$$\text{After-tax rate without tax deferral} = r \times (1 - \text{Tax}) \quad (20.3)$$

For example, an investment growing at 10% per year experiences an after-tax growth rate of 6% when applying a tax rate of 40%. Thus, a dollar placed in a 20-year investment using the same rates would grow to $1 $\times$ (1.06)^{20} = $3.2071.

Deferral of taxation of gains is included by compounding an investment forward at its pretax rate and subtracting taxes on liquidation. For example, $1 growing for 20 years at 10%, with gains taxed at 40% at the end of 20 years, would grow as shown:

$$\text{After-tax future value of \$1} = \$1 \times (1.10^{20} - 1)(1 - 0.40) + \$1 = \$3.4365 + \$1$$
$$= \$4.4365$$

Using these numbers, tax deferral allows accumulation of 55.7% more profit [($3.4365 − $2.2071)/$2.2071]. The general formula for the after-tax rate using an annual taxation of gains that is equivalent to earning r% for T years with tax deferral is shown in Equation 20.4:

$$\text{After-tax rate with tax deferral} = \{1 + [(1 + r)^T - 1](1 - \text{Tax})\}^{1/T} - 1 \quad (20.4)$$

Note that the annual after-tax return for the preceding example can be found as the rate that equates the after-tax future value ($4.4365) to the initial investment $1, as indicated in the following equation:

$$\text{After-tax rate} = (\$4.4365/\$1)^{1/20} - 1 = 7.73\%$$

Tax deferral of gains has the effect of increasing the after-tax gains from 6% to 7.73%. Alternatively, note that the pretax rate equivalent to 7.73% after-tax is found by dividing by $(1 - \text{Tax})$, which generates 12.89%. Thus, tax deferral of gains relative to annual taxation of gains is equivalent to being able to earn 12.89% pretax rather than 10%.

20.1.3 Depreciation, Deferral, and Leverage Combined

As previously indicated, the ability to deduct depreciation as an expense for income tax purposes is, in most cases, tantamount to deferral of income taxes (rather than a reduction in total taxable income). Deferral of taxes is also available to real estate because capital gains are generally not taxed until realized through a transaction, as discussed in the previous section. Finally, leveraged real estate can offer taxable investors the advantage of deducting interest payments on the debt financing of real estate for income tax purposes in the periods an interest payment is made.

Taken together, the income tax benefits of leveraged real estate can be especially valuable to investors in very high tax brackets. Returning to the example of the previous section on depreciation, the potential value of the depreciation tax deduction to a taxable investor, almost $1 million in the example, is especially substantial when leverage is applied. If the building in the example (perhaps worth $12,000,000, including land) is financed with 6:1 leverage, the entire $0.98 million depreciation tax shield can be generated with only $2 million of equity investment.

20.2 LEVERAGE

Leverage is an integral part of most real estate investing. Leverage generally offers tax-deductible financing costs for income tax purposes and can be especially valuable to a highly taxed investor attempting to enjoy the tax benefits of real estate, such as depreciation.

Leverage is discussed in Chapter 19 as a factor in determining the volatility of an equity position. In analyzing the returns of an equity real estate investment, an investor should be aware of the effects of leverage on volatility.

Over a short period of time (i.e., ignoring interest expense), and for small changes in value, the returns of a leveraged equity position, R_{lev}, can be approximated as the product of the return of the underlying assets, R_{assets}, and the leverage or gearing factor L (expressed as the ratio of assets to debt), as shown in Equation 20.5:

$$R_{\text{lev}} = R_{\text{assets}} \times L \tag{20.5}$$

The volatility of the leveraged returns, σ_{lev}, can be derived from the volatility of the asset returns, σ_{assets}, and Equation 20.5, as shown in Equation 20.6:

$$\sigma_{lev} = L \times \sigma_{assets} \tag{20.6}$$

Equations 20.5 and 20.6 ignore the financing costs of leverage for simplicity, since over very short periods of time the costs would be negligible. For example, a rapid drop of 2% in the value of the assets of a position levered 3:1 would cause a 6% drop in the value of the equity. Note, however, that for large changes, the relationship becomes more approximate. Given limited liability, a drop in assets of 40% cannot cause the equity to drop by 120%. Equation 20.6 can be used to approximate that if the volatility of the returns of the assets is 20%, then the volatility of the returns of equity leveraged 3:1 would be 60%. Investors in leveraged real estate should be aware of the potential benefits and costs of leverage, including the impact of changes in asset values over time on leverage.

20.3 AGENCY RELATIONSHIPS

Institutional real estate ownership typically involves agency relationships, which are important drivers of performance. Agents can fulfill two important functions: serving as managers of the operations of each property, and serving as decision makers in purchasing and selling properties.

The size and nature of a portfolio manager's allocations should be based on the investor's abilities to select, monitor, and manage agency relationships, because the success of the real estate investment is substantially driven by the performance of the managers.

There are three reasons that agency relationships are especially important in the selection and management of real estate relative to the management of other investments, such as passive public equities funds:

1. The market for agents such as real estate managers is not highly efficient. In an efficient market, buyers get what they pay for. For example, in a truly efficient market for athletes, a team owner who hires the most expensive athletes will tend to have the greatest athletes. However, in an inefficient market, buyers cannot be confident that they will receive value. To the extent that the market for real estate managers is inefficient, an investor's ability to select superior managers with appropriate compensation levels and schemes can justify higher allocations to real estate.
2. In the case of direct property ownership through partnerships with a small number of investors, the investor's relationship with real estate managers may be important, as the real estate investor cannot rely on other investors to monitor and control the managers. In the case of public equity investing, an investor can remain passive, becoming involved in issues only in limited cases of shareholder activism. Most real estate ownership requires greater contact with real estate managers over the life of the project. Therefore, an investor's ability to have

effective ongoing relationships with managers can justify higher allocations to real estate.

3. In a perfectly efficient market, managers cannot consistently generate abnormal profits or losses. Real estate properties often trade in relatively inefficient markets wherein superior managers can consistently generate superior performance. Therefore, investors better able to select and monitor managers who are successful in assembling portfolios of real estate properties can justify higher allocations to real estate.

These three aspects of private real estate emphasize the importance of superior real estate management. Investors must be able to identify capable managers and maintain successful relationships with those managers. The conclusion is simple: Investors with the contacts, access, and capabilities necessary for successful property acquisition and management should consider overweighting private real estate. However, investors unable or unwilling to acquire and maintain superior management capabilities should consider underweighting private real estate.

Note that investments in large publicly traded real estate markets or other large publicly traded markets do not typically require the ability to select superior managers and to monitor them. In an informationally efficient market, an investor with poor ability to select and monitor managers can earn average market returns by holding a well-diversified portfolio of publicly traded securities. Thus, investors with little or no expertise in real estate or in optimizing agency relationships may do best by holding well-diversified portfolios of REITs or other market-traded real estate securities, such as futures positions in real estate indices. With high levels of diversification and in relatively efficient markets, the investor's performance should closely track the performance of the overall market without requiring superior management capabilities.

20.4 INFORMATION ASYMMETRIES

Due to the uniqueness of most real estate investments, the prices of real estate offered for sale are more likely to vary widely from true economic values compared to homogeneous assets trading in relatively efficient markets. In a more efficient market, such as large markets for public equities, there are numerous well-informed buyers and sellers seeking to buy securities that they perceive to be underpriced and sell securities that they perceive to be overpriced. The large number of such informed investors tends to force market prices toward levels that reflect available information. Therefore, a poorly informed investor can be somewhat confident that transactions in efficient markets will generate normal average returns.

However, investors with poor information (and analysis) should be concerned that transactions in relatively inefficient markets will systematically generate inferior returns. The net result is that investors with access to superior information and analysis of private real estate should consider overweighting private real estate, while those with more limited information and analysis should consider underweighting private real estate.

20.5 LIQUIDITY AND TRANSACTION COSTS

Private real estate is typically highly illiquid. The illiquidity of real estate is driven by uniqueness and transaction costs, among other factors. Real estate transaction costs are relatively high. The costs of acquiring and eventually liquidating properties can include sales commission of perhaps 5% and other costs, including transfer taxes, searching costs, and financing costs, approaching a total of 10%.

The substantial length of the real estate sales process is due to the complexities involved. For instance, sellers will typically have to prepare the relevant documentation and hire a brokerage firm to market a property, and potential buyers will often have to spend a considerable amount of time searching, performing due diligence, and dealing with financing. Furthermore, negotiations between the two parties can take a considerable amount of time.

Large interests in private real estate are often restricted to a fixed size that may be inconvenient to traders, thus limiting the liquidity of the interest (i.e., lumpiness). For example, many direct private equity real estate investments take place with a single institutional investor or a small number of institutional investors serving as limited partners. An investor cannot typically adjust the size of the existing limited partnership to increase or decrease his or her allocation to the interest. Furthermore, in attempting to liquidate the interest, the investor may have difficulty finding a buyer who is both interested in the underlying property and satisfied with the size of the interest being offered.

As a result of their illiquidity, it is argued that total returns generated from real estate investments should reflect a liquidity premium. A **liquidity premium** is the higher expected return required by investors to compensate them for bearing the risks, costs, and inconveniences of illiquidity. This liquidity premium causes private real estate to offer higher expected returns, ceteris paribus, than are offered by liquid investments. Investors who do not require highly liquid portfolios should consider overweighting illiquid assets, including private real estate, to potentially capture liquidity risk premiums that may be available.

20.6 CROSS-BORDER REAL ESTATE INVESTMENT

Cross-border real estate investing offers opportunities for enhanced diversification. Investors often begin real estate investing domestically because domestic opportunities are more available and more familiar than cross-border (international) investing. As investors gain experience, having invested in many appropriate types of domestic real estate opportunities, they often look to other countries for new opportunities. Institutional investors often begin international investing by becoming a limited partner in an international project somewhat similar to the domestic opportunities with which they are already familiar and experienced.

Historically, institutions have dominated commercial real estate investment throughout most markets and most countries, with the vast majority of holdings held domestically. The primary problems encountered with international investment include lack of local knowledge, regulatory restrictions on foreign ownership, complex taxation, small-scale markets, political risks, and access to local services. The growth in the use of funds for real estate investment has had an impact on the increase in cross-border real estate investments. Real estate funds allow investors to enjoy the benefits of diversification into cross-border products with less concern regarding lack of knowledge regarding the foreign markets.

The growth in international real estate investments, while widening the potential pool of properties available for purchase, does not come without challenges. In particular, real estate funds are exposed to foreign exchange risk. Currency exposure is particularly apparent in the case of international real estate investments, given the relative low volatility of property operating income when compared to other asset classes, particularly exchange-traded assets such as stocks.

A U.S. investor receiving an expected cash flow of €10 million faces two risks in terms of the cash flow measured in U.S. dollars: the volatility of the cash flow, and the volatility of the exchange rate. Similarly, the investor can be viewed as facing two risks regarding the value of the real estate holdings: the volatility of the asset in the local currency, and the volatility of the exchange rate. For example, to the U.S. investor, a property currently worth €100 million can be viewed as being worth the product shown in Equation 20.7 at the end of the next period:

$$\text{€}\,100\,\text{million} \times (1+r) \times (1+fx) \approx \text{€}\,100\,\text{million} \times (1+r+fx) \quad (20.7)$$

where r is the percentage change in the property as valued in euros and fx is the percentage change in the value of euros expressed in terms of U.S. dollars. The investor's risk can be viewed as effectively a two-asset portfolio if r and fx are thought of as assets. Analogous to the case of a two-stock portfolio, this international investment's variance can be decomposed as follows:

$$\sigma_d^2 = \sigma_{fx}^2 + \sigma_r^2 + 2\,\text{cov}(fx, r) \quad (20.8)$$

where σ_d^2 is the variance of the international real estate investment return, expressed in domestic currency terms; σ_{fx}^2 is the variance of the foreign exchange rate; σ_r^2 is the variance of the foreign real estate asset return in its currency; and cov(fx,r) is the covariance between the foreign exchange rate and the foreign real estate asset return. Equation 20.8 illustrates the idea that investment in real estate domiciled in a location with a different currency can be viewed as adding foreign exchange rate risk, especially in instances in which revenues are dominated by leases fixed in terms of the foreign currency, and expenses, such as interest expense, are specified in terms of the foreign currency.

This analysis of foreign investment as having added risk due to the operation of the real estate in a jurisdiction with a different currency is based on measuring risk in the currency of the investor's home country. However, it is not clear that investor wealth and risk should be measured with respect to a single currency. Investors who minimize currency risk measured in terms of a single currency are likely maximizing their risk exposure to the risk of unanticipated inflation in that same currency. A strong argument can be made that investors should consider having their wealth exposed to a diversified basket of currencies to avoid concentration of inflation risk in a single currency.

Real estate investors should consider currency risk in making cross-border real estate allocations. Derivatives allow most currency risk exposures to be hedged if desired. To the extent that an investor perceives diversification into nondomestic currencies to be a plus, cross-border real estate investment may be especially attractive and worthy of higher allocations.

20.7 SUMMARY AND CONCLUSIONS

This chapter has reviewed several distinguishing characteristics of real estate that may be considered by an asset allocator in setting the target portfolio weights for real estate and its subclasses. The idea is that investors should consider their own tax situation, tolerances for illiquidity, ability to manage projects or managers, and so forth, in making allocation decisions.

Additional issues with real estate should also be considered. The challenges of accurately estimating true historical volatilities and correlations increase the risk measurement risk of real estate. **Risk measurement risk** is the economic dispersion caused by inaccuracies in estimating the volatilities and correlations of investments. The challenge of inferring volatilities and correlations for real estate using historical data increases the unreliability of applying state-of-the-art portfolio management techniques, such as mean-variance optimization.

With the complexities and challenges of real estate investing come opportunities. Matching the returns of traditional investments such as stocks and bonds can be easily accomplished using passive portfolio management approaches, such as indexation. But optimizing the risk and returns of a well-diversified portfolio of private and public real estate with the liquidity and taxation characteristics appropriate for a particular investment requires expertise and effort. It is especially within the challenging area of real estate that investment professionals can add value.

CHAPTER 21

Farmland and Timber Investments[*]

Institutional investors have recently expressed an increased interest in the returns produced by the direct ownership of real assets, and farmland assets in particular. Global private investment in farmland by financial investors is estimated to be between $10 billion and $25 billion (HighQuest 2010). The rationale for such investment has typically centered around three motivations:

1. *Farmland as an inflation hedge.* As a real asset that is linked to food and energy production, farmland is expected to be a hedge against inflation. Its supply is largely inelastic (in contrast with fiat currency, securities, etc.), and increasing valuations will lead to relatively marginal increases in supply, further reinforcing its value as an inflation hedge.

2. *Farmland as a diversifying source of return.* Being a private market investment subject to its own physical and economic dynamics and an asset that is, for the most part, privately held and often indirectly stabilized by government subsidy, farmland's returns are not, in the short run, directly linked to financial markets. Furthermore, farmland is generally a relatively unlevered asset, further disassociating its returns from financial markets.

3. *Farmland as asset positioning for a food and energy scarcity theme.* Economic and demographic growth is likely to create demand for agricultural products that outstrips current productive capacity, leading to the development of new farmland and price appreciation of existing farmland assets.

While there exists disparate research on each of these themes, only recently has empirical research been conducted to address these questions from the perspective of a capital markets investor.

Most habitable regions of the earth have farmable land in some form; however, this chapter presents an analysis of some of the key characteristics of U.S. farmland

---

[*]This chapter incorporates and adapts independent and original work (1) published by Geman and Martin (2011), which was sponsored by Bunge Global Agribusiness, whose support is gratefully acknowledged, and (2) excerpted from Martin (2012). Without suggesting any intellectual liability, I offer my warm thanks to my co-authors, my colleagues at Wood Creek Capital Management and the Center for International Securities and Derivatives Markets (CISDM), and the investment professionals at Bunge for supportive, intellectual, and practical engagement on farmland investing.

to illustrate the characteristics of farmland as an asset class. This focus is driven by three considerations: (1) U.S. farmland is a relatively stable, mature asset, and its history is free from wholesale disruptions in market structure, organizational form, and political economy; (2) correspondingly, the amount of available data on farmland and agriculture (both time series as well as depth of information) for the United States is greater than for any other country, facilitating the analysis of the long-run investment properties of the asset; and (3) the organizational form of farmland in the United States, which is largely privately held and market-based but subject to meaningful government regulation and activity, generally mirrors, in a mature form, the state of existing international markets for farmland (for example, Brazil, Australia, and, to a lesser extent, Eastern Europe). This background is essential for demonstrating that farmland has relatively stable properties, including its relationship to the macroeconomic factors that are of concern to institutional investors.

The empirical results presented are generally supportive of recent efforts by institutional investors worldwide to gain exposure to farmland via direct investment. The results are also relevant to other economic actors seeking to understand some of the wider risk characteristics of broad-based farmland investments in both the United States and internationally. However, investment opportunities in farmland are evolving and new risks are arising. In particular, potential risks may be arising because of increasing integration (which may be expressed both in price and in risk) between agricultural and energy markets, as elevated fossil fuel prices have made biofuel technologies cost-competitive and sources of marginal demand for agricultural commodities. A risk of great concern to cross-border investors is that of **expropriation**: that a government may steal assets belonging to foreign investors, either by direct action (nationalization or forced asset transfer) or indirect action, such as discriminatory taxation or predatory regulation.

In contrast to recently increasing returns to farmland investment, returns to U.S. timberland investing have undergone substantial compression in the past two decades as financial investors have acquired a large portion of timber assets previously held by integrated wood products firms. As a result, return opportunities for future timber investments are increasingly focused on non-U.S. assets. Return prospects and risks for such non-U.S. opportunities are reviewed in the last section of this chapter.

21.1 GLOBAL DEMAND FOR AGRICULTURAL PRODUCTS

The global demand for agricultural products has experienced consistent growth, and is expected to continue to do so for the foreseeable future. Global growth rates in the demand for agricultural products have been around 2.0% since the late 1960s, and are projected by the Food and Agricultural Organization (FAO) to grow at around 1.5% through 2030. According to the FAO and the Organization for Economic Cooperation and Development (OECD), three macro factors are driving the growth in demand for agricultural products: (1) worldwide population growth, (2) rising incomes in emerging markets that lead to changing diets, and (3) the growing use of biofuels. The increased production that is required to meet this demand will come from a combination of improved agricultural yields and the expansion of cropland.

21.1.1 Population Growth, Income Growth, and Changing Food Demands

The world's population continues to rise steadily, with almost all of the growth projected to occur outside of Europe and the Americas. Long-range population forecasts have historically been more accurate than other variables that are notoriously unreliable, such as gross domestic product (GDP). For example, world population projections for the year 2000 made in the early 1970s by the United Nations Population Division were only 2.3% higher than the actual value observed 30 years after the prediction (Sohn 2007). The current UN projections that global population will continue to rise by approximately 11% from 6.9 billion in 2010 to 7.7 billion by 2020, and there will be a cumulative 20% rise to 8.3 billion in 2030 (United Nations Population Division 2008), can be reasonably relied upon. It is estimated that population expansion accounts for approximately 1% annual growth in demand for agricultural products.

Global per capita GDP has risen at an average annual rate above 4.5% since the 1980s. As the global population becomes wealthier and disposable incomes rise, dietary habits tend to shift. Increases in disposable income lead to increased consumption of meat proteins. This demand shift in turn leads to increased demand for animal feed grains (corn, soybeans, etc.). This is important in the context of land valuation, as it is supportive to the expansion of agricultural land. On a calorie basis, the production of feed grains that are needed for livestock production requires much more land than the production of the same calories in a vegetable form. A vegetarian diet uses between one-quarter and one-half of the land corresponding to a meat-rich diet (Peters, Wilkins, and Fick 2007; Vegetarian Society 2009). However, the number of calories consumed in the form of livestock products varies greatly worldwide.

According to data available to 2007, per capita consumption of livestock products in Europe and North America is currently around six times that of the regions with the lowest consumption, Africa and South Asia (FAO 2009b). This indicates that there is significant room for growth in meat and dairy consumption as per capita incomes rise in those regions. Further, as rapid income growth has occurred, livestock products consumption per capita has risen very rapidly in East and Southeast Asia, with meat consumption growing at an annualized rate of 4.1% from 1995 to 2005 (FAO 2009b). The countries of East and Southeast Asia (China, Indonesia, Japan, Philippines, and Vietnam) combined represented about 2.1 billion people in 2010, or 31% of the world's population. Despite the rapid growth that has occurred, these countries could still increase their livestock consumption by an additional 70% before they reach the average per capita consumption levels of the developed world.

South Asia, mainly comprising the countries of India, Pakistan, and Bangladesh, presents significant uncertainty, with a population of around 1.55 billion in 2010. Meat consumption in the region has remained low, barely rising in 45 years, which may be due to religious or cultural reasons. However, the low growth may also be attributable to the persistently low per capita GDP in these countries ($1,000 per capita for India and Pakistan versus $3,700 for China and $46,000 for the United States). A big unknown for future livestock demand is how the trend will unfold in South Asia as per capita incomes rise. If trends seen elsewhere in Asia repeat themselves in South Asia, over 1.5 billion people could be eating almost four times more meat within 20 years. Compounding this effect, population growth in South

Asia is likely to average around 1.25% per annum, greater than the world average of 1% per annum (United Nations Population Division 2008). In other words, the proportion of the world population living in South Asia, and hence its importance in world demographics, will increase.

Overall, shifting diets toward higher per capita meat consumption will increase demand for feed grains. The degree to which this increased demand cannot be satisfied by improved crop yields will dictate increased pressure for the expansion of farmland.

21.1.2 Biofuels

The increasing use of **biofuels**, defined as the use of agricultural products for producing fuels, has become an increasingly significant factor in agricultural demand. The combination of rising fossil fuel prices, improvements in biofuel production and distribution, and governmental support has created a positive environment for biofuels (i.e., ethanol and biodiesel). As a result, global demand for biofuels has been growing. According to the *OECD-FAO Agricultural Outlook 2010–2019*, global production of biofuels averaged 89.4 billion liters for 2009 and is expected to reach 200 billion liters by 2019, a compounded annual growth rate of nearly 8.4%.

Underpinned by a growing focus on energy security, a desire to limit the growth of greenhouse gas emissions, and a desire to support domestic agricultural producers, government policy has been the key driver in the expansion of biofuels demand.

Further, biofuels growth will be supported by future growth in demand for transportation fuel, the primary use of biofuels. Energy use in transportation (including both passenger and freight transportation) is projected to rise by 1.3% per annum between 2007 and 2020, and continue to grow at that rate to 2030 and beyond (U.S. Energy Information Administration 2010). The use of biofuels is projected to grow at an annual rate of 6% to 2030 (IEA 2009).

The most widely grown feedstocks for biofuels are sugarcane, used for ethanol production in Brazil; rapeseed oil, used for biodiesel in Europe; and, in the United States, corn for ethanol and soybeans for biodiesel (Ajanovic 2010).

The growth in biofuels usage has created additional pressure to expand cropland globally. In 2007, biofuels contributed only 1.5% of the world energy requirement for road transport (IEA 2009), and made no contribution to aviation fuel requirements. These biofuels occupied 1% of global cropland area (FAO 2008). While it is unlikely that the biofuels will provide a large direct demand for agricultural land, the added pressure on production serves to promote expansion and land valuation.

21.2 ACCESSING AGRICULTURAL RETURNS

Capital market investors considering nonoperating investments in agricultural assets have three primary approaches to gain access to those assets:

1. Ownership of farmland to earn lease income
2. Ownership of listed equities in agricultural firms
3. Purchase of agricultural futures or related derivative instruments

Each of these approaches to investing has distinct advantages and disadvantages, and provides access to different points in the agricultural value chain.

Capital market investors have historically accessed futures through index-based products, such as the S&P Goldman Sachs Commodity Index (GSCI). The S&P GSCI is a so-called first-generation commodity index, which focuses narrowly on giving investors liquid exposure to near-term price appreciation or depreciation in commodities, as well as potential benefits (or losses) associated with the roll from front to next-out futures contracts. It also offers an implicit momentum-based strategy associated with an index-weighting scheme based on accumulated value. Since its inception in 1990 until the end of 2010, the S&P GSCI Agriculture subindex has returned an average of –0.1% per annum.[1]

Investors may also access commodity-oriented returns via investment in agricultural equities. Companies with listed equities are active at all points in the value chain. Though various index providers have recently created ex post indices of agriculturally related firms, these indices are of a relatively short time horizon (typically 2000 onward), and suffer from significant survivorship bias or insufficient attention to the changing nature of the non-agriculture-related industrial activity conducted by firms. A further consideration for investors is that a significant component of returns to agriculture-related equity investments is equity market beta, which needs to be either hedged out or accepted as a significant dilution to the expected agriculturally derived risk profile. The best long-term equity index focused on agricultural equities is that created by Kenneth French (KF) from Center for Research in Security Prices (CRSP) and Compustat data. The index is value weighted and rebalanced annually, and requires that a firm have a contemporaneous agricultural sector classification at each rebalancing point, not just a current classification. Average annualized returns to the KF index since 1950 have been 11.9%, with a volatility of 24.4%.

These returns compare to an annualized return of 12.5% for the S&P 500 and a volatility of 17.8% over the same time period, with a correlation of 0.55, and compare, in terms of pure, nonrental returns, to holding U.S. farmland of 6.1%, with a volatility of 6.6%. Rental returns to land are estimated to have a long-run average level of approximately 6% over this time period, although they have more recently been close to 4%. Returns to farmland investing have a correlation with the S&P 500 of –0.26, suggesting greater portfolio diversification benefits from farmland relative to agricultural equities for an investor already holding equities. Kastens (2001) estimates the total return to owning farmland over the period 1951–1999 at 11.5%, against an average return of the KF agricultural index over this time period of 10.7%. Kastens also calculates the returns to operating farms, based on a sample of 2,000 Kansas farms for the period 1973–1999. Operating returns over that period are 6.8% per annum, and all-in land returns are estimated at 8.9% over the corresponding period. This

---

[1] While well known, the S&P GSCI may not be an efficient commodity index, particularly for accessing agricultural returns, and is therefore not fully representative of the agriculturally related returns available via futures markets. There may be other, more efficient indices available. Disclosure: The author has commercial relationships in this area.

compares to an average of 13.3% per annum for agricultural equities as proxied by the KF index.[2]

21.2.1 Direct Ownership of Land: Capturing Improvements in Yield

While equities allow investors to access returns available in the value chain associated with agricultural production, including the sale of inputs like fertilizer, machinery, and genetically modified seeds, as well as agricultural distribution for food, fuel, and feed, **direct ownership of land** has a number of distinct advantages. For example, yield-enhancing technologies, such as the genetic modification of seeds, while raising the costs of specific inputs, allow owners of land to capture the bulk of the economic benefit, particularly outside of Europe and North America (Carpenter 2010). Furthermore, while investing in securities or their derivatives necessarily involves exposure to the financial complex, direct ownership of farmland offers insulation from systemic failure or disruption of the financial system.

More generally, the long-run returns to owning farmland and the short-run returns to owning particular types of farmland require an understanding of crop yield. Crop production is largely a process of transforming solar energy into chemical potential energy; land is the platform upon and through which that process occurs. Assuming no scarcity of water or nitrogen and no extreme temperature (cold or heat), **crop yield** (per unit of land per unit of time) can be decomposed as (Hay and Porter 2006):

$$Y = S \times I \times E \times H$$

where:

Y = yield
S = total solar radiation over the area per period
I = fraction of solar radiation captured by the crop canopy
E = photosynthetic efficiency of the crop (total plant dry matter per unit of solar radiation)
H = harvest index (fraction of total dry matter that is harvestable)

S is largely a function of geography and weather. Over the short run, I is the most variable, as it depends on the extent to which crops have been able to deploy canopy; total dry matter production (absent severe stresses of drought, etc.) is largely a linear function of captured solar radiation. Increases in H have largely accounted for the increase in yields to key grains over the twentieth century, as shown in Exhibit 21.1. E varies little, but is the subject of much research; as for a given species, I and H have been changed for many key crops and are difficult to change further.

---

[2] Based on the author's calculations on data provided by the National Council of Real Estate Investment Fiduciaries (NCREIF), direct ownership of *permanent* cropland averaged returns of 11.3% for the period 1992–2011, compared to lease-based (rent and share) strategies, which returned an average 9.5% over the same time period. Volatility of direct ownership has been 11% versus 8% for lease-based strategies.

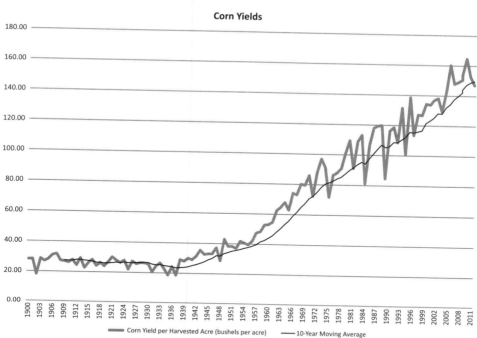

EXHIBIT 21.1 U.S. Corn Yields Are Rising over Time
Source: Author's calculations from U.S. Department of Agriculture (USDA) data.

While yield is an important source of the economics of crop production, the price of harvested crops is the most important and volatile short-run determinant of farming profitability.

A further consideration is the operating overhead of owning and operating a farm. A farm is a piece of scenery unless it is being farmed. The people, expertise, chemicals, machinery, seeds, livestock, and so on needed to make a farm productive have a substantial aggregate ongoing cost. Food processors will earn part of the value created. As an idiosyncratic physical asset, professional fees such as surveying, legal, and other administrative services will add up. Whether these costs are wrapped into a single operator's fees or are paid piecemeal by the investor, the running cost of a farm portfolio is far higher than the custody costs for a portfolio of financial assets, and must be budgeted carefully to arrive at a robust business case to validate an investment.

An examination of Exhibit 21.2 shows that the profits to farming row crops can be quite volatile, as the costs of both inputs and outputs are variable. Should the corn price decline at a time when the costs of fuel, chemicals, and fertilizer rise, farmers will be faced with declining margins or even operating losses.

U.S. farmland has historically been the key point of focus for government-sponsored agricultural support, insurance, and stabilization payments, though with elevated commodity prices, as well as fiscal constraints, the volume of such subsidies is expected to decline in the future, as the nature and amount of any subsidy are liable

EXHIBIT 21.2 Economics of Corn Production: Heartland Corn
Production Costs, 2010

Costs	Dollars per Acre	Percent of Total Cost
Seed	85.07	16%
Fertilizer and chemicals	136.11	25%
Fuel	26.87	5%
Labor	24.29	4%
Machinery	94.33	17%
Land	146.58	27%
Other	32.52	6%
Total	545.77	
Value of product	678.28	
Price	4.4	
Yield	154	
Yield break-even	124	
Yield margin	30	

Source: Author's calculations based on USDA data.

to political or other exogenous pressures. These payments are capitalized into the value of land, tending to raise values and providing a floor to possible price depreciation. Estimates vary widely: Goodwin et al. (2003) quote studies that estimate that between 7% and 69% of farmland values can be attributed to capitalized government payments, with land in the Northern Great Plains most dependent on government payments. However, studies that look at the cross-sectional variation of land prices within particular regions, such as Kirwan and Roberts (2010) and Gardner (2003), find that land prices are not sensitive to government payments. Gardner hypothesizes that this may be because subsidies do not have a commodity-specific impact on land values, since land use is highly flexible, particularly over the long time horizons associated with capitalization. Studies additionally suggest that land rental rates are largely set, except in the worst markets, so that owners of the land can capture such subsidies. Best practice is to run two sets of cash flow projections, one assuming that subsidies continue and the other assuming that subsidies disappear.

21.3 UNDERSTANDING THE RETURNS TO FARMLAND

There are several considerations when evaluating the historical returns to U.S. farmland:

- Pre-Depression (pre-1930s) farmland returns, which represented a period in which there were few government programs aimed at stabilization of agricultural production and incomes, were highly volatile.
- Exhibit 21.3 shows that a strong trend emerged around 1940, starting a period of consistent annual growth averaging 5.85%. Note that this does not include ancillary cash flows, such as lease payments.

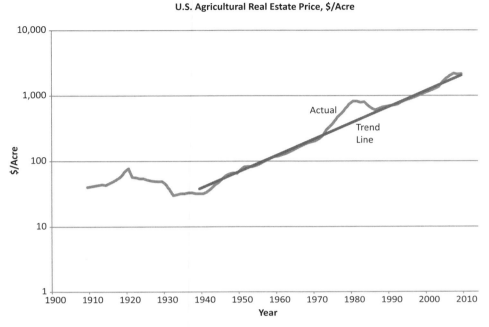

EXHIBIT 21.3 Farmland Prices Are Rising over Time
Source: Author's calculations using USDA data.

- There have been only two deviations from this trend: a strong rising trend starting in 1973, reverting to a lower value in 1986, and a weaker higher trend beginning with the recent commodities boom that began in the early 2000s.

21.3.1 Macroeconomic Factors Explaining U.S. Farmland Returns

The returns to a specific investment in farmland should be driven by the cash flows generated on an investor's land. This cash flow is a function of microeconomic factors that are asset and sector specific (yield, input costs, etc.). Generally these micro factors are a substantial determinant of cash flow; in particular, the quality and experience of management will differentiate one farm from another. Good farm management balances the long-term productivity of land with its near-term yield. Investors acquiring and operating farmland should pay particular attention to structuring economic incentives for the operator that reflect the multiple time horizons of farmland husbandry. In addition to selecting a specific subset of farmland assets that is expected to generate positive returns, the investor will likely want to consider the ramifications of macroeconomic factors on the farmland investment as well as the effects on the existing portfolio. That is, a capital markets investor is keenly concerned with the accumulation of macroeconomic and asset-based factor exposures in the investment portfolio.

An analysis was conducted of the factors that play a part in driving U.S. farmland returns, as proxied by the USDA $/Acre series for the period 1973–2009. Factors

EXHIBIT 21.4 Regression Explaining the Prices of U.S. Farmland, 1973–2009

Variable	Coefficient	Standard Error	t-Statistic	Probability
Constant	0.075840	0.018803	4.033280	0.0004
Wheat	−0.043553	0.047263	−0.921487	0.3644
Corn	0.045586	0.048112	0.947495	0.3512
Yield to worst	−2.549153	0.387147	−6.584451	0.0000
DXY	0.218149	0.073892	2.952271	0.0062
U.S. CPI	3.203890	0.381546	8.397123	0.0000
Industrial production	0.695191	0.198973	3.493893	0.0015
Oil Price	0.031608	0.018895	1.672785	0.1051
R-squared	0.786049	Mean dependent variable		0.065915
Adjusted R-squared	0.734406	Standard Deviation dependent variable		0.079446

Source: Author's calculations from USDA data.

considered included U.S. GDP, U.S. industrial production, U.S. inflation (as proxied by the GDP-deflator or CPI-U), interest rates (as proxied by the yield to worst on the Barclays Aggregate Index and the returns to the Barclays Government Bond Index), strength of the U.S. dollar, European inflation, and the spot price of commodities like oil, corn, and wheat.

A standard regression analysis was conducted to identify the most important factors, after which the model was reestimated (see Exhibit 21.4). The model is statistically significant, with an adjusted R-squared of 0.73. Interestingly, the most significant variables are:

- U.S. CPI, which shows that the returns to U.S. farmland have been a significant hedge against inflation risk.
- Yield to worst, which is an indicator of the level of interest rates with a negative coefficient. This suggests that higher interest rates are associated with lower farmland returns. This association is likely linked to both the business cycle (as higher interest rates are associated with a contraction in monetary policy) and the fact that higher interest rates are likely to put downward pressure on land prices (as increased discount rates bite into the present value of future proceeds from agricultural land).
- Industrial production, which is positive, suggesting that land prices are procyclical and part of a growth story, rather than a store of value dynamic.
- The U.S. Dollar Index (USDX or DXY), which suggests that a stronger dollar is associated with increases in land prices. This may be a proxy for monetary policy, or may actually reflect the impact of increased external demand for U.S. farm products on both land values and the price of the dollar.

In particular, note that the spot prices of commodities, corn, wheat, and oil are not statistically significant determinants.

The robustness of this model can be evaluated in two ways: First, the results predicted by the model (fitted) are compared to the actual farmland returns. From an inspection of Exhibit 21.5, it can be seen that the model fit has been relatively strong over the entire period, and is not driven by outliers or other factors.

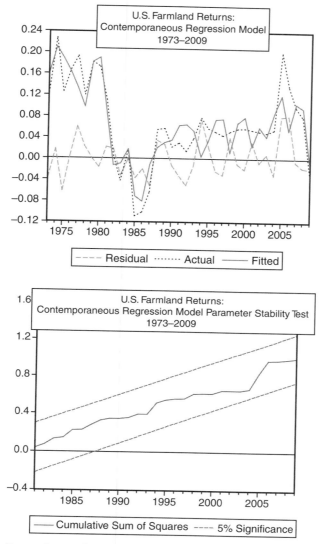

EXHIBIT 21.5 Regression Fit for U.S. Farmland Returns, 1973–2009
Source: Author's calculations from USDA data.

A more formal analysis, based on the cumulative sum of squared deviations from a set of recursive (Durbin) regressions, shows that the regression parameters are statistically stable.

The analysis presented in Exhibits 21.4 and 21.5 was conducted on an overall average of U.S. farmland returns. However, investors seeking to make investments in farmland cannot invest in such an average in particular because, given available investment vehicles, farmland investments are typically made in a small number of states only. The question is: How heterogeneous are farmland returns across U.S. states? The simplest way to evaluate this is to conduct a principal-components analysis for state-level returns for the period 1973–2009. The results suggest, first and foremost, that there is a common factor (first principal component) across U.S. farmland, which explains 56% of the cross-sectional variation in farmland returns. Examining the correlations between the first principal component and state-level returns shown in Exhibit 21.6, Kansas and Missouri returns are observed to be highly correlated (0.90 and 0.91, respectively) with this common factor. Candidates for the CAIA designation are not required to memorize specific statistics from Exhibit 21.6, but should be knowledgeable about the following broad conclusions regarding Midwest versus coastal farmland. The risks and returns associated with Kansas are representative of U.S. farmland returns, and vice versa. Geman and Martin (2011) provide further analysis, which groups state-level farmland returns according to their macroeconomic sensitivities. They find that coastal farmland returns have significantly different macroeconomic sensitivities than core farmland in primarily agricultural states. One major factor that tends to be present in coastal farmland, and which accounts for a portion of this difference, is urbanization and commercial or residential real estate use value. That is, the land in the U.S. Midwest that is used for farmland is farther away from residential development than farmland closer to the U.S. East Coast and West Coast regions. Coastal regions also tend to have higher land and housing prices than the U.S. Midwest. This introduces a speculative element of potential rezoning into the appraisal of the investment characteristics of agricultural land.

The preceding analysis is based on historical USDA data, which does not actually represent returns to farmland investors. The National Council of Real Estate Investment Fiduciaries (NCREIF) publishes data on the actual performance (via transaction and appraisal values) of farmland investments among its members.

- The data are based on reported gross returns (appraisal and transaction based) to institutions investing in U.S. farmland, for agricultural properties only, including permanent, row, and vegetable cropland.
- Only income-producing properties, either wholly owned or in a joint venture structure, are included.
- Investment returns are reported on a nonleveraged basis; while there may be properties in the index that have leverage, returns are reported as if there is no leverage.
- The properties must be owned or controlled by a qualified tax-exempt institutional investor or its designated agent.
- Property is included in the index beginning in the first full quarter it qualifies (properties are generally excluded in the acquisition quarter).

The Farmland Index constructed by NCREIF represented about $2.5 billion in assets as of 2010, which is less than 1% of U.S. farmland value, though this is growing significantly as institutions are deploying capital to farmland. The index itself is currently split between annual row cropland and permanent cropland.

Row cropland, or annual cropland, which comprises approximately 60% of the NCREIF Farmland Index, is used to grow crops that need to be replanted each year, such as soybeans and grains, including corn and wheat. **Permanent cropland,** which comprises approximately 40% of the NCREIF Farmland Index, is used to grow crops that do not need to be replanted annually, such as tree-based crops, including

EXHIBIT 21.6 Principal Components Analysis of U.S. Farmland (by State)

Explained Variance (Eigenvalues)

Value	PC 1	PC 2	PC 3	PC 4	PC 5
Eigenvalue	27.19	4.29	1.86	1.81	1.44
% of variance	56.65	8.94	3.88	3.78	3.01
Cumulative %	56.65	65.59	69.47	73.25	76.25

Component Loadings (correlations between initial variables and principal components)

Variable	PC 1	PC 2	PC 3	PC 4	PC 5
Alabama	0.80	−0.07	−0.08	−0.09	−0.30
Arizona	0.30	0.27	0.27	−0.46	0.23
Arkansas	0.83	0.10	−0.06	−0.11	−0.11
California	0.70	0.13	0.36	−0.04	−0.22
Colorado	0.82	0.09	0.00	−0.18	0.13
Connecticut	0.45	−0.79	−0.09	0.05	−0.13
Delaware	0.60	−0.28	0.46	0.28	−0.01
Florida	0.58	−0.08	0.59	0.06	−0.09
Georgia	0.80	−0.24	0.26	−0.01	−0.05
Idaho	0.85	0.14	0.22	−0.10	0.21
Illinois	0.86	0.25	−0.02	0.29	0.06
Indiana	0.86	0.27	−0.16	0.22	−0.06
Iowa	0.85	0.21	−0.11	0.35	0.12
Kansas	0.90	0.17	−0.10	0.12	0.14
Kentucky	0.87	0.00	0.07	−0.05	−0.18
Louisiana	0.75	0.15	−0.02	−0.14	−0.38
Maine	0.57	−0.61	−0.19	−0.21	−0.06
Maryland	0.68	−0.23	0.45	0.10	−0.21
Massachusetts	0.33	−0.76	−0.13	−0.11	0.03
Michigan	0.82	0.19	−0.14	0.01	−0.23
Minnesota	0.87	0.20	−0.07	0.29	0.02
Mississippi	0.85	0.17	−0.03	−0.07	−0.27
Missouri	0.91	0.11	−0.05	0.05	−0.13
Montana	0.78	0.04	0.15	−0.13	0.29
Nebraska	0.85	0.13	−0.17	0.19	0.20
Nevada	0.62	0.14	0.30	−0.29	0.12
New Hampshire	0.48	−0.73	−0.16	−0.17	0.13
New Jersey	0.47	−0.44	0.22	0.31	0.25
New Mexico	0.78	0.09	0.17	−0.08	0.26
New York	0.63	−0.34	−0.25	0.04	0.18
North Carolina	0.85	−0.02	0.05	−0.08	−0.24
North Dakota	0.80	0.16	−0.19	0.16	0.24
Ohio	0.88	0.13	−0.14	0.18	−0.07
Oklahoma	0.87	0.16	−0.01	0.01	−0.03
Oregon	0.82	0.22	−0.09	−0.20	−0.10
Pennsylvania	0.77	−0.13	−0.07	0.17	0.14
Rhode Island	0.51	−0.59	0.09	0.15	0.19
South Carolina	0.84	−0.04	−0.12	0.06	−0.05
South Dakota	0.82	0.20	−0.07	0.19	0.20
Tennessee	0.88	−0.02	−0.13	0.04	−0.23
Texas	0.65	0.06	0.06	−0.43	0.14
Utah	0.74	0.19	0.00	−0.45	0.16
Vermont	0.53	−0.62	−0.26	−0.27	−0.07
Virginia	0.74	−0.33	0.21	0.14	−0.08
Washington	0.76	0.25	−0.20	−0.09	0.00
West Virginia	0.79	−0.11	−0.04	0.03	0.15
Wisconsin	0.87	0.06	−0.13	−0.05	−0.14
Wyoming	0.80	0.10	−0.17	−0.23	0.18

Source: Author's calculations from USDA data.

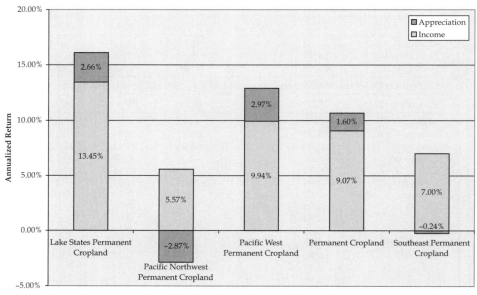

EXHIBIT 21.7   Returns to Permanent Cropland
Source: NCREIF.

apples, oranges, nuts, coffee, and cocoa. As shown in Exhibits 21.7 and 21.8, over the past 20 years, total net returns to row crop land have averaged around 10.5%, split evenly between income and capital appreciation. Returns to permanent crops have been of a similar order of magnitude, but have derived largely from income. Profit margins from row crops may be more volatile than for permanent crops, as row crops use a greater amount of annual inputs, which vary in price over time.

21.4   COMMODITY PRICE VOLATILITY AND ITS IMPLICATION FOR FARMLAND-BASED INVESTMENT STRATEGIES

The case for commodities as a diversifier is largely based on the low correlation between the returns to commodities and the returns to stock and bond investments. However, as the correlation to financial assets or the correlation between commodities increases, the diversification benefits decline. As commodities become more popular as a target of institutional investment, and as agricultural products are increasingly used for the production of energy, there are concerns that these correlations have permanently increased, making commodities less attractive as a diversifier.

Historically, energy and agricultural commodity prices were largely uncorrelated. As shown in Exhibit 21.9, commodity price volatility has undergone substantial spikes as well as secular increases for agricultural commodities like corn, wheat,

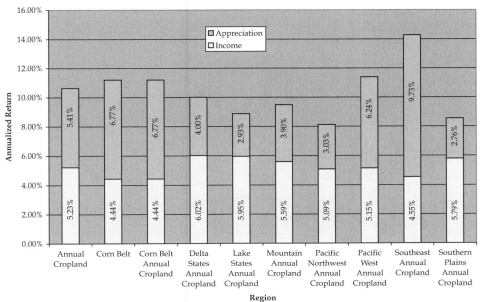

EXHIBIT 21.8 Returns to Annual Cropland
Source: NCREIF.

and soybeans. At the same time, with elevated prices of fossil fuels, biofuel production has become commercially viable. Have linkages between the pricing of energy product and biofuel feedstock increased beyond the increase in commodity price correlation that has come from the so-called financialization of liquid commodity markets? Will the historical diversification benefits of farmland and agricultural investments be eroded by increasing integration with other commodity and financial markets?

To the extent that elevated energy commodity prices will persist, these linkages can be expected to persist and grow stronger as the economic infrastructure necessary to exploit pricing differences becomes more established and more efficient.

But are these linkages evident in liquid futures markets? Are increasing correlations the result of changing causal relationships between commodities, as expressed in futures markets for those commodities? Or are increasing correlations the result of latent factors affecting many or all commodities?

In order to relate economic theory or intuition to observed interrelationships, correlations or regressions can be used to validate or hypothesize. However, hypotheses are usually formulated in terms of causality rather than association; for example, increasing energy prices will cause increases in the price of biofuel feedstocks (such as corn). Causality has a direction; correlation and regression are silent on direction and always symmetric.

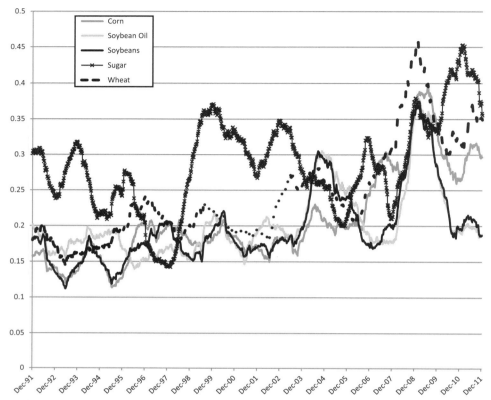

EXHIBIT 21.9   Rolling Price Volatility of Agricultural Commodities
Source: Author's calculations, Bloomberg, Dow Jones–UBS commodity indices.

Correlation interpreted as causality can easily be confounded by latent or observed common factors. For a **causal relationship** to be robust, a measure of association must not disappear when that relationship is conditioned on other variables or factors. Obesity may be linked with both increased propensity to television viewing and toward diabetes, and there may be an observed correlation between television viewing and diabetes in a population, but it would be incorrect to infer that television viewing causes diabetes. Conditioning on obesity, or any other conditioning variable that results in a statistically insignificant partial correlation between diabetes and television viewing, provides a mechanism for determining which variables have an actual causal relationship.

Classical econometric strategies for assigning causal relationships, such as Granger causality, are narrowly focused on intertemporal prediction; however, causality need not have a temporal lag (e.g., obesity and diabetes). Instead, one can employ an approach based on directed acyclic graphs and developed, inter alia, by Lauritzen (1996), Pearl (2009), Spirtes et al. (2001) that can be implemented in software such as Tetrad. The basic approach is to assume that the entire set of candidate variables are casually connected, and then prune relationships by testing for pairwise and conditional independence between all variables. The results of

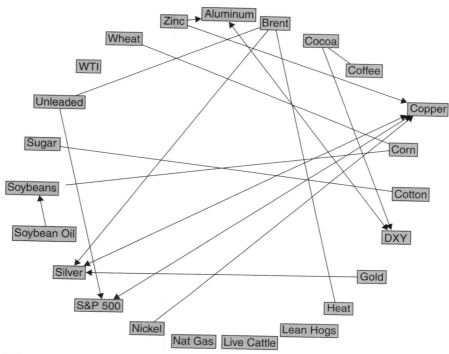

EXHIBIT 21.10   Causal Relationships between Commodity Returns
Source: Author's calculations, Bloomberg, Dow Jones–UBS commodity indices.

the statistical analysis include a set of relationships including independence, directional causality (represented by a line with an arrow), and causality of indeterminate direction (represented by a line without a single arrow).

In applying this approach, weekly individual commodity index return data (2010–2011) from the constituent commodities of the Dow Jones–UBS commodity index were analyzed, and corresponding returns of the S&P 500 and DXY, a trade-weighted index of U.S. currency, were added to provide financial variables that may have causal linkages. As shown in Exhibit 21.10, results of the analysis indicate that the S&P 500 and DXY are not causal as financial variables, particularly for agricultural commodities. However, financial variables are closely linked to energy and metal commodities, as evidenced by S&P 500 adjacent to copper and unleaded gasoline. Price returns of agricultural commodities are still causally independent of energy and metals. West Texas Intermediate (WTI), crude oil located in the United States, has become causally delinked from Brent, crude oil located in Europe, which causally interacts with the energy complex. However, this is a marginal statistical result, as the *p*-value of the correlation between Brent and WTI conditioned on unleaded gasoline and heating oil is 0.08.

The transmission of volatility between commodities and financial markets for the same period of time (2010–2011) can also be estimated and are shown in Exhibit 21.11. The results indicate that there is no causal relationship detected between agricultural price volatility and other nonagricultural commodities or financial assets.

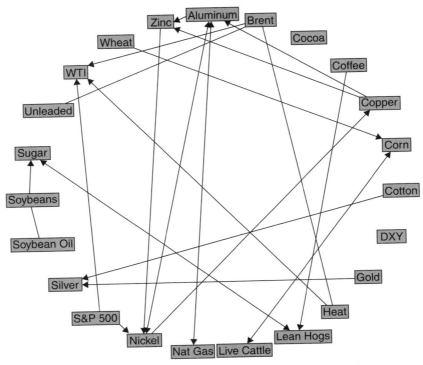

EXHIBIT 21.11   Causal Relationships between Commodity Volatilities
Source: Author's calculations, Bloomberg, Dow Jones–UBS commodity indices.

For example, wheat volatility drives corn volatility. Further, S&P 500 volatility is observed to cause volatility in WTI and nickel; the volatility of DXY is independent. Brent volatility acts through WTI and heating oil during this time period; copper and aluminum serve as a nexus for volatility transmission of other metals.

21.5   GLOBAL INVESTING IN TIMBERLAND

While investors are recently discovering farmland investing, institutional investors have long recognized the benefits of investing in U.S. timberland assets. Institutional investment in timber assets, as proxied by the NCREIF Timberland index, was equal to $24 billion in 2009 (Meketa 2010). This is well documented in a range of articles (Meketa 2010, Healy et al. 2005, and Waggle and Johnson 2009).

 However, as shown in Exhibit 21.12, the past decade has witnessed substantial compression in returns to investing in U.S. timberland, as dedicated institutional and other private capital have acquired an increasing proportion of overall timber assets, in large part from integrated forest product companies. These companies recognized that the returns available from retaining forest land assets in vertically integrated corporate form have been less than that available from the divestiture of such assets to investment capital (Healy et al. 2005 and Lonnstedt and Sedjo 2012). Over the period 2000–2009, an estimated 40 million acres changed hands. This divestiture process

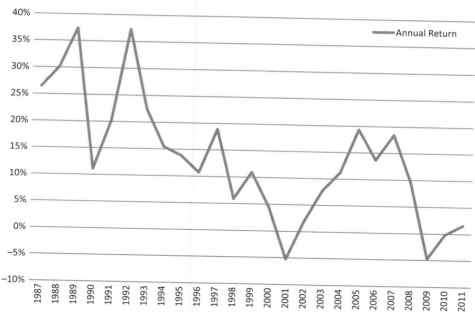

EXHIBIT 21.12   Annual Returns to Timberland Investments
Source: NCREIF.

is not globally uniform, and reflects both cost of capital as well as market structure and regulatory issues. Canada, Finland, and Sweden have seen some divestitures; however, until recently, there have not been substantial divestitures in, for example, Latin America.

This compression in returns has resulted in substantial attention by investors to non-U.S. timber and forest product opportunities. However, little research has appeared in the investment literature on the characteristics of these opportunities, with only an occasional notable exception, such as Akers and Staub (2003), who developed and rely on a factor-based approach to international timber returns and portfolio construction. This lack of academic attention may indicate an underexploited and therefore attractive investment opportunity set. More recently, Cubbage et al. (2010) published a comprehensive set of estimated internal rates of return (IRRs) by species and location, which is illustrated graphically in Exhibit 21.13. These are reinvestment IRRs, which assume that land costs have already been paid.[3] Of particular note, of course, are the relatively low IRRs for U.S.-based species when compared to non-U.S. species. Eucalyptus species tend to have the highest IRRs, in part because of the shorter periods to rotation (15 to 20 years).

Exhibit 21.14 shows the **rotation age** by species. Most species of trees take between 10 and 20 years to reach a size that allows for economically optimal harvesting. Beyond a certain age, the growth rate of trees begins to slow. At that point,

---

[3] The authors abstract from land costs, since such costs are highly variable even within countries; instead, the authors focus exclusively on production and management costs.

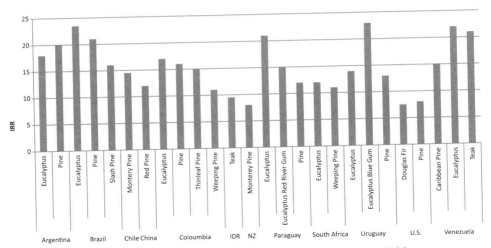

EXHIBIT 21.13   IRRs of Timber Investments by Country and Species, 2008
Source: Cubbage et al. (2010).

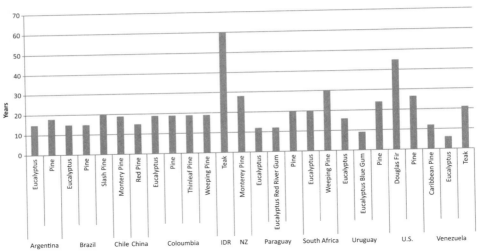

EXHIBIT 21.14   Optimal Rotation Age of Timber Varies by Species and Location
Source: Cubbage et al. (2010).

the forestland may be better used for newly planted trees, as the existing trees are harvested after the peak growth rate has passed.

While the IRRs for species grown outside of the United States are much higher than for U.S. species, the risks to a nonlocal currency investor are substantially greater. In particular, incremental risks that must be considered include:

- *Currency risk.* Typically, currency volatility between developed and emerging market currencies is on the same order as asset price risk in local currency. Given the long-term nature of these investments, currency hedging can be costly, as well as difficult. It is an open question as to whether currency risk between developed and emerging markets pairs involves compensation for risk bearing (Kim 2012).

- *Legal risk.* Land-based assets are typically subject to a unique, and political, set of regulations governing foreign ownership, taxation, environmental obligations, and indigenous rights. Agricultural legislation often includes some of the oldest statutes in any given jurisdiction, and can therefore be among the most idiosyncratic. In particular, plantation-based forestry may be subject to different regulations than would economic use of existing forests.

21.6 KEY POINTS AND SUMMARY CONCLUSIONS

- Global demographic and economic trends support increased demand for agricultural products and correspondingly productive agricultural assets.
- Direct ownership of farmland has been an efficient means for the capital market investor to access returns to agriculture.
- Factor modeling of U.S. farmland shows that at national (and state) levels, farmland has been positively correlated with U.S. inflation, and in that manner constitutes a real asset; farmland has been negatively associated with the level of interest rates and positively associated with measures of economic growth.
- Factor modeling of U.S. farmland shows that core returns to farmland have been available with state-level investments.
- Graph-based causal modeling indicates that causality between commodity markets is greater in return volatility than in returns themselves. Returns on futures on agricultural commodities are not causally linked to other nonagricultural commodities or financial assets.
- Financial market volatility has greater causal effect on commodity markets (primarily via the energy complex) than on commodity price returns.
- Substantial turnover in timberland assets to financially oriented investors has caused compression in timberland returns.
- Many institutional investors are looking toward non-U.S. timber and farmland assets, which offer the prospect of higher returns but also involve incremental ancillary risks, such as currency and legal risks.

CHAPTER 22

Investing in Intellectual Property[*]

A substantial portion of gross domestic product (GDP) is now generated by and comprised of so-called intangible assets, such as **intellectual property** (IP). Like tangible assets, these assets are important ingredients in the production of goods. This chapter provides an overview of IP and details three categories of IP: film production and distribution, artwork, and research and development (R&D).

22.1 CHARACTERISTICS OF INTELLECTUAL PROPERTY

Historically, most intangible assets were bundled with other corporate assets and available for investment through traditional means, such as an equity investment in a software company. However, in recent years, there has been an increased interest in unbundling and isolating intangible assets, IP in particular, for stand-alone investment purposes. Examples of such assets include patent portfolios, film copyrights, art, music or other media, research and development (R&D), and brands.

Unbundled intellectual property is IP that may be owned or traded on a stand-alone basis. Unbundled IP may be acquired or financed at various stages in its development and exploitation. Ex ante, newly created IP may have widely varying value and use. The value of property such as exploratory research, new film production, new music production, or pending patents will typically be widely uncertain prior to production or implementation. Similar to venture capital investments, many of these types of IP may fail to recapture initial investment or costs, though a proportionately small number of cases may capture a large return on investment. For example, De Vany and Walls (2004) reports the received wisdom that "80% of movies lose money"; yet films, on average, are still profitable, and, in the subsample of films studied, far more than 20% are profitable. De Vany and Walls (2004) report that for a sample of more than 2,000 films, 6.3% of the films generated 80% of the total profits.

Mature intellectual property is IP that has developed and established a reliable usefulness. Mature IP will typically have much more certain valuation and a more

---

[*]Portions of this document were derived from Martin (2010) as well as from Wood Creek (2008, 2011). Thanks to my colleagues at Wood Creek Capital Management, especially Jon Rotolo and Brian Egan, for sharing their ongoing insights in these areas, and for personifying the corporate commitment that Wood Creek has to thought leadership in investment in intellectual property and other asset classes.

clear ability to generate licensing, royalty, or other income associated with its use. Such income, to the extent that it has returns and risks that are understood, is likely to be well priced in the marketplace with risk premiums associated with asset complexity, asset liquidity, and variability of asset returns.

Returning to the example of film, Soloveichik (2010) argues that theatrical film should be considered a long-lived asset, with a life span of 80 years, in which 50% of a film's value is lost in the first year after release, and with depreciation in subsequent years occurring at 5% per year. In addition to predictable depreciation, post-box office revenues tend to be correlated with box office revenues. While it is likely somewhat a function of statistical outliers, it's worth noting that De Vany and Walls (2004) finds, perhaps implausibly,[1] that domestic DVD sales and licensing revenues for his sample of films have a correlation of 0.97 and 0.99, respectively, with domestic box office revenues.

To the extent that specific IP is purely a consumption good and largely removed from the capital accumulation process (as is typically the case with pure works of art, such as paintings, or other noncommercialized media), it is less likely to generate sustainable, long-term investment returns. However, the evidence (Nakamura 2009) does suggest that there is substantial capital accumulation for many intangible assets, which implies that intangible assets can represent important investment opportunities.[2]

Evidence also exists that IP may offer substantial investment returns. For example, estimates of the private, pretax returns to R&D expenditures are in the 20% to 30% range (although it is important to note that there are substantial issues in measuring these returns). Furthermore, inclusion of the **spillover effects** elevates the estimated rate of return significantly.[3] The spillover effects of an activity, also known as externalities, represent effects on other entities such as benefits realized by other firms and consumers from the successful R&D of a firm. The National Science Foundation estimates that total corporate R&D in 2007 was $242 billion, with 70% of R&D being conducted by the manufacturing sector. Pharmaceuticals represent about 21% of total R&D expenditures, and computers and electronic products represent another 21%.[4]

---

[1] These high correlations may be the result of nonrobustness of the Pearson correlation to outliers.

[2] There are whole schools of economic thought (e.g., New Growth Theory) that emphasize the central role of intangibles, and, in particular, their nonconvexities, in economic growth. This is in contrast to traditional economic theory, which sees most production technologies as suffering from declining marginal returns to scale. See Cameron (1998) for a survey.

[3] See Congressional Budget Office (CBO 2005). It is worth noting that a divergence in the private returns and social returns to R&D suggests an investment opportunity regarding the social returns. Capturing such an opportunity can be done, for example, through increasing the enforcement and concomitant licensing of IP rights for assets with broad applicability.

[4] Correspondingly, the ratio of R&D to sales for all surveyed firms was 3.5%, with pharmaceuticals at 12.7% and computers and electronic products at 8.4%. Broad survey information on corporate R&D is published by the National Science Foundation's Survey of Industrial Research and Development.

The next three sections discuss three major categories of IP for which there are well-developed bodies of economic research literature: (1) film production and distribution, (2) visual works of art, and (3) patents and R&D.[5]

22.2 FILM PRODUCTION AND DISTRIBUTION

Film production and distribution comprise a subset of IP that often has relatively substantial accounting data availability and that therefore provides a good example of the methodologies for estimating and modeling expected future cash flows and accounting profitability.

22.2.1 Film Production and Distribution Revenues

Film production and distribution falls into the IP category of artwork. Soloveichik and Wasshausen (2011) report that in 2007 the total revenue from the sale and licensing of copyrighted artwork in the United States was $285 billion. Total revenues from film production (including exports of U.S.-produced films and U.S. revenues generated from non-U.S. films), including exhibition, licensing for home media and broadcast, and ancillary income, were estimated to be $37 billion. Film revenues are generated almost exclusively by exhibition, which has a generally stable set and sequence of stages, though not all films will be licensed for exhibition in all forms. Exhibit 22.1 shows the schedule of exhibition venues.

While total revenues from film have demonstrated relative stability, the mix of revenue sources has been changing relatively quickly, due in part due to technology, but also to other financial imperatives, such as the availability (or lack) of capital for new film production. Examples of changing revenue sources include the rise and subsequent relative decline in revenues associated with DVD and other similar exhibition technologies as well as the increasing importance of non-U.S. revenues to overall revenue.

---

[5] For example, CBO (2005) survey results on the significant private and social returns to corporate R&D spending; Lev et al. (2006) find that the returns to "R&D leaders" (defined as greater than average R&D to sales for firms in a given industry) are superior (that is, greater in magnitude and lower in volatility) than returns to "R&D followers"; Hall, Jaffe, and Trajtenberg (2005) study the valuation of corporate patents; Bessen (2008, 2009) estimates the value of patents by owner and patent characteristics; Arora, Ceccagnoli, and Cohen (2008) and Chen and Chang (2010) examine the interaction between patent value and R&D; Goodwin and Ahmed (2006) document the increasing importance of intangible assets relative to earnings in the market valuation of firms; Fazzari et al. (2009) find that corporate R&D spending is sensitive to available sources of corporate finance (retained earnings, debt, and equity) and the attendant frictions, which are more acute for smaller firms and younger firms, suggesting (along with the evidence presented in Hall and Lerner [2009]) that IP in production by smaller firms may offer a richer source of returns to the strategic investor; Barlevy (2007) and Rafferty and Funk (2008) find that R&D spending is procyclical. For a perspective on European intangible assets, see Sandner (2009).

EXHIBIT 22.1   Schedule of Film Exhibition Venues

Exhibition Form	Window	Time after Release
Theatrical	6 months	0
Home video	10 years +	4
Pay-per-view	2 months	8
Pay TV	18 months	12
Network	30 months	30
Pay TV second window	12 months	60
Basic cable	60 months	72
Television syndication	60 months	132

Source: Wood Creek (2011).

22.2.2   Film Production and Distribution Life Cycle

In order to understand the opportunities for generating returns from film production and distribution, especially in a relatively dynamic period, it is helpful to review the life cycle of a film. **Film production stages** include:

- **Story rights acquisition:** Payments to license concepts, books, or screenplays
- **Preproduction:** Script development, set design, casting, crew selection, costume design, location scouting, and budget
- **Principal photography/production:** Compensation of actors, producers, directors, writers, soundstage, wardrobe, set construction, labor, catering, and lodging
- **Postproduction:** Film editing, scoring, titles and credits, dubbing, special effects, soundtrack music rights or composition

22.2.3   Costs and Financing of Film Production and Distribution

Collectively, the costs of film production are often referred to as negative costs. This refers not to the sign of values, but to the fact that these are all costs required to produce what was, in the predigital era, the film negative. These costs are coupled with the substantial cost of prints and advertising (P&A), which is the cost of the film prints to be used in theaters (whether digital or physical) and the film's advertising and marketing costs (see Exhibit 22.2).

Revenues from each of these exhibition forms are used to pay for the financing required to produce and distribute each film. Financing is achieved through equity or debt financing, or a combination of both.

Equity financing structures include:

- **Slate equity financing:** In slate equity financing, an outside investor (e.g., hedge fund or investment bank) funds a set of films to be produced by a studio. These slates typically reflect a set of parameters regarding diversification, risk, the number of films to be released, minimum and maximum budgets for film production and P&A, and genre diversification requirements. Slate deals emerged in order to spread financial risk across a series of films, thus limiting the impact of one

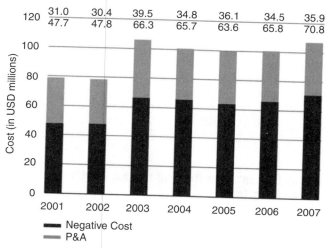

EXHIBIT 22.2 MPAA Member Production and Marketing Costs (per Film)
Source: Motion Picture Association of America (MPAA).

film's losses on a financial investment overall. Slate financings may have further provisions to ensure against moral hazards; such a provision would, for example, deter a studio from assigning films with lower expected return or greater risk to slate financings.

- **Corporate equity:** This is equity fund-raising (private placement or public offering) to fund the activities of a production company.
- **Coproduction:** Two or more studios partner on a film, sharing the equity costs and, correspondingly, the risks and returns.
- **Miscellaneous third party:** Some combination of high-net-worth individuals, institutional investors, and other third-party investors fund costs not covered by other types of financing; this is particularly common for smaller, independent films.

Debt financing structures include:

- **Senior secured debt:** A bank or other financial institution lends funds to a movie studio or producer to finance the production and/or P&A of a film. This loan can come in various structures and forms, backed by specific collateral, such as:
  - *Negative pickup deal.* Film distributor agrees to purchase a film from a producer for a fixed sum upon delivery of the completed film.
  - *Foreign presales.* Before the film is made, the producer sells distribution rights for specific foreign territories for a fixed price; all, or nearly all, of this payment is due upon delivery of the completed film.
  - *Tax credits/grants.* Producer receives tax credits (which are salable) or grants (paid in cash) for filming in a specific state or country.
- **Gap financing:** This covers the difference between the production budget and the senior secured debt, which can be collateralized by sales of unsold territories to distributors.

■ **Super gap financing/junior debt:** This is a second-level of gap debt, often syndicated, representing the final gap that the senior lender or gap financier does not want to risk.

Further, financing may be supported directly or indirectly with royalty participations. These may, in the case of talent, be in lieu of salary or other noncontingent compensation; or, in the case of financial investors, they may be used to lower the cost of up-front financing. These participations are usually assignable (i.e., transferable to third parties) after a film has been produced.

22.2.4 Empirical Evidence on Revenues and Profits to Film Production

Economists have long tried to bring some order to the study of ex ante determination of box office revenues (a world in which, as screenwriter William Goldman famously noted, "nobody knows anything"). The typical focus of this analysis has been on domestic box office revenue (DBOR), since this information is readily available in near real time.[6] More recently international box office revenue (IBOR) data have become generally available; however, detailed information on posttheatrical revenues is typically unavailable to the public on a film-by-film basis, although particular stylized facts are discussed or deduced from aggregates, such as the fact that posttheatrical revenues are typically similar to box office revenues.

Translating revenue numbers into profits is generally impossible without direct knowledge of and participation in the production of particular film assets. However, there are many regularities that arise in contracting, and these can be used to conduct analysis. In particular, it is a relatively conventional (and accurate) assumption that theatrical exhibiters earn roughly 50% of the take at the box office, and this proportion of the take will tend to increase with the length of time that a film is on the exhibitor's display schedule.

A growing literature has looked at the impact of various factors in determining revenue or profit associated with exhibition, with various studies including differing stages of the exhibition life cycle as well as more or less actual cost incurred for big items like P&A. There is empirical evidence, summarized in Exhibit 22.3, that:

■ Bigger budgets tend to lead to bigger revenues, but lower average profitability.
■ Some stars may have a positive impact on movie revenues, but most do not.
■ Sequels tend to generate greater revenues and lower risk.
■ Different genres have different risk-return properties.

Relatedly, there is some question as to whether the returns to a film can be well-determined based on opening box office revenues. De Vany finds they cannot and

---

[6] The transparency in DBOR numbers is high enough that substantial efforts have been made to create a futures market in DBOR results for individual films. Most recently, in the summer of 2010, efforts by the Cantor Exchange to list and trade these futures were stymied by Congress, after being approved by the Commodity Futures Trading Commission (CFTC). See www.cantorexchange.com for more information.

EXHIBIT 22.3 Academic Literature on Factors Determining Revenues/Profits to Film Exhibition

Factor	Study	Dependent Variable	Findings
Budgets	Litman (1983), Litman and Kohl (1989), Litman and Ahn (1998), Zufryden (2000), Elberse and Eliashberg (2003)	Revenues	Budgets are positively associated with revenues.
	John, Ravid, and Sunder (2002), Hennig-Thurau, Houston, and Walsh (2007)	Profits	Movies with larger budgets are less profitable.
Stars	Ravid (2004), Ravid (1999)	Profits	Large budgets may decrease profitability.
	Liu (2006), De Vany and Walls (1999), Ravid (1999), Litman (1983) Basuroy, Desai, and Talukdar (2006), Ainslie, Drèze, and Zufryden (2005), Elberse and Eliashberg (2003), Basuroy, Chatterjee, and Ravid (2003), Neelamegham and Chintagunta (1999), Sawhney and Eliashberg (1996), Sochay (1994), Litman and Kohl (1989)	Revenues	There is no relationship between star power and revenues. There is a positive relationship between star power and opening or total revenues.
	De Vany and Walls (1999), DeVany and Walls (2002), Ravid (1999), Ravid and Basuroy (2004)	Profits	There is no relationship between star power and profits.
Production-studio-related effects	Hennig-Thurau, Houston, and Walsh (2007)		There is a slightly negative association between star power and profits. Top directors increase revenues.
	Litman and Kohl (1989) Ainslie, Drèze, and Zufryden (2005) Hennig-Thurau, Houston, and Walsh (2007)	Revenues	Revenues and market shares vary across studios, due to different levels of expertise in timing of releases and accuracy about predicted competition.
Sequels	Ravid (1999)	Profits	Director power does not guarantee increased profits.
	Ainslie, Drèze, and Zufryden (2005) Basuroy and Chatterjee (2008)	Revenues	Sequels are associated with higher revenues. Sequels are associated with stronger openings. Sequels earn less revenue than originals, but more than contemporaneous nonsequel movies.
	Hennig-Thurau, Houston, and Heitjans (2009) Ravid (1999) Walls (2006)	Profits	Sequels are associated with higher revenue and less risk. Sequels are associated with marginally higher profitability. Sequels have higher expected profitability.
Genres	Elberse and Eliashberg (2003)	Revenues	Literature review concludes that findings with respect to genre are inconclusive.
	Ainslie, Drèze, and Zufryden (2005) Litman (1983) Neelamegham and Chinatagunta (1999)		Very few genre variables are significant. Science fiction genre is associated with higher revenue. Thriller (romance) is associated with higher (lower) revenue.

Source: Adapted from Karniouchina, Carson, and Moore (2010).

provides evidence that there is a critical inflection point, at around six weeks after box office opening, when film attendance either trails off or expands significantly.

22.2.5 Estimating the Relationship of Returns to Film Production

A simple metric of the return to an investment is the ratio of the cash in to the cash out. A return of −1.0 indicates no revenues, an investment with a ratio of 0.0 breaks even (ignoring the time value of money), and a positive ratio indicates a profit. This subsection examines the historical returns (the "cash in to cash out" ratios) to various film categories and fits curves to those returns in an attempt to provide analysts with simplified summaries of their behavior. The challenge is to identify a type of distribution that is able to closely approximate the observed frequencies of various levels of profitability.

For example, profitability of films is widely recognized to be highly skewed to the right, similar to venture capital. In other words, there are many outcomes with little or no profitability and a small percentage of films with very high profitability. Obviously the normal distribution, which is symmetrical, would serve as a very poor distribution with which to model film investments since previous academic work has attempted to model the wildly uncertain character of box-office-related revenues using the fat-tailed stable Paretian distribution.[7] However, the cash flows for box office revenues have been observed to be far more skewed than can be modeled by the stable Paretian distribution.[8]

The four-parameter kappa distribution (K4) of Hosking (1994) is commonly used to model distributions with fat tails. Of particular usefulness is the ability of the K4 distribution to assume a wide variety of shapes with fat tails, including densities with no bounds, lower bounds, or lower and upper bounds. The K4 distribution is parameterized with two shape parameters, one scale parameter, and one location parameter. This subsection demonstrates the use of the K4 distribution to model the returns to films. Data are collected from the Opus Data set for the period 2005–2010, including domestic box office revenue (DBOR), global box office revenue (GBOR), production costs, film genre, and date of release. This includes 981 films. Estimated cash-on-cash returns are modeled by calculating $(1/2) \times (DBOR + GBOR)/$Production costs − 1. P&A spending is not considered on the cost side, while posttheatrical revenues are not considered on the plus side.

---

[7] There are many reasons that this distribution has been adopted in the literature, including the fact that the stable Paretian distribution does not have second-order or higher-order moments, and therefore mimics the extreme uncertainty about box office outcomes. As a practical matter, the absence of second moments means that the variance of an increase sample of outcomes will not converge to specific value. Secondarily, an important reason for the use of this distributional model is the availability of software to estimate stable Paretian models.

[8] As evidenced by the fact that most reported results of estimating stable Paretian distributions for box-office-related revenue have $\beta = 1$, its upper boundary. See Martin (2005) for more discussion on the shape limits of the stable Paretian distribution, as well as the difficulty in estimating β precisely.

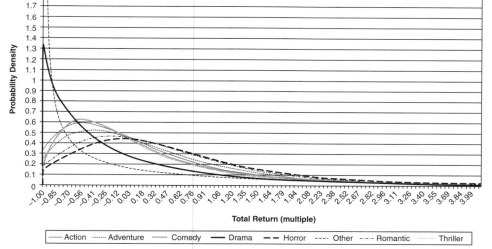

EXHIBIT 22.4   Probability Density of Estimated Total Box Office Returns by Genre (K4 Model), 2005–2010
Source: Authors' calculations.

The probability densities of returns to various film genres are graphed as shown in Exhibit 22.4 using the K4 distribution. In other words, the four parameters of the K4 distribution are econometrically estimated and then used to form the graphs that approximate the relationship between probability and return for various film genres.

From the density functions, action, drama, and "other" have the most skewness. The estimated density functions can also be used to estimate the probability that each genre will fail to break even (i.e., generate a loss). Exhibit 22.5 provides the estimated probabilities of loss for each film genre.

Exhibit 22.5 indicates a range of probabilities for different genres, with horror the least risky and "other" the most risky. While still displaying substantial risk,

EXHIBIT 22.5   Estimated Probability that Films Do Not Break Even

Genre	Prob X < 0
Action	0.56
Adventure	0.49
Comedy	0.53
Drama	0.66
Horror	0.37
Musical	N/A
Other	0.72
Romantic	0.42
Thriller	0.55

Source: Authors' calculations.

the results are much less pessimistic than suggested by the received wisdom.[9] This is partly a result of the growth in outlets for film production, particularly in international markets. It is also likely the result of better segregation of studio overhead from direct production costs, as well as increasing efficiency in the production process, which is associated, in part, with competitive pressures between studios. More generally, because of the asymmetry and fat tails associated with box office returns, traditional investment performance and risk measures (e.g., correlations, Sharpe ratios, regression betas) are generally invalid, and the analyst interested in constructing and monitoring portfolios of such risks must address this directly.

22.3   ART AS AN INVESTMENT ASSET

Over the past 20 years, there has been a growing interest in understanding the **investment properties of art,** due in part to investors' increasing interest in considering art acquisition and holding as part of broader wealth-management strategies. Within IP, art tends to provide better pricing data for analysis of historical returns.

Capgemini (2011) reports that 42% of wealth advisers to high-net-worth families believe that their clients purchase art primarily as a strategy for accumulating wealth. Moreover, there is much practitioner literature emphasizing that the newly wealthy (e.g., families from Brazil, Russia, India, China) have a demand for art that is driving up auction prices for art, particularly for certain styles and traditions.

More generally, there are a number of reasons advanced for considering art as an asset class:

- Long, sustained history of substantial demand by investors and consumers
- Potential for market inefficiency, and therefore mispricing, due to illiquidity and private valuation
- Lack of transparency in auction markets[10]
- No immediate link in valuation between art assets and traditional financial assets

However, the question remains: Does the empirical evidence indicate that the long-run returns to holding broad baskets of art are compelling? In other words, are investors in it for the financial gain or for the entertainment value?

There are a number of immediate issues that arise when trying to understand the investment performance of art as an asset class. In particular, unlike traditional financial assets, which have continuous markets and relatively homogeneous sources of risk, art markets are characterized by infrequent transactions in highly heterogeneous assets. Without some special techniques, merely looking at weighted averages

---

[9] See De Vany and Walls (2004) for other careful evidence that suggests that break-even probabilities on films are substantially greater than the stylized 20% figure.

[10] While art auctions are themselves very public, the extent to which individual art transactions are brought to market and the mechanisms for preventing transactions at adverse, but market-clearing, prices are not always clear. There has also been a significant history of collusion between auction houses in the setting of commissions, which can net the auction house up to 25% of the auction (hammer) price.

of infrequently traded art prices will induce substantial smoothing in returns. Similarly, disproportionate turnover in one subset of art will bias any inference about the prices of the overall universe of art being considered. As a practical matter, index construction methods to deal with these issues can be divided into two groups: (1) **hedonic price estimators**, which use a regression-based methodology to synthetically develop continuous price series by controlling for the unique characteristics (qualities) of each transaction that comes to market, and (2) **repeat-sales estimators**, which use a regression-based methodology that focuses on the returns to artworks that have more than one transaction. Both of these methods, and their extensions, have their origins in the efforts of econometricians to understand other illiquid and heterogeneous assets, such as real estate.[11]

There is a wide range of studies regarding the returns to art, typically by style or geography. For example, Taylor and Coleman (2011) create price and return indexes for Australian Aboriginal art. Ashenfelter and Graddy (2003) offer an extensive review of the literature through the early 2000s, which is broadly representative of subsequent research on returns. The results of the review are summarized in Exhibit 22.6.

It can be seen in Exhibit 22.6 that the median real return to holding art over extended periods of time is 2.2% (return estimates do not vary substantially by estimation methodology). However, most studies of the returns to art investment consider only **hammer prices**. Hammer prices are final auction prices, which do not include commissions to the auction house. Commissions that may be charged to both the buyer and the seller amount up to 15%. If we assume that the typical round-turn transaction cost for a sale is 25%, then it would be expected to take 10 years of price appreciation to cover the transaction costs associated with a piece of art.

Ashenfelter and Graddy (2006) offer a further review of the literature designed to evaluate the presence of two other possible characteristics of the art market that could conceivably form the basis for investment strategies. The first, known as the **masterpiece effect**, hypothesizes that the returns to the most expensive artworks are qualitatively different from the market as a whole. Ex ante, it is not clear if there should be such an effect, and if so, what sign it should have. That said, of six studies reviewed by Ashenfelter and Graddy (2006), only one finds a positive masterpiece effect. The second market characteristic in question is the so-called law of one price: Do transactions in similar artworks across auction houses and/or geographies occur within the bounds set by transaction costs? Of the various studies reviewed, there is mixed, weak evidence that the law of one price does not hold, for example, for transaction prices on the works of Picasso, as they vary systematically between auction locations (London versus Paris).

In a series of related papers, Spaenjers and co-authors offer a current, comprehensive view of the international art market. In particular, Spaenjers (2010) considers data on over one million art transactions across 13 countries from the 1960s onward, accounting for both geographical and currency effects. The results, summarized in Exhibit 22.7, are consistent with the preceding: Annualized real returns to a diversified basket of art have been in the neighborhood of 2%, and do not vary significantly

---

[11] Ginsburgh, Mei, and Moses (2006) offer a broad overview of these methods as applied to art.

EXHIBIT 22.6 Estimated Returns to Art from Various Studies

Author	Sample	Period	Method	Nominal Return	Real Return
Anderson (1974)	Paintings in general	1780–1960	Hedonic	3.3%	2.6%
	Paintings in general	1780–1970	Repeat sales	3.7%	3.0%
Stein (1977)	Paintings in general	1946–1968	Assumes random sampling	10.5%	
Baumol (1986)	Paintings in general	1652–1961	Repeat sales		0.6%
Frey and Pommerehne (1989)	Paintings in general	1635–1949	Repeat sales		1.4%
		1950–1987	Repeat sales		1.7%
Buelens and Ginsburgh (1983)	Paintings in general	1700–1961	Hedonic		0.9%
Pesando (1993)	Modern prints	1977–1991	Repeat sales		1.5%
Goetzmann (1993)	Paintings in general	1716–1986	Repeat sales	3.2%	2.0%
Barre et al. (1996)	Great Impressionist	1962–1991	Hedonic	12.0%	5.0%[a]
	Other Impressionist	1962–1991	Hedonic	8.0%	1.0%[a]
Chanel et al. (1996)	Paintings in general	1855–1969	Hedonic		4.9%
	Paintings in general	1855–1969	Repeat sales		5.0%
Goetzmann (1996)	Paintings in general	1907–1977	Repeat sales		5.0%
Pesando and Shum (1996)	Picasso prints	1977–1993	Repeat sales	12.0%	1.4%
Czujack (1997)	Picasso printings	1966–1994	Hedonic		8.3%
Mei and Moses (2011)	American, Impressionist, and old master	1875–2000	Repeat sales		4.9%
Graeser (1993)	Antique furniture	1967–1986	Neither[b]	7.0%	2.2%
Ross and Zondervan (1993)	Stradivarius violins	1803–1986	Hedonic		2.2%

[a]As many of the surveys report only nominal returns, the authors calculated the real return rates as follows. For the Anderson and Baumol studies, an inflation rate of 0.7% a year was used. This number is based on Baumol's estimate of inflation during the 300-year period of his study using the Phelps-Brown and Hopkins price index. Goetzmann's estimate of inflation during the period of his study (also based on Phelps-Brown and Hopkins) is 1.2%. French price inflation between 1962 and 1992 according to OECD statistics was 7%.
[b]Assumes random sampling within a portfolio of fixed furniture types.
Source: Ashenfelter and Graddy (2003).

across geographies or markets. In addition, the volatility of art indexes has a median of 17% per year. This combination of risk and return compares unfavorably to historical experience in equity markets.

One immediate question that arises is the extent to which these returns are a function of fluctuations in the value of the U.S. dollar. Spaenjers (2010) provides domestic currency returns for the same 13 countries, which have a median return of 1% and a correlation of 0.88 with the annualized returns reported previously. This suggests that currency effects are not a significant driver of art market returns. Spaenjers also looks at quality effects, in which works of better-known artists are considered to be of higher quality. From the adjacent results, a mild **quality effect**

EXHIBIT 22.7 Real Returns to Art

Country	Period	Annual Return	Volume	Minimum	Maximum	Annual GDP	Eq Return
Australia	1971–2007	3.09%	21.15%	−40.40%	66.66%	3.91%	7.56%
Austria	1971–2007	2.53%	17.44%	−38.40%	37.76%	4.11%	5.66%
Belgium	1975–2007	−0.90%	17.41%	−44.30%	38.57%	2.02%	8.42%
Canada	1972–2007	2.36%	16.12%	−27.19%	28.31%	3.03%	5.91%
Denmark	1976–2007	1.75%	15.56%	−41.96%	29.66%	2.70%	9.58%
France	1971–2007	1.14%	18.94%	−61.03%	39.74%	3.50%	8.00%
Germany	1971–2007	1.52%	13.12%	−28.08%	25.87%	1.43%	5.44%
Italy	1971–2007	1.99%	17.67%	−41.80%	36.66%	3.68%	6.75%
Netherlands	1971–2007	2.30%	17.94%	−44.26%	48.74%	4.13%	8.14%
Sweden	1971–2007	2.32%	20.18%	−55.16%	44.56%	2.65%	10.51%
Switzerland	1972–2007	1.99%	18.50%	−38.99%	75.63%	3.41%	7.30%
UK	1971–2007	4.60%	15.79%	−38.66%	30.47%	3.88%	7.94%
US	1971–2007	3.07%	14.31%	−28.73%	33.58%	2.53%	6.19%

Note: Results are USD denominated, deflated.
Source: Spaenjers (2010).

EXHIBIT 22.8   Risk and Return for Art Investments, Sorted by Quality

Country	Period	High Quality		Medium Quality		Low Quality	
		Return	Volatility	Return	Volatility	Return	Volatility
Australia	1980–2007	—	—	4.23%	23.13%	3.98%	17.97%
Austria	1980–2007	—	—	2.37%	20.80%	0.32%	17.25%
Belgium	1980–2007	—	—	0.60%	20.80%	−0.64%	16.57%
Canada	1980–2007	—	—	—	—	2.13%	17.34%
Denmark	1980–2007	—	—	1.32%	20.27%	0.90%	16.26%
France	1980–2007	3.21%	28.94%	1.39%	19.34%	1.57%	19.01%
Germany	1980–2007	—	—	0.96%	13.71%	−0.36%	14.55%
Italy	1980–2007	—	—	2.93%	17.04%	2.83%	18.21%
Netherlands	1980–2007	—	—	2.57%	18.81%	1.28%	14.60%
Sweden	1980–2007	—	—	1.56%	25.33%	−0.05%	19.93%
Switzerland	1980–2007	—	—	—	—	−0.72%	14.82%
UK	1980–2007	5.95%	17.62%	4.75%	15.23%	4.03%	14.06%
US	1980–2007	4.85%	20.95%	3.78%	14.49%	3.25%	11.13%

Note: Results are USD denominated, deflated.
Source: Spaenjers (2010).

is noted, with higher-quality paintings generating higher returns. However, these higher returns were at the expense of higher volatility. Median information ratios for highest-quality paintings are 0.23, with corresponding information ratios of 0.11 and 0.08 for medium- and lower-quality paintings. From an investment perspective, these findings are unattractive.

With such low returns, why might it be that there is significant demand for art? Spaenjers (2010) offers preliminary, but intuitive, evidence, summarized in Exhibit 22.8, that art prices are significantly explained by wealth effects, as proxied by gross domestic product (GDP) growth, lagged equity market effects, and income inequality. While interesting in its own right, these results also suggest that the diversification benefit of art is lower than might otherwise be thought, as most traditional investors already have positive exposure to GDP and equity markets; high-net-worth investors will also have existing positive exposure to wealth inequality.

Forsyth (2012) suggests that high-net-worth investors invest in art as a hedge against inflation or confiscation of wealth by governments. For those with a net worth above $100 million, the goal is to maintain rather than grow wealth. Artworks can protect against monetary debasement, confiscation, and social unrest. Forsyth quotes Richard Morais: "Any private banker will tell you that, as soon as a centi-millionaire in Moscow, Beijing or Sao Paolo makes their fortune, the first thing they do is figure out how they can ferret away large chunks of that wealth to countries that guarantee political and personal freedoms, have sound legal systems, a favorable tax environment, good security and good schools for their kids." A substantial portion of this newfound wealth may be invested in real estate in cities such as New York or London, and in art, which can easily be shipped to the residences in these safe, global cities.

Another explanation of low financial returns to art could be that the investment in art provides a total return that is a combination of the financial return to art (price appreciation) and the aesthetic benefit to being the owner of the art. The aesthetic (nonfinancial) benefit to owning art includes the joy of viewing and otherwise controlling the art. To the extent that competition drives the total return to similar risk-adjusted levels, there is a trade-off between the financial return and the aesthetic benefit. In artwork overall and perhaps in some artwork in particular, prices are driven higher (and expected financial returns are driven lower) in anticipation of the nonfinancial benefits from ownership.

22.4 R&D AND PATENTS

Research and development (R&D) and patents provide important insights into intellectual property (IP) in the context of the establishment and preservation of property rights. Unlike tangible assets, for which property rights are typically indicated by possession and usually clearly established, IP often raises challenges regarding its potential nonexcludability. This section overviews purchasing, financing, contracting, litigating, exiting, and other issues related to investment in patents.

22.4.1 Estimating Returns to R&D

Economists have devoted substantial effort to theorizing and measuring the returns to R&D expenditures. There are several complications that immediately arise. First, R&D is usually bundled with other assets inside an operating firm. Further, much ambiguity is introduced by the fact that R&D expenditure is typically undertaken over many years and therefore represents an accumulated stock of knowledge against which a flow variable, economic return, must be measured.

The theoretical and empirical evidence on the private returns (captured by the investors) and social returns (captured by all players in the market from spillover effects) to R&D is well described in a survey by Hall, Mairesse, and Mohnen (2009). The survey evidence indicates that the private returns to R&D are positive and greater than for other forms of capital investment, and that the social returns to R&D are higher than the private returns.

22.4.2 Accessing R&D through Patents

Investors have historically accessed the returns to R&D through private or public equity investments in operating entities. However, to the extent that patents or other protected IP represents the crystallization of prior R&D, ownership of patents may represent a mechanism for accessing the benefits of R&D without bearing the operational risk associated with broader investments in companies that own such IP. **Investments in patents** can take multiple forms, such as direct acquisition or indirect acquisition through firms or funds that specialize in the acquisition and monetization of IP.

Six key strategies for acquisition of and exit from (monetizing) patent-related IP are:

1. Acquisition and licensing
2. Enforcement and litigation

3. Sale license-back
4. Orphan patent pooling
5. Patent sales
6. Lending strategies

These strategies are detailed in the next four subsections.[12]

22.4.3 Patent Acquisition and Licensing Strategies

Acquisition and licensing strategies are generally built around agreements regarding royalty streams. Examples of key terms between the licensor/grantor and the licensee include:

- **Minimum royalty provision:** If the royalties do not hit the contracted amount within a specified commercialization period, the licensor may either terminate the license or make the license nonexclusive.
- **Field of use provisions:** A licensor may grant an exclusive license for a geographical region or a particular market.
- **Reservation of rights provision:** The grantor may make use of the patent, most often for noncommercial research uses.
- **Improvements provisions:** These are provisions dealing with improvements to the patent whereby a more efficient method is created (but the new method would arguably infringe on the claims of the patent); improvements are a difficult part of the license negotiations, because either the licensor or the licensee may be the originator of the improvement.
- **Audit/reporting/payment due date obligations:** Licensors may want to monitor the licensee's royalty payments.
- **Exclusivity responsibilities:** Generally, the licensor has (sometimes limited) duties to enforce exclusivity, while the licensee has to report infringement cases to the licensor. This varies a great deal from license to license.

In general, license rates are typically specified as a function of revenues associated with products built on the licensed technology.

22.4.4 Patent Enforcement and Litigation Strategies

Ownership of patents may require patent enforcement and litigation to protect the value of the IP. In fact, an IP investment strategy can be to acquire patents or other protected international property that the potential purchaser believes is being infringed upon in the marketplace.

Typically, the investor who believes that her patent is the subject of infringement will approach users of the technology and seek to negotiate a license agreement with infringers. This is usually far more cost effective than litigation. However, should agreement and licensing not be achieved, the owner of a patent may seek litigation.

---

[12] Descriptive information in this section is largely derived or adapted from Wood Creek (2008).

While subject to risks and requiring substantial expertise in addition to the time and cost of the litigation, actual patent litigation tends to proceed in a relatively orderly fashion, with most patent cases being resolved through settlement. For example, Janicke (2007) finds that most patent litigation ($\sim$80%) is resolved through settlement rather than trial. Further, he shows evidence, shown in Exhibit 22.9, that settlement rates have been relatively stable through time.

The difficulty with settlements, however, is that their terms are not generally reported, so it is difficult to evaluate from public data the extent to which settlement-based outcomes generate sufficient risk-adjusted returns. While settlement-based outcomes are difficult to evaluate, it is known that cases resolved through trial generate median awards of $10 million.

In evaluating the returns to litigation, a key factor is the amount of time that it takes to resolve a case, in part because length of time is positively correlated with costs, but also because the longer the case, the longer it takes to redeploy capital in new cases. The timing of resolutions is illustrated in Exhibit 22.10, with the stylized facts that:

- Defaults (represented by the first bar in the Nonsettled Cases 2006 chart) have the shortest time to resolution.
- Summary judgments (represented by the next six bars in the chart) range from 5 months to 35 months in duration.
- Trials (represented by bars 8 to 10 in the same chart) generally take between 35 and 50 months to resolve.
- Late dispositions (shown in the final bar on the chart) take the most time to resolve: upwards of 50 months.

22.4.5 Patent Sale License-Back and Financing Strategies

The patent sale license-back (SLB) strategy parallels the sale lease-back transactions of the real estate world. In an SLB, the patent holder sells one or more patents to a buyer, who then licenses those patents back to the original holder. In doing so, a patent seller is benefiting from the ability to monetize a portion of the intangible assets. The patent buyer then places the patent in a pool of similar technologies for out-licensing to other parties. Often, the patent buyer will participate in the licensing revenue from new licensees. By allowing the patent to be pooled with other patents, the patent owner can benefit from revenue participation generated from the potential synergies of the pooled patents.

There is also a potentially substantial tax benefit if a company lends a patent to an IP holding company in a jurisdiction with a lower tax regime than the previous patent holder. However, it is important to note that SLBs can incur structural problems. A borrower who has transferred title of the patent may have difficulty bringing infringement actions.

Lending strategies backed by patents are typically separated into two classes of transactions, depending on the quality of the underlying IP:

1. *Securitization:* Lending backed by IP collateral; this allows separation of the IP owner's credit risk from the risk of holding the IP through the bankruptcy process.

EXHIBIT 22.9 Outcomes of Patent Litigation

	2006 Results		Comparative Results		
Mode of Disposition			2004: Patent Cases (2,362)	1986: Patent Cases (1,013)	1979: Patent Cases (786)
ADJUDICATED					
Summary judgment	170	(7.0%)	157 (7%)	78 (7.6%)	58 (7.6%)
Jury trial	52	(2.2%)	60 (2.5%)	20 (2.0%)	17 (7.6%)
Bench trial	22	(0.9%)	18 (0.7%)	53 (5%)	66 (7.6%)
Want of prosecution	31	(1.3%)	38 (1.6%)	16	14
No jurisdiction	24	(0.9%)	34 (1.4%)	10	8
Default	28	(1.2%)	26 (1.1%)	23	2
Total adjudicated:	327	(13.5%)	333 (14%)	190 (19%)	165 (21%)
SETTLED					
Consent judgment	124	(5.1%)	144 (6%)	150	140
Voluntary dismissal	611	(25.3%)	617 (26%)	673 (All agreed dismissals included)	481 (All agreed dismissals included)
Dismissal stating settlement	1,045	(43.3%)	931 (39%)		
Other dismissals	309	(12.8%)	337 (14%)	Included	Included
Total settled	2,089	(86.5%)	2029 (86%)	823 (81%)	621 (79%)

Source: Janicke (2007).

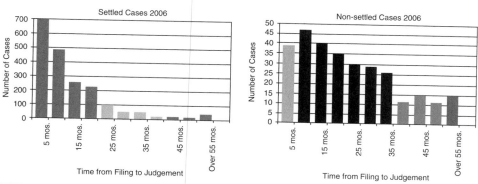

EXHIBIT 22.10   Time to Resolution for Settled Cases versus Non-Settled Cases, 2006
Source: Janicke (2007).

2. *Mezzanine IP lending:* Lending secured by IP collateral; this usually includes warrants or other upside.

22.4.6   Patent Sales and Pooling

Patent owners seeking to divest patents must find buyers. Traditionally, patent buyers have entered the market for one of three reasons:

1. To purchase patents for operational use
2. To purchase patents to use as "trading cards"
3. To purchase a patent for strategic use: In this scenario, the purchaser may use the patent for defensive protection in negotiating with patent dealers.

A fourth (and emerging) class of patent buyers is made up of IP asset managers looking to buy patents for monetary exploitation.

Patent pooling is more complex than in-house licensing because of the need to divide royalty income based on revenue-sharing formulas. This can be a practical solution in industries with set standards and large quantities of patented technologies.

Two recent patent pools that were highly effective at setting industry standards were the establishment of the Moving Picture Experts Group (MPEG) patent pools and the DVD patent pools. Even though multiple pools had to be formed (for different MPEG formats and different DVD formats), it meant that licensees dealt with only one of a couple of pools, rather than a myriad of individual companies. This simplification led to the success of both technologies.

22.4.7   Risks to Investment in Patents

While there are many strategies involving patent assets, there are also many risks:

- *Illiquidity.* IP assets are highly illiquid assets, which often cannot easily be monetized.
- *Technology/operational risk.* For investors buying cash flow streams generated by IP or purchasing debt collateralized by IP, technological risk and operational

risk (which may limit the investors' ability to capitalize on the IP) are major concerns; cash flows depend on successful operation of the asset, particularly when the asset is prone to heavy competitive pressure (e.g., brands or technology in a fast-moving space).

- *Obsolescence*. If new technology displaces current IP, the asset may be rendered worthless.
- *Macroeconomic/sector risk*. If macroeconomic or sector-specific factors drive down an industry, this can have significant effects on the value of a patent or a company's ability to produce cash flows from the patent.
- *Regulatory risk*. IP represents government-issued rights; at any point, the government could change the structure of IP authority or impose regulation on licensing/sales activities.
- *Legal risk*. IP transactions require a thorough understanding of IP law; failure to account for all legal implications of a transaction could result in a loss of IP value.
- *Expiration risk*. A patent's life is 20 years (with some exceptions for extensions, primarily in the pharmaceutical space).

22.5 CONCLUSION

This chapter reviews three primary forms of IP that can serve as the basis for direct investments offering new sources of return as well as salutary effects on an investment portfolio. In the case of film production and distribution, profitability differs according to attributes such as genre, but may generally be viewed as offering return distributions skewed to the right, similar to private equity returns. Art provides a long and plentiful history of transactions data from which estimation of historical risk and return is possible. Art has offered relatively low returns with moderate levels of risk and is subject to high transaction costs. Finally, R&D and patents are emerging as stand-alone investments potentially offering high returns but requiring expertise in the underlying assets.

Commodities

Key Concepts in Commodity Market Analysis

23.1 INTRODUCTION

Commodity investment and analysis often include a number of concepts that are unique to commodities. This is due to the fact that commodities are fundamentally different from many traditional securities. Financial securities are claims on a profit-generating enterprise,[1] while commodities are simply raw materials used in the production of goods and services. Even among alternative investment strategies, commodity strategies are unique. Most alternative investments are trading strategies based on the purchase and sale of traditional securities. For example, hedge funds typically utilize publicly traded stocks and bonds. The valuation methods and risk factors of private equity strategies are closely related to those of public equity strategies. Investment strategies such as those based on earnings per share (EPS) forecasting or value-based investing, which are effective when applied to traditional assets, may not be effective when applied to commodities.

The opposite is also true. Effective commodity strategies based on an understanding of seasonal patterns in commodity demand, market pressures leading to the existence of backwardation and contango, do not always work as well in traditional markets. While some of this is due to differences in the way the commodity and traditional securities markets are organized, it is also due to the fundamental difference between the economic and market factors driving traditional equity and fixed-income securities versus those driving commodities.[2] When we discuss commodity investment, the primary focus tends to be on commodity futures markets for two reasons. First, the large majority of commodity investment is directly or indirectly effected through futures and forwards. Second, and as importantly, futures markets are the primary venue for price discovery in most commodity markets. However, it is important to note that exposure to commodities can be attained through a variety of vehicles ranging from direct ownership of a physical commodity to investment in a

---

[1] In *SEC v. W.J. Howey Company*, the Supreme Court affirmed the definition of a security as "a variety of situations where individuals were led to invest money in a common enterprise with the expectation that they would earn a profit solely from the efforts of the promoter or of someone other than themselves."

[2] The returns in commodity futures investing are due to highly nuanced factors. For background, see Till (2006) and Kazemi et al. (2007).

mutual fund that focuses on commodity-based equities. These investment vehicles will be discussed in greater detail in Chapter 26. This chapter focuses on the key concepts relating to commodity futures and forwards.

23.2 REAL ASSETS AND FINANCIAL ASSETS

Commodities are real assets. **Real assets** are sometimes called economic assets, as they can be used or consumed. They are tangible and intangible assets with intrinsic value that offer a reasonable expectation of inflation protection. Real estate, factories, patents, certain types of real options, and human capital are examples of real assets. Economists distinguish between two types of real assets: durable and nondurable. Durable assets are employed in the production of wealth but are not consumed in the process. Materials are used during production and can be either durable or nondurable. For example, production of airplane travel uses durable assets (airplanes, airports) as well as nondurable assets (jet fuel, roasted peanuts, etc.) that are used up in the production process. Many other inputs are also required for airplane travel, of course, including human capital (pilots, ground crews) and management of these assets by corporate executives.

Financial assets are claims on the income that is derived from the use of real assets. A financial asset may also have an ownership claim on the real assets themselves. For example, the stockholders of an airline company are entitled to share in the income generated by using real assets such as airplanes, jet fuel, and peanuts. If the airline company owns the airplanes, the stockholders will also share in the profits or losses when airplanes are sold.

23.3 THE ROLE OF INVESTORS IN COMMODITY MARKETS

Noncommercial investors in commodity markets have historically been called speculators. The term *speculation* is applied differently in commodity markets vis-à-vis the traditional financial markets, where it has negative connotations because it has often been viewed as a trading activity not based on economic necessity, one that may causes market distortions that harm commercial users of the futures markets as well as other market participants, including certain investors. It is generally accepted that **speculators** in commodity markets play an important economic function because their investment adds liquidity to the market, which makes it easier for other participants to manage risk. This function of speculators is often compared to insurance, in that speculators are willing to accept risks that commercial firms would prefer not to bear. The following definitions of a speculator and of the quantity of a commodity held by a speculator (speculative stocks) come from one of the seminal articles on commodity markets, entitled "Speculation and Economic Stability" (Kaldor 1939).

> *Speculation . . . may be defined as the purchase (or sale) of goods with a view to re-sale (re-purchase) at a later date, where the motive behind such action is the expectation of a change in the relevant prices . . . and not a gain accruing through their use, or any kind of transformation effected in them or their transfer between different markets.*

> *Speculative stocks of anything may be defined as the difference between the amount actually held and the amount that would be held, if other things being the same, the price of that thing were expected to remain unchanged.* (Kaldor 1939)

In Kaldor's view, there were only two types of positions: speculative trades and nonspeculative trades. Speculators always speculate. Nonspeculators buy or sell commodities for reasons that may include an expectation of profit from a change in price, but must include some other reason as well, such as traditional business-related activities like production, transportation, and warehousing. This may also apply to certain noncommercial investors in commodity markets. An investor who holds commodities for reasons other than price appreciation is not speculating. These reasons could include inflation hedging, currency hedging, and hedging against a change in other asset prices. The key, according to Kaldor, is to determine the quantity and variety of commodities an investor would hold if "the price of that thing were expected to remain unchanged." That portion of an investor's commodity holdings would be deemed nonspeculative. The remainder (positive or negative) would be considered speculative stocks.

Another seminal study in this area is Working (1949), which takes an approach slightly different than Kaldor's, defining **hedging** as any futures activity conducted by those who handle the physical commodity, and speculative trading as any activity that is not hedging. The difference between these approaches is subtle but important. While both definitions would reach the same conclusion about the vast majority of hedging and speculative positions, there are some noteworthy exceptions.

23.4 CONVENIENCE YIELD

All real assets have a **convenience yield**, which is the benefit that comes from physical possession of an asset. It is literally a measure of the convenience of having the asset available to use. Alternatively, it is a measure of how much a buyer would pay to avoid the inconvenience of constantly ordering new quantities of the asset and worrying that the supply of the asset will not arrive when needed. It is an economic benefit, not a monetary benefit. Continuing the airline example, the convenience yield of having sufficient fuel for an airplane is quite high if the airline has routes that need to be flown. If the airline has more airplanes than it needs, given travel demand (as in October 2001, for example), the convenience yield of available fuel for an additional airplane is quite low, or possibly almost zero.[3] However, if the number of airplanes held by an airline is equal to traveler demand, the convenience yield for materials such as jet fuel is quite high, since the production of air travel is impossible without it. Convenience yields vary with the level of inventories. As inventories decline, the convenience yield rises, as consumers will pay more to ensure adequate supplies to operate their businesses.

---

[3] Common practice is to require that the convenience yield be nonnegative, except for assets such as nuclear waste that have negative market prices and are not easily disposed. The cost associated with maintaining and storing a surplus airplane is accounted for under carrying costs, not as part of the convenience yield.

Measuring the convenience yield of a real asset is difficult, because it differs for every user and may be different for the same user from one day to the next. Alternatively, what can be measured using market prices is the marginal convenience yield, which is the lowest convenience yield that will match buyers with sellers. Buyers who have a higher convenience yield will earn a **consumer surplus**. A consumer surplus is the difference between the highest price a buyer would be willing to pay (the reservation price) and the actual market price. If the price is lower than the reservation price, the buyer earns a surplus. Because we cannot observe the reservation price of each buyer, we cannot measure the total amount of convenience yield that is earned.

The convenience yield of a commodity is often compared to the dividend stream paid by a stock, because in both cases there is a return that is paid to the owner of the asset that is not paid to owners of derivatives based on the asset. Owners of equity futures contracts or stock options do not receive cash dividends. Similarly, owners of commodity futures contracts do not receive the convenience yield. Owners of stock options and equity futures contracts can earn implicit dividends, since the size and frequency of stock dividends is captured by derivatives pricing models. Similarly, owners of commodity futures contracts implicitly earn a portion of the commodity's marginal convenience yield, because the marginal convenience yield is incorporated into commodity futures pricing equations. However, comparing a convenience yield to a dividend yield overlooks some important differences between commodities and equities. Most significant is that convenience yield is unique to the user of the asset, whereas dividend yield is the same for all holders of a share of stock.

23.5 COST OF CARRY

The **cost of carry** is equivalent to the cost of storing a commodity. The major components of the cost of carry include:

- *Financing costs.* The standard assumption is that storage is fully financed, and that the financing cost is the cost of capital the firm applies to working capital.
- *Storage costs.* These costs include rental of storage facilities, insurance, inspections, transportation costs, and maintenance costs (e.g., cattle feed).
- *Spoilage.* This is the loss of value that may naturally occur through storage.

In Exhibit 23.1, if the commodity is needed three months in the future, in theory it would make no difference to the buyers whether they paid $4.25 today in addition to $0.31525 in storage costs or paid a futures price of $4.56525 for delivery in three months' time. For these calculations, we ignore commissions and transaction costs.

$$\text{Cost of carry} = \text{Financing cost} + \text{Storage cost} + \text{Spoilage cost}$$

If the futures price were higher than $4.56525, the buyer could profit by purchasing more of the commodity than needed and simultaneously selling the additional quantity in the futures market. This trade is known as **cash-and-carry arbitrage**.

If the futures price is below $4.56525, then the buyer may choose to use the futures market for delivery or may choose to purchase the commodity today. The

EXHIBIT 23.1   Cost of Carry Example

		Monthly Carry Cost
Spot price per bushel	$4.250	
Storage cost per month	$0.030	$0.03000
Insurance per month	$0.015	$0.01500
Spoilage rate per month	0.50%	$0.02125
Financing rate per month	0.60%	$0.02550
Total monthly cost per bushel		$0.09175
Transport to or from storage	$0.020	
Total storage costs for three months		$0.27525
Transportation cost (round trip)		$0.04000
Total cost of carry		$0.31525
Break-even futures price (spot + carry)		$4.56525

choice will depend on the buyer's convenience yield. If the buyer's convenience yield is $0.10 per month, then the break-even futures price would be $4.26525 (the spot price plus storage and transportation costs minus convenience yield).

As with the convenience yield, the cost of carry for a commodity varies from user to user. The cost of carry also depends on seasonal factors and on the amount of the commodity in storage at a particular time. For example, when crude oil stocks are low, the cost of storage is relatively low, since there is ample capacity in storage facilities. Conversely, when stocks of oil are high, the cost of storing increases as storage capacity is in scarce supply.

23.6   THEORIES OF COMMODITY FORWARD CURVES

The price of a commodity for delivery in the future can be higher or lower than the price of that commodity for immediate delivery. When the price for delivery in the future (the future price) is higher than the price for immediate delivery (the spot price), we say that the **forward curve** is upward sloping. This is also termed **contango**, as illustrated in Exhibit 23.2.[4] When the future price is below the spot price, we say the forward curve is downward sloping, or in **backwardation**.

The theories for why commodity forward curves slope up or down are similar to theories that try to explain why yield curves slope up or down. In the context of commodity markets, nonspeculative or commercial accounts are typically segregated into producers and users of the commodity. In fixed-income markets, we can think of borrowers as producers of bonds, and lenders as users of bonds. To expand on this

---

[4] This awkward term is nineteenth-century British equity trading jargon for a fee that was paid by the buyer of shares to the seller on the settlement date in order to defer payment for the shares until some future date, a trade similar to today's repurchase agreement. It is assumed to be derived from the word *continuation*. On some occasions, either because of a large short interest that was being rolled or due to dividend payments, the contango fees would be negative, or backwards, which gives us the equally awkward term *backwardation*.

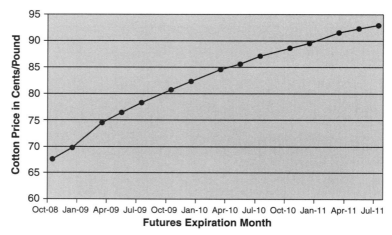

EXHIBIT 23.2   Upward-Sloping Commodity Curve (Contango) ICE Cotton, September 1, 2008
Source: Intercontinental Exchange (ICE).

analogy, borrowers typically have a preferred maturity date in mind when issuing bonds, but are willing to shorten or extend that maturity date if market conditions dictate. Also, a borrower may increase the quantity of bonds issued if the price is attractive. Similarly, buyers of bonds (lenders) typically consider the prices of bonds with differing maturities when making decisions.

Borrowers and lenders also make hedging decisions. A borrower can decide to lock in the interest rate today for a project that will be funded in the future. Alternatively, the borrower can wait until the project begins to issue bonds. These decisions are similar to a commodity producer's decision to sell future production in the forward market or to wait and sell the commodity at the future spot price. The literature on commodity forward curves and yield curves has tended to use different terminology, but both are ultimately trying to explain the interaction among producers, users, and speculators in establishing forward prices.

23.6.1 Rational Expectations

The **rational expectations hypothesis** holds that the price of an asset for delivery in the future must be the same as the market's current forecast of the spot price of the asset on the future delivery date.[5]

Till (1997) quotes the following regarding the work of Hicks, who further developed the hypothesis that commodity futures prices tend to be downwardly biased estimates of future spot prices in his 1939 book, *Value and Capital: An*

---

[5] Rational expectations models have been explored by a number of researchers across many fields, including fixed income and commodity pricing. Hicks (1939) is commonly credited with applying these concepts to forward commodity prices, although according to Evans and Honkapohja (2001), the phrase *rational expectations* was first used in a 1946 article by Hurwicz.

Inquiry into Some Fundamental Principles of Economic Theory. Hicks addressed a key element of economist John Maynard Keynes's hypothesis that it is producers who desire to use the futures markets to hedge unpredictable, volatile spot price risk. This hypothesis raises several questions: What about consumers? Wouldn't they be long hedgers? If one has both long hedgers and short hedgers, why should the futures price be downwardly biased? These questions were answered by Hicks:

> *There are quite sufficient technical rigidities in the process of production to make it certain that a number of entrepreneurs will want to hedge their sales for this reason; supplies in the near future are largely governed by decisions taken in the past, so that if these planned supplies can be covered by forward sales, risk is reduced.*
>
> *But although the same thing sometimes happens with planned purchases as well, it is almost inevitably rarer; technical conditions give the entrepreneur a much freer hand about the acquisition of inputs (which are largely needed to start new processes) than about the completion of outputs (whose process of production—in the ordinary business sense—may be already begun). Thus, while there is likely to be some desire to hedge planned purchases, it tends to be less insistent than the desire to hedge planned sales. If forward markets consisted entirely of hedgers, there would always be a tendency for a relative weakness on the demand side; a smaller proportion of planned purchases than of planned sales would be covered by forward contracts.*
>
> *But for this very reason forward markets rarely consist entirely of hedgers. The futures price (say, for one month's delivery) which would be made by the transactions of hedgers alone would be determined by causes that have nothing to do with the causes ordinarily determining market price; it would therefore be widely different from the spot price which any sensible person would expect to rule in a month's time, and would ordinarily be much below that expected price. Futures prices are therefore nearly always made partly by speculators, who seek a profit by buying futures when the futures price is below the spot price they expect to rule on the corresponding date; their action tends to raise the futures price to a more reasonable level.*
>
> *But it is of the essence of speculation, as opposed to hedging, that the speculator puts himself into a more risky position as a result of his forward trading—he need not have ventured into forward dealing at all, and would have been safer if he had not done so. He will therefore only be willing to go on buying futures so long as the futures price remains definitely below the spot price he expects; for it is the difference between these prices which he can expect to receive as a return for his risk-bearing, and it will not be worth his while to undertake the risk if the prospective return is too small.* (Hicks 1939)

In essence, Hicks's theory is that producers are in a more vulnerable position than consumers, and so will be under more pressure to hedge than consumers. This leads to a "relative weakness on the demand side" of commodity futures markets.

For example, assume that a survey of participants in the copper market (appropriately weighted for the relative impact of each on the overall market) found that the price in one year was expected to fall by 5%. The rational expectations model would predict that the price for delivery of copper in one year would be 5% below the current spot price. Any other price would violate the hypothesis.

Rational expectations models hold up well in laboratory settings, which are, essentially, perfect markets with no transaction costs, taxes, or borrowing constraints, and in markets in which some portion of the traders are risk neutral. Rational expectations models have not proven to be a useful method for explaining commodity forward curves. This does not mean that commodity markets are irrational, but merely that the assumptions about perfect markets and risk neutrality are too strong for these markets.

The mechanism that drives rational expectations models is relative value arbitrage. Speculators who identify prices on the forward curve that deviate from their expected values either can purchase or sell those commodities outright, or can enter into spread trades by purchasing the commodity at one point on the curve and selling it at another.

23.6.2 Normal Backwardation/Preferred Habitat

Keynes argued in 1930 that commodity futures prices should typically be lower than the rational expectations prices defined in the previous section. Keynes defined **normal backwardation**[6] as the tendency of commodity futures contracts to trade at prices below the rational expectations price.

This argument was based on the assumption that producers of a commodity have a strong incentive to lock in a price today for future production by selling futures contracts, but that users of the commodity have a strong incentive to purchase at spot prices. If there is a natural oversupply of futures contracts, then speculators will enter the market to purchase the excess supply, but only at a discount. Alternatively, discounts for future delivery may entice more users to lock in the price.

The economic rationale for this theory is that producers of a commodity have predictable production costs, so locking in a future price for their goods is equivalent to locking in a profit margin. Users, in contrast, prefer the flexibility offered by the spot market.[7] In the fixed-income world, this argument is similar to the **preferred habitat hypothesis**. This hypothesis holds that producers of bonds (borrowers) prefer long maturities, whereas consumers of bonds (lenders) prefer short maturities. Producers offer attractive yields, which would mean low bond prices, to entice borrowers

---

[6] Normal backwardation and backwardation are similar, but not identical, terms. A market is in backwardation if the futures price is lower than the spot price. A market is in normal backwardation if the futures price is lower than the expected spot price. Since the expected spot price cannot be observed, we can never know if a market is in normal backwardation.

[7] This theory is more applicable in markets where costs are easily passed along to final consumers. For example, the owner of a gasoline station has no incentive to lock in the wholesale price of gasoline six months forward, since any price increase is easily passed along to customers. An airline, on the other hand, has a stronger incentive to lock in the cost of jet fuel, since fuel costs are difficult to pass along to buyers of airplane travel.

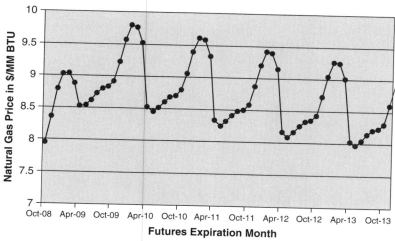

EXHIBIT 23.3 Forward Curve for Natural Gas Illustrates the Storage Effect NYMEX Natural Gas, September 1, 2008
Source: New York Mercantile Exchange (NYMEX).

to extend their maturity, or to induce speculators to borrow at short maturities and lend at long maturities.[8]

23.6.3 Storage Models

The relationship between spot and forward prices for a commodity depends, to a large degree, on the relationship between current storage levels and expected storage levels in the future. Storage models also consider the cost and feasibility of storing a commodity for an extended period of time, and of transporting it to other locations for delivery. Commodities that can be either expensive or difficult to store, such as natural gas and live cattle, can have forward curves with steep positive or negative slopes. This is because relative value arbitrage trades can be very difficult to hedge with physical positions. In the case of natural gas (see Exhibit 23.3), storage is feasible but becomes quite expensive as physical storage capacity limits are approached. Inadequate storage capacity for peak winter demand can result in exceptionally steep positively sloped forward curves during the fall-winter period in the natural gas futures curve (Till 2008b). In comparison, live cattle are arguably nonstorable. The animal degrades after getting to market weight, resulting in a historical tendency for backwardation (Helmuth 1981).

Storage models of a commodity forward curve predict that the curve will be upward sloping when the current inventory levels are beyond the threshold levels of demand, and that it will be downward sloping when inventories are tight. Storage

---

[8] An upward-sloping yield curve is the same as a downward-sloping forward curve for bond prices.

models are unique to real assets. They do not have a corresponding model in fixed income, because storage and transportation of bonds is effectively free.[9] Another factor incorporated into storage models is the risk of **stock-out**. Stock-out occurs when storage drops effectively to zero, and consumption is then dependent entirely on production and transportation networks. The risk of a stock-out typically occurs in markets with peak seasonal demand, such as natural gas or heating oil, or annual crop cycles such as grains. To avoid stock-out, users of a commodity have an incentive to hedge more actively at points on the forward calendar that are most susceptible to stock-out. These would be the months just before harvest for annual crops, and the later part of the heating season for natural gas and heating oil.

23.6.4 Other Models and Special Cases

In certain markets, the users of a commodity rarely use the forward market to hedge future supplies. These particular markets typically exist for products that are directly consumed by the public, such as gasoline. This phenomenon is explained by the **liquidity preference hypothesis**. It is an extreme case of the preferred habitat hypothesis, in which there is an insufficient natural commercial long position in the futures markets, so some long positions must be taken up by speculators in order to balance the market.

Another special case is a **segmented market**. Segmented markets are markets for the same product that, due to geography or other market frictions, operate relatively independently of each other, and consequently the price of the product in one market does not influence the price in the other.[10] A market can be segregated across time as well. For example, the spot market for a product may be dominated by one set of buyers and sellers, and the market for delivery in the future dominated by a different set of buyers and sellers. When this happens, the forward curve for the commodity provides little useful information, as spot market players ignore what is happening in the futures market, and vice versa.[11] In certain markets, the users of the commodity have a stronger need to hedge than the producers have. This is the opposite of normal backwardation, where it is assumed that the producer has the strongest incentive to hedge. When this occurs, the forward curve would be upward sloping, as users of the commodity would need to entice sellers to sell the commodity in the forward market rather than the spot market. An upward-sloping forward curve is termed contango. The natural gas market in the United States may exhibit this property. Utilities are believed to purchase more natural gas in the forward market than they are likely to need, in order to plan for spikes in demand. When this demand does not materialize,

---

[9] The cost of financing a position is a component of both storage models and fixed-income models, but that is not generally considered a storage cost. Storage costs for bonds would consist of custody services.

[10] Good examples of this are the natural gas markets in North America and in Europe. Because the cost of shipping liquefied natural gas (LNG) from Europe to North America is high, the markets are effectively segregated. Markets for water are typically segregated across much smaller geographical regions.

[11] There is reasonable empirical evidence that the long-term market for crude oil (beyond 18 months) is segmented from shorter-term delivery. See Lautier (2005) for a discussion of this research.

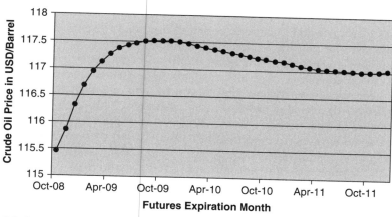

EXHIBIT 23.4 A Humped Forward Curve: NYMEX Crude Oil, September 1, 2008
Source: New York Mercantile Exchange (NYMEX).

the utilities sell the surplus gas in the spot market. This results in an upward-sloping curve, as shown in Exhibit 23.2.

In recent years, the crude oil futures curve has often been humped, which means the market is in contango in the short term, but gives way to inverted markets for longer-maturity contracts (see Exhibit 23.4). Contango refers to the condition when long-term futures prices are higher than short-term futures prices. Since the current spot price can be viewed as a futures contract with no time to delivery, contango can also refer to the idea that futures prices are higher than current spot prices. **Normal contango** refers to the relationship between futures prices and expected spot prices. Specifically, normal contango is when the futures price is believed to be higher than the expected spot price. Since we cannot directly observe the expected spot price, we can only estimate whether a market is in normal contango.

Option-based models of the term structure focus on two types of real options embedded in commodity markets. The first is the option to extract a natural resource. A copper mine can be shut down if the price of copper falls below the marginal cost of production. While there may be times when the spot price of copper falls below its marginal cost of production due to a temporary glut, producers will not sell forward production below cost; they will shut down the mine. The option to extract the resource dampens the volatility of commodity prices for future delivery.

The second real option embedded in the commodity forward curve is related to inventories. Commodity markets generally have higher volatility when prices are rising than when they are falling. This is because shortages tend to cause more problems than surpluses. The volatility asymmetry favors owning physical inventory (or short-dated futures contracts) over longer-dated futures contracts. All other things being equal, this factor will tend to make commodity forward curves flatten.

23.6.5 Speculation and Market Impacts

While much of the regulation of traditional security markets focuses on the use of private information and outright fraud, commodity futures regulation often focuses on market manipulation through excessive position size or order flow. Since the prices of commodities directly impact social welfare, large price increases in commodities (particularly energy and agricultural commodities) tend to generate a great deal of attention (including concerns about price manipulation) from regulators, politicians, academics, and practitioners. For many, the rise in commodity prices may be due in part to speculators, who have historically been defined as traders who take commodity futures positions without the natural hedging needs of the producers and consumers who also trade in physical commodities.

For example, the growth of various commodity prices in 2008 was blamed by some on the existence of speculators who increased their investment in newly created commodity indices (see Masters and White 2008), while academics tended to focus on the impact of fundamental supply and demand pressures (see Till 2009, Plante and Yücel 2011, and Black 2009). It is a matter of debate as to whether institutional investors are speculators in commodity markets, as some believe that these investors may require the use of commodity futures to hedge their natural exposures to inflation risk.

Commodity index investment became viable with the introduction of the Goldman Sachs Commodity Index (GSCI) in 1991. Commodity index investment experienced modest growth through the remainder of the 1990s. However, between 2003 and 2008, commodity index investment grew at a remarkable pace. Since the prices of many commodities experienced extremely large run-ups over the same time period, there was a great deal of concern that the run-up in commodity prices was a direct result of the demand for commodity futures resulting from growth in commodity index investing.

While it is beyond the scope of this section to fully address this issue,[12] there are a number of points that are worth considering in assessing the impact of investors in commodity markets.

As mentioned throughout this chapter, futures markets differ considerably from traditional security markets. With stocks or bonds, a limited number of securities are outstanding at any point in time. In order for new funds to flow into these markets, some investors must be willing to sell their securities.[13] In contrast, since futures markets are derivatives, new futures positions can be generated at any time. When an investor opens a long position in a futures contract, the other side can be an existing long closing a position or a new short opening a position. Thus, there is always a balanced open interest in any futures contract. Furthermore, one must consider the fact that commodity index investors do not take physical delivery of the underlying commodities. They close their futures positions prior to expiration and roll their exposure into new futures with a longer time to expiration. That is not to say that futures prices cannot impact spot prices. In markets in which price discovery is in the futures, it is natural to believe that spot prices will respond to changes in futures prices through the term structure (cost of carry) relationship between them. However, if one believes that commodity index traders put upward pressure on longer-term futures from their long positions, then it makes little sense to ignore the

---

[12] For further reading, see Stoll and Whaley (2011); Pirrong (1994); Till (2009); Masters and White (2008); Tilburg and Stichele (2011); Irwin, Sanders, and Merrin (2009); and Black (2009).

[13] Of course, a firm will issue new stocks and bonds from time to time.

downward pressure they might exert from their selling of short-term futures as the contracts are rolled. Thus, one might argue that the primary impact of index traders may be to increase the slope of the futures term structure. One would expect that this impact would be seen in inventory levels, since increased contango encourages delayed consumption.

Data limitations further complicate the matter. Prior to the introduction of the Disaggregated Commitments of Traders (DCOT) report of the Commodity Futures Trading Commission (CFTC) in 2009, the data for an effective analysis were essentially unavailable. While the release of the DCOT report has fostered a great deal of research in the area, the report is not without its limitations.[14] Since the CFTC has the only direct access to the raw data on which much of the extant literature is indirectly based, it is certainly worth noting the results of their analysis of the data. On May 20, 2008, in his written testimony before the Senate Committee on Homeland Security and Governmental Affairs, Jeffrey Harris, Chief Economist of the CFTC, made the following statements regarding the issue:

All the data modeling and analysis we have done to date indicates there is little economic evidence to demonstrate that prices are being systematically driven by speculators in these markets. Generally, the data shows that:

- *Prices have risen sharply for many commodities that have neither developed futures markets (e.g., Durham wheat, steel, iron ore, coal, etc.) nor institutional fund investments (Minneapolis wheat and Chicago rice).*
- *Markets where index trading is greatest as a percentage of total open interest (live cattle and hog futures) have actually suffered from falling prices during the past year.*
- *The level of speculation in the agriculture commodity and the crude oil markets has remained relatively constant in percentage terms as prices have risen.*
- *Our studies in agriculture and crude oil markets have found that speculators tend to follow trends in prices rather than set them.*
- *Speculators such as managed money traders are both buyers and sellers in these markets. For example, data shows that there are almost as many bearish funds as bullish funds in wheat and crude oil.*

The current literature on whether speculation is helpful or harmful is summarized by the G20 Study Group on Commodities (2011) as follows: "The expansion of market participants in commodity markets increases market liquidity (including in longer-term contracts), thereby accommodating the hedging needs of producers and consumers. ... On the other hand ... increased correlation of commodity derivatives markets and other financial markets suggests a higher risk of spillovers."

---

[14] See www.cftc.gov/ucm/groups/public/@commitmentsoftraders/documents/file/disaggregat edcotexplanatorynot.pdf for an explanation of some limitations of the various formats of the Commitments of Traders reports.

As a final point, while there are many definitions of speculation, the CFTC defines a speculator as: "In commodity futures, a trader who does not hedge, but who trades with the objective of achieving profits through the successful anticipation of outright price movements or through relative price movements in the case of spread trades."[15] However, if investors increasingly demand commodity futures as investable vehicles to reduce portfolio risk, the very concept of speculation may need to be revisited.[16]

---

[15] See CFTC (2008, 69).
[16] For further discussion of current definitions of speculation, see Szado (2011).

CHAPTER 24

Role of Commodities in Asset Allocation

24.1 INTRODUCTION

While it is impossible, in a short synopsis, to convey all of the roles played by commodity investments in asset allocation, this chapter provides a brief outline of the roles of commodity investments and highlights some of the research that has helped foster the interest in commodities as an investment. While a great deal of commodity research dates back 75 or more years, research on the role of commodities in asset allocation began to gain momentum only in the late 1970s. Since then, many publications have shown that commodity investments provide both return enhancement as a stand-alone investment and risk-reduction opportunities for a range of traditional and alternative investments. In addition, commodities have been shown to provide unique investment opportunities relative to investor exposure to inflation and other macroeconomic events. This chapter also discusses the unique sources of returns to commodities and the statistical properties of their returns, as well as the ability of commodities to provide diversification as well as a hedge for inflation risk, business cycle risk, and event risk.

Select Highlights in Commodity Research

1970s	Commodities are viewed as high-risk investments. Most investment is made indirectly, through equities or bonds.
1978	Greer shows that a collateralized basket of commodity futures contracts had lower risk and higher returns than an equity basket (over the time frame of his study).
1980	Bodie and Rosansky illustrate diversification benefits of commodities when added to a stock portfolio.
1988	Fama and French find a strong business cycle component to prices of industrial metals.
1991	Goldman Sachs Commodity Index (GSCI) is introduced.
1995	Froot shows that commodities hedge unexpected inflation.
1997	Bjornson and Carter find that agricultural commodities provide a natural inflation hedge.
1998	Dow Jones–AIG Index is created, later renamed Dow Jones–UBS Index (DJUBSI).
2006	Erb and Harvey and Gorton and Rouwenhorst show that diversification return is a significant contributor to commodity index return.

2008   Many commodities hit high price levels; concern over excessive speculation increases. Schneeweis, Kazemi, and Spurgin find commodity momentum is related to storage and hedging demand.

2011   Stoll and Whaley show commodity index investors are not the primary driver of increasing commodity prices.

24.2 REVIEW OF MAJOR ARTICLES AND STUDIES

It was not until the 1970s that academic studies highlighting the positive role of commodities in institutional portfolios appeared. In a seminal 1978 article published in the *Journal of Portfolio Management*, Greer tackled the issue of perceived risk in commodity futures. He showed that risk in a commodity position could be lowered significantly by full collateralization. Using a data set from 1960 to 1974, Greer calculated the returns of an unleveraged, collateralized basket of commodity futures contracts, including the collateral returns. He showed that such an index had higher returns and a lower maximum drawdown than an index of equities. Greer also pioneered efforts to demonstrate the benefit of diversifying an equities-only portfolio with the addition of commodity futures, showing that a rebalanced portfolio of stocks and commodities provided a steadier and higher rate of return than a stock-only portfolio (Greer 1978). Bodie and Rosansky (1980) echoed Greer's findings, showing that an equally weighted basket of commodity futures (constructed using 1950–1976 data) produced equity-like returns, as long as collateral returns were included. Of equal importance, the mean of the annual loss on the portfolio was significantly lower than if it had held equities only. Furthermore, they found that commodity futures provided valuable diversification benefits for an equity portfolio and were a very effective inflation hedge.

Since then, a steady evolution of research has indicated that commodity investment not only is a good buffer for inflation, but can also provide a profitable source of returns on its own. In addition, and of equal importance, it has been demonstrated that adding commodities to a portfolio can help reduce portfolio volatility. Satyanarayan and Varangis (1994) discussed the issue of portfolio diversification with commodities and its impact on the portfolio's risk-return ratio, or efficient frontier. Specifically, they researched how the efficient frontier changed if commodities were added to international portfolios. Using the recently created Goldman Sachs Commodity Index (GSCI) as a proxy for commodity investments, they found that adding commodities to a portfolio of global stock and bond indices expanded the efficient frontier, providing the same level of return with less risk. Froot (1995) showed that, while a variety of commodity portfolios could effectively hedge a domestic bond portfolio against unexpected inflation, a commodity index must be oil-dominated in order to reduce the risk of domestic equity investments. He found little difference in the hedging effectiveness of spot commodity positions and corresponding commodity futures positions. Furthermore, Froot discovered that commodity-based equities are not effectual hedges, as they act more like equities than commodities. A decade later, Idzorek (2006) showed that the efficient frontier for a diversified portfolio would be improved with commodity futures contracts.

The potential role of commodity investment in institutional portfolios was further clarified by Beenen (2005), who showed that commodities could assist in an institution's pursuit of matching future asset returns against expected liabilities. His study resulted in meaningful allocations to commodities, based on their diversification and risk-reduction potential when combined with other holdings in a pension plan. The diversification potential of commodity investment was further explored by Gorton and Rouwenhorst (2006), who showed that an equally weighted index of commodity futures was negatively correlated with equity and bond returns, but positively correlated with inflation. All of these correlations were found to be most pronounced at five-year holding periods. Gorton and Rouwenhorst also found that the commodities index had roughly the same return and Sharpe ratio as U.S. equities. However, in looking at the equities of firms that produce commodities, they found that the firms' stocks were more highly correlated with the stock market than with the corresponding commodity. This may be reinforced by the fact that an index of the commodity equities underperformed a futures-based commodity index.

Erb and Harvey (2006) took a look at rebalancing (an action that brings portfolio allocations back into line with target allocations), by examining the returns of 16 commodity futures contracts from 1982 to 2004. They found that when correlations are low and asset variances are high, the diversification return from rebalancing can be high. This return from rebalancing (sometimes called **diversification return**) is not unique to commodities. The term was first coined by Booth and Fama (1992), and has been studied for equities, bonds, emerging markets, and multi-asset-class portfolios. Commodities seem particularly well suited for this type of return for two reasons. First, diversification returns are highest when the individual assets in a portfolio are highly volatile and the correlation among those assets is low. Second, frequently rebalancing a portfolio of these assets will result in higher geometric growth rates than infrequently rebalancing. Historically, commodities have satisfied these criteria. To understand the effects of diversification on geometric (i.e., compounded) returns on a portfolio of commodities, consider the approximate relationship between arithmetic return and geometric return. The two figures are calculated as:

$$R_A = \frac{1}{T}(r_1 + r_2 + \cdots + r_T)$$
$$R_G = \sqrt[T]{(1 + r_1)(1 + r_2)\ldots(1 + r_T)} - 1$$

Here, R_A is the arithmetic mean return of the portfolio, R_G is the geometric mean return of the portfolio, and r_i is the annual rate of return on the portfolio for year i. In this case, there are T observations (years). There is an approximate relationship between these two estimates, expressed as:

$$R_G = R_A - \frac{1}{2}Stdev^2$$

The annual volatility (standard deviation) of the return on the portfolio is denoted by *Stdev*. Notice that the arithmetic average return of a portfolio will be equal to the weighted average of the arithmetic averages of returns on n individual commodities futures. That is,

$$R_A = \sum_{j=1}^{n} (w_i \times R_{A,j})$$

Here, $R_{A,j}$ is the arithmetic mean return on commodity j. Therefore, given the arithmetic mean returns on individual commodities, the lower the volatility of the portfolio, the higher the geometric mean return of the portfolio will be. It is well known that the volatility of the portfolio will be low if the commodities included in the portfolio are not highly correlated with each other. Further, if the individual commodities are not highly correlated, the geometric mean return of the portfolio will be significantly higher than the average of the geometric means of the individual commodities. This is because the volatility of the portfolio will be smaller than the average of the volatility of individual commodities. In fact, Erb and Harvey (2006) found that, while the average excess return to individual commodity futures is near zero, the average correlation of commodities with one another is only 0.09. As a result of the low correlation (and relatively high individual commodity volatility), the historical geometric mean of a rebalanced portfolio of commodities is significantly greater than zero. Similarly, Gorton and Rouwenhorst (2006) considered a broad range of commodity futures for the period 1959–2004 and reported that, while the number of commodities with geometric excess returns above zero was about equal to those with geometric excess returns below zero, a portfolio of commodity futures exhibited returns similar to those of equities.

Willenbrock (2011) explained that the diversification return is related to the fact that rebalancing reduces the weight of commodities that have increased in relative value, and increases the allocation to commodities that have declined in relative value. He argued that this return to contrarian trading is a more important driver of the diversification return than the reduction in variance. Frequent rebalancing produces better returns if asset values exhibit mean reversion. Several studies of rebalancing in commodity markets have concluded that the optimal rebalancing window is once every 12 to 18 months, which is consistent with the hypothesis that commodities exhibit long-run mean reversion.[1]

Exhibit 24.1, from Sanders and Irwin (2012), explains diversification return. Consider a 10-period investment in two commodities, each of which has a high volatility but a zero return over the 10 periods. A buy-and-hold investment over the 10 periods will earn a zero return, as the prices at the end of the tenth period are the same as at the beginning of the investment period. However, rebalancing the portfolio produces a different outcome. Rebalancing each period entails the purchase of the underperforming commodity and the sale of the outperforming commodity, returning the portfolio to equally weighted at the end of each period. By the end of the tenth period, the rebalanced portfolio has earned a return of 4%, which can be completely attributed to the diversification return. Sanders and Irwin contend that individual commodity futures markets have long-run returns of zero, but that trading strategies and commodity weights can have a substantial influence on long-term returns.

Till and Eagleeye (2005) suggest that commodities that are difficult to store (either because storage is impossible or expensive or because it is more efficient to leave the commodity stored below ground rather than extracting it) are more likely to be in backwardation and to generate positive returns. In contrast, difficult-to-store

---

[1] Rebalancing returns has been analyzed and discussed by Greer (2000), Gorton and Rouwenhorst (2006), and Till (2006).

EXHIBIT 24.1 Portfolio Diversification Return Example

Time	Price Asset 1	Price Asset 2	Return Asset 1	Return Asset 2	Equal Weighted Return
1	10	ID			
2	20	30	100%	200%	150%
3	30	40	50%	33%	42%
4	40	50	33%	25%	29%
5	50	60	25%	20%	23%
6	50	40	0%	−33%	−17%
7	40	10	−20%	−75%	−48%
8	30	20	−25%	100%	38%
9	20	20	−33%	0%	−17%
10	10	10	−50%	−50%	−50%
	Arithmetic average		9%	24%	17%
	Geometric average		0%	0%	4%

"Diversification return" = 4%

Source: Sanders and Irwin (2012).

commodities tend to exhibit high spot volatility, since the existence of large inventories can dampen price volatility by cushioning the impact of supply-and-demand shocks. Kolb (1996) considered 45 commodity futures markets for the period from 1969 to 1992. Only futures on difficult-to-store commodities had significantly positive returns (crude oil, gasoline, live cattle, live hogs, soybean meal, and copper). These results are consistent with Nash (1997), who states, "The return on a commodity index is proportional to the amount of time the commodity is in backwardation." Gorton, Hayashi, and Rouwenhorst (2007) found that the risk premium of commodity futures varies across commodities and over time, and that a major determinant of the risk premium is the amount of a given commodity held in storage. Using a comprehensive data set on 31 commodity futures and physical inventories between 1969 and 2006, they showed that price measures, such as the futures basis, prior futures returns, and spot returns, reflect the state of inventories and provide useful information about commodity futures risk premiums.

24.3 SOURCES OF RETURN TO FUTURES-BASED COMMODITY INVESTMENT

Returns on commodity futures contracts stem from three sources: a spot return, a risk-free income return or collateral yield, and a roll return.

24.3.1 Spot, Collateral Income, and Roll

The benefits of commodity investment were explained by Anson (1998), who examined the component parts of commodity futures investment return: the spot return, roll yield, and collateral return. Examining data that spanned the years 1985–1997,

Anson showed that the spot return provides a diversification benefit, while the roll yield and collateral return are responsible for the bulk of a commodity investment's total return.

Spot prices increase over time, although historically they have increased less than inflation (Burkart 2006). **Spot returns** result from changes in the value of the underlying cash commodity, and are generally driven by classic market factors, like fluctuations in supply and demand for that asset. These factors can be the result of weather patterns or crop sizes for agricultural commodities, seasonal issues like weather or driving patterns for energy, and growth in real demand for base metals. Anson (1998) pointed out that periods of financial and economic distress can lead to market conditions that are often favorable for spot commodity prices. Because spot commodity prices tend to mean-revert over longer time horizons, spot prices cannot usually be positive sources of return over longer periods (Till 2006).

The **income return** (or **collateral yield**) of a commodity investment results from the return of the cash collateral, which is usually a Treasury bill rate in the United States, although the cash collateral can also be in other forms like Treasury Inflation-Protected Securities (TIPS), money market securities, and other liquid assets. As indicated earlier, most commodity trading programs include a collateral feature.

Because commodity investors generally are not in the market to take ownership of the actual physical commodity they are trading, a futures position needs to be closed out or rolled prior to expiration. Rolling involves selling a futures contract that is close to expiration, and opening a new position in a contract that expires at a later date. Roll return is often mistakenly thought of as a profit or loss occurring at the time of the contract roll. However, **roll return** is defined as the portion of the return of a futures contract that is due to the change in the basis. Roll return actually accrues over time, from the time the investor goes long the futures contract to the time of the roll, much like a bond coupon. While one would expect the roll return to a long futures position to be positive if the forward curve for the commodity slopes down (backwardation) and negative if the forward curve slopes up (contango), the roll return is also affected by changes in cost of carry (interest rates, storage costs, convenience yields, and, for financial futures, dividends).

24.3.2 Scarcity

Scarcity in commodity markets can provide a source of return to commodity investors, but the difficulty can be in determining when this market pattern is occurring. Using the forward curve, relative price differences of futures contracts across delivery months can be measured. If the forward curve is downward sloping, meaning spot prices are higher than those in the futures market, this price pattern can indicate scarcity, as a premium is being offered for the immediately deliverable commodity. This price pattern may also indicate a lack of excess of commodity inventories (Till and Eagleeye 2005).

24.4 THE STATISTICAL PROPERTIES OF COMMODITY PRICES

The historical performance of commodity investments can provide useful information for forecasting future returns, volatility, and correlations with other asset

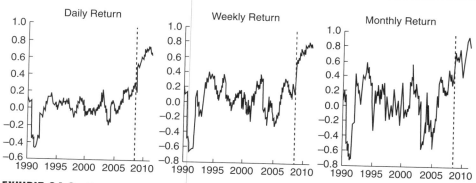

EXHIBIT 24.2 Return Correlation Coefficient between S&P GSCI and MSCI All-Country World Equity Index

Note: The figures show the one-year rolling correlation coefficients between the return of the global equity index (MSCI AC World Index) and that of the commodity index (S&P GSCI).
Source: Bloomberg, Kawamoto et al. (2011).

classes. However, with the growth of the commodity index-based investment, many commodity markets have been transformed from purely commercial markets into markets with a significant investor presence, leading to concerns that the historical track record may be of questionable value in projecting future returns. In particular, much of the case for commodity investment is derived from the low levels of historical correlation between the returns on commodity futures and stock or bond investments. If the correlation is rising over time, commodities may be less diversifying than previously estimated.

Buyuksahin, Haigh, and Robe (2010) addressed this concern. They used dynamic correlation and recursive co-integration techniques to determine whether the relationship between commodity index returns and equity index returns had changed over recent years. They found that the extent of co-movement between the two asset classes had not changed significantly over the period of the study (1991 to 2008). Furthermore, they found that the low correlation actually became negative in the last five years of the study. Even when they restricted their analysis to periods of extreme returns, they found no increase in co-movement between commodities and equities. Chong and Miffre (2008) also discovered that correlations between commodity futures and S&P 500 returns fell over the period from 1980 to 2006.

In contrast, a more recent study by Kawamoto et al. (2011) showed that the correlation between commodity and equity markets has increased sharply since the second half of 2008. (See Exhibit 24.2.) The markets seem to have recently included commodities in the category of risky assets, which are highly correlated with equities in a "risk on, risk off" volatility regime.

Haigh et al. (2007) used a proprietary data set of trader positions in West Texas intermediate (WTI) sweet crude oil futures to consider the impact of the financialization of commodity markets on the term structure of commodity futures. They found an increase in price efficiency and co-integration between near-month futures and long-maturity (one- and two-year) futures as the market presence of commodity swap dealers and hedge funds increased.

The first question researchers ask is whether the long-run return to spot commodity investments has been positive or negative. Evidence is inconclusive. While spot commodity prices have trended higher over the past century in nominal terms, the inflation-adjusted prices of many commodities have actually declined. Gorton and Rouwenhorst (2006) found that over the past half-century (i.e., from 1959 to 2004) spot commodities have not kept pace with inflation. There is conflicting empirical evidence regarding the existence of a long-term positive return in commodity prices. Cuddington (1992) found little evidence to support the view that prices of primary commodities were on a declining path over the long term. However, evidence also fails to support a long-term positive drift in commodity prices. Cashin and McDermott suggest that such evidence of a low long-term expected return may be of little significance, since it is dominated by the variability of prices (Cashin and McDermott 2002; Cashin, McDermott, and Scott 1999). Furthermore, they found a trend of increasing volatility over the 140 years of their study. Another complication arises from currency effects. While most research focuses on performance measured in U.S. dollars, investors who measure performance in different currencies may observe either a long-run positive drift or a negative drift, based on the historical performance of the home currency exchange rate (Black 2009; Till 2008b).

Difficulty in measuring a long-run return is not unique to commodity markets. Commodity investment, like most alternative investment strategies, including hedge funds, managed futures, and private equity, has a relatively short history of clearly defined performance. For example, crude oil futures were first listed on a futures exchange in 1983. Data for energy markets prior to 1983 have been assembled by researchers from over-the-counter sources and from spot market transactions.

Over the past century, there have been long periods of rising commodity prices as well as extended periods of declines. Commodity prices have risen, in real terms, over the past two decades, but observations about the very long-term performance remain inconclusive.[2]

As mentioned earlier, collateralized commodity futures returns can be decomposed into the spot return, the collateral return, and the roll return. Not surprisingly, even if spot returns are zero, an investor might generate positive returns if a futures contract market is in backwardation, by rolling from high-priced to low-priced contracts and riding the term structure. Similarly, an upward-sloping (contango) term structure could result in negative returns. Gorton and Rouwenhorst (2006) found that, while spot commodities dropped in value in real terms from 1959 to 2004, fully collateralized portfolios of commodity futures provided returns and volatilities that were very similar to those of stocks. The average historical risk premium of commodity futures was about equal to stocks at 5% per annum, which is about twice that of bonds. However, with some exceptions, commodities have positive skewness whereas stocks have negative skewness.

Another important question is what factors influence performance. Williams and Wright (1991) studied the implications of storage on the time series of commodity prices. They found that the time series of spot prices for major commodities have two features in common: (1) considerable positive autocorrelation and (2) spikes in prices. Williams and Wright pointed out that both the autoregressive structure of commodity time series and the excess skewness and kurtosis are the natural result of storage.

---

[2] For additional arguments, see Heap (2005) and Till and Gunzberg (2005).

Another area of research on momentum in commodity markets relates to the persistence of volatility shocks. Research finds strong evidence of long memory for the volatility of commodity futures over time (Elder and Jin 2007; Baillie et al. 2007). There is both theoretical and empirical evidence of a positive relationship between volatility and convenience yield. An important part of convenience yield is the risk premium. The risk premium can be positive or negative. For example, Cootner (1960) proposes that hedgers can be net purchasers or sellers of futures (varying cross sectionally and over time). Thus net hedging pressure can result in a positive or negative risk premium to entice speculators to take on the hedgers' risk. All other things being equal, an increase in commodity price volatility will cause the magnitude of the (positive or negative) risk premium to increase. During periods of positive risk premium, a volatility shock will cause the risk premium and convenience yield to rise. In periods of negative risk premium, the risk premium and convenience yield would be expected to decline in response to a volatility shock. So, to the degree that spikes in volatility exist and persist over time and that such spikes in volatility are consistent with the existence of convenience yield, strategies such as momentum models that are positively related to volatility may capture excess returns. As discussed in Chapter 31, it can be difficult to disentangle volatility from momentum, as managed futures funds may actually be long gamma rather than long volatility.

Finally, many active managers in commodity markets employ momentum strategies. The profitability of momentum-based trading rules has been examined for a number of commodity futures markets (Schneeweis, Kazemi, and Spurgin 2008). Empirical research on momentum models that tests for weak-form efficiency in commodity markets dates back several years. A series of articles published more than 30 years ago found evidence of pricing patterns that differed from simple random walks.[3] However, they did not address the theoretical or behavioral causes for the existence of such pricing patterns. In commodity markets, the structural friction that may lead to momentum profits is frequently linked to problems associated with storing and transporting commodities.

Given the importance of storage in many commodities, it is not surprising that recent empirical research (Gorton et al. 2007) has concluded that profitability of momentum and backwardation strategies is related to storage in particular commodities. However, storage is not the only basis for momentum in commodity futures. Similar to the source of pricing patterns in other futures markets, government intervention, macroeconomic shocks, and differing risk appetites among investors may all lead to variations in commodity pricing patterns.

In summary, the historical track record for commodity markets is inconclusive as to whether the long-run risk premium is positive, although it has been positive in recent decades. There is evidence that commodity prices exhibit short-term autocorrelation. There is also evidence of price shocks, which lead to excess kurtosis in commodity returns. There is considerable evidence that volatility in commodity markets varies over time. Researchers have also rejected the hypothesis that commodity markets are weak-form efficient, as simple trading rules based on

---

[3] For example, see Cargill and Rausser (1975), Leuthold (1972), and Peterson and Leuthold (1982).

storage or momentum have been shown to deliver excess returns after adjusting for transaction costs.

24.5 ASSET ALLOCATION

Commodities have been proven to enhance the risk-adjusted returns of diversified portfolios. Commodity returns have low correlations to stocks and bonds, but a higher correlation with inflation, particularly unexpected inflation and the rate of change in inflation. Research has shown that an allocation to commodities can improve the efficient frontier, or risk-adjusted return, of the portfolio. Additionally, research has shown that commodities have a low, sometimes even negative, correlation with one another, and so can offer uncorrelated investment opportunities across various commodity markets. In particular, the energy sector is frequently negatively correlated to the nonenergy sectors, because higher energy prices can weigh on economic growth and depress demand for other commodities. This correlation pattern can potentially help lower the risk of a diversified commodity portfolio (Till and Eagleeye 2005).

Commodity futures returns are positively correlated with inflation, and correlation has been shown to increase over longer time horizons. Because commodity futures returns are more volatile than inflation rates, long-term correlations better capture the inflation-hedging properties of commodity investments. While stocks and bonds are negatively correlated with inflation, the correlation of commodity futures with inflation is positive at all horizons and statistically significant at the longer horizons. Commodity futures' opposite exposure to (unexpected) inflation may help explain why they do well when stocks and bonds perform poorly (Gorton and Rouwenhorst 2006).

The optimal portfolio allocation to commodities will be largely determined by the expected risk premium. The statistical properties of commodities are attractive for most investors, providing diversification benefits and a positive correlation with inflation. For this reason, most investors can justify a commodity allocation even if the risk premium is low.

In addition to providing hedging against unexpected changes in inflation, commodity indices may provide exposure to long-term growth in world demand, which in turn may result in increasing demand and prices for certain commodity products (Greer 2000).

24.5.1 Event Risk Hedging

One of the benefits of commodity investment, from an asset allocation perspective, is the ability of such investments to hedge event risk. Whereas equity prices tend to be impacted negatively by natural disasters and political or economic distress, commodity prices generally react positively to such occurrences. This characteristic of commodity returns is particularly beneficial, since it results in further reduced correlations between stocks and commodities in periods of market stress, which is precisely when diversification benefits are most needed (Chong and Miffre 2008). In addition to offering protection from major market stresses, commodities can provide protection from more narrowly focused events as well as from unanticipated macro trends. For example, Burkart (2006) points out that a strike at a large zinc mine would likely decrease the price of the firm's equity while simultaneously putting upward pressure on zinc prices. In addition, he argues that commodities can provide a hedge against unanticipated global growth. As countries like China, India, Indonesia, South Africa, and Mexico have developed, their equity prices have risen and their bonds have become investment grade. Their economic growth is naturally accompanied by an increase in per capita commodity consumption, placing upward pressure on the spot prices of these commodities. The positive event risk exposure of commodities results in positively skewed return distributions, which investors prefer to the negative skews of equity indices (Jensen and Mercer 2011).

24.5.2   Stock and Bond Diversification

A number of studies have found that commodity index returns and volatility are similar to those of equities (Greer 2000; Gorton and Rouwenhorst 2006). However, of greater importance is the fact that commodities generate these returns with a low correlation to traditional assets. Gorton and Rouwenhorst (2006) found that, for time horizons longer than one month, an equally weighted commodity futures portfolio was negatively correlated with the return on both the S&P 500 and long-term bonds. Although the hypothesis that the correlation of commodity futures with stocks is zero at short horizons cannot be rejected, the authors' findings suggest that commodity futures are effective in reducing the risk of equity and bond portfolios. The negative correlation of commodity futures with stocks and bonds tends to become more negative as the holding period increases. This pattern suggests that the diversification benefits of commodity futures may be realized only at longer horizons (Gorton and Rouwenhorst 2006). Furthermore, Chong and Miffre (2008) found that correlations have been decreasing over time. More recently, Jensen and Mercer (2011) considered the performance of GSCI from 1970 to 2009, and found that commodities provided similar return and risk performance (slightly higher return and standard deviation) to U.S. and non-U.S. equities. They uncovered low correlations between most commodities and equities, and low or negative correlations with fixed income. Their results are provided in Exhibits 24.3 and 24.4.

EXHIBIT 24.3   Investment Performance of Commodities and Equities: Monthly Data, 1970–2009

Index	Mean Monthly Return	Standard Deviation	Skewness	Kurtosis
S&P GSCI	0.979%	5.763%	0.082	2.858
Energy	1.180%	9.315%	0.434	1.873
Livestock	0.768%	5.223%	0.056	1.556
Agriculture	0.523%	5.851%	0.741	3.713
Metals	0.964%	7.038%	0.553	4.164
Precious metals	0.816%	6.692%	1.218	7.732
S&P 500	0.669%	4.497%	−0.458	1.931
EAFE	0.934%	4.947%	−0.323	1.215

Source: Jensen and Mercer (2011).

EXHIBIT 24.4 Correlation Coefficients of Commodities with Traditional Assets and Inflation, 1970–2009

	GSCI	Energy	Livestock	Agriculture	Metals	Precious Metals
S&P 500	0.034	0.112	0.216*	−0.078	0.159	−0.065
EAFE	0.135	0.018	0.419***	0.021	0.260*	0.048
T-bonds	−0.263***	−0.240**	−0.076	−0.211*	−0.322***	−0.220
T-bills	0.021	0.161	0.169	0.064	−0.105	−0.030
Inflation	0.318**	0.588***	0.166	0.372**	0.115	0.411*

*Significant at the 10% level.
**Significant at the 5% level.
***Significant at the 1% level.
Source: Jensen and Mercer (2011).

24.5.3 Inflation Hedging

As has been said, like other real assets, commodities are generally considered to be effective hedges for inflation, particularly for unexpected inflation. Commodity futures also have the added benefit of high liquidity, which many other real assets, such as raw land, lack (Satyanarayan and Varangis 1994). Ankrim and Hensel (1993) argue that commodities provide more effective diversification than most institutional real estate investments, because the revenue stream of such real estate investments makes them act more like equity investments.

Whereas individual commodities vary in their degree of inflation hedging, commodity indices have traditionally been effective hedges for inflation. A number of studies have found precious metals (particularly gold) to have significant inflation hedging abilities (Blose and Gondhalekar 2008; McCown and Zimmerman 2006). Halpern and Warsager (1998) found that, in contrast to stocks, bonds, and real estate, both energy and nonenergy commodities perform well in periods of high inflation. Ultimately, they determined that stocks, bonds, and real estate are negatively correlated with the level of inflation, while energy and nonenergy commodities are positively correlated with inflation. Furthermore, they showed that stocks, bonds, and real estate are negatively correlated with unexpected inflation (proxied by the change in inflation), while energy and nonenergy commodities are positively correlated with unexpected inflation. Thus, commodities provide valuable inflation-hedging properties, particularly in periods of increasing inflation. However, the authors state, "Not all commodities have direct links with measured inflation. Many commodities simply do not have a major economic impact on the price of goods and services. Of the wide range of alternative commodities, energy based commodity products most often have been directly linked as possible inflation hedges." Similarly, Froot (1995) found that commodities (spot prices or futures prices) provide valuable hedging for a diversified portfolio, with oil and oil-biased commodity indices providing the strongest hedges, while commodity-based equities are not effectual hedges, acting more like equities than commodities.

EXHIBIT 24.5 Average Returns by Stage of the Business Cycle, July 1959 to December 2004

Cycle Type	Stocks	Bonds	Commodity Futures
Expansion	13.29%	6.74%	11.84%
Early	16.3	9.98	6.76
Late	10.4	3.63	16.71
Recession	0.51%	12.59%	1.05%
Early	−18.64	−3.88	3.74
Late	19.69	29.07	−1.63

Source: Gorton and Rouwenhorst (2006).

24.5.4 Business Cycle Hedging

Bjornson and Carter (1997) found evidence indicating that agricultural commodities provide a natural hedge against business cycles. Fama and French (1988) uncovered a strong business cycle component for metal futures, consistent with the effect of inventory levels predicted by the theory of storage. Gorton and Rouwenhorst (2006) argue that commodities are unique, in that they are effective diversifiers of systematic (theoretically nondiversifiable) risk. (See Exhibit 24.5.) They found that commodity futures perform well in the early stages of a recession and poorly in later stages of a recession, which is in exact contrast to equity performance. Interestingly, they found that equities and commodities perform similarly, on average, through an expansion and a recession. However, when one considers the phases of recessions and expansions, the results are markedly different. In the early phase of a recession, stocks and bonds exhibit negative returns, while commodity returns are positive. The relationship is the opposite in the late phase of recessions. In fact, the authors determined that commodities outperform stocks and bonds in late expansion and early recession phases.

CHAPTER 25

Methods of Delivering Commodity Alpha

25.1 INTRODUCTION

In contrast to traditional stock and bond markets, research has shown that commodities offer unique risk and return alternatives. These risk and return alternatives are due to the unique supply-and-demand conditions affecting physical spot markets as well as the changing carry and storage relationships that influence futures pricing. When one adds micro market impacts related to unique trading processes in commodity markets, including rollover and delivery impacts, it is evident that there exist numerous potential opportunities to generate profits. The questions remain, however, to what degree commodities can offer returns consistent with their underlying risk exposure, and whether various commodity investment strategies also offer the potential for commodity alpha. Most of these strategies involve trading commodities themselves, or trading the stocks of companies involved with commodities. This chapter provides an overview of these strategies. Many are standard hedge fund or managed futures strategies, and are covered extensively in other sections of this book.

Commodity trading strategies can be separated into two broad groups: directional and relative value. Directional strategies take outright positions based on a forecast of market direction. **Relative value strategies** attempt to identify mispriced assets or securities and to hedge away some or all of the market exposure.

25.2 DIRECTIONAL STRATEGIES

Directional strategies are strategies that express a view on market direction, resulting in either long or short positions. While these strategies can be implemented with traditional assets, such as the equities of commodity firms or commodity-based exchange-traded funds (ETFs), they more often utilize listed commodity futures and options as well as over-the-counter (OTC) derivatives, such as forward contracts or swaps. Some strategies also involve holding physical commodities, though this is much less common. Further details on the investment vehicles available for the implementation of directional strategies can be found in Chapter 26, which discusses accessing commodity beta.

Fundamental directional strategies are based on an analysis of supply-and-demand factors for commodities or commodity sectors. They can be based on macroeconomic factors such as economic growth, interest rate forecasts, and currencies, or on industry-specific factors, such as the number of cattle in feedlots.

Quantitative directional strategies use technical or quantitative models to identify overpriced and underpriced commodities. These strategies are similar to managed futures strategies discussed in Chapters 29 to 32.

25.3 RELATIVE VALUE STRATEGIES

Relative value strategies in commodity markets are best understood as businesses rather than as trading strategies. Relative value managers combine investment capital with expertise in a particular sector to provide economic value-added. They generally compete for profits with vertically integrated commodity firms, merchant banks, shipping companies, and trading firms.

Relative value strategies in commodities can be executed across three risk dimensions: location, correlation, and time. The same commodity can have different prices at different locations in the world. The prices of two similar commodities can diverge from historical norms. The price of the same commodity can be different based on when the commodity is scheduled for delivery. For example, consider a spread trade that is long crude oil for delivery in October in the United Kingdom and short heating oil for delivery in December in the United States. This trade has three risk dimensions: location, correlation, and time.

In contrast, relative value arbitrage strategies in equity and fixed-income markets are generally limited to a single dimension: correlation. A share of stock, when expressed in the same currency, sells at essentially the same price everywhere in the world, so there is no location dimension. Similarly, the price for delivery of a share of stock in the future is determined by its price today and the cost of financing, so there is no time dimension. Commodity traders have more degrees of freedom when designing strategies, leading to a richer set of relative value opportunities than is available in debt or equity markets.

25.3.1 Commodity Futures and Options Spreads

Commodity spreads are strategies that take advantage of trading opportunities that can be executed entirely in derivatives markets. They can involve futures contracts, forward contracts, OTC swaps, and options.

25.3.1.1 Time Spreads Perhaps the simplest strategy is a **calendar spread**, which involves taking opposing positions in the futures market for delivery at different times in the future. These trades can be designed to provide liquidity or insurance against an unforeseen event.

For example, a typical calendar spread trade involves selling natural gas futures for delivery in March and taking a long position for delivery of natural gas in April. This spread could be profitable in a very mild winter, but could lose money in a very cold winter. Utilities purchase more natural gas for delivery in March than they expect to need to ensure adequate supplies. If the winter is mild, they will sell the surplus gas inventories toward the end of the season, which will push down the price for delivery in March. Traders who hold this spread are writing a synthetic weather derivative. They will earn a premium if the weather is mild, but will take a loss if the weather is severe. Traders may also take the other side of this trade by buying natural gas for March delivery and selling it for delivery in April. If a natural gas shortage develops due to an exceptionally cold winter or supply disruptions, this trade will be profitable.

Other common calendar spreads are designed to provide liquidity. For example, in 2005 and 2006, it was common for traders to buy crude oil futures for delivery two months forward and hedge this position by selling crude oil for delivery three months forward. This trade was designed to take advantage of the growth in commodity index investments. Since most commodity index investments are designed to hold futures for near-term delivery, there was a surplus of these contracts on roll dates, when the indices were selling their short-maturity futures positions, and a corresponding shortage of second-deferred futures, when the indices were buying the second-deferred futures positions. Speculators responded by designing a calendar spread that offered liquidity to the indices at prices that could provide a reasonable expected profit to the speculators. A study by Mou (2011) provides evidence that significant alpha can be generated by exploiting the established roll pattern of the S&P GSCI. Mou tested two pre-roll strategies (5 days and 10 days prior to the S&P GSCI roll) on 19 of the commodities included in the S&P GSCI (representing about 93% of the S&P GSCI). Both pre-roll strategies generated significant abnormal returns over the period of 2000 to 2010, with the energy sector providing the best performance. Over the period of 1980 to 2000, however, a period in which there was little to no investment in the S&P GSCI, pre-roll strategies were not able to generate alpha. This result suggests that the alpha found for the pre-roll strategies from 2000 to 2010 is capturing price imbalances caused by the S&P GSCI roll process. Since 2006, however, the profitability of pre-roll strategies has been declining to the point that these strategies now may have average excess returns of close to zero.

Depending on their market views, investors can enter two types of calendar spreads: bull spreads and bear spreads. In a **bull spread**, the investor is long the nearby (near-term) contract and short the distant (long-term) contract. In markets that are in backwardation, the investor is hoping for the spread to widen; in contango markets, the bull-spread investor is hoping for the price difference to narrow. The losses of a bull-spread investor tend to be limited because, in an efficient market, price differences cannot exceed carrying costs. If, at some point, the differences do exceed carrying costs, arbitrageurs would drive prices toward a level reflecting fair carrying costs.

In a **bear spread**, the investor is long the distant (long-term) contract and short the nearby (near-term) contract. In markets in backwardation, the investor wants the spread to narrow, whereas in contango markets the bear-spread investor wants the price difference to widen. If prices move against the investor's position, the bear spread faces unlimited risk, since the nearby contract theoretically can rise without an upper limit; consequently, the bear-spread investor would have to deliver or offset at any price.

Example of Spread P&L Calculation   The profit and loss (P&L) from a spread position can be calculated only after the spread is closed. Assume the following scenario. (See Exhibit 25.1.) In March, a spread trader observes a contango in the crude oil forward curve. Anticipating a flattening of the curve and a narrowing of

EXHIBIT 25.1 Profit and Loss Calculation

	July (1st Leg)	December (2nd Leg)	Total
March, open	Long: −$44.37	Short: +$50.78	
June, close	Short: +$35.18	Long: −$38.16	
Net per barrel	−$ 9.19	$12.62	$3.43

the spread, the trader goes long three July light sweet crude oil futures (traded on NYMEX) at $44.37, simultaneously shorting three December light sweet crude oil futures at $50.78. In April and May, an oversupply of crude in the world markets causes prices to slump across the board. At the beginning of June, the spreader closes out the July contract at $35.18 and the December contract at $38.16.

The profit for the combined position can now be determined. Since the size of the NYMEX light sweet crude oil contract is 1,000 barrels, and the size of the trader's spread position is three contracts, the total gain of his position is $10,290.

$$\text{Position P\&L} = \text{P\&L}_{barrel} \times \text{Contract size} \times \text{Position size}$$
$$= \$3.43 \times 1,000 \times 3 = \$10,290$$

25.3.1.2 Correlation Spreads Processing spreads seek to take advantage of the relative price difference between a commodity and the products produced using the same commodity. For example, processing spread strategies can involve crude oil and its products. A common processing spread involves buying crude oil futures and selling a combination of heating oil and gasoline futures. Another example of a processing spread involves buying soybeans and selling a combination of soybean meal and soybean oil.

Processing spreads are used by producers to lock in favorable margins. For example, a soybean processor may wish to buy the spread (buy soybean futures, sell soybean meal and soybean oil futures). However, there are no natural sellers of this spread. Instead, there are three separate natural participants on the other side of the spread: farmers who sell the soybean futures, livestock feed producers who buy the soybean meal, and vegetable oil consumers who buy the soybean oil. Speculators may provide liquidity by selling the spread to permit the processor to lock in a favorable margin, and then attempt to find buyers or sellers to unwind the individual components of the spread trade. They can also hold the spread intact and hope to unwind the entire transaction at a more favorable price.

In summary, there are two conditions that hold for all producers: (1) producers take long futures positions to hedge against rising input prices, and (2) producers take short future positions to hedge against falling output prices.

It should be noted that futures exchanges set lower margins for bona fide hedging spreads, in which a producer goes long futures on the input and goes short futures on the output. On the flip side, a spread investor who goes long the output and shorts the input is subject to higher margin requirements. A few examples of typical processing spreads follow.

Crack spreads are hedges typically used by oil refineries. The typical producer hedge position would involve going long crude oil futures (to hedge future input purchases) and short gasoline and heating oil (to hedge against potential decreases in the price of the outputs, distillates). The crack spread locks in the refiner's margin, which is the revenue earned for refining each barrel of crude oil.

It is a common practice to express the crack spread in terms of a ratio as $X{:}Y{:}Z$, where X represents the number of barrels of crude oil, Y represents the number of barrels of gasoline, and Z represents the number of barrels of heating oil, subject to the constraint that $X = Y + Z$. Typical crack spreads are 3:2:1, 5:3:2, and 2:1:1; examples of benchmarks include "Gulf Coast 3:2:1" and "Chicago 3:2:1."

Financial intermediaries have custom products that facilitate entering scaled crack positions. For example, the New York Mercantile Exchange (NYMEX) offers virtual crack spread futures contracts by aggregating a basket of underlying NYMEX futures contracts corresponding to a crack spread ratio. It is possible to obtain even more customized products in the over-the-counter market.

Example of Crack Spread 3:2:1   The following example has been partially adapted from New York Mercantile Exchange's publication *Crack Spread Handbook* (2001). An independent refiner is concerned about the possibility of increasing oil costs (input) and falling refined product prices (output). In other words, the refiner is subject to the risk that his refining margin will be less than anticipated. However, using a crack spread hedge, the producer can effectively lock in the current refining margin as demonstrated in the following example.

On June 15, the refiner enters an obligation in the cash market to buy 60,000 barrels of crude oil on July 15 at prevailing market prices. He has also entered an obligation to sell 840,000 gallons (20,000 barrels) of heating oil and 1,680,000 gallons (40,000 barrels) of gasoline on August 27 at prevailing market prices. (See Exhibit 25.2.)

EXHIBIT 25.2   3:2:1 Crack Spread: Three Parts Crude, Two Parts Gasoline, and One Part Heating Oil

Date	Cash Market	Action	Futures Market
June 15	Light, sweet crude oil: $89.58 per barrel	Agrees to buy at prevailing prices: 60,000 barrels of light, sweet crude on July 15	Goes long 60 August light, sweet crude contracts at $88.68 per barrel
	Gasoline: NY Harbor: $2.6548 per gallon ($111.50/bbl.)	Agrees to sell at prevailing cash market prices: 1,680,000 gallons (40,000 barrels) of NY Harbor gasoline on August 27	Shorts 40 September NY Harbor gasoline contracts at $2.6210 per gallon ($110.08/bbl.)
	Heating oil: NY Harbor: $2.6296 per gallon ($110.44/bbl.)	Agrees to sell at prevailing cash market prices: 840,000 gallons (20,000 barrels) of NY Harbor heating oil on August 27	Shorts 20 September NY Harbor heating oil contracts at $2.6558 per gallon ($111.54/bbl.)

Source: Adapted from New York Mercantile Exchange, *Crack Spread Handbook* (2001).

That same day, June 15, the refiner initiates a long hedge in crude oil and short hedges in heating oil and gasoline to fix a substantial portion of his refining margin through a 3:2:1 crack spread. The refiner does this by going long 60 August crude oil futures contracts at $88.68 per barrel, while selling 20 September heating oil contracts at $111.54 per barrel and 40 September gasoline futures contracts at $110.08 per barrel. Each of these contracts is for the equivalent of 1,000 barrels. Crude oil contracts are quoted in dollars per barrel, while products are quoted in dollars per gallon. The price per gallon for gasoline, $2.621, can be calculated as $110.08 per barrel divided by 42 gallons per barrel.

In this case, the futures crack spread is calculated as: [(Number of gasoline futures contracts sold short × Gasoline futures price) + (Number of heating oil contracts sold short × Heating oil futures price) − (Number of long crude oil contracts × Crude oil futures price)]/Total number of crude oil contracts. Thus, the futures crack spread on June 15 is:

$$[(40 \times \$110.08) + (20 \times \$111.54) - (60 \times \$88.68)]/60 = \$21.88/\text{bbl.}$$

In this example, the cash market margin is calculated as: [(Number of gasoline futures contracts sold short × Gasoline cash market price) + (Number of heating oil contracts sold short × Heating oil cash market price) − (Number of long crude oil contracts × Crude oil cash market price)]/Total number of crude oil contracts. Thus, the NY Harbor cash market margin is:

$$[(40 \times \$111.50) + (20 \times \$110.44) - (60 \times \$89.58)]/60 = \$21.56/\text{bbl.}$$

The $21.88 per barrel crack spread has ensured that refining crude oil will be at least as profitable in August as it was in June, regardless of whether the actual cash margin narrows or widens. A decline in the cash margin is offset by a gain in the futures market. Consider the following two scenarios.

Scenario A: Rising crude, falling distillates, and stable basis; refiner puts on the spread shown in Exhibit 25.3A.

EXHIBIT 25.3A   Refinery Example: Rising Crude, Falling Distillates

Date	Cash Market	Action	Futures Market
July 15	Light, sweet crude oil: $90.06 per barrel	Buys 60,000 barrels of light, sweet crude at $90.06 per barrel	Shorts 60 August light, sweet crude contracts at $90.06 per barrel
August 27	Gasoline: NY Harbor: $2.3492 per gallon ($98.66/bbl.)	Sells 1,680,000 gallons (40,000 bbl.) of NY Harbor gasoline for $2.3492 per gallon ($98.66/bbl.)	Goes long 40 September NY Harbor gasoline contracts at $2.3610 per gallon ($99.16/bbl.)
	Heating oil: NY Harbor: $2.4818 per gallon ($104.24/bbl.)	Sells 840,000 gallons (20,000 bbl.) of NY Harbor heating oil for $2.4818 per gallon ($104.24/bbl.)	Goes long 20 September NY Harbor heating oil contracts at $2.4890 per gallon ($104.54/bbl.)

Futures crack spread: [(40 × $99.16) + (20 × $104.54) − (60 × $90.06)]/60
= $10.89 per barrel

Futures profit : Initial crack spread − Closing crack spread = $21.88 − $10.89
= $10.99 per barrel

NY Harbor cash market margin : [(40 × $98.66) + (20 × $104.24)
−(60 × $90.06)]/60 = $10.46 per barrel

Realized margin : Cash margin + Futures profit = $10.46 + $10.99
= $21.45 per barrel

Scenario B: Falling crude, rising distillates, and stable basis; refiner puts on the spread shown in Exhibit 25.3B.

Futures crack spread : [(40 × $122.64) + (20 × $107.42) − (60 × $82.94)]/60
= $34.63 per barrel

Futures loss : Initial crack spread − Closing crack spread = $21.88 − $34.63
= −$12.75 per barrel

NY Harbor cash market margin : [(40 × $121.46) + (20 × $107.00)
−(60 × $82.94)]/60 = $33.70 per barrel

Realized margin : Cash margin − Futures loss = $33.70 − $12.75
= $20.95 per barrel

In summary, the cash market refining margin on June 15 was $21.56. Unhedged, under scenario A, the refiner would have experienced a 50% drop in his refining margin. If the hedge were applied, his loss would have been reduced to less than 1%. On the other hand, the hedge would have eliminated the refiner's potential gain under scenario B. Note that the hedge was not perfect in this case; the imperfection

EXHIBIT 25.3B   Refinery Example: Falling Crude, Rising Distillates

Date	Cash Market	Action	Futures Market
July 15	Light, sweet crude oil: $82.94 per barrel	Buys 60,000 barrels of light, sweet crude at $82.94 per barrel	Shorts 60 August light, sweet crude contracts at $82.94 per barrel
August 27	Gasoline: NY Harbor: $2.8918 per gallon ($121.46/bbl.)	Sells 1,680,000 gallons (40,000 bbl.) of NY Harbor gasoline for $2.8918 per gallon ($121.46/bbl.)	Goes long 40 September NY Harbor gasoline contracts at $2.9200 per gallon ($122.64/bbl.)
	Heating oil: NY Harbor: $2.5478 per gallon ($107.00/bbl.)	Sells 840,000 gallons (20,000 bbl.) of NY Harbor heating oil for $2.5478 per gallon ($107.00/bbl.)	Goes long 20 September NY Harbor heating oil contracts at $2.5600 per gallon ($107.52/bbl.)

was caused by the fact that the refiner had to buy in July and deliver in August, whereas the futures maturities happened in different months.

Crush spreads are hedges typically used by soybean processors. A typical crush spread would involve going long soybean futures (to insure the processor against potential input price increases) and short soybean oil futures and soy meal futures (to insure against potential output price decreases). The reason behind the name of this spread is that, historically, soybeans were crushed to produce oil and meal.

Substitution spreads are trades between commodities that can be substituted for one another. There are two types of substitution. A producer may use the same capital equipment to produce different products. Also, a consumer may be able to substitute one commodity for another based on their relative prices. Examples of producer substitution include corn and soybeans, because land suitable for growing soybeans is usually also suitable for growing corn. Oil refineries can also vary the mix of refined products. A refinery can be adjusted, within limits, to favor production of heating oil, jet fuel, or gasoline depending on seasonal demand. Consumers of commodities can often substitute a less expensive commodity. Utilities can utilize different fuels for electricity generation. For example, in the long run, natural gas can be substituted for oil-based fuels. Cattle and hogs are also substitutes. Substitution spread trades are generally riskier than processing spreads or calendar spreads, since they depend on historical correlations that may not persist in the future.

The general premise of substitute spreads is that the relationship between easily substitutable commodities should be stable. If the price of one becomes too expensive, consumers will switch to the substitute. This results in a price drop for the original and a rise for the substitute, forcing the ratio back to normal. To normalize ratios of contracts with different pricing specifications and contract sizes, one can study natural logs of the ratios of prices. For example, one might look at the natural log of a series of heating oil/natural gas price ratios, such as:

$$\text{Substitute test statistic}_t = \ln\left(\frac{\text{Close price (Heating oil)}_t}{\text{Close price (Natural gas)}_t}\right)$$

For the purposes of illustration, let's assume that the nearest-maturity NYMEX heating oil (HO) yesterday has closed at \$2.5620 per gallon, while the same maturity NYMEX Henry Hub natural gas (NG) has closed at \$8.112 per 10,000 million British thermal units (MMBtu). The HO/NG test statistic for yesterday would be estimated as follows:

$$\text{Substitute test statistic}_{\text{yesterday}} = \ln\left(\frac{\text{HO}_{\text{yesterday}}}{\text{NG}_{\text{yesterday}}}\right) = \ln\left(\frac{2.5620}{8.112}\right) = -1.15$$

To determine whether the spread has experienced a change significant enough to warrant a spread trade, a measure of stability is required. One such measure at traders' disposal is "difference from 100-day moving average," calculated as follows:

$$\text{100-day statistic} = \frac{\text{Close} - \text{100-day moving average of closes}}{\text{100-day standard deviation of closes}}$$

The critical values of the statistic that would trigger entering or exiting a spread position are determined statistically (optimizing over historical series of logs of price ratios of the related securities). For example, assume that the critical value for entry is 2.75, while the critical value for exit is 0. A long entry into the spread would be triggered if the 100-day statistic fell below −2.75, whereas a short position in the spread would be established if the 100-day statistic rose above 2.75. Long spreads are exited when the 100-day statistic rises above zero, and short spreads are exited when the 100-day statistic falls below zero. Note that entering a spread long means going long the product in the numerator of the price ratio and shorting the product in the denominator. The assumption of the long spread position is that the product in the denominator has become too expensive relative to the numerator. Shorting the spread means the opposite: shorting the product in the numerator and going long the product in the denominator. The assumption of the short spread position is that the product in the numerator has become too expensive relative to the product in the denominator.

In practice, though, the price reversion of a substitution spread between natural gas and heating oil would take place in the long term. Consider the discussion in 2012, when U.S. natural gas prices were reaching multiyear lows below $2 per MMBtu, while heating oil was trading for above $4 per gallon at retail fueling stations. There were calls for shipping companies owning large fleets of trucks to convert from using diesel fuel to using natural gas. Even though the difference in fuel costs was substantial at that point in time, there remained significant switching costs. In addition to switching from diesel fuel–powered to natural gas–powered truck engines, the infrastructure of natural gas fueling stations also had to be developed over highways carrying large portions of trucking traffic. Only after these longer-term investments were made could the demand for natural gas increase and the demand for heating oil decrease to the point that the Btu-equivalent price of the two fuels would start a meaningful convergence.

Quality spreads are similar to substitution spreads, except that the spread is across different grades of the same commodity. A common quality spread executable in futures markets involves spring wheat and hard red winter wheat. Most other quality spreads involve OTC transactions. For example, there is a liquid OTC market in jet fuel, which is very similar to diesel fuel/heating oil. Similarly, there are many grades of coffee that are traded OTC, but only a few grades that are listed on futures exchanges.

Quality spread traders provide liquidity to producers in the OTC market, and then hedge by using other OTC markets or listed futures contracts. Most quality spreads have historically had relatively low price risk. There has been little chance that the spread between jet fuel and heating oil would undergo a major structural change, because refineries have easily switched production between heating oil and jet fuel when a demand imbalance takes place. Rather than list separate futures contracts for diesel fuel, jet fuel, and heating oil, liquidity in the futures markets is combined into a single market (heating oil), and users of the other two commodities utilize quality spreads to provide an effective hedge.

25.3.1.3 Location Spreads Location spreads are trades that involve the same commodity but different delivery locations. A common location spread involves Brent crude oil, delivered in the United Kingdom, and West Texas intermediate (WTI) crude oil, delivered in the United States. Location spreads are primarily traded using OTC derivatives, though some location spreads, such as the Brent/WTI spread, can be executed using listed futures contracts (Pringle and Fernandes 2007).

Some location spreads have an arbitrage component. For example, if the Brent crude/WTI crude trade is executed with a one-month lag, then it is possible to take delivery in one location and make delivery in another location. However, if the location spread is made without a lag, then the trade is a correlation trade.

25.3.2 Intramarket Relative Value Strategies

Many of the strategies utilized by active commodity managers and hedge funds combine trading **commodity derivatives** with trading the underlying commodities in the physical or spot markets. These strategies utilize commodity futures markets the same way that commercial users do: as hedging vehicles to minimize the exposure of a particular transaction to unexpected market risk.

Storage strategies utilize leased storage facilities to hold physical commodities for delivery at a later date. These strategies are more complex than futures-based strategies and are both labor and capital intensive. Storage strategies are typically hedged transactions, involving a simultaneous purchase of the physical asset and sale of the commodity in the futures or OTC forward market. The strategy can also be an unhedged or directional trade in anticipation of an increase in the commodity price, though this is less common. A storage strategy is equivalent to a calendar spread in that the transaction involves holding the same commodity over time.

Transportation strategies utilize spot commodity markets to execute location trades. The strategy involves leased transportation services, such as tankers, bulk shipping, or pipelines, to physically move a commodity from a location where the commodity is in surplus to a location where there is a shortage.

Transportation and storage strategies carry risks that futures-based strategies do not. For example, the investors must be willing to assume the attendant credit risk of the OTC counterparties used in these transactions (Till and Eagleeye 2005). The investors must also be prepared to bear the risks associated with storing and transporting potentially hazardous commodities, including the potential headline risk. Market participants must also make sure that these strategies do not give the appearance of physical-market manipulation. Till (2008b) describes a Commodity Futures Trading Commission (CFTC) and U.S. Department of Justice action against a major international oil company, in which the company was fined $303 million for attempting to manipulate one U.S. delivery location's physical propane market. The firm's positions were initially entered into through the forward OTC markets. This case was particularly striking, since the firm had actually failed in this attempted manipulation, and had lost at least $10 million in attempting to carry out this market corner.

25.4 COMMODITY-BASED EQUITY AND DEBT STRATEGIES

Equity-based commodity strategies involve hedging the commodity price risk associated with the share price of a particular company. They can also involve buying the commodity to hedge a production input. An example of this would be buying jet fuel as a hedge for an airline stock.

Commodity-based corporations are typically valued as the sum of the firm's **commodity rights** and its **enterprise value**. Commodity rights reflect the current value of untapped commodity assets, such as oil reserves. The enterprise value is the residual value of corporate assets. If an analyst determines that the enterprise value of a particular firm is overpriced, a common strategy is to sell the firm's equity short and buy commodity futures to hedge out exposure to the commodity rights. Conversely, if the enterprise value is underpriced, the strategy involves buying the equity and selling futures to hedge the commodity rights.

Debt strategies use commodity futures and options to hedge the default risk of commodity producers and consumers. Because default risk is highly nonlinear, commodity options are commonly utilized for this type of hedge. For example, a lender to a copper producer might purchase put options on copper to hedge this exposure. The owner of airline bonds would buy call options on jet fuel to hedge the negative effect on margins of higher fuel costs.

25.5 FUNDAMENTAL ANALYSIS FOR DIRECTIONAL AND RELATIVE VALUE STRATEGIES

Directional and relative value strategies often depend on fundamental analysis for trade identification. Fundamental analysis in commodity investment involves identifying and predicting changes in supply and demand, including changes in inventory levels and cost of carry. The time frame of analysis depends on the horizon of the investment and the characteristics of the particular commodity in question. While much of the analysis may focus on shorter-term patterns (such as harvest season to harvest season), longer-term trends may also be considered, such as global demand growth due to emerging markets. A fundamental understanding of the commodity in question is essential. A brief description of the characteristics of wheat is provided next.

25.5.1 Fundamental Analysis: Understanding the Characteristics of Wheat

Wheat is a member of the grass family. It is the most prevalent cereal grain and provides more nourishment across the globe than any other food. It is believed to have originated near what is now Iraq, and has been consumed by humans since about 10,000 B.C. Although it was grown by colonists in America in the seventeenth century, wheat remained a relatively small crop in the United States until the late nineteenth century, when a hardy strain known as Turkey red wheat was brought to Kansas by Russian immigrants. Wheat is classified by growing season and further segmented by class. It is grown in two distinct growing seasons. Typically, about three-quarters of U.S. wheat production is made up of winter wheat, which is planted in the fall, lies dormant through the winter, grows in the spring, and is harvested in early summer. The remainder is spring wheat, which is planted in the spring, sprouts quickly, and is harvested in late summer or early fall. In addition to the growing season, wheat classes are based on the characteristics of the wheat, such as

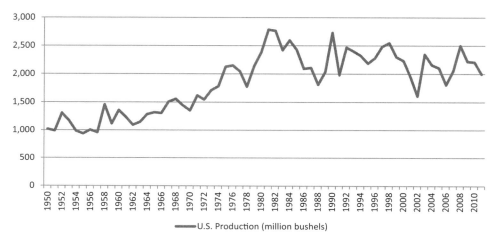

EXHIBIT 25.4 U.S. Wheat Production
Source: USDA Economic Research Service.

hardness and color. In the United States, wheat is classified in two winter classes: hard red winter (highest production and export levels, used for bread) and soft red winter (low protein, used for cakes). It is also classified into four spring classes: hard red spring (highest protein, excellent for breads); hard white (similar to red wheat, mostly consumed domestically); soft white (similar to soft red winter); and durum (hardest U.S. wheat, very little exported, used for semolina). (See Exhibit 25.4.)

Wheat is generally grown in arid regions with relatively poor soil quality. The particular temperature, soil, and rainfall of a region tend to determine which class of wheat is grown. Wheat production climbed significantly from 1950 to 1980, but it has been on a slight decline since 1980. This is partially due to the fact that wheat has no significant uses beyond food and feed production, while other crops, such as corn, have a variety of uses, including energy production. Since farmers will plant crops with the highest yield, the broader demand for corn may result in a reduced supply (and demand) of wheat.

China is the largest consumer of wheat, but the majority of its consumption is produced internally. The United States is the third largest producer of wheat (behind China and India), and the largest exporter of wheat (exporting close to half of its production).

Shortages of wheat during a season can be supplanted with wheat from other regions, since wheat is planted at different times of the year around the world. In addition, since wheat is generally consumed as flour, there are a number of substitutes available. While there are certainly differences in characteristics, flour can be made from corn, rice, beans, rye, and other crops.

Wheat marketing years vary across the globe, depending on a region's harvest date. In the United States, the wheat marketing year runs from June 1 to May 31. Wheat is usually harvested from June to September, progressively moving from Texas northward. Typically, about half of the wheat is sold at or before harvest, while the other half is stored. This excess supply at harvest depresses prices during the summer each year. Prices generally recover after the harvest, until excess supply

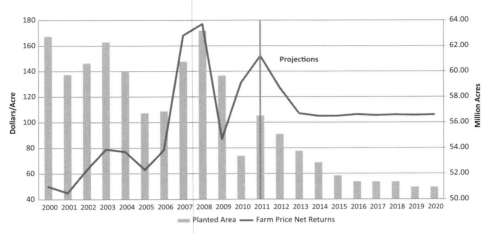

EXHIBIT 25.5 U.S. Wheat Planted Area and Returns
Source: USDA Economic Research Service.

appears again when wheat growers in the southern hemisphere begin their harvest in December.

Wheat futures in the United States trade on the Chicago Board of Trade (CBOT), the Kansas City Board of Trade (KCBT), and the Minneapolis Grain Exchange (MGE). The underlying class of wheat for CBOT wheat futures is generally considered to be soft red winter wheat, although the contract allows delivery of four different varieties of wheat. The KCBT contract specifies hard red winter wheat, while the MGE contract specifies hard red spring wheat. Wheat futures typically trade in contango, which entices producers to retain a portion of the wheat crop in storage throughout the marketing year. (See Exhibit 25.5.)

25.6 LOOKING FORWARD

From a long-term perspective, Waugh (2007) outlines a number of fundamental changes in global supply and demand. Waugh argues that we are approaching a new world order in commodity markets. The recent outperformance of energies and metals will give way to outperformance in agricultural commodities. Similarly, Black (2009) argues that the increased standard of living in Asia is driving an increase in Asians' demand for meat. Since livestock requires significant consumption of feed in the form of grains, demand for grains is driven by the increased demand for meat. Black argues that the growth in demand for biofuels puts further pressure on the price of agricultural commodities. Finally, since many commodities are traded in U.S. dollars, and since American investors are typically interested in U.S. dollar–denominated returns, the value of the U.S. dollar relative to other currencies can have a significant impact on the returns to a commodity portfolio as well as the effectiveness of commodities as return enhancers and portfolio diversifiers.

In March 2012, Bill Gross argued that we are at a turning point that will see an increasing change in focus from financial assets to real assets, such as commodities. Gross stated, "You have to move from financial assets into the world of real assets," because emerging markets such as China are not "looking for financial assets, they're looking to lock up commodities going forward."[1]

Over the past two decades, we have witnessed a rapid growth in the number of commodity-based investment vehicles available to investors, as sources of both commodity beta and alpha. These products will continue to evolve in the future in order to meet unique return and risk demands of investors. The day of the one-size-fits-all commodity index has come and gone. Many subindices and enhanced indices allow investors to more finely tune their commodity exposures. These offerings will undoubtedly continue to grow along with the increasing interest in commodities in the future.

---

[1] See www.cnbc.com/id/46871380/Invest_in_Commodities_Dividend_Payers_Pimco_s_Gross.

CHAPTER 26

Methods of Delivering Commodity Beta: Indices, Swaps, Notes, and Hedge Funds

26.1 INTRODUCTION

The return to commodity beta may be defined as the fundamental risk-based return from holding a passive long position in a commodity. For example, to deliver oil-based commodity beta, an investor can use a number of investment vehicles that capture the price change in a particular oil-based commodity investment. Historically, indirect investments (e.g., equity ownership of firms specializing in direct commodity market production) have been the principal means by which many investors obtain exposure to this asset class. Investment through commodity-based equity firms, however, mixes equity beta with commodity beta. The matter is further complicated by the complex commodity exposures and degree of commodity price risk hedging by commodity-based corporations. However, in recent years, the number of investable commodity indices and commodity-linked investments has increased dramatically. This chapter provides an outline of the wide range of investment products that are currently available to acquire commodity beta exposure. Since most commodity investment is in some way linked to commodity indices, we discuss the characteristics of commodity indices and enhanced commodity indices as well as the calculation of their returns. Finally, the chapter provides an overview of some of the major commodity indices upon which the returns of many commodity investment vehicles are based.

Select Highlights in Commodity Investment Product Development

Pre-1990	Most commodity investment is implemented indirectly through stocks or bonds.
1991	Goldman Sachs Commodity Index (GSCI) is introduced.
1996	Standard & Poor's (S&P) GSCI tracking exchange-traded fund (ETF) is introduced.
2002	PIMCO CommodityRealReturn Strategy Mutual Fund is introduced.
2000s	Long-biased commodity hedge funds grow in popularity.
Mid-2000s	Energy master limited partnerships (MLPs) grow rapidly.
Mid-2000s	Enhanced commodity indices are introduced.
2004	Gold bullion ETF is introduced.
2006	Crude oil tracking ETF is introduced.

26.2 DIRECT PHYSICAL OWNERSHIP OF COMMODITIES

Most investors avoid holding physical commodities, because storage can be cumbersome and expensive. For example, barrels of oil require a storage tank as well as transportation from the purchase site. In fact, some commodities are perishable (e.g., many agricultural and livestock commodities), making them virtually impossible to store for an extended period. Precious metals are an exception. Investors often hold precious metals in the form of bullion or coinage. Gold is especially easy to store, and gold investors have historically preferred to hold physical gold rather than gold derivatives.[1] In short, real assets such as commodities require a degree of active management in order to maintain their value. Furthermore, research suggests that, over the long term, the prices of physical commodities have not kept up with inflation, which is in stark contrast to the returns generated by other forms of commodity investment, such as commodity indices (Gorton and Rouwenhorst 2006). As a result, most commodity investments are made through derivatives contracts, such as futures contracts, forward contracts, swaps, and options. This allows the owner to benefit from price changes in the commodity without the need to store it.

26.3 INDIRECT OWNERSHIP OF COMMODITIES

The most common method of obtaining commodity exposure is through **indirect commodity investments (equity, fixed income)**. Most investors actually have this type of exposure embedded in their traditional investment portfolios. These exposures can be as simple as traditional stock or bond investments in companies that are involved in the production, transportation, and marketing of commodities, or they can be one of a number of more specialized commodity-based investments, as outlined in the following pages. A great deal of institutional investment in commodities takes the form of index-based investments. The primary vehicle used by institutional investors for exposure to commodity indices is commodity index swaps.

26.3.1 Commodity Index Swaps

A **commodity index swap** is an exchange of cash flows in which one of the cash flows is based on the price of a specific commodity index, while the other cash flow is based on an interest rate. Commodity index swaps are the preferred vehicle for most institutional commodity investments. Swaps are competitively priced, with multiple dealers making markets in swaps on several major commodity indices. Competition among vendors ensures liquidity and provides multiple counterparties to spread the default risk that stems from over-the-counter (OTC) swap transactions. Investors sometimes prefer this structure because it allows them to maintain control of their cash. While most indices include a collateral return equal to that of Treasury bills, most investors can achieve higher collateral returns by managing the cash themselves. The cash can also be utilized in portable alpha strategies or, if desired, held in

---

[1] It is worth noting that the SPDR Gold Trust exchange-traded fund (ticker GLD), which holds gold bullion on behalf of its investors, is one of the largest ETFs as measured by assets under management.

Treasury bills. The principal drawback of OTC swaps is that only a small number of investors have access to this market, as it is limited to large, highly creditworthy investors. Most commodity investors are excluded from directly participating in these structures. Also, the secondary market for commodity swaps is not liquid, so early termination or modification of swap agreements typically requires negotiating with the counterparty. Swaps also experience greater counterparty risk than do the commodity futures markets.

26.3.2 Public Commodity-Based Equities

Owning the equity of a firm that derives a significant part of its revenue from the sale of physical commodities is a straightforward way of gaining exposure to commodities. However, not all of these investments have returns that are highly correlated with specific commodities. For example, the returns of integrated oil companies (like Exxon) and gold-mining companies (like Homestake Mining) are generally highly correlated with the prices of crude oil and gold, respectively, but the returns of food companies typically have only a modest correlation with the prices of grains and livestock. However, many of these firms hedge their principal commodity exposures, which can significantly affect the degree of commodity exposure the firm provides to investors. Furthermore, there is evidence that commodity producers engage in selective hedging, in which they actively alter their hedge ratios based on their view of future commodity prices (Stulz 1996). Such hedging activity can result in unpredictable commodity exposures for indirect commodity investors. Indirect commodity investments derive at least some of their returns from the active management of commodities.

The disadvantage of using equities for commodity exposure is that they provide the investor with significant stock market exposure. In addition to the underlying commodity risk associated with direct investment in a given commodity, an investor who takes a position in the equity securities of companies engaged in the sale of physical commodities is also subjected to the company's underlying business risk (Schneeweis 2006). According to the widely read 2006 article by Gorton and Rouwenhorst, "Facts and Fantasies about Commodity Futures," an index of commodity-producing equities had similar long-run returns to an index of commodity futures contracts, and the volatility of the commodity futures index was lower than that of the commodity equity portfolio. However, the returns and volatility tell only part of the story. The study also showed that the portfolio of commodity-based equities had a higher correlation with the S&P 500 than with the portfolio of commodity futures. The authors' conclusion is that commodity company stocks behave more like equities than like commodity futures and thus, in terms of performance, are not a good proxy for an investment in commodity futures. This result is particularly relevant for investors who are interested in accessing commodity exposure to diversify traditional stock and bond portfolios.

26.3.3 Bonds Issued by Commodity Firms

Similarly, investors can gain exposure to commodities through owning bonds issued by firms that derive a significant part of their revenue from the sale of commodities. However, if these are high-grade bonds, the yield on these bonds generally has a low sensitivity to the commodity market in which the company is involved. Specifically, the bond price will fluctuate less with the value of the commodities that provide the basis of the firm's revenue than with economy-wide changes in interest rates and credit spreads. In contrast, for high-yield bonds, where the default or political risk is high, the price of the bonds will tend to be more highly correlated with the commodity being produced by the firm.

26.3.4 Commodity-Based Mutual Funds and Exchange-Traded Products

Other ways to gain exposure to commodities are through commodity mutual funds or exchange-traded products. These vehicles typically use one of four methods to acquire commodity exposure: (1) commodity index funds or swaps, (2) equities of commodities-based companies, (3) physical commodities, or (4) actual commodity futures. Commodity mutual funds are available in different active and passive structures, including commodity-based equity funds and passive commodity index tracking funds. While commodity index tracking mutual funds are generally considered passive funds, they have an opportunity to attempt to outperform the commodity index by actively managing the collateral portion of the investment. Commodity mutual funds have fees and cost structures similar to other types of mutual funds (Burkart 2006).

Commodity-based exchange-traded funds (ETFs) may offer similar exposures to many of the commodity mutual funds. The most obvious difference between commodity mutual funds and commodity ETFs is that ETFs trade on organized exchanges like traditional equities and generally charge lower fees than mutual funds do. ETFs offer a liquidity advantage over other index-linked structures because they are easily arbitraged. If the price of the commodity ETF falls below fair value, it can be profitable for commodity trading desks to purchase shares in the fund and sell the index short to lock in the profit. Long-only commodity index-based ETFs may track broad-based commodity indices (such as the iShares S&P GSCI Commodity-Indexed ETF) or commodity subindices (such as the PowerShares DB Energy Fund). These ETFs generate their returns by directly or indirectly (such as through swap agreements) holding commodity futures contracts. ETFs are also available that track the spot price of individual commodities, such as the SPDR Gold Trust (GLD), which tracks the price of gold bullion. Rather than tracking commodity futures, the GLD ETF holds physical gold bullion. While most commodity ETFs track commodity prices (based on commodity futures or spot commodities), some ETFs track the equity prices of firms engaged in commodity production. For example, the Market Vectors Agribusiness ETF tracks the stocks of agribusiness firms. It is worth noting that equity-based ETFs may provide a less pure exposure to commodity prices than futures-based commodity ETFs provide, since their performance is influenced by factors that drive the equity markets as well as factors that drive commodity prices (Jensen and Mercer 2011).

26.3.5 Public and Private Commodity Partnerships

Some commodity investment vehicles have structures similar to private real estate partnerships or publicly traded real estate investment trusts (REITs). Private commodity partnerships offer long-term ownership of real assets used in mining and energy markets. Whereas real estate vehicles typically own buildings, commodity partnerships might own the extraction rights to a natural gas field, a pipeline, railcars, storage facilities, or refining operations related to natural resource extraction. Partnerships are organized as pass-through entities. The income from ownership of the assets is distributed to the partners, typically without taxation at the corporate level. Income can be in the form of rental income, for example if the partnership owns a pipeline, or from the sale of commodities such as crude oil or natural gas. In either case, the income paid by the partnership is usually correlated with the price of some commodity, so investors see partnerships as a substitute for direct commodity investments.

As with REITs, the principal advantage of the **master limited partnership (MLP)** structure is in avoiding corporate taxation. Income from qualifying MLPs is distributed directly to investors. It is worth noting that the growth in MLPs over the past decade was accompanied by an increasing concentration in energy infrastructure. Currently, about 90% of MLPs are energy related (Ciccotello 2011). Energy-related MLPs typically own midstream assets used to store or transport energy, such as pipelines, storage terminals, or shipping vessels. Upstream assets, such as oil- and gas-producing properties, which are exposed to energy price risk, are more frequently owned in private partnerships than through MLPs.

Most MLPs concentrate on the midstream portion of the energy value chain, which is dominated by long-term, fee-based contracts with price escalators, while a smaller number concentrate on the upstream portion (exploration and production, mainly production), in which a significant amount of commodity price exposure is hedged (Ciccotello 2011). Thus, the commodity exposure of energy-related MLPs may vary significantly, depending on whether they focus on the midstream or upstream portion of the energy value chain. Midstream MLPs, which frequently own pipelines, earn revenue based on the volume of energy products moving through the pipelines. This fee-based revenue is typically more sensitive to the volume of energy transported than to the underlying energy prices.

The publicly traded MLP market has expanded rapidly since 2000. For example, as reported by Alerian Capital Management, the market capitalization of the Alerian MLP index increased from $15.7 billion at the end of 2000 to $250.7 billion at the end of 2011. Demand for all commodity-linked investments increased over the time period, which explains much of the growth. However, other factors are also at play. Infrastructure and other real asset investments have become an important strategic part of institutional portfolios. The long duration of partnership investments is attractive to pension funds. Another factor in the growth of commodity partnerships is the public listing of partnership units. Like REITs, commodity partnerships can be listed on public exchanges if they adhere to regulations governing payout ratios and make appropriate filings with the Securities and Exchange Commission (SEC). This has greatly increased the liquidity and transparency of partnerships, and has expanded the potential investor base.

26.3.6 Commodity Debt Investments

A variety of commodity-based exchange-traded notes (ETNs) are available, which offer the returns of investment strategies similar to those of many of the commodity

ETFs. While the returns and fee levels of ETNs are similar to corresponding ETFs, there are a number of significant differences. ETNs are zero coupon debt instruments. Since an ETN investment is not a claim on a basket of assets, the return to an investment in an ETN is subject to the creditworthiness of the issuer. One disadvantage of ETNs is credit risk exposure. This risk is generally higher than the counterparty risk inherent in a commodity index swap. In a swap contract, the counterparty posts collateral at regular intervals, so counterparty risk is usually no more than a few percentage points of the total notional size of the swap. This extra risk exposure represents a significant difference between ETFs and ETNs. The price of an ETF is based on the assets that the fund holds, so there may be some tracking error versus the index that the ETF is designed to track. In contrast, the price of an ETN is based on a contractually designated relationship with the underlying index.

Investors may face different tax treatment depending on whether they choose to invest in ETFs or in ETNs (Jensen and Mercer 2011). ETNs are frequently referred to as prepaid forward contracts, because the notes are economically equivalent to fully collateralized forward contracts for delivery of the index value. The advantage of the ETN structure is primarily related to taxation. Commodity indices have a high turnover rate, so profits and losses are usually treated as short-term income. However, since an ETN is based on the index value (rather than futures contracts), an ETN may qualify for capital gains tax treatment if held for a long enough period of time.

Fully margined, long-maturity futures contracts on several commodity indices are also available. These are economically equivalent to ETNs, except that they are listed on futures exchanges rather than stock exchanges. The key difference between these contracts and typical commodity futures contracts is that, as said earlier, long-maturity index-linked futures contracts are fully margined. The investor must post 100% collateral at the time of investment (although market makers and other commercial users of these contracts are allowed to post much smaller margin amounts). Index-linked futures contracts offer one of the least expensive solutions for retail investors. Furthermore, there is less credit risk associated with futures exchanges than with ETNs.

The **commodity index-linked note** market is somewhat more expensive than swaps, but offers a number of advantages. These include a secondary market and much smaller minimum investments. Index-linked notes appeal primarily to investors who prefer to hold bonds, often for regulatory purposes. Many investors are obligated to own securities and have difficulty owning futures contracts. Furthermore, futures contracts and swaps require frequent margin and/or collateral postings. Index-linked note structures do not require collateral since the structure is already fully collateralized. Finally, there is a secondary market for index-linked notes. A swap contract cannot generally be transferred, but ownership of notes is easily transferred. It is worth noting that ETNs are index-linked notes that are listed on major stock exchanges.

26.3.7 Commodity-Based Hedge Funds

Hedge funds are active players in the commodity markets. Before 2000, commodity hedge funds were primarily focused on absolute return and relative value strategies. However, in response to the rise in institutional investment in commodities, a number of firms have launched long-biased commodity hedge funds. There are two categories of long-biased funds.

The first group is similar to long-only equity funds. Funds in this group look to identify undervalued commodities to purchase and hold in unhedged portfolios. These funds have been successful in attracting assets that would otherwise be placed in commodity index funds. Active managers may be able to avoid unfavorable rolls and to overweight or underweight commodities based on fundamental or systematic strategies. The fund managers are typically benchmarked to a particular index, with compensation schemes tied to their performance relative to its benchmark. For the most part, these managers hold futures contracts rather than physical commodities. Lockups are short, and liquidity and transparency are high.

The second group of long-biased funds is involved in the physical markets. These funds are engaged in the purchase, storage, and transportation of commodities. Because they limit their use of hedging, their returns are influenced by the direction of commodity prices. These managers tend to specialize in particular commodities or commodity sectors. Investors in these funds are seeking returns generated through a combination of active management (alpha) and commodity beta. Similar to other hedge fund styles, investments with these managers are fairly illiquid, often requiring long notice periods prior to redemptions. Competitors include trading companies, shipping firms, and the commodity trading desks of major financial firms.

Hedge funds that focus exclusively on commodity investment are by no means restricted to long-only funds. Hedge funds are familiar with commodity investments and provide pure alpha, pure beta, and alpha-plus-beta options in various hedge fund products. Hedge fund alpha is available through a number of methods, including cash management, long/short positions, and instrument choice (Burkart 2006). A detailed discussion of the types of strategies used by commodity hedge fund managers can be found in the commodity alpha discussion in Chapter 25. In an actively managed hedge fund, there is no guarantee that a manager will maintain a long position in commodities, as most hedge funds utilize a core risk-management principle of hedging most or all systematic risk (Till and Eagleeye 2005). Commodity hedge funds also utilize market-timing strategies. Historically, the correlation between commodity hedge fund returns and the returns of the underlying commodities has been low.

26.3.8 Commodity Trade Financing and Production Financing

Financing for the production, storage, and transportation of commodities has historically been provided by merchant banks and vertically integrated commodity firms. A number of private investment pools have been organized to compete in the high-margin segments of this business. The strategy can be executed in a number of ways. Most commonly, investment funds will provide financing for the extraction or shipping of bulk commodities, with the commodities pledged as collateral for the loans. Other strategies involve purchasing commodities for future delivery directly from the producers. In effect, the producers are borrowing money that will be repaid with commodities. This provides working capital to the producers and an effective hedge against a decline in the price of the commodity. For the investment funds, these transactions typically have higher margins than are available simply by purchasing commodity futures, as they are custom transactions that frequently involve both default and political risk. Many commodity producers are located in parts of the world with elevated political risk. A commodity futures contract is settled daily and guaranteed by the futures exchange; however, purchasing commodities for future delivery from many producers carries considerable risk. These risks, and the resulting profits, have traditionally gone to multinational banks and other financial intermediaries. As the financial system has become more risk-averse, the opportunities for disintermediation by investment funds have grown.

26.4 LEVERAGED AND OPTION-BASED STRUCTURES

While most commodity investments are delivered through standard index-based beta-one structures such as swaps, ETFs, and structured notes, an array of complex structures, such as principal-protected notes, levered notes, and options, are available to investors.[2]

Most commodity index-based products are designed to provide an unleveraged long exposure to a commodity index; however, there are a variety of ETFs and ETNs designed to provide leveraged (usually two times) long, leveraged short, or unleveraged short exposure to commodity indices. It is worth noting that these funds are designed to provide the levered return on a daily basis, and rebalancing (as well as the associated transaction costs) may be required to achieve the desired levered return over longer time periods, particularly in high-volatility market environments (Hill and Teller 2009).

Many index-linked notes offer leveraged exposure to commodity indices. These are referred to as leveraged notes. A common structure offers three-times-leveraged exposure to a commodity index. Because these notes can lose 100% of their value when a decline of more than 33% in the index is experienced, the issuer and investor can be viewed as having or needing options. The issuer typically purchases option protection against further declines in the commodity. The investor enjoys an implicit protective put through the limited liability of the notes, since the price of the note cannot become negative. The main benefit of leveraged notes is the high commodity exposure. In a three-times-leveraged note, each $1,000 note controls $3,000 of commodity exposure, so an investor can add exposure without committing large amounts of capital. These notes provide a middle ground between an index-linked swap (no up-front capital commitment) and ETN structures (100% collateralized at purchase).

Many investors prefer **principal-guaranteed notes**. These notes offer investors the opportunity to profit if commodity prices rise, combined with a guarantee that the principal amount will be returned at the maturity of the structure. These structures are popular with retail investors but have generated little interest from institutional investors. This is because a steep decline in commodity prices will cause the issuer to shift 100% out of commodities and into bonds. This feature of principal-protected notes ensures that the investor will not lose principal, but if the notes are shifted into bonds, it prevents the investor from benefiting from the diversification properties of commodities. For example, investors holding notes that were shifted into bonds during 2006 would have missed out on the commodity bull market in 2007 and 2008.

---

[2] One can find a myriad of payoff structures in various commodity-linked notes that commercial and investment banks have been issuing via the EDGAR/SEC database.

There are two common structures for principal-guaranteed notes. The first structure is the **cash and call strategy**, in which the principal guarantee comes from an investment in zero coupon notes, while the commodity-linked return comes through call options. A five-year, $1,000 zero coupon note yielding 5% has an issuance price of $783.53, which leaves $216.47 for the purchase of call options on a commodity index. The principal-guaranteed note will return $1,000 at maturity if the commodity index does not settle above the strike price of the option, and the issuer of the note has the cash and credit quality to pay the face value of the unsecured notes at maturity. The notes will have a maturity value of less than $1,000 when the issuer of the note defaults on the obligation and a maturity value of greater than $1,000 when the commodity index settles above the strike price of the option at maturity.

The second structure for principal-guaranteed notes is a **dynamic strategy**, which varies the size of the commodity investment based on the cost of insuring the principal guarantee. Using the previous example, the initial price of the zero coupon bonds is $783.53, which is set as the floor value. This floor value changes over time, as rising yields will reduce the cost of the zero coupon bonds, while the passage of time increases the cost of the zero coupon bonds, as there is less time remaining to earn interest. In the dynamic strategy, commodity investments are held as long as the value of the commodity investments exceeds the cost of purchasing the zero coupon bonds to insure the portfolio. Some strategies will have greater investments, such as 100% of face value invested in commodities when there is a greater distance between the portfolio value and the floor, and smaller investments, such as 30% commodities, when the value of the portfolio is moving closer to the cost of the zero coupon note. Once the commodity portfolio has posted sufficient losses to reach the value of the zero coupon note floor, all commodity assets are liquidated and the principal-guaranteed note will hold 100% of the remaining assets in the zero coupon note until maturity. After the floor value has been touched and the portfolio has been completely moved into zeros, the note will no longer have any exposure to the underlying commodity index.

26.5 COMMODITY INDICES COMPARED TO SECURITIES INDICES

Commodity indices are an effective and efficient means for gaining access to the benefits of commodities. A **commodity index** is a group of commodity futures contracts. Commodity indices provide returns comparable to passive long positions in listed futures contracts. In order to gain long-term exposure, commodity futures contracts must be rolled from one maturity to the next before the expiration of the front-month contract. They attempt to replicate the returns one would generate through holding long positions in agricultural, metal, energy, or livestock futures contracts, without requiring the investor to actively manage the positions. The first generation of commodity indices, which includes the S&P GSCI, are long-only, are infrequently rebalanced, and ignore term structure in their weighting methodology. Second- and third-generation enhanced commodity indices have been developed in an attempt to improve returns by providing unique roll or weighting methodologies, rebalancing more frequently, or implementing rules-based trading strategies that utilize signals derived from futures market characteristics, such as momentum, term structure, and time to maturity.

The number of commodity indices available to investors has multiplied since the 1990s. A wide variety of commodity indices and subindices, both traditional and enhanced, are currently publicly available. While all indices offer a diversified exposure to commodity markets through the use of commodity futures contracts, they differ in composition, commodity selection criteria, rolling mechanism, rebalancing strategy, and weighting scheme. Commodity index performance can be a function of the methodology of the index combined with the impact of market factors on the index components. As a result, commodity index performance can vary across indices and market environments. The methodology of the index can have an impact on volatility and return levels (Kazemi, Schneeweis, and Spurgin 2008).

26.6 SOURCES OF COMMODITY INDEX RETURNS

Commodity indices can benefit from multiple sources of returns, many of which tend to be uncorrelated. These can include spot, roll, beta, momentum, rebalancing, and collateral returns. Additional factors, like diversification, commodity component weighting, and roll schedule, can also impact the index return. We now proceed to explain these return sources.

Commodity beta: For a given market, commodity beta can be defined as the return to holding the active futures contract until the contract roll date, and then rolling to the next active futures contract. With respect to liquidity and transparency, this is the simplest way to hold commodities, and thus is the benchmark against which other methods of holding commodity futures are measured.

Roll return: Roll return, or roll yield, is the profit or loss from holding a futures contract due to the change in the basis. Roll returns have a direct impact on index performance. Roll returns tend to be positive when the commodity forward curve persistently slopes down (backwardation), and tend to be negative when the forward curve persistently slopes up (contango). Some commodities, such as gold, nearly always have a negative roll yield. The cost of carry for gold has been larger than the convenience yield, so the forward curve has been upward sloping. The weighting scheme of an index can have a significant impact on its roll return. Difficult-to-store commodities are more likely to be in backwardation, and therefore generate positive roll returns (Till and Eagleeye 2005). It is worth noting that there are a number of reasons to be wary of designing an index strictly on the basis of roll return. First, roll return for a particular commodity changes over time with changes in interest rates, storage costs, and convenience yields (and for financial futures, dividends). A commodity's forward curve may flip from backwardation to contango with changes in cost of carry. Second, commodities in backwardation typically exhibit high volatility due to their low inventory levels. Finally, focusing strictly on roll return may negatively impact the degree of diversification of the commodity portfolio.

Spot return: The difference between the excess return of an index and the roll return is referred to as the spot return. Since commodities tend to mean revert over longer time periods, spot return is expected to contribute little to total returns over longer periods (Till 2006), with one exception: There can be a rare trend shift in spot commodity prices, as occurred during the early 1970s.

Dynamic asset allocation: Some commodity indices incorporate dynamic asset allocation models. These models determine which commodities to overweight and which to underweight. Momentum is a commonly used asset allocation rule. Momentum models overweight commodities that are increasing in price, and underweight commodities that are declining in price. Another common strategy for dynamic asset allocation includes mean reversion. This strategy reduces the allocation to commodities that have increased in value, and increases the allocation to commodities that have declined in price. Typically, momentum-based asset allocation rules are based on short-term models, while mean reversion strategies are based on price changes over a time horizon greater than one year. Term structure signals can also be used for dynamic allocation. For example Fuertes, Miffre, and Rallis (2008) analyze the performance of long/short strategies that take long positions in backwardated futures markets and short positions in contangoed markets.

Diversification: The greater the number of commodities, the more diverse the index, making it less sensitive to price increases or decreases in a particular commodity or commodity subsector. Diversification is particularly relevant for commodity indices, since commodities tend to have a very low correlation with one another and individual commodities tend to have high volatilities. Erb and Harvey (2006) find that the low correlations and high volatility of commodities can result in significant **diversification returns** from rebalancing the components of a diversified commodity portfolio. This portfolio return effect is further discussed and clarified in Willenbrock (2011).

Commodity weights: Higher index returns may result from overweighting commodity futures that are increasing in value and underweighting those that are falling in value. However, risk and volatility can increase in an index that allocates a large weight to a small subset of commodities. A commodity weighting scheme should also have an economic rationale, to avoid designing an index that optimizes based solely on past performance.

Maturity: Using longer-maturity contracts tends to increase roll returns and consequently total returns, but may not significantly affect spot returns. Investing in longer-maturity contracts can also effectively enhance risk-adjusted returns, as measured by the Sharpe ratio. Long-maturity futures contracts tend to be less volatile. Events that may cause a dramatic change in the spot price of a commodity often have a more subdued influence on the price for delivery six or 12 months in the future. As a result, an index based on longer-maturity futures contracts will be less volatile. The drawback to this approach is that liquidity is much more variable in long-maturity futures contracts, so it may be more difficult to exit a large index position in a short period of time.

Collateral: In total return indices, the notional amount of the investment is held in interest-bearing instruments, often short-term sovereign debt issues. This collateral, which can be used as futures margin, earns interest, which adds to the return of commodity futures-based investments.

26.7 ISSUES IN COMMODITY INDEX DESIGN

There are a number of decisions that need to be made when designing a commodity index. These decisions include weighting and roll methodologies, as well as collateral considerations. Enhanced commodity indices may modify the roll methodology and the choice of contracts traded in the pursuit of higher returns.

26.7.1 Value-Based versus Quantity-Based

Commodity indices can be value-based or quantity-based. A value-based index has fixed component weights. The number of futures contracts in the index changes dynamically to maintain constant weights. A quantity-based index holds a fixed quantity of each commodity, so that the index weights change each day. For example, the S&P 500 stock index is quantity-based, since the number of shares of each company in the index changes only when the index constituents are changed. Conversely, a benchmark that consists of 60% stocks and 40% bonds is value-based.

26.7.2 Total Return versus Excess Return

There are two types of return indices available to investors. A **total return index** is a fully collateralized investment strategy, with the collateralization generally taking the form of Treasury bills. In a total return index, the overall calculation of the index return includes the cash return from the collateral. Generally, total return indices have returns and risk comparable to stock markets. An **excess return index** provides returns over cash and is linked to the price movements of a basket of commodity futures contracts (Blanch and Scheis 2006).

26.7.3 Roll Methodology

Roll methodology can have a significant impact on the returns of a commodity index. In its simplest form, roll methodology involves two primary choices: futures curve positioning and roll procedure. Future curve positioning determines the time to expiration of the futures contracts at the initiation of the position, and the length of time the contract will be held before rolling to a further-out contract. First-generation indices, such as the S&P GSCI, which has an average maturity of less than two months, generally position themselves at the near end of the futures curve and hold their contracts for a short period of time. Many of the newer indices position themselves further out on the forward curve and/or hold their positions for a longer time before rolling. Since forward curves of commodities are generally nonlinear, the impact of contango or backwardation on returns can vary significantly due to the choice of curve positioning strategy. Far more complicated curve positioning strategies exist as well. For example, the JPMorgan Commodity Curve Index (JPMCCI) introduced a new concept in commodity index investing by holding the entire commodity curve as opposed to holding only the front contracts held by the more popular indices. This index holds exposure along the entire commodity curve in proportion to the open interest of each tenor. Further enhancements involve actively varying curve positioning based on the current or expected shape of the forward curve for each commodity.

The actual roll procedure can have a significant impact on returns, particularly for the more popular indices whose sheer volume can move the markets. Typically, extremely large futures positions must be rolled over the period of a few days. In addition, the roll procedure is publicly available and thus entirely predictable. This can result in significant market impact to the detriment of index returns. Many newer indices are designed to minimize the inefficiencies of their roll. For example, the Bache Commodity Index (BCI) rolls a small portion of its positions each day, resulting in a low-impact, almost continuous roll.

26.7.4 Weighting Methodology

Perhaps the largest impact on index returns comes from the weighting methodology. A weighting methodology determines the degree of diversification or concentration on particular commodities or sectors. For example, the S&P GSCI has a very high concentration on energies (about 71% at the start of 2012), whereas the Dow Jones–UBS Commodity Index (DJUBSCI) has a 33% cap on energy sector exposure. There are a number of variables an index provider can use to determine individual commodity or commodity-sector weights. The primary variables are world production (for example, the S&P GSCI is a quantity-based, world production–weighted index) and liquidity (for example, the DJUBSCI uses a combination of liquidity and production measures to assign weights to individual commodities). Liquidity has twice as much influence as production in deciding the overall weights. Index weighting schemes can vary significantly in the degree of diversification they provide. For example, the Deutsche Bank Liquid Commodity Index (DBLCI) consists of only six highly liquid commodities, whereas the Diapason Commodities Index (DCI) is one of the broadest commodity indices available, with 48 components. It is worth noting that many indices use maximum and/or minimum limits on individual commodity or commodity-sector allocations to limit the degree of position concentration. Weighting methodologies can also incorporate more active weights, as well as short positions for long/short or short-biased indices.

26.7.5 First-Generation Commodity Indices

Spot-based commodity indices date back to the 1800s (the *Economist* commodity price index). However, spot indices are of limited use to investors, since most commodity investment is futures based. The Commodity Research Bureau (CRB) Index, established in 1957, has the longest history of all the futures-based commodity indices, but the usefulness of the long track record has been reduced by the high number of revisions in methodology and by the fact that the index was not investable in the early years. The first generation of investable commodity indices began with the introduction of the Goldman Sachs Commodity Index (now the S&P GSCI) in November 1991. The S&P GSCI and the Dow Jones–UBS Commodity Index (introduced in 1998) are by far the most dominant commodity indices and represent the first generation of investable commodity indices.

Overviews of the S&P GSCI and the DJUBSCI, their specific methodologies used, and the factors impacting their performance are provided in the box.

OVERVIEW OF S&P GSCI (SPGSCI)

The S&P GSCI (SPGSCI) is a quantity-based, world production–weighted index that currently holds six energy products, five industrial metals, eight agricultural products, three livestock products, and two precious metals. The index has the flexibility to hold any number of contracts as long as the particular contract meets the liquidity criteria. Contracts are weighted by the average worldwide production in the past five years of available data. The SPGSCI is dominated by energy, with a roughly 71% allocation to the energy sector as of the beginning of 2012. There is also a series of indices that use the same convention and hold the same components as the SPGSCI, including the SPGSCI Reduced Energy, SPGSCI Light Energy, and SPGSCI UltraLight Energy subindices. The SPGSCI Reduced Energy Index uses one-half of the SPGSCI contract production weights for the energy components, while the SPGSCI Light and SPGSCI UltraLight Energy indices use one-quarter and one-eighth of the contract production weights for the energy components, respectively. The SPGSCI Enhanced Commodity Index is another variant of the SPGSCI. It holds the same basket of commodities as the SPGSCI, but tries to address the issue of negative roll yield due to dominance of contango markets in recent years.

Launch date: November 1991.

Roll: The SPGSCI rolls from the front to the next contract between the fifth and ninth business day of the month prior to delivery. Rebalancing of the index takes place once a year, after the weights are reviewed by the index committee. However, these weights typically do not vary much from year to year, due to the five-year evaluation period.

Average maturity: The weighted average maturity of futures contracts in the SPGSCI is less than two months, the shortest average maturity of all commodity indices.

Energy allocation: Because the SPGSCI does not have sector-weight constraints, the index methodology generates the largest energy allocation of any commodity index.

Outperformance: This index is expected to do well in times of rising energy prices. It will also perform quite well when commodity markets are in backwardation, because it holds the shortest average maturity contracts of any major commodity index.

Overview of Dow Jones–UBS Commodity Index (DJUBSCI) (Formerly the DJ-AIG Commodity Index)

The DJUBSCI, a quantity-based commodity index, predefines a set of criteria to prevent any sector from becoming dominant in the index. It limits the maximum weight of any commodity to 15% of the index, any sector to 33% of the index, and any commodity, along with its downstream products, to 25% of the index. This index currently holds 20 commodity futures, of which seven are agricultural products, five are energy products, four are industrial metals, two are precious metals, and two are livestock products. The DJUBSCI had a roughly 33% allocation to the energy sector as of the beginning of 2012. A combination of liquidity and production measures is used to assign weights to individual commodities. Liquidity has twice as much influence as production in deciding the overall weights. Use of the production data has the drawback of underweighting commodities, like gold, that are storable over a longer time horizon.

Launch date: July 1998.

Roll: The DJUBSCI follows a roll strategy similar to that of the SPGSCI, and rolls from the fifth to the ninth business day of the month, from the front to the next contract.

Average maturity: The DJUBSCI has the same average maturity for agricultural markets as the SPGSCI, but longer average energy and metal maturities, because it skips every other expiration in commodity markets that trade on a monthly expiration schedule.

Energy allocation: The DJUBSCI methodology has a cap of 33% on the energy sector, lower than almost all of the other commodity indices.

Outperformance: The DJUBSCI will tend to outperform other indices when agriculture and metals prices rise more than energy prices. This index may also do better when agriculture and metals are experiencing greater backwardation than energy.

Most commodity index-based investment is tied to these two indices; however, they suffer from some limitations, which may result in suboptimal returns. Both the S&P GSCI and the DJUBSCI invest in short-maturity futures, and roll these futures to the next-further-out contract over a relatively short time frame. The sheer size and concentration of the roll of these indices result in a reduction in their returns. For example, as discussed in Chapter 25, Mou (2011) provides evidence that significant alpha can be generated by exploiting the established roll pattern of the S&P GSCI. Mou tested two **preroll strategies** on 19 commodities included in the S&P GSCI, and found that rolling futures contracts before the scheduled roll period generated significant abnormal returns over the period of 2000 to 2010, with the energy sector providing the best performance. Furthermore, the first-generation indices are truly passive, and make no attempt to adjust their exposures in response to the shape of the forward curves or the expected returns of the commodities they invest in.

In the years following the introduction of the S&P GSCI, a wide variety of indices evolved. Many were simply slight evolutions of the first generation, differing by degree of diversification or the focus of their concentrated exposure. For example, while the Thompson Reuters/Jefferies CRB Index (TR/J CRB) has an average maturity and roll methodology similar to the S&P GSCI, it has the largest allocation to agriculture of any index.

26.8 PERFORMANCE ENHANCEMENTS OF ENHANCED COMMODITY INDICES

A variety of enhanced commodity indices are available, which claim to provide return improvements over the first generation of commodity indices without increasing risk. As discussed earlier, enhanced commodity indices may be able to enhance returns by increasing weights to commodities that have recently performed well and underweighting commodities that have recently performed poorly, to capture short-term momentum. They may also seek to maximize roll return by increasing weights in commodities that are in steep backwardation and by underweighting those in steep contango. Furthermore, they could gradually roll their futures contracts or utilize longer-maturity contracts to minimize the price impact of their roll activities or reduce volatility. Unfortunately, validating the performance improvement due to the methodology enhancements of these indices is far from trivial. As Erb and Harvey (2006) point out, commodity futures markets tend to exhibit high volatility and very low correlations with one another. As a result, the returns of commodity indices have been driven by a few commodities that historically performed extremely well. This makes ex-post comparisons between index methodologies difficult, since a high weight in a commodity that happens to perform extremely well can have a large impact on returns.

To analyze the potential improvements of enhanced commodity indices while addressing this issue, Fuertes, Miffre, and Rallis (2010a) compare two first-generation indices (S&P GSCI and DJUBSCI) with enhanced versions of the indices. To create the enhanced versions of the indices, Fuertes et al. utilize the weighting and rolling methodology of the first-generation indices as a baseline, and adjust the weighting or time to maturity of the futures contracts. The weighting is adjusted based on a momentum signal (overweight the winners), term structure (overweight commodities with higher roll return), or a combined momentum and term structure signal to create reweighted enhanced indices. The time to maturity is also altered to create enhanced indices that retain the baseline weights. Fuertes et al. examine the performance of the base indices and the enhanced versions of the indices over the period from October 1988 to November 2008 for the S&P GSCI, and the period from January 1991 to November 2008 for the DJUBSCI. The authors find that all of their hypothetical enhanced versions of the S&P GSCI and DJUBSCI improve the returns of the first-generation indices, providing significant positive alphas. The largest improvement comes from the time to maturity enhancement, with the longer-maturity versions exhibiting the highest performance. As important, the authors find that the enhanced indices provide effective risk diversification and inflation hedging comparable to the underlying first-generation indices.

26.8.1 Second-Generation Enhanced Commodity Indices

The second-generation commodity indices attempt to enhance returns through forward curve positioning. In contrast to first-generation indices, second-generation indices tend to spread the roll period or target different segments of the forward curve. For example, the Bache Commodity Index (BCI) spreads its roll over its entire holding period by rolling a small portion of its positions every day, gradually rolling the entire position of each commodity from one contract month to the next further out.

The Merrill Lynch Commodity Index eXtra (MLCX) differs from the S&P GSCI and DJUBSCI in its longer average maturity. The MLCX rolls over a period of 15 days, from the first to the fifteenth business day of the rolling month, and rolls from next to second next contract (i.e., from the second contract to the third contract) instead of the more conventional front to next contract (i.e., from the first contract to the second contract). Rolling one month ahead of the S&P GSCI and DJUBSCI gives the MLCX an average maturity of about one month longer than the DJUBSCI and six weeks longer than the S&P GSCI.

The Deutsche Bank Liquid Commodity Index (DBLCI) Optimum Yield Index uses fixed commodity weights similar to first-generation indices, but employs a variable curve positioning strategy. The particular contract month selected for each commodity is determined by selecting the contract with the highest implied roll yield from all contracts expiring in the following 13-month period (Dunsby and Nelson 2010).

26.8.2 Third-Generation Enhanced Commodity Indices

The third generation of commodity indices adds yet another enhancement: active commodity selection. Active commodity selection may be algorithmic (such as momentum, inventory levels, term structure signals, etc.) or discretionary. For example, the UBS Bloomberg CMCI Active Index invests in the same commodities as the standard UBS Bloomberg CMCI Index, but varies the weights and tenors of individual commodities based on UBS research analysts' performance expectations for each contract.[3]

26.9 A PRIMER ON COMMODITY INDEX CALCULATION: SPOT, ROLL, EXCESS, AND TOTAL RETURNS

The four measures of return that are commonly published by commodity index providers are *spot return*, *roll return*, *excess return*, and *total return*. Each of these measures of commodity performance has an important use in evaluating the performance of different commodity investment strategies. This section introduces these concepts by calculating a hypothetical commodity index over the course of two trading days. The sections that follow focus on analysis of these return measures. Three index values are calculated: excess return index, total return index, and spot index. The industry convention is to compute index returns in the following way.

Spot return: Percentage change in market value of futures contracts held in the index at the end of the day, after accounting for any index changes. The following expression describes the spot index at time $t - 1$:

$$\text{Spot index}(t - 1) = w_1 \times F_1(t - 1, t_1) + \cdots + w_N \times F_N(t - 1, t_1)$$

where:

$$w_i = \text{number of contract } i \text{ in the index}$$
$$F_i(t - 1, t_1) = \text{futures price of contract } i \text{ at time } t - 1. \text{ The contract matures}$$
$$\text{at time } t_1.$$

---

[3] For further discussion of enhanced commodity indices, see Dunsby and Nelson (2010).

The following expressions describe the spot index at time t for the three different possible states of the index:

Spot index$(t) =$

$$\begin{cases} w_1 \times F_1(t, t_1) + \cdots + w_N \times F_N(t, t_1) & \text{No roll return and no change in contracts} \\ w_1 \times F_1(t, t_2) + \cdots + w_N \times F_N(t, t_2) & \text{Roll and no change in contracts} \\ w_1' \times F_1(t, t_2) + \cdots + w_N' \times F_N(t, t_2) & \text{Roll and changes in contracts} \end{cases}$$

where $w_i' =$ new number of contract i in the index.

At time t, the spot index is calculated as a weighted sum of futures prices. However, compared to time $t - 1$, the index could switch to futures contracts with longer maturity, the number of contracts for each commodity could change, or both. Any of these changes could result in realizing a roll return. The percentage change in the spot index creates the spot return.

Excess return: Percentage change in the market value of the futures contracts held in the index at the end of the trading session but *before* accounting for any index changes:

$$\text{Excess return index}_t = \text{Excess return index}_{t-1}$$
$$\times \left(\frac{w_1 \times F_1(t, t_1) + \cdots + w_N \times F_N(t, t_1)}{w_1 \times F_1(t - 1, t_1) + \cdots + w_N \times F_N(t - 1, t_1)} \right)$$

Note that the numerator and denominator of the terms appearing in the parentheses refer to spot indices at time t and $t - 1$ *before* any change in the index composition. The percentage change in the excess return index creates the excess return.

Total return: Excess return plus the risk-free return (usually Treasury bills):

$$\text{Total return index}_t = \text{Total return index}_{t-1} \times \left(\frac{\text{Excess return index}_t}{\text{Excess return index}_{t-1}} \right)$$
$$\times \left(1 + \text{T-bill rate} \right)$$

The percentage change in the total return index creates the total return.
(Realized) roll return: Excess return minus spot return:

$$\text{Realized roll return}_t = \left(\frac{\text{Excess return index}_t}{\text{Excess return index}_{t-1}} \right) - \left(\frac{\text{Spot index}_t}{\text{Spot index}_{t-1}} \right)$$

There will be a difference between spot and excess return when the index's composition changes, either because a contract is rolled forward or because the weights are changed. For most indices, rolls take place on only a few days per month and weights change once per year, so for most days the realized roll return is zero. On any date when the index changes, the excess return will measure the return on the positions before the changes take place, and the spot index will measure the value of positions after the changes take place. The following example shows the return calculations for a simple commodity index comprised of two commodities. The first

EXHIBIT 26.1 Example of Commodity Return Calculations on a Non-Roll Date

	28-Aug	29-Aug
Contracts		
Crude oil (October)	114.12	115.46
Copper (December)	340.25	338.7
Crude oil (November)		
Copper (March)		
Interest Rate		
T-bill rate (basis points)	0.8	2.41
Number of Contracts		
Crude oil	0.59842	0.59842
Copper	0.07682	0.07682
Indices		
Spot index	94.43	95.11
Excess return index	118.21	119.06
Total return index	231.41	233.14
Returns		
Spot index		0.72%
Excess return index		0.72%
Total return index		0.75%
Realized roll return		0.00%
Index Weights		
Crude oil	72.32%	72.64%
Copper	27.68%	27.36%
Total	100.00%	100.00%

exhibit in the example (Exhibit 26.1) shows return calculations on a date when the index does not change any positions (i.e., does not roll or rebalance). The exhibit shows the values that will be used to calculate index values, returns, and weights for August 29, 2008. The figures appearing in the first column for August 28, 2008, are given.

The key figures are the number of contracts in the spot index. These values are fixed each year in most indices, and represent the number of contracts held for each commodity in the index. Since there is no realized roll return in this example, the spot index uses futures with the same expiration months used in calculating the excess return and total return indices. In the example, the price of copper declined and the price of crude oil rose on the evaluation date (August 29, 2008). Since there were no changes in the index, spot return and excess return are the same, and the roll return is zero. Crude oil has a higher weight in the index, so all three indices gained in value. Note that the weight of crude oil rose in the index as well. This is because the index holds a fixed position in each commodity, so with crude oil rising more than copper, the portion of the index represented by crude oil increased as well.

EXHIBIT 26.2   Example of Commodity Return Calculations
on a Roll Date

	29-Aug	1-Sep
Contracts		
Crude oil (October)	115.46	111
Copper (December)	338.7	330.6
Crude oil (November)		111.38
Copper (March)		328
Interest Rate		
T-bill rate (basis points)	2.41	0.78
Number of Contracts		
Crude oil	0.59842	0.59842
Copper	0.07682	0.07682
Indices		
Spot index	95.11	91.85
Excess return index	119.06	114.94
Total return index	233.14	225.09
Returns		
Spot index	0.72%	−3.43%
Excess return index	0.72%	−3.46%
Total return index	0.75%	−3.45%
Realized roll return	0.00%	−0.03%
Index Weights		
Crude oil	72.64%	72.57%
Copper	27.36%	27.43%
Total	100.00%	100.00%

The next exhibit (Exhibit 26.2) shows the same set of calculations on a date when the index rolls. On a roll date, futures contracts nearing expiration are replaced in the index by new contracts. The changes take place after the futures markets close. In this table, crude oil for October delivery is replaced with a contract for November delivery. Also, copper for December delivery is replaced with a contract for delivery the following March. The changes are assumed to take place after the close of trading on September 1. In this table, the excess return index is calculated based on the original contracts (October crude and December copper). The spot return index uses the new contracts (November crude and March copper). Using these values, the spot return is slightly higher than the excess return (−3.43% vs. −3.46%). The difference of 0.03% (or 2.9 basis points) represents the roll return. Note that on the next day, September 2, both the spot and excess return indices would be calculated using the new contracts.

CHAPTER 27

Macroeconomic Determinants of Commodity Futures Returns[*]

Commodities have enjoyed a renewed interest from both investors and academics in recent years. After the oil price shocks in the 1970s, a period of declining commodity prices followed for the next 20 years, which went along with little attention from the academic side. Currently, prices of many commodities are at a record high in nominal terms and at a high level in real terms.

Most of the literature on commodities concentrates on long-term passive investments in commodity futures. However, a pure buy-and-hold strategy may lead to higher-risk positions and further disadvantages for the investor. On the one hand, investors have no influence on the timing and weights of portfolio constituents, and thus cannot react to market changes. On the other hand, Akey (2005) shows that active management gives the investor the opportunity to minimize risk and take advantage of the market circumstances. In order to be successful, the investor needs a sound understanding of the determinants of commodity prices and the interdependencies between those factors and traditional assets. Commodities are a very heterogeneous asset class, with daily price changes driven mainly by a variety of commodity-specific factors. However, commodity prices are also subject to macroeconomic changes that are common to all commodities.

Pindyck and Rotemberg (1990) find co-movements between largely unrelated commodities that are affected by common macroeconomic shocks. Hence, current and expected values of macroeconomic factors, such as inflation, interest rates, and industrial production, affect the supply and demand for commodities and thus their current and expected prices. The authors show that the demand for commodities can be determined directly, such as through an increase in world industrial production, which will raise the demand for energy as well as for industrial and precious metals. The demand for commodities can also be influenced indirectly through storage costs. For storable commodities, the demand for holding inventories, and hence current prices, is driven by the opportunity costs of holding inventories. For instance, higher interest rates can directly lower commodity prices because of the negative effect on economic conditions in general, and the demand for commodities in particular. At the same time, commodity prices can also decline because of an increase in storage costs.

---

[*]This chapter, authored by Zeno Adams, Roland Fuss, PhD, and Dieter G. Kaiser, PhD, and edited by the CAIA Association, was originally published in F. J. Fabozzi, *Handbook of Commodity Investing* (Hoboken, NJ: John Wiley & Sons, 2008). Used with permission.

Accordingly, the aim of this chapter is to show the relationship between commodities and the macroeconomy.[1]

27.1 COMMODITIES AS AN INFLATION HEDGE

According to Greer (1978), one important property of commodity investments, besides diversification, is that commodities can be used as a hedge against inflation. The value of nominally priced assets, such as bonds and stocks, decreases when both expected inflation and unexpected inflation increase. In theory, stocks represent claims against real assets; however, as companies have nominally fixed contracts with suppliers, workers, and capital, stocks do not react directly to an increase in inflation. Stocks represent company ownership and a share in the payout of dividends. Bonds represent a claim on debt repayment, and, in contrast to stocks, the bondholder receives a predefined stream of cash flows. The present value of the future cash flows depends on the size and timing of the cash flow and the assumed interest rate.

In contrast, commodity futures represent the expected spot price in the future. Therefore, commodities are an **inflation hedge**, as commodity futures prices increase when expected inflation increases. In fact, the increase of commodity prices itself causes inflation, as commodities are part of the basket of goods from which the aggregated inflation of an economy is calculated. Furthermore, because futures represent short-term contracts, they can react to changes in unexpected inflation, as the new information is taken into account when rolling into the next contract. Previous studies show empirically that annual returns of commodity futures are positively correlated with changes in inflation and that commodities provide an effective inflation hedge during periods of high inflation.[2] Gorton and Rouwenhorst (2006) show (for the time period 1959 to 2004) that commodities can be used as a hedge against inflation, so a positive correlation between the total return indices and the U.S. Consumer Price Index (CPI), which ranged from 0.01 for monthly futures to 0.45 for five-year averages of monthly futures, exists. In contrast, the correlation coefficients between stocks, bonds, and inflation range between −0.12 and −0.32, depending on the time period under consideration.

The following empirical analysis employs the excess return indices of the S&P GSCI for energy, industrial metals, precious metals, agriculture, and livestock to construct an equally weighted composite index.[3] The excess return index does not include the return of the collateral, and thus provides a better exposure to commodities than, say, the total return index, which is heavily influenced by the return of the risk-free rate of the collateral. All subindices are normalized to 100 in 1983Q1. After this date, the composite index was not rebalanced, as this would amount, in

---

[1] For empirical evidence that commodities are, on average, affected by the same macroeconomic determinants that also affect stock and bond markets, see Bailey and Chan (1993).
[2] See, for example, Bodie and Rosansky (1980), Ankrim and Hensel (1993), and Froot (1995).
[3] The composite index offered by the S&P GSCI is a production-weighted index, with energy having a weight of around 70%. The equally weighted index has the advantage of not being dominated by the energy sector. However, as mentioned earlier, the index is not rebalanced, so the weights in this passive index can vary according to the magnitude of price changes in the individual commodity sectors over time.

EXHIBIT 27.1 Correlations between Monthly Inflation of Different Countries and Commodity Returns, January 1983 to January 2007

Variable	U.S. Inflation	EU Inflation	Asian Inflation
Composite	0.3131[a]	0.1022	−0.0619
Agriculture	−0.0148	0.0008	0.0301
Energy	0.3405[a]	0.2141[a]	−0.1251[b]
Industrial metals	0.0735	−0.0578	0.0890
Livestock	0.0400	−0.0159	−0.0183
Precious metals	0.0735	−0.0844	−0.0245
MSCI World	−0.0301	−0.0994	0.1044
JPM Global Bond Index	−0.0750	−0.0049	−0.0833

Note: [a] and [b] denote significance at the 1% and 5% levels, respectively.

an active trading strategy, to selling the subindex with increasing returns and buying the subindex with decreasing returns. This approach ensures pure development of commodity prices; that is, performance influences arising from portfolio rebalancing are avoided. Measures of inflation used are the consumer price indices from the United States, Europe, and Asia. Normally, only the U.S. CPI is considered in literature on commodities, but that seems too narrow a perspective.[4] Investors are concerned about inflation in their respective home countries, not necessarily about U.S. inflation. For instance, European or Asian investors shift money into commodities when inflation in Europe or Asia rises. However, while including Asian and European inflation can solve this problem, it raises others. First, inflation measures in those regions are averages of inflation in different countries, which might bias the estimated correlation; and second, European or Asian investors also have to consider exchange rate movements when investing in dollar-denominated commodities, so the effects of exchange rate movements have to be taken into account as well. Exhibit 27.1 shows the correlation coefficients between inflation in the different regions and the commodity index returns for the time period 1983Q1 to 2007Q1.[5] As can be seen, the commodity composite index is positively correlated with U.S. inflation, but the correlation can be almost completely attributed to the energy index.

World stocks and bonds are negatively correlated with U.S. inflation, as the nominally denominated value of those assets decreases when inflation increases. Thus, higher inflation means lower returns for stocks and bonds. European inflation is positively and significantly correlated with energy, but again uncorrelated with the other commodity indices. Asian inflation is negatively correlated with energy returns, which seems puzzling. However, the correlation coefficients may be biased due to exchange rate movements and the problem of averaging inflation over different countries with different levels of economic development. Furthermore, these calculations incorporate short-term market fluctuations that are inherent to monthly data.

---

[4] See, for example, Erb and Harvey (2006).
[5] When denominating commodity indexes in euros instead of U.S. dollars, the relationship to European inflation did not change significantly.

Because short-term price fluctuations could obscure the correlation relationship, averages over longer periods of time provide a better picture of the underlying relationships. If the investment horizon expands to one, three, and five years, the correlation with European Union and Asian inflation shows a more heterogeneous picture. Exhibit 27.2 displays the correlation of U.S., EU, and Asian inflation with commodity returns, averaged and rolled over different time horizons. As can be seen, most commodities are positively and significantly correlated with inflation in the United States, Europe, and Asia. Furthermore, correlations become stronger over a longer period of time, which suggests that short-run correlations are heavily influenced by short-term market fluctuations. In the United States, correlations are particularly high for energy over the one-year period, and for industrial metals and livestock for averages of three and five years. Correlation between the agriculture index and inflation is much stronger in Asia and in Europe than in the United States, and increases with the investment horizon. The European and Asian markets have to be interpreted with caution. The coherence with the agriculture index seems to be strong, especially in Asia. However, other indices are significantly negative. For example, the precious metals index is negatively correlated with inflation. Accordingly, for the European and Asian markets, agriculture and livestock have historically provided a stronger inflation hedge than the composite commodity index.

The drawback of computing correlations between averages is that such computations cannot take into account time periods of highly positive or negative returns and inflation, as the averages smooth the time series. Those periods, however, are of particular interest, as the inflation hedging property becomes especially valuable during periods of high inflation. Additionally, it would be interesting to know if the correlations remain stable over time. For this reason, one-year and five-year rolling correlation coefficients have been computed for the U.S. CPI and the commodity indices in order to show the time-varying behavior. Exhibit 27.3 illustrates the rolling correlation coefficients for the different time periods.[6]

Common to all commodity indices is the fact that the one-year correlation coefficients fluctuate strongly from year to year and range between +0.8 and −0.8, as in the case of industrial metals and the composite index.[7] For this reason, it can be concluded that over short periods of time commodities do not offer efficient inflation protection. Over longer time periods of five years, the correlations are more stable but generally smaller in magnitude, ranging between zero for agriculture and around 0.4 for the energy index.

---

[6] Exhibit 27.2 shows the correlations of returns averaged over one, three, and five years, whereas Exhibit 27.3 shows the monthly rolling correlation coefficients over observation periods of one and five years.

[7] However, it should be noted that the coefficients are in part biased due to the autocorrelation that is generated by the rolling window. In addition, only linear interdependence under the assumption of normality is captured with this measure. Furthermore, the correlation coefficients are meaningful only if the multivariate distribution is elliptic. Since most monthly commodity index returns have a positive skewness and/or an excess kurtosis, the joint distribution is far from being elliptic, and thus the correlation coefficient does not exhaust the full interval [−1; +1].

EXHIBIT 27.2   Correlation of Rolling Average Means for Different Time Horizons

Index	U.S. Inflation			EU Inflation			Asian Inflation		
	1 Year	3 Years	5 Years	1 Year	3 Years	5 Years	1 Year	3 Years	5 Years
Composite	0.532[a]	0.568[a]	0.658[a]	−0.269[a]	−0.323[a]	−0.188[a]	−0.118	−0.025	−0.026
Agriculture	0.058	0.216[a]	0.426[a]	0.114	0.283[a]	0.520[a]	0.407[a]	0.672[a]	0.786[a]
Energy	0.550[a]	0.467[a]	0.332″	−0.064	−0.255[a]	−0.406[a]	−0.255[a]	−0.324[a]	−0.461[a]
Industrial Metals	0.367[a]	0.586[a]	0.743[a]	−0.224[a]	−0.184[a]	0.018	0.108	0.172[a]	0.191[a]
Livestock	0.402[a]	0.694[a]	0.907[a]	−0.051	0.087	0.322[a]	−0.015	0.274[a]	0.394[a]
Precious Metals	−0.312[a]	−0.380[a]	−0.404[a]	−0.706[a]	−0.770[a]	−0.792[a]	−0.272[a]	−0.334[a]	−0.511[a]

Note: [a] denotes significance at the 1% level.

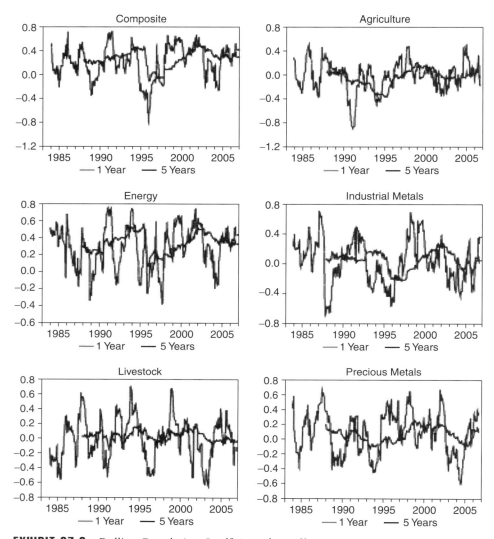

EXHIBIT 27.3 Rolling Correlation Coefficients for Different Investment Horizons

Given these facts, the inflation hedging property often claimed in the literature[8] can be strong yet negative during short time periods, and generally remains unclear when European or Asian inflation is considered. Denson (2006) shows that the rolling correlations for U.S. inflation fluctuate strongly in the short run, but are more stable, and on average positive, when considered over periods beyond three years. Thus, in the long run, a positive relationship between U.S. inflation and commodities exists. In order to test the inflation hedging property in more detail, inflation is decomposed into expected inflation and unexpected inflation. The reason is that expected inflation may already be partially incorporated into prices of stocks and bonds, so the inflation

---

[8] See, for example, Greer (2000).

hedging property becomes especially valuable in the case of unexpected changes to inflation. Thus, the commodity returns are regressed on the two components of inflation according to the following equation:

$$R_t = \beta_0 + \beta_1 E(\pi_t) + B_2(\pi - E(\pi_t)) + e_t \qquad (27.1)$$

where R_t is the return of the respective S&P GSCI commodity excess return index, β_0 is a constant, the term $\beta_1 E(\pi_t)$ is expected inflation whereas $B_2(\pi - E(\pi_t))$ is the remaining unexpected inflation, and e_t is an error term. The coefficients β_1 and B_2 measure the effectiveness of the hedge in the case of expected and unexpected inflation, respectively. A common approximation for the market's expectation of inflation is the short-term interest rate. **Unexpected inflation** is defined as inflation minus the short-term interest rate. Another possible proxy for unexpected inflation, which will be used here, is the change in inflation, $\Delta \pi_t$. Based on the random walk hypothesis, the best expectation of this year's inflation is the inflation of last year.[9] Monthly inflation is computed as the percentage change in CPI, while unexpected inflation is computed as the change in inflation:

$$\pi_t = (\log CPI_t - \log CPI_{t-1}) \times 100 \qquad (27.2)$$

$$\pi_t^{\text{unexpected}} = \pi_t - \pi_{t-1} \qquad (27.3)$$

Exhibit 27.4 shows the estimated coefficients and t-statistics in brackets for the monthly commodity indices. As can be seen, a positive relationship between expected and unexpected U.S. inflation and the composite as well as the energy index exists. For both commodity indices, the effect of unexpected inflation is much larger than for expected inflation, so the hedging property is much higher when inflation is unexpected. In the case of European inflation, the inflation hedging property actually holds only for unexpected inflation. While expected inflation should also be included in the pricing of nominally denominated assets, such as stocks and bonds, it is the hedge against unexpected inflation that makes the commodity investments especially valuable. Erb and Harvey (2006) conclude that commodities that are storable to only a limited extent, such as copper, heating oil, and livestock, provide a better hedge against unexpected inflation than commodities that are very suitable for storage. One reason for this could be that an increase in demand for the former type of commodities increases prices directly, while in the latter case, prices are affected only after the inventory has been depleted.

To a lesser extent, unexpected inflation in the United States also plays a role in the industrial and precious metals indices, where the effects are significant at the 10% level. In the case of Asian inflation, it does not come as a surprise that almost none of the t-statistics are significant, since the correlation coefficients were not significant on a monthly basis.[10] An attempt to explain the inverse relationship between stocks and commodities and inflation is provided by Akey (2005). If it is reasonable to assume sticky output prices, an increase in inflation due to rising commodity prices raises the

---

[9] See Kat and Oomen (2007b).

[10] One exception is the energy index, where the correlations as well as the ordinary least squares (OLS) regression coefficients are negative.

EXHIBIT 27.4 Regression Results for the Inflation Hedging Property

Index	U.S. Inflation			EU Inflation			Asian Inflation		
	β_0	β_1	β_2	β_0	β_1	β_2	β_0	β_1	β_2
Composite	−0.439	2.859[a]	5.532[a]	0.295	−0.021	2.535[c]	0.353	−0.137	−0.321
	[−1.307]	[2.833]	[6.329]	[0.569]	[−0.022]	[2.805]	[1.183]	[−0.373]	[0.257]
Agriculture	−0.063	−1.103	0.198	−0.785	0.903	−0.718	−0.601[c]	0.479	0.095
	[−0.156]	[−0.901]	[0.186]	[−1.310]	[0.816]	[−0.688]	[−1.770]	[1.151]	[0.296]
Energy	−1.393[c]	7.601[a]	12.699[a]	−0.977	3.114	9.249[a]	1.105[c]	−1.141	−1.303[b]
	[−1.909]	[3.469]	[6.691]	[−0.881]	[1.520]	[4.879]	[1.701]	[−1.431]	[−2.119]
Industrial Metals	0.490	0.236	2.274[c]	1.469[c]	−1.896	−0.641	0.122	0.852	0.556
	[0.945]	[0.151]	[1.686]	[1.918]	[−1.341]	[−0.481]	[0.281]	[1.604]	[1.356]
Livestock	−0.311	1.637	0.104	0.133	−0.057	−0.365	0.198	−0.164	−0.075
	[−0.832]	[1.460]	[0.107]	[0.810]	[0.955]	[−0.380]	[0.633]	[−0.426]	[−0.254]
Precious Metals	−0.248	−0.276	2.033[c]	0.783	−2.271[b]	−0.679	−0.294	−0.096	−0.143
	[−0.615]	[−0.228]	[1.933]	[1.312]	[−2.060]	[−0.654]	[0.339]	[−0.230]	[−0.446]

Note: [a], [b], and [c] denote significance at the 1%, 5%, and 10% levels, respectively.

costs for firms that buy commodities as inputs for production. Higher costs reduce the profits of such firms, and thus put downward pressure on stock prices. Over time, higher commodity prices lead to the entry of new commodity-producing firms into the market.[11] This raises the supply of commodities while firms reduce their demand for commodities due to the higher costs. Both effects decrease commodity prices and, as the central bank works to reduce inflation to more normal levels, profits of firms. In turn, stock prices increase again.

Another, possibly more relevant, explanation is proposed by Greer (2000). When inflation increases, the central bank is expected to raise interest rates, which reduces the present value of future cash flows and thus lowers stock and bond prices. Commodity prices, however, already incorporate the new inflation rate, giving investors an incentive to move out of stocks and bonds and into commodities.

27.2 COMMODITIES AND EXCHANGE RATES

Commodities account for a quarter of merchandise trade, which again accounts for a quarter of the world gross domestic product (GDP). Since many developing countries depend on the export of only a few commodities, it is important to understand the effects of exchange rate deviations on commodity prices. Many commodities are denominated in U.S. dollars, so exchange rate movements vis-à-vis the dollar affect the prices for exporters and importers of commodities. Thus, in addition to the market risk, investors also face exchange rate risk.

However, the effects of a volatile exchange rate go beyond the investors' risk. A general depreciation of the dollar increases dollar-denominated commodity prices, as commodity exporters from other countries demand a higher price in return for the exchange rate loss, and vice versa.[12] Exchange rate movements of single currencies can have substantial effects on the profits of commodity-producing firms as well as on supply changes.[13] One prominent example is the case of South Africa, where the rand depreciated against the dollar by 35% in 2001, while at the same time the gold price in dollars actually decreased by 2.9%. This raised profits of South African gold companies, which expanded production in the following period. However, it should be noticed that the supply of nonstorable commodities is fixed in the short run, since investment in commodity infrastructure can take years, so price movements can be caused by either changes in the U.S. dollar or changes in demand. Only in the long run do further investments in commodity production lead to an increase in supply. The short-run supply of storable commodities is somewhat more elastic, as long as commodity-producing firms still have inventories. The relationship between supply and demand is shown in Exhibit 27.5, which displays a falling demand curve, D, in reaction to higher prices and fixed short-run supply curves, $S^s(ns)$ and $S^s(s)$. If demand increases, the supply of nonstorable commodities, $S^s(ns)$, is fixed in the short run or increases marginally in the case of storable commodities, $S^s(s)$, so that

---

[11] Some commodity-producing firms, such as oil companies, have considerable sunk costs, so supply may be very inelastic, even in the long run.

[12] See Keyfitz (2004).

[13] Exchange rate movements may come into effect with a lag, since this kind of risk is often hedged for the near future.

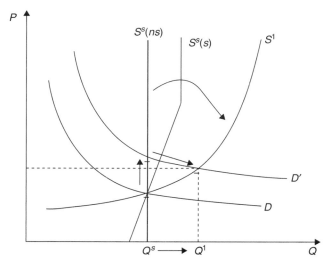

EXHIBIT 27.5 Short-Run and Long-Run Responses to Changes in Demand

prices mainly increase. Over time, the long-run supply, S^1, responds to changes in the price level, resulting in an increase in output and a slight decrease in prices.

This makes it difficult to predict commodity price movements in the future. On one hand, if world demand remains high in the coming years, if new investments in commodities are not yet completed, and if the U.S. dollar continues to depreciate, commodity prices will remain high or increase even further in the near future. On the other hand, an appreciating U.S. dollar and a higher supply would tend to cause commodity prices to mean-revert toward the long-term real price level, which in theory is the cost of production. The relationship between the dollar and the commodity composite index can be seen in Exhibit 27.6, where the dollar exchange rate index is a weighted average of the foreign exchange value of the dollar against a subset of broad index currencies. The weights are computed as an average of U.S. bilateral import shares from, and export shares to, the issuing country.[14] In order to illustrate the negative relationship more clearly, the exchange rate index is measured on the left axis in inverted scale and the commodity index is measured on the right axis.

As can be seen, the negative relationship holds for most of the observed period, with deviations during the late-1980s as well as during the past few years, when the commodity index strongly increased while the exchange rate remained relatively stable. In the face of high growth in emerging markets, especially in India and China, this suggests that the latest increase in commodity prices is due to higher world demand rather than movements in the exchange rate. Exhibit 27.7 shows the monthly correlation coefficients between the weighted exchange rate index and the individual commodity index returns.

[14] The index is provided by the Federal Reserve Bank; see www.federalreserve.gov/pubs/bulletin/2005/winter05_index.pdf.

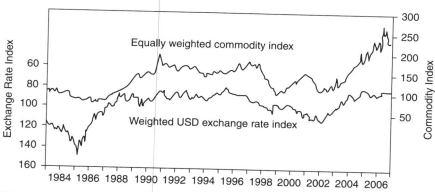

EXHIBIT 27.6 The Relationship between the Weighted Dollar Exchange Rate and Commodity Prices
Note: Exchange rate is measured in inverted scale on the left axis and the commodity index on the right axis; based on 289 monthly observations from January 1983 to January 2007.

As can be seen, while most correlation coefficients have the expected negative sign, they are significantly negative only in the case of industrial and precious metals. This supports the argument that an increase in the exchange rate, which corresponds to an appreciation of the dollar, decreases commodity prices (and vice versa), although not all commodities are affected in the same magnitude.

27.3 COMMODITIES AND THE BUSINESS CYCLE

The Federal Reserve Bank targets the core inflation rate, which excludes the very volatile energy and agriculture indices. When commodity prices increase to very high levels, however, the effects start to show in the core inflation, which induces a reaction from the central bank in order to keep inflation under control. This is why the interdependencies between monetary policy and commodity prices need to be discussed. The effect of a contractive monetary policy can be thought of as a continuation of the inflation effect and, perhaps, the start of a recessionary phase of the business cycle. As discussed previously, an increase in inflation raises commodity prices as investors take advantage of the inflation hedging property and increase their demand for commodities. Higher inflation then induces the central bank to increase

EXHIBIT 27.7 Correlations between Commodities and the Exchange Rate (January 1983 to January 2007)

Variable	Composite	Agriculture	Energy	Industrial Metals	Livestock	Precious Metals
Δ Exchange Rate Index	−0.122	0.058	−0.084	−0.339[a]	0.026	−0.384[b]

Note: [a] and [b] denote significance at the 1% and 5% levels, respectively.

interest rates in order to decrease inflation. The following period of disinflation reduces the demand for commodities, so their prices return to their long-run levels. Armesto and Gavin (2005) find evidence that commodity futures markets respond positively to an unexpected increase in the federal funds rate target by raising the inflation rate expected by the market participants for the next three to nine months. Jensen, Johnson, and Mercer (2002) analyze the effects of monetary policy in the United States by distinguishing between subperiods of expansive and contractive monetary policy.[15] For the time period 1973 to 1999, the authors find significantly higher commodity returns during periods of restrictive monetary policy and relatively low returns during an expansive period. This seems to be especially true for energy and industrial metals, whereas livestock exhibits inverse but insignificant coefficients. Similar effects have been found by Kat and Oomen (2007b), who consider single commodities instead of aggregated indices.

Frankel (2006) proposes an arbitrage model, in the style of the overshooting exchange rate model of Dornbusch (1976), in order to explain the inverse relationship between the real interest rate and commodity prices. The main arguments are that high real interest rates increase the opportunity costs of investors who hold commodities in storage, which leads to a temporary reduction in the demand for storable commodities.[16] Furthermore, during times of higher interest rates, speculators have higher incentives to move out of commodities and invest in fixed-income assets. Both effects reduce the demand for commodities and thus decrease commodity prices. In the theoretical model, a monetary contraction increases nominal interest rates i and, often at the same time, decreases expected inflation, so that the ex ante **real interest rate** $r = i - \pi^e$ increases while commodity prices decline. The decline continues until commodities are generally considered undervalued, at which point it is expected that commodity prices will appreciate by more than the costs of holding commodities in storage. Accordingly, investors are now willing to hold commodities in storage, so demand for commodities increases again. In the long run, the contractive monetary policy also reduces both inflation and the increase in real money growth, whereas the real interest rate and commodity prices remain unchanged.

The effects of inflation and the real interest rate suggest a cyclical pattern for commodities. In a period of strong expansion, consumer demand is high, unemployment is low, and wages increase more than under normal circumstances. This increases inflation, which in turn raises commodity prices (as long as commodities exhibit the inflation hedging property). In addition, high economic activity also means an increase in the demand for commodities, as most commodities are required as an input to firms' production. The increase in inflation induces the central bank to raise the real interest rate in order to prevent the economy from overheating.

---

[15] A change in monetary policy is observed if the Federal Reserve Bank changes the direction of interest rate movements after a prolonged period of interest changes in the same direction. For example, a contractive monetary policy is observed if the Fed increases the interest rate after a foregoing period of decreasing interest rates.

[16] On the one hand, holding commodities in storage gives the investor the return of an appreciation of the commodities in the future as well as a convenience yield, which is the assurance of having a critical supply in case of a negative supply shock. On the other hand, the investor has to pay the opportunity costs, that is, the real interest rates as well as storage costs, as well as a risk premium for the uncertainty of future price changes.

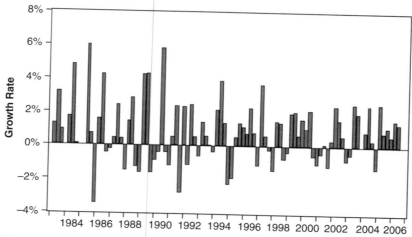

EXHIBIT 27.8 Quarterly Changes in World Industrial Production

When the increase in the real interest rate takes place, the expansion reaches its peak before growth slows, since investments decline due to higher financing costs. With a lag of several months, the higher real interest rate reduces the demand for commodities, which in turn leads to a decrease in commodity prices. During recessions, commodity prices are expected to behave analogously: At the beginning of a recession, the demand for commodities is low, which reduces commodity prices; when the real interest rate is cut by the central bank, commodity prices are expected to increase again.[17]

An empirical examination of the business cycle behavior is complicated by the fact that the change in the real interest rate does not always take place at the same point in the business cycle; that is, the lag between changes in the real interest rate and the effect on demand for commodities can vary, while other factors that are not strongly related to the business cycle (such as exchange rate movements) might further obscure the relationship.[18] Exhibit 27.8 shows the quarterly changes in world industrial production for the time period 1983Q1 to 2007Q1.[19] On the one hand, industrial production is not perfectly correlated with the business cycle. An increase in economic activity leads firms to reduce their inventories before increasing production, while a recession fills storage up before firms reduce production. On the other hand, industrial production has the advantage of a closer correlation to commodity demand, especially for energy and industrial metals, than has world GDP, for which the linkage to commodity demand may not be as direct.

---

[17] For further literature on the relationship between commodity prices and the business cycle, see, for example, Bjornson and Carter (1997) and Fama and French (1988), among others.
[18] Furthermore, business cycles are far from recurrent regular patterns. In fact, many economists believe business cycles to be only stochastic fluctuations of the market. See, for example, King et al. (1991).
[19] The proxy for world industrial production includes all Organization for Economic Cooperation and Development (OECD) countries plus Brazil, Mexico, India, and China. China is included in the index from 1990Q1 on.

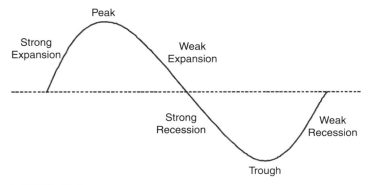

EXHIBIT 27.9 Business Cycle Phases

The quarterly changes in industrial production over the **business cycle** are now divided into subperiods: strong expansion, weak expansion, strong recession, and weak recession. A strong **expansion** is defined as a period in which growth is positive and increasing for at least two quarters. A weak expansion corresponds to the same time period with positive but decreasing growth. A strong **recession** occurs when growth becomes increasingly negative for at least two quarters, and a weak recession corresponds to two consecutive quarters of negative but increasing growth. Exhibit 27.9 displays the four phases of the business cycle.

Strong and weak expansions covered the majority of the time period between 1983Q1 and 2007Q1, as industrial production follows a positive long-term growth path. Exhibit 27.10 shows the average returns of the individual commodity indices as well as the average returns for stocks and bonds under the respective phase of the business cycle. The clearest result can be seen for the energy index, which may be most strongly affected by changes in industrial production. In a strong expansion, energy demand is especially high, driving up energy prices, while prices decrease during recession periods. The other index expected to show a strong reaction to the business cycle is industrial metals. Returns are positive during a strong expansion yet decrease otherwise, though less so for the strong recession. If the outlier

EXHIBIT 27.10 Return Properties During Different Phases of the Business Cycle

Index	Strong Expansion	Weak Expansion	Strong Recession	Weak Recession
Composite	7.09	2.62	−3.52	−9.99
Agriculture	−5.81	−6.43	−1.76	−12.76
Energy	37.37	10.03	−7.45	−4.89
Industrial metals	4.12	−4.39	−5.73*	−6.30
Livestock	−4.03	5.79	−1.06	−9.76
Precious metals	−1.79	1.21	−13.87	−13.77
JPM Bonds	7.77	7.58	−4.74	5.04
MSCI World	15.86	6.17	6.37	2.69

return of 39.32% in Q1 1989 is removed, the return becomes a more reasonable −5.73%.[20] It is worth noticing that the returns for the energy and industrial metals indices are much lower during weak expansions than during strong ones. On the one hand, this may be due to lower demand during these phases. On the other hand, it could be due to increased interest rates, which lower commodity prices as well. In fact, if a strong expansion precedes a weak expansion, the weak expansion may occur because of increased real interest rates. The agricultural and precious metals indices show negative returns for almost all periods, as those indices generally declined during the period under consideration. For the precious metals index, however, the returns are more negative during recession periods than during expansive periods.

Many commodity indices, such as agriculture, industrial metals, and livestock, show less negative returns during strong recessions than during weak recessions. This could be due to the effect of a lower real interest rate during recession periods. During strong recession periods, the bond index exhibits negative returns, which means the lower real interest rate might induce investors to shift part of their capital into commodities. In this case, the lower demand during those periods is partly compensated for by the gain in relative attractiveness of commodities.

Combining the demand effects from the business cycle and the exchange rate effects discussed previously, an estimation equation can be expressed by the following regression:

$$R_t = \alpha + \beta_1 \times \Delta IPW_{t-1} + \beta_2 \times \Delta EXC_t + e_t, \qquad (27.4)$$

where R_t denotes the quarterly return of the individual commodity index, ΔIPW_{t-1} is the percentage change in world industrial production from the previous quarter, and ΔEXC_t is the percentage change in the weighted exchange rate index. The lag in world industrial production takes into account that most commodities are storable to some degree, which means higher demand for commodities does not increase commodity prices until the following quarter. Exchange rate movements affect commodity prices directly and impact Equation 27.4 in the current period. Exhibit 27.11 displays the regression results for the time period 1983Q1 to 2007Q1. The coefficient β_1, in the case of the composite index, shows that an increase in world demand for commodities by 1% increases commodity prices on average by 0.6%, with a lag of one quarter. The effect is significant for the energy index but insignificant for other indices.

Exhibit 27.11 illustrates that a general appreciation of the U.S. dollar by 1% decreases commodity prices by around 0.6% in the case of precious metals, and by around 1% for industrial metals. Thus, a higher value of the dollar has a negative effect on commodity prices.

---

[20] Including this outlier return, the starred observation in Exhibit 27.10 would show a return of 22.14% for industrial metals in a strong recession.

EXHIBIT 27.11 The Effects of World Demand and the Exchange Rate on Commodity Returns (1983Q1 to 2007Q1)

Variable	Composite	Agriculture	Energy	Industrial Metals	Livestock	Precious Metals
α	−0.106	−0.577	−1.059	1.023	0.296	−1.234[c]
	[−0.162]	[−0.655]	[−0.583]	[0.799]	[0.334]	[−1.871]
β₁	0.600[c]	−0.750[c]	3.060[a]	0.312	0.102	0.265
	[1.816]	[−1.681]	[3.325]	[0.481]	[0.227]	[0.795]
	−0.182	0.08	−0.324	−1.048[a]	0.041	−0.603[a]
β₂	[−1.182]	[0.386]	[−0.755]	[−3.478]	[0.195]	[−3.882]

Note: [a] and [c] denote significance at the 1% and 10% levels, respectively; based on quarterly data (96 observations).

27.4 CONCLUSION

This chapter presented an overview of macroeconomic influences on commodity prices and has provided empirical evidence for the relationship between commodity prices and inflation, monetary policy, exchange rate movements, and the business cycle. Although commodities are a very heterogeneous asset class, some effects apply to all indices: Most commodities exhibit an inflation hedging property when compared with U.S. inflation. For European and Asian inflation, and when considering different time horizons, the inflation hedging property becomes more ambiguous, so the general effect is unclear. Closely linked to inflation are the changes in the real interest rate. An increase in the real interest rate decreases real commodity prices, with a lag of two or more quarters as investors react to increasing opportunity costs and shift part of their financial capital out of commodities. Exchange rate movements can have considerable effects on the supply of and demand for commodities, since most commodities are denominated in U.S. dollars. A general depreciation of the dollar increases commodity prices, as export countries demand higher prices in order to compensate for the exchange rate loss. Changes in the return patterns of commodities over time are reflected in different phases of the business cycle. In a period of economic expansion, the demand for commodities increases. At the same time, the central bank is likely to raise real interest rates, which decreases the demand for commodities. Whereas the former increases commodity prices, the latter decreases them, so a decomposition of the effects would be necessary and remains to further research. The overall picture, however, is that commodity returns are higher during expansive periods and lower or negative during recessions, which means that the demand effect is stronger than the real interest rate effect.

CHAPTER 28

Effective Risk Management Strategies for Commodity Portfolios*

There are fundamental differences between commodity markets and equity, bond, and currency markets. This chapter highlights those differences by outlining six operational guidelines that should be part of a firm's best practices when trading commodities as well as what an investor should know before investing in commodity trading firms.

The data and conclusions presented in this chapter are drawn from the author's experience advising commodity trading firms, and build upon a case study surveying best practices among three top commodity trading firms.

28.1 MARKING THE NET ASSET VALUE

Commodity traders can execute trades in the futures market, the physical market, or the over-the-counter (OTC) market. Commodity futures contracts are easy to value, as prices are available in real time and each exchange publishes daily settlement prices. In contrast, valuation of OTC contracts, which are traded through a network of brokers and dealers, can be notoriously opaque. Consequently, since OTC data are not available through exchanges, it is difficult if not impossible to accurately mark the book and know precisely at any given time what the market is trading at. Even if OTC contracts are cleared through an exchange, derivatives are typically valued using forward curves that often are not traded on exchanges. As such, the value of these derivatives depends on the OTC forward prices of the contracts. In order to independently value positions, it is imperative for a risk manager or investor to have access to accurate and independent forward curves. This is because if exchange-traded contracts or New York Mercantile Exchange (NYMEX)-cleared prices are used as a proxy to the OTC market, investors and risk managers may be lulled into a false sense of security, believing that they have the market data to price OTC derivatives and to obtain an accurate net asset value.

To illustrate the danger of not incorporating appropriate market data into risk-management practices, note the differences in Exhibit 28.1 between exchange data

---

*This chapter, authored by Moazzam Khoja, CFA, and edited by the CAIA Association, was originally published in F. J. Fabozzi, *Handbook of Commodity Investing* (Hoboken, NJ: John Wiley & Sons, 2008). Used with permission.

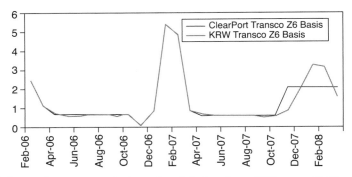

EXHIBIT 28.1   Exchange versus Independent Market Data: IF Transco Z6 Basis
Forward Curve
Source: NYMEX ClearPort and Kiodex Global Market Data.

and an independent source. The forward prices shown are for IF Transco Z6 (exchange data) versus OTC broker data on the same natural gas location. As a result, two firms using a similar average price for a winter strip, but with different assumptions for seasonal patterns based on the curve of OTC broker data versus exchange data, will arrive at two different net asset values for the same set of positions. A volume-weighted average price in a shaped curve will differ from a flat curve when trade quantities are uneven.

Exhibit 28.2 shows the difference in the net asset value that would be reported using hypothetical volume positions, contrasting exchange prices with independent market data.

Getting the right data is paramount to ensure an accurate net asset value. Without high-quality independent market data, a commodity trading firm will not accurately know its net asset value and may overstate or understate its risk. Using the Transco Z6 example, a firm could underreport its net asset value based on long winter spreads for Transco Z6, given the uneven volumes shown.

EXHIBIT 28.2   Difference in Net Asset Value Given Hypothetical MMBtu

	Position in MMBtu	Net Asset Value ClearPort Prices	Net Asset Value Kiodex Global Market Data
Nov-07	300,000	$ 630,000	$ 254,752
Dec-07	620,000	$1,302,000	$1,202,796
Jan-08	620,000	$1,303,000	$2,041,658
Feb-08	280,000	$ 588,000	$ 881,944
Mar-08	310,000	$ 651,000	$ 496,579
	Total	$4,473,000	$4,877,729

Note: MMBtu is the unit of natural gas contract that trades as the unit of energy produced by the given heat content of that natural gas.

28.2 MEASURING EVENT RISKS

Event risk, defined as a catastrophic unforeseen event, often leads to unusual market anomalies. One of these anomalies, seen during Hurricane Katrina, was the breakdown of intercommodity correlations. Basic economic relationships between commodities, for example, crude oil prices and refined oil prices (crude is a major input to the refinery process), ensure that certain commodity markets generally correlate with each other. Similarly, one would expect power and natural gas to be closely correlated, since natural gas fuels power plants. But after Hurricane Katrina, natural gas prices, which usually move in tandem with power prices, became less correlated. The effect of this type of event is illustrated in the following example.

In the oil market, a crack spread is the profit earned by a refiner for processing crude oil into diesel fuel or gasoline. In the electricity market, the **spark spread** is the profit earned by a power plant operator for generating electricity from natural gas. Assume that a fund had a short position on 500 MW/hour spark spreads between PJM Western Hub and NYMEX Henry Hub on August 26, 2005 (three days before Hurricane Katrina hit the Gulf). This position, with a $13 million notional, would require a 10% margin (i.e., economic capital), equal to $1.3 million in cash investments. Because Hurricane Katrina caused an unusual breakdown in the NYMEX natural gas and PJM power price correlation for a few days around August 29, 2005, the spread position experienced an unusual level of stress. This is illustrated in Exhibit 28.3, which shows that the daily movement of PJM prices was not matched by corresponding movement in NYMEX natural gas prices.

Exhibit 28.4 continues this example, showing the change in profit and loss (P&L) resulting from the effect of Katrina: a net loss to the fund of about $2.8 million within three days. In this scenario, the unusual market anomaly associated with Hurricane Katrina more than doubled the loss of total capital invested.

Although it is impossible to predict event risk, a firm can test the impact of an event on a portfolio. By measuring the impact on the portfolio, the firm can assess its liquidity situation should an event occur. The next section details how to test the effects of events on the portfolio.

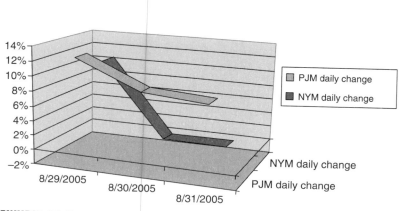

EXHIBIT 28.3 NYMEX and PJM Daily Movement, August 29 to 31, 2005

EXHIBIT 28.4   Loss as a Percent of Capital Calculation

| | | Notional | $(13,023,920) | | | |
| | | Capital | $ 1,302,392 | | | |

Date	PJM	IF Transco Z6	Mark to Market	P&L Change	PJM Daily Change	NYMEX Daily Change
8/26/2005	$ 77.52	$10.3210	−$ 47			
8/29/2005	$ 87.20	$11.4120	−$ 256,166	−$ 256,166	12.48%	10.57%
8/30/2005	$ 94.76	$11.4120	−$1,522,560	−$1,266,393	8.68%	0.00%
8/31/2005	$102.41	$11.4095	−$2,806,972	−$1,284,412	8.07%	−0.02%
		Loss as percentage of capital		−215.52%		

28.3   STRESS TESTING USING VALUE AT RISK

Commodity markets are more exposed to the effects of events than are other as-set classes. One way of managing a commodity firm's risk is to use value at risk (VaR). VaR quantifies the amount of risk capital needed to support a fund. As part of an application to the credit management process, VaR can be used to identify the maximum potential credit exposure due to a commodity derivatives operation. VaR can also be used as a means of allocating risk capital via limits to different traders within a firm. However, VaR should not be the sole measure for managing a commodity firm's risk, as it cannot identify unforeseen catastrophic events, such as Hurricane Katrina.

For example, a 5% VaR, which measures the risk of a 5% worst-case scenario loss to a portfolio, cannot account for events when historical correlation patterns break down. The only way to address such events is to conduct stress tests. There are three ways to stress-test a portfolio. First, shift forward curves arbitrarily and see the resulting change in the net asset value. Second, simulate price movements to mimic a historical event, such as a hurricane. Third, use the **front-month equiv-alent** (FME) for each commodity and create a matrix of price movements with different correlations.

FME is a statistical measure that defines the entire position of a commodity in an equivalent front-month contract. Relative prices, correlations, and standard deviations are used to value the FME. The FME equivalent distills all the positions in different months into an equivalent position in the front-month contract. Because later-maturity contracts are typically less volatile than front-month contracts, the FME of later-maturity contracts is less than one. The FME can then be shocked with different assumptions of intercommodity correlations.

For example, consider the FME of NYMEX heating oil and NYMEX unleaded gasoline, shown in Exhibit 28.5. The FME of 11,813 long heating oil barrel equiva-lents and FME of 11,882 short unleaded gasoline barrel equivalents can be shocked in a matrix, as illustrated in Exhibit 28.6. This process allows a firm to examine the associated changes in net asset value.

In Exhibit 28.6, assuming a large $3.00 per gallon change in price for both heating oil and unleaded gasoline, the resulting change in the net asset value of

EXHIBIT 28.5 FME of NYMEX Heating Oil and NYMEX Unleaded Gasoline

	NYMEX WTI		NYMEX HO		NYMEX UNL		Total	Total
Month	Delta (bbl.)	Position (bbl.)	Delta (bbl.)	Position (bbl.)	Delta (bbl.)	Position (bbl.)	Delta (bbl.)	Position (bbl.)
Total	366,507	500,000	11,813	11,905	−11,813	−11,905	366,507	500,000
FME	366,507	—	11,813	—	−11,882	—	366,438	—
Jan-06	366,507	500,000	11,813	11,905	—	—	378,320	500,000
Feb-06	0	—	0	—	−11,813	−11,905	−11,813	—

Source: Data from Kiodex Risk Workbench.

EXHIBIT 28.6   Price Changes Affecting Net Asset Value

Price Change Scenario	$3.00		
	FME	Correlation 1	Correlation −1
NYMEX heating oil	11,813	35,439	−35,439
NYMEX unleaded gasoline	−11,882	−35,646	−35,646
Change in net asset value		−$207	−$71,085

the firm can be observed using two different correlation assumptions. A correlation of −1 is highly unlikely; it assumes that the price of heating oil and unleaded gas will move in opposite directions. Nonetheless, one can see the impact such an event would produce on the value of the portfolio, and can measure corresponding liquidity constraints, if any. Conducting stress tests should be considered a best practice for any risk-management process to assess the potential impact of a catastrophic event to the portfolio. This should be done with a view to identifying a firm's liquidity needs should such a scenario occur.

28.4   MEASURING LIQUIDITY RISKS

As a part of the risk-management process, a fund manager needs to estimate the fund's ability to survive the sudden liquidation of positions. To do so, the risk manager must understand the concentration of positions as well as the size of positions, in each market, that would be expensive and time-consuming to liquidate. This is critical, as the inability to liquidate positions caused the Long-Term Capital Management crisis in 1998 and is widely believed to have been the major cause of the Amaranth and MotherRock debacles in 2006. For a trader with a large concentrated position, a market impact cost is incurred in order to unwind.

Market impact cost is the percentage loss incurred by a portfolio during the unwinding of a large position. The analysis in Exhibit 28.7 uses five-minute interval data to calculate the coefficient of price changes for unusually large volumes on a NYMEX Henry Hub Natural Gas Prompt contract. This scenario assumes a regression on five-minute interval price and volume data, and shows that unwinding a large order (defined as an order size equal to two times the standard deviation of the usual volume for each five-minute interval) could incur a 0.00025% impact cost. In

EXHIBIT 28.7   Impact Cost Calculation

Number of contracts	5,000
Total MMBtu	50,000,000
Coefficient for change in price	0.00025%
Impact cost per MMBtu	1.2449%
Price per MMBtu	$8.00
Possible impact cost	−$4,979,406

Source: Data from Globex.

other words, assuming the fund has a position of 5,000 open contracts, a cost of nearly $5 million would be incurred to unwind this position.

Risk managers should calculate impact costs for each contract. Next, they should set maximum open position limits, based on the impact cost and the firm's tolerance. A firm will be able to survive a liquidation event if the manager forces a maximum open position limit.

$$\text{Total MMBtu} = \text{Number of contracts} \times 10,000(\text{NYM HH})$$

$$\text{Impact cost per MMBtu} = \text{Total MMBtu} \times \text{Coefficient for change in price}$$

$$\text{Possible impact cost} = \text{Impact cost per MMBtu} \times \text{Price per MMBtu} \times \text{Total MMBtu}$$

Liquidity cost is often overlooked when managing commodities funds. This can have dangerous consequences. A fund manager must measure liquidity cost and impose maximum open position limits on traders to ensure that the fund can survive a catastrophic liquidity event.

28.5 PERFORMANCE ATTRIBUTION

Exhibit 28.8 illustrates that changes in forward curves, volatilities, time, and interest rates can all impact profits and losses (P&L). A risk manager must be able to attribute the P&L to its components: It is important to know which strategy made money, as well as whether the firm made money by adhering to its strategy or if there was a strategy drift.

As an example, assume a fund invests in three strategies: directional speculation, speculation on spreads, and speculation on implied volatility. Profits from hypothetical positions in each of the strategies for January 2006 contracts are shown in Exhibit 28.9. For each of the strategies, the change in mark to market (MTM) for different days is calculated. For the volatility strategy, the change in MTM is further broken down between changes in the forward curves and changes in the implied volatilities. The returns are calculated on capital invested (i.e., the margin required) to open these positions on NYMEX.

A few interesting insights are drawn from Exhibit 28.9. The volatility strategy, which should have demonstrated P&L based on the volatility changes, is, in fact, showing most of its profits due to the changes in the forward curves. Although it is a very good return on investment, investors and risk managers should be wary of this

EXHIBIT 28.8 Impact of Various Strategies on P&L

Portfolio	Total Quantity	Total P&L	Forwards	Volatility	Time	Interest Rates
Trader A	N/A	−916,171	−893,599	4,131	−17,596	−1
Trader A outright	500,000	−339,833	−339,994	0	203	−2
Trader A spread	500,000	−10,779	−10,774	0	−4	0
Trader A vol strategy	500,000	−565,559	−542,832	4,131	−17,795	0

Source: Data from Kiodex Risk Workbench.

EXHIBIT 28.9   Forward and Volatility Strategies

Date	Changes Due to Directional and Spread Speculation		Changes Due to Implied Volatility Speculation	
	Directional	Spread	Option Forward	Option Volatility
11/29/2005	50,780	1,587	−202,446	13,782
11/30/2005	423,697	−14,776	192,070	871
12/1/2005	219,334	−3,576	335,869	−9,365
12/2/2005	450,427	−2,036	291,891	−21,653
12/5/2005	−135,004	12,651	227,057	−19,636
12/6/2005	−85,197	−7,542	12,173	−333
12/7/2005	105,138	−12,754	−288,079	−14,633
12/8/2005	644,860	−7,544	605,416	−1,900
12/9/2005	−339,833	−10,779	−542,832	4,131
12/12/2005	263,751	−943	879,378	23,937
12/13/2005	267,772	32,329	34,152	2,480
12/14/2005	348,594	11,473	−256,211	3,976
12/15/2005	−447,890	−14,057	−424,184	—
Total P&L	1,069,241	−15,967	864,254	−18,343
Std. deviation	36.48%	7.98%	41.52%	
Capital	$810,000	$145,238	$847,500	
Return on capital	132.01%	−10.99%	99.81%	
Return on std. dev.	3.62	(1.38)	2.40	

Source: Data from Kiodex Global Market Data and Multifactor Model.

performance, since the return was due to the change in the forward curves rather than volatility.

The spread and outright strategies also show interesting dynamics. Although the spread strategy lost money in the period, its standard deviation was very low. Presuming the investor intended to allocate a portion of the fund to a less volatile strategy, this objective was achieved. Return per unit of standard deviation is a good means of assessing a strategy's efficiency post facto.

Fund managers must be able to explain their P&L. If they do not know how the firm is making or losing money, they cannot adequately evaluate the success of the trading strategy. If the P&L can be explained, corrective measures can be taken to ensure that resources are allocated to winning strategies.

28.6 MITIGATING OPERATIONAL RISKS

Often, firms that have lost money attribute their losses to lax operational controls. One area that is particularly prone to operations mistakes is the accurate setting of energy commodity attributes. There are thousands of energy commodities (defined by physical market product or location), most of which have unique settlement mechanisms, holiday calendars, and OTC averaging conventions. Due to the sheer number of variables at play, transaction risk materially increases. To mitigate this risk, a firm needs an auditable process of trade recording. This process should include reconciliation with the primary broker and OTC confirmations. Trade recording and confirmations or reconciliations should be performed by different people within an organization to ensure objectivity and serve a gatekeeping function. All amendments to trades must also be recorded and documented. Therefore, Microsoft Excel is not an adequate risk-management system. A risk-management process needs to include an auditable risk-management reporting system into which all trades are entered. Any separation of the trade entry and confirmation process may cause the firm to misreport its risk and net asset values to stakeholders.

28.7 CONCLUSION

The low correlation of commodity markets to stock and bond markets provides an opportunity for return enhancement and risk reduction. When an investor performs careful due diligence, investing in a commodities trading fund can be highly lucrative. This chapter highlights six golden principles of risk management:

1. An independent source of market data should be used to calculate net asset value. Confirming position valuation with an independent pricing source can reduce the chance of fraud and misrepresentation.
2. Unexpected events, such as Hurricane Katrina, may be the greatest threat to a commodity trading firm. Although events can't be prevented, a firm can assess the impact of a catastrophic event on its viability.
3. A commodity trading firm that is prone to huge shocks, and where traders can take highly leveraged positions, should not rely exclusively on VaR as a measure of potential risk. Furthermore, a firm's inability to liquidate positions can have undesirable consequences. The Long-Term Capital Management and Amaranth disasters are attributed to the funds' inability to quickly liquidate large positions at a reasonable cost.
4. Funds should have a mechanism for measuring the market impact cost of liquidating positions. Concentration limits help ensure that a firm will have the capital necessary to pay all liquidation costs.
5. A good fund not only measures profitability, but also keenly measures its performance attributes. The fund knows how profits are earned as well as which strategies are more versus less profitable.
6. None of these guidelines are effective unless a firm has proper controls and accurately records and reports its transactions on a timely basis.

There is no guarantee that a fund will not suffer catastrophic losses. But, if a firm adheres to these guidelines, the chances of such an event occurring are considerably reduced.

Hedge Funds and Managed Futures

Structure of the Managed Futures Industry

The term **managed futures** denotes the sector of the investment industry in which professional money managers actively manage client assets using global futures and other derivatives as investment instruments.[1] In the United States, managed futures managers are also known as commodity trading advisers (CTAs) or commodity pool operators (CPOs). The first managed futures fund started in 1948; significant growth in managed futures began in earnest in the 1980s.

Managed futures, through their ability to take both long and short investment positions in commodity, equity, fixed-income, and currency futures and forward contracts, offer risk and return patterns not easily accessible through traditional asset classes (such as long-only stock and bond portfolios) or other alternative investments (such as hedge funds, real estate, private equity, or long-only commodities).

29.1 INVESTING IN CTAs AND CPOs

Investors may choose to invest in CTAs using either individual managed accounts or a fund structure. Most CTAs prescribe minimum account sizes in order to commence trading in a particular investment program. Investors are often required to select a **futures commission merchant (FCM)**, an **introducing broker (IB)**, or a brokerage house with which they will maintain their account.[2] An investor's choice of firm is very important, as it must have the capacity to handle complex trades, which can have a material effect on overall performance. Although CTAs may not have authority over the choice of the FCM or arrangements between the investor and the FCM, they must nevertheless be acceptable to the CTA. The FCM generally has custody of investor funds and is responsible for furnishing investors with confirmations of all transactions, monthly statements showing information about trading activities in their account, as well as other account statements. The CTA will, of course, have authority to execute trades in customer accounts. In a managed account structure, management and incentive fees charged by CTAs are generally deducted directly from the brokerage account.

---

[1] Examples of derivatives are various swaps, options, and forward contracts.
[2] The bankruptcy of MF Global, a large FCM, highlights the counterparty risks associated with an FCM. These are further discussed later in this chapter and in Chapter 32.

Investors can also access the managed futures industry by investing through a **commodity pool**, a commingled investment vehicle that is managed by a **commodity pool operator (CPO)** (which resembles a fund of funds), in which the CPO invests in a number of underlying CTAs. Investments from a number of investors are pooled together and then invested in futures contracts either directly by the CPO or through one or more commodity trading advisers. CPOs may be either public or private. The requirements for investing in public futures funds generally differ from state to state as well as among each offerings.

Currently, several managed futures indices publish returns on a daily basis, including the Dow Jones Credit Suisse (DJCS) Managed Futures Index, the WisdomTree Managed Futures Strategy Fund, and the Newedge CTA Index. Returns on these indices closely approximate returns on an investable product. Each index has specific distinguishing characteristics. For example, the constituent weights of the DJCS Managed Futures Index are calculated based on the assets under management (AUM) of each fund and rebalanced semiannually, while the Newedge CTA Index is an equally weighted index of CTA managers who are open to new investments. These indices are based on portfolios of actively managed programs, but there are also a few passively managed indexes that could be used to represent the returns to the underlying investment strategy. These include the MLM Index created by Mount Lucas Management LP, and the MFSB Index created by the Institute for Global Asset and Risk Management.[3] The MLM Index is based on actual market prices for a basket of passively traded futures contracts consisting of commodities, global bonds, and currencies. However, as discussed in Chapter 31, the tracking error between the MFSB and MLM indices and CTA indices can be quite large.[4]

29.2 INDUSTRY REGULATION

Asset growth in the managed futures industry has moved in tandem with the growth of regulatory oversight.[5] The U.S. Congress acted in 1974 to create the U.S. **Commodity Futures Trading Commission (CFTC)** as a federal regulatory agency for all futures and derivatives trading. The CFTC's efforts were later joined by the U.S. futures exchanges and the **National Futures Association (NFA)**, an independent, industry-supported self-regulatory body created in 1982.

The NFA, in regulatory partnership with the CFTC, provides the primary oversight in the auditing of member firms. The NFA, as a self-regulatory organization, acts as the principal overseer of FCMs, IBs, CPOs, and CTAs. It carries the primary responsibility to conduct audits, though the CFTC conducts audits as well. The NFA also provides an arbitration program for resolving disputes in the futures industry.

Foreign exchange is one area of the managed futures industry that remains largely unregulated. Futures trading in international currencies came under the purview of the CFTC in 1972, when the International Monetary Market (IMM) was founded

---

[3] See https://www.mtlucas.com/ and www.ingarm.org/.
[4] Other approaches to passive indices include those described in Spurgin (1999) and Jaeger, Cittadini, and Jacquemai (2002).
[5] This section briefly offers an example of a regulatory structure based largely on the current U.S. system; rules in other countries will differ.

EXHIBIT 29.1 CTA, CPO, FCM, and IB Definitions

CTA	Commodity trading adviser	A person who, for pay, regularly engages in the business of advising others as to the value of commodity and financial futures or options or the advisability of trading in commodity and financial futures or options, or issues analyses or reports concerning commodity futures or options
CPO	Commodity pool operator	A person engaged in a business similar to an investment trust or a syndicate who solicits or accepts funds, securities, or property for the purpose of trading commodity and financial futures and options contracts and who either makes trading decisions on behalf of the pool or engages a commodity trading adviser to do so
FCM	Futures commission merchant	An individual, association, partnership, corporation, or trust that solicits or accepts orders for the purchase or sale of any commodity for future delivery on or subject to the rules of any exchange and that accepts payment from or extends credit to those whose orders are accepted
IB	Introducing broker	A person (other than someone registered as an associated person of an FCM) engaged in soliciting or accepting orders for the purchase or sale of any commodity for future delivery on an exchange who does not accept any money, securities, or property to margin, guarantee, or secure any trades or contracts that result therefrom

in Chicago. The great majority of currency trading is conducted in the over-the-counter (OTC), interbank spot, and forward markets, which are subject to only limited regulation.

As noted, there are a number of regulated entities that participate in the managed futures industry. Some of these are shown in Exhibit 29.1.

It is useful to distinguish the roles and responsibilities of CTAs versus CPOs. Exhibit 29.2 delineates some of these responsibilities.

EXHIBIT 29.2 CTAs and CPOs Compared

CTA Responsibilities	CPO Responsibilities
• Developing trading strategies • Monitoring performance and reporting to investors • Ensuring the completion of audited financial statements for submission to the NFA • Ensuring that funds and managed accounts meet the requirements of the CFTC and the NFA • Ensuring that the investors meet all necessary regulatory requirements • Complying with all rules and regulations of the CFTC and the NFA	• Selecting CTAs and determining the size of allocations to each • Monitoring pool performance and reporting to investors, and monitoring the performance of individual CTAs • Ensuring the completion of audited financial statements for submission to the NFA • Ensuring that the pool meets the requirements of the CFTC and the NFA • Ensuring that the investors meet all necessary requirements • Complying with all rules and regulations of the CFTC and the NFA

If a CTA or a CPO has U.S. investors, it is subject to CFTC regulations and must register with the NFA. If a futures trading firm does not have any U.S. investors, it is not regulated by the CFTC nor is it required to register with the NFA, even if the investments are being traded on U.S. exchanges. Other exemptions to CTA and CPO registration exist. For a current listing, see the CFTC's website (www.cftc.gov).

Trading on behalf of U.S. investors in futures contracts listed on an exchange outside the United States must be approved by the CFTC, but approval is not required for trading outside the United States on behalf of non-U.S. investors. However, those trading on exchanges outside the United States may be subject to the local or national regulatory agencies that oversee those exchanges. For example, the Financial Services Authority (FSA) in London regulates all investment products traded in the United Kingdom, including derivatives such as futures and options.

A firm's registration (CTA or CPO) is dependent on the activities in which a company is engaged. A firm that trades directly for U.S. investors registers as a CTA. In contrast, CPOs pool investors' funds into a collective vehicle, such as a fund or a limited partnership, and then allocate the funds to the underlying managers. These investment vehicles are typically investment companies and are organized in a range of countries. Popular jurisdictions to register fund vehicles include the British Virgin Islands, the Cayman Islands, Luxembourg, and the Channel Islands. These investment companies may or may not be listed on a stock exchange. The Irish Stock Exchange, for example, is used to list a number of these non-U.S. investment companies.

29.3 BENEFITS OF CTAs

CTAs provide a number of benefits in terms of risk-return trade-offs to investors.[6] These include the following:

Diversification: Managed futures constitute an alternative asset class that has achieved strong performance in both up and down equity, commodity, and currency markets, and has exhibited low correlation to traditional asset classes, such as stocks, bonds, cash, and real estate. Managed futures, when used in conjunction with traditional asset classes, may reduce risk while potentially increasing portfolio returns.

Performance: Historically, managed futures have provided risk-return profiles comparable to those of many traditional asset classes and superior to those offered by long-only investments in commodities. For example, the historical Sharpe ratio of a diversified portfolio of managed futures could be four times higher than that of a long-only portfolio of commodities.

Access to multiple markets: There are more than 150 liquid futures products across the globe, including stock indexes, currencies, interest rates, fixed income, energies, metals, and agricultural products. CTAs are able to take advantage of potential opportunities in various asset classes in many geographical locations. The fundamental law of active management states that the information ratio of an investment increases as the breadth of the investment strategy increases (holding other

---

[6] For discussions of these benefits, see Schneeweis (2009) and Burghardt and Walls (2011).

variables constant). This means that CTAs have the potential to provide performance with a superior risk-return profile.

Transparency: Futures prices are determined competitively and are marked to market daily. The fact that futures prices tend to be determined in single-price discovery markets in which everyone can see the limit order book and in which the settlement prices are, in most cases, tradable makes them more accurate and more reliable than prices determined in nearly any other market. The prices used to mark portfolios to market are not stale. There are no "dark pools" of liquidity, like those found in equity markets. There are no interpolation methods similar to those of some bond markets, in which only a handful of bonds actually trade on any given day. And there are no models needed to determine the value of structured securities. As a result, the returns experienced are real and have not been smoothed.

Liquidity: Liquidity has already been mentioned, but only in the context of liquidating positions and extracting cash. In fact, transaction costs in futures are lower than in their underlying cash markets. As a result, the benefits of the kind of active management and trading that CTAs implement are available with less drag from market impact than one would incur with the same type of trading in underlying markets.

Size: As an investment alternative, managed futures have been available since the 1970s and experienced significant growth over the past several decades. According to the National Futures Association, as of 2011 the size of the market was estimated to exceed $200 billion.[7] This means the market has reached a level at which it can accommodate allocations from institutional investors.

No withholding taxes: In a number of the world's stock and bond markets, foreign investors are taxed more heavily than are domestic investors. With futures, all of the tax benefits that accrue to domestic investors can be passed through to those who use futures in the form of simple cash/futures arbitrage.

Very low foreign exchange risk: Futures on foreign assets or commodities have little exposure to foreign exchange risk. A futures contract has no net liquidating value. As a result, a long position in a European equity index futures contract has no exposure to the change in the price of the euro, while an investment in European equities exposes the investor not only to changes in the price of European stocks but to changes in the price of the euro as well. In the case of futures, the investor's currency risk is limited to the comparatively small amounts of margin that must be posted at exchanges around the world and to any realized profit or loss that has not yet been converted back into the investor's home currency.

29.4 MARGIN REQUIREMENTS

The industry standard for determining minimum margin or collateral requirements is known as **Standard Portfolio Analysis of Risk (SPAN)**. The system was originally designed by the Chicago Mercantile Exchange to integrate positions that included both futures and options on those futures by performing scenario or what-if analysis as a way of dealing with the nonlinear risks in options. It has since been expanded and extended to allow for the effects of diversification on risk in a futures portfolio.

---

[7] See www.nfa.futures.org.

SPAN evaluates overall portfolio risk by calculating the worst possible loss that a portfolio of instruments might reasonably incur over a specified time period (typically one trading day). This is done by computing the gains and losses that the portfolio would incur under different market conditions. The basic objective of SPAN margins is to make sure that on most days the amount of margin on hand would be enough to cover the day's losses.

In fact, the minimum margin on a globally diversified portfolio would be more than enough to meet this objective, because allowances for diversification are made only within a given clearinghouse. In a typical CTA portfolio, several clearinghouses in various countries may be involved, with each assessing margins that cover the risks in the contracts that it clears without regard to positions held in other markets.

In practice, each clearinghouse requires that margins be posted in their local currency. One way for the trading client to handle this, of course, would be to maintain pools of appropriate collateral denominated in each of these currencies. The chief advantage of securing one's positions this way would be the elimination of transaction costs associated with daily conversions of one currency into another to keep all positions square. The chief disadvantage would be the exposure to changes in foreign currency prices associated with the cash positions one would have in each of these currencies.

The solution to multicurrency margining from the client's standpoint is known as **single currency margining**. With this approach, as the name suggests, the trading client can post the full margin in the form of dollars (or euros or any other allowed currency). Under this arrangement, the clearing firm is responsible for converting the client's cash into collateral that is acceptable to the various exchanges around the world.

As previously discussed, for a well-diversified CTA portfolio, the passing of each trading day produces gains and losses in various currencies. In futures markets, it is standard practice to settle all gains and losses in cash every day. These daily cash settlements of gains and losses are known as **variation margin**. The clearinghouse's main responsibility is to stand between buyers and sellers of futures contracts, acting as a seller to the buyers and a buyer to the sellers. This arrangement is intended to eliminate counterparty risk between market participants. Additionally, customer funds are supposed to be segregated, ensuring payment of obligations. Part of the clearing broker's job is to handle these cash flows efficiently on a daily basis. Margin requirements, as set by clearinghouses, are adjusted to reflect the risks of various contracts. Therefore, during periods of increased volatility, the margin requirements for futures contracts could be increased by a clearinghouse.

29.5   UNDERSTANDING RETURNS

The purpose of this section is to bridge the gap between the world of conventional money management, in which return has a natural and well-understood meaning, and the world of futures, in which the idea of return, by itself, is rather unclear. The disconnect between the two markets is simply this: Real assets tie up real cash. To buy a portfolio of stocks, for example, one invests cash. The stocks then spin off dividends, which constitute part of the return, and the prices of the stocks rise or fall, which constitutes the rest. The resulting gains or losses are converted into a percentage return using a denominator equal to the value of the cash invested in the stocks.

Once one leaves the world of fully invested, conventional assets, estimating returns becomes more of a challenge. What, for example, is the return to a long/short strategy in which the market values of positions are exactly offsetting? This is, in fact, the case with futures, which behave like fully leveraged or geared positions in the underlying commodity. Their purpose in applied finance is to capture changes in the price of the underlying market, which allows them to be used equally well for both hedging and trading. In the hands of CTAs, futures contracts are building blocks from which highly diversified portfolios of positions, both long and short, in the world's financial and commodities markets can be built.

Although futures are like forwards in the sense that they both behave like fully leveraged positions in the underlying commodity, the futures industry has much stricter counterparty risk- and cash-management practices than does the over-the-counter derivatives market. The way futures markets approach risk has important implications for the way CTAs do business and for the way one may choose to invest in these markets. As discussed in the CAIA Level I curriculum, (1) futures markets require gains and losses to be settled in cash daily, (2) futures contracts have no net liquidating value, and (3) futures markets require participants to post collateral to cover potential daily losses.

The first point has important consequences for the way an investor organizes the investment in CTAs. The practice of settling gains and losses every day in cash produces an ongoing stream of small transaction costs. Minimizing these costs is an important objective for CTAs and their investors. The cash that flows into or out of an account also affects the ultimate return earned by the investor. Cash that flows in can be invested, while cash that flows out must be financed, either explicitly or out of pocket.

The second point actually follows from the first and is truly fundamental. Because all gains and losses are settled in cash daily, futures contracts never have any net liquidating value except for whatever they accumulate over the course of a single trading day. As a result, there is no natural denominator for estimating the return on a futures position.

The importance of the third point also becomes apparent when one decides how to structure an investment in CTAs. The decision process that allows an investor to compare an investment in CTA funds with an investment in managed accounts or with a hybrid investment using a CTA investment platform is examined in Chapter 32. Interest earned on any cash or collateral invested in a fund or posted as collateral in a managed account is part of the total return. The investor must always care about the security of the cash investment.

To cope with these features of futures markets, the CTA industry has adopted three specialized terms that investors must know: (1) trading level, (2) funding level, and (3) notional level.

Trading level is simply the choice of denominator. It determines the size of the actual positions that the CTA takes in futures markets, depending on the CTA's leverage goals. It is the account value that the CTA uses to translate futures profits and losses into percentage returns. It is also the account value that the CTA uses to calculate management and incentive fees.

Funding level is the total amount of cash or collateral that the investor posts or invests to support the trading level. The rock-bottom minimum funding level for any futures position or portfolio is the total value of margin collateral required by the various futures exchanges.

EXHIBIT 29.3 Sample Futures Portfolio (March 2010)

Market and Contract Position			
Equity		**Foreign Exchange**	
CAC 40	−731	Australian dollar	1,499
DAX	−214	British pound	−1,812
Euro Stoxx 50	−969	Canadian dollar	1,899
FTSE 100	499	Euro	−1,114
Hang Seng	−242	Japanese yen	1,466
IBEX 35	−267	Mexican peso	4,223
KOSPI	473	New Zealand dollar	−1,935
MIB	−241	Swiss franc	−1,570
NASDAQ-100 Mini	1,271		
Nikkei 225	325	**Commodities**	
Russell 2000 Mini	573	Cocoa	−358
S&P 500 E-mini	744	Coffee	−545
SPI 200	−499	Copper	135
Swedish OMX	3,110	Corn	−1,972
		Cotton #2	553
Interest Rates		Crude oil	−461
Australian 3-month	1,083	Gold	760
Australian 10-year	1,566	Heating oil	−420
Euro 3-month (Euribor)	6,475	Lean hogs	654
German 5-year (BOBL)	2,197	Live cattle	−810
German 10-year (BUND)	1,412	Natural gas	−527
German Schatz	5,206	RBOB	426
Japan 3-month	990	Silver	−584
Japan 10-year (JGB)	261	Soybean oil	−952
UK 10-year (Gilt)	−1,023	Soybeans	−875
UK short sterling	3,435	Sugar #11	2,688
U.S. 3-month rate (Eurodollar)	4,989	Wheat	−1,001
U.S. 2-year	2,853		
U.S. 5-year	2,265		
U.S. 10-year	1,474		
U.S. 30-year	−971		

Source: Burghardt and Walls (2011).

Exchange margins tend to be small relative to the face value or portfolio equivalent value of the underlying contracts. In a diversified portfolio of futures contracts, the actual day-to-day risk in the portfolio can be smaller still. As a result, funding levels can be lower than trading levels. If they are, the difference between the trading and funding levels is known as the **notional level**, or the amount being notionally funded.

As an example, consider Exhibit 29.3, which represents the diversified portfolio of a hypothetical CTA. The figures refer to the numbers of futures contracts held in the portfolio.

The example in Exhibit 29.3 shows how one can have exposure to a broad range of financial and commodities markets within the CTA product. In this case, the

EXHIBIT 29.4 Margin, Collateral, and Cash Summary for Hypothetical CTA

Market by Currency	Margin ($) March 9, 2010	P&L ($) March 10, 2010	Margin ($)	FX Rates ($/FX) March 9, 2010	March 10, 2010
U.S. dollar	83,229,369	−6,166,098	83,229,369	1.00000	1.00000
Australian dollar	7,370,730	−74,492	7,370,730	0.91345	0.91585
Euro	18,076,360	2,275,928	18,111,974	1.35945	1.36530
Swedish kroner	0	4,198,500	0	1.49870	1.49800
British pound	3,578,829	483,818	3,578,829	0.12885	0.12885
Hong Kong dollar	15,584,800	605,000	15,584,800	0.01112	0.01105
Japanese yen	281,580,000	17,672,500	281,580,000	0.14015	0.14045
Korean won	7,727,164,500	47,300,000	7,727,164,500	0.00088	0.00089
Converted total	131,845,567	7,739,779	132,028,927		

Source: Burghardt and Walls (2011).

contract mix covers equity, interest rates, foreign exchange (FX), and commodities. The mix of contracts within each sector has been chosen to give roughly equal volatility weighting to each contract. The sizes of the four sectors have been chosen in this example so that roughly 30% of the portfolio's return volatility comes from each of the three financial sectors, and 10% of its volatility comes from commodities. The overall position sizes have been chosen to produce a return volatility of approximately 15% per year on a $2 billion portfolio, although the numbers of contracts in each market have been limited to no more than 1% of open interest and 5% of average daily volume in their respective markets.

Exhibit 29.4 shows how much margin would have been required in various currencies for such a portfolio on March 9, 2010. The total dollar margin shown in the exhibit is $131,845,567. This is the minimum value of the collateral that the various exchanges would require the clearing broker to post to guarantee performance. The trader's clearing broker is free to require more.

Next, consider the question of turning these profits and losses into rates of return. As explained, this particular collection of futures contracts was chosen to produce an expected volatility of returns of 15% on a $2 billion portfolio. Suppose the account started the year with $2 billion, and the resulting year's arithmetic return was 8.83%, with an annualized standard deviation of 13.89%, which was close to the 15% target.

The choice of $2 billion as the denominator is arbitrary, of course, and could just as easily have been $1 billion or $4 billion, in which case the annualized return volatilities could have been almost 28% or just under 7%.

In this case, the $2 billion denominator, if that is what the CTA chooses, is known as the trading level. There remains, then, the question of the actual funding level and its complement, the notional funding level. In many CTA funds, one would be fully invested in cash, thus making the investor's funding level equal to the investor's trading level. In fact, however, the trading program does not require this much cash. For example, in Exhibit 29.4, the minimum exchange margin for a similar portfolio was $131.8 million, which is far less than $2 billion.

In fact, one of the advantages of managed accounts and of CTA investment platforms, which is discussed at length in Chapter 32, is that they allow investors to economize on the use of cash. In the fully invested program, investors count on the CTA to invest the excess cash wisely. In a managed account, the excess cash is invested in whatever way best suits the investor. In a managed account, the funding level is negotiated, and the difference between the trading level and this mutually agreed-upon funding level is known as the notional funding level. The CTA does not actually have the cash, but the sum of the actual and notional funding levels produces the hypothetical trading level on which all return and fee calculations are based.

29.6 FOREIGN CURRENCY EXPOSURE

One benefit of using futures to take market positions is that they come with a built-in currency hedge. This is because futures contracts have no net liquidating value. As a result, a position in Euro Stoxx futures makes or loses money only when the index rises or falls. A change in the dollar price of the euro would, by itself, produce neither a gain nor a loss, because the investor has no cash position in euros.

In contrast, the U.S. dollar return to a fully funded, currency-unhedged investment in Euro Stoxx would be, to a first approximation, the sum of the return on Euro Stoxx, as viewed by a euro-based investor, and the dollar return on the euro. Conventional money managers are well aware of the problems raised by currency risk because currency volatility is potentially very large. During periods of increased uncertainty in global markets, the currency volatility may contribute as much to the risk of a fully funded position as the volatility of the underlying asset, Euro Stoxx in this example.

For CTAs, the only foreign currency risk associated with using futures to trade comes from the value of cash or collateral balances that are the result of either posting margin collateral or accumulating gains or losses in currencies in which the contracts are denominated. Because these balances tend to be small relative to the notional values of the positions taken, foreign currency risk is, for all practical purposes, separate from the risks associated with the underlying assets or commodities. This decoupling allows CTAs to take much more nuanced views on currency exposure than would be possible for most conventional money managers, for whom hedging currency exposure can be costly.

29.7 COLLATERAL INCOME AND SEGREGATION ISSUES

The collateral posted by the customer of the clearing broker remains the property of the customer and is supposed to be segregated from the clearing broker's funds. In principle, then, customers stand to earn interest or dividends on whatever collateral they have posted. Just how much, though, is limited by the costs of managing cash and the type of collateral that the various clearinghouses require. Unless the trading client posts exactly the kind of collateral that each clearinghouse requires in exactly the right amounts, the clearing broker will incur costs in converting whatever the client has deposited into whatever the clearinghouse requires. In addition, the daily settlement of gains and losses will require that collateral be bought and sold in various currencies, which also entails costs. As a result, customers face a steady tension between maximizing income and minimizing costs, which occupies a great deal of time, energy, and attention in managing a futures portfolio efficiently.

The difference between a good CTA and an excellent CTA may come down to the way they handle the complexities of collateral, segregated funds (various forms and provisions), and single currency margining, as well as the costs and noise involved in managing foreign exchange balances. Exchanges have well-defined ideas about the kinds of collateral they accept, while many investors have strong ideas of their own about the kinds of collateral they want to post. Segregation of funds is common in the futures industry, but the regulatory meaning of segregation can vary in hugely important ways across jurisdictions. Futures clearing firms can provide single currency margining for their clients but extract a fee for the service. CTAs can be highly attentive to their control of foreign currency exposure or they can be relaxed. All of these considerations can have important effects on the investor's rate of return and on the safety of the investor's cash and collateral investments.

How and where cash and collateral are managed and held are important considerations in whether the investor is comfortable with an investment in a CTA's fund or with a managed account. With a fund, the CTA or CPO controls an investor's cash; with a managed account, the investor controls the cash. Each approach has its strengths and drawbacks, and examples like those provided here and in Chapter 32 can be used as a foundation for evaluating the two approaches.

On October 31, 2011, MF Global, a futures commission merchant (FCM), declared bankruptcy, the eighth largest in U.S. history. Even under the best of circumstances, the bankruptcy of an FCM is likely to cause some disruptions in the trading activities of its clients, including CTAs and other traders. However, the bankruptcy of MF Global led to major disruptions and potentially significant losses for its customers. Following MF Global's bankruptcy, it was alleged that over $1 billion of customer funds were missing. This was not supposed to happen, as it was required that each customer's funds be segregated from those of MF Global.

In contrast to CPOs, in which investors' funds are pooled together, thereby giving a CPO substantial authority over the management of its investors' funds, CTAs do not pool their customers' funds. In the **segregated account structure**, the margins required for each futures contract are supposed to be kept in the customer's name. In the case of MF Global, it is alleged that some of these customer funds were transferred to other financial institutions by MF Global without the knowledge of its customers. If these funds cannot be recovered, the losses will have to be absorbed by MF Global's customers. In addition, because of this alleged transfer of funds, only portions of the cash balances and margins initially posted by its customers were transferred to the new FCMs following MF Global's bankruptcy. As a result, many customers received margin calls at the new FCMs, requiring them to post additional margins to their accounts. Many customers were not able to meet the additional margin calls at the new FCMs, and thus their positions were liquidated. Forced liquidations left a number of investors either unhedged or worse

(Mallon 2012). Investors in traditional stocks and bonds do not face such a risk in the United States, as the Securities Investor Protection Corporation (SIPC) insures their accounts.[8] There is no similar protection for investors' accounts in the case of futures contracts.

As the MF Global bankruptcy is processed, there are already a number of proposed regulations to eliminate or reduce similar risks and to help restore confidence to the managed futures industry. In the meantime, investors need to be aware of the financial health of their FCMs and take the necessary steps to protect their capital should their FCMs face financial difficulties.

29.8 MARGIN-TO-EQUITY RATIOS

One consequence of having to settle gains and losses daily is that cash flows into and out of an account as it makes or loses money overall. This leads to a practical question about how much collateral the client will be asked to leave with the clearing broker or how much collateral the client will want to leave with the clearing broker.

The **margin-to-equity ratio** is the proportion of client assets required for margin deposits, simply, margin to equity equals exchange-required margin/client equity. For example, if a CTA fund with $100 million AUM executes trades requiring $25 million in margin, the margin-to-equity ratio is 25%. More conservative managers may build portfolios with margin-to-equity ratios between 5% and 10%, while more aggressive managers may have a margin-to-equity ratio above 20%. Margin to equity is closely correlated to fund volatility, as the implied leverage of higher margin-to-equity ratios leads to greater levels of fund volatility.

From the clearing broker's perspective, the task is one of posting the minimum amounts of margin at the various exchanges. If a client has lost money at any clearinghouse, additional collateral must be posted to make up the loss. In contrast, if a client has made money, collateral may be freed up. If required margins exceed the value of the client's account with the clearing broker, the clearing broker is required to incur a capital charge. Therefore, it is in the clearing broker's interest to have a collateral cushion that allows losses to be covered in a timely way.

From the trading client's perspective, there is a clear advantage of maintaining control over collateral, but there is an ongoing cost to wiring money in and out of an account on a regular basis. Therefore, it is in the trading client's interest to maintain a cash buffer with the clearing broker that absorbs typical flows of cash into and out of the account on a daily basis.

Just how large the buffer should or must be is the result of the clearing broker and the trading client balancing risks and costs. Whatever the outcome, though, it is common for the trading client's equity (i.e., open trade equity) to exceed the margin required by the various clearinghouses. This results in a margin-to-equity ratio, or margin/equity ratio, that is less than 1.0.

---

[8] The amount of insurance is currently limited to $500,000 for securities and $250,000 for cash.

29.9 CONCLUSION

Perhaps the toughest question asked by investors who are considering CTAs or managed futures investments for the first time is why CTAs should make money. After all, investments in most hedge funds in general and CTAs in particular are not investments in conventional assets such as stocks, bonds, and real estate. Stocks, bonds, and real estate represent ownership claims on assets that generate real yields or income. That is, investors expect to earn a positive rate of return in the long run for holding these assets. Issues related to the sources of return to CTAs, historical performance, and benchmarking of CTAs and construction of portfolios consisting of CTAs are discussed in the next three chapters.

CHAPTER 30

Managed Futures: Strategies and Sources of Return

The sources of return to managed futures are essentially different from those related to traditional stocks, bonds, or even hedge funds. For instance, futures, swaps, and forward contracts can provide direct exposure to underlying financial and commodity markets but often with greater liquidity and less market impact. Futures and options allow traders to take short positions without the need to borrow the securities from other investors. This allows traders to actively allocate assets between long and short positions within the futures/options market-trading complex. In addition, options traders may also directly trade market/security characteristics, such as price volatility, that underlie the contract. The unique return opportunities of managed futures may also stem from the global nature of futures contracts available for trading and from the broader range of trading strategies.

It is important to note that many managed futures strategies trade primarily in futures markets, which are **zero-sum games**. This means that each futures contract involves two counterparties, in which the gains by one party result from equal losses by the other party. Ignoring transaction costs and the return to margin accounts, the total return from the futures contract to the parties is therefore zero. If CTAs were only trading against other CTAs, then one may conclude the following:

- The total rate of return to the entire managed futures industry should be less than the riskless rate (i.e., the return on the margin account) or even negative due to transaction costs and fees.
- Only the most skilled managed futures managers could possibly show positive return on a consistent basis.
- A significant number of CTAs should disappear, because if some CTAs are making money for their investors, other CTAs must be losing money and therefore leaving the industry.

Futures markets are not zero-sum games if one considers that many participants have positions in cash markets and that losses in the futures markets may be offset by gains in cash markets. In other words, some spot market participants may be willing to lose money in futures markets because the loss is offset by gains in other parts of their operations. These gains could be in the form of higher income or lower risk. The classical case of a corn farmer who hedges and is willing to experience a small loss on her futures contract in exchange for avoiding exposure to fluctuations in future corn prices highlights this scenario. Without a hedge, this farmer could lose her entire business if the price of corn unexpectedly declines. Thus, she would be willing to suffer a small loss in the futures market to avoid the risk of ruin.

Some may suggest that the return and risk opportunities available to actively managed portfolios of futures contracts are entirely dependent on the skill set of CTAs. However, as will be shown in Chapter 31, passive algorithm-based managed futures indices exist that represent the return process of actively managed systematic futures programs. It is important, therefore, to realize that the performance of managed futures programs is not based solely on a manager's skill set. One can think of managed futures returns as a combination of the return to the manager's skill and the return to the underlying strategy.

The performance of an individual manager can be measured relative to an active-manager-based CTA benchmark or a passive algorithm-based investable benchmark. If a manager's performance is measured relative to the passive algorithm-based managed futures index/benchmark, then the differential return may be viewed as the manager's alpha (return in excess of a similar non-manager-based replicated portfolio). If a manager's performance is measured relative to an index of other active managers, then the relative performance simply measures the over- or underperformance to that index of manager returns.

30.1 INVESTMENT STRATEGIES

Investment strategies of CTAs can be broken into three distinct groups: (1) trend following, (2) relative value, and (3) discretionary. However, various academic and industry studies have shown that there exists one dominant factor explaining a large portion of CTA returns, and this dominant factor appears to be highly correlated with basic trend-following investment strategies. In other words, trend followers dominate the CTA industry, and even discretionary traders may employ some type of trend-following strategy within their portfolios of investment strategies.

Trend-following strategies are rather similar to the market-timing strategies used in the equity markets, in which the investment manager takes long (or short) positions in those futures contracts that are trending up (or down). There are, however, two subtle differences between market-timing and trend-following strategies. First, market-timing strategies may involve some degree of fundamental analysis. For instance, a market timer may examine changes in credit spreads, money supply, and the term structure of interest rates to forecast a change in the direction of equity markets. A trend follower's actions, however, are predominantly based on technical analysis, using data on past prices and volume to determine whether recent price changes constitute a trend in futures prices. Second, a market timer wants to anticipate a change in the market's direction, while a trend follower wants to determine if the most recent changes in futures prices represent a trend and, if so, whether that trend is strong enough to warrant an allocation to one or more futures contracts. Therefore, a trend follower may miss the early part of a trend and may maintain the same position for a short time even after the trend has changed direction.

Trend-following strategies are referred to as systematic strategies because various quantitative models are used to identify trends, and there is little discretion in the timing of the futures market positions taken by traders. However, other aspects of the trading strategy, such as the size of the position and the degree of leverage, may allow for some degree of discretion.

Trend-following strategies themselves can be divided into at least three different categories—short-term, medium-term, and long-term—depending on the length of the trends that the CTA manager is attempting to exploit. Aside from higher transaction costs and perhaps the greater market impact associated with short-term trend-following strategies, research shows that these strategies have different degrees of success in different markets. For instance, short-term trend-following strategies do not produce the desired results when applied to equity markets but appear to produce reasonable results in currency markets (Burghardt and Walls 2011; Covel 2009).

Relative value strategies are more heterogeneous than trend-following ones. The most common form of relative value strategy is rather similar to a pairs trading strategy employed in equity markets. The strategy considers the relative values of two related futures prices, and positions are taken to profit from anticipated relative changes in those futures prices. In futures markets, relative value strategies are applied to contracts whose underlying commodities have well-known economic relationships. For instance, there should be a close relationship between the futures price for heating oil and that for gasoline. A relative value trader may use historical prices of these two products to determine their long-run equilibrium relative prices. If the relative prices of these products are substantially away from their equilibrium values, then a trader will take positions in the two futures contracts to benefit from the convergence of the two prices toward their relative equilibrium prices. For instance, if the difference between the futures price of gasoline and the futures price of heating oil is significantly higher than its equilibrium value, a trader will take a short position in gasoline futures and a long position in heating oil futures. In this case, the trader will profit if the two futures prices converge and the difference between them narrows. Furthermore, the return from this trade is essentially independent from the trend in the two prices; the important factor is the relative changes in the two prices. Since divergences can last longer than expected, or even widen far beyond historical extremes, risk control is the most important determinant of long-term success of a relative value strategy.

Discretionary strategies are not as well defined. For instance, a discretionary trader may use signals from a technical trading system along with fundamental analysis of demand for and supply of commodities to form an opinion about expected changes in futures prices. However, these signals and analysis are not employed in a systematic manner to generate trading models, and it is up to the trader to use all available information to implement the trading strategy. For this reason, in a due diligence process it may be difficult to identify the sources of return to a discretionary trading strategy.

Systematic trading may hold some significant advantages over discretionary styles. For example, one of the challenges faced by a discretionary trader is the control of emotions during critical points of market activity or personal performance. In contrast, systematic trading programs are emotionless and do not suffer from this issue. Furthermore, firms that employ systematic trading programs benefit from a reduction in key person risk. The maintenance of systematic programs can be transferred from one person to another; however, the same cannot necessarily be said of discretionary trading prowess. In addition, trading systems are inherently far more scalable because they are, by nature, almost or entirely automated and can thus far more readily accommodate new markets or new investor capital. Additionally, systematic programs are typically more broadly diversified than discretionary traders, both in the number of markets analyzed and in the types of strategies employed (Park, Tanrikulu, and Wang 2009).

Some studies have shown that systematic trend-following strategies tend to outperform discretionary strategies on a risk-adjusted basis (Aldridge 2009). These studies show that on the basis of absolute monthly returns, systematic funds outperform discretionary funds whenever the relevant markets are falling. When markets are rising, however, discretionary funds tend to deliver higher absolute returns than do systematic funds. Across a variety of metrics, systematic funds perform better than discretionary funds. In particular, on an ex post basis, systematic funds produce less extreme drawdowns, higher Sharpe ratios, and higher Jensen's alpha (measured against traditional asset classes). Furthermore, systematic funds exhibit lower skewness and kurtosis than do discretionary funds. Results suggest that much of systematic funds' outperformance comes from a better ability to manage extreme events, performing better than discretionary funds in crisis conditions.

Managed futures managers, and trend followers in particular, are supposed to be able to time their chosen markets (e.g., currencies or commodities). A recent study investigated the return and volatility market-timing ability of CTAs and examined whether there is a difference in market-timing abilities between systematic and discretionary traders (Kazemi and Li 2009). For this purpose, a set of risk factors was developed based on returns from the most heavily traded futures contracts. The study concluded that:

- CTAs exhibit both return and volatility market-timing ability in markets that they have declared to be their focus, most notably for currencies, interest rates, and commodities. However, CTAs display negative return timing in equity markets.
- Systematic traders are generally better market timers than are discretionary traders. Systematic traders show timing ability for currency futures and physical product (corn, crude oil, natural gas, gold) futures.

30.2 ECONOMICS OF COMMODITY FUTURES MARKETS

This section briefly discusses two prominent theories that have been put forward to explain the relationships among futures prices, current spot prices, and expected future spot prices. Understanding these relationships is essential in explaining the potential sources of returns to CTAs and, in particular, trend-following strategies.

30.2.1 Theory of Storage and Convenience Yield

The theory of storage, as initially developed by Kaldor (1939), attempts to explain the relationship between futures prices and current spot prices. The theory emphasizes the importance of holding inventory and the potential benefits derived from the ownership of physical commodities as opposed to having a claim to commodities through forward and futures contracts.[1] Ownership of commodities has economic value because it allows owners to absorb demand and supply shocks. Owners can meet an unexpected rise in demand and can avoid production disruptions resulting from supply shocks. The benefit of this ownership is often referred to as convenience yield, which is analogous to the equity dividends received by owners of equity shares and not by owners of futures contracts or other derivatives instruments.

Because commodity markets are volatile, both producers and consumers seek ways to hedge their risks. Derivative markets, such as futures and options, for commodities represent one venue through which producers and consumers of commodities can hedge their risks. Alternatively, they can hedge some of their risks by holding inventories of physical commodities. Indeed, some risks can be reduced only through the physical holding of a commodity. For instance, a manufacturer that uses an industrial commodity such as copper in its production process can hedge against a disruption in the supply of copper only through holding an inventory of copper.

On the other hand, a supplier of copper may also wish to carry an inventory of copper in order to hedge against the risk that there may be an unexpected increase in demand, which in the absence of the inventory can be met only through costly changes in the production process. Academic studies have shown that the convenience yield depends on two primary variables for extractable industrial commodities: (1) the level of inventories and (2) the volatility in commodity prices. The convenience yield increases as the level of inventories declines. Both producers and consumers hold inventories in order to be able to reduce the cost of adjustment to demand or supply shocks. As inventories decline, the risk of not being able to absorb demand or supply shocks increases, leading to an increase in the level of convenience yield. In addition, the convenience yield increases as the volatility of commodity prices increases. The reason is that demand for inventories increases as volatility in demand and supply increases, which in turn leads to an increase in the convenience yield. Of course, higher volatility of demand and supply naturally leads to higher price volatility.

Clearly, the level of convenience yield is also subject to commodity-specific factors. For example, the size of the convenience yield is affected by whether or not there are close substitutes for the commodity and by the amount of time it takes to respond to demand shocks and increase production of the commodity. Therefore, convenience yield is likely to behave differently for industrial and agricultural commodities than for financial products, which tend not to have any convenience yield.[2]

30.2.2 Cost of Carry Model

In additional to the convenience yield, there are other variables that affect the relationship between futures prices and cash prices of the same commodity. These include the cost of storage and the opportunity cost of capital. The cost of carry

---

[1] For surveys of the literature on the theory of storage, see Gray and Rutledge (1971) and Carter (1999).
[2] For further discussion, see Pindyck (2001), Sørensen (2002), and Feldman and Till (2006). In addition, a number of papers have modeled convenience yield as a call option on stock-out; see Milonas and Thomadakis (1997) and Zulauf, Zhou, and Robert (2006).

model has been developed to present the impact of all of these factors on the relationship between spot and futures prices. To present this model, let $F(t,T)$ denote the futures price observed at time t on a contract that will mature at time T, and let $P(t)$ denote the cash price of the same commodity. If cash and futures markets are free of frictions, such as transaction costs and limits on shorting commodities, then the difference between futures price and spot price of the same commodity (i.e., the basis) can be written as follows:

$$F(t, T) - P(t) = P(t) \times (r + s - c) \times (T - t) \tag{30.1}$$

Here, r is the annual rate of interest and represents the cost of funding the cash position in the commodity; s is the annual rate of storage cost; and c represents, on an annual basis, the benefits of holding the commodity, including any potential income from owning the commodity as well as the convenience yield associated with having an inventory of the commodity. Finally, $(T - t)$ measures the time to maturity of the contract in terms of years.

Example: Suppose the current cash price of one barrel of Brent crude oil is $100, while the three-month futures price is $98 per barrel. If the annual cost of funding is 4% and the annual storage cost is 5%, the implied convenience yield can be calculated with the following equation:

$$98 - 100 = 100 \times (0.04 + 0.05 - c)\frac{3}{12}$$

which can be solved as follows:

$$4\left(\frac{98 - 100}{100}\right) = 0.04 + 0.05 - c$$

$$c = 0.04 + 0.05 + 0.08$$

Thus, the implied convenience yield is 17% per year. The fact that the convenience yield is rather large and positive in this example leads to a negative total cost of carry:

$$\text{Net cost of carry} = (0.04 + 0.05 - 0.17)\frac{3}{12} < 0$$

This makes the spot price greater than the futures price. Similarly, if the total cost of carry is positive, then the spot price will be smaller than the futures price. Furthermore, assuming a constant per-period interest rate, storage cost, and convenience yield, these figures imply that longer-maturity futures contracts will have lower prices than will shorter-maturity contracts. Together these figures point to a term structure of futures prices that is downward sloping. In this case, the futures market is said to be in backwardation. On the other hand, if total cost of carry is positive (i.e., the convenience yield is smaller than the cost of funding and storage), then the term structure of futures prices will be upward sloping; in this case, the futures market is said to be in contango.

Since convenience yield is likely to be large and positive when inventory levels are low, one should expect to see a downward-sloping term structure of futures prices when inventory levels are low and commodity prices are displaying higher than normal volatility. Available empirical evidence appears to support the proposition that backwardation in futures markets is generally observed when the levels of inventories are abnormally low and price volatility is high.

It should be clear from the previous analysis that certain adjustments must be made to the cost of carry model depending on whether it is applied to financial futures or to storable commodities.

Convenience yield plays almost no role in describing the relationship between the spot and the futures price when it comes to financial futures. If the underlying financial asset of a futures contract pays a regular income, such as coupon or dividend payments, the potential income will be included in the cost of carry model. However, unlike the convenience yield associated with storable physical commodities, the dividend or coupon income from holding financial assets does not depend on the level of inventory or volatility in the price of the financial assets.

The important implications of the theory of storage (Geman 2005) can be summarized as follows:

- The volatility of commodity prices tends to be inversely related to the level of global inventories. Lower levels of inventory mean that any demand or supply shock has to be absorbed through changes in commodity prices leading to increased volatility.
- Changes in commodity prices and changes in the volatility of commodity prices tend to be positively correlated. The reason is that demand and supply shocks generally lead to spikes in commodity prices when the levels of inventory are low, which is also associated with higher price volatility. This is the opposite of what is observed in equity markets, where higher price volatility is normally associated with lower equity prices.
- Spot prices are more volatile than are futures prices because changes in the levels of production reduce the impact of demand and supply shocks on forward and futures prices. This effect tends to be more pronounced for industrial and energy commodities, where production is not affected by seasonal factors.
- An inventory-dependent convenience yield is an important variable that is increasingly employed by traders and researchers to explain changes in the shape of the term structure of futures prices.

30.2.3 Futures Prices and Expected Future Spot Prices (Theory of Normal Backwardation)

The relationship between the futures price and the expected future spot price of the same commodity has been the subject of many studies. Keynes, credited with the first rigorous examination of this relationship, proposed that futures prices should generally rise through time in order to provide enough incentive for speculators to take long positions in futures contracts. According to Keynes (1930), most hedgers in commodity markets are producers of commodities and therefore have net short positions in futures markets. This requires speculators to take the opposite side of the market and therefore have a net long position in these markets. Speculators will take such a position only if they expect to earn a profit from their long positions, which requires that the futures price rises over time. Since spot and futures prices must be equal at the maturity date of the futures contract, the futures price initially tends to be less than the expected future spot price (assuming that the spot price does not display any trend). The difference between the futures price and the expected future spot price is referred to as the risk premium, which represents the return required by speculators. In this case, one can think of speculators as supplying insurance to hedgers.

This condition is referred to as normal backwardation. Notice that the term *backwardation* refers to the term structure of futures prices, while the term *normal backwardation* refers to the relationship between current futures prices and the expected future spot prices. In particular, it refers to the conditions in which the futures price is less than the expected future spot price.

Under normal backwardation, a speculator who has a long position in a futures contract would expect to earn a profit if the actual future spot price is, on average, equal to what the market participants expected to see. On an ex post basis, the speculator would make money as long as the actual spot price is not lower than the expected spot price by more than the risk premium embedded in the futures price. To see this, consider the following expression, which follows normal backwardation theory:

$$\text{Risk premium} = E\left[P(T)\right] - F(t, T)$$
$$= E\left[F(T, T)\right] - F(t, T) = \pi > 0$$

Here, $E\left[P(T)\right]$ is the expected future spot price, and π is the risk premium. Notice that at maturity, the futures prices will be equal to the spot price, $P(T) = F(T, T)$. In this expression, π represents the expected profit to a speculator who takes a long position in the futures market. On an ex post basis, the profit earned by the speculator would be $P(T) - F(t, T)$. If the expected future spot price, $E\left[P(T)\right]$, is added to and subtracted from this expression, the profit earned by the CTA will depend on the risk premium and the difference between the actual spot price and the expected future spot price.

$$\text{Ex post profit of long futures} = P(T) - F(t, T)$$
$$= (P(T) - E[P(T)]) + E[P(T)] - F(t, T)$$
$$= (P(T) - E[P(T)]) + \pi$$

Example: The current spot price for Brent crude oil is $90 per barrel, while the three-month futures price is $95 per barrel. If the three-month expected future spot price is $105 per barrel, the implied risk premium would be $\pi = 105 - 95 = 10$. Three months later, the actual spot price for Brent crude is $100. The ex post profit of a long position in a futures contract will be $100 – $95 = $5 per barrel. Suppose the actual spot price turns out to be $89 per barrel, which is $16 less than the expected future spot price, $105. The speculator with a long position would lose $6 per barrel ($89 – $95 = –$6).

It is important to note that one cannot directly test the theory of normal backwardation because the risk premium is not observable. All that can be observed is the ex post gains or losses from futures contracts. Of course, if the theory of normal backwardation is indeed a good representation of futures markets, then one should expect to see positive profits in the long run from taking long positions in the futures market.

The theory of normal backwardation is consistent with both backwardation and contango in the term structure of futures prices. However, empirical observations tend to show that a backwardated term structure is generally associated with the theory of normal backwardation (Gorton, Hayashi, and Rouwenhorst 2008). Note that term structure will be negatively sloped only if the convenience yield is rather large. Furthermore, a large convenience yield is associated with low inventory levels, which generally lead to volatile commodity prices. Because volatile commodity prices tend to increase the demand for hedging, speculators will have to be offered a larger premium in order to take long positions in futures contracts. Therefore, a downward-sloping futures curve is generally more consistent with the presence of a positive risk premium in futures prices.

Keynes's theory of normal backwardation assumes that hedgers are mostly producers of commodities and are, therefore, net short in the futures markets. However, consumers of commodities may have the desire to hedge their risk, which will require them to take a long position in futures contracts. Therefore, to the degree that consumers are eager to hedge their risk, producers of commodities will not need to provide speculators with the incentive to take long positions in futures markets; thus, the risk premium associated with normal backwardation may cease to exist. In fact, if hedging demand by consumers of a commodity is large enough, then speculators will need to be net short in the futures markets. Therefore, hedging pressure could increase the futures price such that it is greater than the expected future spot price. In this case, the risk premium would be negative, and speculators would earn a positive return by being short futures contracts. Given this discussion, one can argue that one way a trend-following strategy could earn a profit would be to identify whether hedgers are net long or net short in futures markets and then establish the opposite position. Furthermore, one could argue that the technical analysis tools employed by trend followers are created to identify changes in hedging pressures and the ensuing trends that may take place.

Academic and practitioner research provides support for this view; that is, in order to generate consistently positive risk-adjusted returns, traders should take long or short positions in commodity futures markets, depending on market conditions. These studies show that strategies that take long positions in futures contracts when markets are in backwardation and short positions when markets are in contango tend to outperform long-only positions on a risk-adjusted basis.[3]

30.3 EFFICIENT MARKET HYPOTHESIS AND RETURNS TO CTAs

At first glance, the presence of trends (negative trends in particular) in futures markets appears to violate the basic tenets of the **efficient market hypothesis**. According to

---

[3] See Erb and Harvey (2006), Miffre and Rallis (2007), and Gorton and Rouwenhorst (2006).

the efficient market hypothesis, investors should not be able to earn abnormally high returns in perfect financial markets, because prices incorporate all available information, and therefore profitable opportunities are arbitraged away. This means that systematic trend-following strategies employed by most CTAs should not allow investors to earn abnormally high rates of return. In this context, an abnormally high return is defined as a rate of return on invested capital that is in excess of what the riskiness of the investment strategy would imply.[4]

Before discussing the implications of this theory for investors who allocate to CTAs, additional details about the efficient market hypothesis must be provided. The efficient market hypothesis proposes three forms of efficiency. The most basic form is referred to as **weak form efficiency**, which proposes that past prices cannot be used to predict future price changes such that the investor could earn abnormally high rates of return. This clearly implies that any type of technical analysis cannot be used to create profitable trading opportunities. Next follows **semistrong form efficiency**, which proposes that past prices as well as currently available public information cannot be used to create profitable trading opportunities. In equity markets, public information includes firm profitability and competitive positioning, while in commodity markets, information about inventories is publicly available. This form of market efficiency, therefore, rules out both systematic and discretionary trading strategies as possible sources of positive risk-adjusted return by CTAs. Finally, **strong form efficiency** suggests that even private information cannot be used to create profitable trading strategies. This form of market efficiency is generally not relevant to CTAs, as private information does not play an important role in the macro markets where CTAs actively trade.[5]

First, it is important to note that the presence of trends in futures prices does not necessarily violate any form of market efficiency. Stock and bond prices display positive trends that are considered to be consistent with market efficiency. For example, the total rate of return on an equity investment can be broken into two separate parts: (1) compensation for the time value of money, which is measured by the short-term nominal riskless rate, and (2) compensation for various types of systematic risks related to an equity investment. Thus, even if one ignores the risk premium, one should expect to observe a positive trend in equity prices simply due to the time value of money.

With regard to futures prices, since a position in an equity futures contract requires no cash outlay (ignoring the collateral associated with a futures contract), the return to a position in equity futures would represent only the compensation for systematic risks of equities. This means that if the risk premium is of the same sign (e.g., positive) for an extended period, a trend in the equity futures prices should be expected. Therefore, CTAs could earn a positive return reflecting the risk premium associated with systematic risk of the underlying asset even if markets are efficient. However, that rate of return is not in excess of the risk assumed by the trading strategy. Finally, while there are sound economic reasons to argue that trends in futures prices on equity and fixed-income assets are consistent with the efficient

---

[4] This implies that often one needs a model of risk and return before it is determined whether a particular market is efficient.

[5] Private information could be relevant if the trader takes positions in stocks and stock options.

market hypothesis, the case for the presence of trends in commodity futures and, especially, currency futures is rather weak. Notice that while spot exchange rates may display some trend to reflect differences in interest rates, currency futures prices should be trendless because the differences in interest rates are already reflected in currency futures prices. Empirical evidence regarding the presence of systematic risks in commodity and currency prices is inconclusive.[6] This means that in the absence of satisfying the needs of hedgers, returns to holding long or short positions in currency and commodity futures should be zero on average.

The fact that an entire asset management industry has been created around actively managed investment portfolios represents a strong argument that not all market participants believe that financial markets are always efficient. Indeed, there is no consensus in the academic community that markets are always efficient and that opportunities for earning abnormally high profits may not exist. There is a large body of academic and industry research on **market anomalies**, which represent research outcomes that appear to violate the basic tenets of the efficient market hypothesis. Further, it turns out that one of the most documented incidents of an anomaly is the profitability of momentum-based trading strategies.

30.4 PROFITABILITY OF MOMENTUM-BASED AND OTHER TREND-FOLLOWING STRATEGIES

Having briefly described the three broad strategies followed by most CTAs and the economic forces that affect futures prices, we now examine the potential sources of returns to CTAs. The goal is to go beyond the easy but unsatisfactory response that CTAs make money because they are smart or skilled in identifying trends in futures prices. This is unsatisfactory for a number of reasons. First, as was previously discussed, systematic trend following is the dominant trading strategy among CTAs, which means that pure skill is not an important component of the dominant strategy. Second, if skill is the sole source of return for a CTA, potential investors will have a difficult time separating skill from luck as the major contributing factor behind the historical performance of the CTA. Unless a trader has a long track record and is able to clearly describe his skill set, investors will have difficulty estimating the contribution of various factors to the CTA's ex post alpha. Thus, potential investors cannot be sure how persistent the future performance of the CTA will be. The objective of this section is to see if there are other sources of return that can be verified during a typical due diligence process.

Futures and forwards trading are referred to as zero-sum games, since every price change of a futures contract leads to equal gains and losses. If all futures traders had positions only in futures contracts and traded only with one another, no trader would be expected to display consistent positive performance unless the trader had a set of skills not available to other market participants. This is in contrast to a cash market, such as single-stock equities, in which an up move in the stock market would create net wealth if there were a net long position among all participants. The concept of

---

[6] For empirical evidence on sources of risk premium in futures prices, see Fama and French (1987), Bessembinder (1992), and Kat and Oomen (2007b).

a zero-sum game depends on the assumption that all futures traders have positions only in futures markets. In fact, many participants in futures markets are hedgers who operate businesses that require them to hedge commodity, currency, and interest rate risks. Thus, the expected payoff to trading in futures markets for speculators as a whole is in fact nonzero in practice. Systematic and discretionary trading strategies attempt to capture the risk premiums offered by hedgers.

30.4.1 A Momentum Strategy for Storable Commodities

In its simplest form, a momentum-based strategy uses past performance of an asset class to decide whether a long or short position in that asset should be established. For instance, a momentum strategy applied to commodities would invest in those that have performed well in the past and would short those that have performed poorly. Strategies based on this simple concept have shown to produce abnormally high returns.[7]

The presence of momentum in storable commodities has been linked to the observation that inventory adjustments cannot be implemented instantaneously and may take several months to complete, which could create short- to medium-term trends in commodity prices. For instance, suppose that as the result of a demand or a supply shock, inventories move away from their optimal levels. Consumers and producers will attempt to restore their inventories to optimal levels by changing their purchase and production policies. Since changes in the production level may take a considerable amount of time to implement, deviations of inventories from optimal levels are expected to be persistent. In addition, because large changes in spot prices in the past are signals of past shocks to inventory levels and changes in the risk premium, momentum in futures prices will be created. That is, the initial unexpected spot price spike due to a negative shock to inventories will be followed by a temporary period of high, expected futures returns for that commodity.[8]

This discussion indicates that when inventory levels are abnormally low, one should expect to observe positive momentum in storable commodity futures prices. For example, Erb and Harvey (2006) argue that since low inventory levels are associated with markets that are in backwardation as well as markets in which futures prices contain a positive risk premium, the return to the strategy that buys backwardated futures contracts and sells contangoed futures contracts should earn a positive return. This strategy, which is applied to 12 storable commodities by the authors, is shown to be profitable.

Miffre and Rallis (2007) examine the profitability of 56 momentum and contrarian strategies in commodity futures markets. For their momentum strategies, they buy the commodity futures contracts that have performed above average in the recent past and sell the commodity futures contracts that have performed below average in the past. These two positions are held for up to 12 months. For their contrarian strategies, they do the opposite: They buy the commodity futures contracts that have performed below average in the past and sell the commodity futures contracts that have performed above average in the past. In this case, the two positions are

---

[7] See Schneeweis, Kazemi, and Spurgin (2008).
[8] See Gorton, Hayashi, and Rouwenhorst (2008).

held for up to five years. Although their contrarian strategies do not work, they identify 13 profitable momentum strategies in commodity futures markets. Tactically allocating wealth toward the best-performing commodities and away from the worst-performing ones generates an average return of 9.38% a year. Over the same period (1979–2004), a long-only equally weighted portfolio of commodity futures lost 2.64%.

The authors also examine whether the presence of momentum in futures prices is related to the shape of the term structure of futures prices. Not surprisingly, they report that there is indeed significant overlap between a momentum strategy and a strategy based on the slope of the term structure of futures prices. They report that markets for commodities that require long positions in a momentum-based strategy are typically in backwardation, whereas markets for commodities that require short positions in a momentum-based strategy are typically in contango.

These two studies are examples of several that have used signals from the term structure of futures prices or signals from past prices to implement profitable long/short strategies in commodity futures markets. Fuertes, Miffre, and Rallis (2010b) compare and contrast the returns from these two strategies; furthermore, they examine the performance of a strategy that uses both signals to take long and short positions in futures markets. They report positive ex post annual alphas between 10% and 12% for each strategy, while the ex post annual alpha increased to 21% when the strategies were combined.

These and many other results reported by academic and industry research highlight the following points:[9]

- Unexpected demand or supply shocks in storable commodities cause inventories to deviate from their optimal levels.
- To bring inventories to their optimal levels, consumers and producers adjust their purchase and production policies, leading to persistent changes in commodity prices.
- Commodity futures prices may display short- to medium-term momentum, which is typically preceded by unexpected demand and supply shocks.
- Convenience yield and volatility of commodity prices increase when inventory levels are low, leading to backwardated futures prices.
- Positive risk premiums in commodity futures prices are associated with low inventory levels and volatile commodity prices.
- Excess returns to momentum-based strategies and strategies based on the shape of the term structure cannot be explained by traditional sources of risks, such as the Fama-French factors used in equity markets and discussed in Chapter 37.

Given this discussion, it can be concluded that there are sound economic reasons for CTAs to generate positive excess returns using momentum- or term-structure-based trading strategies. However, some words of caution should be provided. First, although the returns to these strategies are not correlated with traditional sources of risk, it does not mean that they do not have exposures to other sources of risk.

---

[9] For a summary of academic and industry research on returns to momentum strategies, see Schneeweis, Kazemi, and Spurgin (2008).

For example, momentum returns have been shown to have significant exposure to changes in market liquidity and to be negatively skewed.[10] Second, these studies report ex post alphas and do not claim that ex ante alphas will be of the same magnitude going forward. Third, these studies could suffer from **data mining**. That is, researchers may have examined hundreds of strategies to discover what would have worked in the past, but there may be little reason to believe that those strategies would work going forward. Fourth, in addition to data mining, the strategies could suffer from **data snooping**. In this case, researchers are influenced by past findings, and therefore the sample selections employed in these studies are not entirely random. Finally, some studies may fail to take into account transaction costs or the price impact of implementing the strategy in less liquid markets.

30.4.2 Momentum Strategies for Financial Futures

The previous section linked the presence of momentum in prices of storable commodities to demand and supply shocks and subsequent inventory adjustments by producers and consumers. The same framework may not be applicable to financial futures in which inventory adjustments play little or no role at all.

There is strong evidence supporting the presence of momentum in equity and currency markets. Many published studies have reported that relatively simple trading strategies based on past stock returns produce significant abnormal returns. These studies show that there are reversals at long horizons of three to five years, which could be employed to implement profitable contrarian strategies. Furthermore, momentum strategies that rely on the behavior of equity returns over the intermediate horizon of 1 to 12 months are shown to be profitable as well. Returns to momentum strategies appear to be robust to the methodology employed and do not appear to be highly time dependent.[11]

The explanations for the presence of momentum or contrarian profits have been the subject of numerous academic papers. In general, three primary explanations have been advanced in the literature. First, it is argued that momentum profits simply represent fair compensation for risk. For instance, momentum profits are highly skewed, and the market beta of a momentum strategy can change significantly during market cycles. For example, the beta could increase when equity markets are experiencing sharp declines. Also, returns to momentum are highly correlated with changes in market liquidity.[12] Second, it is argued that momentum returns are due to differences in cross-sectional returns. That is, because high-beta stocks are supposed to produce higher returns than low-beta stocks, momentum profits result from positive allocation to high-beta stocks and negative allocation to low-beta stocks. Third, it is argued that momentum profits result from under- and overreaction of investors to firm-specific news. This implies that investors are not entirely rational, and therefore markets may not be completely efficient. For example, recent research shows that changes in investors' sentiment and overconfidence have a strong influence

---

[10] See Daniel (2011).

[11] Of course, profitability of momentum strategies could vary significantly from year to year. See Jegadeesh and Titman (2011) and Daniel (2011).

[12] See Daniel (2011) and Asness, Moskowitz, and Pedersen (2009).

on the profitability of momentum-based strategies. These strategies are shown to be more profitable when taking advantage of potential overpricing of assets (investor sentiment is high) (Stambaugh, Yu, and Yuan 2011).[13]

Most academic studies examine returns to momentum strategies using individual stocks. CTAs, however, invest in futures contracts that represent broad market indices. Therefore, CTAs would profit from momentum in equity markets to the degree that momentum at the individual stock level spills over into broad market indices. Of the three explanations provided here, the under- and overreaction of investors is the only one that is compatible with the presence of momentum in broad equity indices. If during a specific period investors generally underreact to positive news about various firms, then the overall market will display positive momentum, and therefore taking a long position in equity indices that have displayed a positive return during the past several months should produce positive returns. By the same token, if during a specific period investors underreact to negative corporate news, then one should observe negative momentum. This indicates that shorting equity indices that have performed poorly during the past several months should generate positive returns.

If momentum in broad equity indices is a result of investors' under- and overre-actions to news, then there is perhaps little reason to believe that such behavior will continue to be displayed in the future. Also, available evidence indicates that the re-turn to momentum strategies when applied to broad equity indices is not as strong or persistent as return to momentum strategies when applied to individual securities or to commodities, fixed-income instruments, and currencies (Park and Irwin 2010). In addition, the theoretical basis for the presence of momentum in broad equity indices is much weaker than what was presented for commodities earlier in this chapter. As was stated, momentum in commodities arises from slow adjustment of inventories to demand and supply shocks and the demand for hedging by producers or consumers. In particular, since commodities are either used in production processes or consumed by the public, the hedgers might be willing to pay an insurance premium to reduce the risk to their business. In other words, there are certain sources of return to hold-ing commodities that are still available to a fully hedged position. The same cannot be said about equity futures. Equities are assets that are held for their potential cash payoffs. Since the return to a fully hedged position in equities would be the riskless rate, a significant and natural hedging demand in the equity futures market does not exist, and consequently the case for the presence of momentum in equity futures is much weaker.[14]

Although the case for the presence of momentum in equity indices is weaker than the case regarding commodities, there is strong empirical evidence that currencies tend to display momentum.[15] Empirical evidence shows that the long/short strategy of buying the most attractive currency and shorting the least attractive currency earns significantly positive average excess returns. One can argue that there are

---

[13] See also Cremers and Pareek (2011).

[14] Equity long/short hedge funds and other investors who possess stock-picking skills may want to hedge the market risk of their portfolios using equity futures. However, demand by these hedgers is not large enough to generate substantial hedging pressure.

[15] See Okunev and White (2003) and Asness, Moskowitz, and Pedersen (2009).

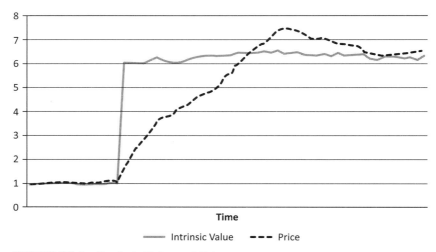

EXHIBIT 30.1   Intrinsic Value and Price

natural hedgers in currency markets who might be willing to pay a premium to avoid currency risks. These hedgers typically earn profits in other markets (e.g., importers or exporters of products or investors in foreign currency–denominated assets), and therefore it may be economical for them to pay an insurance premium to those who are willing to take the other side of the trade. In addition, the possibility of intervention by national governments in currency and government bond markets could lead to momentum in currency and interest rate futures.

30.4.3   Trends and Behavioral Finance

In recent years, empirical evidence accumulated by academics and practitioners has supported the hypothesis that market participants do not always act in the rational manner described by the efficient market hypothesis. That is, market participants display certain biases on a consistent basis, and these biases could cause prices to deviate from their intrinsic values for an extended time and to display trends.[16] In the context of this discussion, these biases provide a basis for profitable trend-following and momentum strategies.

Exhibit 30.1 is used to explain the behavioral foundations of trend-following strategies.[17] As can be seen at the beginning, the price and intrinsic (or fundamental) value of an asset closely follow each other. Then, due to some event, the intrinsic value of the asset increases. For example, a supply shock or a change in the central bank's policy could cause this sudden change in the intrinsic value of the asset. Market participants realize that there has been a change in the intrinsic value of the

---

[16] This research was pioneered by Tversky and Kahneman (1974).

[17] The following discussion is based on the results appearing in Daniel, Hirshleifer, and Subrahmanyam (1998); Hong and Stein (1999); Hurst, Ooi, and Pedersen (2010); and Berger, Israel, and Moskowitz (2009).

asset, but they underreact to the new information; according to behavioral finance, this can be caused by two biases:

1. *Anchoring.* Research has shown that when people make quantitative estimates, their estimates are heavily influenced by previous values of the item. For example, in Exhibit 30.1, **anchoring** causes market participants to use the initial price as an anchor; as a result, their estimates of the new intrinsic value are not sufficiently adjusted in reaction to new information. Anchoring can cause investors to underreact to new information.

2. *Disposition effect.* The **disposition effect** leads market participants to close their profitable positions too quickly and hold their losing positions for a longer period. In the context of Exhibit 30.1, the initial increase in the price of the underlying asset causes those participants who have held long (profitable) positions to close them rather quickly, putting downward pressure on the price. In contrast, those who have held short (losing) positions would tend to keep those positions open longer; therefore, they would not put upward pressure on prices. The disposition effect causes the price to react slowly to changes in the intrinsic value of an asset.

These two behavioral biases can lead market participants to underreact to the initial good news, thus creating an upward trend in the market. Next, behavioral models predict that other biases would eventually lead market participants to overreact to the news, and thus the price could overshoot the intrinsic value of the asset. This is displayed in Exhibit 30.1 when the price line moves above the intrinsic value line. This overreaction may be caused by the following biases:

- *Herding and feedback.* **Herding** refers to a group of investors who, after observing the price trend, decide to come to the market to take advantage of the trend. This herding effect could feed on itself, leading the price trend to continue and to overshoot the intrinsic value. For example, herding could arise if market participants are concerned about their performance relative to their peers. In this case, those participants who did not have long positions when the trend began may become concerned about their performance relative to their peers who had long positions in the market and may decide to join the crowd. This will put upward pressure on the price, encouraging more participants to come to the market.

- *Confirmation and representativeness.* **Confirmation bias** leads market participants to favor information that confirms their initial beliefs. In **representativeness bias,** participants tend to look at past prices to form their beliefs. Together, these two biases imply that market participants would look at the recent trend as a confirmation of their initial beliefs, leading them to increase the sizes of their positions. This will reinforce the trend and could eventually lead the price to overshoot the intrinsic value of the asset. These two biases generally lead participants to believe that the current trend will continue.

At some point, the overreaction will come to an end and the price will revert to the intrinsic value of the asset. This could result from another event, from slow realization by participants that the price has moved too far away from the intrinsic value, or because all potential capital has been allocated to the long position and therefore very few potential participants have been left on the sidelines.

To the degree that technical analysis and trend-following tools can identify various turning points in the movements of futures prices, CTAs could establish profitable trend-following strategies. The key is to identify the trends quickly and to exit the market such that only a small portion of the accumulated profit is lost when the trend ends.

30.4.4 Limits to Arbitrage

Although many alternative investments can claim that several sources of return, ranging from illiquidity (e.g., private equity or other real assets) to market inefficiency (e.g., distressed debt, venture capital, or mortgage-backed securities), contribute to their total returns, it is not possible to rely on these sources of return to explain the performance of CTAs; this is because they operate in very liquid and transparent markets. Recent academic research argues that certain sources of abnormal return may continue to exist and that the normal argument that sources of abnormal profit are arbitraged away may not always hold.

The standard models of finance predict the well-known relationship between risk and expected return, which appear to be contradicted by the presence of numerous anomalies in financial markets. Leading anomalies are (1) short-term momentum in prices of commodities, fixed-income securities, currencies, and equities; (2) long-term reversal in equity markets; (3) the outperformance of value stocks relative to growth stocks; (4) the high volatility of asset prices relative to the volatility of their fundamentals (e.g., dividend payments); and (5) the post–earnings announcement drift (the tendency of stock earnings surprises to predict future stock returns).[18]

According to Gromb and Vayanos (2010), understanding why anomalies arise and persist requires a careful study of the process of arbitrage: Who are the arbitrageurs, what are the constraints and limitations they face, and why can arbitrage fail to remove profit opportunities represented by these and other anomalies? Empirical evidence shows that arbitrageurs face a number of **limits to arbitrage** that may prevent them from taking advantage of available profit opportunities. First, arbitrageurs must raise the capital needed to implement a trading strategy that attempts to exploit the apparent mispricing. Second, even if the needed capital is raised, the strategy may not become profitable immediately. This means the arbitrageur has to convince investors to maintain their investments and not to withdraw their funds. Third, certain structural constraints, such as restrictions on short selling or the size of the position, may make the implemented strategy less profitable. Fourth, significant leverage may be needed to exploit strategies with small profit margins. Financial markets may not be willing to provide the needed leverage to arbitrageurs. Fifth, even if arbitrageurs face no capital constraints, they may not wish to commit all available capital in order to maintain liquidity and for the fear of losing out on profitable opportunities that may arise in the future. Finally, mispricings and arbitrage

---

[18] See Gromb and Vayanos (2010).

opportunities typically arise during periods of market stress. These are exactly the times during which arbitrageurs will face significant capital and leverage constraints (Griffoli and Ranaldo 2011; Mitchell, Pedersen, and Pulvin 2007).

30.5 EMPIRICAL EVIDENCE ON TECHNICAL TRADING RULES

Systematic trend-following strategies represent a subset of technical analysis as applied to futures contracts. Substantial academic and practitioner research on the profitability of technical analysis has been published. Though some may place technical analysis in the same category as astrology, there are sound theoretical explanations for the profitability of trend-following systems.

As previously discussed, arbitrageurs help move prices toward their fundamental values but are unable to fully move the market due to risk aversion, capital constraints, or position limits. The result is that the price may display trends that can be detected through technical analysis. The common argument for trend-following prices is based on a delayed movement toward equilibrium after new information enters the marketplace.

Before discussing the available empirical evidence, we summarize the three basic building blocks of technical analysis.[19]

1. *Moving average–based systems.* **Moving average–based systems** are the most simple and popular trend-following trading systems among practitioners.[20] In a simple moving average–based system, long or short positions are taken depending on whether the current price is above or below a given moving average of past prices of the same asset. In a dual crossover moving average–based system, trading signals are generated by comparing the current value of a short-term moving average to the current value of a long-term moving average.
2. *Price channels.* The **price channel**, which is also referred to as a **trading range breakout** or support and resistance, is also extensively used. The fundamental characteristic underlying price channel systems is that a market's movement to a new high or low suggests a continued trend in the direction established. Thus, all price channels generate trading signals based on a comparison between today's price level and price levels at specified days in the past. More specifically, this system generates a buy signal anytime the closing price trades above the highest price in a channel length (specified time interval), and generates a sell signal anytime the closing price trades below the lowest price in the price channel.
3. *Relative strength index.* The **relative strength index (RSI)** is also referred to as a **momentum oscillator system**. Momentum oscillator techniques derive their name from the fact that trading signals are obtained from values that oscillate above and below a neutral point, usually given a zero value. In its simplest form,

---

[19] For more detailed discussion of these rules, see *CAIA Level I: An Introduction to Core Topics in Alternative Investments*, 2nd ed. Also see Park and Irwin (2004).
[20] See Kestner (2003).

the momentum oscillator compares today's price with the price of n days ago. When the price moves up very rapidly, at some point it is considered to be overbought; when it moves down very rapidly, at some point it is considered to be oversold. In either case, a reaction or reversal is imminent.

Earlier studies of the profitability of technical rules, which are summarized in Park and Irwin (2004), were completed before the 1980s. The results of these studies, which examined the profitability of technical trading rules in various markets, varied greatly from market to market. Typically, various technical rules proved to be ineffective when applied to stock markets. However, moving average and relative strength approaches outperformed buy-and-hold strategies in physical commodity and currency markets.

These early studies had a number of limitations. First, they typically concentrated on a few trading rules; thus, the results were affected by data snooping. Second, absolute or relative returns to strategies were estimated with no adjustments for risk. Third, in most cases the statistical significance of the resulting profits was not tested; therefore, although the reported performances may have been economically significant, it is unclear whether they were statistically significant.

Recent studies concerning the profitability of technical rules have attempted to avoid these limitations. These studies typically examine a large number of trading rules to check whether the trading systems could produce positive gross returns, returns above transaction costs, and returns above transaction costs plus returns to risk. The trading systems generally consist of channels, moving averages, momentum oscillators, filters (or trailing stops), and a combination system, some of which are known to be widely used by fund managers and traders. The results of trading simulations normally show that a majority of the systems generate statistically significant monthly gross returns. Many of these studies have examined the performance of trading rules in currency markets. Relative to equity markets, these studies generally find stronger support for the efficacy of technical analysis in foreign exchange markets. For example, moving averages tend to generate positive portfolio gains for currency trading, and the gains are much larger than those in the stock market. In addition, the profits earned using moving average rules resulted from the central bank's "leaning against the wind intervention." That is, central bank interventions created profit opportunities that trading rules were able to detect.[21] A recent paper by Neely et al. (2011) examines the role of technical analysis in estimating the risk premium in equity markets. The paper shows that while macroeconomic variables such as credit spread, slope of the term structure, economic growth, and inflation rate have not demonstrated consistent predictive power about the risk premium in equity markets, the addition of technical signals significantly improves the predictive powers of the model. The paper finds that technical indicators display statistically and economically significant out-of-sample forecasting power and generate substantial gains; moreover, technical indicators tend to detect the typical decline in the equity risk premium near cyclical peaks. This and similar recent papers appear to indicate that a model combining fundamental and technical models could predict changes in the size of the equity risk premium.

---

[21] See Menkhoff and Taylor (2007).

In short, studies show that technical rules such as moving average, trading channel, and relative strength tend to produce positive risk-adjusted returns when applied to foreign currency and interest rate markets and, to a lesser degree, commodity markets. The performance of these trading rules is less consistent when applied to equity markets. However, a combination of technical and fundamental analysis appears to provide some information about the future performance of equity indices. Finally, the performance of trading rules applied to commodity markets improves if additional information such as the shape of the term structure is taken into account.[22]

30.6 CONCLUSION

This chapter has examined the economic foundations for the sources of returns to trend-following strategies. It has argued that futures markets are not strictly zero-sum games if one considers the positions that some market participants have in the spot markets. In other words, some market participants may be willing to accept losses in the futures markets when those losses are offset by gains in other markets. This can be one potential source of return to trend-following strategies. The chapter also discussed the potential behavioral reasons for the presence of trends in futures prices. Investors may not always behave in the rational manner assumed by supporters of the efficient market hypothesis. Under some circumstances, such behavior could lead to trends in security prices, and systematic CTAs may be in a position to take advantage of these trends.

---

[22] See Park and Irwin (2004) and Fuertes, Miffre, and Rallis (2010b).

CHAPTER 31

Risk and Performance Analysis in Managed Futures Strategies

Managed futures strategies have the same elements of risk found in all investment strategies. Much of the work that has been done to provide a framework for measuring investment risk can also be applied to managed futures products. However, the managed futures industry has developed some ways of measuring and describing risk of managed futures programs that are unique to the industry, and it is worthwhile to discuss some of these. Commodity trading advisers (CTAs) are commonly described as strategies that should be held in a portfolio because they tend to perform well when traditional asset classes, especially equities and high-yield bonds, perform poorly. This chapter closely examines this property of CTAs. Finally, most institutional investors seek benchmarks to measure the performances of the asset classes that comprise their portfolios. Because of the wide variety of trading processes employed, it is generally difficult to create single passive investable benchmarks for CTAs. This chapter examines the existence of investment benchmarks, the separation of beta and alpha in CTA returns, and volatility exposures of CTAs.

31.1 RISK MEASUREMENT

Because futures contracts are exchange-traded instruments, CTAs need to satisfy the rules and restrictions put forth by these exchanges. One of these rules pertains to the amount of collateral or margin that a party to a futures contract must put up: the **margin requirement**. The amount of **initial margin** is the amount of cash or Treasury bills that must be in an account at a broker or futures commission merchant (FCM) in order to initiate a trade in a specific futures contract. Minimum initial margins are set by the exchanges for each futures contract. This initial margin, which is generally only a small percentage of the notional value of the futures contract, is related to the volatility of the assets underlying the futures contract and can change over time. More volatile contracts require larger margins. Futures exchanges have the ability to change margin requirements at any time. Margin requirements are often increased after a sharp rise in prices or price volatility. Exhibit 31.1 displays the initial margin and maintenance margin requirements for selected futures contracts as of March 1, 2012. The **maintenance margin**, which is typically lower than the initial margin, is the amount of margin required to carry previously initiated positions. If a customer's margin account drops below the level required for the maintenance margin, then

EXHIBIT 31.1 Initial and Maintenance Margin Requirements for Selected Futures Contracts (March 2011)

Contract	Exchange	Initial Margin ($)	Maintenance Margin ($)	Contract	Exchange	Initial Margin ($)	Maintenance Margin ($)
Grains and Oilseeds				**Currencies**			
Corn	CBOT	2,363	1,750	Australian $	IMM	3,780	2,800
Soybeans	CBOT	3,375	2,500	British pound	IMM	2,025	1,500
Wheat	CBOT	3,038	2,250	Canadian $	IMM	2,295	1,700
Meats				U.S. $ Index	NYBOT	1,254	1,140
Live cattle	CME	1,620	1,200	Euro FX	IMM	5,400	4,000
Feeder cattle	CME	2,025	1,500	Japanese yen	IMM	4,860	3,600
Lean hogs	CME	1,688	1,250	**Softs**			
Metals				Sugar #11	NYBOT	1,595	1,450
Gold	COMEX	10,125	7,500	Cocoa	NYBOT	1,980	1,800
Silver	COMEX	21,610	16,000	Coffee	NYBOT	3,905	3,550
Copper	COMEX	6,750	5,000	Cotton	NYBOT	1,870	1,700
Palladium	NYMEX	5,775	5,250	**Interest Rates**			
Energy				U.S. T-bond	CBT	5,738	4,250
Crude oil	NYMEX	6,885	5,100	10-year notes	CBT	1,485	1,100
E-mini crude oil	NYMEX	3,443	2,550	Eurodollar	CBT	439	325
RBOB gas	NYM	8,100	6,000	**Indices**			
Heating oil	NYM	7,155	5,300	S&P 500	CME	25,000	20,000
Natural gas	NYM	2,835	2,100	E-mini S&P 500	CME	5,000	4,000
E-mini natural gas	NYM	709	525	NASDAQ 100	CME	17,500	14,000
				E-mini NASDAQ 100	CME	3,500	2,800
				Nikkei 225 stock index	CME	5,313	4,250

Source: CBOT, CBT, CME, COMEX, IMM, NYBOT, NYM, and NYMEX.

the customer has to add funds to restore the margin account to the level of the initial margin.

In certain circumstances, the initial margin may be less than the sum of the initial margins of the individual futures contracts. Futures exchanges take into account the fact that the manager is holding both long and short positions in related contracts. Since such spread positions may have less risk than outright directional positions, the exchanges apply a lower spread margin. For instance, a relative value trader might be long a nearby futures contract (e.g., long March corn) and short a distant contract (e.g., short September corn). In such cases, spread margins would apply.

The **margin-to-equity** ratio is expressed as the amount of initial margin as a percentage of the net asset value of the investment account. If the equity invested in a futures portfolio is valued at $1,000,000 and the total margin required by various exchanges is $61,000, then the margin-to-equity ratio would be 6.1%. It is often difficult to interpret margin-to-equity ratios. High levels could indicate highly levered trading; for instance, a margin-to-equity ratio of 100% means that the invested equity is just enough to cover the margins, indicating that the maximum amount of leverage provided by the contracts is employed. However, high levels of the margin-to-equity ratio could equally result from a portfolio diversified across many futures markets where margin offsets are not available (e.g., partially offsetting positions at different exchanges). The margin-to-equity ratio is a popular measure of CTA risk because it tells investors roughly how much of their investment could be used for margin purposes. This number will fluctuate from day to day for a given manager, but investors can obtain the average range. It should be noted that the exchange sets the margin to reflect the riskiness of the futures contract. The greater the exchange's estimate of the risk associated with a contract, the higher the level of the margin required by that exchange on the particular contract.

Managed futures traders normally employ stop-loss rules in their trading programs. These stop losses are specific prices at which the strategy will exit a futures position should the price move adversely. In the case of reversal systems, stops are effectively the price at which the system liquidates an existing directional position and establishes a new position in the opposite direction. **Capital at risk (CaR)** represents the total loss that would be incurred should each position hit its stop-loss price level on that day. Exhibit 31.2 displays the CaR of a sample portfolio of long futures positions. It assumes that each stop loss is set at 1% of the notional value of each contract (i.e., the position would be liquidated upon a 1% adverse price move).

The usefulness of CaR is dependent on the stop-loss level established for individual futures positions. If this level is very close to the current market price, the CaR might underestimate the real risk of loss, since unanticipated price volatility could lead the futures price to gap through the stop-loss level, resulting in a greater loss than that being reported by the CaR. This is a particularly important risk in less liquid markets, such as futures on agricultural commodities. In another sense, though, CaR often overstates a portfolio's risk, since it does not account for the possibility that a portfolio may hold both long and short futures positions, which might offer some offset should significant price moves occur. That is, it is unlikely for all positions to hit their stop-loss levels simultaneously. Finally, a typical investor does not have the transparency to the CTA's positions that is needed to calculate CaR. The exception is when the investor uses a managed account platform to invest in a CTA program. Under the managed account platform, the investor has access

EXHIBIT 31.2 Leverage and Capital at Risk (CaR) of a
Sample Portfolio

Contract	Notional Contract Value	Loss at 1% Price Change
S&P 500 stock index	$ 207,250	-$ 2,073
Corn	$ 17,913	-$ 179
Soybeans	$ 47,475	-$ 475
Eurodollars	$ 987,650	-$ 9,877
U.S. long bond	$ 126,640	-$ 1,266
Crude oil	$ 40,320	-$ 403
Gold	$ 90,166	-$ 902
Japanese yen	$ 139,636	-$ 1,396
Size of notional positions	$1,657,050	
Total CaR value		-$16,571
Assumed account value	$1,000,000	
Notional leverage	165.71%	
Capital at risk	-1.657%	

Source: Authors' calculations.

to the positions and can therefore calculate the CaR of a portfolio. The advantages and disadvantages of managed account platforms and other approaches to accessing CTA programs are discussed in Chapter 32.

Value at risk (VaR) is a method of measuring potential loss in an investment portfolio given a particular holding period, with no changes to the portfolio during the holding period, and at a particular confidence level. The most common confidence levels used are 95% and 99%. A portfolio's one-day VaR of $3 million at a 95% confidence level means that there is a 95% probability that losses sustained by the portfolio over the next day will not exceed $3 million and, thus, a 5% chance that losses will be greater than $3 million. In other words, during 100 trading days, losses exceeding $3 million are expected in only five trading days. If the value of the portfolio is $100 million, then the VaR could be expressed as 3%.

For example, using the portfolio shown in Exhibit 31.2 (i.e., one long contract in each of the individual markets), a one-day VaR can be computed over a continuous 60-day period. At a 99% confidence level, the one-day VaR could be $9,453, or approximately 1% of the assumed portfolio of $1,000,000. That is, one would expect that 99% of the time, the daily loss on this portfolio would be less than $9,453.

There are several methods for estimating the VaR of an investment. The simplest and most common method is the parametric approach. In the **parametric approach** to calculating an investment's VaR, one assumes that return on the investment follows a known distribution (typically normal). Then in order to estimate the VaR of the investment, one has to estimate the parameters of the distribution (typically, mean and standard deviation). In fact, to obtain an accurate estimate of VaR, it is crucial to obtain an accurate estimate of the return volatility. There are several methods for estimating the return volatility, and in general the higher the frequency of available observations, the more accurate the estimated volatility.

The most common method for estimating volatility is to obtain daily returns on an investment, say a CTA, and then perform the following procedure on the data to obtain an estimate of daily volatility:

$$\sigma_T^2 = \frac{1}{T-1} \sum_{r=1}^{T} (\mu - R_t)^2$$

Here, σ_T^2 is the estimate of the current daily variance, R_t is the daily rate of return, T is the number of observations, and

$$\mu = \frac{1}{T} \sum_{t=1}^{T} R_t$$

is the estimated daily mean return. In this method, all observations have the same weight. An alternative to this method is to assign larger weights to the most recent observations and smaller weights to observations that occurred many periods ago. The **exponential smoothing method** is a simple and popular method in this area. Under this approach, the estimated value of the variance is obtained using the following expression:

$$\sigma_T^2 = (1 - \lambda) \times \sigma_{T-1}^2 + \lambda(\mu - R_T)^2$$

Here, $0 < \lambda < 1$ is a parameter that is selected by the user. The larger the value of λ, the higher the weight assigned to the most recent observations.

Once an estimate of the standard deviation is obtained, the user needs to specify the desirable level of confidence. The higher the selected level of confidence, the higher the estimated value of VaR will be. After the desirable confidence level is selected, the critical value of α is calculated as follows:

$$\Pr\{Z \le \alpha\} = 1 - \text{Confidence level}$$

Here, Z is a standard normal random variable.[1] This means α is the value for a standard normal random variable where the probability of observing a value less than α is equal to 1 minus the selected confidence level. To determine the value of α, one may use either a table of standard normal random variables or a spreadsheet program. Once this critical value is calculated, the VaR of the portfolio can be estimated using the following expression:

$$VaR_\alpha = \alpha \times \sigma_t + \mu$$

The VaR obtained using this expression is typically a negative number. However, it is customary to report the absolute value of this figure. In addition, since the daily mean, μ, is likely to be very small, it is common practice to ignore it.

---

[1] For example, using Microsoft Excel, one can obtain an estimate of α using the following function: NORM.S.INV(1–Confidence Level).

Example: Daily returns for a CTA are used to obtain estimates of daily volatility, σ_t, and daily mean return, μ, of the CTA. These are reported to be 1.8% and 0.03%, respectively. What is the daily VaR of this CTA at 95% confidence level?

First, the critical value of α for the 95% confidence level is −1.6448. That is, $Pr\{Z \leq -1.6448\} = 1 - 0.95$. Thus, the daily VaR at 95% confidence level will be calculated as follows:

$$VaR = -1.6448 \times 1.8\% + 0.03\% = -2.93\%$$

There is 5% probability that the daily loss experienced by this CTA will exceed 2.93%.

As can be seen in the example, one of the critical assumptions was that the probability distribution of the portfolio's daily return is approximately normal. If the probability distribution deviates from normality, then alternative methods to estimate the VaR must be used.[2]

As a method of calculating risk, VaR is useful but should be used in conjunction with additional risk-measurement techniques. Its reliance on specific estimates of correlations and volatilities makes it prone to underestimating potential tail risk during periods of increased financial stress.

Maximum drawdown is calculated as the relative value of the last peak price to the all-time low price since the peak was reached. For example, using performance figures covering January 2008 through December 2011, the maximum drawdown for a CTA can be estimated using the following expression:

$$\text{Maximum drawdown} = \left[\min\left(\frac{NAV_{t+i}}{NAV_t} \right) - 1 \right] \times 100$$

where t is any date between January 2008 and December 2011 and $t + i$ is any date between t and December 2011. For example, suppose the NAV of a CTA at the end of June 2009 was 120 and the NAV of the same fund was 90 at the end of August 2010. The ratio would be (90/120) = 0.75, which turns out to be the lowest value that can be obtained using the fund's NAVs between January 2008 and December 2011. In this case, the maximum drawdown of the fund is calculated to be −25%.

Maximum drawdown is a useful measure of risk because it shows how sustained the losses experienced by a manager are, and may be used to determine if the manager has the skill to reevaluate the model and make appropriate adjustments when losses are increasing. Risk managers may also use maximum drawdown. For example, a risk manager may follow the maximum drawdown of a fund and decide that whenever the fund's maximum drawdown reaches some predetermined level, the fund should significantly reduce its leverage or reevaluate the fund's trading system.

Many factors affect the maximum drawdown of a manager. The most important factors are volatility of the returns, mean of the returns, and length of time during which the maximum drawdown is calculated. In particular, everything else being constant, maximum drawdown will be higher for CTAs with higher return volatility, whereas maximum drawdown will decline as the average return on the

---

[2] See *CAIA Level II: Current and Integrated Topics.*

EXHIBIT 31.3   Portfolio Stress Test: Eight-Standard-Deviation Price Move; Doubling of the Initial Margin

Contract	Notional Contract Value	1-Standard-Deviation Move in Price	Price Move	Initial Margin Requirement
S&P 500 stock index	$ 207,250	1.24%	−$20,559	$30,938
Corn	$ 17,913	1.68%	−$ 2,408	$ 2,025
Soybeans	$ 47,475	1.45%	−$ 5,507	$ 4,725
Eurodollars	$ 987,650	0.08%	−$ 6,005	$ 1,485
U.S. long bond	$ 126,640	0.63%	−$ 6,383	$ 4,320
Crude oil	$ 40,320	2.17%	−$ 7,000	$ 8,100
Gold	$ 90,166	1.26%	−$ 9,089	$ 5,399
Japanese yen	$ 139,636	0.66%	−$ 7,373	$ 4,860
Total loss from 8-standard-deviation price move			−$64,322	
Total required initial margin				$61,852

Potential Total Cash Demand
8-standard-deviation price move	$ 64,322
Initial margin at 2 × levels	$ 123,704
Total	$ 188,026
Assumed account value:	$1,000,000
Potential total cash demand as %	18.80%

Source: Authors' calculations.

CTA increases. Holding everything else constant, there is greater chance of a large drawdown as longer time periods are used to calculate the drawdowns.

A **stress test** or **scenario analysis** is a market simulation applied to a portfolio to determine how it will perform under different market scenarios. Commonly, these try to focus on extreme market events, both those historically encountered (e.g., the financial crisis in the fall of 2008) and simulated financial stress. Often this technique is used in conjunction with VaR, since it examines scenarios in which volatility and correlations are assumed to change.

Exhibit 31.3 illustrates a stress test under simplified assumptions. It analyzes the demand on cash in an investment account should a set of futures positions have an eight-standard-deviation adverse price move and, at the same time, should futures exchanges double the required initial margins on these same positions. For example, previous calculations may have shown that this portfolio has a margin-to-equity ratio of 6.1%, a CaR of 1.66%, and a VaR of 1%. However, under the conditions assumed in the stress test, the portfolio could lose over 6.4% on that day (6.4% = 64,322/1,000,000). This is significantly higher than indicated by the CaR or the VaR. In addition, the doubling of the initial margin creates a further demand on cash of 12.4% of the account value. The combined impact would be an 18.8% use of cash in the portfolio over one day. Although this may be an unlikely scenario, the purpose of stress tests is to examine the potential impact of low-probability events. It has been seen in the past that these low-probability events do occur (e.g., failures of Long-Term Capital Management and Lehman Brothers). Similar to the

EXHIBIT 31.4 Hypothetical Monthly Return (Target Rate = 4% per Year)

	Realized Monthly Return	Above Target Return	Below Target Return	Upper Partial Moment	Lower Partial Moment
January 2011	18.55%	1	0	18.22%	0.00%
February 2011	−18.62%	0	1	0.00%	18.95%
March 2011	8.58%	1	0	8.25%	0.00%
April 2011	−4.68%	0	1	0.00%	5.01%
May 2011	1.69%	1	0	1.36%	0.00%
June 2011	−3.50%	0	1	0.00%	3.83%
July 2011	−13.07%	0	1	0.00%	13.40%
August 2011	−21.47%	0	1	0.00%	21.80%
September 2011	−4.91%	0	1	0.00%	5.24%
October 2011	8.13%	1	0	7.80%	0.00%
November 2011	2.66%	1	0	2.33%	0.00%
December 2011	−5.27%	0	1	0.00%	5.61%
Average				3.16%	6.15%
Omega					0.51
Target					4%

CaR calculation, an investor who has allocated to more than one CTA is not in a position to calculate these stress figures unless the investments are made using managed account platforms.

Omega ratio is a more general measure of risk that takes the entire distribution of an investment (e.g., a CTA) into account. Traditional measures of risks and risk-adjusted returns such as VaR, Sharpe ratio, Treynor ratio, and information ratio have been questioned by researchers because of their reliance on specific and sometimes restrictive assumptions about the distribution of returns. Omega is an alternative to these and provides a better assessment of downside risk and upside potential relative to a target return. The target level could be zero for an absolute return product such as a CTA or a hedge fund, while other rates, such as the inflation rate or a short-term nominal riskless rate, could be selected for a product that is supposed to protect the real value of an investor's portfolio.[3]

The omega ratio is the ratio of the average realized return in excess of a given target return relative to the average realized loss relative to the same target return. Exhibit 31.4 contains the hypothetical annual returns on a CTA. In this example, a 4% annual return (0.333% monthly return) is the stated target. For each realized monthly return, it is determined whether the realized return is greater or less than the target level. These differences are presented in two columns called upper partial moment and lower partial moment. For example, the January 2011 figure in the upper partial moment column is given by the following:

$$18.22\% = \max(18.55\% - 0.333\%, 0)$$

---

[3] See Shadwick and Keating (2002) and Kazemi, Schneeweis, and Gupta (2003).

and the February 2011 figure in the lower partial moment column is given as follows:

$$18.95\% = \max(0.333\% - (-18.62\%), 0)$$

The averages of these upper and lower partial moments are calculated to be 3.16% and 6.15%, respectively. Finally, the omega ratio is calculated to be 0.51, the ratio of these two figures (3.16/6.15). Mathematically, omega is given by the following expression:

$$\Omega = \frac{\text{Upper partial moment}}{\text{Lower partial moment}}$$

$$= \frac{\dfrac{1}{N} \sum_{i=1}^{N} \max(R_i - T, 0)}{\dfrac{1}{N} \sum_{i=1}^{N} \max(T - R_i, 0)}$$

where R_i is the rate of return on the investment in period i, N is the total number of observations, and T is the target rate.

When the omega ratio is less than 1, it means the investment has provided fewer opportunities to earn a return that exceeds the target level. Furthermore, it can be shown that higher volatility, lower skewness, and higher kurtosis will, in general, reduce the omega of a portfolio (Kazemi, Schneeweis, and Gupta 2003). In addition, increasing the target return will reduce the omega of the investment product. For instance, in the previous example, the omega will decline to 0.48 if the target return is raised to 8% per year (0.666% per month). Using historical performance figures, studies have shown that for a target level of zero, the omega of a diversified portfolio of CTAs would be around 4, and the omega measure of MSCI World Equities would be around 2.

Understanding investment risk in any portfolio requires constant interpretation of multiple risk factors. This is no less true in managed futures. However, doing so in managed futures is made somewhat easier because these strategies typically only trade futures contracts listed on major exchanges or liquid over-the-counter foreign exchange markets. In both cases, pricing of these instruments is transparent and continuous, thereby permitting the risk of these portfolios to be monitored and measured on a real-time basis.

31.2 HISTORICAL PERFORMANCE OF CTAs

This section provides some evidence regarding the historical performance of CTAs both as stand-alone investment products and within the context of diversified portfolios of traditional asset classes (the role of CTAs in diversified portfolios is further examined in Chapter 32). In addition, the benefits of CTAs as risk diversifiers, especially during periods of market stress, are presented.

Exhibit 31.5A presents basic statistics of two CTA indices, the Barclay Trader Index Discretionary and the Barclay Trader Index Systematic, along with similar

EXHIBIT 31.5A Estimates of Statistical Properties of Returns on Indices of CTAs and Other Investments

Index (Jan. 2000–Dec. 2011)	Barclay Trader Index Discretionary	Barclay Trader Index Systematic	World Equities	Global Bonds	U.S. High Yield	Commodities
Annualized arithmetic mean	5.8%**	5.5%**	1.7%	6.4%**	7.6%**	7.8%**
Annualized standard deviation	4.1%	8.6%	16.9%	6.2%	11.0%	24.7%
Skewness	0.6**	0.2	−0.6**	−0.1	−1.0**	−0.5**
Kurtosis	1.2**	0.3	1.1**	0.3	6.3**	1.2**
Sharpe ratio	0.8	0.3	−0.1	0.6	0.5	0.2
Annualized geometric mean	5.7%	5.1%	0.3%	6.2%	7.0%	4.8%
Annualized std (auto correlation adjusted)	3.9%	8.6%	20.1%	6.5%	14.8%	29.0%
Maximum	4.7%	7.4%	11.2%	6.2%	12.1%	19.7%
Minimum	−2.7%	−5.6%	−19.0%	−3.8%	−15.9%	−28.2%
Autocorrelation	−03.1%	−00.2%	18.7%**	05.7%	32.0%**	17.5%**
Max drawdown	−4.0%	−10.1%	−54.0%	−10.1%	−33.3%	−67.6%

**Significant at 95% confidence level.
Source: Authors' calculations and Bloomberg data.

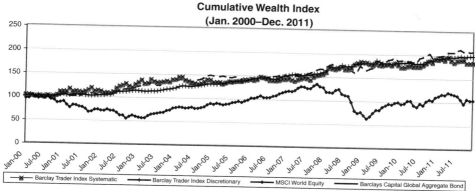

EXHIBIT 31.5B   Growth of $100 Invested in CTA Indices and Other Asset Classes
Source: Authors' calculations and Bloomberg data.

statistics reported for two traditional asset classes (equities and bonds). Several issues must be addressed in connection with the results reported here. First, the CTA indices represent equally weighted portfolios of CTAs; therefore, their volatility, skewness, and kurtosis are not necessarily representative of the properties displayed by individual CTAs. For instance, according to Exhibit 31.5A, the annual volatility of the discretionary index is less than 50% of the volatility of the systematic index. However, if the average volatility of discretionary CTAs is examined, it will be seen that it is only slightly less than the average volatility of individual systematic CTAs. The reason for the difference is this: Because discretionary CTAs are less correlated with each other, a portfolio consisting of a large number of discretionary CTAs will have a relatively small volatility.

Second, both discretionary and systematic CTA indices display zero-to-positive skewness during this time period. This is in contrast to the properties displayed by many hedge fund styles and traditional asset classes during the same period.[4] As was previously stated, many CTAs use stop-loss orders to control their downside risk. The depth and liquidity of many futures markets allow CTAs to exit their positions without significant price impact. More importantly, because CTAs do not generally invest in individual securities, market illiquidity and large bid-ask spreads are not significant issues for CTAs during periods of market stress. Exhibit 31.5B displays the growth of two CTA indices, MSCI World Equity index and Barclays Capital Bond index.

Exhibit 31.5C   displays the exposures of CTAs to various factors in both multivariate and univariate settings. The important points to take from this exhibit are the low levels of exposures of CTAs to equity, interest rate, commodity, credit, and volatility risk factors. As will be demonstrated in Chapter 32, these low exposures are the basis of the diversification benefits provided by CTAs. In addition, a smaller percentage of volatility of the discretionary index (15.72%) is explained by these

---

[4] It is important to realize that many of the reported properties are time specific and may change significantly over short periods of time, especially when market conditions change.

EXHIBIT 31.5C Exposures of CTAs to Various Risk Factors (January 2000–December 2010)

Multivariate Betas	World Equities	Global Bonds	U.S. High Yield	Commodities	Annualized Estimated α	R^2
Barclay Trader Index Discretionary	0.05*	0.11*	–0.12**	0.04**	3.15%**	15.72%
Barclay Trader Index Systematic	–0.07	0.52**	–0.20**	0.10**	1.30%	24.50%

Univariate Betas	World Equities	Global Bonds	U.S. High Yield	Commodities	%Δ Credit Spread	%Δ VIX
Barclay Trader Index Discretionary	0.03	0.13**	–0.03	0.05***	0.01	–0.01
Barclay Trader Index Systematic	–0.05	0.46**	–0.14**	0.08**	0.01	0.01

Correlations	World Equities	Global Bonds	U.S. High Yield	Commodities	%Δ Credit Spread	%Δ VIX
Barclay Trader Index Discretionary	0.13*	0.20**	–0.07	0.29**	0.09	–0.09
Barclay Trader Index Systematic	–0.11*	0.33**	–0.18**	0.24**	0.07	0.05

* Significant at 90% confidence level.
** Significant at 95% confidence level.
Source: Authors' calculations and Bloomberg data.

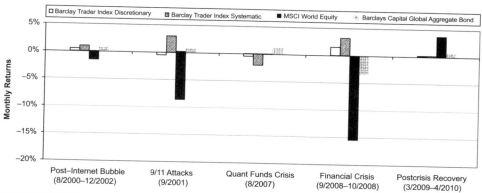

EXHIBIT 31.5D   Performance of CTAs during Specific Market Events
Source: Authors' calculations and Bloomberg data.

factors when compared to that of the systematic index (24.50%). This confirms the initial statement in Chapter 30 that discretionary CTAs are more heterogeneous, and unlike trend-following CTAs, no single strategy dominates this space.

Finally, Exhibit 31.5D highlights a major benefit of CTAs in providing downside protection during periods of market stress. Both CTA indices provided positive returns during the post–Internet bubble (8/2000–12/2002) and the peak of financial crisis, represented by Lehman Brothers bankruptcy (9/2008–10/2008). This issue is examined further later in the chapter.

31.3   RESEARCH ON PERFORMANCE AND BENEFITS OF MANAGED FUTURES

A more direct way to examine the attractiveness of a managed futures investment is to analyze the performance of managed futures traders. In 1983, John Lintner presented one of the first academic papers on this topic. His analysis was designed to examine the risk-return characteristics of managed futures accounts or funds. In this study, Lintner concluded that "the combined portfolios of stocks (or stocks and bonds) after including judicious investments . . . in managed futures accounts (or funds) show substantially less risk at every possible level of expected return than portfolios of stocks (or stocks and bonds) alone."

Lintner's work provided an initial academic basis for investing in managed futures. Other early studies that followed his research both challenged and supported his results. A series of studies by Elton, Gruber, and Rentzler (1987, 1989, and 1990), known as the EGR studies, examined public commodity pools and found little evidence of the benefits of managed futures. Other analyses of managed futures supported the inclusion of managed futures in investment portfolios.[5] Some of these later analyses attempted to address data issues in the EGR studies. The EGR studies looked at public commodity pools, known to have been a very expensive way to

---

[5] See McCarthy, Schneeweis, and Spurgin (1996); Edwards and Park (1996); and Schneeweis, Spurgin, and Potter (1997).

invest in managed futures. Later analyses directly examined the returns of managed futures traders and found evidence that, on average, managed futures provide attractive risk-adjusted returns, especially if the performance is measured in the context of a diversified portfolio of stocks and bonds.

Unlike previous studies that examined the benefits of CTAs as a stand-alone investment or in the context of portfolios consisting of traditional asset classes, Kat (2002) examines the possible role of managed futures in portfolios of stocks, bonds, and hedge funds. He finds that allocating to managed futures allows investors to achieve a very substantial degree of overall risk reduction at limited costs in terms of lower returns or skewness. Apart from their lower expected returns, managed futures appear to be more effective diversifiers than hedge funds. The paper concludes that adding managed futures to a portfolio of stocks and bonds will reduce that portfolio's standard deviation more and quicker than hedge funds will, and without the undesirable side effects in terms of lower skewness and higher kurtosis. Finally, Kat observes that overall portfolio standard deviation can be further reduced by combining both hedge funds and managed futures with stocks and bonds. Again, it is worth repeating that these results are, to some degree, time dependent and can change dramatically over short periods of time.

One of the major difficulties in evaluating the performance and benefits of CTAs and hedge funds is the lack of a central database of individual CTA and hedge fund performance. This problem is discussed in Bhardwaj, Gorton, and Rouwenhorst (2008). They note that there is no single repository of performance data for managed futures traders. Instead, there are multiple data vendors, with each reporting performance figures of individual managers. The set of managers covered by these databases may have significant overlap, but they would also include managers that are unique to each database. Performance reporting to these data vendors by CTAs and hedge funds is voluntary. Some managers may report to only one database and not to others; some report only to their investors and not to any database. As a result, analyses of managed futures may differ depending on which data source is used for the analysis.

Beyond the data source issue, several other problems encountered in analyzing the performance of managed futures should be mentioned. Again, these problems stem from the lack of uniform standards in collecting and reporting performance data. There are a number of potential sources of bias in hedge fund/CTA databases that should be noted. The first is **selection bias**. This stems from the voluntary nature of the data reporting process. Funds that achieve strong performance may choose to provide data to one or more databases, while those with weak performance may choose not to report at all. Similarly, successful managers may discontinue reporting their performance as their need to attract new investment capital decreases. As a result, it can be difficult to assess the representativeness of the database. Selection bias will affect the performance of published indices because the managers that are used to create the index may not be representative of the entire industry.

A second issue is the **look-back bias**. This also results from the voluntary nature of performance reporting. For example, a fund may stop reporting after a period of poor performance. If performance improves, the fund may begin reporting to the vendor again; however, if poor performance persists, the fund may not report any further results. This pattern of selective reporting after knowing performance results may create an upward performance bias in average performance of the managers that report to a database. Note that the look-back bias is not likely to affect published indices that are based on these databases, because most index providers do not revise the history of their index as managers decide to report their past performance.

A third issue relates to **survivorship bias**. This occurs when a fund's performance data is removed from the database as a result of the fund shutting down (or, perhaps, as a result of the fund requesting that its data be removed from the database). The effect of such a removal is that the database reflects only the performance results of the surviving funds. That is, it includes the performance of only those funds that continue to stay in business, presumably at least in part due to better-than-average investment performance. Of course, funds that reach their capacity and decide to close to new investors may stop reporting to a database. Therefore, it is an empirical question whether the funds that have stopped reporting did so because of poor performance. Available results seem to indicate that funds that stop reporting to databases underperform remaining funds by about 3% per year. Again, similar to look-back bias, this bias is not likely to impact the performance of published indices.

The last issue is that of **backfill bias** or **instant history bias**. Backfill bias occurs when a fund that decides to provide its investment performance data to a vendor provides not only figures from that date forward but also data on its past performance. The reasonable concern here is that backfilled returns will be stronger for funds that eventually report to a database than for funds that might have existed over the same time period but never reported their performance data (again, presumably due to poor performance). Again, this bias is not likely to affect the published values of most indices. Note that an index may have an instant history bias if the index is created in, say, January 2000, but the index provider decides to create a history going back to 1990. However, going forward, the index will not suffer from this bias unless the index provider decides to revise the history of the index (a rather uncommon practice).

These biases combine to make it difficult to conduct a comprehensive analysis of the performance results of all hedge funds, including managed futures. It is an issue that needs to be understood in interpreting the results of any performance analysis.

31.4 BENCHMARKING OF CTAs

Over time, there have been three approaches to benchmarking managed futures performance. The first has been to use an index of long-only futures contracts. Because CTAs are as likely to be short as to be long, this approach has not been found to be particularly useful. Schneeweis and Spurgin (1997) note that there appears to be little connection between the absolute returns of major indices and the returns of CTA indices, and the results presented suggest that CTA-based indices provide a better benchmark for an actively managed futures portfolio than either passive or active long-only commodity-based performance indices.

The second approach is to use peer groups. In this case, managed futures are most commonly benchmarked to indices representing active or passive futures trading. Active benchmarks of futures trading reflect the actual performance of a universe of CTAs. As previously noted, there are a number of issues that one needs to be aware of when using hedge fund databases, including those reporting CTA performance. Recall that many funds report to only one of these providers and not others. Indeed, some of the best CTAs have no incentive to report to any database. A major problem with using an index reflecting the actual performance of CTAs is that the benchmark is not investable. For traditional asset classes, construction of investable indices is common; relatively inexpensive investable products such as indexed mutual funds and exchange-traded funds (ETFs) are available to investors. In contrast, construction of truly investable indices in the CTA space is complex and may not result in a truly investable index that is an accurate representation of the industry.

Within the second approach, a few indices composed only of managers who invest through managed accounts at a specific firm have recently become available. This would be true of the Newedge CTA Index or the WisdomTree Managed Futures Strategy Fund. These investable indices may suffer from access bias, which could have an adverse impact on the performance of these indices. **Access bias** arises because some managers may not wish to be part of an investable index due to the restrictions that such indices may impose on them. For example, a manager may be prevented from increasing or decreasing leverage outside a predetermined level, or a manager may have to agree to reduce fees. Therefore, only those managers who have difficulty raising funds outside the investable index platform may agree to be part of the platform.

Finally, CTAs may be compared to passive benchmarks of futures trading. These passive indices represent the performance of an individual algorithmic-based trading system, as opposed to the performance results of CTAs themselves.[6] In managed futures, passive indices have been created primarily for trend-following strategies. The oldest and most prominent of these is the MLM Index. Mount Lucas Management has published the MLM Index since 1988. Another passively managed futures index with a reasonable track record is that of the Institute for Global Asset and Risk Management.[7]

The MLM Index represents the daily performance of a 252-day moving average trend-following system applied to 22 futures markets. Such an algorithmic-based index can be quite useful because it provides the return that can be achieved from a simple trend-following trading model. This return can then be compared to the performance of active trend-following managers in order to examine the value-added of more active (and expensive) strategies.

Although benchmarking trend-following CTAs can be a reasonably straightforward exercise due to the high correlation among trend-following strategies, the same is not true of other managed futures trading styles, such as non-trend-following and relative value. There is considerable heterogeneity among managers in both of these styles. For example, one fund of funds manager noted that among 30 trend-following CTAs examined, the average paired correlation was 0.56, but of 25 non-trend-following CTAs examined, the average paired correlation was zero, indicating no common trading style among these managers. Finding or creating useful indices to benchmark non-trend-following CTA styles remains a significant

---

[6] The case for creating passive indices and the associated methodology are described in Spurgin, Schneeweis, and Georgiev (2001).

[7] See www.ingarm.org.

challenge. A recent paper by Kazemi and Li (2009) examines the performance of both trend-following and non-trend-following managers using portfolios of futures contracts. The portfolios are created using the Sharpe style analysis approach, whereby returns of individual CTAs are regressed against total returns of a set of futures contracts. Kazemi and Li report that the resulting portfolios have significant explanatory power when the performance of trend-following managers is analyzed (the R-squareds are as high as 45%). On the other hand, the performance of non-trend-following managers can hardly be explained with an average R-squared of about 6%. However, non-trend-following managers displayed higher alphas in comparison to trend-following managers.

31.5 ALPHA-BETA SEPARATION USING PASSIVE INDICES

As previously discussed, a number of index providers are now offering indices based on transparent systematic trend-following strategies. Similar to the procedure adopted in traditional asset classes, one can use these indices to separate sources of CTA returns into beta and alpha. In this section, the performance of the MLM Index is compared to that of the Barclay Trader Index Systematic to estimate the beta sources of return to trend-following CTAs.

Exhibit 31.6A displays the basic statistics of the MLM Index and the Barclay Trader Index Systematic. The MLM Index has provided a lower return at lower volatility than the CTA index. Interestingly, the MLM Index displays significant autocorrelation compared to the CTA index. This may be an artifact of the time period examined rather than some inherent property of futures prices or the MLM Index.

Exhibit 31.6B displays exposures of the MLM and CTA indices to traditional asset classes as well as a long-only commodity index. There are two important

EXHIBIT 31.6A Statistical Properties of Active MLM and CTA Indices

Index (January 2000 to December 2011)	MLM Index	Barclay Trader Index Systematic
Annualized arithmetic mean	4.3%**	5.5%**
Annualized standard deviation	6.3%	8.6%
Skewness	0.3	0.2
Kurtosis	3.2**	0.3
Sharpe ratio	0.3	0.3
Annualized geometric mean	4.1%	5.1%
Annualized standard deviation (autocorrelation adjusted)	7.0%	8.6%
Maximum	7.8%	7.4%
Minimum	−5.9%	−5.6%
Autocorrelation	12.0%*	−0.2%
Maximum drawdown	−8.9%	−10.1%

*Significant at 90% confidence level.
**Significant at 95% confidence level.
Source: Authors' calculations and Bloomberg.

EXHIBIT 31.6B Exposures of Active MLM and CTA Indices to Various Risk Factors

Multivariate Betas

	World Equities	Global Bonds	U.S. High Yield	Commodities	Annualized Estimated α	R²
MLM Index	−0.08*	0.11	−0.13**	0.05**	1.54%	13.34%
Barclay Trader Index Systematic	−0.07	0.52**	−0.20**	0.10**	1.30%	24.50%

Univariate Betas

	World Equities	Global Bonds	U.S. High Yield	Commodities	%Δ Credit Spread	%Δ VIX
MLM Index	−0.10**	0.03	−0.16**	0.02	0.03**	0.01
Barclay Trader Index Systematic	−0.05	0.46**	−0.14**	0.08**	0.01	0.01

Correlations

	World Equities	Global Bonds	U.S. High Yield	Commodities	%Δ Credit Spread	%Δ VIX
MLM Index	−0.26**	0.03	−0.29**	0.06	0.17**	0.13*
Barclay Trader Index Systematic	−0.11*	0.33**	−0.18**	0.24**	0.07	0.05

*Significant at 90% confidence level.
**Significant at 95% confidence level.

EXHIBIT 31.6C   Relative Performance of Active CTA Indices Compared to MLM Index

1990–2011	Correlation vs. MLM Index	Beta vs. MLM Index	Annualized Alpha	R^2
Barclay Trader Index Discretionary	16.78%	0.13	0.75%	2.6%
Barclay Trader Index Systematic	37.51%	0.66	2.16%	13.5%

Sources: Bloomberg and Author's Calculations.

observations with regard to the results displayed in this exhibit. First, the MLM Index displays a positive alpha when benchmarked against a combination of traditional asset classes and a long-only commodity index. Furthermore, the annual alpha of the MLM Index is rather close to the alpha of the active CTA index. Second, the long-only commodity index has very little explanatory power when it comes to these two trend-following indices. This is consistent with the fact that trend-following strategies involve long and short positions in both commodities and financial futures.

Exhibit 31.6C examines the sources of returns to active CTA indices using the passive MLM Index. First, the passive MLM Index is relatively more correlated with the index of trend-following CTAs. This is confirmed by the relatively high beta (0.66) and R-squared of the regression, relating excess returns on the index of systematic CTAs to excess returns on the MLM Index. Second, the index of systematic CTAs displays a positive alpha when benchmarked against the MLM Index (2.16% per year). Since the annual mean excess return on the systematic CTA index during this period was 3.51%, this means that the beta of a trend-following strategy is responsible for less than 50% of its total excess return (beta return is 1.35% while total excess return is 3.51%). The remaining 2.16% is ex post alpha associated with active trading strategies of trend-following CTAs that comprise the index. Although the MLM Index appears to be a reasonable benchmark for systematic CTAs, it does not appear to be a suitable benchmark for discretionary CTAs. Finally, even in the context of trend-following CTAs, the MLM Index does not appear to be a suitable index during various market cycles. For example, Exhibit 31.6D shows that in the

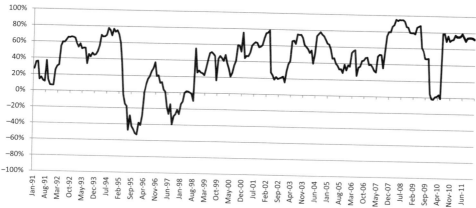

EXHIBIT 31.6D   Twelve-Month Rolling Correlation of Trend-Following Systematic CTA Index versus the MLM Index, 1991–2011
Sources: Bloomberg and Authors' calculations.

later 1990s and more recently in 2009, the correlation between the MLM Index and the trend-following index was negative.

These results lead to the following conclusions:

- Passive trend-following indices, such as the MLM Index, can provide a reasonable benchmark for trend-following CTAs.
- Less than half of the historical excess return earned by trend-following CTAs is due to their beta exposure to passive trend-following indices. More than half of the returns cannot be captured by such passive indices.
- Trend-following CTAs display low exposures to traditional asset classes as well as long-only commodity indices.
- Discretionary CTAs display low exposures to traditional asset classes as well as long-only commodity indices.
- Peer groups appear to be the most suitable benchmark for discretionary CTAs.

31.6 PERFORMANCE OF CTAS DURING PERIODS OF FINANCIAL STRESS

Numerous studies have examined the benefits of CTAs in terms of providing downside protection during periods of financial stress.[8] Since CTAs have access to multiple markets and can easily take long or short positions in these markets, they are able to take positions that will benefit from increased uncertainty and financial distress in markets. For example, a decline in equity prices could benefit CTAs who are (1) short equity indices, (2) long short-term Treasuries which benefit from a flight to safety, (3) long USD which typically benefits from turbulence in financial markets; and (4) long implied or realized volatility derivatives.

31.6.1 Are Trend-Following CTAs Long Volatility?

Some argue that CTAs are long volatility, and since equity volatility appears to be the most dominant factor affecting volatility in other markets, CTAs are expected to benefit whenever equity market volatility spikes.[9] As will be discussed further, CTAs are not long volatility in the same way that a holder of a volatility swap or a straddle would benefit from an increase in volatility. CTAs, in general, do not directly invest in derivatives that are closely linked to volatility. Therefore, if CTAs are able to produce positive returns when there is a spike in equity market volatility, it has to be the result of their trading strategies in financial and commodity futures.

It is a well-known empirical observation that sharp declines in equity prices are associated with sharp spikes in equity volatility (Black 1976; Baillie and DeGennarro 1990; Bekaert and Wu 2000). Furthermore, this relationship is asymmetric in the sense that sharp increases in stock markets are not associated with equally sharp declines in equity market volatility. A number of reasons for this relation have been discussed, including the following: (1) A stock price decline increases the debt/equity

---

[8] See Schneeweis (2009) and Kat (2002).
[9] See Gregoriou et al. (2004).

ratio of firms, leading to higher volatility on equity returns; (2) a stock price decline creates forced selling by those who have purchased stocks on margin, leading to increased volume and higher volatility; (3) an initial increase in volatility (e.g., due to an exogenous event) increases risk aversion among investors, leading to a decline in stock prices; and (4) an increase in volatility (e.g., due to an exogenous event) increases the equity risk premium, leading to lower stock prices. Whatever the reason, changes in volatility and changes in stock prices are highly negatively correlated. For example, between 1990 and 2011, the correlation between changes in the monthly volatility of the rate of return on the S&P 500 and the monthly rate of return on the same index has been about –0.35.

As stated in previous chapters, a majority of CTAs employ long-term trend-following strategies. These investment managers benefit from orderly directional trends in markets on which they focus and suffer losses in random and directionless markets. These characteristics of price behavior are not directly related to volatility levels or volatility changes.

The notion that CTAs are long volatility comes from available empirical evidence that appears to show that CTAs perform relatively well when the level of equity volatility is high and when equity volatility is increasing. Given the preceding discussion, a downtrend is likely to be associated with higher volatility, and a trend follower who is short equities would benefit. Another factor contributing to this issue is a set of academic research showing that CTA returns share similar properties with a long position in a **straddle**.[10] In a typical straddle, the trader takes long positions in both call and put options on the same underlying asset. The trader will profit if the underlying asset of the straddle makes large moves in either direction. In addition, the sensitivity of the position (i.e., its delta) increases as the underlying asset of the straddle continues its move in the same direction.

The notion that CTAs are long volatility is not very precise. As stated by Malek and Dobrovolsky (2009), volatility exposure would mean different things to different traders employing different systematic trading strategies. Furthermore, it is not clear what is meant by "volatility exposure." First, it could mean that CTAs provide higher returns when the level of volatility is high. Second, it could mean that CTAs provide higher returns when the level of volatility is increasing. Equally important, one needs to be precise whether conditional or unconditional volatility is being discussed. As will be shown shortly, the way volatility is measured has important implications for estimating the volatility exposures of CTAs.

To gain a better understanding of volatility exposure of CTAs, terminology from option pricing is used to analyze the behavior of a typical trend-following CTA.[11] Suppose the market is directionless and a CTA has no positions. In this case, the CTA's directional market exposure (i.e., its delta) is zero. Once the market starts to move and begins a trend, the CTA starts adding to its positions. When the market moves up, the CTA increases its long position (i.e., its delta becomes positive and increases), and when the market goes down, the CTA increases its short position (i.e., its delta becomes negative and decreases). This behavior is exactly what makes the trend-following CTAs' return profiles similar to those of a long position in a straddle. However, this return profile is not the result of any exposure to volatility; rather,

---

[10] For example, see Fung and Hsieh (1997).
[11] This section follows closely the arguments set forth in Malek and Dobrovolsky (2009).

it is a result of being long **gamma**. Using option terminology, gamma measures the rate of change in the delta of an option as the price of the option's underlying asset changes. This means that the sensitivity of a position that is long gamma increases as the price of the underlying asset increases, and the delta decreases as the price of the underlying asset decreases. Therefore, trend-following strategies are characterized by being long gamma, and relative value strategies are characterized by being short gamma. As a result, even though return profiles of trend-following CTAs are similar to return profiles of straddles, it does not follow that CTAs are long volatility simply because straddles are long volatility.

Option premiums are most sensitive to volatility when the options are at-the-money. When they are deeply in-the-money, they behave similarly to long or short positions in their underlying assets; when they are deeply out-of-the-money, they become almost worthless. Thus, a straddle displays volatility exposure only when it is close to being at-the-money. As the underlying price moves away from its strike level, the straddle's sensitivity to volatility declines. This means that a trend-following CTA that is trying to take advantage of a trend behaves like a deeply in-the-money straddle and, as a result, can be characterized as being long gamma.

31.6.2 Empirical Evidence on the Volatility Exposure of CTAs

This section presents some empirical evidence on the exposure of CTAs to the level of volatility as well as changes in volatility. In addition, CTA behavior is examined during periods of financial stress, as represented by extreme changes in credit spreads and government bond prices. Since CTAs, and particularly trend-following CTAs, do not invest in instruments that provide direct exposure to volatility, they can provide downside protection if, on average, they have short positions in equity markets when there are sharp declines in stock markets. During periods of financial stress (drops in equity prices or increases in credit spreads), there is typically a flight to safety, leading to higher prices for short-term and medium-term government bonds and higher prices for safer currencies (e.g., the U.S. dollar). Therefore, it could be argued that CTAs have on average long positions in government bonds and safe currencies during periods of financial stress.

Exhibits 31.7A through 31.7C display the performance of CTAs, including systematic and discretionary CTAs, during periods of sharp declines and increases in equity prices (Exhibit 31.7A), high-yield bond prices (Exhibit 31.7B), and hedge fund net asset values (NAVs) (Exhibit 31.7C). For instance, Exhibit 31.7A shows that between 1990 and 2011 during the worst 24 months for MSCI World Index, the index declined by 8.78% per month while all three CTA indices showed positive average return during the same 24 months, with systematic CTAs performing the best. Interestingly, during the best 24 months for the MSCI World Index, all three CTA indices were essentially flat. Exhibit 31.7C shows that CTAs could also offset the downside risk of hedge funds. During the worst 24 months for the HFRI Fund Weighted Composite Index, the index declined by 3.12% per month, while all three CTA indices were profitable, with the systematic CTA index displaying the best performance.

CTAs, particularly trend-following CTAs, tend to perform well during periods of financial stress and therefore have the potential to provide downside protection

EXHIBIT 31.7A Performance of CTAs during Worst and Best Months for Equities

	Average Monthly Return	
1990–2011	24 Worst Months of MSCI World	24 Best Months of MSCI World
MSCI World Index U.S. Currency TR	−8.78%	8.05%
HFRI Fund of Funds Composite Index	−1.35%	1.47%
HFRI Fund Weighted Composite Index	−2.37%	2.82%
Barclay Trader Index CTA	1.90%	0.02%
Barclay Trader Index Discretionary	1.02%	0.56%
Barclay Trader Index Systematic	2.54%	0.02%
Barclays Capital U.S. Corporate High Yield	−3.49%	2.78%
VIX end-of-month	33.77%	24.30%

Source: Authors' calculations and Bloomberg.

to portfolios consisting of traditional assets as well as certain hedge fund strategies. Exhibit 31.8A shows that most CTA strategies have historically provided their highest returns during months in which the S&P 500's volatility is reportedly very low. In addition, the next best performance is generally observed during months in which the S&P 500's volatility is reportedly very high. Exhibit 31.8B examines the sensitivity of various CTA strategies to changes in the level of volatility. In most cases, the best performance is not observed when the S&P 500's volatility shows the largest increase. However, when the index's volatility experiences the smallest changes, CTAs tend not to perform as well as they do in response to larger changes in the index's volatility. The results presented in these two tables seem to support the conceptual discussion presented in the previous section that CTAs are not long volatility but behave as if they are long gamma.

Exhibit 31.9 shows three different price behaviors for a hypothetical asset. In all cases, the price starts at 10 and remains constant for the first 25 observations. Next, the price follows three different trends. In one case, the price increases by the

EXHIBIT 31.7B Performance of CTAs during Worst and Best Months for High-Yield Bonds

	Average Monthly Return	
1990–2011	24 Worst Months of High-Yield Bonds	24 Best Months of High-Yield Bonds
Barclays Capital U.S. Corporate High Yield	−4.96%	5.41%
MSCI World Index U.S. Currency TR	−6.70%	4.08%
HFRI Fund of Funds Composite Index	−1.58%	0.92%
HFRI Fund Weighted Composite Index	−2.60%	2.39%
Barclay Trader Index CTA	1.74%	−0.37%
Barclay Trader Index Discretionary	0.95%	0.33%
Barclay Trader Index Systematic	2.23%	−0.54%
VIX end-of-month	31.83%	25.41%

Source: Authors' calculations and Bloomberg.

EXHIBIT 31.7C Performance of CTAs during Worst and Best Months for Hedge Funds

1990–2011	Average Monthly Return	
	24 Worst Months of Hedge Funds	24 Best Months of Hedge Funds
HFRI Fund Weighted Composite Index	−3.12%	4.20%
HFRI Fund of Funds Composite Index	−2.16%	2.97%
Barclays Capital U.S. Corporate High Yield	−3.90%	3.07%
MSCI World Index U.S. Currency TR	−6.84%	4.82%
Barclay Trader Index CTA	1.25%	1.67%
Barclay Trader Index Discretionary	0.64%	0.81%
Barclay Trader Index Systematic	1.65%	2.09%
VIX end-of-month	31.08%	21.20%

Source: Authors' calculations and Bloomberg.

EXHIBIT 31.8A Sensitivity of CTAs to the Volatility Levels of the S&P 500 Index

1990–2011	Intramonth Volatility of S&P 500			
	Lowest	Low	High	Highest
Barclay Trader Index CTA	1.03%	0.29%	0.23%	0.52%
Barclay Trader Index Discretionary	0.51%	0.35%	0.23%	0.57%
Barclay Trader Index Diversified	1.39%	0.40%	0.29%	0.71%
Barclay Trader Index Systematic	1.26%	0.39%	0.18%	0.63%
MSCI World Index U.S. Currency TR	1.68%	1.13%	0.62%	−1.28%
Barclays Capital U.S. Corporate High Yield	1.09%	1.02%	1.23%	−0.34%
S&P 500 total return volatility	8.11%	11.81%	16.32%	28.87%

EXHIBIT 31.8B Sensitivity of CTAs to Changes in the Volatility Levels of the S&P 500 Index

1990–2011	Changes in Intramonth Volatility of S&P 500			
	Lowest	Low	High	Highest
Barclay Trader Index CTA	0.21%	0.43%	0.76%	0.57%
Barclay Trader Index Discretionary	0.46%	0.41%	0.38%	0.39%
Barclay Trader Index Diversified	0.35%	0.54%	0.96%	0.84%
Barclay Trader Index Systematic	0.19%	0.52%	0.93%	0.71%
MSCI World Index U.S. Currency TR	3.05%	1.73%	0.83%	−3.28%
Barclays Capital U.S. Corporate High Yield	1.76%	1.20%	0.76%	−0.68%
Bloomberg Generic USD LIBOR 1-Month	3.67%	4.01%	4.05%	3.80%
Changes in S&P 500 total return volatility	−4.59%	−1.12%	0.64%	5.06%

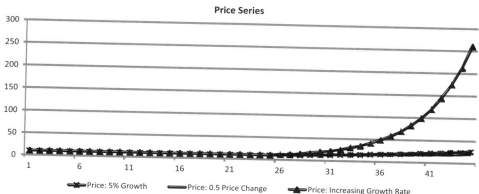

EXHIBIT 31.9 Three Price Behaviors for a Hypothetical Asset
Source: Authors' calculations.

same percentage (5%) during each period; in another case, the price increases by the same amount (0.5) during each period; and in the final case, the price increases at a predictably increasing rate during each period. Thus, in all three cases, the trends are predictable and therefore conditioned on the trend; the true (i.e., conditional) return volatilities are zero, and there is no uncertainty about the future price if one can observe the current price and identify the trend. For example, given the observed value of price in, say, period 30, one can perfectly predict the price in period 31, provided that one is able to identify the trend.

In Exhibit 31.10, the unconditional volatilities of the rates of return on these three price series are calculated and displayed. These volatilities are estimated using a 10-day rolling window. That is, the volatility in day 30 is calculated using data

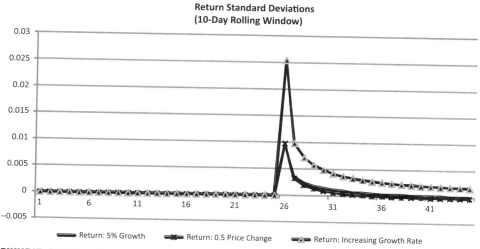

EXHIBIT 31.10 Estimates of Volatilities for a Hypothetical Asset
Source: Authors' calculations.

from day 20 through day 30. These are the same estimated volatilities that will be reported by an observer who uses the return series to calculate the volatility. It can be seen that once the price breaks out and follows a predictable pattern, the estimated value of the unconditional volatility will increase. Therefore, if the observer is not aware that the price has broken out and a new trend has emerged, the estimated volatility will be significantly different from the true volatility of prices (in this case, the true volatility is zero). This means that at least a portion of the reported exposures of CTAs to changes in volatility is due to the fact that reported volatilities do not take the emerging trends into account. Therefore, because price breakouts and emergence of new trends are associated with increases in estimated volatilities as well as increases in the profitability of CTAs, it may appear that CTAs are long volatility.

31.7 CONCLUSION

To understand the risk-return properties of CTAs, one needs to apply special measures designed to account for special characteristics of CTAs. The fact that CTAs allow investors to gain exposure to a variety of markets with minimal investments and that the margin requirement for each contract is closely linked to the riskiness of the underlying market means investors should carefully examine the amount of margin that a CTA is carrying. In addition to the margin-to-equity ratio, investors should use other metrics, such as volatility, VaR, and CaR, to gain a better understanding of a CTA's risk profile.

One important issue that investors need to address is the lack of proper benchmarks for CTAs in general, and discretionary CTAs in particular. Although passive strategies have been developed to mimic the risk-return properties of trend-following CTAs, no such passive strategies have been developed for discretionary CTAs. The MLM Index represents one such attempt to produce a passive and investable benchmark for systematic CTAs. The performance of this index can be used to estimate the returns on CTAs due to their beta exposures to a passive trend-following strategy. The results presented in this chapter showed that less than 50% of the return earned by trend-following CTAs is due to their beta exposure to a passive trend-following index.

This chapter has also examined the role of CTAs in providing downside protection for traditional asset classes, such as equities and high-yield bonds, as well as alternative assets, such as hedge funds. It was argued that though CTA return profiles give the appearance that they are long volatility, it is more appropriate to characterize CTAs as being long gamma. This gives the appearance that CTAs are long volatility while what trend-following CTAs do is increase the delta of their positions as prices move in their favor, the basic characteristic of a long gamma position.

CHAPTER 32

Structuring Investments in CTAs*

T his chapter outlines a process often used by investors to identify and analyze individual managed futures traders. The discussion is not meant to be comprehensive, but rather to highlight certain steps and issues common to the process. In addition, the chapter examines the potential benefits of adding commodity trading advisers (CTAs) to portfolios of traditional and alternative assets, the issues related to investing in a single CTA rather than a portfolio of CTAs, and four different methods for investing in CTAs. Finally, it discusses the potential costs associated with actively managing a portfolio consisting of CTAs or other active managers.

32.1 SOURCING MANAGERS

There are several approaches to sourcing potential investment candidates in the managed futures industry. One of the best ways is through referrals from knowledgeable industry participants. These referrers could be individual managers themselves who are willing to suggest others in the industry, fund of funds managers, or consultants whose business it is to follow the managed futures industry. Obviously, the referral approach requires that a potential investor already have a network to draw on when considering an investment in this asset class.

   Beyond individual referrals, potential investors can look at public information sources, such as publications and futures brokers, to assess potential investment candidates. For instance, *Absolute Return* magazine, a publication of Hedge Fund Intelligence, reports the monthly returns of several CTA investment programs. Newedge Financial Inc. makes available to its clients the monthly performance of several hundred CTAs. However, a more common way to source managers is through subscription to one or more database services, such as BarclayHedge, Hedge Fund Research (HFR), or Morningstar/CISDM, which offer performance indices of CTAs.

---

*Portions of Chapters 29 to 32, were originally published in Galen Burghardt and Brian Walls, *Managed Futures for Institutional Investors: Analysis and Portfolio Construction* (Hoboken, NJ: Bloomberg Press, 2011).

32.2   ISSUES IN STRUCTURING A CTA INVESTMENT PROGRAM

Once investors decide to make an allocation to managed futures, they must tackle the problem of just how to structure the investment. To do this, they will need to follow a decision process that proceeds along the following lines.

First, the investor must determine how many CTAs he/she wants in the portfolio. Many family offices, and even some larger institutional investors, will decide to invest in a single CTA. This decision has the virtue of simplicity and is possible to implement by choosing one of the large, diversified trend-following CTAs, whose performance correlates highly with a trend-following benchmark. If the investor decides to utilize this approach, the focus should be on the examining differences between investing in a fund sponsored on behalf of the CTA versus a managed account.

Generally, the single-CTA route exposes the investor to a greater amount of risk. In this scenario, the results depend on the performance of a single manager, have concentrated risk to a single organization, and may be exposed to a limited number of trading models. To avoid these constraints, the investor is well advised to form a diversified portfolio of CTAs.

Second, the investor must decide how to create a diversified portfolio of CTAs. Initially, the most cost-effective approach to achieving diversification is to allocate to a multi-CTA fund. Then, as the size of the allocation to CTAs increases, more options become available to the investor. Eventually, the investor must decide whether to assemble an in-house team to manage the portfolio or to use a managed account platform. There are cost issues associated with each choice. Related to the size of allocation to CTAs, two issues arise as the investor decides on the best approach to creating a diversified portfolio of CTAs.

The first issue is related to the level of allocation at which it becomes cost effective to move from a multi-CTA investment program to assembling an in-house team to create and manage a diversified portfolio of CTAs. While no exact figure exists for this cost threshold, it is primarily affected by four factors:

1. The extra layer of fees that the investor will have to pay the multi-asset fund
2. The cost of assembling a team of analysts who can construct and manage a CTA portfolio
3. The minimum size of the investment that CTAs are willing to accept
4. The number of CTAs that should be included in the portfolio to achieve diversification

In order to achieve a reasonable degree of diversification, a portfolio must consist of at least six CTAs. Since the minimum investment size for large institutional quality funds is assumed to be $5 million, an investment of at least $30 million is required to make it cost effective to create a portfolio of CTAs. The management fee associated with a $30 million portfolio is $300,000 to $450,000. This amount may not be enough to create a team that can select and manage a portfolio of CTAs.

The second issue is related to the next level of allocation, in which it becomes viable for the investor to use a **managed account platform**. Managed accounts offer a number of very important advantages over CTA funds, including transparency, security of collateral, and ease of opening and closing positions. However, they require the investor to have experienced people and reliable systems in place, which can be costly.

Some of the questions that investors should ask when considering allocating to a CTA include:

- How many managers should the investor choose?
- What are multi-CTA funds, and how do they differ from CTA funds?
- What are managed accounts?
- What are platforms?
- How does an investor compare and contrast these choices?

32.3 HOW MANY MANAGERS SHOULD ONE CHOOSE?

The question lends itself to an interesting analysis of what an investor is trying to accomplish. For example, an investor may want to create a portfolio that tracks a diversified CTA index (e.g., Barclay CTA Index or Newedge CTA Index). This is a plausible goal, because these indices are widely used benchmarks. Further, in some cases the CTAs whose returns make up these indices are among the largest in the business and, in the case of the Newedge CTA Index, are open for business and provide daily returns. In examining the construction processes for CTA portfolios, Burghardt and Walls (2011) use the returns reported by CTAs that are part of the Newedge CTA Index in order to see how quickly the return on a portfolio of CTAs converges to the return on the index.

Exhibit 32.1 demonstrates the range of returns realized on randomly formed and equally weighted portfolios that include anywhere from one to 20 CTAs. The gray bars indicate the two middle quartiles while the black lines are related to the

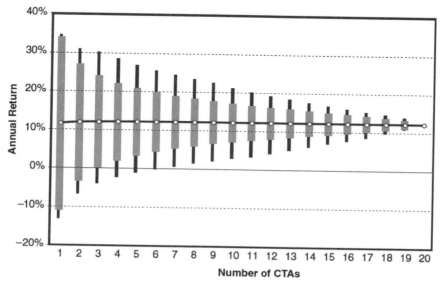

EXHIBIT 32.1 Annual Return on Randomly Formed Portfolios of CTAs
Source: Barclay Hedge, Newedge Prime Brokerage Research, 2008.

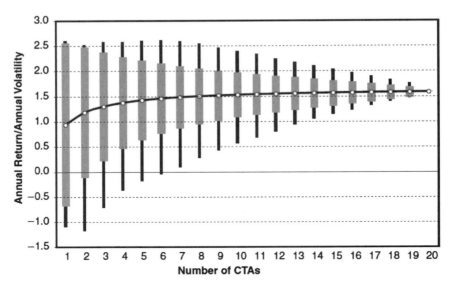

EXHIBIT 32.2 Information Ratios of Randomly Selected Portfolios of CTAs
Source: Barclay Hedge, Newedge Prime Brokerage Research, 2008.

bottom and top quartiles. The index return in 2008 was about 12%. This exhibit shows that the main effect of increasing the number of CTAs in the portfolio is a decrease in the amount by which an investment might outperform or underperform the index. With a single-CTA portfolio, an investor might outperform the index by as much as 22%; however, the investor could also lose money on the investment, even if the industry is, on average, making money. From there, the main question is how much tolerance the investor has for slippage. In this example, it would take 10 CTAs to bring the range of outperformance or underperformance down to 5%. Further, with five or six CTAs, the chance of losing money when the industry is making money is reduced nearly to zero.

Another consideration is the risk-adjusted return. The effects of diversification will, as shown in Exhibit 32.2, tend to bring up the ratio of expected return to the volatility of returns. For the index, the ratio of return to standard deviation of returns was about 1.6. With a single adviser, the expected risk-adjusted return would have been less than 1.0. It is apparent from the curve that most of the expected gains from diversification are realized by the time the portfolio contains five or six CTAs. After this, diversification still helps, but less so.

Still another issue is the outright expected return, irrespective of risk. The reason for bringing this into the discussion is shown in Exhibit 32.3, which illustrates the returns for each of the 20 managers in the Newedge CTA Index. For the purposes of this exhibit, trend-following CTAs are organized alphabetically first, with non-trend-following CTAs listed alphabetically second. Thus, Aspect through Winton are found in the first group, with Boronia through QIM in the second group.

In examining the two groups, it becomes apparent that trend-following CTAs tend to target a higher return volatility than non-trend-following CTAs, who strive for more diversity. In this example, the only way to earn more than 10% would be to focus the portfolio on trend-following CTAs. Even then, given the variability of

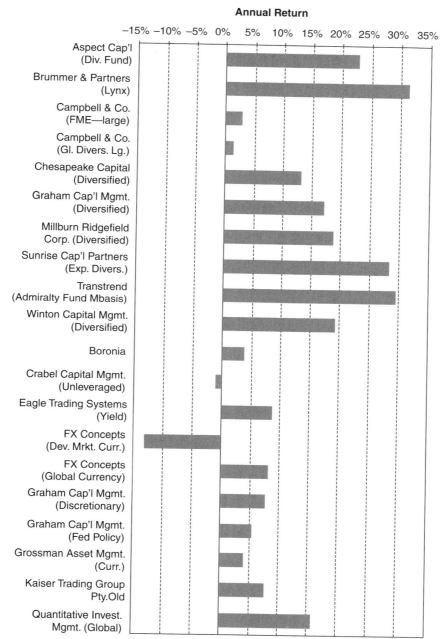

EXHIBIT 32.3 Returns on CTAs in the Newedge CTA Index (2008)
Source: Barclay Hedge, Newedge Prime Brokerage Research.

this group's returns, four or five CTAs would be needed to gain confidence in the portfolio's outcome.

In short, five to six is about the minimum number of CTAs an investor would want in a portfolio of CTAs. This number affords the investor some protection from tracking error, provides some diversification, and would likely produce a risk-adjusted return similar to the index. From six on up, the investor makes smaller, but possibly important, improvements in how the portfolio performs.

32.4 CTA FUNDS AND MULTI-CTA FUNDS

A **CTA fund** is a separate legal corporation with a board of directors that assigns trading authority to the single-manager CTA's investment management company. With a CTA fund, the investor turns the money over to the company organized by the CTA manager by filling out a subscription form and wiring the money to the account. Investors have limited liability for the fund manager's actions. Some oversight is provided by the board of directors and third parties, such as auditors, brokers, and regulators, because of the fund's status as an independent company. Additionally, for the manager's flagship fund, industry analysts, reporters, and other investors in the fund will pay attention to performance, effectively providing additional oversight.

Fund investors have a broad choice of managers, because most managers have funds, and funds are more likely to accommodate smaller investors than managed accounts. (A handful of managers will only take managed accounts, but they are unusual.) Managers like dealing with investors through funds because there are standard terms for risk, return, and liquidity.

However, a fund has less transparency for an investor than a managed account, and the amount of transparency can be variable. It is customary to provide monthly returns and a performance commentary. Liquidity can be just as variable, though, with managers offering different schedules for withdrawals, ranging from daily to annual, and requiring notice in advance of the scheduled withdrawal period.

Most CTA funds are managed through offshore accounts. A typical fund is set up as a Cayman Islands limited liability corporation (LLC). In this scenario, it is possible to appeal to the British court system if necessary, but only after local courts are consulted on disputes. Outside directors are chosen by the manager, and have varying amounts of experience in corporate governance and investments.

These accounts generally utilize a **master-feeder structure**. Under a typical master-feeder arrangement, two funds feed into a single master account. One feeder is for U.S. investors, while the other is for investors overseas. Money from both feeder funds is combined in the master fund, which opens trading accounts at the brokerage firm. This setup is established for tax purposes, enabling non-U.S. investors to avoid dealing with U.S. tax authorities, while American investors receive the documentation they need to report to the U.S. tax authorities. Both sets of investors receive the same performance.

Some funds are structured with different share classes. The classes may differ in fee structure and withdrawal rights. For example, someone who wants daily liquidity might be willing to pay a higher management fee than someone willing to accept annual liquidity. New investments may be held in a temporary share class until it reaches the same high-water mark as the rest of the fund. Some classes may be invested in additional assets that are not part of the main fund.

Multi-CTA funds are known variously as CTA funds of funds or commodity pools. From the investor's standpoint, both accomplish the same thing: They provide a single vehicle for investing in a diversified portfolio of CTAs. The differences are chiefly regulatory, relating to the way the funds are structured and where they are offered. Commodity pool operators (CPOs), for example, create vehicles that are distributed in the United States. They are common investment vehicles for retail investors, high-net-worth individuals, and even some small institutions. Some funds launch offshore funds and tend to attract larger institutional investors. The expression *fund of funds* derives from a time when the primary investment vehicle at the individual CTA level was a fund. As the industry has evolved, multimanager funds have migrated to the use of managed accounts.

The primary benefits of a multi-CTA fund structure are accessing the expertise the fund manager has in choosing the managers, structuring the portfolio, performing both investment and operational due diligence, performance reporting, risk monitoring, and accounting. In addition, the fund manager performs less obvious tasks, such as collecting data, meeting many managers, running background checks, analyzing performance and strategies, negotiating contracts and fees, and then monitoring performance and rebalancing the portfolio as necessary. From an investor's perspective, the investment offering and services of such a structure consolidate much of the work into choosing and reviewing a single organization. Because different multi-CTA funds have different investment objectives, investors need to find a fund that is consistent with their needs for risk and return as well as for reporting and transparency.

With a multi-CTA fund, the manager assembles a portfolio of CTAs and then accepts investments in the entire portfolio. The multi-CTA manager charges a fee for the portfolio construction and oversight services. Each of the managers in the fund charges a fee as well. Although investors negotiate contracts and fees with the multi-CTA manager directly, and the investment is consolidated into a single organization, investors still have due diligence and monitoring obligations.

The fees charged by multi-CTA managers raise important questions about how to structure the investment. If the level of allocation is relatively small, the investor would likely invest in CTA funds. However, if investors intend to allocate a large amount to CTAs, they might be better advised to save the fees that would be paid to a multi-CTA manager and simply hire the staff and consultants needed to select CTAs, perform the due diligence, construct the portfolios, and so on. Managed accounts, which are the vehicle of choice for most multi-CTA managers, are a much bigger undertaking than CTA funds. To warrant the work involved in setting up brokerage accounts, negotiating agreements, monitoring the accounts, reconciling trades, complying with anti-money-laundering regulations, managing cash flows, and so forth, a reasonable break-even point is an investment in CTAs of around $500 million.

32.5 MANAGED ACCOUNTS

Managed accounts are brokerage accounts, held by a brokerage firm that is also registered as a futures commission merchant (FCM), in which investment discretion has been assigned to the CTA manager. The investor is responsible for opening and maintaining the account; reconciling brokerage statements and maintaining cash controls; and negotiating contracts with managers, including investment management agreements and powers of attorney. The limited power of attorney gives the manager authority to trade on the investor's behalf, but the money has to remain in the investor's account. The investor controls the terms of the power of attorney, including the right to revoke trading privileges.

The key advantage to a managed account is complete control. By pulling trading privileges, the investor has the ability to manage the cash and liquidate the account at any time. Managed accounts, then, avoid the lockup provisions frequently found in hedge fund investments. In theory, this gives the investor better than daily liquidity, as the account can be liquidated whenever the market is open. That alone is enough to make some investors demand managed accounts, especially investors with in-house staff to handle the paperwork.

Managed accounts have other advantages. The money is in the investor's control, not the fund manager's, at all times. The accounts offer complete transparency. The investor can see the positions, trades, and details at any time. Managed accounts, then, virtually eliminate the risk of fraud, as the transparency and security of managed accounts prevent the manager from misstating leverage, manipulating returns, or stealing the investor's assets. The investor can choose the parameters for leverage based on the targeted volatility of returns. The choice of leverage makes it easier for the investor to manage the underlying cash. In fact, this type of CTA account structure is often looked at as an overlay on the cash position in an investor's portfolio, rather than as a separate asset class.

Of course, these advantages come at a cost. The first is the reduced pool of managers to choose from. Many large managers do not accept managed accounts, while those that do require a large minimum investment and other administrative requirements. In addition, the previously mentioned transparency and control come with the responsibility for establishing and maintaining brokerage accounts that require legal, administrative, risk, and investment oversight in accordance with each organization's investment standards. Further, unless procured by the investor, there is no administrator or auditor.

Managed accounts can be set up several different ways to meet different portfolio policy requirements. The limited partnership structure of hedge funds limits investor liability to the amount invested. For example, an investor who allocates $10 million to a failed hedge fund cannot lose more than $10 million, even if the hedge fund is highly leveraged and sustains losses greater than the amount of contributed client assets. Managed accounts, however, do not automatically have a **limited liability structure**. Especially in futures markets, where the required margin is much smaller than the notional value of contracts, investor losses in high margin-to-equity investments can be larger than the amount of contributed capital. Therefore, managed accounts must be carefully designed with a legal structure that ensures that limited liability is obtained. Structures offering limited liability vary by legal jurisdiction, but may include limited liability companies, limited partnerships, special purpose vehicles (SPV), or bankruptcy-remote entities. Each structure is designed to limit investor losses to the amount of cash invested, even if trading activity incurs greater losses.

The examples in Exhibits 32.4A to 32.4D show some of the more common structures observed in the marketplace.

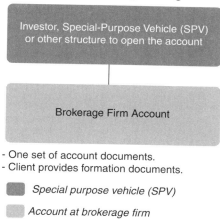

EXHIBIT 32.4A Managed Account Structures (Example 1, Allocation to a Single Manager)
Source: Newedge Prime Brokerage Research.

In many managed account situations, the investor starts by setting up an SPV or other holding entity to fence off any trading liabilities from the rest of the money that the investor controls. It is not a necessary step, however, as there are other ways to manage the potential liability. If an SPV is used, the account would look like the first three examples, Exhibits 32.4A to 32.4C.

In Exhibit 32.4A, allocation to a single manager, the investor uses the SPV to open an account at a brokerage firm where the CTA manager has trading authority. The investor gives the manager the authority to trade in the account.

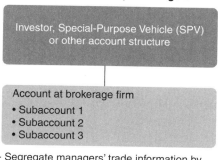

EXHIBIT 32.4B Managed Account Structures (Example 2, Allocation to Multiple Managers)
Source: Newedge Prime Brokerage Research.

Allocation to Multiple Managers

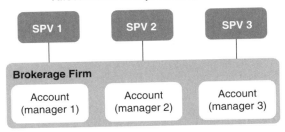

- Segregate investments by forming separate SPVs.
- Each SPV opens an account.
- Each SPV completes account documents.
- Each SPV provides formation documents.
- No cross-liability between the accounts–no cross-collateral.

■ *Special purpose vehicle (SPV)*

▢ *Account at brokerage firm*

EXHIBIT 32.4C   Managed Account Structures (Example 3, Allocation to Multiple Managers)
Source: Newedge Prime Brokerage Research.

Allocation to Multiple Managers

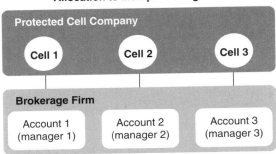

- Segregate managers by forming a protected cell company (PCC) with multiple cells.
- The PCC completes one set of account documents and provides addendums for each cell.
- The PCC provides one set of formation documents.
- No cross-liability between subaccounts if the PCC and cells are formed correctly.

■ *Protected Cell Company (PCC)*

▢ *Account at brokerage firm*

EXHIBIT 32.4D   Managed Account Structures (Example 4, Protected Cell Company)
Source: Newedge Prime Brokerage Research.

In Example 2, allocation to multiple managers, a single investment account is set up by the SPV at the futures brokerage firm. The account has subaccounts allocated to different trading managers with three different powers of attorney, but there is just one legal entity. This is a simple way to set up several managed accounts, requiring paperwork and credit checks to be done only once. Net margining across the accounts is allowed because one legal entity owns them all. As there is no firewall between the different accounts, the performances and values of the accounts are netted together.

Example 3 is an expansion of Example 1. It allows for allocation to multiple managers by setting up three different SPVs; each SPV opens an account using a different CTA manager. Each account requires its own paperwork and credit check, and the performance of the managers is separated.

Example 4 is an allocation to multiple managers in the form of a protected cell company (PCC), an account structure that is allowed in many regulatory jurisdictions, including the United States. This structure allows for a simplified account setup, with firewalls between the money managers trading for it. This is becoming the most common way to set up a multiple-manager CTA account, replacing Examples 1 and 2. A PCC structure combines the simplicity of opening one account with the ability to separate performance in order to evaluate the effects of manager selection better. It allows for greater customization of the CTA investment.

32.6 PLATFORMS

The third way to structure a CTA investment is through a platform. This is a relatively new product, offered by a handful of financial services firms. It operates almost like a multi-CTA fund, except that investors can select their own leverage and create their own portfolios from the mix of funds offered through the platform.

Platform companies argue that a key advantage of their structure is having objective, independent boards of directors and vendors that are selected by the platform company, not a manager. The platform structure may also reduce custody concerns. Usually, these platforms pass on some of the advantages of managed accounts, such as transparency, liquidity, and customized leverage.

Investors can have a series of fund investments in the platform's participating money managers, receiving consolidated performance information as well as consolidated subscription and redemption paperwork from the platform. It is relatively easy to move money from one manager to another. Because of the transparency and liquidity, these are a hybrid of managed accounts and CTA funds.

32.7 COMPARISON OF APPROACHES TO STRUCTURING
A CTA INVESTMENT

Exhibit 32.5 consolidates much of the previous discussion into a summary table. It provides answers to the primary questions for the four different categories of investment structures: CTA funds, multi-CTA funds, managed accounts, and platforms. While there are definitely exceptions to the answers in this table, it should serve as a good starting point when considering an investment structure.

EXHIBIT 32.5 CTA Fund, Multi-CTA Fund, Managed Account, and Platform

	Liability	Liquidity	Funding and Leverage	Oversight and Control of Assets	Terms and Fees for Service Providers	Maintenance	Position and Trade Transparency	Availability	Due Diligence Burden
CTA Fund	Limited	Monthly	Manager determined	Directors selected by manager	Directors selected by manager	Low	Usually not	Most managers offer flagship fund.	Medium
Multi-CTA Fund	Limited	Weekly/monthly	Manager determined	Directors selected by manager	Directors selected by manager	Low	Usually not	Most managers offer flagship fund.	Low
Managed Account	Unlimited	Daily	Customer determined	Investor	Investor	High	Yes	Not all managers accept managed accounts.	High
Platform	Limited	Weekly/monthly	Hybrid	Directors selected by platform	Directors selected by platform	Medium	Varies; manager determined	Not all managers have an established relationship with a platform.	Low

Source: Newedge Prime Brokerage Research.

Where possible, specific answers, such as who appoints directors, are given. When it comes to the cost of resources or the difficulty of a function, simple rankings of low, medium, and high are offered. It is useful to look at these answers together. An investor following the path of managed accounts might not have considered the high cost of maintenance or the problem of limited manager availability. Investors would be well served to have a more thorough dialogue with multi-CTA funds or platforms to see if their structuring needs can be accommodated. Ultimately, if full control of the assets and daily liquidity is necessary, investors may have to accept the costs of a managed account.

32.8 QUANTITATIVE ANALYSIS OF MANAGERS

According to Burghardt and Walls (2011), the research on sources of risk and return to CTAs has important implications for those who perform due diligence or evaluate portfolios for a living. However, obtaining relevant information through research has its challenges. First, because luck dominates skill over the kinds of horizons that investors usually work with, track records are very weak tools for evaluating the performance of a manager (running a portfolio of strategies) or a fund of funds (running a portfolio of managers). Therefore, historical track records produce imperfect estimates when used to approximate the statistical properties of returns needed to determine portfolio weights. As a result, there are serious limits on what investors can hope to accomplish by reviewing track records of investment managers. Second, once portfolios are formed, the ensuing track records produce sampling errors that make it very hard to determine whether the manager was selected successfully. It can be argued that short-term to medium-term track records tell us essentially nothing about the way a trader or investor makes money. However, investors often cannot afford to wait four or five years for the longer-term results needed to make reasonably good evaluations. Therefore, qualitative research regarding a manager's trading strategy, including its foundations, plays a critical role in manager selection process.

The limitations regarding track records hold true for evaluating CTAs. Extensive research exists on the performance persistence of CTA managers, which may be used to shed more light on the usefulness of track records. However, available empirical research provides mixed results in this area. Several earlier studies found little support for performance persistence among CTAs, and reported that past returns cannot be used to predict future returns of individual CTAs. However, other studies have uncovered some evidence of performance persistence. In particular, it appears that multi-CTA funds display more persistence than single-adviser CTAs.[1] Furthermore, Gregoriou, Hübner, and Kooli (2010) found that studies using longer time periods and examining persistence across various market cycles reported increased persistence in performance. In short, when investors are considering managers who possess long track records, past performance can be used as an indication of future performance over a relatively long period of time.

---

[1] For examples, see Irwin, Zulauf, and Ward (1992); Irwin (1994); McCarthy, Schneeweis, and Spurgin (1996); Schneeweis, Spurgin, and McCarthy (1997); Brorsen (1998); Goetzmann and Park (2001); and Edwards and Caglayan (2001).

A lack of strong performance persistence among CTAs does not mean investors should give up on quantitative analysis of CTA performance in the absence of long track records. Financial theory and statistics suggest that estimates of expected returns may be improved. For instance, Chapter 30 examined the conditions under which commodity futures prices are likely to display trends. In addition, the CAIA Level I material discusses quantitative methods that could be employed to verify the statistical significance of estimates. More importantly, while absolute levels of performance of CTAs do not display significant persistence, other properties of their return distributions tend to display significant persistence. For example, volatile funds tend to remain volatile, while funds that are not correlated with other trend followers tend to maintain their low correlation through time.

There are a number of different approaches to quantitatively analyzing the performance of individual managers. Each approach focuses on the time series of a manager's performance, and may include any of the following:

- *Composite track record of many programs rather than an individual investable program.* Since firms often offer multiple investment products, it is not uncommon for them to publicize a composite performance series. However, it is still necessary to analyze the performance of the specific product or fund under consideration.
- *Actual track record of an individual product or fund.* This approach focuses on the performance series of the investment product under consideration. While always appropriate to analyze, such records may be somewhat short, particularly in the case of new managers.
- *Pro forma or simulated track records.* New investment managers often put together **pro forma, or backtested, performance records.** In systematic trading, these records are created by applying a current trading system to a series of historical prices, and then computing the results as if the system had been trading at that time. While the performance data generated by such an analysis is useful and may be the only data a manager is able to show, it should be reviewed with a great deal of caution. Most importantly, pro forma results are always subject to the issue of data fitting. That is, the performance results reflect a system whose trading parameters work over the time period tested, but may not be profitable over other time periods. Even in the case of discretionary managers, pro forma records are often presented. Sometimes these represent a carve-out of a manager's track record when working for another firm (e.g., an investment bank). These results are very difficult to assess because concrete information is typically lacking, such as the manager's actual capital base at the previous firm, whether the manager had total discretion over the trades being shown, or whether any trades were excluded from the track record.

The analysis of any performance track record can be straightforward or relatively complex. At one end of the scale is an analysis that looks at common performance measures such as return, standard deviation, drawdown, and risk-adjusted returns. At the more complex end, the quantitative analysis might examine the full distribution of returns, the importance of single months or periods in overall return, and the role of performance as a function of specific market conditions. Increasingly, various forms of factor analysis have been applied to managed futures performance.

EXHIBIT 32.6 Performance Evaluation of Three Hypothetical Managers

1990–2011	Manager A	Manager B	Manager C	MSCI World Equity Index	Barclays Global Aggregate Bond Index
Annualized mean return	9.60%	13.20%	14.00%	6.55%	7.07%
Annualized standard deviation	14.00%	15.90%	15.90%	15.68%	5.59%
Sharpe ratio	0.40	0.58	0.63	0.16	0.55
Skewness	0.35	−0.10	0.32	−0.61	−0.02
Kurtosis	1.40	0.38	0.15	1.25	0.43
Maximum drawdown	−26.80%	−23.10%	−17.20%	−54.03%	−10.08%
Best single month	14.00%	14.50%	12.90%	11.22%	6.21%
Worst single month	−7.70%	−14.00%	−12.60%	−18.96%	−3.81%
Average positive month	3.51%	3.26%	3.90%	3.46%	1.50%
Average negative month	−2.70%	−3.40%	−3.10%	−3.64%	−1.12%

Source: Bloomberg and authors' calculations.

This practice has gained momentum as researchers apply investment replication techniques in their analyses.

Exhibit 32.6 provides a simple performance analysis of three managed futures traders for the period January 1990 through December 2011. Included in this table is the performance of the MSCI World Equity Index and Barclays Global Aggregate Bond Index for the same period. In the example, Manager A is a relative value trader, Manager B is a non-trend-following trader, and Manager C is a long-term trend follower. Annualized returns for these managers range from 9.6% to 14.0%; risk, as measured by standard deviation, ranges from 14.0% to 15.9%; and risk-adjusted returns, as measured by the Sharpe ratio, range between 0.40 and 0.63. The performances of these three managers compare quite favorably against the MSCI index, with Sharpe ratios similar to that of the Barclays index over the same period. Not surprisingly, these managers exhibited little correlation to equities and bonds over this period (see Exhibit 32.7). Correlations of managers A, B, and C to the

EXHIBIT 32.7 Correlation Matrix of Three Hypothetical Managers

	Manager A	Manager B	Manager C	MSCI World Equity Index	Barclays Global Aggregate Bond Index
Manager A	1				
Manager B	0.24	1			
Manager C	0.3	0.26	1		
MSCI World Equity Index	−0.05	−0.37	−0.35	1	
Barclays Global Aggregate	0.01	−0.15	0.2	0.30	1

Source: Bloomberg and authors' calculations.

MSCI index are −0.05, −0.37, and −0.35, respectively, while correlations to the Barclays index were 0.01, −0.15, and 0.2, respectively.

The outperformance of these three managed futures traders relative to equities over this period is quite striking, as illustrated in Exhibit 32.6. One might think that, since they all outperformed equities so strongly, they followed similar strategies. However, the correlation matrix in Exhibit 32.7 demonstrates that this is not the case. Here, one can see that the correlations of these managers' returns to each other are quite low.

There are other aspects of the return and risk profile of these three managers, and all managers in general, that are important to analyze. In particular, it would be illuminating to learn, to the fullest extent possible, which market conditions contributed to the managers' returns. Through a thorough analysis of performance relative to specific market conditions, one might begin to develop insights into the probabilities of future outcomes that would support individual and portfolio investment decisions.

32.9 INVESTMENT AND OPERATIONAL DUE DILIGENCE PROCESSES

After analyzing individual managers, both qualitatively and quantitatively, most firms eventually proceed to a formal investment recommendation. While investment firms, such as funds of funds, have proprietary, formal processes for recording these recommendations, most would include:

- General manager information
  - Name of firm and contact information
  - Name of specific investment fund/product being recommended
  - Assets under management of the firm and the fund/product
- Description of the management company and regulatory registrations
- Biographical information of key staff
- Investment references
- Description of the investment strategy, including markets traded, liquidity, time frames, and full discussion of investment style
- Quantitative review of the investment strategy
- Discussion of investment risk
- Discussion of current portfolio activities
- Subscription/redemption terms of the fund along with its fee structure, and information about whether investments can be "side pocketed" or redemption restrictions (gates) imposed
- Specific amounts to be invested
- Evidence of investment recommendation approval (i.e., authorized signature)

Again, the specific information and level of detail included in a formal investment recommendation differs from firm to firm. However, the existence of a formal process, backed by independent due diligence, is widely felt to be a required best practice in the industry.

Firms, such as funds of funds, have increasingly separated investment due diligence from operational due diligence. An **operational due diligence** review focuses on the legal documents of an investment vehicle as well as the back office operations and trading systems of an investment firm. The skills required for an operational due diligence review, such as legal, accounting, and operational risk assessment, often differ from those used to assess the investment strategy of a manager. **Investment due diligence**, which assesses the investment strategy, will require knowledge of markets as well as the macroeconomic environment, and involve a fair degree of sophisticated quantitative analysis. These are different skills than those required to review managers' documents or accounting systems.

The formal due diligence process begins with a review of all of the documents and counterparties involved in an individual investment. It also includes a review of the internal procedures of the investment manager. As an example, the operational due diligence process is likely to review the following fund documents:

- **Offering documents:** Offshore and onshore hedge funds are marketed to investors through an offering document, referred to as an Offering Memorandum or Private Placement Memorandum. This document summarizes the terms of the investment product, including a description of the fund's structure (e.g., where it is domiciled, what laws govern it, and whether it is listed on an exchange), as well as investment goals and objectives, management team, fees and expenses, and subscription and redemption terms. The offering document serves a marketing purpose and is not the legally operative document of a fund.

- **Subscription agreement:** Investors in a hedge fund need to complete a subscription agreement. This includes detailed information about the investor. As anti-money-laundering rules have been adopted in many legal jurisdictions, subscription agreements have increasingly asked for proof of the investor's identity. In the case of U.S. investment products, subscription agreements include a number of questions designed to ascertain whether the investor is qualified, that is, whether the investor has sufficient income and/or assets to legally qualify as eligible to participate in certain investments.

- **Redemption form:** A redemption form, given to investors at the time of their initial investment, provides information about redemption terms and restrictions. Such information includes the frequency of allowed redemptions (e.g., monthly, quarterly, or annually); the notice period required for a redemption (e.g., 90 days before the redemption date); special terms, such as whether a penalty can be imposed on redemptions of investments not held for minimum periods of time (e.g., a 5% redemption penalty on investments held less than one year); and lockup periods (e.g., periods of time after the initial investment during which no redemption is permitted), as well as whether redemptions may be suspended and, if so, under what conditions.

- **Investment advisory agreement:** For offshore funds, the investment manager signs an investment advisory agreement with the fund itself. The agreement describes the obligations of the investment manager with regard to the investment vehicle. In the case of a U.S. limited partnership, the investment manager typically acts as the general partner, and the obligations are set forth in the partnership agreement.

- **Administration agreement:** Most offshore funds, and increasing numbers of U.S. limited partnerships, use outside administrators for certain tasks. Such tasks include receiving subscriptions into the funds and paying out redemptions. In addition, and importantly, administrators are also responsible for valuing the fund on a periodic basis, most commonly on a monthly basis. For managed futures, this valuation process is normally straightforward, since most of the instruments traded are readily priced on a transparent futures exchange.

- **Audited financial statements:** Both offshore funds and onshore partnerships undertake an annual audit. These audits are provided to current and prospective investors. It is common for prospective investors to request at least three years of audits prior to formally deciding to invest. These audits are reviewed to verify information provided by the manager, to assure that there is an unqualified audit letter, and to discern whether there has been a change in auditor over this period. While there are often simple explanations as to why an auditor has been replaced, prospective investors usually wish to discuss the reasons with a manager, and often with the audit firm directly.

32.10 COST OF ACTIVE MANAGEMENT

After an allocation to a managed futures trader is made, most firms institute a specific formal monitoring and review process. Although individual firms may have proprietary processes, most include the following central elements:

- *Quantitative comparison.* On a regular basis, each investment will be quantitatively compared on the basis of its realized return and its risk, as well as on the basis of its correlation structure to its history, to designated peers, and to manager benchmarks. During this process, deviations from expectations and/or historical performance are identified.
- *Idiosyncratic behavior monitoring.* While quantitative comparison is usually done on a continuous basis, any idiosyncratic performance among managed futures traders typically leads to a more formal review, which is conducted on a periodic (generally semiannual or annual) schedule. At that time, other aspects of the investment are also reviewed, particularly regarding changes in any of the following areas: strategy, markets traded, key personnel, risk, operations, liquidity, or counterparties.
- *Due diligence review.* Also on a periodic basis (usually annually), a due diligence review is performed. At that point, the investment can be formally reapproved for the next investment horizon.

The previous examples of an investment monitoring process are presented as an illustration of practices found in firms allocating to managed futures traders. They do not differ materially from the practices one would find in other hedge fund investment styles.

As a result of monitoring, or stemming from the desire to actively manage a portfolio of CTAs, an investor may decide to redeem a CTA or change allocations among CTAs. While there may be benefits to either action, there are also associated costs. The most important costs in actively managing a portfolio of CTAs are forgone loss carryforward and costs associated with liquidation and reinvestment: dormant cash, opportunity losses, and slippage from transaction costs.

32.10.1 Forgone Loss Carryforward

This cost is borne by every investor. It arises from the asymmetric fee structure that is typical in the alternative investment world of hedge funds and CTAs. That is, the manager collects performance fees only when net asset value is above the most recent high-water mark at the end of the relevant accounting period. For a manager who is underwater (that is, whose net asset value is below the most recent high-water mark), all gains are free from performance fees until a new high-water mark is achieved. By replacing a poorly performing manager with another manager, the cost of loss carryforward can be isolated. Going forward, the return realized from the poorly performing manager will be gross of fees, while the return earned on the investment with the new manager will be net of fees. This means the new manager will need to outperform the old manager by the amount of the performance fee just to break even. If the drawdown of the current manager is large, the investors collect gross of fees returns for several periods. For example, if a manager experiences a drawdown of 25%, then the next 33.3% return ($0.75 \times 1.333 = 1.0$) generated by the manager is passed on to investors gross of performance fees. Assuming a performance fee of 20%, the new manager has to earn 41.67% $[0.333/(1 - 0.2)]$ for the investor just to break even.

32.10.2 Costs of Liquidation and Reinvestment

In addition to giving up the benefits of loss carryforward, the process of liquidating and reinvesting incurs three additional costs, two of which might go unexamined unless benchmarks and investment opportunities are well defined. These include forgone interest on dormant cash, forgone excess returns on uncommitted cash, and the market impact costs of closing out one position and opening another.

Exhibit 32.8 provides a rough schematic of the steps involved in redeeming from one manager and investing in another. The key lesson from this exhibit is that investors have to deal with several leads and lags when making a decision to take money from one manager and to give it to another.

The first lag is identified as L1, and represents the time it takes to review a manager's results and make a decision about redemption. This might take anywhere from a few days to, in some complex cases, several months. The second lag is identified as L2, and represents the time between the notification deadline for a withdrawal and the time when a net asset value is struck. This can take several weeks. The third, L3, is the time between the striking of net asset value and the receipt of the first round of cash. Finally, the fourth, L4, represents the time that passes between the receipt of the first round of cash and the final round of cash.

The two net asset value series in Exhibit 32.8 serve as a reminder that while investors are gathering information, making decisions, redeeming cash, and reinvesting the proceeds of any cash received from an existing manager, things are in motion. The net asset value of the existing manager (i.e., Manager A) is changing with each passing month, as is the net asset value of any manager to whom the investor might direct future allocations (i.e., Manager B).

One cost associated with liquidation is the forgone interest on dormant cash. This cost is borne chiefly by investors in funds, and depends entirely on a fund's

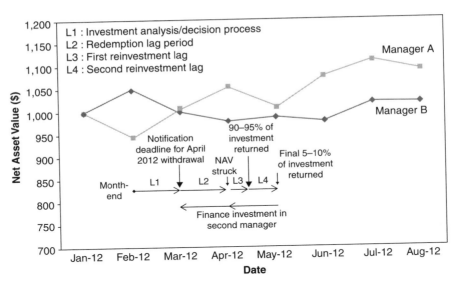

EXHIBIT 32.8   Liquidation and Reinvestment Process
Source: Newedge Prime Brokerage Research.

practices with regard to interest payments on cash balances. Industry practices vary a great deal, but it is not uncommon to find that funds do not pay interest on the value of cash balances. In these cases, the cost of forgone interest depends on how quickly cash is returned to the investor.

A second cost associated with liquidation and reinvestment is **opportunity losses.** These losses stem from the intervals during which investments are not committed to enterprises that promise returns in excess of market interest rates.

The third and final cost associated with liquidation and reinvestment relates to transaction and administrative fees. Closing out old positions and opening new positions entails transaction costs in the form of bid-ask spreads and brokerage commissions. The total amount of these costs could vary, depending on the liquidity of the positions that have to be closed. This cost is borne, most obviously, by investors in managed accounts. It is also borne, but in a more diluted way, by investors in funds that incur transaction costs as a normal part of doing business and, as a result, share these costs with all other investors in funds. In addition to costs associated with closing positions, investors will incur administrative costs related to due diligence on new managers.

32.11   CONCLUSION

Available evidence suggests that CTAs benefit investors by providing meaningful diversification benefits to portfolios consisting of traditional asset classes as well as hedge funds. To achieve these benefits, investors need to consider the various ways that CTAs can be accessed. Further, to mitigate risks associated with investing in a single manager (e.g., model risk, key person risk, firm risk, etc.), the investor should consider investing in a portfolio of CTAs. Another consideration is whether to pay an additional layer of fees in order to outsource the construction of this portfolio to a multi-CTA fund or to assemble an in-house team that could select and construct the portfolio. Finally, for those investors who plan to make a substantial allocation to CTAs, a managed account platform will provide substantial transparency, control, and customization of the CTA investment program.

CHAPTER 33

Hedge Fund Replication

33.1 INTRODUCTION

This chapter discusses hedge fund replication methodologies and potential applications of products developed using these methodologies. The subject of hedge fund replication was first examined by academics in the early 2000s while attempting to develop performance benchmarks for hedge funds. Later, in 2007, following initiatives by major investment banks (such as Merrill Lynch, Goldman Sachs, Credit Suisse, and Morgan Stanley) and other firms to introduce investable hedge fund replication products, there was renewed interest in the subject among academics and practitioners.

This chapter examines, from both a theoretical and an empirical standpoint, the respective benefits and limits of the three different approaches to hedge fund replication, which are referred to as factor-based replication, payoff-distribution replication, and bottom-up replication (also called algorithmic replication). The chapter examines the potential benefits that replication products could offer investors, and provides a brief summary of some of the empirical evidence regarding the performance of these products.

33.2 AN OVERVIEW OF REPLICATION PRODUCTS

Fundamentally, **hedge fund replication products** (also called clones or trackers) are created to capture the traditional and alternative betas underlying the expected return and risk of a hedge fund benchmark. **Alternative betas** refer to those sources of return that are not normally available through investments in traditional assets or, if they are available, are commonly bundled with other risks. For instance, publicly traded equities have exposures to a number of factors, including volatility and commodity price risks. These last two risks are generally considered as alternative sources of risk but, in the case of common stocks, are bundled with pure equity risk, which dominates the behavior of common stocks. Other examples of alternative betas are risks associated with currency investments, momentum or trend-following strategies, and structured products.

Available replication products are based on statistical techniques (e.g., factor-based and payoff-distribution approaches) or bottom-up (algorithmic) trading models. The latter approach attempts to trade the underlying securities in a manner consistent with the trading approach taken by most active managers within a particular strategy. To the degree that tracker products are designed to track active manager-based benchmarks, they are designed to capture a significant portion of the common strategy return of fund strategies, and to reflect fund managers' common beta exposures to various traditional and alternative sources of risk. Additionally, these tracker products are designed to capture the common strategy alpha earned by managers, as represented by the excess return of the fund strategy relative to a passive benchmark consisting of traditional sources of risk (e.g., S&P 500 index). In other words, if the overall strategy, rather than just the top managers, generates alpha, then replication products may be able to capture all or some of that alpha.

33.3 POTENTIAL BENEFITS OF REPLICATION PRODUCTS

Before discussing the various approaches to hedge fund replication, the potential benefits that one may receive from using a replication product must be examined. The term *using* is employed, rather than *investing*, because investors may benefit from these products even if they do not make any allocations to them, as replication products can lead to a better understanding of the underlying risks of hedge funds and allow investors to build better benchmarks against which to measure their hedge fund investments. The reason that investors may allocate to hedge funds in the first place needs to be understood. In other words, why is it of some potential value to replicate hedge funds?

As discussed in the CAIA Level I and Level II curriculum, to understand the potential benefits of investing in hedge funds, one must distinguish among various strategies. Some strategies have significant systematic risks, and therefore allow investors to earn relatively high risk-adjusted return through exposure to directional market risks. Equity long/short funds and some global macro funds fall into this category. The primary benefit that investors seek in investing in these **return enhancers** is to improve the risk-adjusted return of their portfolios. This benefit can come from earning alpha, or by investing in alternative beta exposures that are underweighted in the investor's traditional portfolio. The alpha is typically measured relative to the performance of all underlying beta exposures, whether traditional betas or alternative betas. Alternative beta exposures may include those taken by a global macro fund that invests in global equity and foreign currency markets, while managing the risks of these investments. Liquidity risk is another important alternative source of return not available through investments in traditional assets. For example, liquidity risk is one of the primary sources of return to a distressed securities strategy. Finally, a time-varying traditional source of beta could be considered an alternative source of beta. For instance, a passive equity index has a constant and positive equity beta, while an equity long/short manager is likely to have a time-varying beta, which could even become negative during bear markets. Equity beta is considered a traditional source of return, while a dynamic beta that results from an actively managed portfolio is considered an alternative beta, and, assuming that the manager has some market-timing skill, serves as a source of alpha.

Some strategies, however, have less systematic exposure to equity, fixed-income, or commodity markets, and are classified as **risk diversifiers**. Some commodity trading advisers (CTAs) and global macro funds, and most relative value funds, such as convertible and merger arbitrage, fall into this category. These funds provide returns that are not highly correlated with returns on traditional assets, and, therefore, can help reduce the overall risk of a portfolio. Similar to return enhancers, a secondary benefit provided by risk diversifiers is exposure to alternative sources of risk and return. For instance, convertible bond arbitrage funds provide exposures to risks associated with implied volatility, credit, and illiquidity, earning a relatively low rate of return while reducing the overall risk of a traditional portfolio.

33.4 THE CASE FOR HEDGE FUND REPLICATION

Prior to the bear market that began in 2000, there was a widely held market belief that the returns to actively managed alternative investment funds were composed primarily of alpha (excess return above that available in an equally risky passive investment product) and small amounts of beta (return due to a fund strategy's exposure to investable market factors). Since then, the return streams associated with passive investable indices, active managers, and other alternative or structured products have severely challenged this belief system. In the traditional mutual fund arena, research continues to question the existence of manager alpha (Bodie, Kane, and Marcus 2010). Even in the alternative investment area, where greater amounts of informational inefficiencies may be expected, studies have shown that the alpha of many hedge fund strategies has declined since 2000 (Fung and Hsieh 2007). Similarly, Fung et al. (2008) document that hedge fund of funds products did not deliver any alpha between 2000 and 2004, and Naik et al. (2007) have shown that the levels of alpha associated with various investment strategies have substantially declined over the period 1995 to 2004.

Exhibit 33.1 displays a one-factor estimate of the rolling beta and rolling alpha of the Hedge Fund Research (HFR) Funds of Funds index, where the S&P 500 index

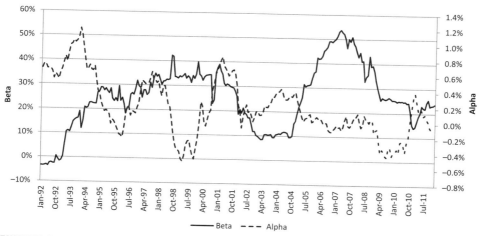

EXHIBIT 33.1 Twenty-Four Month Rolling Estimates of Betas and Alphas of the HFR Funds of Funds Index Relative to the S&P 500 Index, 1992–2011
Source: Bloomberg and authors' calculations.

is used as the benchmark. Both the beta and the alpha are estimated using a 24-month rolling window. The alpha is estimated using the following expression:

$$\overline{R}_{t,HFR} - r_t = \alpha_t + \beta_t \left(\overline{R}_{t,SP} - r_t \right) \tag{33.1}$$

Here, $\overline{R}_{t,HFR}$ is the estimated mean return of the HFR Funds of Funds index, $\overline{R}_{t,SP}$ is the estimate mean of the total return on the S&P 500 index, β_t is the estimated beta of the HFR index to the S&P 500, α_t is the estimated alpha of the HFR index, and r_t is the monthly rate for 30-day London Interbank Offered Rate (LIBOR). All variables are estimated using a 24-month rolling window.

From Exhibit 33.1, it can be seen that since 1992 there has been a general rise in the beta of the HFR index and a corresponding decline in its alpha. In fact, the estimated alpha was close to zero, and even negative, between 2006 and 2011.

The studies previously cited, as well as others, put forth various explanations for the increase in beta and the decline in alpha: changes in trading strategies, increased liquidity, technological advances that have all but eliminated information premiums, or regulatory intervention. These explanations have given rise to three alternative hypotheses:

1. The fund bubble hypothesis
2. The capacity constraint hypothesis
3. The increased allocation to active funds hypothesis

The **fund bubble hypothesis** assumes that successful hedge fund managers can earn substantially greater incomes than successful fund managers in the traditional space. Investment bubbles provide an opportunity for less-skilled traditional fund managers to become hedge fund managers. The fund bubble hypothesis simply states that as the supply of investment capital to hedge fund space increased, so did the number of less qualified managers who entered the industry and who, correspondingly, provided inferior returns that diluted the overall performance of the industry.

The **capacity constraint hypothesis** argues that most alpha is a zero-sum game. Therefore, only a few managers can offer alpha on a consistent basis. In short, the growth in assets under management has sharply reduced the per capita amount of alpha available in the marketplace. In addition, unless new strategies or sources of alpha are discovered, further declines in alpha can be expected.

The **increased allocation to active funds hypothesis** argues that as hedge fund investment becomes more popular, the performance of hedge funds will be adversely affected by the trading decisions of investors who have allocations to these funds as well as to traditional assets. In other words, the systematic risks or betas of hedge funds increase as more capital flows into them. In particular, during periods of financial stress, investors may be forced to liquidate both their traditional and their alternative investments, increasing the correlation between traditional asset and alternative asset classes.

The common theme flowing through these three hypotheses is that while star managers exist and their ability to provide meaningful returns is not questioned, the investment management universe also includes managers who either are mandated to invest in accordance with a given benchmark or do not have the skill to surpass that benchmark. Note that the lack of manager outperformance is not necessarily manager induced. For example, some managers may be constrained by the mandates of their contracts; in this case, often the clients have made an asset allocation decision that requires the manager to remain within certain limits. Client intervention, however, plays a very limited role within absolute return vehicles, whereas the decline of alpha is pronounced and without very many mitigating factors. The real question in the replication or tracking literature remains the degree to which the representative benchmark is investable, and the degree to which the investable replication or tracker fund adequately reflects the risks and returns of the representative benchmark.

33.4.1 Replication Products as a Source of Alpha

It is commonly argued that replication products cannot possess alpha because they are not managed by skilled managers. However, replication products that track a benchmark consisting of one or more actively managed funds may be able to capture the alpha provided by the benchmark. In the extreme case, if a replication product can perfectly replicate the return properties of the benchmark, then by definition it will capture the alpha provided by the benchmark as well. If the benchmark consists of a group of top managers, then, in theory, the replication product may even be able to capture the alpha provided by top-tier managers. Whether, in practice, one can create such a perfect replication product will be discussed later. The point of this discussion is that, a priori, one cannot dismiss the possibility that a replication product could be a source of alpha. Further, since hedge replication products carry lower fees than actively managed portfolios, the possibility of providing alpha to investors who allocate to these products increases. On the other hand, if the replication product cannot gain access to certain sources of returns used by managers in the underlying benchmark, then replication products will not be able to generate the level of alpha provided by managers. In short, whether replication products can generate alpha is an empirical question.

33.4.2 Replication Products as a Source of Alternative Beta

Replication products have the potential to give investors access to some of the alternative sources of beta. Whether this potential can be realized in practice depends greatly on the set of securities used to create the replication product. For example, if liquid publicly traded securities are used to create the replicating portfolio, then clearly the product cannot provide exposure to illiquidity risk. This, in turn, means any return that can be attributed to illiquidity risk will not be present in the replicating product's performance.

As new passive investable products, such as exchange-traded funds (ETFs), are created, replication products are given a greater chance to offer investors access to many sources of alternative betas. For example, ETFs based on convertible bonds and volatility have recently become available. These ETFs make it possible to create investable products that would track convertible bond arbitrage and volatility trading strategies. An interesting question that arises is whether these can still be considered sources of alternative beta now that they are available through traditional investment vehicles to all investors. To the degree that these new investment products bundle an alternative source of beta with other traditional sources of risk, they may still be considered alternative assets. For example, a convertible bond ETF provides exposure to the options embedded in convertible bonds, while at the same time exposing investors to credit, equity, and interest rate risks. Some of these risks are commonly hedged away by active managers, and thus a convertible bond arbitrage fund may have little exposure to equity or interest rate risks. Therefore, the embedded option of a convertible bond and its implied volatility can still be considered as potential sources of alternative beta. Finally, as discussed in the previous section, time-varying betas associated with traditional sources of risk could be considered alternative betas. Therefore, to the degree that a replicating product can capture the dynamic beta of a hedge fund, then the product could be a source of alternative beta.

33.5 UNIQUE BENEFITS OF REPLICATION PRODUCTS

In the previous sections, it was argued that replication products have the potential to provide many of the benefits that motivate investors to allocate to hedge funds. Namely, they could act as both return enhancers and risk diversifiers. This section examines the benefits that are somewhat unique to replication products and are generally not offered by most hedge funds. These represent the strongest rationales for the development of various replication products and the reasons why some investors consider allocating to them. Whether the unique benefits provided by hedge fund replication products makes a strong case for increased allocations to these products depends, primarily, on the investor's initial reason for investing in hedge funds. If access to some unique sources of risk premium (e.g., illiquidity) and skills displayed by top-tier managers are the main reasons, then replication products will not be considered viable alternatives to hedge funds. On the other hand, if the goal is to capture the alpha and the beta that are represented by the benchmark that underlies the replication product, then these products may be attractive to some investors. The two key questions in this discussion are:

1. Can one identify top-tier managers a priori, and do managers display significant persistence in their performance?
2. Can hedge fund replication products track performance of various strategies during different market cycles?

Regarding the first question, academic and industry research provides mixed results. Some studies show that top-tier funds do display return persistence, but their outperformance is partially eroded through time. The reason is that capital flows to top-performing funds, leading to some erosion of their superior performance.[1] Other studies show no performance persistence among hedge fund managers, or, if there is any, it tends to disappear after a few months.[2] The second question is discussed later

---

[1] See Jagannathan, Malakhov, and Novikov (2012).
[2] Brown, Goetzmann, and Ibbotson (1999) and Bares, Gibson, and Gyger (2003).

in this chapter. First, we examine the unique benefits that hedge replication products are supposed to provide.[3]

Liquidity: Tracker products invest primarily in liquid instruments (e.g., ETFs or futures), and are therefore able to offer liquidity terms (both purchase and redemption) to investors that most fund managers cannot match. Most replication products do not have lockup periods or the ability to erect gates to slow investor withdrawals. Though it is difficult to quantify the redemption premium required by fund investors, evidence from the secondary market for hedge fund investments[4] shows that, during periods of market distress (e.g., 2007–2008), investors were willing to accept a discount of 20% of the net asset value (NAV) of their hedge fund investments in order to exit a fund. Even though this reflects the cost of a liquidity premium during a market crisis, the cost of redemption liquidity, even under normal market conditions, is likely to be a few percentage points.

Hedge fund investors are bound by the redemption policies of the hedge funds. An investor in a hedge fund often has to manage liquidity by attempting to anticipate the behavior of other investors, who may decide to redeem quickly, leaving the long-term investor with the least liquid (and least attractive) remnants of a fund's portfolio. An investor who executes a replication strategy does not face these problems. The investor will enjoy whatever liquidity is on offer from the actual market, and is not hurt because other investors decide to exit early.[5]

Hedge fund investors can achieve some degree of liquidity and reduce exposure to the behavior of fellow investors by using a managed account platform. The key advantage to a managed account is complete control by the investor. By pulling trading privileges, the investor has the ability to manage the cash and liquidate the account at any time. In theory, this gives the investor better than daily liquidity, as the account can be liquidated whenever the market is open. Of course, these advantages come at a cost. For example, one cost is the reduced size of the pool from which managers are selected. Many large managers do not accept managed accounts, and those that do require rather large minimum account sizes and other additional administrative requirements.

Transparency: Replication products can afford to be highly transparent in terms of their trading strategies, including security holdings. Moreover, since replication products operate primarily in the most liquid segments of the markets (e.g., exchange-traded securities), trades implemented by them tend to have negligible price impact when trading is focused on the most liquid ETFs. Further, since trades are often primarily algorithmic, suppliers of tracker products can disclose a significant amount of information about the trading process. As discussed previously, hedge fund investors could receive a high degree of transparency by using a managed account platform. However, while such an approach increases transparency in terms of portfolio positions, it may not provide complete transparency in terms of the trading process of the portfolio manager.

Flexibility: Most replication products can be very flexible in terms of the risk profile they offer investors. An investor may able to specify a particular hedge fund

---

[3] The following discussion is partly based on Crowder, Kazemi, and Schneeweis (2011).
[4] See www.hedgebay.com.
[5] Kamel (2007).

strategy benchmark that the product is designed to track, as well as its volatility and other desired statistical properties. These products are especially suited for use in separate accounts designed to meet individual investors' unique requirements. Funds of funds may be able to put investors' assets to work rather quickly by investing in a replication product.

Lower fees: Replication products charge lower total fees than hedge funds. The fees for replication products may offset the higher gross returns that individual hedge fund managers may generate, reducing the differential net-of-fees returns generated by both products. Further, once other costs, such as market impact, due diligence, monitoring, and liquidity, are taken into account, replication products can offer net returns that are comparable to those offered by individual funds and funds of funds. The results in Exhibit 33.2 for a given hypothetical level of return indicate that the higher expenses in both direct hedge fund and funds of funds investments require a hedge fund–based product to produce a substantially higher gross return, compared to that of a replication product, if investors are to receive the same net return. The higher expenses generally involved in hedge funds and funds of funds set a high gross return hurdle if their net returns are to exceed those of comparable replication products. In Exhibit 33.2, only 62.78% and 50.47% of the gross returns earned by a hedge fund and a fund of funds, respectively, flow to the investors. In contrast, 83.33% of the gross returns of replication products are earned by investors. Further, if these products are used in structured products, structuring fees applied to tracker investments would be significantly lower due to their transparency and liquidity.

Hedging: If replication products are created using liquid financial instruments, then it should be possible to short the replication product. This creates a number of potential opportunities for investors. For example, if an investor cannot reduce her allocation to a hedge fund, she might be able to hedge some of its risks by shorting a replication product that is designed to mimic its strategy.

Lower due diligence and monitoring risks: Recent experience has shown that hedge funds and funds of funds have significant due diligence and operational risk

EXHIBIT 33.2 Gross and Net Return Comparisons

	Hedge Funds	Funds of Funds	Replication
Net return assumed to be earned by investors	7.00%	7.00%	7.00%
Management fee—fund level	2.00%	2.00%	1.00%
Performance fee—fund level	20.00%	20.00%	
Estimated operating expenses—fund level	0.40%	0.40%	0.40%
Management fee—FoF level		1.00%	
Performance fee—FoF level		10.00%	
Estimated operating expenses—fund level		0.40%	
Gross return required to achieve comparable net return	11.15%	13.87%	8.40%
% of gross return earned by investors	62.78%	50.47%	83.33%

Source: Crowder, Kazemi, and Schneeweis (2011).

exposure. Replication products entail lower operational risk, imposing substantially lower due diligence and monitoring costs on their investors. In addition, hedge funds and funds of funds may deviate from their expected investment styles, exposing investors to style drift risk. Since replication products are calibrated to a defined hedge fund strategy benchmark, investors have minimal exposure to style drift.

Diversification: In some replication approaches, diversified factors, such as the returns on ETFs or futures contracts, are used to create portfolios that mimic the performance of hedge funds. This creates replication products that are highly diversified. Even when the product's positions are concentrated in a few economic sectors or countries, diversified instruments such as ETFs and futures are normally employed to gain these exposures. Diversification benefits offered by replication products also reduce the risk of both large drawdowns and high volatility associated with investing with a small number of managers or securities. Investors can achieve the same degree of diversification by investing in a portfolio of hedge funds or in a diversified fund of funds. However, both alternatives entail added costs in terms of either increased monitoring costs or extra layers of fees.

Benchmarking: The benefits just listed would accrue only to investors who allocate to replication products. The benchmarking benefit does not require any allocation to the replication product. If a replication product were able to capture the properties of the returns to a given hedge fund strategy, then it would represent an investable benchmark, which can be used by investors to estimate the value added by their managers. In addition, the investor may be able to negotiate incentive structures that are tied to the manager's performance relative to a replication product.

33.6 FACTOR-BASED APPROACH TO REPLICATION

As discussed in the first section, there are three broad approaches to hedge fund replication: (1) factor-based, (2) payoff distribution, and (3) bottom-up or algorithmic.

The underlying assumption behind the **factor-based approach** is that a significant portion of a fund's returns can be explained by a set of asset-based factors. This approach involves construction of a portfolio, composed of long and/or short positions in a set of suitably selected risk factors that minimizes the tracking error with respect to the predefined benchmark being replicated. The benchmark may consist of a single manager or, more commonly, an equally weighted hedge fund index. The following issues must be addressed in constructing a replication product:

- *Choice of benchmark.* The benchmark to be replicated must be selected carefully. The most common practice is to use a publicly available index, such as one of the HFR or Center for International Securities and Derivatives Markets (CISDM) strategy indices. It is also possible to create a custom-made benchmark that meets certain criteria. If a strategy index (e.g., equity long/short) is used as a benchmark, the investor may want to ensure that only those managers that clearly follow such a strategy are added to the benchmark, rather than relying on the self-declared strategy of managers. Hedge fund indices are investable or noninvestable. Tracking products have a much better fit with investable hedge fund indices, as the underlying hedge funds are available for investment and may invest in more liquid securities. Noninvestable hedge fund indices often have higher returns than investable hedge fund indices, perhaps due to investments in less liquid securities or because highly successful managers have closed their funds to new investors.

- *Choice of factors.* The factors should be readily investable. Otherwise, the replication product will fail to serve its main purpose. In addition, investors should decide whether a fixed set of factors will be used, or whether statistical methods (e.g., stepwise regression) will be used to identify the most suitable set of factors.
- *Length of estimation period.* The parameters of the model have to be estimated using historical performance data. In general, a longer data series means smaller errors in the estimated values of the parameters. However, when there are significant changes in the characteristics of the benchmark and/or the factors, longer estimation periods may lead to a mimicking portfolio that reflects the market conditions of several months ago, rather than the current market conditions.
- *Number of factors.* Using a large set of factors will generally lead to a better in-sample fit, but is likely to lead to poor out-of-sample performance. Using a small set of factors, on the other hand, may prevent the creation of a tracking portfolio with low tracking error and poor in-sample and out-of-sample performances. One should use factors that represent different sources of return and, if possible, sources most relevant to the strategy being replicated.

Aside from these basic choices, there are many other technical choices, such as adjusting the benchmark's return series for stale prices, adjusting net returns for fees, and selecting the appropriate econometric technique to be employed. Once the initial setup is complete, the analyst will need to estimate the parameters of the following equation:

$$\tilde{R}_{t,HF} - r = \beta_1 \times \left(\tilde{F}_{1t} - r\right) + \beta_2 \times \left(\tilde{F}_{2t} - r\right) + \cdots + \beta_K \times \left(\tilde{F}_{Kt} - r\right) + \tilde{\varepsilon} \qquad (33.2)$$

Here, $\tilde{R}_{t,HF}$ is the total rate of return on the benchmark that is to be replicated, r is the short-term riskless rate (e.g., 30 LIBOR), $\tilde{F}_{it}$ is the random total rate of return on factor i, β_i is the exposure of the benchmark to factor i, and $\tilde{\varepsilon}$ is the return on the benchmark that cannot be explained by the factors. Note that (1) all factors should represent investable assets, and (2) returns in excess of a riskless rate must be used on both sides of the equation. The factors must be investable because the resulting portfolio needs to be investable. Excess returns are used because the requirement that the betas should add up to 1.0 will be relaxed. For instance, excess returns on a number of equity, fixed-income, and commodity ETFs can be used to represent the factors. Many ETFs trade in liquid markets, provide immediate access to various sources of return, and represent diversified portfolios.

Once the betas are estimated, the weight of the replication product in cash is given by:

$$\beta_{Cash} = 1 - \sum_{i=1}^{K} \beta_i$$

If the weight of cash is negative, then it means the product will use leverage to create the mimicking portfolio. The parameters of the preceding equation are estimated using T observations; that is, $t = 1, \ldots, T$. Then, the return on the replicating portfolio, which is invested for the period $T + 1$, is given by the following expression:

$$R_{Re, T+1} = \hat{\beta}_{1,T} \times \tilde{F}_{1, T+1} + \cdots + \hat{\beta}_{K,T} \times \tilde{F}_{K, T+1} + \hat{\beta}_{Cash, T} \times r$$

Note the weights (betas) were estimated using data up to time T. The portfolio is constructed at the beginning of period $T + 1$ and is held for one period. The process is repeated next period, as new observations on the performance of the benchmark and the factors are obtained.

The in-sample fit of the model is estimated using the R-squared of the regression, which is calculated using this expression:

$$\left(1 - Var\left[\tilde{\varepsilon}\right] / Var\left[\tilde{R}_{t, HF}\right]\right)$$

If the variance of the error term from Equation 33.2 is small, then the in-sample R-squared would be high. However, even if the in-sample R-squared is close to 1.0, it does not mean that the out-of-sample tracking error will be small. In fact, most hedge funds are relatively active, meaning their allocations to various securities and asset classes change through time. Therefore, the estimated weights are likely to have significant estimation errors, leading to poor out-of-sample performance.

Two common questions arise in the context of factor-based replication. First, how can hedge fund returns be replicated using a relatively small set of factors? After all, each hedge fund may invest in hundreds of securities, and thus several hundred securities will underlie an index. Second, how can the appropriate weights of the mimicking portfolio be estimated if the weights of the actively managed product change over time? If managers are dynamically changing the weights of their portfolios, then the true values of the betas are changing constantly, and, thus, can only be estimated with significant errors. In addition, the estimated betas would reflect what the managers were holding several months ago, not necessarily what they are holding now.

Two key concepts help to answer these questions.[6] The first concept, referred to as **view commonality**, is related to the fact that when individual hedge fund managers' views (measured by their exposures) are aggregated in a hedge fund index, they tend to cluster into common themes that drive the overall performance of the index. For instance, if most equity long/short managers have positive views about energy stocks, they may attempt to exploit this view by allocating assets to various energy companies. In the index, these views are aggregated, and are represented by increased exposure of the index to energy sector, which could be captured by the replication product through increased allocations to an energy ETF.

The second concept, referred to as **exposure inertia**, attempts to explain why the overall weights of an index consisting of actively managed portfolios can be empirically estimated. The idea here is that the large number of decision makers in a

---

[6] Drachman and Little (2010).

hedge fund index reduces the speed at which the common views or exposures change over time. If the core themes that drive hedge fund returns change rapidly, then the factor-based replication models would not be able to identify the appropriate weights of the mimicking portfolio. This is particularly true when monthly data are used to estimate the parameters of the model. With rapidly changing factor exposures, monthly returns would not be able to transmit much information about the behavior of the factor exposures of hedge fund indices. While one hedge fund may actively change its exposures through time, the index is likely to display a more stable behavior because its exposure is the aggregate of many single exposures.

33.6.1 Research on Factor-Based Replication[7]

There is much academic and industry research in the area of factor-based benchmarking and replicating of hedge funds. Karavas, Kazemi, and Schneeweis (2003) examine the replication of equally weighted portfolios of European-based hedge funds for five strategies: funds of funds, convertible arbitrage, fixed-income arbitrage, event driven, and long/short equity. The in-sample period is a rolling 24-month window, and the out-of-sample period is the month immediately following the sample window. The factors selected are European market factors that include equity market risk, interest rate risk, credit risk, and volatility risk. The authors obtain in-sample R^2 of 29.2% for fixed-income arbitrage, 31.9% for convertible arbitrage, 54.3% for funds of funds, 67.7% for long/short equity, and 85.8% for event driven. The explanatory power of the different factors, by strategy, is low in the in-sample period, generally below 70%. Out-of-sample results are in line with the disappointing in-sample results. The correlation in performance between strategies and clones ranges from 12% to 91%, but is mainly below 50%. Only one strategy, event driven, reveals a satisfying correlation of 90% with the multifactor analysis. Overall, the replicating models considerably underperform hedge funds. Moreover, they are generally more volatile.

Studying eight strategies, Agarwal and Naik (2004) use a multifactor model in which the risk factors are buy-and-hold and option-based. The buy-and-hold risk factors are equities (four indices), bonds (three indices), currencies (one index), and commodities (one index). The authors add the Fama-French size and book-to-market factors, momentum factor, and a credit risk factor. The option-based risk factors are at-the-money (ATM) and out-of-the-money (OTM) European call and put options on the S&P 500. First, a stepwise regression is conducted to identify the significant factors from 1990 to 2000 for eight HFR indices. Second, the authors examine whether the replicating portfolios based on these factor loadings can do a good job of mimicking the out-of-sample performance of hedge funds. A replicating portfolio is constructed, and the accuracy of the return replication is tested. The authors obtain in-sample adjusted R^2 ranging from 40.5% to 91.63%, while the one-year out-of-sample results are too short to draw meaningful conclusions.

Lo and Hasanhodzic (2007) attempt to replicate the return distributions of 11 strategies covered by the TASS Hedge Fund database: convertible arbitrage,

---

[7] This part is partly based on Amenc et al. (2007, 2008).

dedicated short bias, emerging markets, equity market neutral, event driven, fixed-income arbitrage, global macro, long/short equity, managed futures, multistrategy, and funds of funds. This constitutes a sample of 1,610 funds. Factor exposures of each strategy are measured by regressing returns onto six factors. These factors are the U.S. Dollar Index, the Lehman Corporate AA Intermediate Bond Index, the spread between the Lehman Corporate BAA Bond Index and the Lehman Treasury Index, the S&P 500, the Goldman Sachs Commodity Index (GSCI), and the first difference of the end-of-month value of the Chicago Board Options Exchange (CBOE) Volatility Index (VIX). The authors select these factors because they can be proxied by liquid instruments, such as forwards or futures contracts. The factor exposures are calculated from February 1986 to September 2005.

Hasanhodzic and Lo implement a 24-month rolling-window approach, which involves dynamic rebalancing of the portfolio. They report highly contrasting results. Equal-weighted portfolios of rolling-window clones underperform equal-weighted portfolios of their respective funds in six strategies, outperform them in four, and have comparable returns in one. Focusing on volatility, equal-weighted portfolios of fixed-weight clones generate higher volatility than equal-weighted portfolios of their respective funds in eight strategies, and similar volatility in three. Equal-weighted portfolios of rolling-window clones display higher volatility than equal-weighted portfolios of their respective funds in nine strategies, and similar volatility in two. The replication of the correlation with market indices is of particular interest, because it can be seen as an indication of the diversification power of hedge funds. The authors analyze the replication of the correlations with 28 market indices, from February 1986 to September 2005. The results, using rolling-window linear clones, indicate that returns earned on the clone and an equally weighted portfolio of hedge funds have similar signs in 71% to 96% of cases and absolute difference in correlation ranging from 9% to 19%. Again, the replication is not perfect, and it introduces significant deformation in the diversification properties.

Overall, a review of the studies that attempt to replicate hedge fund return distributions through a factor replication approach leads to the conclusion that replication accuracy is not satisfying. In-sample R^2 is not sufficiently high to indicate satisfactory in-sample fit, while out-of-sample results suggest that hedge fund return replication is approximate at best.

The factor models discussed so far represent a small sample of research performed to explain hedge fund returns using linear relationships between hedge fund returns and some risk factors. Amenc et al. (2010) use a **nonlinear approach to replication**. The idea behind this approach is that hedge fund managers have the skill to time the market, and therefore will increase their portfolios' exposure to a factor if the return from that factor is expected to be positive, and decrease exposure when factor returns are expected to be negative. The linear factor model of Equation 33.2 can be adjusted in the following manner:

$$\tilde{R}_{t,HF} - r = \beta_1 \times \left(\tilde{F}_{1t} - r\right) + \beta_2 \times \left(\tilde{F}_{2t} - r\right) + \cdots + \beta_K \times \max\left(0, \tilde{F}_{Kt} - r\right) + \tilde{\varepsilon}$$

$$(33.3)$$

It can be seen that, for the last factor, it is assumed the hedge fund will have an exposure only if factor K is expected to have a positive excess return. Amenc et al. estimate Equation 33.3, along with two other approaches.[8] They report that, while the nonlinear models produce a better in-sample fit, their out-of-sample performance is not that different from the linear model discussed in Equation 33.2. The authors attempt to fine-tune their models by selecting factors that are most relevant to each strategy. This results in relatively small improvements in the performances of the models. They conclude that none of the methodologies generate fully satisfactory results, and that, in fact, the factor approach to hedge fund replication faces a series of formidable challenges. These challenges notably include the difficulty in identifying the right factors, as well as the difficulty in replicating, in a robust manner, the time-varying exposures of hedge fund managers with respect to these factors.

33.7 PAYOFF-DISTRIBUTION APPROACH

The payoff-distribution approach was developed by Amin and Kat (2003), based on initial theoretical work done by Dybvig (1988) that was later applied by Robinson (1998). The objective of this methodology is far less ambitious than the one pursued in the factor-based approach to hedge fund replication. While the factor-based approach aims to produce a portfolio whose per-period returns match those of the underlying benchmark, the **payoff-distribution approach** aims to produce a return distribution that matches that of the benchmark. The following simple numerical example can highlight the difference.

Exhibit 33.3 displays the monthly returns on a hypothetical hedge fund and the returns on two replicators: a factor-based replicator and a payoff-distribution replicator. Exhibit 33.4 displays some basic statistics related to the performance of these three investment products. The factor-based replicator does a reasonable job of tracking the performance of the hedge fund on a monthly basis. In fact, the correlation between the two is about 80%. However, this replicator cannot produce the same mean return, standard deviation, skewness, and kurtosis as the hedge fund. On the other hand, the payoff-distribution replicator exactly matches the higher moments of the distribution of the hedge fund's return, but does a poor job of tracking the monthly returns on the hedge fund. It can be seen that its monthly return has almost no correlation to the monthly return on the hedge fund. Another important point is that the payoff distribution cannot, and does not try to, match the mean return on the hedge fund. There are two reasons for this.

First, while higher moments (e.g., standard deviation, skewness, kurtosis) of the distribution of most investments tend to be rather stable, the first moment (e.g., mean) is highly unstable and unpredictable. Thus, it is difficult to create a portfolio that would match the mean return of the benchmark with high probability. The other reason is related to the methodology employed to create the clone. The clone is created using a dynamic strategy similar to the one employed to delta hedge an options position. When delta hedging is used to replicate an option, one of the assets employed to create the portfolio is an underlying asset of the option. Thus, one is assured that the mean return on the replicator and the option will be very close. In

---

[8] The other two approaches are Kalman filtering and Markov regime switching.

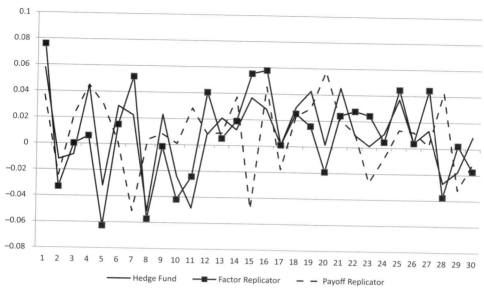

EXHIBIT 33.3 Hypothetical Returns on a Hedge Fund and Two Different Replicators
Source: Authors' calculations.

the case of hedge fund replication, one has to use an asset other than the underlying hedge fund to replicate the hedge fund. Thus, one is not assured that the mean returns would match. In fact, the higher moments of a hedge fund's return distribution may not be matched if they are highly unstable for the underlying assets used to replicate the hedge fund.

The payoff-distribution approach attempts to replicate the payoff distribution of the hedge fund, rather than to match its monthly return as closely as possible. That is, the factor-based and payoff distribution–based approaches use the term *replication* in different forms.

First, the return on the hedge fund and return on the clone are said to be equal, in terms of probability, if their values agree with probability 1; in other words, when for all time periods that $\Pr(R_{t,HF} = R_{t,Clone}) = 1$. This is precisely what the factor-based approach attempts to achieve; the actual results, as was discussed previously, have had limited success.

EXHIBIT 33.4 Statistics of Hypothetical Hedge Fund and Two Replicators

	Hedge Fund	Factor Replicator	Payoff Replicator
Mean	0.90%	0.84%	0.85%
Standard deviation	2.76%	3.46%	2.75%
Skewness	−0.47	−0.219	−0.48
Kurtosis	−0.22	−0.36	−0.22
Correlation vs. hedge fund	100.0%	78.6%	7.4%

Source: Authors' calculations.

Second, the return on the hedge fund and the return on the clone are said to be equal in distribution if their probability distributions are identical; in other words, when for all values of x that $\Pr(R_{HF} < x) = \Pr(R_{Clone} < x)$. As is obvious from the previous definitions, while equality in probability almost surely implies equality in distribution, the converse is not true. Hence, equality in probability almost surely appears as a stronger, more ambitious, definition of replication.

The payoff-distribution approach was initially used to measure the performance of hedge fund managers; that is, to create a benchmark. The underlying philosophy of this approach is that when buying fund participation, an investor acquires a claim to a certain payoff distribution. If one is able to replicate the payoff distribution under consideration through a particular trading strategy, the cost of the replicating strategy could be compared to that of a direct investment in the hedge fund. This, in turn, could be used in assessing whether the manager is really adding value.

The principle of payoff replication is very simple, and is inspired from derivative pricing theory. It is based on the following steps.[9] First, one needs to collect return data on the fund to be replicated and on the reserve asset (i.e., the asset that will be used to replicate the hedge fund). Second, the data are analyzed to infer the distribution of the fund return, which is referred to as the desired distribution. Third, the same process is applied to the return on the reserve asset to obtain its probability distribution, referred to as the building block distribution. Fourth, the cheapest payoff function that can turn the building block distribution into the desired distribution is determined. Finally, the required allocations to the reserve asset and cash that would create the payoff function must be derived.

Here, the process employed to create the payoff function is outlined. The payoff function, which is denoted by $G(R_r)$, maps the return of the reserve assets, R_r, onto a hedge fund return. Once this function is determined, the cost of creating the portfolio and deriving the dynamic trading strategy that would create the desired payoff distribution needs to be estimated. This step is rather similar to the procedure recommended by Merton (1973) for the hedging and pricing of equity options.

There is one key difference between the process used to obtain the payoff function, $G(R_r)$, and the standard option pricing. In the case of hedge fund replication, the payoff function is created synthetically, so as to match the hedge fund return distribution, as opposed to being exogenously given, as in the case of a standard option pricing problem.

The process for determining $G(R_r)$ is as follows. Suppose the cumulative probability distribution of the hedge return is given by $F_{HF}(x)$, which gives the probability that the hedge fund could produce a return less than x. That is,

$$\Pr(R_{HF} < x) = F_{HF}(x)$$

Next, find the value of x, where the probability of earning less than x is 10%; that is, find the value of x that satisfies the expression $F_{HF}(x) = 10\%$. This requires the inverse of the function $F_{HF}(x)$. If the inverse of $F_{HF}(x)$ is denoted by H, then $H(10\%) = x$.

---

[9] Kat and Palaro (2006).

Example: Suppose the distribution of the hedge fund return is uniform between a and b. This means that the hedge fund return can take any value between a and b with equal probability. In this case, the cumulative distribution of hedge fund returns will be:

$$F(x) = \frac{x-a}{b-a} \qquad \text{For } a \leq x \leq b$$

The inverse of this function will be:

$$H(y) = a + y(b-a)$$

In general, if $F_{HF}(x) = y$, then $H(y) = x$.

Next, let $F_R(R_r)$ denote the cumulative distribution of the reserve asset. That is,

$$\Pr(R_r < x) = F_R(x)$$

Given these definitions, the payoff function is now calculated:

$$G(x) = H(F_R(x))$$

What has been created is a function that uses the return on the reserve asset to produce a payoff distribution that would closely follow the payoff distribution of the hedge fund.

The next step is determined by how much it costs to match the desired distribution and how to manage the reserve asset through time. The process in this step is rather similar to a classical option pricing model. In the present case, the reserve asset could be a portfolio consisting of a liquid risky asset (e.g., S&P 500 index) and a safe asset, which are rebalanced frequently to produce the desired payoff distribution.

One of the early criticisms of the payoff-distribution approach was that it ignored a primary reason for investing in hedge funds, namely, the diversification benefits. Thus, it is not enough to match the return distribution of a hedge fund. It is equally important to match its correlations to other assets as well. Kat and Palaro (2006a, 2006b) tackled this problem. They proposed a procedure that, in theory, would create a payoff function that not only matches the distribution of a hedge fund's return, but also its correlation to the investor's current portfolio.

33.7.1 Empirical Evidence on Payoff Distribution

Amenc et al. (2008) performed straightforward tests of the payoff-distribution approach. They attempted to replicate the payoff distributions of 13 hedge fund indices, from January 1997 to December 2006. For reserve assets, they used the nearby futures contract on the S&P 500 index and on the Eurodollar over the same period.

The out-of-sample period starts in January 1999 (i.e., they used the first two years of data to calibrate the model). To check the quality of their replication process, they employed various tests. The first one consisted of analyzing the difference between the first four moments of the observed and replicated returns. The results differed depending on the strategy. First, the average returns on the clones were, in most cases, very different from that of the index to be replicated. This was to be expected, since the methodology does not aim to replicate the first moment (i.e., mean return) of the hedge fund return distribution. Interestingly, however, the average return obtained for the clone was always lower than that of the index in the out-of-sample period. This result suggests that extreme caution should be used in choosing the reserve asset, and that the performance results of the replicating strategy are not robust with respect to the choice of the risky asset involved and the sample period considered.

Second, the volatility values obtained for the clones were relatively close to those obtained for the hedge fund indices. In addition, the authors reported mixed results regarding the equalities of estimated skewness and kurtosis values for the clones and those of the observed returns on the hedge fund indices. Going beyond individual moments, they also tested the equality of the entire distributions. The best replication process was obtained for the short-selling index, and the worst was obtained with the equity market neutral index. The payoff-distribution approach was able to match the distribution in less than half of the cases.

These results imply that, even if one is willing to ignore the differences in mean returns, not all hedge fund distributions can be matched with relative satisfaction. Finally, the authors reported the value of the Sharpe ratio and the historical 95% value at risk (VaR). In all cases, the Sharpe ratio was higher for the observed indices, which was to be expected, given their higher mean returns. The VaR measure, by contrast, was fairly similar for the clones and the indices.

Another important point is that the good results obtained for at least some hedge fund strategies were displayed only when a long out-of-sample period was used. In some cases, it took close to eight years to obtain payoff distributions that matched the return distribution of the hedge fund indices. For an investor with more limited patience, the payoff-distribution approach to hedge fund replication can lead to disappointment. These results suggest that the payoff-distribution method produces satisfying results only if the investor is willing to wait a long period before assessing the quality of the replication. Finally, the authors show that the replicating portfolio performs poorly in terms of matching the correlation of hedge fund indices with other assets.

33.8 BOTTOM-UP OR ALGORITHMIC APPROACH

The **bottom-up or algorithmic approach** is substantially different from the previous two, as it is suitable only for well-defined strategies that involve systematic trading and exclude manager discretion as a significant source of return. Examples of relatively well-defined strategies are merger arbitrage, convertible arbitrage, trend-following, and a subset of equity long/short (i.e., momentum and value-growth).

The approach does not rely on a predefined benchmark; it involves implementing a simple version of the actual trading strategy employed by funds that follow the particular strategy. For instance, the most basic type of merger arbitrage strategy involves taking long positions in target firms and short positions in acquiring firms. Therefore, merger arbitrage is a strategy that can be implemented by buying a portion of all announced mergers and shorting the acquiring firms. The strategy would perform well if a large number of the announced mergers included in the portfolio are completed.

The simple version of the convertible arbitrage strategy involves purchasing a portfolio of convertible bonds and then hedging out the equity risk of the convertible bond portfolio by using short positions in the underlying equity. In addition, the strategy can be expanded further by using interest rate futures to hedge out the interest rate risk of the convertible bond portfolio. The strategy will perform well if the implied volatility of the options embedded in the convertible bonds is less than realized volatilities on a consistent basis.

There is substantial academic and industry research on the profitability of momentum and trend-following strategies, which are discussed in Chapters 30 and 31. A simple version of a momentum strategy involves a long position in a portfolio of stocks, commodities, or currencies that have outperformed over the previous periods, and a short position in a portfolio of the stocks, commodities, or currencies that have underperformed over the previous periods. This strategy has been shown to produce a positive rate of return in the long run.[10] Similar to the momentum strategy, the value-growth strategy involves taking a long position in a portfolio of value stocks and a short position in a portfolio of growth stocks. Value stocks are typically defined as those stocks with low price-to-earnings ratios and high book-value-to-market-value ratios. Similarly, growth stocks are defined as those stocks with high price-to-earnings ratios and low book-value-to-market-value ratios.

Systematic algorithmic trading strategies can typically be implemented in a bottom-up approach, to the degree that a systematic trading process representing the fund strategy can be developed and monitored. The bottom-up approach may not offer some of the benefits of replication, like liquidity and flexibility, since they essentially hold some of the same securities as the hedge funds that are being replicated. In times of market distress, as evidenced during the most recent financial crisis of 2007 and 2008, bottom-up replication managers face significant difficulty meeting redemption requests, which adversely affect the value of their funds. However, if liquidity risk and event risk are significant contributors to the alpha of hedge fund strategies, investing in hedge funds or bottom-up replication products may be the only way to access this portion of returns.

33.9 CONCLUSION

Hedge fund replication products are based on three different approaches: factor-based, payoff distribution, and algorithmic. The factor-based approach attempts to take advantage of the fact that beta exposures of hedge funds have increased in recent years, and therefore a larger portion of their returns can be explained by traditional sources of risk and return. In addition, in recent years, financial innovations have given investors expanded access to alternative sources of return. Consequently, carefully constructed portfolios of liquid securities may be able to capture a large portion of the returns earned by a portfolio of hedge funds. The payoff-distribution approach attempts to match the return properties of a hedge fund by implementing dynamic

---

[10] Asness, Moskowitz, and Pedersen (2009).

EXHIBIT 33.5 Overview of Replication Products

Promotor	Product	Launch Date	Replication Target	Methodology
AlphaSwiss Aquila Capital	AlphaSwiss Alternative Beta Fund AC Spectrum Fund	2005 2008	Composite Newedge CTA Index	Algorithmic Payoff Distribution
Arrow Funds	Arrow Alternative Solutions Fund	2007	Composite (hedged equity + fixed income arbitrage + managed futures)	Factor-based + algorithmic
BlueWhite Alternative Investments	BlueWhite Alternative Beta Fund	2007	Portfolio of thousands of hedge funds	Factor-based
Credit Suisse	Liquid Alternative Beta Index (Event Driven, Equity Long/Short, Managed Futures, Merger Arbitrage)	2010	Directional equity, relative value arbitrage, and tactical trading	Factor-based + algorithmic
Desjardins Global Asset Management	DGAM-Synthetic Alternative Investment Fund	2007	Hedge fund index	Payoff Distribution
Deutsche Bank Fulcrum Asset Management	DB Absolute Return Beta Index Fulcrum Alternative Beta Plus	2007 2007	HFRI Fund of Funds Composite Index Composite	Algorithmic Algorithmic
Goldman Sachs IceCapital Fund Management Company	Goldman Sachs Absolute Return Tracker IceCapital Alternative Beta	2006 2007	Portfolio of thousands of hedge funds Composite	Factor-based Factor-based
IndexIQ	HedgeIQ Composite HedgeIQ Long Short HedgeIQ Market Neutral HedgeIQ Fixed Income Arbitrage HedgeIQ Global Macro HedgeIQ Multi Strategy HedgeIQ Emerging Market	2007	CS/Tremont Investable Hedge Fund Index CS/Tremont Investable Long Short Index CS/Tremont Investable Market Neutral Index CS/Tremont Inv. Fixed Income Arbitrage Index CS/Tremont Investable Global Macro Index CS/Tremont Investable Multi Strategy Index CS/Tremont Investable Emerging Market Index	Factor-based + algorithmic

Company	Product	Year	Index	Type
Innocap	Salto MSCI Hedge Fund Composite Synthetic Tracker	2007	MSCI Hedge Fund Composite Index	Factor-based
JPMorgan	JPMorgan Alternative Beta Index	2007	HFRI Fund of Funds Composite Index	Factor-based
Morgan Stanley	Altera	2007	MSCI hedge fund indices	Factor-based + algorithmic
Merrill Lynch	Merrill Lynch Factor Index	2006	HFRI Fund Weighted Composite Index	Factor-based
Partners Group	Partners Group Alternative Beta Strategies	2004	CTA, equity hedge, equity market neutral, fixed-income arbitrage, volatility arbitrage, event driven, global macro, emerging markets	Factor-based + algorithmic
Rydex Investments	Absolute Return Strategies Fund	2005	Composite	Algorithmic
Rydex Investments	Hedged Equity Fund	2005	Long/short equity	Algorithmic
SGAM Alternative Investments	T-Rex	2007	HFRI Fund Weighted Composite Index	Factor-based
State Street Global Advisors	Hedge Fund Beta Strategy	2007	HFRI Fund of Funds Composite Index	Factor-based
Stonebrook Capital Management	Stonebrook Alternative Beta Fund	2007	HFRI Fund of Funds Composite Index	Factor-based

Source: Amenc et al. (2008) and authors' calculations.

trading strategies similar to those employed in a traditional option-replication strategy. Finally, the algorithmic approach attempts to implement a simple and transparent version of a well-defined hedge fund strategy. For example, a simple version of the merger arbitrage strategy would require an investor to take a long position in a portfolio of target companies and a short position in a portfolio of the acquiring companies. Exhibit 33.5 displays some basic information about a number of the replication products introduced since 2005.

CHAPTER 34

Convertible Arbitrage

34.1 EVOLUTION OF THE CONVERTIBLE ARBITRAGE STRATEGY

Convertible arbitrage is a classic arbitrage strategy that attempts to exploit inefficiencies in the pricing of convertible bonds relative to their underlying stocks. Initially, convertible arbitrage started as a niche business for dedicated proprietary trading desks in large investment banks. Convertible arbitrageurs typically bought cheap convertible bonds and hedged their market risk by selling short the underlying stocks. Subsequently, thanks to the development of sophisticated option pricing models and the availability of credit derivatives, the strategy expanded to include volatility and credit trading elements. As of year-end 2011, Hedge Fund Research (HFR) reports that dedicated convertible arbitrage funds represent less than 3% of the assets managed by hedge funds. Though quite small in comparison to, say, equity long/short, convertible arbitrage shares important features common to a variety of hedge fund strategies and serves as a valuable example.

In its simplest form, the convertible arbitrage strategy involves purchasing convertible bonds and hedging away various risks associated with the instrument, including equity risk, credit risk, and interest rate risk. The ultimate objective is to isolate underpriced options embedded in convertible bonds. Naturally, the question arises as to why corporations should issue underpriced securities. The answer is simple. In addition to raising capital through the issuance of debt, corporations have the potential to raise capital through the issuance of equity. When a corporation issues convertible bonds, convertible arbitrage managers will short the underlying stock, effectively increasing the supply of shares. If the firm performs well and the convertibles expire in-the-money, the increase in the number of shares will become permanent as the convertibles are exchanged for shares. In this scenario, the firm has effectively raised capital by issuing new equity without incurring the administrative costs associated with a straight equity issue. For firms that typically issue convertible bonds, raising capital through straight bonds or equity may prove to be too expensive. For example, the straight bonds might have to carry a very high coupon, which would negatively affect the cash flow of the firm. Though raising capital through equity alone may not have the same negative cash flow impact, the size of the issue might have to be so large that it would dilute the ownership of current shareholders. In short, convertible arbitrage managers provide a service to issuing corporations and get paid for this service. This provides a partial economic explanation for the potential source of alpha found within the convertible arbitrage strategy.

This raises yet another question: Why wouldn't other investors step in to purchase these underpriced securities? The answer lies in the very nature of convertible bonds. They are neither stocks nor bonds but a hybrid of the two. As such, many traditional money managers do not have a natural place in their portfolio for them. Furthermore, taking advantage of the mispricing of convertible securities requires managers to hedge a number of risks. This requires special skills, which traditional money managers may not possess. In addition, the investment strategy may not fall within the mandate of many traditional investment managers.

34.2 TERMINOLOGY

Convertible bonds give holders the right to exchange the bonds for common shares of the issuer at a stated ratio during a particular period. They are complex securities that blend the characteristics found in equity, debt, and option securities. As a result, traders and arbitrageurs have developed specialized terminology to describe various aspects of the marketplace. For the sake of simplicity, assume it is now January 1, 2012, and that a hypothetical convertible bond is denoted as XYZ convertible 2% 2016. Exhibit 34.1 describes the various parameters that characterize this convertible bond.

EXHIBIT 34.1 Summary of the Terms Offered by the XYZ Convertible 2% 2016 Bond

Fixed-Income Features

Issuer	XYZ Company Inc.
Rating	BBB
Coupon	$C = 2\%$ (annual)
Issue date	January 1, 2012 (today)
First coupon date	December 31, 2012 (in one year)
Accrued interest	0
Maturity	December 31, 2016 (in $T = 5$ years)
Nominal value	$1,000
Risk-free rate	$R_f = 4\%$ per year
Issuer credit spread	$CS = 400$ basis points (bps) above the risk-free rate

Equity Features

Issuer	XYZ Company Inc.
Stock price	$S_0 = \$100$ per share
Stock price change volatility	$\sigma = 30\%$ per year
Stock dividend	None

Conversion Features

Conversion ratio	$CR = 8$
Conversion price	$125.00
Call protection	None

Market Valuation

Convertible market price	90 (i.e., 90% of face value)
Parity	80 (i.e., 80% of face value)
Conversion premium	12.50%

The fixed-income features of the convertible bond are as follows:

- The *issuer* is the XYZ Company Inc., a company with a BBB *rating*.
- The convertible bond has a five-year *time to maturity*.
- The convertible bond pays a 2% *annual coupon*, with the first coupon paid in exactly one year.
- There is no *accrued interest*; the bond has just been issued.
- The *nominal* or *par value* of each bond is $1,000. This is the amount for which each bond can be redeemed at maturity.[1]

The convertible bond can be converted into shares of the stock of the issuer. These shares have the following characteristics:

- The issuer is the XYZ Company Inc., the same issuer as for the convertible bond.
- The stock price is currently $100 per share.
- The volatility of the stock price is 30% per year.
- The stock pays no dividend.

The terms of the conversion are fixed in the convertible bond's indenture as follows:

- The **conversion ratio** denotes the number of shares obtained if one converts $1,000 of the face value of the bond. In this example, each bond with a $1,000 face value can be converted into eight ordinary shares. The conversion ratio is therefore 8. This number usually remains fixed through the life of the instrument unless stock splits, special dividends, or other dilutive events occur.
- The **conversion price** denotes the price at which shares are indirectly purchased via the convertible security. It is equal to the par value of the convertible security divided by the conversion ratio, or $1,000/8 = $125.
- **Call protections** grant the issuer the right to call back the convertible bond before its stated maturity. This can be either a *hard call*, in which the issuer can call the bond at a prefixed price regardless of any other circumstances,[2] or a *soft call*, in which the issuer can call the bond only if the equity price has risen significantly above the strike price or some other hurdle rate. In this example, for the sake of simplicity, it is assumed that there is no call protection.

The valuation parameters of the convertible bond are observable in the market as follows:

- The **convertible price** denotes the quoted price of the convertible bond, which is usually expressed as a percentage of the nominal value (consistent with the traditional bond market). In this example, the convertible is quoted at 90% of its face value.

---

[1] The nominal value of convertible bonds is often 1,000 euros in the euro-convertible bond market and ¥1,000,000 in the Japanese domestic and euro-yen markets.

[2] Typically, the issuer must give public notice of its intention to redeem a convertible bond prior to maturity, and bondholders are given a limited period of time to decide whether to convert their convertible bonds into shares.

- **Parity** is the total market value of the shares into which the bond can be converted. In this example, it is calculated as 8 shares per bond × $100 per share = $800. Parity is normally quoted as a percentage of the par amount of the bond; that is, $800/$1,000 = 80%, or simply 80. Note that for a convertible bond to be **in-the-money**, its parity must be higher than 100.
- The **conversion premium** is the difference between the convertible bond price and parity, expressed as a percentage of parity. In this example, the conversion premium is (90 − 80)/80 = 12.5%. The premium expresses how much more an investor has to pay to control the same number of shares via a convertible. This premium also gives an indication of how a convertible should perform in relation to the underlying shares. All else being equal, convertibles with very low premiums will be much more sensitive to movements in the underlying share price (i.e., parity) than convertibles with higher premiums.

In addition to these standard features, convertible bonds may have more complex characteristics, some of which are described here:

- Zero coupon convertible bonds are typically issued at a deep discount to par value and are redeemable at par. The most famous examples of such bonds are liquid yield option notes (LYONs), which are both callable (redeemable prior to maturity by the issuer) and puttable (redeemable prior to maturity by investors).
- Mandatory conversion securities (MCSs) are convertibles whose conversion is mandatory at some stage. They tend to trade and behave like shares, although some may have additional features; for example, a preferred equity redemption cumulative stock (PERCS) is a mandatory preferred convertible with a preset cap level, above which the conversion ratio is adjusted to keep the total return payoff constant (i.e., as the underlying stock price rises, the PERCS becomes convertible into fewer and fewer underlying shares).
- Convertible preferred shares are preferred stocks that include an option for their holder to convert them into a fixed number of common shares, usually following a predetermined time span.

In the following example, these complex features are largely ignored, with the focus on the arbitrage of plain-vanilla convertible bonds.

34.3 VALUATION OF CONVERTIBLE SECURITIES

To identify convertible bond arbitrage opportunities, one must be able to calculate the fair value of a convertible bond.

34.3.1 Component Approach

The component approach is the most intuitive valuation approach for simple convertible bonds. It essentially divides the convertible bond into a straight bond component and a call option:

Convertible bond = Straight bond + Call option on the underlying stock

EXHIBIT 34.2 Expected Cash Flow (CF) Decomposition for a Convertible Bond

Time (Years)	0	1	2	3	4	5
Cash flows		$20	$20	$20	$20	$1,020.00
PV(CF) @ 8%		$18.52	$17.15	$15.88	$14.70	$ 694.19
Total PV	$760.44					

The straight bond component refers to the pure fixed-income portion of the convertible bond. It ignores the conversion possibility, and its value is easily obtained by discounting all future expected cash flows (coupons and final repayment) at an appropriate discount rate (the risk-free rate plus a credit spread). The discount rate of 8% is composed of a 4% risk-free rate added to the credit spread of 4%. Exhibit 34.2 illustrates the computation using a discount rate of 8% to calculate the total present value (PV) of the XYZ convertible bond as $760.44. Notice that the coupon rate of interest, 2%, is far below the discount rate of 8%. Issuing convertible bonds rather than straight debt reduces the current-year interest expense of the firm, as investors are willing to earn a lower coupon rate of interest in exchange for the value provided through the embedded equity call option.

This pure bond price is, in a sense, the minimum value of a convertible bond. It is unaffected by the stock price level unless the latter falls so much that the issuer's ability to face its debt obligations is called into question.

The option component considers the conversion features of the convertible bond only. It is essentially an option to buy a certain quantity (the conversion ratio) of shares of stock by paying the value of the convertible bond. Option prices are frequently calculated using the Black-Scholes formula, which is presented in the appendix to this chapter.[3] The theoretical price for the option component of the XYZ bond is $202.23. The theoretical price of the convertible bond is obtained by summing the theoretical prices of its components: $760.44 + $202.23 = $962.67, or 96.27% of its face value.

The major drawbacks of the outlined component approach are threefold: (1) it uses the Black-Scholes model, which is valid only for European options and cannot deal with early termination (call and put) clauses, (2) it does not take the credit risk of the issuer into consideration, and (3) it does not account for special conditions and contractual covenants (e.g., callability).

34.3.2 Binomial Model

In another approach to price convertible bonds, the possible evolution of the underlying stock price is modeled. The binomial tree approach introduced by Cox, Ross, and Rubinstein (1979) is widely used in practice because it can deal with a wide range of contractual specifications while still remaining relatively simple.

---

[3] Note that since the price of the bond is not constant, the Black-Scholes model provides a very crude approximation for the price of the convertible bond. As seen in the following section, the preferred approach is to use a binomial model.

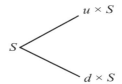

EXHIBIT 34.3
Possible Stock Price
Movements (One
Period)

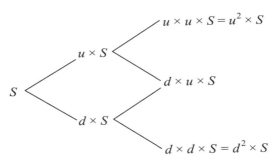

EXHIBIT 34.4   Possible Stock Price Movements
(Two Periods)

Let us assume that the stock price process follows a binomial random walk. That is, over the next period, the stock price can either go up by a multiplicative factor u or go down by a multiplicative factor d, where $u > d$ (see Exhibit 34.3).

This process can be repeated as many times as needed and is made manageable by its recombining prices. For instance, over two periods, the tree in Exhibit 34.4 is obtained, representing the evolution of discrete possible underlying stock prices into three ending prices.

The parameters u and d are proportional to the volatility of the underlying asset and must be specified. As suggested by Cox, Ross, and Rubinstein (1979), set $u = \exp(\sigma\sqrt{t})$, where t is the length of one period in the tree, σ is the volatility of the stock returns and $d = 1/u$. This ensures that the resulting expected volatility of percentage changes in the stock price is σ.

Returning to analyze the XYZ convertible bond, the life of the tree is set equal to the life of the convertible bond (five years). For the sake of simplicity, consider a tree made of $N = 5$ periods of $t = 1$ year, which implies that the convertible bond pays its coupon each period.[4] The size of the up move is $u = \exp(0.30) = 1.3499$, while the down move is calculated as $d = 1/u = 0.7408$. The resulting stock price tree is given in Exhibit 34.5.

---

[4] In practice, a five-year time to maturity would need to be divided into several hundred periods to obtain an accurate bond price.

EXHIBIT 34.5   Binomial Tree for the Stock Price

$t = 0$	$t = 1Y$	$t = 2Y$	$t = 3Y$	$t = 4Y$	$t = 5Y$
					448.17
				332.01	
			245.96		245.96
		182.21		182.21	
	134.99		134.99		134.99
100.00		100.00		100.00	
	74.08		74.08		74.08
		54.88		54.88	
			40.66		40.66
				30.12	
					22.31

As suggested by Cox, Ross, and Rubinstein (1979), given the riskless interest rate, R_f, this binomial tree can be used to extract the **risk-neutral probability** of the stock price increasing (p) or decreasing $(1 - p)$. This probability is as follows:[5]

$$p = [\exp(R_f) - d]/[u - d] = 0.4926$$

and

$$1 - p = 0.5074$$

The conversion value of the convertible bond is given by the stock price times the conversion ratio; thus, the associated parity tree can be easily constructed, as shown in Exhibit 34.6.

At time $t = 5$ years, the pure bond price of the convertible bond is its repayment value ($1,000) plus the last coupon ($20). Conversion should only occur if the conversion value is higher than $1,020. It is easy to verify that this is the case when the final stock price is $448.17, $245.96, or $134.99 (i.e., for the top three end nodes in Exhibit 34.5). For the bottom three end nodes, no conversion should occur. Therefore, at time $t = 5Y$, there is a 100% probability of converting for the top three nodes, and a 0% probability for the bottom three nodes.

For each node before time $t = 5Y$, the conversion probability can be calculated using backward induction (right to left) and the risk-neutral probability p. This probability is as follows:

$$\text{Prob.Conv.} = p \times \text{Prob.Conv.}_{up} + (1 - p) \times \text{Prob.Conv.}_{down}$$

where Prob.Conv.$_{up}$ and Prob.Conv.$_{down}$ are the probabilities of converting in the next up node and down node, respectively. The resulting conversion probability tree is given in Exhibit 34.7.

---

[5] Note that R_f (4%) is used for r here, not $r = \ln (1 + R_f)$, as in the Black-Scholes example.

EXHIBIT 34.6   Binomial Tree for the Parity

$t = 0$	$t = 1Y$	$t = 2Y$	$t = 3Y$	$t = 4Y$	$t = 5Y$
					358.54
				265.61	
			196.77		196.77
		145.77		145.77	
	107.99		107.99		107.99
80.00		80.00		80.00	
	59.27		59.27		59.27
		43.90		43.90	
			32.53		32.53
				24.10	
					17.85

Let us now find the theoretical value of the convertible bond. The only remaining complication is the choice of the discount rate used in conjunction with the tree. Fortunately, the conversion probability at each node can be used to determine the relevant discount rate. If conversion will occur with 100% probability, the discount rate should be the risk-free interest rate. But if the conversion is highly unlikely, the discount rate should reflect the credit spread (CS) of the issuer. In general, the discount rate is calculated as follows:

$$\text{Discount rate} = [\text{Prob.Conv.} \times (1 + R_f)] + [(1 - \text{Prob.Conv.}) \times (1 + R_f + CS)] - 1$$

The resulting credit-adjusted discount rate tree is given in Exhibit 34.8.

As expected, the credit-adjusted discount rate increases as the stock price decreases. Next, proceed with the calculation of the theoretical value for the convertible bond using backward induction. The value of the convertible bond at expiration is already known. At any given node prior to expiration, the convertible bond value

EXHIBIT 34.7   Binomial Tree for the Conversion Probability

$t = 0$	$t = 1Y$	$t = 2Y$	$t = 3Y$	$t = 4Y$	$t = 5Y$
					100%
				100%	
			100%		100%
		86.93%		100%	
	67.63%		74.25%		100%
48.61%		48.88%		49.26%	
	30.14%		24.26%		0%
		11.95%		0%	
			0%		0%
				0%	
					0%

EXHIBIT 34.8 Binomial Tree for the Credit-Adjusted Discount Rate

$t = 0$	$t = 1Y$	$t = 2Y$	$t = 3Y$	$t = 4Y$	$t = 5Y$
					4.00%
				4.00%	
			4.00%		4.00%
		4.52%		4.00%	
	5.29%		5.03%		4.00%
6.06%		6.04%		6.03%	
	6.79%		7.03%		8.00%
		7.52%		8.00%	
			8.00%		8.00%
				8.00%	
					8.00%

is equal to the expected convertible bond value of the next two nodes discounted at the credit-adjusted discount rate of the current node, plus the coupon:

$$\text{Convert.Value} = \frac{[p \times \text{Convert.Value}_{up} + (1 - p) \times \text{Convert.Value}_{down}] + \text{Coupon}}{1 + \text{Discount rate}}$$

The tree for the convertible bond value is shown in Exhibit 34.9.

According to the basic binomial tree approach, the theoretical value of the convertible bond is 103.36% of its face value. Of course, one could argue that the fictitious XYZ bond was extremely simple. In reality, it is relatively easy to modify the tree to incorporate specific features and terms, such as put and call clauses, reset features, and varying interest rates and credit spreads.

EXHIBIT 34.9 Binomial Tree for the Convertible Bond Value

$t = 0$	$t = 1Y$	$t = 2Y$	$t = 3Y$	$t = 4Y$	$t = 5Y$
					358.54
				267.82	
			201.00		196.77
		155.05		147.88	
	124.11		120.14		107.99
103.36		102.88		100.98	
	91.38		94.20		102.00
		88.24		96.44	
			91.30		102.00
				96.44	
					102.00

34.3.3   Convertible Bond Behavior at Various Stock Price Levels

The overall profile of a convertible bond can be obtained by calculating the theoretical prices of its components for various levels of the stock price.

As illustrated in Exhibit 34.10, there are four possible states for a convertible bond:

1. **Junk** or **distressed** (area 1) occurs when the stock price is so low that it indicates substantial doubt about the issuer's ability to meet its debt obligations. The call option is worth zero, and the convertible trades like a distressed bond would. The parity is typically between 0% and 30% of the face value. The convertible is said to be **deep-out-of-the-money**.
2. **Busted** (area 2) occurs when the stock price is low enough that conversion is unlikely. The value of the call option is negligible, and the convertible bond trades essentially similar to a straight bond with no equity sensitivity. The parity is typically between 30% and 80% of the face value. Such convertibles are said to be **out-of-the-money**.
3. **Hybrid** (area 3) occurs when the stock price is high enough that the option to convert gains value. The parity is typically between 80% and 120% of the face value, and the convertible is said to be **at-the-money**.
4. **Equity proxy** (area 4) occurs when the stock price is extremely high, making conversion likely. The convertible trades more like a stock than a bond. Its equity sensitivity is high, while its fixed-income sensitivity is low. The parity is typically above 130% of the face value, and the convertible is said to be **deep-in-the-money**.

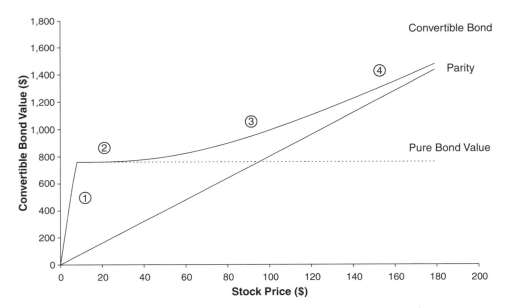

EXHIBIT 34.10   Behavior of a Convertible Bond at Various Stock Price Levels

It may be recalled that the price of a call option can be broken into two parts: the intrinsic value and the time value (i.e., the optionality value). The optionality value tends to be highest for at-the-money options. For this reason, convertible arbitrage managers generally prefer hybrid convertibles that exhibit both fixed-income and equity sensitivities. Hybrid convertibles tend to have greater profit potential because the optionality value of a convertible bond is highest when the embedded option is at-the-money.

34.4 THE GREEKS

The Greeks are measures that represent the sensitivities of convertible bonds in relation to a variety of factors. These measures got their name because the parameters are often denoted by Greek letters.

34.4.1 Delta and Modified Delta

Delta measures the sensitivity of the value of a derivative security (e.g., a convertible bond) to changes in its underlying asset (i.e., its stock price or parity level). Mathematically, it is the first-order partial derivative of the convertible bond value with respect to the underlying stock price. (Note that the following expression is strictly correct if the conversion ratio is 1. More precisely, delta measures the sensitivity of the bond to changes in its parity value.)

$$\text{Delta} = \Delta = \frac{\partial \text{Derivative price}}{\partial \text{Stock price}}$$

Since the underlying asset of a convertible bond is the stock price times the conversion ratio, the delta of a convertible is calculated using the sensitivity to parity. When using a binomial tree, the delta is also easily obtained by comparing the changes of the convertible value to the changes in parity in the next two nodes. For instance, if the trees in Exhibits 34.6 and 34.9 are used, the delta of the initial node is determined as follows:

$$\text{Delta} = (124.11 - 91.38)/(107.99 - 59.27) = 0.672$$

This means that a one-point movement in the convertible's parity level will generate a 0.672-point movement in the convertible bond value.[6] By repeating this procedure for each node prior to maturity, it is possible to build the delta tree shown in Exhibit 34.11.

Note that as one moves along the convertible price curve, the value of delta varies between 0 and 1, which are the two bounds for the delta of a call option. At-the-money options generally have deltas of approximately 0.50. Deep-in-the-money call options have deltas that approach 1.0, while out-of-the-money call options have

---

[6] Although delta (and gamma) are calculated in terms of changes in the parity level here, the numerical result would be similar if the earlier definition of delta (and gamma) were used as a function of the change in the stock price.

EXHIBIT 34.11 Binomial Tree for the Delta of the
Convertible Bond

$t = 0$	$t = 1Y$	$t = 2Y$	$t = 3Y$	$t = 4Y$	$t = 5Y$
					1.000
			1.000		
		0.911		1.000	
	0.793		0.713		
0.672		0.532		0.123	
	0.406		0.126		
		0.108		0.000	
			0.000		
				0.000	

deltas near 0.0. As the underlying stock price moves, the embedded option becomes further in- or out-of-the-money, changing the delta of the convertible bond.

Graphically, delta corresponds to the slope of the convertible bond price curve, as illustrated in Exhibit 34.12. A steeper slope indicates a higher sensitivity to the underlying stock price. When a convertible bond gets very deep-in-the-money, it begins to trade like the stock, moving almost dollar for dollar with the stock price (area 4, delta = 1). Meanwhile, out-of-the-money convertibles do not move much in absolute dollar terms (area 2, delta = 0), unless there are some serious bankruptcy concerns (area 1).

So far, it has been implicitly assumed that nothing else is changing, such as the volatility of the underlying stock, interest rates, or the passage of time. In reality, changes in any one of these quantities can affect the delta of the convertible bond, even if the price of the underlying stock remains the same. In fact, the more

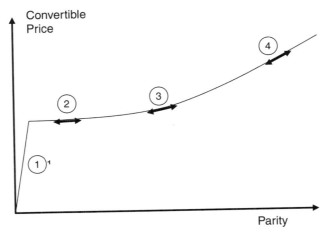

EXHIBIT 34.12 Delta as the Slope of a Tangent Drawn on the Convertible Price to Parity Curve

in-the-money or out-of-the-money the embedded option is, the less sensitive the delta is to changes in volatility or time to expiration.

Delta is a critical variable for convertible arbitrageurs, for it indicates how many shares of stock one should sell short to hedge the equity risk of a long position in the convertible bond.

It is worth noting that some arbitrageurs use a modified delta rather than the original delta. The modified delta is defined as follows:

$$\text{Modified delta} = \frac{1}{2}\left[\frac{\text{Change in convertible value}}{\text{Positive change in stock price}} + \frac{\text{Change in convertible value}}{\text{Negative change in stock price}}\right]$$

For instance, an arbitrageur could set a 5% increase in the stock price, determine the convertible price change, and obtain the first term of the modified delta. Repeating the process with a 5% decrease in the stock price would provide the second term. The average would be the modified delta, which is no longer a pure delta since it implicitly incorporates the impact of other Greeks in the calculation, in particular the gamma (discussed next).

34.4.2 Gamma

Delta only provides a linear approximation for the change in the convertible bond value. It is relatively accurate for small variations of the underlying stock price, but it fails to capture the nonlinearity of the convertible bond profile. To correct for this, it is necessary to introduce a convexity adjustment.

Gamma measures the rate of change of the delta as the stock price changes. Mathematically, it is the second derivative of the convertible bond value with respect to the underlying stock price (assuming a conversion ratio of 1):

$$\text{Gamma} = \Gamma = \frac{\partial^2 \text{ Convertible value}}{\partial \text{Stock price}^2} = \frac{\partial \text{Delta}}{\partial \text{Stock price}}$$

When using a binomial tree, the gamma is easily obtained by looking at the change of delta in the next two nodes relative to the changes in parity. For instance, if the trees of Exhibits 34.6 and 34.11 are used at the initial node, the initial delta is 0.672, and there is an upside delta of 0.793 and a downside delta of 0.406. The gamma is therefore as follows:

$$\text{Gamma} = \Gamma = (0.793 - 0.406)/(107.99 - 59.27) = 0.00794$$

This indicates that the delta will change by 0.00794 for each point change in parity level.

Gamma is very important for convertible arbitrageurs, as it indicates how much delta changes with regard to changes in the stock price. If gamma is large (i.e., delta is very sensitive to the underlying price), the portfolio will need to be frequently adjusted to maintain delta neutrality. If gamma is small (i.e., delta changes slowly), the portfolio will need to be adjusted less frequently to keep the portfolio delta neutral.

Just as delta changes, so does gamma. Gamma is normally larger for at-the-money convertibles and gets progressively lower for both in- and out-of-the-money convertibles. This means that the delta of **at-the-money convertibles** changes the most when the underlying stock price moves up or down. In the case of distressed convertibles, gamma can even become negative.

In addition, gamma also changes as time passes and volatility changes, but in a more complex way than delta; time passing or volatility decreasing normally increases the gamma of at-the-money convertibles but decreases the gamma of in-the-money and out-of-the-money convertibles.

34.4.3 Vega

Vega measures the sensitivity of the convertible bond value to changes in the volatility of the underlying stock. Mathematically, it is the derivative of the option value with respect to the volatility of the underlying stock:

$$\text{Vega} = \nu = \frac{\partial \text{Convertible value}}{\partial \text{Volatility}}$$

Note that vega is always positive, as an increase in volatility will raise the value of all options on an asset, while a decrease in volatility will lower their value. Convertibles that are trading near their conversion price are most sensitive to volatility and therefore display the highest vega.

34.4.4 Theta

Theta, also known as time decay, is the change in the convertible price due to the passage of time. Mathematically, it is the derivative of the option value with respect to time:

$$\text{Theta} = \theta = \frac{\partial \text{Convertible value}}{\partial \text{Time}}$$

Conventionally, theta is expressed as the percentage change in the convertible price for the passage of one day, other things being equal. Theta is used to estimate the degree to which a convertible bond option's time value is whittled away by the always constant passage of time. For an at-the-money convertible, theta will be negative if the time decay of the option element outweighs any upward drift in the bond floor.

Recall that the value of the straight bond component of the convertible serves as the floor for the price of the convertible bond because the value of the embedded option can never be negative.

34.4.5 Rho

Rho is an estimate of the sensitivity of a convertible value to movements in interest rates. Mathematically, it is the derivative of the option value with respect to interest rates:

$$\text{Rho} = \rho = \frac{\partial \text{Convertible value}}{\partial \text{Interest rate}}$$

Conventionally, rho is expressed as the change in convertible price for a given one-basis-point move in interest rates (a parallel shift in the whole yield curve). Rho also evolves along the convertible curve, increasing when parity decreases (i.e., as the convertible starts trading more based on its fixed-income characteristics).

34.4.6 Other Greeks

Convertible bond traders use additional Greeks to measure the sensitivities of their positions to other market parameters:

- Chi is an estimate of the rate of change of a convertible's value to changes in the spot exchange rate.
- Omicron is an estimate of the rate of change of a convertible's value to changes in the credit spread.
- Upsilon is an estimate of the rate of change of a convertible's value to changes in the credit recovery rate.
- Phi is an estimate of the rate of change of a convertible's value to changes in the underlying stock's dividend rate.

The Greeks of mandatory convertibles behave very differently from those of ordinary convertibles. A mandatory convertible has a required conversion or redemption feature. Either on or before a contractual conversion date, the holder must convert the mandatory convertible into the underlying common stock. These securities offer higher yields to compensate investors for the additional risk incurred under the mandatory conversion structure. For mandatory convertibles, delta may actually increase as stock prices decline and decrease as stock prices rise; in addition, gamma may turn negative for some stock price ranges. Therefore, hedging such convertibles requires a precise analysis of the dynamics of the Greeks.

34.5 AN ARBITRAGE SITUATION

The example XYZ convertible bond had a theoretical value of 103.36% according to the binomial model. For the sake of illustration, let us assume that the XYZ convertible bond is quoted by the market at 90% of par. Given the current price and the estimated volatility of the underlying asset (stock), the convertible bond is clearly undervalued. The question is: How can one exploit such a mispricing? Buying the cheap convertible is clearly part of the solution, but it is not sufficient. Simply waiting for market prices to adjust is not an arbitrage because the long convertible position comes with a variety of risks that could easily wipe out the expected gains.

To arbitrage, it is necessary to buy the cheap convertible *and* hedge its risks, a dynamic process that is very similar to what option arbitrageurs do all day long.

The primary risk of holding a long convertible position comes from the potential variations in the underlying stock price. This equity risk can easily be eliminated by selling short an appropriate quantity of the underlying stock. This quantity corresponds to the convertible's delta multiplied by the number of shares into which the bond may be converted. If the stock price gains $1, the convertible bond will gain approximately delta dollars and the short stock position will lose delta dollars, so that the overall variation will be nil. Conversely, if the stock price drops by $1, the convertible bond will lose approximately delta dollars and the short stock position will gain delta dollars, leaving the overall variation again at nil. In both cases, the overall position's value will no longer depend on variations in the stock price.

The delta of the XYZ convertible bond was 0.672. To hedge the equity risk, an arbitrageur would therefore need to sell short (delta × the conversion ratio) 0.672 × 8 = 5.376 shares of stock per $1,000 face value of the convertible bond bought. For a small change in the price of the stock, the arbitrageur's position will be hedged. However, if the stock price changes by a large amount, the delta of the convertible bond will no longer be 0.672, and therefore the **net delta** of the position will no longer be equal to 0. In order to keep the position delta hedged, a rebalancing of the hedge (rehedging) is needed.

As the stock price increases and the option component moves further in-the-money, the convertible bond becomes more equity sensitive (see Exhibit 34.13). The delta of the convertible bond increases, so the arbitrageur must adjust the hedge by shorting more shares. Conversely, as the stock price declines and the option moves out-of-the-money, the delta of the convertible bond declines and the arbitrageur must reduce the hedge by buying back some shares. In any case, the hedge needs to be rebalanced repeatedly as the stock price moves. This investment approach, referred to as **dynamic delta hedging** in options terminology, is the most common way of extracting value from convertibles without taking directional views on the underlying stock.

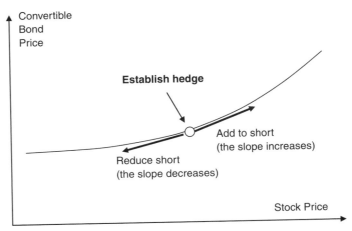

EXHIBIT 34.13   Delta Hedging a Convertible Bond

A key question for most arbitrageurs is how often they should rebalance their hedges. Theoretical delta hedging assumes that rehedging is done continuously; that is, infinitesimally small stock transactions are made for every infinitesimally small stock price movement. This is not feasible in the real world, as stock prices change in finite increments and fractional shares are normally not traded, and even if they were, transaction costs would skyrocket along with the number of transactions. In practice, therefore, arbitrageurs rehedge at discrete times, usually based on a time or price formula. In the former case, rehedging takes place at prespecified time intervals, such as every day or every hour. In the latter case, rehedging takes place whenever the stock price changes by a certain amount (e.g., every $1 move or every 1% move in the stock price) or when the size of the necessary adjustment reaches a certain threshold. If the selected rehedging interval is small enough, the risk of running a poorly hedged position is limited. Of course, a combination of the two approaches can also be implemented; in practice, however, the optimal choice of rehedging strategy often varies, not only from stock to stock but also over time, depending on market conditions.

Of particular interest to convertible bond arbitrageurs is the asymmetric valuation profile generated by large movements in the underlying stock price. Due to the nonlinear nature of their payoff, most at-the-money convertible bonds exhibit a desirable property known as positive convexity, or high gamma. That is, they appreciate in value more than they depreciate with respect to the same absolute change in the underlying stock price. Consequently, the delta-hedged position will actually benefit from *any* large movement in the underlying stock. In other words, the position tends to become underhedged when the price of the stock (and, consequently, the convertible bond) increases, which is a good thing, and becomes overhedged when the stock price decreases, another good thing. Convertible securities that demonstrate this property are attractive in volatile markets; all else being equal, the more volatile the stock price, the greater the expected profit of the position.

Exhibit 34.14, which shows the expected profit and loss of the hedged position as a function of the stock price, may give the impression that there is a pure arbitrage. The worst outcome seems to be a zero profit in the case of an unchanged stock price, whereas a positive profit occurs in any other case. Unfortunately, this is not strictly true. Stock price variations have been considered, but other aspects of the convertible position have been ignored, in particular the loss of time value of the option component.[7] This time decay offsets the convexity gains to such an extent that the expected return on the continuously delta-hedged position actually equals the risk-free rate if expected stock volatility equals the implied volatility of the convertible bond. The curve in Exhibit 34.13 should therefore be shifted down to reflect the possibility of a loss around the current stock price.

Once the exposure to the underlying stock price is neutralized, the profitability of the transaction will be affected by a series of other factors, such as the volatility level of the embedded option, the general level of interest rates, the cash flow stream

---

[7] This is understandable if one considers that a long-term American call option is always worth more than a short-term American call option with the same exercise price. Other things being equal, as the maturity of the option draws closer, the option value decreases.

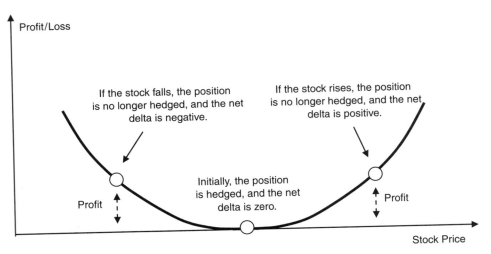

EXHIBIT 34.14 Profit on a Delta-Hedged Position (Long Convertible, Short Stock)
Note: The **net delta** is the slope of the curve.

generated by the position, and the credit spread inherent in the bond resulting from the issuer's credit quality.

Saying that a convertible bond is cheap is equivalent to saying that its implied volatility is too low. The exact shape of the profit-and-loss curve will therefore also depend on the *realized* volatility of the stock price versus its implied volatility. Every rebalancing trade is expected to be profitable, as the strategy is selling more stock as the price rises and buying more stock as the price falls (i.e., buying low and selling high). Since convertible bond arbitrageurs have paid to purchase the embedded call option, they are naturally long volatility. Any increase in the volatility of the stock's price should result in profits for the strategy. And if the realized volatility is higher than the implied volatility, the delta-hedged position will make a profit in excess of the risk-free rate. Conversely, if the realized volatility is below the implied volatility, the loss due to time decay will outweigh the profit made from the realized volatility, and the position will underperform a risk-free investment, perhaps even incurring a loss. When the realized volatility exceeds the implied volatility, the gamma trading is profitable, as the accumulated profits from the rebalancing trades are greater than the cost of the time decay of the long options position embedded in the convertible bond.

Convertible arbitrageurs who are not willing to be exposed to volatility risk can hedge against volatility fluctuations. This is called **vega hedging**, or making the portfolio vega neutral. Vega hedging in practice involves buying and selling other options or convertible bonds, since only these instruments exhibit convexity and hence have vega.[8] These options positions need to be adjusted on a regular basis, as the vegas of both the hedged convertible bond and the options position change continuously. Alternatively, arbitrageurs may opt to vega hedge by using volatility

---

[8] Note that the delta and gamma of these other options would need to be hedged as well.

futures, such as Chicago Board Options Exchange (CBOE) Volatility Index (VIX) futures contracts, which provide a pure play on the implied volatility of the S&P 500 equity index, independent of the direction and level of stock prices.

The interest rate factor is also important. A simple long convertible bond position is typically long duration and long convexity and will lose money if interest rates rise. Here again, if they want to, arbitrageurs can easily hedge this risk by either selling interest rate futures contracts or entering interest rate swaps.

The cash flow generated by the position is usually positive for arbitrageurs. Arbitrageurs receive the coupon payment from the bond and the **short stock rebate,** which is the interest earned on the proceeds from the stock sale. This income is reduced by any costs associated with borrowing the stock, such as the repayment of dividends owed to the purchaser of the shorted stock.

Credit considerations are also essential and are discussed in the next section.

34.6 CONVERTIBLE ARBITRAGE IN PRACTICE: STRIPPING AND SWAPPING

Once equity, volatility, and interest rate risks have been eliminated from the convertible position, the arbitrageur is left with credit risk, or the possibility of changes to credit spreads. This risk is important because the majority of convertible issuers are below investment grade, at least in the United States. Moreover, many convertible bonds are unsecured, subordinated, and issued by firms with high earnings volatility, high leverage, or intangible assets. These bonds are particularly sensitive to the business cycle, so the arbitrageur cannot ignore credit risk.

Short selling the stock provides a partial hedge against credit risk, for as spreads widen, stock prices generally decline. However, this hedge is imperfect and difficult to calibrate precisely. Moreover, to entirely eliminate the credit-spread risk with a short stock position, the arbitrageur would need to short considerably more stock than the delta hedge calls for, placing the position at considerable risk should spreads not widen and stock prices appreciate. One alternative is to sell short a straight bond of the same issuer. This is usually an effective hedge against credit risk, but it is feasible only if other bonds from the same issuer are still actively traded and can be borrowed easily. This is clearly not the case for all issuers. Using credit default swaps might also be considered, but this practice exposes the arbitrageur to a serious call risk if the bond is callable; arbitrageurs who wish to unwind a default swap are reliant on finding a counterparty, but if the deliverable convertible bond has been called, there is unlikely to be a market. A workaround is to buy credit default swaps that mature before the call date, but there is no guarantee that the arbitrage profit will be realized by the call date.

Until recently, it was almost impossible to properly hedge the credit risk of a specific convertible bond issuer. However, it is important to remember that real arbitrageurs are not really interested in the fixed-income/credit portion of convertible bonds. They are just keen to purchase the associated cheap equity call options, which they can offset against either the equity or other equity-linked securities. On the other hand, many investment banks and prime brokers have clients who are interested in the fixed-income portion of convertible securities but have no real desire to hold the associated call option. Once again, financial innovation comes to the rescue: The

Convertible Market

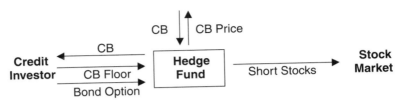

EXHIBIT 34.15 Typical Flows in an Asset Swap on a Convertible Bond (CB)

asset swap is a key development that has boosted the demand for convertible bonds in recent years. This new instrument offers the ability to split a convertible bond into its two components: the fixed-income portion and the equity call option. Most of the time, the asset swap involves a credit seller, who will keep the equity option, and a credit buyer, who will acquire the fixed-income component. This unlocks the theoretical value of the convertible bond and greatly facilitates the implementation of arbitrage strategies.

Although asset swap arrangements can be technically complex, their basic construction is simple (see Exhibit 34.15); the process can be summarized in the following two steps:

Step 1: A hedge fund manager identifies an undervalued convertible bond (CB). He verifies with his prime broker that the underlying stock can be borrowed. If so, he purchases the convertible bond, which generally bears a fixed-rate coupon and an option for its holder to convert into equity. In terms of risk, the manager is now exposed to rising interest rates, falling equity prices, declining volatility, and widening credit spreads.

Step 2: The hedge fund manager enters into an asset swap with a credit investor. This swap is usually made up of two transactions:

1. The fund manager sells the convertible bond to the credit investor at a large discount to its market price. The selling price is typically set at the **bond floor** value, or the present value of the bond's future cash flow (coupons and repayment), discounted at LIBOR plus a fixed credit spread.

2. In exchange for the discount on the sale price of the convertible bond, the credit investor gives the fund an over-the-counter call option. This option allows the fund to purchase the convertible bond back at a fixed exercise price. This is typically set at the present value of the bond's future cash flow (coupons and repayment), discounted at LIBOR plus a fixed recall spread. The recall spread is tighter than the one used for calculating the bond floor value both to discourage rapid turnover of positions and to deliver a minimum return to the credit investor. For instance, the swap terms could allow for a call at par value at the maturity of the bond.

Before proceeding further, verify that the asset swap has left each party with only their desired exposures. The hedge fund, for its part, still has the equity upside exposure inherent in the convertible bond by virtue of owning the call option, but it is no longer exposed to the risk of widening credit spreads. This option is useless when the convertible bond remains out-of-the-money but allows for participation in the upside potential of the stock when the convertible bond is at- or in-the-money. Because the convertible bond is purchased below fair value and the straight bond component is sold at fair value, the hedge fund is left holding an option whose final purchase price is lower than its theoretical value. To capture the price difference, most hedge funds will simply delta hedge this option until it returns to fair value. Note that the hedge fund's loss is limited to the premium of the option, whose strike price depends on the credit spread initially agreed on in the asset swap. On the other hand, the hedge fund can benefit if the credit trades to a tighter spread by calling the initial asset swap and simultaneously establishing a new one at a tighter spread.

After entering the asset swap, the credit investor holds a synthetic straight callable bond.[9] She has no equity exposure but now faces credit risk and interest rate risk. If she is solely interested in betting that the credit quality of the issuer will improve in the future, she can eliminate the interest rate risk by entering into another swap in which she pays a fixed rate equal to the convertible bond coupon and receives a floating rate, typically LIBOR plus a spread. This leaves her with only the credit exposure of the original convertible bond.

Now consider what can happen at expiration. There are five basic cases to be considered:

1. If the convertible bond matures out-of-the-money, the hedge fund manager lets his option expire. The credit investor redeems the convertible bond and is repaid at par by the issuer.
2. If the convertible bond matures in-the-money, the hedge fund manager calls back the convertible bond and pays the par value to the credit investor. The hedge fund manager then exercises the conversion option and receives the parity value, which is higher than his payment to the credit investor.
3. If the convertible bond is called out-of-the-money by the issuer, the hedge fund manager lets the option expire. The credit investor is then repaid at the call price by the issuer.
4. If the convertible bond is called in-the-money by the issuer, the hedge fund manager calls back the convertible bond and pays the agreed call value to the credit investor. The hedge fund manager then exercises the convertible bond and receives the parity value, which is higher than his payment to the credit investor.
5. If the issuer defaults, the hedge fund manager lets his option expire. The credit investor receives the recovery value of the convertible bond, if any, from the issuer.

In practice, asset swaps may take several forms, but their basic function remains the same: to split the convertible bond into its two core components. Convertible bond arbitrageurs use these asset swaps to gain equity exposure to a company while avoiding credit and interest rate risk exposure.

---

[9] The term *synthetic* is used because the position is not a straight callable bond but behaves exactly like one.

34.7 LEVERAGE AND CONVERTIBLE ARBITRAGE

Historically, convertible arbitrage and fixed-income arbitrage hedge funds have used a much greater degree of leverage than have many other hedge fund strategies. Ineichen (2003) estimates that convertible bond arbitrage funds routinely use leverage between 2 and 10 times fund assets, while fixed-income arbitrage strategies may employ more than 20 times leverage.

Ideally, the amount of leverage used in a strategy should be positively related to the degree of liquidity of the assets underlying the strategy. For example, managed futures and global macro strategies have the ability to use a large degree of leverage due to the high degree of liquidity in global futures markets. However, convertible bonds and mortgage-backed securities tend to have varying degrees of liquidity, with much less liquidity than desired during times of market stress.

Consider the example of 2008, when the Dow Jones Credit Suisse Core Convertible Arbitrage Hedge Fund Index fell by over 30%. Convertible arbitrage hedge fund managers had obtained leverage through prime brokers. The prime brokers extended loans to the hedge funds, which were secured by their convertible bond holdings. (Generally speaking, hedge fund managers need to carefully understand their relationship with prime brokers, as prime brokers typically reserve the right to liquidate whichever positions they deem necessary to reduce the leverage of a fund, and to change credit limits on short notice.) In 2008, both stock prices and corporate bond prices were falling rapidly, while many investors in convertible arbitrage hedge funds sought to withdraw assets from these funds. Convertible arbitrage hedge funds were required to liquidate assets both to meet redemptions and to reduce leverage as the price of convertible bonds declined. The liquidation included the sale of convertible bonds, the sale of put option hedges, and the covering of equity short sales. This massive selling pressure by convertible arbitrage hedge funds drove bond prices even lower, which necessitated further selling, as the asset value was declining as the prime brokerage loan balances remained stable, which was increasing the leverage multiple. Finally, prime brokers reduced the amount of leverage available. If a prime broker reduced the maximum leverage from 10 times to 5 times assets, a fund manager would be required to sell half of the fund's positions in a matter of hours or days. This forced selling led to catastrophic losses at highly leveraged convertible arbitrage funds. The mispricing of convertible bonds became so extreme that the convertible bonds of some firms were priced at below the option-free debt of the same firm, essentially offering the valuable stock option for a negative price.

APPENDIX

European options can be valued using the Black-Scholes (1973) formula, where S_t is replaced by the conversion ratio times the price of one share, and the strike price is set equal to the price of the straight bond to be delivered in exchange for the shares. The call option value is calculated as follows:

$$\text{Call option} = S_t e^{-q(T-t)} N(d_1) - K e^{-r(T-t)} N(d_2)$$

where:

$$d_1 = \frac{\ln\left(\dfrac{S}{K}\right) + \left(r - q + \dfrac{1}{2}\sigma^2\right)(T - t)}{\sigma\sqrt{T - t}}$$

$$d_2 = d_1 - \sigma\sqrt{T - t}$$

Note that $r = \ln(1 + R_f)$ is the continuously compounded risk-free rate, q is the continuous annual dividend yield, and $N(.)$ is the cumulative normal distribution function. All of the Greeks can be derived using the Black-Scholes formula. Delta is given as follows:

$$\text{Delta} = e^{-q(T-t)} N(d_1)$$

Gamma is given by $\gamma = \frac{\partial(\text{Delta})}{\partial S}$ (partial derivative of delta with respect to stock price):

$$\text{Gamma} = \frac{e^{-q(T-t)} N'(d_1)}{S\sigma\sqrt{T - t}}$$

When using the Black-Scholes formula, rho is given as follows:

$$\text{Rho} = \rho = K(T - t)e^{-r(T-t)} N(d_2)$$

Vega is given as follows:

$$\text{Vega} = S N'(d_1)\sqrt{(T - t)} e^{-q(T-1)}$$

And finally, theta is given as follows:

$$\text{Theta} = -\frac{\left[S N'(d_1)\sigma e^{-q(T-t)}\right]}{2\sqrt{T - t}} - r K e^{-r(T-t)} N(d_2) + q S N(d_1) e^{-q(T-t)}$$

CHAPTER 35

Global Macro and Currency Strategies

Global macro managers have been around for more than 30 years, but their golden era culminated in the early 1990s, when their strategy represented more than half of worldwide hedge fund assets. This was the time when legendary managers such as George Soros (Quantum Fund) and Julian Robertson (Tiger Fund) were running multibillion-dollar funds involved, primarily, in leveraged directional trades. Today, this strategy represents between 10% and 15%, or over $400 billion, of the hedge fund industry's assets under management. While macro assets have grown over time, they have grown at a slower rate than other hedge fund strategies. Investors' appetite for global macro funds fell in mid-2000, when high-profile operators such as George Soros and Julian Robertson shut down their macro funds and retired after posting disappointing performance numbers.[1] Other fund managers returned capital to investors because they were losing their edge in large liquid markets, yet were too big to operate in illiquid markets. More importantly, by 2005, the lack of volatility across global markets had made it difficult for global macro funds to make money. Lastly, the number of liquid bond and currency markets (and hence opportunities) was drastically reduced with the introduction of the euro.

After a long dry spell, the global macro strategy came back in favor in the second half of 2007 and in 2008, when global market volatility soared and the fear of a U.S.-led global recession became a real threat. Short dollar positions and long commodity trades became clear winners for global macro funds. But the global macro funds of today are very different from those of prior generations. Leverage is still employed, but the focus is more on consistency of returns and effective risk management.

35.1 INTRODUCTION TO THE MACRO STRATEGIES

Global macro hedge funds have the broadest mandate of any of the major fund strategies. Their mandate often has no limitations in terms of types of instruments,

---

[1] At their peaks, Soros and Robertson had assets of about $22 billion. Soros Fund Management announced a revamping of the Quantum Fund amid steep losses in technology stocks, billions in redemptions, and the departure of two top managers, Stanley Druckenmiller and Nicholas Roditi. Robertson announced in March of 2000 that he was liquidating his funds and closing the doors on Tiger Management after his bets on value stocks backfired.

asset classes, markets, and geographies. They can dynamically allocate capital to the asset class, sector, or region in which they think the best opportunities currently lie, hence the term *global*. The second term, *macro*, reflects the fact that these managers apply macroeconomic views to global markets. Instead of analyzing microeconomic events affecting companies or assets, they view the world from a top-down perspective. Their goal is to anticipate global macroeconomic changes and themes, detect trends and inflection points, and profit by investing in financial instruments whose prices are likely to be impacted most directly. They can go long or short, be concentrated or diversified, with or without leverage. While some funds trade single stocks in anticipation of macro themes, most funds concentrate trading in forwards, futures, and swaps on macro markets, including commodities, currencies, equities, and interest rates.

There are probably as many approaches to the strategy as there are global macro hedge fund managers, but they share a common desire to identify and exploit markets in severe disequilibrium. It is only when prices are perceived as being more than one or two standard deviations away from fair value that macro traders deem that the market presents a compelling opportunity. Ideally, macro managers will be able to find trades with an asymmetric risk-reward profile, offering minimal potential losses and large potential gains.

35.1.1 Discretionary versus Systematic

Discretionary global macro managers usually perform intensive fundamental research. They continuously analyze information from varied sources, such as central bank publications, survey data, confidence indicators, asset flows, liquidity measures, forecasting agencies, political commentators, and personal contacts. They look for markets that do not match the macroeconomic realities, identifying situations that are unsustainable or asset classes that are likely to follow predictable trends. They spend hours forming their views on likely market scenarios while assessing the probabilities of alternative scenarios. Once interesting risk-reward opportunities have been identified, global macro managers determine appropriate entry points, often by applying traditional technical analysis. The overall result is completely discretionary and highly dependent on the particular skills of the manager.

By contrast, **systematic global macro managers** apply a highly structured, disciplined, and repeatable investment process. They replace subjective macroeconomic analysis with a systematic way of looking at economic data, and rely on mathematical models to evaluate markets, detect trading opportunities, generate signals, and establish entry and exit points. Many of them seek to identify specific fundamental data and key economic drivers that explain the long-term behavior of various markets, and combine these elements with assessments of the current economic conditions and market forecasts. Others focus on identifying directional trends in markets that can be traded in large volumes, and where capital is capable of moving quickly. Their systems can be based on moving averages, breakout systems, pattern recognition, or any combination of these. Some investors like to call them global trend followers, as they are very close in spirit to trend-following commodity trading advisers (CTAs), particularly when they focus on longer-term trends.

The reality is that CTAs and some global macro funds share a fundamental source of returns, namely, long-term secular shifts in capital flows. Generally, both tend to participate in large trends in major equity, fixed income, and foreign exchange markets, and, to a lesser extent, the energy, commodity, and precious metals markets. But they participate in these trends in different ways:

- Global macro funds are often anticipatory, whereas CTAs are reactive. They therefore often overlap in the middle part of a well-established trend, but their entry and exit points are fundamentally different.
- CTAs are purely price-based in their analysis, and follow their systematic models regardless of fundamentals. Global macro managers prefer to look at the big picture and stand aside when market fundamentals do not appear to properly explain a trend.
- CTAs tend to exhibit the same views on markets at the same time as each other, because their inputs and systems are similar. By contrast, global macro managers can be quite different from one another in how they evaluate data and make trading decisions.
- CTAs are generally momentum (technically driven) traders, whereas their global macro counterparts focus on such fundamentals as inventories in commodity markets or interest rate differentials in currency markets.

These disparities in approach help explain the disparity of returns and return volatility.

35.1.2 Schools of Thought

Alternatively, one may want to distinguish the sources of returns that global macro funds are trying to tap. In this case, according to Ahl (2001), there are essentially three possible schools of thought to be considered:

Feedback-based global macro managers assume that markets are rational most of the time, but that there can exist periods of severe irrationality. Such periods can arise either because people have made money too easily and become complacent or because they have lost money too quickly and become stressed or distressed. As a result, feedback-based global macro managers attempt to read the financial market's psychology, sell in bursting bubbles, and buy into postcrash recoveries.

Information-based global macro managers rely primarily on collecting micro-level information to better understand the global macro picture. Their hypothesis is that an information gap is created by the delay in release of official macro statistics. This gap then opens the door for pricing inefficiencies, which will persist until the macro information has been disseminated into the public domain.

Model-based global macro managers rely primarily on financial models and economic theories to analyze market movements, detect policy mistakes of central banks and governments, or extract implied market expectations and compare them to sensible estimates. As discussed by Safvenblad (2003), examples of trades or models commonly used include:

- Carry trades (i.e., using interest rate differentials as indicators of positive carry positions) involve holding long-maturity bonds against shorter instruments, or long high-yielding currencies against low-yielding ones.

- Yield curve relative-value trades involve identifying the undervalued or overvalued part of the yield curves, or trading the slope of one yield curve against the slope of another.
- Purchasing power parity (PPP) models are often used by global macro funds to assess the relative value of currencies.
- Valuation models, such as the dividend discount model used in trading equity markets, are usually applied bottom-up, at each company level; expected returns for each company are then aggregated and weighted to derive a market-level expected return at a country level.
- Option pricing models provide the market's implied views about the future volatility of some underlying asset.

35.1.3 Multistrategy Global Macro Funds

Investing large sums of money is usually not an issue for global macro managers, given their flexibility and the depth and liquidity of the markets they trade in; however, the reality is that, past a certain fund size, it becomes prudent to add more traders and strategies. Thus, it should come as no surprise that the larger global macro-oriented hedge funds have migrated to a multistrategy model, which in turn has increased their correlations with funds of hedge funds. In such a case, identifying precisely which school of thought a manager belongs to may be difficult. For this reason, this chapter approaches the global macro universe from a trading perspective, rather than from a classification perspective.

35.2 DIRECTIONAL CURRENCY TRADES

One would be remiss, in discussing the global macro strategy, to neglect to mention George Soros and the Exchange Rate Mechanism (ERM) crisis of 1992–1993. (See Exhibit 35.1.) This was likely the first time the general public became aware of the existence of global macro funds and their actions. This case study explains the discretionary, fundamental, information-based style of macro trading. In this case, the information used focuses on central bank policies and the level of currency reserves held by each country.

The European Monetary System (EMS) was formed in 1979, by several European countries, to coordinate their monetary and exchange rate policies. Among other things, the EMS created a fictitious accounting unit called the European Currency Unit (ECU), using guidelines established by the ERM agreement. The ERM was essentially a managed floating exchange rate system, where the currencies of participating countries were allowed to fluctuate, within prespecified bands, around a reference point (±2.25% for most countries; ±6% for Italy, Spain, Portugal, and the United Kingdom). Central banks were charged with taking appropriate measures, whenever needed, to keep the exchange rate within these bands. Since the ECU was fictitious, in practice the unofficial reserve currency, the German mark, turned out to be the most stable currency of the group. That is, the bands were effectively maintained with respect to the German mark, and central banks typically intervened by selling or buying marks against their respective domestic currency. In a sense, the

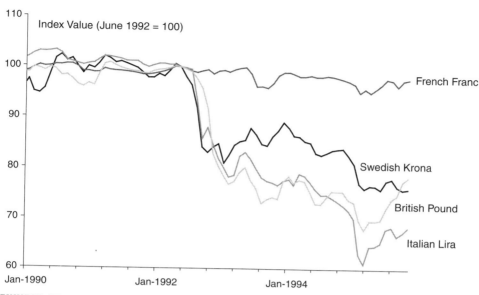

EXHIBIT 35.1 Evolution of Exchange Rates around the 1992 Crisis

role of Germany within the ERM was similar to that of the United States within Bretton Woods. Since there were only 10 direct exchange rates among the 11 member countries, Germany was free to set its monetary policy, often forcing other countries to follow its lead, even when doing so ran counter to domestic interests. In practice, the countries had effectively lost all control over their own monetary policies. When an exchange rate approached one extreme of the preset bands, the respective central bank was forced to intervene, using the country's reserves to maintain the band.

Since its creation, the EMS had achieved its main objectives to a large extent. In 1992, however, the policy interests of Germany and the rest of Europe began diverging dramatically. German reunification created strong domestic growth, which drove German interest rates higher and ultimately pushed other European currencies to the bottom of their respective bands. By contrast, the United Kingdom was in its worst recession since the end of World War II, with unemployment rates well in excess of 10%. In the absence of the ERM agreement, the United Kingdom would have resorted to an expansionary monetary policy or a devaluation to get out of the slump. Unfortunately, its actions were constrained by the fixed exchange rate system.

While most market participants thought that it was impossible to build up enough pressure to force the British authorities to abandon the bands, a few speculators, led by George Soros and his Quantum Fund, decided to launch a speculative attack. In the summer of 1992, they sold a huge amount of British pounds in exchange for other currencies. The Bank of England rushed to defend the band through intervention, but rapidly depleted its foreign currency reserve holdings in the process. On September 3, to replenish these lost reserves, the Bank of England was forced to borrow 10 billion ECUs (i.e., approximately $14.3 billion) on the international market. At the same time, speculators began attacking the Italian lira, forcing the

Bank of Italy to raise its discount rate from 12% to 15%. The Italian central bank may have raised interest rates to attract new capital flows and to increase the cost of holding short positions in the lira.

Speculation against the pound culminated on September 16, subsequently referred to as Black Wednesday.[2] Exacerbated by uncertainties over a French referendum on European construction, massive speculative flows continued to disrupt the functioning of the Exchange Rate Mechanism. The Bank of England responded by raising its base lending rate from 10% to 12%, then to 15% the next day, but both announcements had little impact on the intense speculative pressure. Massive interventions in the foreign exchange markets proved futile as well. Ultimately, Germany agreed to lower its discount rate by 50 basis points and its Lombard rate by 25 basis points, but by then it was too late. Although the Conservative government had repeatedly vowed otherwise, the Bank of England was forced to suspend participation of the pound in the ERM. Italy soon followed, causing a rapid and massive depreciation of both currencies. Spain was also pressured to devalue its currency by 5% and impose capital controls. The speculative attacks continued well into 1993, when the bands of several ERM currencies were widened temporarily to 15%, which meant they were effectively floating currencies. For George Soros and his $10 billion Quantum Fund, the result was a profit of more than a billion dollars in this directional bet against the British pound.

Twenty years later, there are still opportunities to trade currencies with a view toward changing governmental policy. In 2012, many investors have long positions in the Hong Kong dollar (HKD), anticipating that the HKD is undervalued and likely to break its peg to the U.S. dollar (USD) and revalue the currency from its official trading range of 7.75 to 7.85 HKD/USD. Other macro traders are attracted to the currencies of the Gulf Cooperation Council (GCC) countries (United Arab Emirates, Saudi Arabia, Qatar, Oman, and Bahrain). The Saudi riyal has long been pegged at an official rate of 3.75 to the USD. As energy prices rise and capital flows into the region, pressure may rise on these countries to move to floating currencies, likely rising in valuation versus the USD.

35.3 THE CASE OF EMERGING MARKETS

The 1997 Asian currency crisis brought to the foreground concerns about global macro funds and their possible role in exacerbating financial market volatility and disrupting emerging markets. Some Asian government officials explicitly accused hedge funds of attacking their currencies and causing their downfalls. Specifically, Malaysia's prime minister, Mahathir Mohammad, argued that by accumulating very large and concentrated short speculative positions (referred to as big elephants in small ponds), hedge funds had destabilized the foreign exchange, money, and equity markets of Thailand, Malaysia, Indonesia, and the Philippines. Several governments also raised concerns about aggressive and manipulative tactics used by some global macro hedge funds, which might have compromised market integrity and interfered with a normal price-discovery process (see Brown, Goetzmann, and Park [1998] for further discussion).

---

[2] Euro-skeptics like to call it White Wednesday.

While the trading activity of hedge funds may have sped up the devaluation process, there was no doubt that many of these currencies were fundamentally weak. Black (2004) explains how the supply and demand for currency can be monitored using the balances of the current account and capital account balances as well as the level of official reserves. For freely floating currencies, a country with net capital inflows would likely see an appreciating currency, while depreciation would be expected with net capital outflows. The current account measures the balance of trade in goods and services, while the capital account measures the net flow of financial transactions. For most countries, there will be a balance of payments, as the capital account and current account will have offsetting flows, such as when a current account deficit is offset by a capital account surplus. In a fixed-rate or pegged currency, net capital outflows cause the central bank to purchase the domestic currency. Once the central bank has exhausted its official reserves, there are no assets left to support the currency at the pegged price, and the currency must be devalued to a point where the central bank is no longer required to purchase the currency to support its value. Many Asian currencies in 1997 and 1998 were pegged at levels above fair value, and the devaluations that were profitable to hedge funds were ultimately the result of both trade imbalances and investment outflows.

The International Monetary Fund (IMF) responded to the charges of market manipulation by examining the role of hedge funds in the Asian currency crisis. In the resulting study, Eichengreen et al. (1998) found no evidence that hedge funds played a major role in the events leading up to the Asian crisis, but many governments contested these conclusions as not fully coming to grips with the role played by hedge funds.

Political sensitivities aside, it can be difficult to fully assess the role and impact of hedge funds in emerging markets. First, many hedge funds operate through over-the-counter (OTC) foreign exchange and money markets, which are very opaque. Second, hedge funds themselves are opaque, as they are not subject to mandatory reporting requirements. As a result, any assessment of the impact that hedge funds may have had in Asia in the late 1990s necessitates access to private information (e.g., trading and position data) or market intelligence (such as off-the-record meetings with various prime brokers and traders), or requires one to make assumptions in order to build an econometric model.

Brown, Goetzmann, and Park (1998) investigated the changing positions of the top 10 global hedge funds vis-à-vis the Malaysian ringgit. They concluded that there were periods when hedge funds had large long and short currency exposures, but that changes in these positions had no relationship to exchange rate movements. In their opinion, there was no evidence to support a claim that hedge funds in general, or any hedge fund in particular, led the charge against Asian currencies.

Using data on the returns of 27 large hedge funds during the Asian currency crisis, Fung, Hsieh, and Tsatsaronis (2000) attempted to infer the currency positions held by the funds. They compared those inferred positions with the total capital flows for the Asian countries, based on balance-of-payments accounts. They concluded that aggregate hedge fund positions were too small to have caused the collapse of the Asian currencies.

Last, the 2000 Financial Stability Forum Report of the Working Group on Highly Leveraged Institutions also attempted to assess the impact of hedge funds in Asia during the crisis. It expresses some concerns about the apparent large size and concentration of macro hedge fund positions and their implications for market dynamics, especially during unsettled market conditions. It provides evidence on the aggressive activities of some hedge funds ("talking their books"—making statements supporting one's investment positions, spreading rumors, aggressive trading at illiquid times, etc.), which could be seen as efforts to move markets. But it also points to the downside risk of using size to move a market. Large players, such as global macro hedge funds, face strong incentives to tailor the size of a position to market size and liquidity in order to avoid moving prices too far when unwinding positions.

35.4 FOUR MODELS FOR CURRENCY TRADING

Pojarliev and Levich (2008) describe four models for currency trading: carry, trend following, value, and volatility. Rather than assuming that all profits from currency trading are alpha, their research shows that manager skill, for currency and global macro managers, should be measured as the returns in excess of those earned from beta exposure to each of these four factors. From 1990 to 2006, Pojarliev and Levich calculated total returns to the four currency strategies combined at 62 basis points per month, with the risk-free rate accounting for 37 basis points and with 25 basis points per month remaining as the excess return of the strategies. The 25 basis points of excess return were concentrated in the years prior to 2000. In fact, after 2000, the excess return to the four strategies declined to just 8 basis points per month. The carry and trend factors were profitable, but the value and volatility strategies had returns near zero over the full time period. With a monthly standard deviation of excess returns of 3.04%, all four strategies combined had a very low information ratio. The trend and volatility return factors had the highest volatility, while the carry and value factors had much lower volatility. Their regression models of the returns of a basket of currency managers on the four strategy factors had an R-squared of 0.66, meaning that the majority of returns to currency funds were attributable to these four factors. In their analysis of individual manager returns, approximately one-quarter of the individual managers had the majority of their returns explained by the four factors. Further, approximately only one-quarter of the currency managers had a positive and statistically significant alpha after adjusting for the four factor returns and for fees.

Both carry and momentum strategies appear to be relatively simple to implement and yet, surprisingly, have shown to be profitable on average. Naturally, this raises the question about the sources of the profitability of these two strategies. The common answers to this question are:

1. The profitability of these two strategies represents fair compensation for the systematic risk to which they are exposed.
2. The profitability is not real, and will disappear when transaction costs and market impacts are accounted for.
3. The profitability is highly unpredictable, which limits arbitrage on the part of traders.
4. The profitability results from trading against central banks that intervene in currency markets.

Of these four explanations, the first does not provide a satisfactory explanation, as academics and practitioners have not been able to identify the specific sources of systematic risks associated with these two strategies. That is, exposures to credit risk, equity risk, interest rate risk, and so on do not seem to explain returns to these two strategies.

The second explanation does provide a partial answer as far as returns from momentum strategies are concerned. Research shows that momentum strategies are most profitable when applied to thinly traded currencies. Therefore, the actual profitability of a momentum strategy will be lower because of the transaction costs associated with trading the currencies of smaller economies. These results do not apply to the carry trade, as this strategy has been profitable when applied to the most active liquid markets.

The third explanation applies to both strategies, and may provide an explanation for the persistence of the profitability of these two strategies. Historically, both strategies have been profitable, but there have also been periods of significant losses. Both strategies tend to attract large pools of capital, which means their trades could become crowded, leading to large losses when trends reverse. For example, the carry trade involving the Japanese yen was very popular in 2007 and early 2008. However, when these trades began losing money in the first quarter of 2008, the rush by traders to close their positions exacerbated the situation, leading to large losses.

The fourth answer does explain some profitable trades (e.g., the famous trade by George Soros against the Bank of England, which reportedly netted Quantum Fund $1 billion in profits). However, central bank interventions do not appear to be widespread enough to explain the persistent profitability of these two strategies.

35.4.1 Carry Models for Currency Trading

A **carry trade** is a very simple yet popular global macro strategy. In its simplest form, a carry trade in currency markets consists of borrowing in a low-interest-rate currency and lending in a high-interest-rate currency, without hedging the **exchange rate risk**. The goal of such a trade is to capture the interest rate differential, which can be quite substantial. As an illustration, if the funding currency carries an annual interest rate of 0.5% versus 5.25% in the target currency, a trader would borrow in the funding currency, convert the proceeds into the target currency, and buy bonds using the target currency. This would earn the trader a positive carry (or profit) of 4.75%, as long as the exchange rate does not change. If the exchange rate does change, carry trading remains profitable as long as the target currency does not depreciate by more than the interest rate differential. This explains why global macro funds often establish carry trades between currencies that display both high interest rate differentials and low exchange-rate volatility.

Currencies such as the Japanese yen and, more recently, the Swiss franc have been popular choices for the borrow side of carry trades due to their low interest rates. For instance, one can borrow yen at rates as low as 0.5%. By contrast, high-yielding currencies, such as the South African rand, the New Zealand dollar, the Brazilian real, or the Icelandic krona, have been attractive currencies in which to invest.

To some extent, the profitability of a carry trade can be reinforced by the flows they generate. For instance, a yen-financed carry trade requires the trader to sell the borrowed yen to convert them into higher-yielding assets, in order to earn a profit. As large amounts of yen flow out of Japan into the global trading system, the yen weakens (all else being equal) while the target currency appreciates, thus reinforcing the cycle. However, at some point the carry trades will unwind. That is, traders will sell the assets in the target currency and convert the proceeds into the funding currency, in order to pay back their initial loan. This typically occurs when one or more of the following three things happen:

1. The funding currency interest rate rises, thereby increasing borrowing costs.
2. The funding currency appreciates against the target currency.
3. The target currency investment does not yield as much as initially expected. This risk is particularly important in more aggressive carry trades, where the investments made using the target currency consist of high-yielding assets, such as non-investment-grade corporate bonds or even equities.

When performed on a large scale, the unwinding of carry trades may be brutal, and can lead to significant amounts of financial market volatility, especially if many traders exit en masse from the same positions at the same time. Carry trades frequently unwind during times of elevated systemic risk, experiencing losses at the same time as long investments in equity markets and arbitrage strategy hedge funds. For instance, in the summer of 1998, the Japanese yen, which had been depreciating versus the dollar for three years, started appreciating. Traders rushed to sell their high-yielding assets and their underlying currencies against yen in order to pay back their yen-denominated loans. Not only did the Japanese currency appreciate very sharply in early October as investors scrambled to buy yen, but prices of high-yielding assets depreciated quickly, forcing the U.S. Federal Reserve to cut the federal funds rate twice (for a total of 50 basis points) in the subsequent month to restore liquidity to the financial markets.

To understand carry trades, two related models of currency markets must be explained. The first model, referred to as **covered interest rate parity**, is similar to the cost of carry model of commodity markets, and it relates the spot and forward exchange rates to differences in short-term interest rates in the two countries.

To explore this concept in mathematical terms, let S_t denote the spot value of domestic currency unit (DCU) per unit of a foreign currency unit (FCU). Also, let r_{DCU} and r_{FCU} denote annualized short-term riskless interest rates on instruments denominated in DCUs and FCUs. Finally, let F_t denote the current forward rate on a one-year forward exchange rate contract. According to covered interest rate parity, the covered (hedged) return from investing in the FCU-denominated instrument should be equal to the rate of return on the DCU-denominated instrument. That is,

$$(1 + r_{FCU}) \times \frac{F_t}{S_t} = (1 + r_{DCU}) \tag{35.1}$$

The left-hand side of Equation 35.1 is the hedged return from investing in the FCU instrument, while the right-hand side represents the return from investing in the DCU instrument.

Example: Suppose annual short-term interest rates in the United States and Japan are 2% and 1%, respectively. In addition, the current spot rate and one-year forward rate for yen versus USD are 0.0125 and 0.012377, respectively. Does covered interest rate parity hold, assuming zero transaction costs?

In this case, the yen is the DCU and the dollar is the FCU. Thus,

$$(1 + 0.02) \times \frac{0.012377}{0.012500} = (1 + 0.01)$$

It can be verified that this equality holds, and covered interest parity is satisfied.

If covered interest rate parity does not hold, then traders can take advantage of the situation by investing in the instrument that has the higher hedged rate of return. For example, if the short-term rate in Japan were 1.1%, then traders could generate an arbitrage profit by shorting U.S. bonds and using the proceeds to purchase Japanese bonds, while hedging against currency risks in the forward market. This would have generated a one year riskless arbitrage profit of 0.1%, not including transaction costs. Because potential profits are essentially riskless, there are rarely meaningful deviations from covered interest rate parity.

Uncovered interest rate parity is similar to covered parity, with the transactions left unhedged. Using the same notation, uncovered interest rate parity holds if the following equality holds:

$$(1 + r_{FCU}) \times \frac{E[S_{t+1}]}{S_t} = (1 + r_{DCU}) \tag{35.2}$$

In the previous example, it was stated that there should be no arbitrage profit from borrowing in one currency and investing the proceeds in another currency while hedging against currency risk in the forward market. According to the uncovered interest rate parity model, even if the transaction is not hedged against currency risk, the profit is expected to be zero.

Example: Suppose annual short-term interest rates in the United States and Japan are 2% and 1%, respectively. In addition, the current spot rate for the yen versus the USD is 0.0125. What is the implied expected future spot rate in one year according to uncovered interest rate parity, assuming zero transaction costs? According to the uncovered parity model, the income from investing in USD and Japanese bonds should be the same after adjusting for currency changes. The yen return on an investment in U.S. bonds is:

$$(1 + 0.02) \times \frac{S_{t+1}}{0.0125}$$

The yen return on an investment in Japanese bonds is 1%. These two returns are expected to be equal to each other according to uncovered interest rate parity. This means that:

$$(1 + 0.02) \times \frac{S_{t+1}}{0.0125} = (1 + 0.01)$$

$$S_{t+1} = \frac{1 + 0.01}{1 + 0.02} \times 0.0125 = 0.012377$$

That is, the yen/USD spot rate is expected to be 0.012377. The implication is that the currency of the country with the higher interest rate, USD in this case, should decline versus the currency of the country with the lower interest rate. At first, this appears to be counterintuitive, as one would think the currency of the country with the higher interest rate should be more attractive and therefore should appreciate. If that were the case, the return from investing in the currency of the high-interest-rate country would be highly profitable, because the investor would enjoy not only the benefits of the higher interest rate, but also that of an appreciating currency.

The carry trade is, in fact, based on the belief that uncovered interest rate parity does not hold on average, and that currency of the high-interest-rate country does not depreciate enough to completely offset the benefits of the higher interest rate. In particular, a carry trade is implemented using the following rule: borrow in terms of currencies with lower interest rates, and invest the proceeds in instruments that are denominated in the currencies with higher interest rates. The trade will be profitable as long as the high-interest-rate currencies do not depreciate enough to offset the differentials between the borrowing rates and the returns on the investments. In this case, gains or losses from the carry trade can be expressed using the following rule:

$$
\text{Profits/losses from carry trade} = \begin{cases} (1 + r_{FCU}) \times \dfrac{S_{t+1}}{S_t} - (1 + r_{DCU}) & \text{If } r_{FCU} > r_{DCU} \\[3mm] (1 + r_{DCU}) - (1 + r_{FCU}) \times \dfrac{S_{t+1}}{S_t} & \text{If } r_{DCU} > r_{FCU} \end{cases}
$$

Example: Suppose short-term rates in Brazil and the United States are 4% and 2%, respectively. The current value of the Brazilian real (BRL) versus the USD is 0.53. Suppose that after one year the spot value of BRL versus USD is 0.51. Has the carry trade been profitable, assuming zero transaction costs?

First, because the short-term rate is higher in Brazil than in the United States, the carry trade requires an investor to borrow short-term in the United States at 2% per year and invest the proceeds in BRL-denominated instruments earning 4% per year. Suppose the investor borrows $1 million. After conversion into BRL, the investor invests (1/0.53)million in BRL-denominated instruments. After one year, this investment will grow to $(1/0.53) \times (1 + 0.04)$ million BRL, and after conversion into USD, it will be:

$$
(1/0.53) \times (1 + 0.04) \times 0.51 = 1.0007 \text{ million USD}
$$

This sum is less than what the investor will need to repay the loan acquired in the United States: 1.02 million USD. In this case, the decline in BRL has more than offset the gain from investing in higher-yielding instruments denominated in BRL. This carry trade has generated a loss.

The carry trade can also be implemented using forward and futures contracts. Given the results reported by covered interest rate parity, it can be seen that the return from investing in higher interest rate currencies would be similar to taking a long position in a futures contract on the higher-interest-rate currency, while taking a short position in the futures contract on the lower-interest-rate currency. In other words, take a long position in FCU if $F_t < S_t$ or a short position in FCU if $F_t > S_t$.

The long strategy will be profitable if the future spot rate, S_{t+1}, turns out to be greater than the current forward rate, F_t. Similarly, the short strategy will be profitable if the future spot rate, S_{t+1}, turns out to be less than the current forward rate, F_t. When forward or futures contracts are used to implement the carry trade, gains or losses can be calculated using the following rule:

$$\text{Profits/losses from carry trade} = \begin{cases} F_t - S_{t+1} & \text{If } F_t < S_t \\ S_{t+1} - F_t & \text{If } F_t > S_t \end{cases}$$

Empirical academic and industry studies have shown that, on average, carry trades have been a profitable strategy. For example, a study by Burnside, Eichenbaum, and Rabelo (2011) shows that a strategy that had invested in the currencies of high-interest-rate countries between 1976 and 2009 would have earned an average return of 4.6% per year. This may not appear to be a significant figure in economic terms, but when it is noted that the strategy could be implemented using futures contracts, where capital commitments are relatively small, this becomes economically significant. Further, the Sharpe ratio of this strategy is more than twice as large as the Sharpe ratio of a buy-and-hold strategy using the S&P 500 index.

35.4.2 Trend-Following and Momentum Models for Currency Trading

A momentum strategy is concerned with the past performance of currencies, rather than with interest rate differentials. To implement this strategy, an investor would examine the relative performance of a set of currencies, then take long positions in those currencies whose values have appreciated in the recent past and short positions in those currencies whose values have depreciated in the recent past. Using the notation employed earlier, the gains and losses from a currency momentum strategy can be calculated using the following rule:

$$\text{Profits/losses from momentum trade} = \begin{cases} S_{t+1} - S_t & \text{If } S_t > S_{t-1} \\ S_t - S_{t+1} & \text{If } S_t < S_{t-1} \end{cases}$$

This means if the FCU has increased in value during the recent past, one would take a long position in the FCU, and thus the strategy would show a profit if the trend continues and $S_{t+1} > S_t$. In contrast, the long strategy would show a loss if the trend reverses and the FCU declines next period; that is, $S_{t+1} < S_t$.

Empirical academic and industry studies have shown that, on average, currency momentum trades have been profitable. For example, the same study by Burnside et al. (2011) shows that a strategy that took long positions in a portfolio of appreciating currencies and short positions in a portfolio of depreciating currencies between 1976 and 2009 would have earned 4.5% per year. The return on a momentum strategy is more volatile than the return from a carry trade strategy and therefore has a lower Sharpe ratio of 0.62. Further, studies have shown that a significant portion of profits generated by a momentum strategy come from currencies of smaller countries, which may suggest that the profits are compensation for the risk of holding these currencies. As determined by Menkhoff, Sarno, and Schrimpf (2011), transaction costs may significantly reduce the reported profits of the momentum strategy.

35.4.3 Value and Volatility Models for Currency Trading

While momentum models may explain a large portion of currency returns in the short run, value models may be more successful at explaining long-run returns to currencies. In the carry trade anomaly, when currencies with high interest rates and high inflation rates may appreciate relative to currencies with lower interest and inflation rates, currency prices tend to move slowly away from the long-term value, as predicted by PPP. When carry trades fail, currencies move very quickly toward the long-run PPP value.

There are three versions of PPP: relative PPP, absolute PPP, and the law of one price. The **law of one price** states that, absent transaction and transportation costs, the same item should have the same cost in all countries adjusted using current exchange rates. The most famous illustration of the law of one price is that of the Big Mac Index. According to the Big Mac Index, in 2008, the euro was overvalued by 47% against the U.S. dollar (USD) (i.e., a Big Mac sold in Europe at a price 47% greater than its price in the United States, when converted into the same currency), while many Asian currencies were extremely cheap vis-à-vis the dollar. However, one could argue that these numbers are not necessarily reliable, because they are calculated on the basis of a single perishable good that cannot be bought and sold by all market participants at the same price.

Rather than using just one good to determine the value of currencies, **absolute PPP** compares the price of a basket of goods across countries. Absolute PPP is a much more reliable indicator of the exchange rate that would equalize the purchasing power of one currency (amount of goods and services that can be purchased with the currency) with that of another currency. One could then compare this PPP level with the current exchange rate level to identify possible future currency movements. For instance, the International Comparison Program of the United Nations collects data on the prices of goods and services for virtually all countries in the world, and publishes PPP exchange rates for all currencies. Comparing these PPP levels with current spot levels allows one to calculate the deviation from PPP, and thus rank currencies based on their level of expected overvaluation or undervaluation.

Another interesting currency relationship is defined by **relative PPP**, which provides a one-to-one link between inflation differential and exchange rate changes. Essentially, relative PPP states that, over time, the change in the exchange rate between two countries should reflect the relative changes between local prices or, equivalently, the difference between the inflation rates of the two countries. Mathematically, this can be written as:

$$\frac{e_1}{e_0} = \frac{1 + \text{Inflation}_{\text{Domestic}}}{1 + \text{Inflation}_{\text{Foreign}}}$$

where e_t is the foreign exchange rate at time t (value of one unit of foreign currency in terms of the domestic currency). How can global macro managers use this relationship? Say, for instance, that the current spot exchange rate is 1.3600 USD = 1 EUR, and that the anticipated inflation rates for next year are 3% in the United

States and 5% in Europe. Therefore, $1.3600 \times 1.03/1.05 = 1.3341$ USD $= 1$ EUR. This means that, over time, one should expect the euro to depreciate against the U.S. dollar. The next issue is to determine the timing and to identify a potential catalyst for this to happen.

Volatility models of currency trading typically involve the trading of options. Managers can profit from long options positions in times of rising volatility, and from short options positions during times of declining volatility. Managers who are short options can also profit from the time decay of options during times of stable volatility, as the price of options declines as time passes and expiration approaches.

35.5 A MORE COMPLEX TRADE: CONTINGENT YIELD CURVE STEEPENING

Beyond the simple directional and relative value trades just presented, global macro funds often look for unusual price fluctuations that can be referred to as far-from-equilibrium market conditions. These situations usually occur when a market's perceptions differ widely from the actual state of underlying economic fundamentals. They open the door to potentially profitable trades, provided that fund managers can find the adequate instruments to express their view.

As an illustration, consider the following trade. In February 1999, following the 1998 Russian default and the collapse of Long-Term Capital Management, financial markets were still experiencing tremendous volatility. The U.S. Federal Reserve had already lowered the federal funds rate twice in an effort to restore confidence and liquidity, but the European Central Bank (ECB) did not initially follow the second Fed cut. Although there was a high probability of further easing of interest rates in Europe should markets fail to stabilize, the implied volatility on two-year and 10-year German interest rates was priced at the same level. This essentially implied that markets had no opinion about whether the yield curve would steepen or flatten on a sell-off. This was clearly a statistical anomaly, as illustrated in Exhibit 35.2.

To arbitrage this situation, several global macro funds started selling out-of-the-money puts on the two-year swaps, and buying out-of-the-money puts on the 10-year swaps. The result was essentially a zero-cost bet on the yield curve steepening between two and 10 years. There were essentially four possible outcomes to this trade:

1. German bond prices could continue to rally on the expectation of further cuts by the ECB. In this case, both option positions would remain out-of-the-money and the trade would expire worthless.
2. German bond prices could sell off in a parallel fashion. In this case, the gains on the 10-year swap puts would be offset by losses on the two-year swap puts.
3. The world could stabilize and German bond prices sell off led by the long end. This is the optimal case, as it leads to high profits for the strategy.
4. The world could stabilize and markets sell off led by the short end (i.e., rate hikes). The last scenario was highly unlikely, given the market environment.

The overall result was therefore essentially a free contingent claim on the yield curve steepening. Global macro fund managers love these positions, because they have very little downside and very large potential upside.

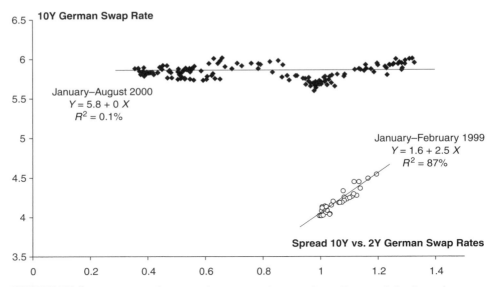

EXHIBIT 35.2   Regression between the 10-year German Swap Rate and the Spread between the 10-Year and Two-Year German Swap Rates

What was the final outcome of that position? As the international environment stabilized, yield curves began to steepen. Ultimately, the ECB did deliver a 50 basis point insurance cut, which dramatically steepened the yield curve between very short-term instruments and two-year notes. Global macro funds were able to repurchase their short two-year put positions at almost no cost, leaving them long deep-in-the-money put positions, which they ultimately monetized for a gain of up to 10%.

35.6   RISK MANAGEMENT AND PORTFOLIO CONSTRUCTION

In their youth, global macro funds were primarily one-person shops placing directional bets with a lot of leverage and very few risk controls. Their volatility was extremely high, and large losses were frequent. For example, the Quantum Fund gained $1 billion against the British pound in 1992, but lost $2 billion during the Russian crisis of 1998. However, this old-style school of global macro fund gradually disappeared after the 1990s. Today's global macro managers still enjoy a high degree of flexibility, but risk management and a disciplined investment approach have become essential components of their activities.

The risk management culture has definitely changed the way global macro strategies are implemented. Most modern global macro managers aim to optimally diversify their portfolio holdings in order to reduce and control risk. In doing so, they often use a combination of value-at-risk measures and stop-loss orders. The former quantifies the estimated loss at different levels of probability and time horizons, and has the advantage of being applicable across all asset classes and instruments as well as at the portfolio level. It is used to allocate risk capital across trade ideas and traders. The latter, stop losses, are intended to impose rational and disciplined behavior, forcing a manager to exit from losing trades regardless of conviction. As summarized by Bruce Kovner (the manager of Caxton Associates LP), stop losses should be set "at a point that, if reached, will reasonably indicate that the trade is wrong, not at a point determined primarily by the maximum dollar amount you are willing to lose." Stop-loss orders, though, are not guaranteed to be executed at the stop loss price, so losses can far exceed expectations during turbulent market conditions.

CHAPTER 36

Fundamental Equity Hedge Fund Strategies

Equity hedge fund strategies may be differentiated by the extent to which positions are determined using discretionary techniques rather than systematic techniques. **Discretionary techniques** usually rely on fundamental analysis, while systematic techniques rely more on technical analysis. Furthermore, discretionary techniques often depend on qualitative analysis, while systematic techniques depend more on quantitative analysis. This chapter provides an in-depth review of fundamental and qualitative equity hedge fund strategies. Chapter 37 discusses equity hedge fund strategies that are more quantitative and systematic.

Equity hedge fund strategies also form spectrums regarding the typical directional bets that are taken, the extent to which the directional bets are allowed to vary in an attempt to time markets, and the use of leverage. Common equity hedge fund strategies are short bias, equity market neutral, long/short, and leveraged strategies, such as 130/30 funds. This chapter focuses on fundamental equity hedge fund strategies in the context of equity long/short strategies, although fundamental strategies can be deployed throughout the directional and leverage spectrums of equity hedge funds.

36.1 VARIATIONS WITHIN EQUITY LONG/SHORT FUNDS

Fundamental equity long/short, typically referred to as long/short, is an investment strategy associated with hedge funds whose managers buy equities that are expected to rise in value and sell equities that are expected to fall in value. This strategy is typically implemented through fundamental stock selection and, to a lesser extent, by varying total net exposure, also known as market timing. Note that in practice, the classification of a long/short hedge fund is somewhat subjective, and therefore caution should be used when a hedge fund is categorized as such.

36.1.1 Investment Opportunity Set, Cash and Leverage, and Market Timing

Since long/short managers typically invest in stocks, the investment opportunity set is all possible combinations of stocks. For simplicity, this discussion excludes derivatives and any private investments, though some managers may employ derivatives.

Given that long/short managers can buy and sell short, all combinations of long and short stock positions need to be included. Additionally, long/short managers can be underinvested and have a positive allocation to cash, or be overinvested by borrowing cash to leverage. The possible number of combinations grows very large when we consider the continuum of allocation choices across long stocks, short stocks, and cash/leverage. Moreover, long/short managers can vary their exposures across time by increasing and decreasing total leverage while holding the portfolio's composition constant, by changing the composition of the portfolio while holding the leverage constant, or by engaging in a combination of both.

36.1.2 Portfolio Concentration and Turnover

Long/short equity hedge fund portfolios are typically highly concentrated in a relatively small number of stocks, with core positions ranging from three to 10 stocks, and noncore positions ranging from 20 to 40 stocks. This is much more concentrated than equity market neutral or statistical arbitrage portfolios, which may have hundreds or even thousands of positions. Long/short managers typically have much lower turnover, with longer holding periods than those of equity market neutral and statistical arbitrage managers. Long/short managers may hold positions for many years. It is not uncommon to hear that the investment horizon for these managers is on the order of three to five years.

36.1.3 Value, Growth, and Blend Approaches

Long/short managers vary with regard to investment style classifications analogously to how mutual funds differ in terms of styles, such as value, growth, and blend. **Value long/short managers** employ traditional valuation metrics, such as book-to-market ratios, price-earnings (P/E) ratios, dividend yield, and the ratio of P/E to earnings growth rate (i.e., the PEG ratio), to look for undervalued companies. Managers following this approach tend to be contrarians and to invest in companies that are temporarily out of favor. Empirical evidence shows that value stocks tend to outperform growth stocks through many business cycles.[1]

The **growth approach** to fundamental long/short equity investing is to look for companies with strong growth potential. Long/short growth managers are attracted by top-line growth numbers and are willing to look past weak current earnings in the presence of aggressive sales growth. Often they invest in small high-tech companies, because large companies in mature industries generally lack the same growth opportunities. Paying a reasonable price for growth companies is known as the growth at a reasonable price (GARP) approach.

The blend approach to fundamental long/short equity investing employs both approaches. Managers vary their investment process depending on the macroenvironment. Value stocks tend to have low betas relative to growth stocks. When anticipating down markets, managers may take a value investment approach, but in anticipation of rising markets, they increase their allocations to growth companies, thereby blending the two approaches.

---

[1] For data on the performance of value versus growth stocks as well as return to momentum strategy, see http://mba.tuck.dartmouth.edu/pages/faculty/ken.french/.

36.1.4 Bottom-Up versus Top-Down Approach

Fundamental equity long/short managers can also be classified as bottom-up versus top-down. Most fundamental equity long/short managers are **bottom-up** investors. They are essentially stock pickers who tend to have concentrated portfolios. These investors are less concerned with market timing and forecasting macroeconomic trends or relative industry performance. Rather, they are concerned with opportunities and threats faced by individual companies and subsequently focus on their strengths and weaknesses. This framework is referred to as a SWOT analysis (strengths, weaknesses, opportunities, and threats).

The goal of bottom-up fundamental analysis is to determine the value of a company's stock based on forecasted sales, expenses, and earnings. These forecasts provide an estimated cash flow stream, which is discounted to arrive at a value of the company. The equity value is found after subtracting the value of the company's debt. Given that forecasting the future is challenging at best, analysts may generate a set of valuations based on good, medium, and bad scenarios, and then use the weighted average of these valuations where they correspond to the probability of the scenarios occurring. An example of a good scenario could be assuming high growth in company sales; a bad scenario could be assuming low growth.[2]

It is common for bottom-up long/short managers to spend substantial time away from their offices checking distribution channels, evaluating production lines, examining traffic at retail stores, and so on. Bottom-up managers often have researchers on the ground ferreting out any useful information that is not included in public documents. They perform detailed due diligence on the companies they hold and in which they intend to invest. For example, managers may ask industry experts about their views on the company's products and processes, competitive advantages, patents, and political and regulatory risks. Typically, this strategy focuses on companies that have limited analyst coverage, based on the idea that limited competition for information may indicate investment opportunities in which public information is not fully reflected in the market price of the equity.

Some long/short managers apply a **top-down** investment approach, driven by a few broad investment themes. Managers seek to forecast macroeconomic forces that would drive a sector's return, and implement their views through diversified portfolios and exchange-traded funds (ETFs). They tend to have strong views on the current stage of the business cycle, inflationary expectations, and monetary and fiscal policies. Influential economy drivers are important to top-down managers, who spend less time on company-specific analysis. Following are some examples of the types of inquiries these managers may make:

- If the euro disintegrates, how will equity markets react?
- If gold is trading at an all-time high, will increased supply or reduced demand cause a reversal?
- What impact might Chinese government actions have on the economies of other nations?

---

[2] For a very sound and useful resource on this approach, refer to the website run by Professor Aswath Damodaran of New York University: http://pages.stern.nyu.edu/~adamodar/.

- Are nations such as Brazil, Russia, India, and China going to fuel global economic growth?
- If oil prices rise or fall substantially, what are the implications for equity markets and various industries?
- What is the impact of expansionary monetary policy on global financial institutions?

Top-down long/short managers have a strong understanding of macroeconomic forces and their impact on financial markets. They understand various interactions among different segments of capital markets: lead-lag relationships between fixed-income, currency, commodities, real estate, and stock market sectors.

36.1.5 Sector-Specific Investment Approach

Long/short managers may be broken into two groups: generalists and sector specialists. **Generalists** invest across a wide universe of stocks, whereas sector specialists tend to stay within a specific equity sector, such as financials, health care, or technology. Additionally, generalists may focus on a particular country or region. Some emerging market long/short hedge fund managers may market themselves as emerging country specialists with a local market presence. This would mean that they have analysts within a given emerging market country who know the local dialect, have an extensive network into companies, and may even have a deep understanding of the market's capital structure and dynamics. Sector funds are typically run by **sector specialists** who at one time were sector analysts for investment banks and brokerage firms. Most of these managers have been following a group of stocks within their industry specialization for many years. Portfolios are constructed by buying the stronger players within a given sector and selling the weaker ones. Popular sector funds focus on areas in which highly specialized skills are necessary, such as finance, health care, biotech, technology, real estate, and energy. In addition to the generalist/sector specialist distinction, long/short managers employ various strategies, such as sector momentum, day trading, and market timing.

36.1.6 Corporate Governance (Activist) Approach

Activists are long/short managers who take a very public stance on their investments. Activist strategies rely on corporate governance changes to unlock value. Activists are open about confronting and criticizing senior management and boards of directors of public companies. Research has shown that they are quite effective in changing the composition of a company's board of directors, and they generally get management to adopt recommended changes to the corporate structure. Corporate governance changes can favor one group of stakeholders over another. For example, an activist manager may recommend increasing dividends, benefiting shareholders to the detriment of bondholders.

36.2 BACKGROUND OF THE LONG/SHORT EQUITY HEDGE FUND

In 1949, Alfred Winslow Jones pioneered the hedge fund industry and the long/short strategy in particular, with the creation of A.W. Jones & Co. However, neither the industry nor the strategy was immediately popularized. This section gives an overview of the rise in popularity of the long/short equity hedge fund strategy.

36.2.1 A Short History of Fundamental Analysis and Long/Short Funds

Benjamin Graham is often referred to as the father of fundamental analysis, and the techniques he pioneered in the 1940s have remained popular over the decades. Value-investing techniques were further popularized by the writings of Graham and David Dodd of the Columbia Business School. Tiger Management Group's Julian Robertson popularized the long/short strategy in hedge funds. His successful implementation of value investing propelled the growth of the long/short hedge fund sector to substantial levels. Some of Robertson's top employees left the company to start their own long/short hedge funds. Some of these former employees (referred to as "Tiger Cubs") have enjoyed success with their funds, presumably employing strategies similar to those of Tiger, and some of these funds went on to spawn new hedge funds when their employees departed.

It is likely that only a few of the top long/short managers have mastered the implementation of these techniques. Finding truly talented long/short managers is a challenging task. Disentangling alpha from beta in long/short returns is difficult due to the dynamic nature of their trading activities and positions.

36.2.2 Size of the Long/Short Market

According to Hedge Fund Research, Inc., the hedge fund industry had approximately $2 trillion of assets under management (AUM) as of year-end 2011. Long/short (equity hedge) had approximately 27% of the total hedge fund assets, roughly $540 billion of AUM. This represents a decline of about 7% from its allocation in 1990. At that time long/short had approximately 37% of the total hedge fund assets.

Over time, the allocation to long/short has changed dramatically. According to Credit Suisse estimates, long/short peaked in late 2000, when it represented over half of the AUM within the hedge fund industry (see Exhibit 36.1). Since then, however, it has fallen out of favor with investors, though it still represents a substantial component of hedge fund assets.

36.3 MECHANICS OF THE STRATEGY

This section discusses the mechanics of the traditional long/short investment process. Though the steps taken by any one manager will vary, essentially all long/short managers begin with an investment idea and end with portfolio risk management.

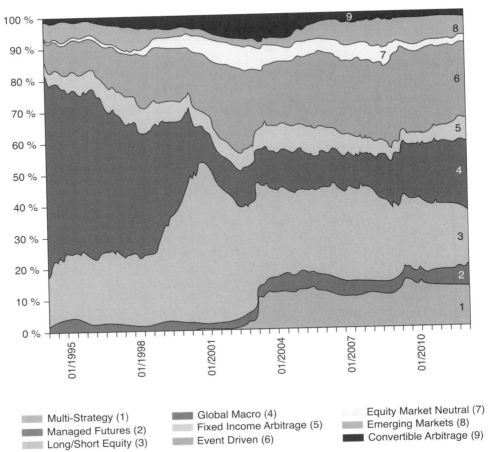

Multi-Strategy (1)
Managed Futures (2)
Long/Short Equity (3)
Global Macro (4)
Fixed Income Arbitrage (5)
Event Driven (6)
Equity Market Neutral (7)
Emerging Markets (8)
Convertible Arbitrage (9)

EXHIBIT 36.1   Historical Sector Weights of the Dow Jones Credit Suisse Hedge Fund Indexes
Source: Dow Jones Credit Suisse hedge fund indexes.

36.3.1 Idea Generation

The first and by far the most critical step is to generate good investment ideas. Some managers screen the universe of stocks based on fundamental ratios or technical indicators so as to reduce the total number of stocks to a manageable size. Others read industry newsletters, research reports, market commentary, academic research, or other written sources of information to gain investment insights. Additionally, some managers attend investment conferences, trade conferences, and idea luncheons/dinners to develop new ideas. The value of a solid network of colleagues cannot be overestimated in uncovering and refining new ideas. Some may talk to friendly CEOs or CFOs, while others may scrutinize forms required by regulators such as Form 13F reports for ideas. Any source that is publicly available can be employed for idea generation.

36.3.2 Optimal Idea Expression

The next step, instinctive to seasoned long/short managers, involves deciding how to best express an idea—in other words, determining the best investment decisions that can be made based on the investment idea. During this process, the manager may make the following inquiries:

- What trade should be executed to extract the highest return from the idea?
- What price level will either confirm or negate the idea's validity?
- Will the stock price move straight up and become range-bound, or will it move slowly upward over many months?

For example, suppose a manager believes that the soon-to-be-released earnings of Company XYZ will exceed the consensus forecast. The manager must decide whether to buy the stock, buy call options, sell put options, or express the trade through sector ETFs. In the interest of executing the optimal trade, the manager must further consider the downside risk and time frame.

36.3.3 Sizing the Position

The next step works in conjunction with the previous step. Typically, a long/short manager has existing positions, so she needs to understand how the new position will fit within the context of her current portfolio. Sizing the position may require resizing the other opportunities within the portfolio. Positions are generally sized according to the level of the manager's conviction regarding the idea. If the long/short manager's conviction is high, she is likely to take a large position. If her conviction is low, she may build a toehold position to see whether the idea is a good one. She may then increase the size of the position if her conviction increases.

36.3.4 Executing the Trade

Many long/short managers will execute their own trades. That is, they will physically place the trade into the market via an electronic trading system or through their broker. The majority of long/short managers have extensive trading experience. They also tend to have a strong understanding of intraday technical indicators and have experience attempting to determine when the technical environment is favorable for entering or exiting positions. When executing their trades, they need to consider whether they should buy aggressively (lift offers), sell aggressively (hit bids), or trade passively (join bids or offers). Other important considerations when executing trades include the following:

- The liquidity of the underlying security at the time of execution
- Whether there is a major announcement due out that may move the market
- The availability of the stock to be borrowed in the case of a short

Successful managers should possess a keen sense of the trade's potential market impact. Depending on the impact, there may be a trading cost associated with it. If a manager has a large order and tries to execute it all at once, he may move the market so violently that the ultimate average price paid would be very expensive. However, if he splits up the order into smaller pieces or executes at either a time-weighted average price (TWAP) or a volume-weighted average price (VWAP) throughout the day, he may achieve a better or worse average price. The trade-off between alpha decay and order completion should be evaluated by determining what opportunity costs arise by waiting to execute. If the manager executes quickly, how much does he influence the market? For instance, the impact would be much greater for thinly traded stocks than for liquid stocks. Additionally, long/short managers should have a firm understanding of the costs of commissions and exchange fees. Upon execution of the trade, long/short managers will usually examine their slippage reports (either generated internally or provided by the prime broker). Some trades may not be fully executed, requiring long/short managers to deal with the consequences.

Fund managers, or more particularly head traders, will often examine the average daily volume of each stock in an attempt to assess the underlying liquidity of each position. Some constraints may be enforced (such as never having more than X% of the average daily trading volume) to ensure the ability to exit the position quickly when necessary. This average may be computed over time periods of various lengths, known as rolling window analysis. However, such attempts at managing portfolio liquidity become increasingly challenging as the manager's AUM increases, typically due to successful performance or fund-raising. As the AUM increases within a given long/short fund, the slow creep into larger-capitalization stocks in search of higher liquidity may become more and more difficult to avoid.

36.3.5   Understanding and Managing the Risks of Long/Short Investing

Once the order has been executed and the confirmations are checked, portfolio positions are examined closely to see whether the investment idea is working. **Corporate actions**, such as merger announcements, spin-offs, and divestitures, require monitoring because they may change the risk profile of the company. Many long/short managers work with risk managers, who go well beyond simply reporting net and gross exposure of the fund. Many employ sophisticated risk models from various risk vendors, such as Barra, Northfield, and Advanced Portfolio Technologies (APT), which assist fund managers with the estimation and daily reporting of factor exposures. Additionally, standard risk reports are typically generated using value at risk (VaR) analysis, in which the portfolio and all of the various ways it can be sliced—longs, shorts, sectors, regions, liquidity buckets—are examined. Furthermore, **scenario analysis** can be helpful in understanding the behavior of the portfolio in stressed markets (such as, "What if this portfolio had been held during the tech crash of 2000?"). Some of the smaller long/short managers may default to using their prime broker's risk reports, since hiring a seasoned risk manager is expensive.

A brief commentary on the short position in a long/short portfolio is in order. Though short selling is a defining characteristic of a successful long/short manager, long/short managers typically run net long. Empirical research has shown that, on average, long/short managers have positive net exposures to the overall market, with a market beta around 0.5. Theoretically, a **short position** may lead to unlimited losses. Additionally, when a short position goes against the manager, it is far more painful than when a long position goes against the manager. This is best illustrated in the following example.

Suppose a long/short manager has two investments, A and B, and suppose she holds a long position of $100 in A and a short position of $100 in B. If both positions go against her by 10% in one day (A goes down from $100 to $90, and B goes up from $100 to $110), the manager loses $10 on the long A position and $10 on the short B position. Now, if both positions go against her the next day by another 10%, she will lose $9 in A as A goes down from $90 to $81, and $11 in B as B goes up from $110 to $121.

Notice that the dollar losses in a long position become mitigated as the base decreases, whereas the dollar losses in a short position become magnified as the base increases. This subtle difference makes short selling stocks more risky than buying stocks.

Long/short managers pay much more attention to their short positions than they do to their long positions. The **process of short selling** is very different from purchasing stock. In many countries, short sales can be executed only on an uptick. This makes execution much more difficult and market impact much larger when stock prices are falling, as the stock may tick lower for a number of trades before the first small increase in price occurs, at which time the stock can be sold short. Stock must also be borrowed from an owner of the stock before it can be sold short. The short seller may be forced to cover the stock if he is no longer able to borrow the stock; this most frequently occurs when the owner of the borrowed stock sells the stock, which requires the lender of the stock to deliver it to the new owner. **Short squeezes** are another unique risk of short selling, in which the stock price rises rapidly and short sellers are forced to cover their positions for risk-management purposes. In heavily borrowed stocks, short squeezes are rumored to come through a concerted effort by some stockholders who would like to see the stock move sharply higher. Those stockholders buy the stock rapidly, hoping to maximize the market impact of their trades and to force the short sellers to cover their positions and add to the buying pressure, driving the stock significantly higher.

Other risks of short selling include regulatory measures aimed at limiting or preventing short sales.

36.4 MANAGERIAL EXPERTISE AND SOURCES OF RETURNS

Two closely related issues in analyzing fundamental equity hedge fund strategies such as long/short are managerial expertise and sources of returns.

36.4.1 Expertise of Equity Long/Short Fund Managers

Fundamental equity hedge fund managers should have an intimate knowledge of their stocks. For each stock within their portfolio, they are expected to know the company's business model, revenue generators, costs and expenses, product lines, comparative advantages, market opportunities, competition, and recent changes to the corporate structure. In addition, they should be aware of the company's weaknesses, threats to their business model, and new threats in technology and possible innovations. In establishing long positions, equity long/short managers look for solid companies with a defendable competitive advantage that are trading at a discount to estimated fair value. It is common to hear long/short managers describe their strategy as "value with a catalyst" or "growth at a reasonable price."

Fundamental equity long/short managers are well trained in fundamental analysis, often with previous experience at a large hedge fund (e.g., Tiger Management Group) or as research analysts at top investment banks. Some long/short managers may come from long-only mutual fund complexes or from successful private equity shops. Regardless, these managers must be well equipped to analyze balance sheets and income statements and to make projections about a company's future earning prospects in order to build discounted free cash flow models. These models are often updated daily or at least weekly.

Many fundamental equity hedge fund managers are strong value investors, who, like Warren Buffett, look to invest in real businesses. These managers are often well versed in analyzing income statements and balance sheets, and understanding their associated footnotes. They listen to company conference calls, perform independent research, and have a strong grasp of what it takes to run a successful company. Some have strong accounting backgrounds and others have law degrees, but the common skill among these long/short managers is that they can analyze a business in depth. Once they understand a business, they put together a forecasting model that predicts future earnings and future cash flows. They value the company by determining an appropriate rate (commonly using the weighted average cost of capital [WACC]) to discount projected future cash flows. They then compare this valuation with the market's assessment of the company. If the market's assessment is lower, the manager would buy the stock; if assessment is higher, the manager would short it. A very important advantage for long/short managers is to have access to timely information through a strong network of contacts.

Large-cap stocks are well covered by equity analysts, making mispricings less likely. As a result, value-oriented equity long/short managers tend to focus their research on small- and mid-cap companies. This is consistent with the empirical evidence indicating that these managers have a positive bias toward small-cap stocks. Additionally, lesser-known names having more inefficiencies when it comes to their potential misvaluations is consistent with informational efficiency theories of equilibrium-based models conditional on participation of agents.

36.4.2 Sources of Returns from a Fundamental Long/Short Strategy

One potential source of returns is **firm-specific informational inefficiency**. If capital markets are informationally inefficient at the semistrong level, then fundamental analysis may generate superior risk-adjusted returns by establishing long positions in underpriced equities and short positions in overpriced equities. Equity long/short hedge fund managers may attempt to exploit informational inefficiencies by either locating information not generally used by other investors or being better at evaluating information that is commonly considered.

Fundamental equity hedge fund managers tend to be value focused and, as discussed previously, are drawn to smaller equities and equities that attract less attention from large institutional investors. This empirical observation is consistent with the idea that returns may result from exploiting capital market inefficiencies in small equities. Because small-cap stocks are not otherwise monitored by major institutions, their market prices may deviate substantially from their appropriate values based on careful analysis of all publicly available information.

Another potential source of returns is **factor-based informational inefficiency**. The idea is that superior fundamental analysis may identify equity return factors (e.g., size) that differentiate groups of stocks into higher-performing firms that should be held long (e.g., small stocks) and lower-performing firms that should be sold short (e.g., large stocks).

The seminal research of Fama and French indicated that realized U.S. equity returns were driven by factors related to the size of each firm and the extent to which the firm appeared to offer value versus growth. Furthermore, average and perhaps even expected equity returns appear to be related to these factors. Specifically, small stocks seem to outperform large stocks, and value stocks seem to outperform growth stocks. Accordingly, fundamental equity hedge fund managers may have been earning higher returns through their focus on small-capitalization value stocks. These higher returns would be driven by a net long bias, along with the high returns attributable to the size and value factors.

Numerous questions remain unresolved. Were the higher observed returns of small stocks and value stocks compensation for bearing a higher risk, or were they alpha? Were the higher past returns of small stocks and value stocks a random outcome, or did they occur because small stocks and value stocks offered consistently higher expected returns? Finally, even if the high historical returns reflected superior expected returns in recent decades, will small stocks and value stocks offer higher expected risk-adjusted returns in future decades? With regard to the last question, if capital markets were informationally inefficient in the past with regard to size and growth/value, is there reason to believe that the same markets will continue to be informationally inefficient and continue to offer superior risk-adjusted returns based on these factors?

A few recent works have examined the equity mispricing within developed and emerging countries. Results show a wider range of valuations over time within emerging countries than within developed countries, which would imply that such theories could be justified, at least superficially, given the initial limited empirical support. Somewhat analogously with large stocks versus small stocks, prices in small, emerging markets may have a lower degree of informational efficiency than prices in large, developed markets. Smaller, emerging markets may offer higher returns as compensation for higher risk, as compensation for lower liquidity, or as an incentive for investors to perform the extra fundamental analysis required to invest in relatively inefficient markets (i.e., a complexity premium).

The potentially higher returns of emerging markets might make a reasonably good case for adding fundamental long/short emerging market managers to the common mix of long/short opportunities. A less obvious motivation would be to avoid the home-country biases affecting allocation decisions. Although it may be easier to have due diligence meetings within one's region/location and in one's mother tongue, the advantage of including emerging market managers may be substantial diversification benefits.

An example of potential information that may be used by a fundamental equity manager is observation of trading by other managers. Knowledge of another manager's holdings may be an important piece of information for an investor to use in evaluating the manager. Such knowledge is, to some degree, readily available for some of the hedge funds operating in the United States pursuant to the Securities and Exchange Commission's mandatory reporting rule, otherwise known as Form 13F. **Form 13F filings** are required of institutional investment managers having discretion over $100 million in 13F securities. A 13F security includes exchange-traded (NYSE, AMEX) or NASDAQ-quoted stocks, equity options and warrants, shares of closed-end investment companies, and certain convertible debt securities. It does not, however, include shares of open-end investment companies (mutual funds). The reporting rule requires managers to disclose the names and positions of all 13F securities held long in their portfolios on a quarterly basis within 45 days after the quarter. To the extent that long/short managers do not change their positions frequently, the information obtained through the 13F reports will be current and relevant.

Seasoned long/short fund-of-funds managers examine 13Fs for top positions prior to meeting new long/short managers. Recently, there has been a proliferation of companies who attempt to capture and commercially present this information to clients. Many websites are available that will provide this information to end users for a fee. Additionally, investment products based on 13F positions of popular hedge fund managers have emerged. However, it should be noted that some funds employ legal techniques in order to sidestep this disclosure requirement.

A study by Brav et al. (2008) reports that between 2001 and 2006, activist hedge funds in the United States proposed strategic, operational, and financial remedies to the firms in which they had taken significant positions, and attained success or partial success in two-thirds of the cases studied. The excess (abnormal) stock returns experienced by the target firms upon the announcement of the proposal were approximately 7%, with no reversal during the subsequent year. Furthermore, it was reported that the target firms experienced increases in payout, operating performance, and higher CEO turnover after activism.

36.5 LONG/SHORT RETURN ATTRIBUTION

The benefits and costs of short selling differ between retail investors and institutional investors, and the particular terms and conditions available to various institutional investors vary based on their size, the markets and securities involved, the selection of a prime broker, and so forth. Retail investors must typically post cash collateral on a short sale and are not able to earn interest on the sales proceeds received when shares are sold short. Institutional investors are typically able to earn interest on collateral or to post securities as collateral. Thus, a long/short equity manager could typically post the long positions as collateral on the short positions, thereby generating earnings on the collateral.

The institutional short seller typically receives a **short stock rebate** on the proceeds of the short sale. The rebate is typically an index-linked variable interest rate (e.g., the federal funds rate) minus the borrowing costs (e.g., 0.15% or 0.25% per year) that the borrower earns on the proceeds of the short sale. In unusual cases of very low interest rates or special-situation securities in which the demand for borrowing is very high, the borrowing costs can exceed the interest revenue, resulting in a negative rebate to the short seller. From the security lender's perspective, the lender is able to borrow money at the rebate rate, a rate below a riskless index, which can presumably be invested at a positive spread relative to the rebate.

The following example is stylized and is intended to represent an analysis of typical, simplified benefits and costs.

Total returns for long/short managers can be decomposed and attributed to the following four components from the long positions and four components from the short positions:

- Returns/costs from long positions:
  1. Price appreciation/depreciation
  2. Dividends received
  3. Margin interest cost of longs if leveraged
  4. Interest earned on any excess cash or any cash posted as collateral
- Returns/costs from short positions:
  1. Price depreciation/appreciation
  2. Interest earned on proceeds of short sale
  3. Cost of borrowing shares, depending on difficulty to borrow
  4. Dividend payments to buyers of borrowed shares

Consider a highly simplified example of a long/short manager with $100 of assets under management and only two positions:

1. Long $100 of Company XYZ, which pays a $2 dividend
2. Short $50 of Company ABC, which pays a $1 dividend

Suppose that the objective is to attribute the total performance of this long/short fund over the specific period of one year. Also, assume that no other trades were executed over that year, that XYZ's share price rises 10% over the year, and that ABC's share price declines 5% over the same year. Assume that the short rebate of 1.5% is composed of the rate of return paid to the fund on the proceeds of the short sale (2% per year) and the cost to borrow the ABC shares (0.50% per year). Finally, assume that the fund is able to post its long shares as collateral for the short sales. Note that there is no excess cash. Exhibit 36.2 illustrates the cash flows.

In the scenario illustrated in Exhibit 36.2, the investor would have earned a gross return of 14.25%, which is the profit of $14.25 divided by investor capital of $100. In unlevered, fully invested funds, long positions equal the amount of investor capital. In the example, the long side is fully invested and unlevered, so there is no interest income earned on cash and no margin interest expense.

The prime broker will normally examine a portfolio's characteristics to determine appropriate terms, with more favorable terms, such as lower borrowing and higher rebate rates, generally offered to larger funds. There have been periods in which prime brokers cut back on the leverage they provided their hedge fund clients, which requires leveraged funds to reduce position sizes during volatile markets.

EXHIBIT 36.2   Illustration of Cash Flows from Long and Short Positions

Dollar returns from long position (XYZ):	
1. Price appreciation/depreciation	+ $10.00 ($110.00 − $100.00)
2. Dividends received	+ $2.00
3. Margin interest cost of longs if leveraged	$0.00
4. Interest earned on cash	$0.00
Total dollar change from long position	+ $12.00
Dollar returns from short position (ABC):	
1. Price depreciation/appreciation	+ $2.50 ($50.00 − $47.50)
2 & 3. Short rebate	+ $0.75 (0.015 × $50.00)
4. Dividend payments	− $1.00
Total dollar change from short position	+ $2.25
Total dollar return	+ $14.25

If a long/short fund is fully invested, is unlevered, earns competitive rebates on securities with minimal borrowing costs, and has long securities with similar dividends to the securities it shorts, the returns from a long/short manager should typically be dominated by the price appreciation/depreciation corresponding to the underlying long and short positions, directly reflecting the manager's stock selection skills. Managers can also add value through market timing, when net long positions are larger during rising markets and smaller, or even net short, during falling markets.

CHAPTER 37

Quantitative Equity Hedge Fund Strategies

This chapter focuses on the more quantitative and systematic approaches to managing equity hedge funds. **Systematic approaches,** also known as quantitative equity market neutral (EMN) strategies, employ more computer resources and extensive use of data in their selection of investments. Quantitative equity market neutral strategies are often birthed from academic, empirical, and financial anomalies or minor/major modifications along this vein of the research. Practitioners often attempt to extract economically substantial profits from these known empirical anomalies by rigorously considering transaction costs and capacity constraints.

This chapter focuses on equity market neutral strategies as premier examples of quantitative equity hedge fund strategies. The analysis of this chapter covers essential information on equity market neutral strategies but leaves the technical details in citations for those who wish to investigate further.

37.1 VARIATIONS OF QUANTITATIVE STRATEGIES

At the heart of every equity market neutral strategy is the attempt to establish long positions in securities when their expected returns are relatively high and to establish short positions in securities when their expected returns are relatively low. Quantitative equity market neutral strategies can be divided based on underlying information (technical factors vs. fundamental factors) or trading frequencies.

37.1.1 Quantitative Strategies Focused on Technical Analysis

Quantitative equity market neutral strategies trade equities in a systematic fashion. Common techniques are based on sorting stocks given a particular indicator. The underlying indicator may be based purely on past prices and volume (i.e., technical analysis). An example would be the identification of a **pairs trade** between two stocks that have a high long-term correlation but recently experienced a sharp diversion in returns, widening the spread between the prices of the two stocks. A typical trading decision would be to establish a long position in the stock that had recently underperformed and a short position in the stock that had recently outperformed. The motivation for the trade would be the expectation that the stocks would converge to similar valuation levels based on their observed tendency to share similar returns and valuation levels. The trader would be speculating that the divergence in returns was temporary, perhaps based on the execution of a large order. A pairs trade is typically structured on a market neutral basis. Not only is the market beta offset, but industry and size factors are often neutralized in pairs trading.

The exact forms of technical analysis used to identify trades vary tremendously. However, the approaches are often distinguished by assuming either mean reversion or momentum (trending). **Mean reversion** is a tendency to return to typical historical relationships or levels, while momentum is a tendency of returns or valuation levels to persist in recently observed directions.

A popular statistical modeling approach is **co-integration**. Co-integration, as described in laymen's terms by Murray (1994), is analogous to the relationship between a drunken person and that person's dog, both walking aimlessly. Because the dog is on a leash, there is a limit to the distance between the person and the dog. Though both may appear to meander randomly and wildly over time, they move less wildly and widely as they continually adjust their positions closer to each other as they try to reunite. Thus, the two are co-integrated. The key to applying a co-integration approach is statistically identifying a relationship that persists.

Applying co-integration or a similar statistical approach to securities typically involves a daunting scale. For example, consider the possible combinations of securities in the S&P 500 index. The number of pairs is solved by "500 choose 2" or by thinking about it this way: given the matrix 500×500, exclude the diagonal (500), divide by 2, and take only one diagonal. So, $[(500 \times 500) - 500]/2 = 124,750$ possible pairs. For each pair, the approach involves identifying the extent, if any, of the co-integration. A fund manager may establish potential patterns based on past data and then monitor the possible opportunities of each pair over time. Monitoring this number of co-integrated pairs over time may be a useful exercise to gauge the opportunity set for generic pairs trading. Obviously, one would have to account for many other issues, such as nuances of defining distance between pairs, transaction costs, market impact, short availability, and rebates. But as a simple exercise, such a barometer of the opportunity set may be useful.

Other techniques include decomposing the contents of a large variance-covariance matrix or correlation matrix into components that explain the main structure. Typically, this decomposition leads to statistically constructed orthogonal factors. For example, if one takes all the stocks in the S&P 500 and looks at the first principal component, chances are that it will look quite similar to the long-only market portfolio. That is, empirically, the first factor resembles the buy-and-hold S&P 500. The second principal component is more difficult to identify, but by construction, it is rendered orthogonal to the first component. Some **statistical arbitrage funds** (stat arb funds) attempt to model and trade higher-order components, or at least those that have some mean-reversion properties. That is, they will not trade the first principal component or the long-only market; they will try to model and trade higher-order factors. Once again, the bet is that ultimately, when things get stretched (when the drunken person and the dog are far away from each other), there will be a time when there is a convergence (the person and the dog will eventually move closer to each other). Measuring distances and timing are very important, and stat arb managers find taking a scientific approach useful in defining the needed terms.

Stat arb managers as a group are typically made up of doctorate-level scientists, mathematicians, and statisticians from leading academic institutions, all of whom have a strong background in analyzing large data sets. Common issues faced by these experts involve the most efficient clustering techniques, the newest machine-learning methods, and principal/independent component analysis. Generally, the goal becomes finding stable distributions or, if distributions are unstable, ways to detect this change of regimes so that positions correctly anticipate transitions to a new regime. With stable distributions, it is increasingly likely that the approach will eventually generate profits, much like the house at a casino will win in the long run if it sets up the payoff of the games correctly. Stat arb managers have the law of large numbers working in their favor if they are placing numerous bets over long periods of time on relationships that they are able to successfully identify and predict as being stable.

The most advanced techniques are often borrowed from other disciplines, such as econometrics and time-series analysis. Successful stat arb managers often have very little fundamental knowledge of the underlying stocks that they hold in their portfolios. These managers fall at one extreme end of the spectrum compared to long/short fundamental managers, who are more likely to have intimate knowledge of their companies.

37.1.2 Quantitative Strategies Based on Fundamental Factors

The underlying information driving trading decisions may be based on fundamental factors. Common **fundamental indicators** are book-to-market-value (B/M) ratio, earnings-to-price (E/P) ratio, cash-flow-to-price (CF/P) ratio, size, and so forth. The primary approach is to identify securities with abnormally high or low expected returns based on fundamental factors and an analysis of past return tendencies. For example, research may show that a particular combination of indicators has cross-sectionally differentiated average returns. A fund manager may assume that the fundamental factors can be used to predict relative expected returns, with long positions being established in those securities forecasted to offer higher expected returns, and short positions being established in those securities forecasted to offer lower expected returns. Some quantitative managers use a combination of technical and fundamental indicators in their trading models. One of the most frequently used model combinations is value plus momentum (discussed in a later section).

The underlying assumption of the use of fundamental factors to establish positions is stability in the relationship. Specifically, the fund manager is assuming that the past relationship between indicators and returns is likely to hold over time, such that relative future expected returns can be predicted. However, the risks are (1) that the observed relationship in the past was a random outcome with no predictive value, (2) that the observed relationship in the past has been corrected through increased informational efficiency or through fundamental changes in underlying economic relationships, and (3) that during periods of stress and other extreme conditions, the historically observed relationship unravels and reverses.

A distinction between a quantitative EMN strategy based on fundamental factors and the fundamental equity hedge funds discussed in Chapter 36 is the extent to which the analysis is based on extensive computational analysis of past returns and current prices. Fundamental equity hedge funds tend to perform extensive fundamental analysis on individual securities based on economic reasoning. Alternatively, quantitative analysts rely more on computerized analysis of large data sets for historical relationships between returns and fundamental factors, typically to predict short-term return differences. Fundamental analysts may screen data and organize data with computers, but their trading decisions are typically based on close examination of smaller data sets to project longer-term valuations.

37.1.3 Quantitative Strategies Differentiated by Trading Frequency

An important distinction between quantitative EMN funds is the trading frequency. The **trading frequency** is generally described as the typical length of time that positions are held (i.e., the **holding period**). Trading speed is calculated in terms of how fast one's model is able to take input information, create the signal, and then submit the orders into the markets for execution.

Exhibit 37.1 describes the spectrum of trading frequency among quantitative equity hedge funds. On the left end of the spectrum is **high-frequency trading** (HFT), in which trades are detected and executed in milliseconds and held possibly for only seconds. The challenge faced by most HFT approaches is generating greater speed than competitors in identifying and executing trades. The idea that drives each trade is typically rather simple; for example, one trading approach is a market-maker

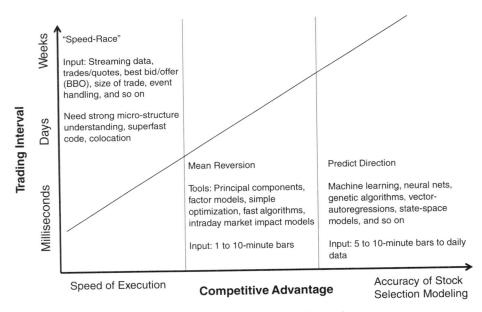

EXHIBIT 37.1   Competitive Advantage versus Trading Interval
Note: A millisecond is 1/1,000 of a second.

approach that identifies temporary price disequilibria presumably caused by large order executions. Another approach is to exploit slow security price responses to new information.

In the middle of Exhibit 37.1 are less rapid trading approaches that typically rely on mean reversion. These approaches require moderate speed and moderately advanced idea generation. On the right side of Exhibit 37.1 are the more directional approaches, which depend little on speed and most on accuracy of the economic modeling of future returns. These approaches are discussed further in a subsequent section.

37.2 BACKGROUND ON QUANTITATIVE STRATEGIES

This section begins with a brief history of quantitative equity hedge funds. The remainder of the section discusses several aspects that are common to many of these hedge funds.

37.2.1 Short History of Quantitative Equity Hedge Funds

One of the most successful hedge funds of all time is based on a quantitative trading strategy: James Simons's Renaissance Medallion Fund. Very little is understood about its actual methodology, given the secretive nature of the fund; however, the founder's prior successes in the field of mathematics may have led to its tremendous success. The fund has generated an annual Sharpe ratio of over 2.5 for over 20 years on an asset base of over $1 billion, and has had a minimum annual performance over its long history of 21%. The fund is currently closed to new investment.

A distinction between Renaissance Medallion and other HFT funds is that it has done this consistently on a very large asset base. One may often encounter smaller shops with less than $100 million of assets under management (AUM) that can boast a high Sharpe ratio, often over a few years at most. On the other end of the spectrum, one may find a larger hedge fund with extremely high annual returns—for example, more than 30% per year over perhaps three to five years. However, if skill is measured over a long period of time on a large asset base, then Renaissance Medallion is arguably the best hedge fund across all categories, from quantitative to discretionary.

37.2.2 Screening the Universe of Equities

Equity market neutral managers often apply a quantitative screening process to the universe of stocks. These screenings are generally based on self-constructed proprietary rankings of various firm characteristics. Typically, these rankings employ historical balance sheet and income statement information variables, as well as analysts' estimates of each firm's future profitability. For example, it is not uncommon to use estimates of earnings, estimates of cash flow, estimates of sales, earnings surprises, and the strength of the analyst's prediction record in the construction of the final ranking. Analysts' ratings of stocks may also be part of the initial inputs, such as Value Line and *Investor's Business Daily* ratings for U.S. stocks. Once the inputs have been determined, z-scoring and Winsorizing techniques are often performed in order to standardize firms' characteristics across the different measurement scales. Long/short managers will employ their own proprietary weighting schemes on the normalized variables and sort stocks belonging to their investment universe to obtain a short list of stocks for further examination.

37.2.3 Z-Scoring of Data and Controlling for Outliers

Z-scoring is a common technique that transforms the original data into standardized dimensionless quantities. Standardization occurs as original variables are transformed by first subtracting the sample mean and then dividing this differential by the sample standard deviation. Practitioners often refer to z-scores as normalized variables because the variables have a mean of zero and a standard deviation of one. For instance, price-to-earnings ratios and price-to-sales ratios are significantly different in terms of scale. To rank stocks along these two dimensions, all price-to-earnings and price-to-sales ratios are normalized across all firms. Thus, a firm with a price-to-earnings score of zero is considered to be at the mean of this valuation dimension, as is a firm with a price-to-sales score of zero.

Z-scores become very useful when one needs to combine many indicators—for example, converting each indicator into its z-score, then combining the z-scores by weighting them. This combination of z-scores becomes a coveted secret, and the weights are fiercely protected against other inquisitive minds (thus, the smoke screen that suddenly materializes in the midst of a friendly conversation). For example, consider an equal-weighted three-factor model. With an earnings-to-price score of $+1$, a cash flow-to-price of $+2$, and an earnings surprise of $+3$, the combined model score would be $+2$, making the stock a very attractive candidate for purchase.

A potential problem with data, including normalized data, is that empirical results may be disproportionately driven by outliers (very extreme values). **Winsorizing** is designed to limit the influence of outliers. For example, a z-score above 3 or below -3 may be Winsorized by setting outliers back to 3 or -3, respectively. For example, suppose that upon z-scoring, we get values of -1.0, 2.4, 3.3, and -5.0 for the price-to-earnings ratio of four different firms. After Winsorizing, we would get z-score values of -1.0, 2.4, 3.0, and -3.0. Winsorizing the outliers is a common procedure employed to account for variables that are too extreme. The extreme outliers cause difficulties when z-scored variables are combined to produce a final score.

Some managers exclusively use quantitative factors in their stock selection process. These systems are designed to profit from factor risks but are blind to idiosyncratic risks. Therefore, purely quantitative managers need to hold a large number of positions in order to diversify away the idiosyncratic risks. Some analysts criticize purely quantitative processes, as stocks may be mispriced on a factor-risk basis due specifically to idiosyncratic risks, such as accounting issues that make the financial statements unreliable or product liability lawsuits that could risk the assets of the firm.

For some long/short managers, quantitative screens are commonly the first step in the investment process. This step yields a short list of companies that are subject to further investigation by the portfolio manager and the research team, which seeks to further screen out companies with high degrees of idiosyncratic risk. Some other approaches to portfolio construction discussed here may be considered part of the more general quantitative approach. For instance, value and momentum approaches to portfolio construction are considered to be a type of quantitative investment approach by Asness, Moskowitz and Pedersen (2008).

37.2.4 Momentum-Based Equity Approaches

Academics have documented that one of the stronger existing anomalies is sector and company **price momentum**. Price momentum exists when the market prices of companies or sectors that have performed well (or poorly) in the past continue to perform well (or poorly) in the future. Academics have extended the analysis of momentum to include international sectors and companies. Some long/short momentum managers have apparently capitalized on this persistence in good and bad performance by creating funds that aim to trade momentum across sectors.

A key issue involves the time period over which momentum is identified and the time horizon over which it is projected. Evidence indicates that over given historical time periods, markets can be shown to vary among exhibiting momentum, exhibiting mean reversion, and exhibiting neither, depending on whether the returns are short-term or long-term. In other words, ultrashort time intervals such as tick-by-tick data may show mean reversion, monthly returns may show momentum, and returns over many years may show mean reversion. Further, observed tendencies may desist or change over time.

Although individual stock momentum has been well documented using historical data in the academic literature, it appears that much of any momentum-based alpha at the stock level disappears once real-world trading costs and constraints are added. Given that single-stock momentum tends to be a high-turnover trading strategy, much of the alpha vanishes once transaction costs and market impact costs are taken into account. The academic literature has also shown that trying to scale up such a strategy is very difficult, since much of the alpha comes from thinly traded stocks, which limits the capacity of a single-stock momentum strategy. Managers who base their strategies purely on technical indicators such as trend, countertrend, momentum, and relative strength may be considered momentum investors.

37.3 MECHANICS OF QUANTITATIVE STRATEGIES

This section describes a generic 10-step quantitative investment process. This process outlines the basic steps that may aid in building quantitative investment models.

37.3.1 Step 1: Gather Data

Any good model begins with having clean input data. The expression "garbage in, garbage out" resonates poignantly for those who have wasted much time struggling with their models, only to discover that the original raw data set had problems. Some common data-set problems are corrupted data or misaligned time stamps.

Data will typically be a function of available resources within the fund or organization, as gathering and cleaning tick data could be the responsibility of another department or a required responsibility of the group. Note that cleaning tick data is much more difficult than gathering, cleaning, and storing daily trade data.

Many vendors offer numerous data services for a fee. Additionally, most exchanges provide prepackaged bundling of data services. If proprietary data exist, such as a difficult-to-obtain information source, chances are likely that the more unique and unmined the data are, the greater the potential benefits. As such, even the source of the input data is proprietary information.

The industry has recently witnessed some models that incorporate news data from social media sources such as Twitter feeds and popular financial blogs, thereby going beyond the traditional news-feed data available from Reuters or Bloomberg. There is at least one hedge fund promoting itself as a Twitter fund. The natural language processing industry appears to be the recent hotbed of activity as quantitative managers attempt to map text into sentiment and then into future movements of tradable securities.

37.3.2   Step 2: Examine and Clean Data

In this step, the fastest way to find problems with a piece of data is to visually inspect it. Even tick data when graphed will reveal many problems associated with bad or stale quotes, trades, volume, and so on. Intraday data are usually meaningful only if there are reasonable volumes associated with the time period examined. For example, some argue that in terms of information content, after-hours trading data on thin volume are less relevant than peak-time trading data. If one believes that trading reveals information to market participants, then the information revealed when heavy trading occurs should be much more important and meaningful than the information leaked when thin trading occurs.

The time during which European and U.S. markets are both open is most important for global markets, especially for foreign exchange (FX) intraday models. When examining data, a keen sense of when the concurrent liquid trading time across markets occurs should be accounted for in a proper manner.

Finally, the dreaded "fill-forward" filter is hotly debated for the uninitiated, for what can be done if there are no data observations at a particular time? A slight mistake in filling backward will incorporate a tremendous flaw into any backtest of the now corrupted database. Such details on the timing of data are very important for the integrity of future model construction and should be thoroughly examined.

37.3.3   Step 3: Determine Model (Mean Reversion or Momentum)

Once data are gathered, examined, and cleaned, the fund manager must next decide which model to use. Technical models generally fall into two main categories: mean reversion or momentum. One can think of this as countertrend or trend. Mean-reversion models have the inherent assumption that relationships will get pushed too far in the short run, only to revert back to normalcy, whereas momentum models are based on a continuation of the "trend is your friend" movement.

Mean-reversion models are constructed with the bet that any deviations from normalcy will revert accordingly. Thus, there is the risk that the market will not revert and values will diverge further. That is, the movement will persist. As a very rough rule of thumb, 70% to 80% of the time, equity markets are range-bound and mean-reversion models tend to perform well; 20%–30% of the time, however, momentum really takes off. Unfortunately, what the environment will be on any given day can be very difficult to predict.

One way to overcome the uncertainty of model selection is to diversify across strategies so as to have multiple mean-reversion and momentum models. Switching between mean-reversion and momentum models or directly combining the two are possible solutions employed today. In addition, depending on one's holding period, the data tend to favor one type of model over the other. For example, if one's horizon is weeks to months, momentum models tend to be easier to build than mean-reversion models. As the horizon becomes shorter (e.g., intraday minutes or seconds), mean-reversion models become more interesting. For the purposes of these sample steps, it is assumed that a mean-reversion model is mandated. Equity prices have historically shown mean reversion at both short and long time periods (under one month and over four years), while momentum has tended to persist in medium time periods (longer than one month but shorter than four years).

37.3.4 Step 4: Define Residuals

In a linear regression, a residual is typically that component that is assumed to be noise, or the error left over once the model has been specified. In security selection, the residual may be viewed as an indication of mispricing. The primary driver of individual equity returns is the first principal component, or overall market returns. EMN managers often attempt to build portfolios that are neutralized to the first component, so whether the overall market goes up or down, the resultant EMN portfolio return behavior is not affected. It is well known, however, that when an extreme event occurs, the normal historical relationship tends to break down, and the seemingly hedged portfolio can become unstable. Accelerating betas can cause the longs to lose much more money than was gained from the shorts, so the net portfolio may suffer.

The interesting question to answer is whether one can construct an EMN portfolio such that the residuals are well behaved. That is, the residual may be broadly defined by some difference of similarly behaving securities, portfolios, and so on, such as the difference between two stock returns, log prices, stock versus portfolio returns, or portfolio versus portfolio returns. The ability to creatively construct long/short portfolios such that the resultant residuals behave well when tail events occur becomes the edge for successful EMN managers.

Avellaneda and Lee (2009) model the cumulative residual from a time-series regression as an Ornstein-Uhlenbeck process. Many others have taken the simpler approach of modeling two securities as co-integrated. In any case, there exists a growing body of research on these approaches. Interested readers are referred to Pole (2007).

37.3.5 Step 5: Generate Signal

Once the residual is properly defined and modeled, the next step is to construct a signal to tell the algorithm (algo) when to trade. In a very basic sense, the algo will be long, short, or flat with no position. Although it may build or reduce positions over time, the basic step is to convert the residual information into some useful space, typically mapped into z-scores.

37.3.6 Step 6: Convert Signal to Positions

The z-score value is subsequently converted into actual positions, calculating the number of shares to be held long or short. Ultimately, the model needs to output the positions needed, as traders or exchanges care only about the position size and direction (i.e., long or short).

This important step contains many degrees of freedom. For example, a model may use a z-score greater than 1.67 as a buy, whereas another may use it as a sell. A mean-reversion model may tell the trader to sell if the z-score is greater than 1.9 and to buy if the z-score is less than –1.9. Another model may set the range of 0.5 to 1.9 as the sell region, with an asymmetric buy region from –0.4 to –2.1. The combinations here are extremely numerous, and the tendency to overfit models to data has become a well-known hazard.

37.3.7 Step 7: Examine Performance (Realized versus Forecasted)

Profit and loss, gross and net of fees, become integrated at this point. Transaction costs generally consist of the sum of two components: (1) fixed (known) costs, and (2) variable (lesser-known) costs. Fixed costs are known to all participants and comprise exchange fees, ticket charges, regulatory charges, possible rebates, and so on. The variable costs are less apparent and include not just direct commissions but also the costs from market spreads and trading impact. The variable costs may be a function of trade size and liquidity/volatility of the underlying security. Much time and effort go into the process of estimating variable costs correctly, typically from prior trade results. Cynical quant managers may even reveal in private that their job is to "game" transaction costs, or to find enough alpha to overcome the total transaction costs.

There are many iterations happening between steps 4, 5, and 6. The more quickly one can evaluate the benefits of new adjustments to the algorithms, the more efficiently a researcher can fine-tune one's model.

37.3.8 Step 8: Enter Model into Production

In this step, the model will be put into production with live capital. Often, small allocations will be assigned to the model prior to sizing it up. Alternatively, some models may launch with large-sized capital in the hope that the alpha will still hold up and not decay too quickly, only to see the allocation reduced over time.

37.3.9 Step 9: Monitor the Model

Once real-time evaluation of the model begins, actual results are typically compared to simulated results. If the model performs very poorly in real trading, this might suggest that the data may have been mined too much and that the model was overfitted. Also, any bugs in the code will reveal themselves very quickly at this stage.

37.3.10 Step 10: Adjust the Model

Any alpha will decay over time, either rapidly or slowly. Presumably the decay is attributable to increased market efficiency with respect to the information being used in the strategy. The EMN manager will subsequently have to research and generate ideas continuously to improve on the model. Some approaches to improving the model include adding different signals at different horizons, attempting to expand the cross-sectional number of securities traded, or attempting to go global (i.e., trade the same model in other countries).

With performance success, the number two person will often be lured out of the shop to run his own group elsewhere. There are many active employment recruiters who map out organizations in an attempt to find talented EMN quants who may want to move and run their own books. At the end of each year, after bonuses have been paid out, the EMN migration begins, and successful managers flock to more fertile opportunities.

37.4   SOURCES OF RETURNS

Some quantitative equity hedge fund strategies appear to have had success in the past but these previously profitable strategies eventually become extremely difficult to successfully implement. As market participants move from company to company, knowledge dissipates very rapidly across the industry. It is not uncommon for quantitative equity managers to join a firm, attempt to implement a model, experience a drawdown, and be shown the door, all within six months. The high turnover within the industry lubricates the knowledge-transfer mechanism. This section begins with a discussion of potential strategies.

37.4.1   Latency Arbitrage

One example of arbitrage trading is **latency arbitrage**, whereby a manager who has a deep understanding of the technology infrastructure of the exchanges can identify trading opportunities. For example, in the FX markets, it is well known that across electronic exchanges, globally refreshed quotes are not in sync, as some exchanges refresh quotes in real time, while others refresh quotes every 100 milliseconds. So, if one has linked all the distinct exchanges when a given currency rate moves quickly, taking offsetting positions on both the slower-refreshing exchanges and the faster-refreshing exchanges may provide opportunities. For example, if a price moves up on a quickly changing exchange, the latent arbitrageur can simultaneously sell the security on the quickly responding exchange and buy the security on the more slowly responding exchange, with the intention to close both positions out once the slowly responding exchange posts the corrected caught-up prices. Another way to think about this arbitrage is that there are inherent stale-pricing issues relevant within the millisecond frequency. These issues have nothing to do with informational advantage but are largely due to the mechanism of trading on platforms across the world. Market participants that have outdated trading infrastructure can lose money to an HFT. The successful HFT can earn arbitrage profits at the expense of participants using stale prices until those participants are forced to use more timely pricing. The arbitrageur obtains profits while bringing market prices to more efficient levels and, in so doing, ensures better allocation of society's resources.

37.4.2 Exchange-Traded Fund Arbitrage

In the equity markets, most exchange-traded funds (ETFs) have mechanisms by which shares in the fund can be created or redeemed based on the fund's underlying portfolio value. Arbitrageurs tend to drive ETF prices toward their net asset values. When leveraged and inverse-leveraged ETFs emerged, many participants did not fully understand their complex pricing during periods of volatility, when leverage is adjusted. This offered substantial opportunities for high-frequency traders, who had a strong understanding of the underlying economics and mechanics. Activities of arbitrageurs eventually drove prices of leveraged ETFs to better reflect their underlying net asset values. Other arbitrageurs have combined futures positions, ETFs, and cash positions into arbitrage strategies that keep all related prices within the bands formed by the level of transaction costs. In all such cases, arbitrageurs increase informational market efficiency; improve the ability of prices to efficiently allocate resources; and, in so doing, earn quick and low-risk profits.

One of the lesser-known forms of arbitrage, cross-border arbitrage, occurs across geographic regions as newer exchanges compete to gain trading volume. A common approach in this category is to identify a similar asset, such as gold, and attempt to extract profits from short-lived dispersion across different futures exchanges of various countries for contracts with very similar specifications.

37.4.3 Returns to a Momentum Factor

Chapter 36 discussed the potentially higher returns related to stock size and value. The role of size and value versus growth were made famous by the work of Fama and French. Many quantitative models base trading strategies on momentum. The role of a momentum factor was demonstrated in the work of Carhart.

What are the sources of returns to strategies based on these factors? Are there natural risk premiums attached to the stocks that are exposed to these factors, or are the sources of returns the result of market inefficiency? Some argue that size, value, and momentum are associated with risk factors, and thus returns to these three factors are consistent with efficient markets. Others argue that returns to these factors represent market anomalies and thus are not consistent with efficient markets. Therefore, these returns may disappear once investors learn about them. Finally, some would argue that there are no systematically significant returns to these investment strategies, and that observed returns either are too small to cover transaction and market impact costs or are simply the result of data mining and will not be present going forward.

Asness, Moskowitz, and Pedersen (2008) argue that historical evidence is too strong to support the last argument and therefore rules it out. However, it is not possible to use available historical evidence to convincingly reject any of the other arguments. Asness provides evidence that a momentum strategy based on buying stocks that have performed well during the past 12 months and shorting the stocks that have performed poorly during the same period has outperformed broad equity indices by about 150% between January 1990 and December 2008. Furthermore, these gains have been rather consistent during the period. On the other hand, a value investment strategy based on buying stocks with high book-to-market ratios and shorting stocks with low book-to-market ratios has outperformed broad equity indices by 50% for the same period. This strategy, however, performed poorly during the tech bubble of 1998–2000.

Asness, Moskowitz, and Pedersen (2008) have argued that combining momentum and value strategies is much more effective than employing momentum or value strategies separately. Given that these strategies are not perfectly correlated, diversification benefits are realized over time through the 50/50 combined portfolio of momentum and value strategies. A 50/50 combination of the two strategies ends up with a higher compounded rate of return because of the lower volatility of the combination (the combination's outperformance is 200% over the same period). Furthermore, they state that momentum and value work not only across stocks but also across bonds, currencies, and commodities. However, as pointed out, these results are likely to overestimate the performance of these two strategies because they do not account for transaction costs and market impact. Furthermore, leverage has to be used to create these results. The interest cost of leverage is accounted for in generating these performance figures; however, the possibility that leverage may not be available at all times or that leverage may have to be reduced during periods of market stress has not been taken into account.

For evidence supporting the presence of momentum, see Carhart (1997); Chan, Jegadeesh, and Lakonishok (1996); and Asness (1997). For evidence on momentum in international markets, see Rouwenhorst (1998), Ngo and Jory (2008), and Liew and Vassalou (2000). For references on the limits of momentum, see Conrad and Kaul (1993) and Lee and Swaminathan (2000).

37.4.4 Sharpe Ratio, Assets under Management, and Capacity

A meaningful exercise to better understand quantitative strategies is to examine the relationship between the Sharpe ratio of a successful fund and its capacity for assets under management. Exhibit 37.2 expresses a hypothesized framework that should provoke reflection for those who are not very familiar with the quantitative investing industry.

On the vertical axis is the Sharpe ratio of a given quant strategy assuming that the fund is successful. On the horizontal axis is the corresponding capacity of the fund in billions of dollars of assets under management. Generally, the relationship between the Sharpe ratio and capacity is a decreasing function. The driver of this negative relationship is the role of trading speed.

For those strategies with a high trading speed, positions are entered and exited very quickly. The size of the trades is generally smaller when the speed is quicker. Thus, although high-frequency traders make numerous trades, the size of the long and short positions at each point in time is much smaller when the trading speed is much higher. Conversely, traders with a slower speed have time to establish and hold numerous large positions simultaneously. Thus, the size of the long and short positions at each point in time is much larger when the trading speed is much lower.

The net result is that in quantitative equity hedge funds, the anticipated Sharpe ratio of a successful trader should be higher when the capacity is lower. Unsuccessful high-frequency traders should have low capacity and low (or negative) Sharpe ratios.

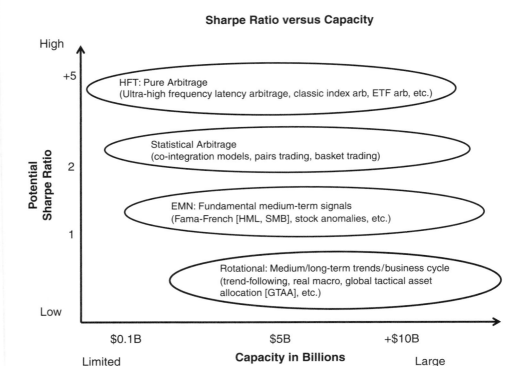

EXHIBIT 37.2   Sharpe Ratio versus Capacity

The most successful HFT strategies may typically be closed to outside investors due to their high Sharpe ratios and their modest need for capital. A high-frequency trader cannot put additional capital to use based on the limited capacity.

It should be noted that the relatively high Sharpe ratios for the HFT strategies in Exhibit 37.2 and the relatively low Sharpe ratios for the lower-speed strategies should not suggest that the HFT strategies are more profitable than the lower-speed strategies. Simply put, funds with high capacity and slow speed may offer more total profits than HFT strategies due to the greater assets being deployed. High-frequency traders may earn small total profits relative to the slow-speed funds due to their small capacity. Nevertheless, institutional investors may miss out on high-percentage profits by being closed out of the strategies that are most profitable on a percentage basis. The issue is analogous to the conflicting signals of the internal rate of return (IRR) and net present value (NPV) methods in evaluating investment projects that differ in scale.

HFT strategies have generated the highest Sharpe ratios across the quant strategies. Often these strategies will have only enough capacity for a partner's capital, so they may not seek outside investments. Interestingly enough, HFT shops often offer their lower-frequency strategies with lower Sharpe ratios to institutional investors. Though their average Sharpe ratios may be lower, such strategies have higher capacity and can provide the diversification benefits typically required by institutional investors.

EXHIBIT 37.3 Cumulative Buy-and-Hold Returns of Factors and Equally Weighted Portfolio

Weekly data from June 26, 1964, to November 25, 2011				
	Mkt-RF	SMB	HML	EW
Ann.Ret	4.5%	2.2%	4.2%	3.6%
Ann.Std	16.1%	8.6%	8.8%	6.0%
Ann.Ret/Ann.Std	0.28	0.26	0.48	0.61
Correlation	Mkt-RF	SMB	HML	
SMB	0.06			
HML	−0.31	−0.13		
EW	0.78	0.47	0.15	

37.5 A STYLIZED QUANTITATIVE EQUITY STRATEGY

This section contains a simple exercise that highlights some useful techniques currently employed within a quantitative equity market neutral strategy. The Fama-French three-factor model is one of the tenets that EMN managers should understand. The model consists of three factors: Mkt-RF, SMB, and HML. Mkt-RF represents excess returns on the market (or excess returns from the market proxy, typically the S&P 500). SMB is a size strategy, with a long portfolio of small-capitalization stocks and a short portfolio of large-capitalization stocks. HML is a value strategy, with a long portfolio of high book-to-market stocks and a short portfolio of low book-to-market stocks. Further, EMN managers should understand the momentum factor as reported by Carhart.

This exercise begins with the three factors: Mkt-RF, SMB, and HML. The potential benefits of combining these strategies have been demonstrated by the historical low correlation across strategies and the improved overall portfolio returns per risk. EW is a portfolio that represents an equally weighted or neutral exposure to the three factors. The EW portfolio is rebalanced once a week.[1]

Exhibit 37.3 demonstrates the improved reward-to-risk ratio (Ann.Ret/Ann.Std) results of the EW portfolio relative to the returns of the three portfolios that are highly exposed to the three return factors (market, size, and value). Notice the low correlations of weekly returns across the three factors (0.06, −0.31, and −0.13). This low correlation drives the improved return-to-risk ratio of EW compared to the others.

The cumulative returns to the three factors are plotted in the graph in Exhibit 37.4. The graph shows periods in which HML vastly underperformed the market factor, namely in 1999–2000, only to recover strongly a few years later. In addition, SMB performed better after 2000 than it did in the 1980s and 1990s. The time

---

[1] Data from Ken French's weekly website series are employed. To simplify the analysis, assume no transaction costs or market frictions. Although this assumption is strong, strategies using weekly data and longer holding periods are less sensitive to transactions costs. See http://mba.tuck.dartmouth.edu/pages/faculty/ken.french/data_library.html.

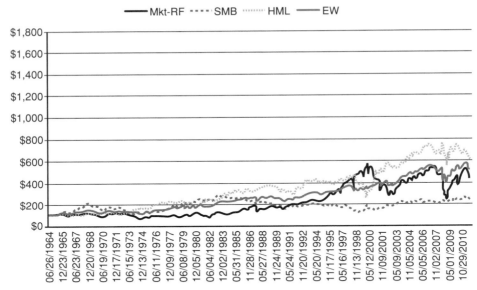

EXHIBIT 37.4 Cumulative Returns of Factors and Equally Weighted Portfolio of Factors

variations of these factors should be noted, as they are not necessarily consistent every year; but over the long run, these factors tend to have positive drift.

37.6 THE GREAT QUANT MELTDOWN OF AUGUST 2007

One of the most insightful summaries of the quant meltdown of August 2007 comes from a Columbia Business School case study by Ang (2008), which discusses the buildup and the eventual meltdown that occurred.

What happens when quant strategies get too crowded? And how much impact could a group of quants[2] actually have on financial markets? Quants are likely to have lofty academic backgrounds—for example, PhDs in mathematics, statistics, physics, economics, or finance. Some quants are internationally renowned research scientists who later ventured into the financial markets. Arguably, the grandfather of all quants is Edward Thorp, who had a successful career playing blackjack prior to his success in hedge funds (Thorp 1962).

As discussed in previous sections, all quant strategies are not the same, differing in holding periods, alpha sources, markets traded, and so on. Quants are also a minority when compared to all the other types of hedge fund managers; such a relatively small group of players would seemingly have a rather limited impact on the financial markets. Interestingly enough, however, the crowded quant strategies

---

[2] *Quant* is a term used to describe hedge fund managers (and proprietary traders) who employ technical methodologies that require a lot of data analysis and statistical tools in an attempt to extract profits from liquid global markets.

caused much financial market turmoil, although it appears to have largely been limited to the destruction of other quant funds and not the overall market.

In 2004, approximately $10 billion was invested in quant funds (according to Hedge Fund Research, Inc.). By June 2007, that number had quadrupled to $40.7 billion. With the backdrop of declining housing markets, subprime funds started to buckle. The first high-profile hedge fund to fail was a Bear Stearns subprime mortgage-backed hedge fund on June 19. Then, without missing a beat, the UK's Cheyne Capital announced large subprime losses on June 26. By the collapse of Sowood Capital on July 31, the stench of fear was pervasive in the markets. These events led to a need for cash by many multistrategy hedge funds to meet redemptions or margin calls. Some funds probably raised cash by liquidating their quantitative trading strategies.

Much can be learned from the reflections of a few prominent quants.

Cliff Asness at AQR Capital wrote in his investment letter: "This isn't about models, this is about a strategy getting too crowded, as other successful strategies both quantitative and non-quantitative have gotten many times in the past, and then suffering when too many try to get out the same door. We knew this was a risk-factor but, like most others, in hindsight, we underestimated the magnitude and the speed with which danger could strike."

Brian Hayes explained: "By de-levering together, possibly in response to a re-pricing of credit risk and recent underperformance of value stocks, quant equity funds manufactured the August turbulence. Although U.S. equities are a liquid market, the overall size of quant equity funds and their bias toward smaller-cap stocks made it difficult for the market to absorb their rapid de-levering in August. These funds were just too large to get out of their own way."

Vadim Zlotnikov, CIO for growth equities at AllianceBernstein at that time, was quoted as saying: "We essentially have 10,000 PhDs looking at the same data."

The discovery that quants were doing similar things was not a surprise, since many had trained at the same school under the same advisers, and most of them knew one another as classmates, work colleagues, and, at some point in time, competitors. What was astonishing was what happened when everyone rushed for the same door at the same time.

Interestingly enough, many of the fundamental-factor models the quants were running were based on the empirical results that a long/short neutral portfolio with zero market exposure had positive drift over the long term, and it was therefore assumed to have positive expected returns. Many of these factor-mimicking portfolios were well known (e.g., HML and SMB) across the financial academic communities, as well as in the industry. As competition eroded returns, some quant funds probably increased their leverage to enhance returns.

Additionally, prior empirical evidence revealed that these factors had generally low correlation to one another. As such, combining these factors into a portfolio of factors was an interesting exercise and at the core of many of the quants' fundamental models. Knowing the weightings across these factors was a closely guarded secret as well as the strategy for varying factor weights over time. However, what the quant crisis of August 2007 revealed was that none of the quants were betting against these fundamental factors; namely, they were playing the long/short factors all the same way. That is, they were betting on the positive drift for each factor to continue as well as the low correlation structure to hold. A key assumption was that if some factors did not work, others would. Tragically, not only did the factors behave perversely so they had negative performance, but it happened all at once, and much faster than could have been anticipated.

As an aside, it should be noted that the ultra-HFT quants, or those who ran models that started in cash at the beginning of the day and ended in cash at the end of the day, generally had strong performance in August 2007. Most of this meltdown occurred in the fundamental-factors space (interestingly enough, fundamental factors have much larger capacity than do HFT models).

The precise origins of the quant meltdown are unknown. However, the generally accepted theory is originated by Rothman (2007a, 2007b, 2007c). Ironically, Dr. Rothman has a finance PhD from the University of Chicago and seemingly many friends who are top quants. As the story goes, he hypothesized, apparently over a sushi dinner, that the quant meltdown started with a large multistrategy fund liquidating its most liquid strategies, likely to post margins on mortgage losses or other parts of its book that were experiencing difficulties. As more than a few multistrategy funds were experiencing simultaneous losses and margin calls, this liquidation event eventually snowballed out of control.

During this time, other quants started to notice that their once positively drifting factors were beginning to generate extremely negative performance. In alarm, they made major adjustments. Typically, if a strategy begins to perform poorly, the author of the strategy must justify why such a strategy should continue to be funded. Historical tests are typically conducted to determine normal patterns for a particular strategy, such as the historical maximum drawdown, worst one-day performance, worst one-week performance, and worst one-month performance. When limits are reached, or if the drawdown is much more severe than what had been experienced in the past, a strong argument can be made for the strategy to be liquidated. Clearly, such an environment can no longer be categorized as normal conditions. Such arguments were likely to have been made, and more than a few quant books were forced to liquidate.

It appears that the events of August 2007 unfolded as hypothesized. The strongest support comes from Khandani and Lo (2007, 2008) and Ang (2008). Khandani and Lo (2007) confirm that common quant strategies had a very difficult time during the first few weeks in August. They conclude that "the main driver of the losses in August 2007 was the firesale liquidation of similar portfolios that happened to be quantitatively constructed."

In a follow-up paper, Khandani and Lo (2008) simulate five well-known factor-based strategies: three value factors based on B/M, E/P, and CF/P and two factors based on price and earnings momentum. Additionally, they construct intraday mean-reversion strategies that serve as proxies for market-making activities.

They fine-tune their conclusions as follows: "The quant meltdown of August 2007 was the combined effects of portfolio deleveraging throughout July and the first week of August, and a temporary withdrawal of marketmaking risk capital starting August 8th." In July 2007, fundamental factors such as SMB and HML began a downward trend, which led to an eventual decline of liquidity during the second week of August 2007.

They also discuss the similarities of the quant meltdown of August 2007 to the Long-Term Capital Management implosion of August 1998, whereby funds employing similar strategies had to cut risk in response to losses, which led to the death spiral. Many of the top quant strategies saw their demise after August 2007. The surviving quant funds ended up even stronger, as they won back market share from their defunct competitors.

The aftermath of the quant meltdown of August 2007 has rekindled an aversion to quantitative investing across the industry. It is fascinating to observe the cyclical nature of investor preferences with regard to quant investments. This love-hate relationship will probably continue well into the future. An important lesson to note is that when certain quant strategies enjoy prolonged success and become crowded, it is prudent for investors to understand the tremendously large and inherent risks that are accumulating in those strategies and, heeding the past, anticipate another magnificent meltdown. This lesson may explain investor aversion to **black box strategies** (a common reference to quantitative trading strategies) and manager aversion to transparent systems that can be easily emulated by competing funds.

CHAPTER 38

Funds of Hedge Funds

A t the end of 2011, Hedge Fund Research reported that all 2,001 funds of funds (FoFs) managed $629.6 billion, while 7,552 single-manager funds controlled $2,008.1 billion. With FoFs controlling 31% of all hedge fund assets under management (AUM), they are significant allocators into underlying hedge funds.

38.1 APPROACHES FOR ACCESSING HEDGE FUNDS

There are three approaches for investors to obtain hedge fund exposure in their portfolios: self-managed (directly accessing hedge funds), delegated (investing through FoFs), and indexed (investing in index-type products).

The self-managed approach consists of investing directly in a series of hedge funds. Unfortunately, this approach may be a bit difficult for smaller investors, who may be constrained by the minimum wealth levels and sophistication standards required by regulators in many countries to invest in hedge funds. In addition, with more than 7,000 hedge funds globally, this approach requires extensive resources to research the market, as well as sufficient experience and expertise to determine the appropriate blend of strategies and managers, and to monitor them. However, even with these obstacles, more and more institutional investors are choosing to invest directly into hedge funds for a variety of reasons. These reasons include the avoidance of the extra layer of fees charged by a fund of funds, as well as the ability to gain greater control and transparency in the asset allocation and due diligence process than would be possible in the delegated approach.

The delegated approach consists of buying shares in an FoF. Funds of funds serve the following functions:

- *Portfolio construction.* Once the strategies and managers have been selected, the FoF manager has to decide on how much to allocate to each strategy and manager. The allocation will depend on the risk and return characteristics of the individual managers and the expected correlations between funds, as well as other fund features, such as the lockup period, the liquidity of the positions, the size of the fund, and the length of each manager's track record.
- *Manager selection.* The FoF manager is responsible for selecting the strategies and the managers that will represent those strategies. FoF managers may have access to closed managers as well as insights regarding strategies that are likely

to perform better going forward. Recently, however, the dissemination of FoF knowledge and expertise across the industry has rendered an FoF's access to closed managers less meaningful. Many of the largest institutional investors and their investment consultants have teams dedicated to finding, vetting, and investing directly into hedge funds.

■ *Risk management and monitoring.* The FoF manager will monitor each hedge fund to ensure that its performance profile is consistent with the fund's overall objectives. Some FoFs employ sophisticated risk-management processes to monitor the underlying hedge funds' positions. Other FoFs may employ multifactor sensitivity analysis to gauge the risk exposure to various market factors and to analyze the funds' potential tail risk.

■ *Due diligence.* For hedge fund investing, due diligence is the process of monitoring and reviewing the management and operations of a hedge fund manager. This is perhaps one of the more important functions and value-added features of an FoF manager when deciding between a direct and a delegated hedge fund investment program. Unfortunately, many of the large FoFs have been marred by blowups and fraud scandals, which have caused some institutional investors to become wary about the value of an FoF's due diligence process. There is, however, some academic evidence justifying the payment of an additional layer of fees in return for operational due diligence. Operational due diligence is the process of evaluating the policies, procedures, and internal controls of an asset management organization. Brown, Fraser, and Liang (2008) estimate that, net of fees, the largest FoFs tended to outperform the smallest FoFs by a statistically significant +2.69% per year from 1995 to 2006. Larger FoFs may outperform because their scale allows them to invest greater resources in due diligence and risk-management processes.

Investors who are uncomfortable with their hedge fund and FoF selection skills have a third option: the indexed approach. In this case, an investor simply has to select a representative hedge fund index and buy a financial product (e.g., an FoF, a certificate, or a structured product) that aims to replicate the performance of that index. The advantages and disadvantages of each of these three approaches are discussed in the following pages.

Exhibit 38.1 shows the tremendous growth of the FoF industry, increasing AUM over seven times, from $102.5 billion to $798.6 billion from 2001 to 2007. Since the end of 2007, the size of the FoF industry receded to $629.6 billion at the end of 2011. This decline in AUM was a result of withdrawals of $179.1 billion and net investment profits of $19.1 billion. An explanation for these outflows may be that institutions are showing a preference to invest directly into hedge funds rather than through FoFs. Over the same time period, single-manager hedge funds experienced net outflows of $159.5 billion.

Exhibit 38.2 displays inflows and outflows to single-manager funds and FoFs. Interestingly enough, flows on a net basis were negative for FoFs in Q4 2011, with outflows at 80.49% of funds compared to inflows at 19.51% of funds. Over this same period, the majority of single-manager funds, 59.44%, experienced outflows while 40.56% of funds experienced inflows. If this trend continues, FoFs may have to adapt their business model as investors opt for the self-managed approach.

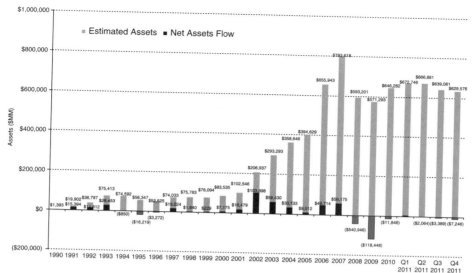

EXHIBIT 38.1 Growth of Assets and Net Asset Flow for Funds of Funds, 1990–2011
Source: HFR Global Hedge Fund Industry Report, © Hedge Fund Research, Inc. 2012,
www.hedgefundresearch.com.

38.2 CHARACTERISTICS OF FUNDS OF HEDGE FUNDS

An FoF is essentially an investment vehicle that pools the capital of a number of
investors and allocates the capital to many different hedge funds with the goal of
diversifying across a range of styles, strategies, and managers. When investing in an
FoF, investors delegate the management of their portfolios to the FoF.

The FoF manager is in charge of selecting individual hedge funds, performing
a complete due diligence on each manager, obtaining capacity, monitoring risk and

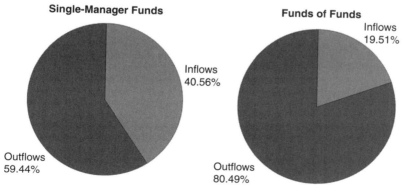

EXHIBIT 38.2 Percentage of Funds with Inflows versus Outflows, Q4 2011
Source: HFR Global Hedge Fund Industry Report, © Hedge Fund Research, Inc. 2012,
www.hedgefundresearch.com.

return, managing the overall portfolio, and reporting performance and other information to the investors.

According to Hedge Fund Research, there were 2,001 FoFs reporting to their database at the end of Q4 2011, versus 80 FoFs at the end of 1990 and 538 FoFs at the end of 2000. These FoFs controlled over $629 billion by the fourth quarter of 2011, which is almost one-third of the hedge fund industry's assets (estimated at $2,008.1 billion). Their success was initially fueled by smaller investors who did not have the capital and resources to invest directly in hedge funds. More recently, the interest has been fueled by institutional investors that are new to the alternative investment industry (e.g., pension funds, endowment funds, private banks, and family offices). These investors may prefer to use an FoF for their first allocation as a way to learn about the portfolio construction and due diligence processes required to build a direct hedge fund portfolio. As these investors gain experience, they may leverage their relationship with the FoF to make direct investments in the underlying hedge fund managers, moving the FoF closer to the role of consultant rather than asset manager.

Asset flows into the FoF industry have been unevenly split between large and small managers. More than 80% of the assets run by FoFs are managed by less than 10% of the funds. (See Exhibit 38.3.) As a result, many of the smaller funds may have to close due to their inability to attract or retain adequate investment levels.

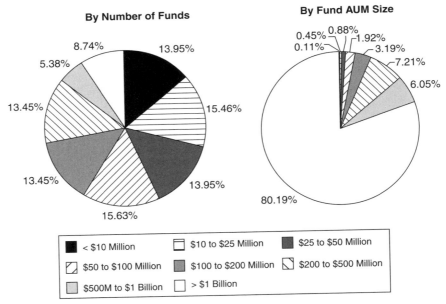

EXHIBIT 38.3 Asset Concentration of FoF Industry, Q1 2009
Note: The left side is the number of funds; the right side is the distribution of assets.
Source: HFR Global Hedge Fund Industry Report, © Hedge Fund Research, Inc. 2009, www.hedgefundresearch.com.

According to Xiong et al. (2007), FoF performance, fund flows, and asset size are closely related. Not surprisingly, the authors find that FoFs that have better performance experience greater capital inflows. The worst-performing FoFs experience net capital outflows, while the top-performing FoFs experience net capital inflows. Moreover, 18-month Sharpe ratios have more explanatory power for capital inflows than do Sharpe ratios measured over other durations or average raw returns. These findings seem to suggest that small funds with poor performance may struggle to survive.

The approach to diversification is also a distinguishing characteristic in the universe of FoFs. Broadly speaking, FoFs can be grouped based on their number of underlying strategies or their number of underlying hedge fund managers:

- A **single-strategy FoF** allocates its assets across several hedge funds following the same strategy, theme, or group of strategies. Its goal is to provide exposure to a particular subset of the hedge fund universe. Popular objectives for single-strategy FoFs include funds that allocate exclusively to long/short equity managers or managed futures funds.
- A **multistrategy FoF** attempts to diversify its portfolio by allocating assets to a number of hedge funds that follow different strategies and are expected to be somewhat uncorrelated to one another.
- A **concentrated FoF** typically allocates assets to a small number of hedge fund managers (i.e., five to 15 managers).
- A **balanced FoF** invests in a large number of hedge fund managers (i.e., typically 30 to 40 managers).

Fund of funds assets and performance are tracked by commercial databases. These service providers greatly facilitate information gathering and performance comparisons. Moreover, many experts feel that returns measured by FoF databases are usually of a much better quality than data on individual hedge funds. In particular, some of the usual hedge fund biases are significantly reduced or even eliminated when applied to FoFs (see Fung and Hsieh [2002]):

- *Little or no hedge fund survivorship bias.* FoFs provide audited track records that include allocations to historical winners and losers, regardless of their individual reporting situation vis-à-vis a particular hedge fund database. For instance, the historical track record of a hedge fund that stops reporting to databases will remain included in the track record of all FoFs that have invested in that fund.
- *No selection bias.* An individual hedge fund may choose not to report to databases, but its track record will be embedded in the performance of any FoF invested in it. As a result, looking at FoF databases increases the potential universe of funds captured.
- *No instant history bias.* When an FoF adds a new hedge fund to its portfolio, the historical track record of that hedge fund will not be included in the historical track record of the FoF. Returns from FoFs are less susceptible to measurement biases.
- *Selection bias.* Most FoFs have an incentive to report their performance numbers to several databases in order to be on the radar screens of consultants and to attract new assets.

■ *Survivorship bias.* The mortality rate of FoFs is much lower than the mortality rate of individual hedge funds. The performance differential between surviving and liquidated FoFs is also smaller than those of single hedge funds. According to Liang (2003), the annual survivorship bias for hedge funds is 2.32% per year, while the bias is 1.18% for FoFs.

As a result, FoF returns are more likely to deliver a more accurate estimate of the actual investment experience of hedge fund investors than are single hedge fund returns or hedge fund indices.

38.3 FUND OF FUNDS PERFORMANCE

From January 1990 to November 2011, FoF indices have earned average annualized returns between 6.4% and 7.6%, with 4.0% to 6.1% annual standard deviations, as proxied by the following indices: HFRI FOF: Conservative, HFRI FOF: Diversified, HFRI Fund of Funds Composite, CISDM Fund of Funds Diversified, and CISDM Fund of Funds. (See Exhibit 38.4.) Annual returns are computed by compounding monthly returns. Standard deviations are annualized by multiplying the standard deviation of monthly returns by the square root of 12. Sharpe ratios employ one-month LIBOR as the risk-free rate of return. Over this period, the best years for FoFs were 1993 and 1999, with returns ranging from 16.3% to 28.5%. Clearly the worst year was 2008, with FoFs down between −16.8% and −21.4%.

The period from 1990 to 1999 was much more profitable for FoFs than was the period from 2000 to November 2011. (See Exhibit 38.5.) Average annual returns fell from the range of 10.53% to 12.56% in the period from 1990 to 1999 to the range of 2.94% to 4.22% in the period from 2000 to November 2011. Additionally, Sharpe ratios fell from the range of 0.898 to 1.355 to the range of 0.063 to 0.315, respectively. FoF investors may find it wise to temper their expectations going forward.

38.4 FUND OF FUNDS PORTFOLIO CONSTRUCTION

Constructing a portfolio of hedge funds as an FoF may initially appear to be a very daunting task. Questions arise, such as: What are the top-down allocations to each strategy? Is this optimal? Are these strategies' definitions exhaustive? Where does one even start? Such questions are forever being debated within thoughtful FoFs. This section highlights some issues that may be encountered when portfolios are weighted using some overly simple allocation methods.

Unlike many standard allocation processes, employing AUM weights with the largest funds receiving the largest allocations may lead to suboptimal allocations. If hedge funds are earning alpha or excessive risk-adjusted returns when capital flows into a given hedge fund strategy, then under the backdrop of efficient markets, the alpha should eventually disappear. Following this reasoning, an allocation process whereby the largest allocation goes to the most popular strategies or the strategy with the most AUM may not be optimal. In fact, some FoFs even argue that a better

EXHIBIT 38.4 Fund of Funds Performance by Year

Year	HFRI FOF: Conservative Index	HFRI FOF: Diversified Index	HFRI Fund of Funds Composite Index	CISDM Fund of Funds Diversified Index	CISDM Fund of Funds Index	S&P 500	LIBOR
1990	14.2%	17.0%	17.5%	7.5%	7.5%	-3.1%	8.6%
1991	11.8%	13.8%	14.5%	11.0%	11.3%	30.5%	6.0%
1992	7.3%	10.3%	12.3%	12.0%	11.9%	7.6%	3.8%
1993	16.3%	25.4%	26.3%	23.3%	24.2%	10.1%	3.3%
1994	-1.2%	-3.1%	-3.5%	-4.4%	-4.4%	1.3%	4.7%
1995	13.1%	7.8%	11.1%	12.5%	12.2%	37.6%	6.1%
1996	13.7%	12.8%	14.4%	16.8%	16.7%	23.0%	5.6%
1997	15.0%	13.7%	16.2%	17.1%	17.2%	33.4%	5.8%
1998	-1.6%	-5.5%	-5.1%	1.7%	1.6%	28.6%	5.7%
1999	18.9%	28.5%	26.5%	22.4%	16.2%	21.0%	5.4%
2000	5.8%	2.5%	4.1%	7.3%	7.4%	-9.1%	6.6%
2001	3.1%	2.8%	2.8%	5.0%	5.2%	-11.9%	3.8%
2002	3.6%	1.2%	1.0%	0.6%	1.1%	-22.1%	1.8%
2003	9.0%	11.4%	11.6%	10.0%	10.2%	28.7%	1.2%
2004	5.8%	7.2%	6.9%	7.2%	7.1%	10.9%	1.6%
2005	5.1%	7.5%	7.5%	6.4%	6.5%	4.9%	3.5%
2006	9.2%	10.2%	10.4%	7.8%	9.1%	15.8%	5.3%
2007	7.7%	9.7%	10.3%	9.5%	8.7%	5.5%	5.3%
2008	-19.9%	-20.9%	-21.4%	-16.8%	-17.0%	-37.0%	2.6%
2009	9.6%	11.5%	11.5%	10.5%	10.3%	26.5%	0.3%
2010	5.1%	5.5%	5.7%	4.8%	6.1%	15.1%	0.3%
2011*	-2.2%	-1.8%	-2.8%	3.8%	0.9%	7.8%	0.2%

1990–2011*	HFRI FOF: Conservative Index	HFRI FOF: Diversified Index	HFRI Fund of Funds Composite Index	CISDM Fund of Funds Diversified Index	CISDM Fund of Funds Index	S&P 500	LIBOR
Annual return	6.41%	7.02%	7.47%	7.61%	7.33%	8.21%	3.97%
Annual standard deviation	4.03%	6.09%	5.91%	4.97%	4.75%	15.25%	0.65%
Sharpe ratio	0.581	0.491	0.577	0.725	0.701	0.292	0.000

*Monthly data from January 1990 to November 2011, 263 observations.
Source: CISDM, Hedge Fund Research, Bloomberg.

EXHIBIT 38.5 Subperiod Fund of Funds Performance Statistics

	HFRI FOF: Conservative Index	HFRI FOF: Diversified Index	HFRI Fund of Funds Composite Index	CISDM Fund of Funds Diversified Index	CISDM Fund Fund of Funds Index	S&P 500	LIBOR
1990–1999							
Annual return	10.53%	11.59%	12.56%	11.69%	11.17%	18.21%	5.49%
Annual standard deviation	3.52%	6.56%	6.04%	4.96%	4.62%	13.43%	0.39%
Sharpe ratio	1.355	0.898	1.125	1.227	1.211	0.966	0.000
2000–2011*							
Annual return	2.94%	3.19%	3.24%	4.22%	4.15%	0.90%	2.66%
Annual standard deviation	4.21%	5.49%	5.57%	4.82%	4.71%	16.37%	0.61%
Sharpe ratio	0.063	0.094	0.102	0.315	0.308	−0.106	0.000

Source: CISDM, Hedge Fund Research, Bloomberg.

approach would be allocating to hedge fund strategies in which flows are shrinking or receding.

According to the HFR Global Hedge Fund Industry Report, macro funds had the largest allocation of 39.30% in 1990, while event driven funds had the smallest allocation of 9.75% (with equity hedge of 37.07% and relative value of 13.88%). (See Exhibit 38.6.) In Q4 2011, macro funds had the smallest allocation of 22.07%, with event driven funds having the second smallest allocation of 24.84% (with equity hedge of 27.47% and relative value of 25.62%). The dynamic nature of assets flowing across hedge fund strategies makes following AUM weights challenging over time. The cost of accessing this data and the fact that one vendor may monitor a hedge fund universe that vastly differs from that of another vendor complicates the situation. Therefore, even the AUM numbers are a bit suspect and may be biased to include only those hedge fund managers who may be looking to raise more assets. Moreover,

**Estimated Strategy Composition by Assets under Management
1990**

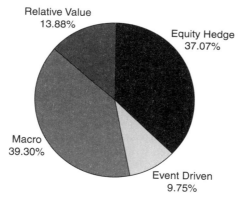

**Estimated Strategy Composition by Assets under Management
Q4 2011**

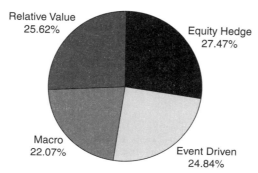

EXHIBIT 38.6 Asset Allocation across HFR Universe by Strategy, 1990 versus Q4 2011
Source: HFR Global Hedge Fund Industry Report, © HFR, Inc. 2012, www.hedge fundresearch.com.

most FoFs will have much more than just four strategy buckets in which to allocate capital.

Consider also that, given the vast differences in strategy definitions for hedge funds, even classifications are a bit fuzzy. For example, a multistrategy hedge fund with a large convertible arbitrage allocation may be initially put into the convertible arbitrage bucket. Over time, if convertible arbitrage opportunities wane, the fund may increase allocations to long/short and event driven strategies. It may not always be clear that the classification system will account for such changes.

As a hedge fund has initial success from its original strategy, assets will flow into its fund. As AUM increases, the fund may branch out and add even more hedge fund strategies. Since hedge fund strategies are not perfectly correlated, this diversification process adds benefits on two important fronts by (1) lowering overall fund volatility and (2) increasing overall fund capacity. The largest hedge funds, therefore, often look more like multistrategy hedge funds than single-strategy managers. This typical style drift may not be properly accounted for by data vendors. Also, if a new hedge fund strategy attracts a large amount of assets and the vendor does not have that particular strategy classification defined, there may be a significant amount of time before the new classification is defined. These are just some of the issues that have to be thought through carefully before pursuing an allocation process based on predefined strategy AUM.

Throughout this section, the challenge of allocating assets across strategies is discussed. Once the strategy weights are determined, investors need to fill the allocations with underlying hedge fund managers.

Typically, FoFs will be organized across strategy experts, such as the portfolio manager who covers long/short hedge funds and the portfolio manager who covers global macro/commodity trading adviser (CTA) funds. Portfolio managers are generally supported by analysts and are responsible for finding individual managers to satisfy the targeted allocations to each strategy.

In the following example, eight HFRX strategies are used to demonstrate the process of weighting strategies within an FoF portfolio. These strategies include equally weighted, equally risk-weighted, unconstrained mean-variance optimization, and mean-variance optimization with constraints on higher moments exposures.

38.4.1 Equally Weighted

The easiest way to allocate across these strategies is to give an equal allocation to each strategy as in in column (1) of Exhibit 38.7. Since there are eight strategies, each strategy gets 1/N, or 1/8 weight. In this overly simplified example, assume no transaction costs and the ability to liquidate or trade any strategy each month. Both are very strong assumptions, since it is well known that many hedge funds have lockup periods and redemption schedules and may impose gates against redemptions. In any case, creating an equally weighted portfolio across eight strategies serves as a very easy starting point.

The equally weighted portfolio has an annualized return of 4.27% and an annualized standard deviation of 5.31%, resulting in a Sharpe ratio of 0.804 (assuming 0% as the risk-free rate). Typically, an equally weighted allocation process across strategies provides a good base case on which to improve. The next sections explore several methodologies that may be able to improve on these results.

EXHIBIT 38.7 Possible Allocations in FoF Portfolios

January 1998 to November 2011 (167 observations) Strategies	(1) Equally Weighted	(2) Equally Risk-Weighted	(3) Mean Variance Unconstrained	(4) Mean Variance Constrained 30% (Maximum)	(5) Skew = 0	(6) Excess Kurtosis = 0
HFRX Convertible Arbitrage Index	12.50%	6.69%	0.00%	0.00%	0.00%	1.45%
HFRX Distressed Securities Index	12.50%	10.80%	0.00%	2.93%	2.74%	0.00%
HFRX Equity Hedge Index	12.50%	9.22%	0.00%	0.00%	0.00%	0.00%
HFRX Equity Market Neutral Index	12.50%	19.92%	0.00%	29.28%	32.75%	0.00%
HFRX Event Driven Index	12.50%	11.76%	0.00%	0.00%	0.00%	0.00%
HFRX Macro Index	12.50%	9.02%	12.32%	22.35%	41.41%	45.89%
HFRX Merger Arbitrage Index	12.50%	21.65%	87.68%	30.00%	13.65%	52.66%
HFRX Relative Value Arbitrage Index	12.50%	10.93%	0.00%	15.45%	9.45%	0.00%
Annual return	4.27%	4.26%	6.07%	4.47%	4.55%	6.20%
Annual standard deviation	5.31%	4.45%	3.65%	3.52%	4.42%	4.92%
Skew	−2.67	−2.14	−0.98	−0.72	0.00	0.23
Kurtosis	14.15	9.04	2.26	1.74	0.79	0.34
Sharpe ratio ($R_f = 0\%$)	0.804	0.956	1.663	1.271	1.028	1.261

38.4.2 Equally Risk-Weighted

Equally weighting across strategies does not account for the differing volatility (or annualized standard deviation) across strategies. A high-volatility strategy will get the same weight as a low-volatility strategy. One procedure to normalize for the differing volatilities would be to size the allocations inversely proportional to the volatility. For example, highly volatile strategies get less weight, and less volatile strategies get more weight. In practice, some analysts may employ rolling standard deviations, but then the choice of window length and frequency of data comes into question. Should one use the data at daily, monthly, or annual frequency, and how many observations should be used? When hedge funds have experienced several months of extremely poor performance, including or excluding one monthly data point will have a profound influence on the rolling inverse risk allocation at certain times. This instability may become problematic, as actual allocation across strategies may not change as quickly as necessary.

Given that there are many different ways to compute volatility, this process has many avenues to follow. Standard deviation is an imperfect measure of volatility because it penalizes upside deviations as much as downside deviations. One of several alternatives to standard deviations when estimating and sizing allocations is semideviations.

Equally risk-weighted allocations are reported in column (2) of Exhibit 38.7. These allocations are constructed by taking the inverse of each strategy's whole-period annualized standard deviations. The sum of the inversed standard deviations is the denominator, and the strategy's inverse standard deviation is the numerator. Thus, the weights sum to 1 and can be directly compared to the equally weighted allocations.

$$\text{Equal risk weight } i = \frac{\text{Annualized standard deviation } i}{\sum\limits_{i=1}^{n} \text{Annualized standard deviation } i}$$

The HFRX Merger Arbitrage Index has a substantially greater allocation of 21.65% compared to 12.5%, given the low historical volatility as estimated by this data. Also, the HFRX Convertible Arbitrage Index has the lowest risk weight of 6.69% compared to 12.50%, given the substantial losses in 2008: September −16.55%, October −34.86%, and November −10.5%. Excluding a few of these monthly observations would substantially affect the allocations across strategies.

38.4.3 Mean Variance

Probably the best-known allocation methodology is based on mean variance in columns (3) and (4). That is, finding the optimal allocations across strategies that increase the ex post Sharpe ratio. Employing HFRX data, the unconstrained optimization employing all the data yields an 87.68% allocation to the HFRX Merger Arbitrage Index and a 12.32% allocation to the HFRX Macro Index. Some have argued that mean variance is error maximizing, as it overly favors historically strongly performing investments and overly emphasizes prior diversification benefits. Both are legitimate reasons to be wary of the mean-variance allocation approach, which can create optimal but not practical or feasible portfolios. Constraints are often employed to reduce the dominant weights that unconstrained optimization may suggest for some strategies. Results such as those with a 30% maximum constraint or some alternative reasonable constraint are common. Unconstrained and constrained at 30% results for mean variance are reported in columns (3) and (4), respectively.

38.4.4 Skew and Excess Kurtosis

Mean-variance optimization may not be appropriate when the returns to hedge fund strategies are not normally distributed, as is evidenced by negative skewness and excess kurtosis. Black (2006, 2012) documents skew-reduction techniques by including the Chicago Board Options Exchange (CBOE) Volatility Index (VIX) in a hedge fund portfolio. In the same vein, this section looks at the allocation across hedge fund strategies by optimizing the allocations in an attempt to force skew and excess kurtosis equal to zero. Results are in columns (5) and (6), respectively. Interestingly enough, the underlying strategies have sufficient distributional characteristics that zero skew and excess kurtosis can be independently achieved. A larger allocation to the HFRX Macro Index coupled with a smaller allocation to the HFRX Merger Arbitrage Index appears to help bring the skew to zero. Finally, to bring the excess kurtosis close to the normally distributed level of zero, the HFRX Macro and Merger Arbitrage indices receive large weights. Limiting the maximum weight on a strategy, such as is done in column (4), will bring more diversification to the low excess kurtosis allocations.

There are a large number of objectives that can be employed with portfolio optimization, including minimizing standard deviation, minimizing drawdown, or minimizing the correlation to equity market returns. Optimization methodologies rely on the stability of the return distribution over time. This assumption is well known to be broken in tail events, especially across hedge fund strategies, so much caution should be taken when pursuing this line of methodologies.

38.4.5 Personal Allocation Biases

It is important to note that the allocations in column (3) to (6) have been made ex post, so the returns could not have been realized. These portfolios were created with hindsight, meaning the results are not realistic or achievable by any investor. This exercise was purely for the purpose of offering insight into alternative portfolio allocation processes typically employed in the FoF industry. In the end, such outputs would typically be generated and a group discussion would ensue within the FoF's investments and risk committees. Ranges are often given rather than hard numbers, and allocations may depend on available managers who have been identified for allocations, as well as on many other nonquantifiable biases. In addition, this analysis should be performed ex ante and account for the underlying hedge funds' liquidity terms.

Finally, when an FoF manager has had a very bad experience with a given strategy, typically due to performance, the manager's personal biases will have a direct influence on asset allocation decisions. Some FoFs avoid mortgages altogether, while others may exclude all quant strategies. Institutional investors may have written mandates to avoid certain strategies that may have blown up in the past. Such biases are conspicuously present across asset allocation methodologies in practice, as legacy experiences weigh in on current decisions.

38.5   MANAGER SELECTION

There are many different ways to fill up the strategy allocation buckets. Typically, the portfolio manager or strategy expert searches for the hedge fund manager who can best meet the goals of the FoF manager. This process, however, involves many difficulties, such as whether the identified hedge fund manager is even open to new investment. Unlike mutual funds, which are easy to access for investors, hedge funds are not always open for new investments. Some of the best hedge funds are closed to new investors after reaching the manager's **capacity constraint**, the AUM level beyond which the manager believes that additional capital will increase market impact and reduce potential returns. Also, the returns to some strategies can be closely tracked with just a few managers, while other strategy buckets may require a larger number of managers. Subsequently, the portfolio managers will constantly be on the lookout for improving strategy buckets with a priority list of possible hedge fund managers. If preferred hedge fund managers are not accessible, the portfolio manager works down a list of alternative managers.

There are times when a hedge fund manager needs to be replaced. Replacing a hedge fund manager consists of coordinating redemptions as well as reallocating capital. Once again, the portfolio manager will rely on a list of potential managers to fulfill this task. FoF portfolio managers are constantly attending conferences and capital introduction events, networking, and so on, all in an effort to keep their short lists of backup managers fresh with talented hedge fund managers.

FoFs will also subscribe to data vendors and may set up quantitative screens to help make their searches more efficient. An example of such a methodology is the Bifurcated Fund Analysis Model (BFAM) by Liew, Mainolfi, and Rubino (2002). This model helps determine whether a potential hedge fund manager's return characteristics are a good fit from two vantage points: (1) the attractiveness from a mean-variance perspective and (2) the rankings from a flexible peer group scoring methodology.

38.6   RISK MANAGEMENT

This section presents the current mind-set with regard to risk management in FoFs (which also extends to hedge funds).

38.6.1   Institutional-Grade Risk-Management Policy: Is It Possible in Practice?

Any robust institutional investment process must be complemented with a proper risk-management policy. The vast array of possible trading strategies and the ability to employ leverage and derivatives make evaluating the risk associated with hedge fund investments (or, for that matter, a portfolio of hedge funds or FoFs) a challenging task.

An investment committee's due diligence on a hedge fund typically consists of following a predetermined process. While this process may vary across investors, it frequently includes examining the portfolio manager's background, the organizational structure of the fund, legal documents (e.g., private placement memorandum and subscription documents), and the internal risk-management policy.

The examination of the risk-management policy often includes looking at the current portfolio's risk characteristics as summarized on recent prime-broker or third-party risk-aggregation reports, or even reviewing the actual underlying positions. Additionally, policy limits may exist on the position, sector/industry, and gross/net exposures. Finally, quantitative analysts use a number of other risk measurements, including value at risk (VaR), conditional VaR, stress tests, DV01s, and Greeks. A DV01 is the dollar value of an oh-one, which is the portfolio's dollar change in valuation given a one-basis-point decline in interest rates.

Most of this analysis, while thorough, misses the critical issues of a proper risk-management policy, argued for by Halpern and Liew (2012): (1) actionable risk management, (2) fraud responsibilities, and (3) hidden risks.

38.6.1.1 Actionable Risk Management

The role of risk management within a hedge fund or an FoF must include the actual reduction of risk. The ultimate risk manager is someone who possesses such an aversion to losses that he cuts any position, strategy, or book with absolutely no regrets.

In practice, many hedge fund and FoF risk managers either do not have the authority to do their job or do not cut risks when appropriate. Many risk managers will not take an unpopular stance against a highly profitable portfolio manager, as they may not consider it part of their fiduciary responsibilities.

An effective risk policy is one in which the CEO or chief risk officer (CRO) (1) has the mandate to tell any portfolio manager to cut risk and (2) has the ability to cut risk himself when appropriate. Both are critical. The CEO, whose fiduciary duty is to both run an organization and protect it, should have the authority to force any portfolio manager to reduce risk rather than merely hoping that the portfolio manager can be convinced to cut risk. Therefore, when doing due diligence, the following three questions should be asked:

1. Who has authority to cut risk?
2. Has that person ever done it?
3. How many times and when?

In the case in which the CEO is also a portfolio manager, the CRO should have the right to tell the CEO to cut risk, but in practice that may not always work, given the ultimate authority of the CEO. The best way to address this is to have a documented risk-management policy that spells out specific risk parameters that, if violated, authorize the CRO to cut the CEO's positions. However, even given such a policy, it is virtually impossible to predict every possible portfolio scenario in advance. The bottom line, therefore, is whether the CRO has advised the CEO/portfolio manager to cut risk, and what the results have been.

38.6.1.2 Fraud Responsibilities

Risk managers should always be concerned about the unknowns, especially fraud. In the past, no matter how much due diligence one conducted on an organization, it was still difficult to detect fraud at a corporate entity or hedge fund. Institutional investors have recently been moving toward managed account platforms, whereby position-level data may be monitored to help reduce the risk of fraud. If fraud does occur, the risk manager needs to assume that the entire investment in a single security or fund may be lost.

At the hedge fund level, this means assuming that the value of the underlying goes to zero for the highest exposure to any single corporate entity. If this would result in a loss of, say, 10% to the portfolio, which is more than can be explained to investors, then the exposure needs to be reduced. At the FoF, this means assuming that the value of the investment in that hedge fund goes to zero for the highest exposure to any particular hedge fund.

Hedge funds and FoFs should not make the mistake of assuming that there is a minimal probability of fraud occurring. Portfolio managers and risk analysts should evaluate each hedge fund or corporate security in a portfolio to determine the probability that its value will be destroyed by fraud. There is rarely a justifiable reason for the market value of any corporate security to ever represent more than 10% of the net present value (NAV) of a hedge fund or for any hedge fund to represent more than 10% of the NAV of an FoF. There exist numerous cases of funds that suffered substantially from violating this basic principle.

38.6.1.3 Hidden Risks   Similar to unknown risks to a portfolio, such as fraud, there are hidden risks that could in fact be measured and therefore be known. One of the most effective tools found to detect and reduce such hidden risks is to assess and rank the correlation of the current portfolio to each of 50 or more markets in which a significant adverse move could take place. It is critical to note, however, that this analysis cannot be accomplished simply by calculating the correlation of the fund's realized returns with each of the markets. Rather, as positions and position sizes change within the current portfolio, the correlation with each of the 50 markets must be reestimated.

It is important to understand that a portfolio might move very closely with a market, even though the portfolio has no outright positions in that market. For example, one could have a portfolio consisting only of equities and corporate bonds, with no outright positions in copper futures, that turns out to have a surprisingly high correlation with copper futures. At the same time, the portfolio could have relatively high turnover, and the realized returns of the portfolio might not demonstrate significant correlation with copper futures.

To take the analysis a step further, based on their qualitative market-based insights, the CRO and portfolio manager might project that certain equity positions would be much more sensitive to an extreme move in copper futures than they have been in recent history. These projections can be incorporated into a stress test or scenario analysis that evaluates the impact an extreme move in copper prices would have on the value of the portfolio.

38.7   DUE DILIGENCE ISSUES ARISING IN THE CONTEXT OF FUNDS OF FUNDS

When selecting a single FoF from more than 2,000 active FoFs in existence, prospective investors need to have a clear due diligence process. A useful tool in this process is the Alternative Investment Management Association (AIMA)'s Illustrative Questionnaire for Due Diligence of Fund-of-Funds Managers. Most FoFs have adopted this questionnaire to provide investors with answers to standard questions. While this questionnaire offers a starting point for due diligence, most investors will modify the standard questions to incorporate information that is needed to assess the strategy and risks of a given investment manager.

The AIMA questionnaire is divided into the following 10 areas:

1. *Background.* Investors should review the history of the FoF management firm and validate its business model. This requires reviewing items such as the following:
   a. The key milestones and significant events
   b. The total assets under management and their evolution over time
   c. The main clients and their types
   d. The ownership and its evolution
   e. The size of the staff and any recent staff changes
   f. The activities performed by the staff (via organizational chart)
   g. The qualifications of the staff to perform its duties (e.g., education and professional background)
   h. The sources of revenue and operating costs—some firms may have multiple business lines or run multiple products
   i. The compensation scheme for key employees
2. *Product information.* Investors should verify that each FoF they are considering is compatible with their requirements and risk/return objectives. This requires reviewing product characteristics such as the following:
   a. Investment objective (including target return and target risk)
   b. Target investors for the product
   c. Current size
   d. Date of inception
   e. Fee structure
   f. Liquidity
3. *Performance.* Investors should obtain performance documentation for the FoF they are considering, along with an explanation of what the performance represents. Typical matters of concern include the following:
   a. Pro forma versus actual returns
   b. Net of fees versus gross of fees
   c. Rebalancing assumptions
   d. Use of leverage and its cost
4. *Asset allocation/style.* Investors should understand how asset allocation decisions at the strategy level are made by the FoF manager.
5. *Due diligence/manager selection.* Investors should review and validate the manager-selection process of the FoF. When possible, they should examine the reports and notes from the due diligence process in detail to better understand how a fund has been selected or rejected. Typical items to investigate include the following:
   a. The minimum criteria a manager has to meet, if any, to pass the due diligence process
   b. The time taken to perform due diligence on a manager

   c. The number of managers analyzed every year, and the success ratio

   d. The process of verifying information provided by hedge funds

   e. The frequency of on-site visits with the managers

   f. The analysis of third-party service providers (e.g., administrators)

   g. The number of approved hedge funds

6. *Portfolio construction.* Investors should understand how and why underlying hedge fund managers are hired and fired. Items to review include the following:

   a. Annual turnover in the portfolio

   b. Reasons that warrant firing of a manager

   c. Use of quantitative tools

   d. Use of qualitative inputs

7. *Risk management.* Investors should review and validate the risk management guidelines of the FoF. This includes items such as the following:

   a. Minimum number of underlying managers

   b. Maximum allocation per manager

   c. Maximum allocation per strategy (in terms of assets or the FoF risk budget)

   d. Maximum allocation into illiquid hedge funds, side pockets, and so on

   e. Maximum leverage at the FoF level, if any

     Investors should also understand how risks are identified and what actions are taken to reduce unwanted risk.

8. *Administration/operations.* Investors should review and validate the activities performed in-house versus the activities delegated to external and independent service providers. Auditors and administrators are crucial with respect to valuation, and their exact duties should be cautiously examined.

9. *Client information/reporting.* Prospects should always review the information they will obtain if they become investors and verify that it is sufficient for their needs. The easiest way to do this is by looking at sample reports.

10. *Compliance/legal.* This covers items such as the registration of the FoF manager with its local regulatory and supervisory bodies; the results of the last inspection, if any; and the existence of a compliance officer. Investors should also validate the alignment of interests between the fund manager and his investors and the avoidance of conflicts of interests.

Although this list appears comprehensive, it is only a set of guidelines, and FoF due diligence should not stop once the investment has been made. Monitoring must continue to make sure the FoF complies with the investment parameters and objectives specified during the initial due diligence process.

38.8 BENEFITS OFFERED BY FUNDS OF FUNDS

Diversification: Prudent investing dictates that portfolios should be well diversified. Some investors lack the necessary asset size and expertise to invest directly in hedge funds to reach an appropriate level of diversification and risk reduction. By contrast, through a single FoF investment, investors can access a well-diversified portfolio in terms of managers or strategies.

However, the diversification level of an FoF portfolio is not necessarily a straightforward function of the number of underlying funds or strategies. This is because hedge funds are not single securities. Instead, they are already-diversified portfolios of securities.

Numerous researchers have studied the impact of increasing the number of funds in an FoF portfolio on various risk measures using a naïve diversification approach (i.e., random selection and equal weighting of the underlying managers). For a single-strategy FoF,[1] an equally weighted portfolio consisting of approximately three to five hedge funds is usually highly correlated with its respective hedge fund strategy index. Moreover, such a portfolio reduces the overall strategy-specific portfolio risk to the level of the universe from which the funds are drawn. This clearly supports the idea, say researchers, of running relatively concentrated single-strategy FoFs. The same has been found to be true for multistrategy FoFs. Lhabitant and Learned (2003, 2004) suggest that an equally weighted portfolio of only 10 to 15 hedge funds is sufficient to diversify away most of the underlying manager-specific risk. Researchers conclude that this also supports the strategy of running relatively concentrated multistrategy FoFs.

Accessibility and economies of scale: The price of entry for investing in a single hedge fund is often $1 million, which makes doing so unaffordable for most individual investors. By comparison, minimum investment levels for FoFs are relatively low. This allows more individual investors and small institutions to gain access to hedge funds even though their capital base is comparatively small. Moreover, investors essentially share the costs associated with the manager-selection process, reporting, and analysis with their FoF co-investors.

Information advantage: Because of their role as asset allocators, FoFs have the ability to access, collect, and interpret data gleaned from various channels, such as data providers, prime brokers, and industry contacts. This gives them an informational advantage over nonprofessional investors.

Liquidity: Investments in hedge funds are relatively illiquid, due to lockups, potential redemption gates, notice periods, and limited redemption dates. By comparison, the liquidity terms offered by FoFs are seen by some as more compelling. Most FoFs offer quarterly or monthly liquidity in normal market conditions.[2] Some FoFs even offer daily liquidity, either through a listing on an exchange or via an over-the-counter secondary market that matches demand and supply.

Access to certain managers: Access to the best talent and ideas in the hedge fund community is a scarce resource. The most desirable hedge funds are often closed to new investments. Most institutional investors do not have the necessary networks and protocol for obtaining investment capacity in these funds when it becomes available. Buying shares of an existing FoF that is already allocated to these desirable hedge funds is the fastest way to immediately participate in their performance.

Negotiated fees: Thanks to the power of their collective assets, some FoFs have successfully negotiated access to certain managers at reduced fees. This is normally beyond the capabilities of most individual investors.

---

[1] See, for instance, Lhabitant and Learned (2003); Schneeweis, Kazemi, and Karavas (2003); or Schneeweis, Karavas, and DuBose (2005).

[2] Note that many FoF managers have gating provisions in their documents to limit redemptions when necessary.

Regulation: In order to facilitate their distribution to a wider audience, some FoFs choose to register in regulatory jurisdictions that offer better investor protection than their underlying investments, even though the cost and administrative and operational burdens may be higher. This can often be reassuring for first-time investors and can ensure that they receive sufficient transparency, oversight, and quarterly reports.

Currency hedging: While the currency of choice in the hedge fund world is the U.S. dollar, several FoFs offer share classes denominated in various currencies with the currency risk hedged. Although institutional investors often wish to manage their own currency risks, many small or private investors prefer to be shielded from currency fluctuations and thus delegate the hedging aspects to professional managers.

Leverage: Some FoFs provide leverage to their investors. They borrow money in addition to the capital provided by their investors and invest it into a portfolio of hedge funds. This allows them to produce higher returns in low-volatility periods than would an unlevered FoF, as long as the interest costs incurred are surpassed by the unlevered returns of the underlying hedge fund portfolio.

Educational role: Many first-time hedge fund investors look at FoFs not simply as an investment vehicle but as a way of learning about hedge fund strategies and hedge fund managers. These investors typically switch to direct investments in hedge funds after a few years.

38.9 DISADVANTAGES OF FUNDS OF FUNDS

Double layer of fees: FoF managers effectively pass on to their investors all fees charged by the underlying hedge funds in their portfolios, while also charging an extra set of fees for their own work as well as for an additional layer of service providers. As an illustration, Ang, Rhodes-Kropf, and Zhao (2008) estimate that in the TASS database, the average FoF charges a 1.5% management fee and a 9.2% performance fee on top of the average underlying hedge fund management fee of 1.4% and incentive fee of 18.4% for hedge funds. Due to economies of scale, institutional investors making large allocations have recently been paying much lower fees to funds of funds managers than 1 and 10.

Performance fees on portions of the portfolio: In an FoF, the investor must pay performance fees for each of the underlying hedge funds, regardless of the performance of the overall portfolio. Thus, if half the managers are down 10% and the other half are up 10% on a gross basis, the investor will still have to pay a performance fee to the positive performers despite no positive returns at the aggregate level.

Taxation: Because of their offshore registration, many hedge funds and FoFs may be tax-inefficient for certain investors in certain countries. As an illustration, in Germany, most FoFs invest in hedge funds that fail to meet the extensive notification and disclosure duties requested by the German authorities. As a result, their gains are subjected to heavy taxation penalties, which ultimately affect the investor.

Lack of transparency: Some FoF managers do not disclose the content of their portfolio or their asset allocation. They contend that it represents what is colloquially called the special sauce that they bring to the table, and they are reluctant to reveal its ingredients. In such cases, it becomes relatively difficult for their investors to understand what is really happening in terms of risk and returns beyond the stream of net asset values.

Exposure to other investors' cash flows: FoFs commingle the assets of a number of investors. As a result, investors are affected jointly by inflows and outflows, since co-investors in the same fund may trigger cash increases or decreases or undesirable leveraging to finance redemptions. Custom portfolios for a single investor (managed accounts) are not exposed to this type of problem. Furthermore, to satisfy investors' requests for redemption, the FoF manager will typically sell the most liquid funds first, leading to a potential change in the FoF's style.

Lack of control: In an FoF, investors give up control over how the assets are invested. Moreover, they lose the direct relationship with the hedge funds in which the FOF invests.

Lack of customization: Direct investment in hedge funds allows investors to create allocations that fit their overall portfolios. For example, the pension fund of a bank may not wish to have exposure to distressed credit instruments because of the business risk of the pension fund's sponsor.

38.10 FUNDS OF FUNDS VERSUS INDIVIDUAL HEDGE FUNDS

One of the most important debates with respect to FoFs concerns whether they deserve their fees on fees and added value with respect to a randomly selected portfolio of, say, 20 to 40 hedge funds. In practice, there are essentially three ways for an FoF manager to add value:

1. *Strategically allocate to various hedge fund styles.* Running an FoF is not just simply a matter of assembling a large collection of good managers. Having such a collection can still result in a concentration of risks, with somewhat illusory diversification if there is a high level of correlation in the trades or underlying exposures of these managers. The first and most important choice that an FoF manager must make when organizing a portfolio is the long-term strategic asset allocation. This normally implies analyzing the long-term risk and return profiles of the different strategies, as well as examining the correlation of their observed and expected returns. The goal is then to determine an initial portfolio allocation consistent with the fund's long-term objectives and constraints. This task determines the long-run beta of the fund with respect to various sources of risks.

2. *Tactically allocate across hedge fund styles.* Tactical asset allocation refers to active strategies that seek to enhance portfolio performance by opportunistically shifting the asset allocation in response to the changing environment. Many FoFs argue that they follow a top-down tactical allocation process. In theory, this involves making three key decisions periodically: (1) what to do (i.e., overweighting or underweighting a particular investment style); (2) when to do it (i.e., implementing the changes based on levels of certain indicators or factors); and (3) how much to do (i.e., deciding whether the overweight should be, for example, 1% or 3%). In practice, however, an FoF is limited because of the underlying hedge funds' liquidity constraints, unless it invests only in the most

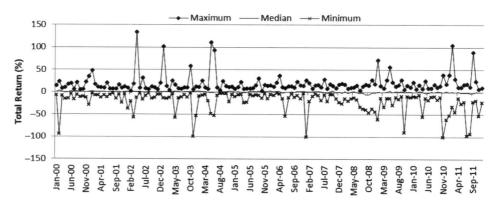

EXHIBIT 38.8 Dispersion of Fund of Funds Returns (2000–2011): Maximum, Median, and Minimum
Source: Center for International Securities and Derivatives Markets (CISDM).

liquid areas of alternative investments or uses managed accounts. This task therefore determines how the FoF adjusts its long-term exposures in response to changes in market environment.

3. *Select individual managers.* This involves the selection of individual managers within a strategy, as well as the decision of how much money to invest with each of them. While this seems very similar to a traditional stock selection activity, the reality is that FoF managers often have to make a trade-off between their ability to add value through dynamic manager allocations in highly liquid funds and the potential contribution of less liquid funds (those with lockups, etc.). This task is the main source of added value for an FoF manager.

Do these methods work in practice? As suggested by Ineichen (2002), the potential to add value in a given market is often inversely proportional to the informational efficiency of the market or the liquidity of the underlying instruments. The hedge fund market may be relatively inefficient, at least from an information perspective, and relatively illiquid. The result is a wide dispersion of returns between managers (see Exhibits 38.8 and 38.9) that seems to increase over time. Investors that lack the informational edge that allows them to select above-average hedge fund managers are more likely to benefit from delegating the hedge fund selection to intermediaries with a competitive advantage.

To analyze whether actively managed FoFs have, on average, generated substantial added value over noninvestable hedge fund indices, the performance of the CISDM Fund of Funds Index [3] or the CISDM Fund of Funds Diversified Index can be compared to the performance of the CISDM Equal Weighted Hedge Fund Index (see Exhibit 38.10).

---

[3] While original FoFs were built around the concept of diversification, single-strategy FoFs allocate up to 100% of their capital to a portfolio of funds following a specific hedge fund strategy. The CISDM Fund of Funds Index is used as a benchmark for such specialized hedge funds.

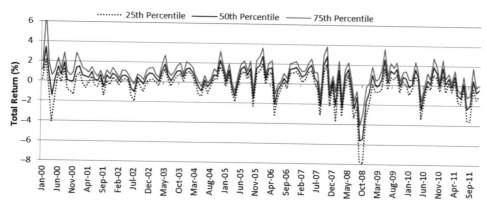

EXHIBIT 38.9 Dispersion of Fund of Funds Returns (2000–2011): 25th, 50th, and 75th Percentiles

Source: Center for International Securities and Derivatives Markets (CISDM).

Funds of funds provide significant diversification potential because they have fairly low drawdowns and standard deviations. This is particularly true of FoFs compared to individual hedge funds. This suggests that a fiduciary who is primarily concerned about the downside risk associated with hedge fund investment should consider an FoF vehicle. However, this risk reduction comes at the cost of lower annualized returns, because average returns on FoFs are only a little more than half of those of single hedge funds over the same period. This is in line with the empirical literature and can be explained by the so-called double layer of fees and the survivorship impact that creates an upward bias in the reported performance of individual hedge funds.

On a risk-adjusted basis, research also indicates that FoFs offer a slightly lower information ratio. This suggests either that FoF managers have not done a particularly good job at selecting superior hedge funds or that the fees they charge wipe out the benefits they deliver. Several studies have confirmed these results and tend to confirm that on average, FoFs underperform hedge funds after fees; see Ackermann, McEnally, and Ravenscraft (1999); Amin and Kat (2002); Brown, Goetzmann, and Liang (2004); Capocci and Hubner (2004); and Fung and Hsieh (2004).

These results should be taken with caution, however. Comparing average risk-adjusted returns or alphas across two asset classes is valid only if they are directly comparable. Single hedge funds and FoFs are, however, not directly comparable. As stated by Ang, Rhodes-Kropf, and Zhao (2008), the average hedge fund is not an investable quantity. This is because the best hedge funds are often closed to new investors. Even if an investor meets the high minimum requirements for investing in hedge funds, there is no guarantee that a successful hedge fund will take that investor as a client. Additionally, hedge funds are hard to find, evaluate, and monitor. Because they are relatively secretive and are legally prevented from marketing, gathering information on them can be costly.

Ang, Rhodes-Kropf, and Zhao (2008) built a model that assumes that FoF managers are skillful. Skilled investors with large amounts of capital and expertise directly invest in hedge funds, while unskilled investors with little capital or no

EXHIBIT 38.10 Analyzing Funds of Funds versus Single Hedge Funds

1990–November 2011	Annualized Mean	Annualized Standard Deviation	Skewness	Information Ratio	Maximum Drawdown	Correlation to CISDM Fund of Funds Index
Barclays Capital Global Aggregate Index	7.06%	5.42%	−0.02	1.30	−10.08%	0.08
S&P 500 Total Return Index	9.09%	14.57%	−0.56	0.62	−50.95%	0.57
MSCI Emerging Markets Index	9.62%	23.95%	−0.70	0.40	−62.67%	0.68
MSCI EAFE U.S. Currency TR Index	5.22%	16.94%	−0.43	0.31	−56.68%	0.54
CISDM Fund of Funds Diversified Index	7.50%	5.05%	−0.78	1.48	−17.50%	0.98
CISDM Fund of Funds Index	7.20%	4.81%	−1.24	1.50	−17.74%	1.00
CISDM Equal Weighted Hedge Fund Index	11.98%	7.36%	−0.61	1.63	−21.71%	0.88
CISDM Merger Arbitrage Index	8.96%	4.17%	−1.00	2.15	−5.75%	0.69
CISDM Global Macro Index	10.05%	6.02%	1.22	1.67	−8.22%	0.61
CISDM Event Driven Multi-Strategy Index	10.46%	5.98%	−1.52	1.75	−20.19%	0.83
CISDM Equity Market Neutral Index	7.98%	1.97%	−0.52	4.05	−2.79%	0.61
CISDM Equity Long/Short Index	11.05%	8.33%	−0.29	1.33	−17.22%	0.76
CISDM Distressed Securities Index	11.42%	6.93%	−1.32	1.65	−21.22%	0.71
CISDM Convertible Arbitrage Index*	9.12%	4.74%	−3.74	1.92	−22.47%	0.67

*Data from January 1992 to November 2011.
Source: CISDM and Bloomberg.

expertise choose to use FoFs. Thus, the hedge funds that can be observed in databases are funded either directly by skilled investors or indirectly through skilled FoFs.

However, if there were no FoFs, all unskilled investors would be forced to directly invest in hedge funds, including the bad ones. These bad hedge funds would not receive any funding in a world where FoFs exist. As a result, most hedge funds receive funding either from skilled investors or from skilled FoFs. The hedge funds observed in databases may therefore be biased upward compared to the full hedge fund universe that would have existed if there were no FoFs. That is, by their mere presence, FoFs discourage bad hedge funds from being formed or, if formed, from staying in business for too long, providing an important monitoring and due diligence function for the industry. This funding bias of hedge funds is very different from reporting biases. Many of the usual hedge fund database biases are based on whether funded hedge funds report or do not report to a database. By contrast, this funding bias involves the unobserved unfunded set of hedge funds.

According to Ang, Rhodes-Kropf, and Zhao (2008), a true FoF benchmark should include both funded and unfunded hedge funds available to unskilled investors. In addition, investors experience significant costs when accessing hedge funds, including search and due diligence costs, which are hard to measure but should nevertheless be estimated and factored in. When these elements are taken into account, Ang, Rhodes-Kropf, and Zhao conclude that FoFs, on average, deserve their fees on fees; that the more skilled investors are, the less likely they will be to find FoFs valuable; and that the less risk-averse an investor is, the less value an FoF will provide. The conclusion is that FoFs have a constituency effect. Investors with lower wealth, less skill, and greater risk aversion are natural clients for FoFs. Institutions with larger assets, greater skill, and less risk aversion are more likely, in the long run, to build a portfolio of direct hedge fund investments.

38.11 HEDGE FUND INDICES

In the universe of traditional assets, indexing has long been an ideal method of achieving broad-based, low-cost passive exposure to global equity and bond markets. As a result, there are countless investment vehicles based on the idea of tracking broad market indices, many of them with large assets under management. Until recently, indexing has not been applied to the world of hedge funds, since hedge funds were historically marketed as following predominantly alpha-oriented strategies (i.e., a rationale of absolute returns). It is only with increasing demand for hedge funds from institutional investors that the thinking has progressively shifted from alpha generation to beta exposure (i.e., a rationale of risk diversification). Not surprisingly, this shift has also generated a greater focus on how to capture the so-called hedge fund beta through indexation and passive strategies.

Liew (2003) argues the case against hedge fund index investing. First, he shows that aggregate hedge fund index exposure is unwarranted, since only one-third of hedge funds have statistically significant skills when employing a single-factor summed beta capital asset pricing model (CAPM). Next, he presents evidence to show that diversification benefits of hedge fund indices disappear in extreme market conditions. Finally, simulations reveal that with even a reasonable degree of discernment, a portfolio of hedge funds can be constructed to outperform most hedge fund indices.

38.11.1 Desirable Properties

Before discussing hedge fund indices in detail, let us recall the desirable properties of investment indices in general. Hedge fund indices that are used as yardsticks for investments should have the following characteristics:

- *Unambiguous.* The hedge funds included in the index must be specified with regard to their weight in the index, style, general partner, adviser, domicile, and so on.
- *Verifiable.* Users should be able to verify all information and calculations used to construct the index. This is greatly facilitated when the construction methodology is publicly available.
- *Accountable.* The construction and the revisions of the index follow exact guidelines, which should be approved by an independent committee.
- *Investable.* Investors should be able to replicate the index with reasonable costs and tracking errors. Note that investability may be a subjective criterion, as it might require large amounts of capital to access the index.
- *Reasonable.* The index should contain only funds that are reasonable investments for a typical client and that are consistent with the investor's risk preference. The weighting and rebalancing rules should be compliant with the underlying investments or funds.

In addition, hedge fund indices should be *representative*. That is, they should accurately reflect either the whole universe of hedge funds or a universe focused on a particular style. In this regard, a potential conflict arises. While it is not difficult to create representative investable indices of traditional assets such as stocks and bonds, this goal is not attainable in the hedge fund world. Investments in hedge funds are lumpy, which means a truly diversified and representative investable index would require an enormous amount of capital to fund and monitor each manager. Even if the funding were available, some hedge fund managers might refuse to join an index platform. As a result, index providers have to strike a delicate balance between representativeness and economic efficiency.

38.11.2 Noninvestable Hedge Fund Indices

In theory, passive hedge fund investing could offer advantages over the FoF approach. Indexing should off-load much of the research and monitoring costs of FoFs, as well as remove the additional layer of fees and expenses charged by actively managed FoFs. Additionally, an investment in a hedge fund index should protect investors from manager selection risk. Just like indices for stocks or bonds, hedge fund indices deliver the normal returns of the asset class or investment style, which can be called the hedge fund beta. By contrast, selecting individual hedge funds exposes investors to the risk of significantly underperforming the aggregate return of the hedge fund industry. Indeed, both hedge funds and FoF dispersions have historically been extremely high, and both exhibit a clear widening trend. A wrong selection decision could, therefore, have a large impact on performance.

Unfortunately, identifying a representative hedge fund index is not a trivial task. The variety of index construction approaches and databases results in the extreme heterogeneity of performances among these indices. For instance, Amenc and Martellini (2003) analyzed 13 different style indices drawn from major index providers and observed a difference in performance of up to 22.04% in a single month for global long/short equity indices. In addition, some indices that were supposed to measure the same strategy were negatively correlated to each other during certain periods. This is clearly confusing for investors and casts serious doubt on the possibility of using such broad-based hedge fund indices as yardsticks in performance measurement. But the challenges for passive hedge fund investors do not end there.

Gaining exposure presents another significant hurdle, as tracking broad-based noninvestable hedge fund indices is complicated by the following issues:

- Most noninvestable hedge fund indices are not transparent. They do not disclose the list of their components, their weights, or even their construction methodology. This significantly complicates the work of a third-party indexer, unless the indexer possesses privileged information from the index provider.
- Most noninvestable hedge fund indices are partially made up of funds that are already closed to new investment or will be closed at some point in the future, once they reach their maximum capacity. A full replication (i.e., buying all the components in the index) is therefore often not feasible.
- Traditional indexing approaches (i.e., regularly rebalancing a portfolio of hedge funds to minimize the tracking error with respect to some index) are not applicable in practice because of the lack of liquidity of the underlying funds (lockups, redemption notice periods, lumpy investments).
- Attempts to replicate the returns of noninvestable hedge fund indices by dynamically trading traditional assets such as stocks and bonds, or even futures and options, usually result in significant tracking errors, essentially because the target is an index of actively managed portfolios. Thus, although the funds in the index do not change, the funds' individual securities and their key characteristics change continuously.
- Most broad-based hedge fund indices often report their net asset value with a considerable delay, such as three weeks after the end of the month. This means that a third-party index always rebalances with considerable lag.

For all these reasons, several providers have recently decided to start from scratch with a new methodology and created *investable* hedge fund indices.

38.11.3 Investable Hedge Fund Indices

The first investable hedge fund indices were launched in January 2001 by Zurich Financial Services and Schneeweis Partners[4] and were soon followed by several

---

[4] These indices were later reintroduced under the name of Dow Jones Hedge Fund Indices.

EXHIBIT 38.11   Key Characteristics of Investable Indices

Index Provider	Launch Date	Start Date	Number of Indices	Strategy Weighting	Fund Weighting	Rebalancing
DJ CS	August 2003	January 2000	10 + composite	Asset weighted	Asset weighted	Semiannual
EDHEC	April 2005	April 2002	5	N/A	Optimized weights	Quarterly
FTSE	April 2004	January 1998	11 + composite	Investability weighted	Investability weighted	Annual
HFRX	March 2003	January 2000	8 + composite	Asset weighted	Optimized weights	Quarterly
RBC	July 2005	July 2005	9 + composite	Representative of each strategy in the universe	Equal weighting	Monthly

others. All investable hedge fund indices share the goal of offering investors the opportunity to hold the entire hedge fund market at a relatively low cost. But as illustrated in Exhibit 38.11, their construction rules, weighting, and rebalancing policies differ widely, resulting in significant variations in their performances.

As mentioned previously, index providers face a trade-off between including more funds to be more representative and using fewer funds to facilitate index tracking. Indeed, to be investable, hedge fund indices must select only a limited number of liquid and open hedge funds. The process of selecting hedge funds based on certain criteria leads to access bias. That is, it is likely that the hedge fund managers who are willing to belong to an investable index would have characteristics different from those of the universe of all managers. Access bias is likely to lead to lower returns for the index, because it is often assumed that top-performing managers are less likely to agree to belong to an index. Most index providers impose strict selection criteria (e.g., minimum track record, minimum assets under management, sufficient liquidity, absence of a lockup period, daily or weekly valuation, minimum transparency, willingness to accept additional investors, and commitment to provide sufficient capacity) in order to select the funds that are eligible to enter their index. Several index providers go one step further and have signed partnerships with managed account platforms or have developed their own platforms in order to secure maximum capacity and liquidity on the components of their indices.[5] Other providers have attempted to circumvent the problem by using quantitative methodologies, which typically partition the hedge fund universe into clusters and use various algorithms to select the funds that are most representative of each cluster.

But regardless of the approach, the objective is to construct a representative sample of the hedge fund universe. As illustrated by Lhabitant (2007), the set of all investable indices included only four of the largest 25 hedge funds worldwide,

---

[5] A managed account is a discretionary account in which a client has given specific written authorization to a hedge fund manager to select securities and execute trades on a continuing basis and for a fee. Most of the time, the managed account closely mirrors the main fund of the manager. Of course, the difficulty is that the number of fund managers willing to offer managed accounts is extremely limited and usually restricted to the most liquid strategies.

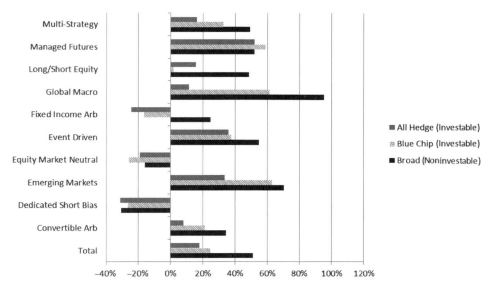

EXHIBIT 38.12 Total Return Achieved from October 2004 to December 2011 by Dow Jones Credit Suisse Investable and Noninvestable Indices
Source: Dow Jones Credit Suisse.

despite the fact that those funds managed more than $300 billion. Hedge funds with superior performance may find no need to be included in an investable index, as they are already capable of attracting investors, while less successful hedge funds may be more willing to comply with strict selection criteria (e.g., more transparency, guaranteed capacity, and better liquidity) to increase their assets.

Beyond the question of representation, several criticisms of the selection process used by investable index providers have been raised. Since investable hedge fund indices are created with the implicit goal of launching a tracking vehicle, it is essential that their historical pro forma performance looks attractive to potential investors. Therefore, index providers have a tendency to select index members among the funds with good track records. However, this does not guarantee good performance in the future. For most strategies and providers, a simple comparison between noninvestable and investable indices *after* the creation date of the latter illustrates the underperformance of the investable index versus its noninvestable cousin (see Exhibit 38.12).

CHAPTER 39

Regulation and Compliance

39.1 A SUCCINCT HISTORY OF HEDGE FUND REGULATION IN THE UNITED STATES

Investors allocating assets to alternative investment managers need to be aware of the regulatory environment. Regulatory issues are an important part of the due diligence process, as investors need to ensure that fund managers have designed processes to comply with all applicable regulations. Investors also need to ensure that their own operations comply with all required regulations. While this chapter focuses on the regulatory environment of the United States, similar regulations are in place in many countries worldwide.

39.1.1 Private Adviser Exemption

In the United States, hedge funds have historically enjoyed little government interference, oversight, or scrutiny. Hedge funds have typically been exempt from the registration and disclosure requirements of federal securities laws, including the Securities Act of 1933, the Securities Exchange Act of 1934 (Exchange Act), the Investment Advisers Act of 1940 (Advisers Act), and the Investment Company Act of 1940. To qualify for the myriad of exclusions and exemptions, hedge funds have to accept investments only from certain sophisticated or accredited investors and cannot advertise to the general public. (Non-U.S. hedge funds are likewise restricted in terms of who can be solicited to invest in them.) Despite these regulatory perks, hedge fund managers must still comply with general federal securities laws, such as the prohibition against fraud and insider trading. And since a hedge fund manager is considered a legal fiduciary under the Advisers Act, managers must put the interests of their clients before their own.

The most coveted of all the federal securities law exemptions for hedge funds was the private adviser exemption in the Advisers Act, which allowed investment advisers to claim an exemption from registration if they (1) had fewer than 15 clients during the previous 12 months, (2) did not publicly hold themselves out as investment advisers, and (3) did not advise registered investment companies.[1]

---

[1] Advisers Act, § 203(b)(3), 15 USC § 80b-3(b)(3).

39.1.2 Elimination of the Private Adviser Exemption

The global financial crisis caused regulators to examine the role hedge funds played in the financial debacle; this time, they did so with a much heavier hand. In July 2010, Congress passed the **Dodd-Frank Wall Street Reform and Consumer Protection Act of 2010 (the Dodd-Frank Act)**,[2] which is widely accepted as one of the most comprehensive pieces of financial legislation ever enacted. The Dodd-Frank Act makes many changes to the registration, reporting, and record-keeping requirements of investment advisers under the Advisers Act. Most importantly, the Dodd-Frank Act eliminates the so-called private adviser exemption, which many hedge fund managers have relied on to escape Securities and Exchange Commission (SEC) registration. Exemptions from registration are now available only to advisers who exclusively advise venture capital funds or private funds with less than $150 million in assets under management (AUM) in the United States, foreign private advisers, and advisers to licensed small business investment companies. All other investment advisers had to register with the SEC by March 30, 2012 (extended from July 21, 2011).

39.1.3 How the Dodd-Frank Act Changes the Investment Adviser Landscape

Aside from requiring hedge funds with assets under management of $150 million or greater to register with the SEC, the Dodd-Frank Act made other important changes with regard to hedge fund managers:

- It revised the definition of **accredited investor**: An accredited investor, under Regulation D of the Securities Act of 1933, is a natural person who has a net worth exceeding $1 million. The Dodd-Frank Act revised the definition of *accredited investor* to exclude the value of a person's primary residence in calculating an investor's net worth.
- Form 13F filers must report short sales: The SEC is expected to adopt rules requiring Form 13F filers to report information about short sales of securities on Form 13F. The information will then be collected and published monthly, so as to make this information public.
- It increased liability for aiding and abetting: Whereas prior to the Dodd-Frank Act the SEC had to establish knowing and substantial assistance to the primary violator to convict a person of aiding or abetting, the SEC now merely has to show recklessness. In addition, the person who aids or abets a violation by another person is now liable to the same extent of fines and penalties as the primary violator.

Registration with the state or the SEC imposes substantial disclosure and regulatory requirements on a hedge fund manager. These requirements are examined further in the next section.

---

[2] Dodd-Frank Wall Street Reform and Consumer Protection Act, Pub. L. No. 111-203, 124 Stat. 1376 (2010) (to be codified at 15 USC § 780-7).

39.2 REGISTRATION AND REGULATION IN THE UNITED STATES

SEC or state registration: A hedge fund manager who is unable (or chooses not) to rely on a registration exemption must register as an investment adviser with either a state commissions agency or the SEC. The amount of assets an investment adviser has under management will determine whether the adviser must register with the SEC or one or more states. This calculation of assets is referred to as **regulatory assets under management (RAUM)** and differs from the calculation of assets under management (AUM) made in Form ADV 2A, which is a disclosure document made available or given to clients. RAUM is defined as the securities portfolio (i.e., a portfolio in which at least 50% of the total value consists of securities, cash, and cash equivalents) to which the adviser provides continuous and regular supervisory or management services. The securities portfolio includes proprietary assets, assets managed for no compensation, and assets of foreign clients.

Under the Dodd-Frank Act, hedge fund managers must now use the following guidelines to determine whether and with which government agency they must register:[3]

Register with the SEC	Register with a state commission
Manages hedge funds whose AUM is between $25 million and $100 million and maintains a principal office and place of business in a state that does not require the registration of investment advisers Manages hedge funds whose AUM is between $25 million and $100 million and maintains a principal office and place of business in a state where the hedge fund would not be subject to examinations as an investment adviser by that securities commissioner Manages only hedge funds whose AUM is greater than $100 million and maintains managed accounts Manages hedge funds whose AUM is greater than $150 million and does not maintain managed accounts	Manages hedge funds whose AUM is between $25 million and $100 million and maintains a principal office and place of business in a state that requires the registration of investment advisers

Hedge fund managers with AUM between $25 million and $100 million are considered midsize advisers and are given a $10 million buffer so they do not have to continually switch back and forth from state and SEC registration as their AUM fluctuates. The rest of this chapter focuses on analyzing investment advisers' obligations once they register with the SEC, as state securities laws vary from state to state.

---

[3] Section 410 of the Dodd-Frank Act.

Overseas hedge funds with more than 15 U.S. clients and investors with assets under management of more than $25 million will have to register with the SEC under the Dodd-Frank Act.[4] Once a hedge fund determines whether it must register with the SEC, it must complete and file Form ADV. The form consists of two parts, along with various schedules and disclosure reporting pages. Part 1 provides information about the hedge fund, its manager, and all associated persons, and is primarily designed for use by regulators for administrative purposes. Part 2 requires information that must be provided to the fund's clients and is thus intended primarily for them (e.g., the types of advisory services provided, advisory fees charged, the fund manager's affiliations with other securities professionals, whether the fund manager effects securities transactions for clients, how securities are analyzed, whether the fund manager has brokerage or investment discretion, and potential conflicts of interest). In many cases, most of the information required in Part 2 is already provided in the fund's private placement memorandum or other offering documents.

Many hedge funds typically deliver Form ADV, Part 2A, or a written document containing the information found in the form, to their clients at the time the investment advisory contract is entered into, in order to satisfy the requirement that registered investment advisers provide certain written disclosures to existing and prospective clients.

39.2.1 Compliance Culture and Policies and Procedures

A registered investment adviser is required under the Advisers Act to adopt and implement compliance policies and procedures reasonably designed to prevent violations of the act by advisers or their supervised persons.[5] Further, the SEC expects that senior management will be proactive in creating a culture of compliance by emphasizing the importance of compliance to their supervised persons and supporting it with adequate resources. The adviser must also appoint a chief compliance officer (CCO) to administer the compliance policies and procedures. The duties of the CCO are described in the next section.

There are several steps that a hedge fund manager needs to take to create a culture of compliance. The most critical component is the commitment and proactive involvement of senior managers, as they need to set the tone at the top to trickle down to the rest of the organization. Senior management must also make it known that all personnel have direct access to them for any concerns that arise regarding compliance issues. The CCO must also be given a role of authority within the organization, be able to discuss important issues with senior management, and be given sufficient resources to carry out the CCO's mandate. From there, the fund manager and CCO must document the entire compliance process, from identification of risks to written policies and procedures designed to mitigate the risks, and to forensic testing conducted as part of the implementation of policies and procedures.

---

[4] Many critics abroad point out that most small hedge funds won't be able to bear the cost of registration and compliance, and thus the scales will tip in favor of larger hedge funds.

[5] Section 206(4)-7 of the Advisers Act.

The SEC has not enumerated specific elements that must be included in the adviser's written compliance policies and procedures. The SEC does, however, recommend that each adviser use a two-step process: (1) identify conflicts of interest and other compliance factors that create risk exposure for the firm and its clients in light of the firm's particular operations, and (2) design policies and procedures to address those risks. The policies and procedures should address a number of issues. The most important are:

- Portfolio management processes, including consistency of portfolios with clients' investment objectives, disclosures by the adviser, and applicable regulatory restrictions
- Trading practices:
  - A best execution policy that includes selection criteria for executing brokers and provides for identification and review of such criteria by the CCO, the best execution committee (if applicable), or senior management
  - A procedure for the prompt and accurate recording of transactions, and a trade error policy
  - Trade allocation policies, such as those regarding allocations among funds and managed or proprietary accounts, where applicable
  - A policy for the use of soft-dollar arrangements and bundled commissions (e.g., review of the adviser's use of soft dollars for consistency with what is being disclosed to investors)
- Accuracy of disclosures (e.g., monthly performance letters) made to investors, clients, and regulators

The advisers, in order to design a list of policies and procedures to prevent violations of federal securities laws, cannot neglect to review their conflicts of interest. Conflicts of interest are an inherent part of business, financial or otherwise, and must be identified and addressed.

The adviser should document the identified conflicts of interest and any new conflicts as they develop, as well as how the conflicts were addressed and the effectiveness of the policies and procedures in addressing those conflicts.

39.2.2 Role of the Chief Compliance Officer

According to the SEC, the **chief compliance officer** of an investment firm should be competent and knowledgeable regarding the Advisers Act and should be empowered with full responsibility and authority to develop and enforce appropriate policies and procedures for the firm. Subsequently, a CCO needs to have sufficient seniority and authority in the firm to see that the compliance program is taken seriously and others are compelled to adhere to its policies and procedures.

The CCOs of hedge funds find themselves in a unique position within the organization. Whereas the other executive officers and employees are counted on to be loyal to the hedge fund adviser, CCOs must maintain a great deal of objectivity and detachment if they are to do their job properly. A CCO's role in the organization is essentially to create a culture of compliance by making sure everyone understands and follows the rules and by being willing and able to discipline anyone who violates any of the policies and procedures. Needless to say, the CCO may not be the most popular person in the firm. And though popularity is something the CCO can do without, respect and commitment from senior management are not. The CCOs cannot effectively carry out their SEC-mandated role if senior management does not give them sufficient resources, support, and authority. Senior management must make it clearly known to the entire organization that compliance is a priority and a day-to-day business for all employees. Furthermore, the compliance program must be integrated into every level and function of the organization.

39.2.2.1 Duties of the Chief Compliance Officer
In addition to setting the general tone about the importance of compliance in conjunction with senior management, the CCO is responsible for the following specific duties in administering the compliance program:

Compliance (or forensic) testing and reporting: Once the compliance policies and procedures are in place, the CCO is responsible for testing the effectiveness of such policies and procedures and reporting the results to senior management. This process is critical to maintaining the health of the compliance system, identifying new issues, and addressing them effectively. The general areas in which the CCO should test and document are:

- Performance management and trade allocation
- Brokerage arrangements and best execution
- Valuation
- Personal trading
- Advertisements and communications with investors

Review of all marketing materials and other documents: The SEC regulates advertising by hedge fund managers by generally prohibiting an investment adviser from engaging in fraudulent, deceptive, or manipulative activities.[6] It should be noted that this prohibition applies to both registered and unregistered investment advisers. The term *advertisement* includes any written communication addressed to more than one person, or any notice or other announcement in any publication or by radio or television, which offers any analysis, report, or publication regarding securities; any graph, chart, formula, or other device for making securities decisions; or any other investment advisory services regarding securities.[7] Electronic advertisements are also included in this definition. Some examples that fall under this broad definition are marketing presentations, monthly performance letters to investors, an offering memorandum, and any document designed to maintain existing clients or solicit new ones.

In order for a hedge fund manager to refrain from violating the rule against fraudulent, deceptive, or manipulative activities, the CCO must review all documents that communicate information to investors to make sure they conform to regulatory

---

[6] Section 206 of the Advisers Act.
[7] Advisers Act Rule 206(4)-1.

guidelines. There are at least two important issues to consider. First, hedge fund managers are not allowed to use testimonials or endorsements from investors. Second, performance must be presented over long time periods, not highlighting specific time frames or only successful trades.

When fund managers include performance results in advertisements or written communications, they must also provide the following to avoid misleading investors:

- The effect of material market or economic conditions on the results portrayed (e.g., it would be misleading to report that the fund manager's equity accounts increased 10% without disclosing that the equity market was up 40% during the same period)
- Performance net of fees (e.g., advisory fees, brokerage commissions, and other expenses that a client or fund would have paid), with exceptions: (1) gross performance figures may be presented if they are given side by side with net figures, (2) custodial fees need not be netted out, (3) performance results may deduct the highest fee charged to a client or fund as long as disclosure is made explaining how the performance was calculated, and (4) gross performance results may be presented in one-on-one presentations to wealthy individuals, pension funds, universities, and other institutions.

Record keeping: Registered investment advisers have extensive obligations with regard to record-keeping rules, and the CCO is responsible for making sure that all supervisory persons understand their obligations in the proper maintenance of certain books and records. The CCOs will also find that documenting nearly every issue and concern that arises during the course of business is critical to their success in running an airtight compliance program and having peace of mind in the event of a possible SEC inspection. In addition to keeping typical business accounting records, a hedge fund manager must generally maintain certain books and records required by the SEC in light of the special fiduciary nature of the business.

Annual review: On an annual basis, an investment adviser must review policies and procedures to determine their effectiveness. (A more frequent review of the compliance program is also appropriate if certain events necessitate immediate changes.) The CCO will conduct the review, which should take into account and give a detailed report of the following:

- The compliance matters that arose during the previous year, including any violations of the policies and procedures
- Any changes in the business activities of the adviser or the adviser's affiliates
- Any changes in the Advisers Act or other applicable regulations that might impact the business and necessitate an amendment in the policies and procedures

Code of ethics: A registered hedge fund manager must establish, maintain, and enforce a written code of ethics. The CCO is responsible for drafting the code of ethics, having it approved by senior management, effectively communicating the code to all supervisory personnel (e.g., in an initial presentation), implementing and enforcing the code, and amending the code periodically as issues arise. The **code of ethics** must include, at a minimum, the following:

- Standards of business conduct for supervised persons that require them to comply with applicable federal securities laws
- Provisions that require access persons[8] of the registered fund manager to report personal securities transactions periodically and require the fund manager to review these reports
- Provisions that require supervised persons to report violations of the code of ethics to the CCO or another designated person
- Provisions that require that each supervised person be provided with the code of ethics and acknowledge receipt of it

39.2.3 SEC Inspection Program

The consummate test of a registered investment adviser's compliance program is undergoing an SEC inspection. Under Section 204 of the Advisers Act, all records required to be maintained by registered investment advisers are subject at any time, or from time to time, to reasonable periodic, special, or other examinations by the SEC. The SEC's inspection program, therefore, is part of the SEC's mandate to regulate investment advisers.

The primary purpose of such inspections is to ensure that (1) the hedge fund manager is in compliance with the Advisers Act and other applicable federal securities laws, and (2) the manager's business activities are otherwise consistent with the information disclosed in Form ADV. The SEC also seeks to curb compliance problems before they become too severe or systematic and help foster strong compliance practices that will help prevent problems from occurring in the first place. Since a fund manager has no legal grounds to refuse an inspection by the SEC, it is wise for the fund manager to simply cooperate as much as is reasonably practicable.

39.2.3.1 Three Types of SEC Inspections   Regular inspections: The SEC categorizes registered investment managers into two general groups for purposes of inspections: high risk and low risk. Investment managers whom the SEC deems to be high risk (e.g., those with custody of client assets, those with discretionary trading, larger advisers, those with weak internal controls, or those with a history of compliance violations) can reasonably expect more frequent inspections. SEC staff aims to conduct routine examinations of higher-risk managers every three years. Lower-risk managers are not examined on a routine basis but are instead chosen randomly for

---

[8] Access persons generally include a fund manager's supervised persons who have access to nonpublic information regarding clients' purchases or sales of securities, or nonpublic information about the portfolio holdings of a registered investment company managed or underwritten by the manager or certain of its affiliates. Access persons also include supervised persons who are involved in making securities recommendations to clients or have access to nonpublic recommendations. In general, the SEC presumes that all directors, officers, and partners of a fund manager are access persons.

inspection.[9] If a newly registered fund manager has a high-risk profile, however, SEC staff will likely plan for an inspection within 12 months of the manager's registration.

Routine exams are often focused in scope and will concentrate on areas that have been identified as posing the greatest compliance risk, as well as areas that may pose compliance risk for the particular firm being examined. In general, the following factors contribute to a high risk profile for a hedge fund manager:

- Large amounts of assets under management
- Questionable responses on Form ADV
- Retail client base
- Affiliated broker
- Multiple affiliates
- Fund manager or employees with disciplinary history relating to securities violations
- Performance-based fees
- Weak compliance program

The SEC will interview members of senior management and other personnel. The CCO will normally sit in on these interviews so that she can provide information to the staff as needed and also be cognizant of what areas in the fund's business are causes for concern with the SEC. Although a fund manager should expect that every document relating to his investment activities and the operation of the fund will be subject to inspection, the SEC will at some point furnish the CCO with a document request list.

Cause inspections: The SEC will initiate a cause inspection when it suspects a fund manager may be violating the federal securities laws. Cause inspections may arise from a client complaint, a tip, rumors of trouble, and so on. The SEC maintains a website for filing complaints at www.sec.gov. The SEC also accepts complaints in paper form.

Sweep inspections: In a sweep inspection (or theme inspection), the SEC typically focuses on a number of investment advisers in a particular geographic area or engaged in certain activities. For example, the SEC may want to gather information on how hedge funds are handling the conflict of interest that soft dollars present and thus select a sample of hedge funds to inspect regarding this compliance issue. Sample sizes can range from hundreds of firms to less than 10, depending on the issue. With the increased globalization of investment advisers, the SEC and its corresponding regulators in other countries try to coordinate examinations of advisers with global operations so that inspections can occur simultaneously in advisers' offices in several countries.

39.2.3.2 Aftermath of an SEC Inspection

If the fund manager and the CCO have survived an SEC inspection more or less unscathed by the mountains of documentation they have had to produce, then they will conclude the on-site portion of the exam with an exit interview with SEC staff. The SEC will then continue its analysis of the fund manager's documents and information received in its offices and may

---

[9] See Richards (2008).

follow up with phone calls to the fund manager for clarification of information or to discuss additional issues not discussed in the exit interview. SEC examiners aim to conclude an inspection 120 days after they have finished the on-site exam.

The best result the fund manager can hope for is that the SEC, having found no problems, sends the fund manager a no-further-action letter. The next-best scenario is that the SEC finds a violation or a possible violation of the federal securities laws and sends the fund manager a deficiency letter. This letter describes the practices or activities in question and requires the fund manager to respond in 30 days of receipt of the letter, explaining what measures the manager has taken in response to the violation (the fund manager may also dispute the alleged violations in the response to the deficiency letter). The worst scenario for a fund manager, short of enforcement proceedings, is that the SEC finds a multitude of significant violations, at which point the fund manager should brace himself for another follow-up inspection. In this case, the SEC will send the fund manager a deficiency letter enumerating all the deficiencies found, which must be addressed immediately and certainly prior to the next regular inspection.

39.3 VARIOUS REPORTING REQUIREMENTS FOR HEDGE FUNDS

Hedge funds are facing increasing demands by the SEC to comply with a variety of reporting, disclosure, privacy, and information-protection requirements, many of which are in addition to those imposed on registered investment advisers.

The Exchange Act requires the filing of the disclosure reports listed below.[10]

- Section 13(d) requires an adviser who beneficially owns more than 5% of a class of publicly traded equity securities to file disclosure reports within 10 days of the acquisition of those securities, identifying, among other things, the source and amount of funds used for the acquisition and the purpose of the acquisition.
- Section 13(f) requires a fund manager with investment discretion of $100 million or more of publicly traded equity securities to file quarterly reports disclosing these holdings and the type of investment and voting authority exercised by the manager.
- Section 13(g) provides an alternative short form to the beneficial ownership reporting scheme for acquisitions by qualified institutional investors and passive investors who acquire securities in the ordinary course of their business and not for the purpose of changing or influencing controls of the issuer.
- Section 13(h) requires certain fund managers with investment discretion who are engaging in certain large levels of purchases and sales of national market system (NMS) securities to file with the SEC and also provide certain identifying information to broker-dealers who, in turn, must provide transaction-related information to the SEC on its request.

---

[10] Rule 13d-1(c) under the 1934 Act.

■ Section 16 applies to fund managers who, investing for their own accounts or for the purposes of changing or influencing control of the issuer, own more than 10% of a class of a publicly traded company's outstanding equity securities.

Form PF: The Dodd-Frank Act, for the purpose of assessing the systematic risk that hedge funds pose, has given the SEC and the Commodity Futures Trading Commission the mandate to adopt one of the most onerous reporting obligations required of investment advisers, Form PF.[11] Registered investment advisers with at least $150 million of assets under management are required to file the new Form PF. These advisers will have to file either quarterly or annually, depending on their level of assets or, in some cases, the types of assets managed.

Large fund advisers must provide more detailed information on Form PF than must smaller advisers. Larger advisers fall into one of three categories:

1. *Large hedge fund advisers.* These advisers have at least $1.5 billion in assets under management attributable to hedge funds, and must file Form PF on a quarterly basis within 60 days after the end of each fiscal quarter.
2. *Large liquidity fund advisers.* These advisers have at least $1 billion in assets under management attributable to liquidity funds and registered money market funds, and must file Form PF on a quarterly basis within 15 days after the end of each fiscal quarter.
3. *Large private equity fund advisers.* These advisers have at least $2 billion in assets under management attributable to private equity funds, and must file Form PF on an annual basis within 120 days after the end of each fiscal year.

Smaller fund advisers (those who are not considered large fund advisers) must file Form PF on an annual basis within 120 days after the end of each fiscal year. The information required consists of fund size, leverage, investor types and concentration, liquidity, and fund performance. Hedge fund managers must also include information regarding their investment strategy, counterparty credit risk, and use of trading and clearing mechanisms.

Hedge funds are not required to furnish investors with any particular type of information aside from the disclosures necessary to prevent misleading investors (discussed previously). Institutional investors, however, are growing increasingly more demanding for hedge fund transparency because they owe fiduciary duties to their own investors. The transparency allows for these institutional investors to conduct the necessary due diligence and monitoring of the fund's activities to ensure that the fund adheres to its investment strategies and risk parameters. In order to meet the demands of these investors, hedge funds typically provide the following types of information to their investors:

■ Inspection of fund books and records
■ Quarterly or periodic letters
■ Annual audited financial statements

---

[11] Form PF can be found on the SEC website at www.sec.gov/rules/final/2011/ia-3308-formpf .pdf.

39.4 THE GLOBAL REGULATORY ENVIRONMENT FOR HEDGE FUNDS

Hedge funds have become global investment products. As the number of funds and the amount of assets managed has grown, so have the efforts to regulate hedge funds. Managers need to consider the regulatory environment of jurisdictions worldwide, such as those in Europe and Asia.

39.4.1 Hedge Fund Regulation in Europe

In November 2010, the European Parliament passed the **Alternative Investment Fund Managers Directive (AIFMD)** in order to regulate the marketing of alternative investment funds in the European Union (EU). Once the AIFMD takes effect in July 2013, all alternative investment funds, including hedge funds, will be able to be marketed to EU investors only if the fund's manager is authorized by a relevant EU regulator or if it complies with its relevant member state's private placement regimes.[12]

The AIFMD's most significant effect on alternative investment funds is the requirement of increased disclosure to investors and regulators. The AIFMD introduces the novel concept of an EU-wide passport that is available only to EU-based hedge fund managers. The passport allows each hedge fund manager to market funds to professional investors across member states under the authorization of a single member state. Non-EU hedge fund managers are required to use the revised private placement regime under the AIFMD.

The rights of both EU and non-EU firms to distribute offshore products within the EU to professional investors[13] and the depositary rules that apply to such firms are described in the AIFMD.

The effect on hedge funds by the passage of AIFMD is the increased costs of compliance with increased investor disclosure and regulatory reporting requirements. The additional reporting is for the purpose of aiding government regulators in monitoring the potential buildup of systematic risk in the financial system, which may arise from the use of leverage by hedge fund managers. Other areas that will contribute to the increased cost of doing business in the EU are the requirement to appoint a depositary for EU alternative investment funds, the uncapped liability on valuers (administration costs will rise), and specific requirements for hedge funds to conduct and maintain due diligence documentation and ongoing monitoring of delegated activities.

The regulation of hedge funds varies widely across Europe. On one end of the spectrum lie Ireland and Luxembourg, where hedge funds are allowed listings on the stock exchange. On the other end of the spectrum lies France, which places severe restrictions on hedge funds and strongly discourages offshore investing. As the United Kingdom is the epicenter of hedge fund activity in Europe (roughly 80% of Europe's

---

[12] The AIFMD is at present inconsistent as to how a non-U.S. fund manager may identify its member state.

[13] A professional investor is defined as an investor who either is considered to be a professional client or is, on request, treated as a professional client within the meaning of the financial markets framework AIFMD, known as MiFID (Markets in Financial Instruments Directive).

hedge funds are based in the UK), it is of particular importance how hedge funds are regulated there. The primary government body responsible for regulating the financial services industry in the United Kingdom is the Financial Services Authority (FSA).[14] The Financial Services and Markets Act 2000 (FSMA) and the Public Offers of Securities Regulations 1995 (POS Regulations) are the statutes that govern UK-based hedge funds. The FSMA contains rules regarding the marketing of hedge funds (i.e., collective investment schemes) that parallel the rules in the United States, such as those regarding the number of shareholders and limits on advertising. The POS Regulations contain rules regarding the structure of a hedge fund's private placement.

Unlike in the United States, in the United Kingdom (and in most of Europe), almost all hedge fund managers must acquire authorization from the FSA prior to carrying out regulated activity. There are four steps to obtaining authorization:

1. *Submission of an application to the FSA.* The firm application is generally seen as being tremendously time-intensive and complex and is required to be supplemented with additional documentation. The application can be downloaded from the FSA website at www.fsa.gov.uk. The requirements for basic financial resources and additional liquid capital requirements will depend on the category into which the hedge fund falls (typically an investment management firm).

2. *Submission of key-person applications.* Key executives, employees, and controllers of the firm (a controller is generally anyone who owns, directly or indirectly, 10% or more of the firm or is able to exercise significant influence over its affairs) must also individually submit an application to become an approved person. In addition, all persons who perform specified key functions (known as control functions) must be approved by the FSA. Approval of an applicant as being fit and proper to perform a particular function depends on the individual's honesty, integrity, reputation, confidence, capability, and financial soundness, as well as how the applicant performs on separate training and competence requirements of the FSA.

3. *Interview prior to approval.* Upon receipt of application, the FSA will visit the fund manager's office to interview the key personnel. If the fund manager passes the interview, then the FSA may decide to grant authorization to the manager in principle and require the fund to then capitalize in line with the FSA's financial resources requirements.

4. *Postauthorization.* Once fund managers have received formal authorization and notice that they will thereafter be subject to the FSA's rules, they must familiarize themselves with the rules and issue a compliance manual to their employees. In doing so, the managers must make a reasonable effort to ensure that their employees are made aware of and adhere to all of the FSA's rules, including those on insider dealing and anti-money-laundering requirements.

39.4.2 Hedge Fund Regulation in Asia

Most Asian governments have recently become more desirous of attracting hedge funds to their shores and have been designing their regulatory regimes accordingly. Hong Kong and Singapore, in particular, seem to want to become the next center

---

[14] The FSA will be replaced by the Financial Conduct Authority (FCA) in 2013.

for hedge funds to rival those of New York and London. Hong Kong and Singapore require hedge funds to register with the appropriate government regulatory body, but the costs of starting and running a hedge fund in these two countries are much lower than those in New York (as are the income tax rates). Where Singapore is more innovative and proactive in its oversight, however, Hong Kong is more conservative and wields tighter regulations. Asia is slowly opening up to the idea of foreign investments. South Korea has recently allowed onshore hedge funds for the first time. By contrast, Taiwan does not allow investments by offshore hedge funds, and Shanghai is largely off-limits to investors outside mainland China. Western hedge funds will find procuring investments from Asia to be far more challenging than the process is in Europe because each Asian country has different regulations (there is no unifying EU AIFMD-like policy regulating Asian hedge funds).

In Hong Kong, the Securities and Futures Commission (SFC) is the primary regulator of hedge funds. Under the Securities and Futures Ordinance (SFO), a hedge fund manager may operate in Hong Kong if it meets a number of requirements. In addition to licenses for the firm and individuals, hedge funds must follow these requirements:

- *Capital requirements.* The fund manager must meet capital requirements and pass a licensing examination. Under the SFO, a hedge fund licensed for asset management is normally required to have paid-up capital of HK$5,000,000 and to maintain liquid capital of at least HK$3,000,000. The requirements differ if the fund does not hold client assets.
- *Relevant experience.* A responsible officer must have at least three years of experience in the management of public funds (i.e., collective schemes sold to the public), proprietary trading, alternative investments, or investment research.
- *Authorization for public offerings.* Hedge funds must be authorized by the SFC prior to offering or inviting the public to acquire shares or interests in the hedge fund. Alternatively, a hedge fund can seek to qualify for an exemption.

As the EU AIFMD is gradually implemented, Asia may feel the greatest impact because the proposed rules prohibit non-EU fund managers from marketing within the EU unless the managers are able to show that they are subject to a regulatory regime of equivalent rigor in their home country. Hong Kong is likely to pass this rigor test since it follows a regulatory model similar to that of the United Kingdom in requiring registration by hedge fund managers and some basic reporting standards. The other Asian regulatory regimes, however, may not fare so well. Regardless, as China, whose alternative investing is thus limited mainly to private equity funds, loosens its market access rules and continues to grow while European economies stagnate, investors will be drawn east.

CHAPTER 40

Operational Due Diligence

This section examines operational due diligence in the context of hedge fund investments. Operational due diligence is an extremely important part of any institutional-grade investment process. This due diligence process should highlight and document potential areas of operational risk. The International Association of Financial Engineers (IAFE) defines **operational risk** as "losses caused by problems with people, processes, technology, or external events."

An investor must understand the operational risk prior to committing to an investment decision, as operational risk is as important as investment risk. Operational due diligence should be an ongoing process thereafter, as organizational structures and businesses change over time, and investors need to be vigilant in defining, monitoring, and accessing their operational risk exposures.

The strength of a hedge fund's operations often follows the fund's level of assets under management (AUM). Larger hedge funds have much more resources to invest in risk management and reporting systems and to hire world-class chief operating officers, chief compliance officers, business development managers, back-office and middle-office personnel, lawyers, accountants, and so on. Smaller hedge funds are more limited in their abilities to hire such qualified staff. In any event, one of the key points of performing operational due diligence will be to understand the hedge fund manager's state of mind in regard to building and maintaining her operations.

This section examines the operational risk of a hedge fund as defined by the IAFE and is delineated as follows: (1) people, (2) investment process, (3) technology (or infrastructure), and (4) external events. A thoughtful operational due diligence process will continually incorporate best practices regarding these categories. To that end, a brief section summarizing some of the more important best practices for operational due diligence has been included at the end of this discussion.

There are a variety of vendors in the marketplace who offer their services in assisting with operational due diligence. A fund of funds or institutional investor with deep financial resources may outsource much of the work necessary for operational due diligence to such vendors. Operational due diligence is an expansive topic; too large to cover in a single chapter. So for practical purposes, the scope of this chapter is limited to the most effective measures for preventing operational risks with regard to hedge fund investments.

40.1 OPERATIONAL DUE DILIGENCE

Hedge fund due diligence is the process by which a potential investor obtains a sufficient understanding of a hedge fund in order to make an informed decision in regard to investing. Issues typically considered during the due diligence process include the hedge fund's investment strategy, the character of the organization, the way the fund operates, the management of its associated risks, and the credibility of its business model. Not surprisingly, due diligence is considered by many as the most critical stage in hedge fund investing due to regulators' relatively light oversight of hedge funds, the general lack of transparency regarding hedge fund portfolio positions, and the difficulty of establishing reliable performance benchmarks. If performed well, due diligence can reduce risk, increase returns, and make investors more secure in their investment. On the other hand, if performed poorly, it can put investors' capital at risk.

Although there appears to be a wide variation in due diligence standards between different hedge fund investors, most generally agree that due diligence should include a review of the fund's marketing materials, investor correspondence, legal/audit documents, regulatory and professional records, background checks, and investment performance. Generic due diligence questionnaires are usually a good starting point in understanding how a hedge fund operates. To be effective, however, due diligence must involve significantly more than just a check-the-box approach. Interviews with key professionals of the fund and discussions with current investors are just as critical as reviews of the documents.

How long does a typical hedge fund due diligence process take? The length of the due diligence process varies widely, since it depends on the complexity of the fund, its geographic location, the size of the organization, the availability and quality of the information supplied by the manager, and the sophistication and knowledge of the investor. According to Anson (2006), a thorough investor should expect to spend 75 to 100 hours in reviewing a hedge fund manager before investing. In 2007, Andrew Golden, president of the Princeton University Investment Company, testified that his organization spends at least 400 hours on initial due diligence before investing in a hedge fund, and then approximately 70 hours per year on ongoing due diligence. A conservative estimate of the cost of due diligence is typically $50,000 to $100,000 per hedge fund, an amount that puts small funds of funds at a competitive disadvantage.

Overall, due diligence is a complex and iterative process that requires judgment, experience, and a variety of skills. Ideally, one needs to possess the skills of an accountant, a trader, an investment analyst, a psychotherapist, a business manager, a human resources manager, and a headhunter. Due diligence also requires a healthy dose of skepticism, combined with strong common sense. Investors may conduct due diligence themselves or use the services of consulting firms, law firms, accounting firms, or other third-party service providers.

40.1.1 Losses Caused by Problems with People

Hedge funds are managed by people. The people who manage hedge funds differ in their degree of integrity, intelligence, and passion for investing. It would be unadvisable to invest with a manager who is intelligent and passionate but possesses no integrity. Such an allocation carries a very high risk of disaster. The importance of integrity, therefore, is paramount.

When investors look at candidate managers, they need to attain insight into the manager's level of integrity. This key insight must be stressed at the onset of the due diligence process. Integrity in an organization trickles down from the tone at the top; thus, the emphasis on ethical behavior must originate with the fund manager. Finding managers with tremendous integrity helps mitigate potential operational risks. Investors want to be assured that when conflicts of interest arise, as they so often do during the course of business, the managers will carry out their fiduciary duty by acting in the interest of the investor and not themselves.

For illustrative purposes, let us create a hypothetical hedge fund with minimal operational risk. First, the hedge fund manager has ironclad integrity. This manager builds a world-class organization by spending a great deal of time and consideration hiring the most qualified people for the operational side of the business. These highly qualified employees go on to build a world-class infrastructure, with proper procedures for checks and balances in place. They also apply best-practice policies and procedures in all areas of the business. Every aspect of the operational due diligence is extremely transparent as the manager has already anticipated a thorough due diligence process by investors. This fund is preemptive in answering operational questions. The reputation of the manager and the hedge fund is well known and the manager is highly regarded among brokers, consultants, vendors, and other hedge fund managers. This is the ideal manager with minimal operational risk. Unfortunately, since many hedge funds are not this well prepared, much work needs to be done before investing.

Interestingly enough, when evaluating hedge funds, insight may be gained by looking at where the manager first learned and practiced investing. Was it at a top investment bank that had sophisticated compliance rules/checks and balances in place, or was it at a "swing for the fences" day-trading shop riddled with bandits? Many times, managers develop their behavior and level of business integrity based on where they were trained in their early days, so each aspect of a manager's past experiences needs to be closely examined. Granted, there are cases in which hedge fund managers begin their careers at a top investment bank's proprietary trading desk only to later derail under the stress of managing money and to start cutting corners, spiraling downward. As entertaining as such stories may be, it is hoped that managers who gained experience in a firm with an ethical culture would be more likely to continue that ethical culture in their own fund than would managers who spent their formative years in a less ethical firm.

There is a dependable correlation that the higher the integrity of a manager, the lower the likelihood of fraud. Fraud is the hedge fund risk that results in the most sensational headlines and could very likely terminate careers, even for a chief investment officer at a large pension fund. Fraud is likely the biggest fear for institutional investors who claim to have a rigorous due diligence process. An institutional investor that fails to detect fraud while being staffed with a large operational due diligence team may be accused of incompetence or negligence.

One needs only to browse the business section of a financial newspaper to see that hedge fund fraud risk is real; investors are periodically being duped by unscrupulous hedge funds or investment managers. Operational due diligence teams would do well to follow the old adage: "If it's too good to be true, it's probably not true." This common sense too frequently loses out to the desire to pick the next great hedge fund manager.

Why would an investor not follow through with conducting thorough due diligence? The following are the most common circumstances for when an investor becomes lax in this area:

- Small family offices or high-net-worth investors may not have the necessary resources to do the proper amount of due diligence on a given manager. They ask friends and trusted advisers about which hedge fund managers they should consider rather than undertaking a substantive due diligence process themselves.
- A highly sought-after manager that has been closed for many years is suddenly open to new investors. An investor's eagerness to invest with the manager trumps the seemingly tedious operational due diligence process and shortcuts are taken, with the investor relying on the fund manager's previous track record.

Due diligence team leaders do not typically possess strong or type A personalities, such as that of an overly eager fund-of-funds (FoF) portfolio manager; rather, they are trained with strong middle-office and back-office experiences and are generally much more detailed oriented. Given the time-consuming process of due diligence and the coordination among accountants, lawyers, analysts, and so forth, an impatient FoF portfolio manager's desire to make an investment may override the well-supported and documented doubts of the due diligence manager.

Of course a hedge fund manager who spends a lot of time in the gray area in terms of integrity can also put up the best risk-adjusted returns. A few successful hedge fund managers have been censored or investigated by the regulatory agencies for walking a fine line between compliance and violation of the federal securities laws by too aggressively pursuing opportunities or structural inefficiencies to deliver alpha. This merciless pursuit of alpha has generated tremendous benefit to investors. These hedge funds, however, come with issues. Therefore, a balance has to be struck between managers with clean backgrounds and the generation of returns.

40.1.2 Confirm Biographies

The process of doing due diligence on a given manager begins by examining the biographies reported in the presentation materials. Investigators should confirm degrees from business school, undergraduate programs, professional certificates, and so forth. Since biographies are examined extensively and sometimes used to build credibility for the manager, some managers may inflate certain accomplishments. It's also possible that marketing staff may rewrite biographies to give a much more positive spin to the manager's prior experiences and accomplishments. There are many vendors who will confirm degrees, run criminal checks, provide credit scores, and so forth on a given manager. Some larger FoFs and institutional investors have been known to procure private investigators to give a detailed account of a manager's past.

40.1.3 Triangulation

After the most superficial level of investigation, manager biographies, investors may attempt to triangulate the manager. **Triangulation** is the process of attaining deeper useful information about a manager from a source that is familiar with the manager. That is, an investigator will try to find someone in the manager's network who may personally know the manager and is willing to answer the investor's questions about the manager.

Many times there are conference calls centered around the strengths and weaknesses of the hedge fund manager, discussing whether the manager has integrity, is a moneymaker, is a good or a very difficult person, and so forth. Some of the best managers have very strong personality traits. Some managers may demand extremely long hours at work, others may force their employees to think exactly like them, and others may subject potential employees to a personality test to ensure they will fit into the organization. Hedge fund organizations naturally run the gambit of different cultural nuances, considering the many colorful characters and strong idiosyncrasies of their founders.

40.1.4 Personnel Turnover

Managing people and building a business are skills that can prove to be drastically different from finding great investments or generating alpha. Often, a great hedge fund manager may not have the requisite skills to manage people. Growing a business, therefore, becomes difficult for such a manager. Careful monitoring should be in place as a hedge fund evolves over time. Is the manager self-aware enough to understand that hiring a world-class operations manager could contribute to more success? Contrast that to a manager who tries to wear all the hats in the organization and ends up with very weak operations.

It may be relatively easy to manage a small team with less than $100 million of AUM. Once success propels a firm's AUM above $100 million, the firm becomes a very different organization. As the business grows, due diligence staff should be constantly updating the questions asked, such as whether the right people are in place, and whether the operations of the hedge fund are growing accordingly.

Just as there are some people who are good at the start-up phase of a business and others who are better at managing a large organization, hedge fund managers should be expected to be aware of the different stages of their business growth cycle. Due diligence staff will have to readjust their focus as the hedge fund business grows. Another way to think about this is that the due diligence on a start-up hedge fund is vastly different from the due diligence on a larger, established fund. It is important, therefore, to understand at what development stage the hedge fund is at the time the investor initiates due diligence.

40.1.5 Prior Employees

Contacting individuals who have left the hedge fund can be a great source of insight into the organization. Ex-employees will typically have fewer motives to paint a bright and rosy picture of the organization and may be more likely, therefore, to give a straightforward answer to most questions. Some caution must be exercised in contacting ex-employees, however, because their prior bad experiences may bias their opinions of the organization. Emotions may have been implicated as they left the organization, and the effects may not have waned. Nonetheless, proper due diligence requires contacting people who have previously worked at the hedge fund and documenting any criticism of the organization.

It is important to know not only why an employee has left the hedge fund but also who replaced the employee, especially if the employee is part of senior management or has compliance duties. Clearly the investor should see red flags if the ex-employee left because the hedge fund lost its largest client or the books were marked too aggressively or senior management was behaving inappropriately. Even if the departure was due strictly to personal reasons, the investor must analyze how the replacement of personnel impacts the operations of the fund.

40.1.6 Losses Caused by Problems with Processes

This section focuses on operational processes of a hedge fund. How has the hedge fund been legally organized? Who really owns the hedge fund? What is the firm's AUM, and how many funds does it manage? What are the organizational conflicts of interest? The answers to these questions will clarify what potential conflicts of interest exist within the hedge fund.

An organized hedge fund that prioritizes minimizing violations of federal securities laws will have very transparent operational procedures. The most compliance-minded of hedge funds will have a written set of operational policies and procedures in place and will conduct regular testing to ensure their effectiveness. In general, operational procedures change as an organization grows or contracts. This proves to be another important reason as to why investors must be sensitive to the changes in an organization and perform due diligence continually.

When a well-funded hedge fund launches with a tremendous amount of AUM, the fund can afford world-class operational teams and support. It can also afford the priciest legal team, accountants, and custodians. On the other side of the spectrum, many hedge funds start out with a shoestring budget, and may have used legal documents prepared for another fund just to get started. As such, understanding each component of the organization, from its origins to the current development, may be a daunting task.

Process due diligence requires the assistance of the hedge fund manager and its employees. The more each side warms up to each other, the more easily information will flow from the hedge fund to the investor. The investor warms up by seriously considering investing in a particular hedge fund. At times, however, the hedge fund may be oversubscribed and will only accept investments from investors who will not tax the hedge fund resources with an unnecessarily long due diligence process. In these instances, the hedge fund may be cagey in disclosing information about its internal processes. This means that the investor must figure out a way to obtain sufficient comfort with the investment while being more or less forced to use an abridged due diligence process. This trade-off between confidence with the sufficiency of an abridged due diligence process and access to a hot manager occurs frequently, especially when flows into hedge funds are very active.

How many times will a hedge fund take a call from an investor for the purpose of due diligence? Generally speaking, once a good relationship is established with a given hedge fund and after an allocation has been made, having remaining questions answered on the operational side becomes much easier. The monitoring may become even more transparent, as most hedge funds are very appreciative of their investors and provide all information needed to satisfy the investor. Hedge funds understand that their investors have to perform their requisite due diligence on an ongoing basis and that they may even be obligated to report to a pension fund board or other investors (as is the case in a fund of funds). Hedge funds also generally favor informed investors who take an active interest in the hedge fund's internal workings, as these types of investors tend to stick with the fund through the difficult periods. Investors who have a more superficial understanding of the operations of the hedge fund are quicker to redeem at the first sign of poor performance.

40.1.7 Organizational Structure

A hedge fund is typically organized as a pooled investment vehicle in which the general partner (GP) is responsible for the operations of the fund, and limited partners (LPs) may make investments into the partnership but limit their liability to the paid-in amount. Generally, there is a minimum of one GP and one LP. Due diligence should cover both the GP and the LPs through inquiries, such as the following:

- Is there a dominant GP, or is the ownership spread out over several main partners?
- Are the LPs high-net-worth families who maintain secrecy over their identity, or do they consist of institutional investors with a record of a thorough due diligence process?
- Are the LPs approachable to answer questions about the fund?

A hedge fund reveals most of the information needed to understand its organizational structure through its subscription agreement, offering memorandum, due diligence packages, one-page summary, investor presentation, and so on. Unfortunately, some hedge funds maintain very complex organizational structures. These organizations may have had prior changes in GPs due to retirement of founders, reorganizations, or a refocus of products. These hedge funds are much more difficult to understand, as typically the history of the GP's ownership and funds or product lines have experienced many changes. It becomes very difficult to re-create the historical changes in the organization without proper guidance.

Note that the due diligence process starts with a snapshot of what the hedge funds look like at the present moment. As the due diligence process unfolds and the investor spends more time interacting with hedge fund personnel, the increased familiarity will lead to a better and deeper understanding of the fund's operations. In turn, the hedge fund will likely become increasingly transparent to the due diligence requests of the investor.

40.1.8 Ownership

Understanding the ownership structure is no doubt a key component and will give tremendous insight into the underlying motives of the parties of interest. Also, ownership provides insight into the possible turnover of staff at the hedge fund. Figuring out who owns what is very challenging, as an investor may not be given information about the equity breakdown (as this is naturally a sensitive subject to the GP). In some instances, due diligence reports will be unable to give any specific information regarding ownership and will have to either vaguely state that the majority of the fund is owned by the partners or give some other general reference as to who owns the GP.

Some hedge funds may obscure the ownership structure by stating that the principals own the majority of the GP. However, if an investor is seriously considering relatively large investments, hedge funds will often provide such information in a confidential manner.

There are times when the ownership may change abruptly, such as when hedge fund managers suddenly leave or are otherwise unable to perform their duties in the funds. Since some hedge funds revolve around a single individual who makes the discretionary calls on investments, some institutional investors have minimized their risks by demanding a side letter with a key-person provision. A key-person provision gives investors more flexible redemption terms (e.g., a shorter notice period or a waiver of a lockup or holding period) if a key person is no longer part of the hedge fund. By being allowed to redeem, investors do not have to keep their money invested in a fund for which they have not had a chance to undertake due diligence on the replacement of the key person. It must be noted that a side letter, which puts into writing a special arrangement between the investor and the hedge fund that is not available to all investors, raises a number of concerns, such as fairness to other investors, and thus a hedge fund may be reluctant to grant a side letter.

40.1.9 Assets under Management

The previous section contained some discussion of the evolution of the organization as its AUM increases or decreases. What do the changes in AUM mean to an investor? Decreasing AUM typically signals a potential reduction in staff, as AUM is determinant of revenues generated by the fund (in the form of management fees). These projections help the hedge fund determine the number of employees it is able to hire and maintain. As AUM diminishes and staff size shrinks, tasks and responsibilities are simply taken on by the remaining employees. In such situations, the investor should keep in mind that the remaining staff, if disgruntled by the increased workload and stagnant pay, may be looking for other employment opportunities. On the other hand, increasing AUM typically signals that the hedge fund may bring on board seasoned staff to help grow the business and make it more institutional grade. Additionally, the organization may implement more structure as it increases the sophistication of its operations (e.g., implementing a formal compliance program or compiling a written set of operational policies and procedures). Substantial changes in AUM may also raise other concerns. Are redeeming investors expressing concern about the fund manager, or are their redemptions solely due to rebalancing or normal trading activity? When AUM rises, will the liquidity and the inefficient pricing of the targeted securities decline and reduce the fund's potential alpha?

40.1.10 Fee Structure

Hedge funds typically charge investors a management fee of 1% to 2% of assets and a 20% incentive fee (subject to a high-water mark), but there are many variations from this common fee schedule.

Typically, the management fee is deducted before calculating the fund's returns so that it may more accurately reflect the appreciation of the investor's investment. In addition, assets held in so-called side pockets are generally not included when the hedge fund calculates performance fees. Since investors may invest in a hedge fund at different times throughout the years, many funds, particularly offshore funds, employ different approaches that serve to allocate the appropriate portion of a performance fee or high-water mark to each investor.

40.1.11 Redemption Terms

During the due diligence process, investors must acquire information about the limitations to redeem their investments from the hedge fund. Most hedge funds use the following mechanisms to limit an investor's ability to withdraw assets:

40.1.11.1 Initial Lockup Periods
Some hedge funds do not allow investors to withdraw any part of their investments in the fund until at least 12 months have passed and will apply this restriction to each part of the investment (i.e., if an investor makes an investment in the fund on January 2011, the investor cannot redeem the investment until January 2012; if the investor makes a second investment on March 2011, that portion of the investment has a lockup until March 2012). Hedge funds that hold particularly illiquid securities, such as distressed or activist funds, may have an even longer lockup period. **Hard lockup provisions** do not allow redemptions for any reason during the lockup period. Other funds may offer a **soft lockup provision,** in which the hedge fund will allow withdrawals during the lockup period if the investor pays a penalty to the fund to compensate other investors for the trading costs caused by the liquidation of the exiting investor's holdings.

40.1.11.2 Withdrawals and Redemptions
During the financial crisis of 2008, many investors attempted to redeem their shares in some hedge funds, only to experience their first gate. A **gating provision,** which should be disclosed in the prospectus, is a restriction placed by the hedge fund that limits the amount of withdrawals during a redemption period. Some gates will allow only a certain percentage of assets to be redeemed in each period. Others will allow redemption on a first-come, first-served basis, or offer some pro rata distribution. In any case, gates caused many investors severe heartache during 2008. Hedge funds impose gates in the investment terms to prevent a run on the fund. In a run scenario, most of the fund's assets are withdrawn, which can force the sale of positions at distressed prices. The argument is that if a large number of redemptions occur and the hedge fund has to liquidate a big position, the subsequent forced sell-off may hurt the remaining investors.

A hedge fund will usually permit withdrawals or redemptions from the fund only at specified intervals (enumerated in the offering documents) by providing written notice 30 days or more in advance.

40.1.12 Client Profile

To whom do hedge funds cater? If a given hedge fund's client list includes many high-net-worth investors who are limited in their ability to conduct proper due diligence, then that should be well documented. Compare this to a hedge fund that primarily pursues institutional investors, who are generally known to undertake painstakingly long and detailed due diligence on hedge funds. The client base of the hedge fund subsequently sheds light on a very important detail of the fund.

Many institutional investors share experiences and notes with other institutional investors, especially about their hedge fund experiences. Building a relationship with other investors who have undertaken arduous due diligence processes (and maintained very detailed notes) and have established an intimate relationship with hedge fund managers is exceedingly important. Having a strong and extensive network of friends in the institutional investment community is extremely helpful.

40.1.13 Follow the Cash

One of the important questions in due diligence has to do with who has the power to move cash. Does cash movement require one person to sign, or does it require a dual signature? A small amount of cash can typically be moved by a single signature, most often that of the COO. A large movement of cash should require a dual signature.

Following the cash begins by taking a very skeptical opinion of the manager. Assume that he is a thief with intent to defraud investors at every opportunity. Assuming this, focus on how he would be able to steal investor funds. Finally, review the hedge fund's policies that respond to the possible risk of asset theft and decide whether those policies are sufficient and consistently examined for effectiveness.

Note that if the hedge fund's operational policies allow for any opportunity for the commingling of accounts, this is a critical risk that needs to be prominently documented. Following the cash through the organization, from the investment stage to withdrawals and redemptions, must be thoroughly understood. Strong internal controls should be in place for any institutional-grade hedge funds.

40.1.14 Valuation, Administration, and Prime Brokers

Parallel to following the cash, due diligence should be conducted by following a trade from idea origination to confirmation and settlement. For exchange-traded securities such as stocks, exchange-traded funds (ETFs), and futures, this process should be particularly transparent, since valuations are typically done on the closing prices or last trade as printed on the exchange. Once less liquid securities or over-the-counter (OTC) products are involved, important questions of proper valuations arise.

As a general rule, if a hedge fund's returns are far from average, then the investor should immediately investigate the hedge fund's operations, specifically the direction of trades and the valuations. For example, if a mortgage-backed hedge fund is consistently earning returns of $+1\%$ each month while all other mortgage funds are contemporaneously flat, alarms should be ringing and questions should be asked of the hedge fund: Was it net short mortgages while others remained net long, or does the valuation process have any bearing on the performance?

The due diligence process should also monitor the process of subscriptions and redemptions for the hedge fund. In other words, how fluid and transparent is the relationship between the given hedge fund and the administrator of the fund? Typically, **fund administrators** maintain the hedge fund's books and records and facilitate any subscription/redemption requests. In particular, the administrator role includes (1) maintaining the fund's financial books and records, (2) computing the net asset value

(NAV) of the fund, (3) paying/receiving the fund's expenses/income, (4) reconciling the daily and monthly brokerage statements, (5) settling daily trades, (6) pricing securities, (7) calculating and paying dividends and distributions (when necessary), and (8) (possibly) supervising the liquidation and orderly dissolution of the fund.

A hedge fund that has a good working relationship with a well-known administrator gives more confidence to potential investors. If a hedge fund employs a small or unknown administrator, then this relationship should be vetted closely before investing. Errors in NAV calculations and deficiencies in accounting controls and procedures should be recorded and closely monitored.

Hedge fund relationships with **prime brokers (PBs)** are a key source of understanding the firm. After the collapse of Lehman Brothers, many hedge funds attempt to diversify PB concentration by having relationships with multiple PBs. Investors will often find newer hedge funds through PB capital introduction events. Beyond introducing hedge funds to investors, PBs typically serve the following additional services: (1) global custody, (2) securities lending, (3) facilitating leverage, (4) portfolio reporting and risk reports, (5) specific operational support, (6) office leasing and servicing, (7) capital (human capital) introduction, and (8) consulting and advisory services.

Prime brokers have tremendous access to the hedge fund flow of information. Such information includes new launches, capital movements, and concentrated positions. Therefore, having a few trusted PB contacts can help build key insights into the hedge fund industry. Many times PBs will have covered the given hedge fund manager at prior positions, as these relationships often survive firm changes on either side.

40.1.15 Idea Generation

It is critical to understand how ideas are generated, because there is a risk that the hedge fund will run out of great investment ideas. Though this may not be directly related to operational risk, it is related to the investment process. Suppose a hedge fund starts to run out of investment ideas that generate returns. Out of desperation, the hedge fund managers or analysts start attending idea dinners. Now suppose that at one of these dinners, there is consensus that a given company is excessively overvalued, after which many attendees begin to build a short position on the company. While these managers may be correct, it is an irrelevant fact for the purposes of this illustration because the unfortunate consequence of so many acting on this belief in the market leads to the trade becoming very crowded very quickly. Such crowded trades will continue to be one of the most tragic self-created risks for hedge fund managers.

As an example, take the Volkswagen (VW) and Porsche short squeeze that occurred in October 2008. At the time, Porsche had a reasonably large position in VW. By most fundamental analysis, VW was expensive, and under normal conditions the price of VW should have eventually reflected the fundamentals. It was well known that many hedge funds had short positions in VW. What was not well known, however, was that Porsche was employing options to covertly build an even larger position in VW. On October 28, 2008, short sellers got caught short and propelled VW to become Germany's largest company by market capitalization as frantic short covering ensued. Porsche surprised the markets with an announcement that it had gained control of 74% of VW's voting shares. On January 25, 2010, the *New York Times* ran an article entitled "Hedge Funds Sue Porsche for Billion Lost on VW." What should be noted was that the four hedge funds that sustained losses did so on their short positions in VW. The losses amounted to hundreds of millions of dollars per hedge fund.

The ability to generate unique ideas away from mainstream sources is one way to mitigate the risk of investing in overcrowded positions. Alternatively, investors could supplement their analysis by employing Form 13F reports or cross-referencing other managers' positions.

40.1.16 Losses Caused by Problems with Technology

Technology constantly changes because business operations are tempted to include the latest and greatest technologies. But upgrades in operational systems, however marginal, may introduce risks. For example, when upgrades occur, slight changes may cause email systems to go down or result in loss of computer access. Even with third-party vendors, outages due to power loss may render technology useless for some time. Additionally, more serious technology problems may occur if the trading desk or trading platform malfunctions. Backup systems should be well understood, and business continuity and contingency plans should be in place.

Investors can reasonably expect a hedge fund to have a backup system and a fully functioning disaster recovery site. Another important area of concern is the flexibility of virtual private network (VPN) access from home, as this may compromise security. This risk is elevated for more quantitatively driven hedge funds, which typically rely on proprietary code and algorithms.

Recently, some hedge funds have dabbled in employing cloud computing, for which end users do not need to know the physical location and configuration of the systems that deliver these computing services. One of the advantages this presents for a hedge fund is cost-efficiency when hedge fund managers want to outsource most of their information technology (IT) responsibilities. Questions remain about the security of such systems and the risks if the cloud goes down. As hedge funds embrace new and different technologies, investors should craft new questions to understand and analyze the changes. The main point here is that as technology infrastructure changes the business process of a hedge fund, investors need to be perpetually aware of these developments and the potential risks they pose to their investment.

40.1.17 Losses Caused by External Events

December 21, 2012, according to the Mayan calendar, is considered an external event. Will hedge funds be prepared for the end of the world? Will recovery sites come through and back up all the critical information? What happens if a comet knocks out the northeastern U.S. electricity grid and all the backups fail? Will investors have enough information to recover their investments? Thinking about these kinds of external events, regardless of how rare and unrealistic they may be, must yield some credible answers. At a minimum, the operations of the hedge fund should have some documented contingency plans.

External events are very difficult to anticipate, since they often occur when and where most people least expect them to occur. Suppose a hedge fund that worried about sensitive information about clients, portfolios, algorithms, and so on, sets up an impenetrable firewall around its internal servers to prevent hackers or cyber attacks. Then one day, an attack is launched on an exchange where this hedge fund exclusively trades. Alternatively, what happens if this hedge fund's administrator is attacked and exposes or loses sensitive account information? There are many unanticipated scenarios that leave hedge fund operations exposed to external risks.

Since natural disasters have occurred and are expected to occur, it is vitally important to understand how the organization is set up to respond to such events. The bulk of the costs in preparing for disaster are attributed to the location of the backup recovery center. If someone has a hedge fund in New York City and the backup recovery center is located in New Jersey, what happens if the whole northeastern electric grid goes down? Unfortunately, building a backup center in California would be too cost prohibitive for most hedge funds. When risk-control decisions are made due to external events, does the organization examine the options through a fiduciary lens, or are decisions made strictly on the basis of minimizing costs? These are just some of the issues that need to be well understood when assessing losses caused by problems from external events.

40.1.18 Current Best Practices for the Hedge Fund Industry

On January 15, 2009, the Asset Managers' Committee (AMC) published a report to set new standards of best practices in answer to the President's Working Group on Financial Markets. The report attempts to reduce systemic risk and foster investor protection.

AMC identified five key areas where best practices would result in a reduction of systemic risk and increase investor protection:

1. *Disclosure:* Strong disclosure practices that provide investors with the information they need to determine whether to invest in a fund, to monitor an investment, and to make a decision whether to redeem their investment
2. *Valuation:* Robust valuation procedures that call for a segregation of responsibilities, thorough written policies, oversight, and other measures for the valuation of assets, including a specific focus on hard-to-value assets
3. *Risk management:* Comprehensive risk management that emphasizes measuring, monitoring, and managing risk, including stress testing of portfolios for market and liquidity risk management
4. *Trading and business operations:* Sound and controlled operations and infrastructure, supported by adequate resources and checks and balances in operations, to enable a manager to achieve best industry practice in all of the other areas
5. *Compliance, conflicts, and business practices:* Specific practices to address conflicts of interest and promote the highest standards of professionalism and a culture of compliance[1]

---

[1] Full report available at www.amaicmte.org/Public/AMC%20Report%20-%20Final.pdf.

AMC's recommendations are very detailed and probably more relevant for a larger multistrategy hedge fund with lots of resources to apply to the operational side of the business. In any case, it is a solid framework to build on.

40.2 STRATEGY-SPECIFIC DUE DILIGENCE

This section focuses on strategy-specific issues arising in a due diligence process. Rather than being exhaustive, this section concentrates on the major hedge fund strategies and discusses some specific questions related to each of them. Beyond hedge funds, strategy-specific risks should be discussed with all asset managers, whether in traditional investments, private equity, or real assets.

40.2.1 Long/Short Equity

Long/short equity is one of the larger hedge fund categories, both in number of funds and in assets under management. It primarily involves buying equities that are expected to increase in value and selling short equities that are expected to decrease in value.

Essential due diligence questions for a long/short equity fund should include the following:

- *What is the exact strategy of the fund?* Whenever a strategy could have several substrategies, the investor should seek to understand the precise substrategy that the manager follows. Long/short equity funds now retain a large variety of strategies (e.g., bottom-up stock pickers, equity market timers, long biased concentrated activists, long/short sector specialists, and event driven equities). It is essential to know how the hedge fund can be categorized as well as how its strategy changes over time, if at all. The substrategy followed by the manager will indicate the investment universe that the manager follows. Some long/short equity managers will focus on one sector, country, or market capitalization range, while others will adopt a generalist perspective and invest on a global basis. Knowing the investment universe is useful for both manager assessment and portfolio construction.
- *How is the portfolio constructed?* Portfolio construction provides great insight into the thought process and risk-management attitude of the fund manager. Some long/short equity managers take separately outright positions on the long and short side, and hedge the residual risks at the portfolio level. Others are split into sectors, where each sector is run (and hedged) as a mini hedge fund. Still others use a pairs trading strategy, with a short position for each corresponding long position.
- *Do the manager and the team have sufficient shorting experience?* Many long-only managers who shift to hedge funds underestimate the skills necessary to sell short. First, short selling requires the ability to identify flaws in a business before its share price drops, which is contrary to the aim of traditional managers. Second, short sellers need to borrow shares from willing lenders via their broker, manage collateral exposure, deal with dividend payments, and handle the risk

that the lenders may recall their stock at any time. Third, short selling exposes the portfolio to additional risk of loss. Losses in a long-only portfolio are limited to what was paid for the stock; when going short, losses are technically unlimited, as the price at which stock can be bought back rises ever higher above the price at which it was sold. All of these risks tend to make short selling more difficult than holding a security long. While examining the manager's skill in managing the short positions of the portfolio, attention must be paid to the role of the prime broker or brokers in providing the manager with borrowed shares. It must be determined whether the manager uses one or more sources for borrowed shares and whether those sources are able to secure hard-to-borrow shares.

- *Is the manager doing naked short selling, covered short selling, or both?* **Naked short selling** refers to short sales by persons who, at the time of selling, neither are the owner of the relevant security nor have put appropriate arrangements in place to meet their borrowing and delivery obligations. It is much riskier than **covered short selling**, particularly in terms of settlement risk. By contrast, a covered short seller will first secure the borrowing of the stock before selling it. In many countries, naked short selling is restricted or even prohibited.

- *What are the typical ranges for gross and net exposures?* **Gross exposure** represents the absolute level of investment bets and is measured as the total of the long and short positions. **Net exposure** represents the implicit amount of directional market risk that resides unhedged in the portfolio. It is defined as the total of the long minus the total of the short positions. For instance, a manager who is 120% long and 50% short would have a gross exposure of 170% and a net exposure of 70%. Knowing the gross and net exposures of a fund is essential to understanding its investment style as well as the possible downside risk and market exposures that the fund is taking.

- *What are the expected sources of return?* This question could be asked of all hedge fund managers regardless of their style. In most cases, there are multiple sources of returns. In the case of long/short equity managers, the key concern is the role of market risk (beta) as a source of return. Long/short equity managers have three primary sources of returns in their portfolios:
  - **Static returns** are the gains of the portfolio in the absence of change in the price of the underlying stocks. These are essentially dividends and earnings on the proceeds of the short sales minus borrowing costs to leverage and the dividends paid to the lender of borrowed stocks.
  - **Market-linked returns** are coming from the residual net long or net short market exposure.
  - **Manager alpha** can arise because of stock picking or market timing activities.

In examining the sources of returns of the hedge fund, one must also determine if the manager uses short positions as a source of returns or whether short positions are primarily used to hedge the risk of long positions. Understanding the sources of returns is essential because static returns and market-linked returns can easily be obtained with relatively simple replicating portfolios at a fraction of the cost charged by hedge funds.

- *How liquid are the stocks in the portfolio?* The liquidity of underlying assets of a hedge fund is always a source of concern for investors. Recent hedge fund failures have highlighted the danger of hedge funds running large positions in relatively illiquid stocks. When the fund buys an illiquid stock, its price can rise dramatically. This could have a great impact on the fund's overall performance. In these cases, selling these positions without affecting their price is almost impossible, which means that the paper gains may never be realized. In that respect, liquidity should always be considered as having three dimensions: (1) how much of a stock the fund can trade in normal market conditions, (2) how quickly it can sell its position, and (3) how much the price will move as a result. Related to liquidity is the issue of the uniqueness of the manager's strategy. If managers follow some of the better-known strategies (e.g., momentum or book to market), then they may face the systemic risk that if a large number of hedge funds operating in the same space decide to liquidate their positions, they will encounter a market where it will be hard to find buyers or sellers. This is exactly what happened in August 2007, when stocks that were considered to be highly liquid were negatively impacted by the mass liquidation of a few large equity long/short and market neutral funds.

- *What is the manager policy regarding nonlisted stocks?* The case of nonlisted stocks must be carefully analyzed, with particular attention paid to such issues as liquidity, valuation, and deal flow access. The latter is particularly relevant for shares in companies that are privately owned or being prepared for initial public offerings (IPOs). Do the key investment professionals possess the specialized knowledge and experience to invest successfully in such securities?

- *Is the fund restricted in some positions?* Investment restrictions are mandatory as soon as private information is made available to the fund manager. This is typically the case if the manager sits on the board of a company and means that the position cannot generally be traded as easily as others.

- *Which types of derivative instruments are being used?* Some long/short equity funds make heavy use of derivatives to implement their views or hedge their positions. While this may be perfectly rational from an investment perspective, the use of derivatives in a hedge fund portfolio may have three impacts that need to be assessed:

  1. They may create excessive leverage. When buying derivatives such as call options, the fund pays only a premium and benefits from the implicit leverage of the option.

  2. They may create excessive liabilities. When selling call or put options, the fund pockets a premium but needs to consider the resulting potential risk of future losses.

  3. They create counterparty risk. Several funds use OTC derivatives such as swaps to enter in positions either for regulatory reasons (e.g., easier access, possibility to create synthetic short positions) or for tax reasons (e.g., to avoid a stamp tax). But this exposes the fund to the risk of the default of its counterparty.

- *How is foreign exchange risk managed?* Funds investing abroad face the risk of having net foreign currency exposures. Some managers systematically hedge their foreign exchange exposure. Others consider it a potential additional source of returns. In the latter case, one needs to ask what expertise the manager has to make these bets.

- *Is the fund manager engaged in shareholder activism?* In the recent past, some hedge funds have engaged in shareholder activism, arguing that they lack some of the conflicts of interest that have deterred traditional institutional shareholders from becoming active in corporate governance. Activism often implies owning significantly large positions for long periods of time and ultimately being restricted in terms of trading.
- *Are there stop-loss rules in the portfolio? How are they set and adjusted?* **Stop losses** are predetermined rules that automatically reduce a portfolio's exposure after reaching a certain threshold of cumulative losses. Trailing stop losses are stop-loss orders that are adjusted upward as a stock moves higher. These rules are commonly used by some hedge fund managers to limit the downside risk of their investments, but other managers do not like them because they automatically lock in losses and prevent participation in a rebound.
- *Does the manager file Form 13F reports with the SEC?* In the United States, investment managers who exercise investment discretion over $100 million in assets must make quarterly disclosures of their holdings on Form 13F with the SEC. Form 13F is publicly available and contains the names and class of the securities, the CUSIP number, the number of shares owned, and the total market value of each security. Form 13F filings can provide insight into the various securities owned by a hedge fund as well as changes in their positions.

40.2.2 Convertible Arbitrage

As previously discussed, the convertible arbitrage strategy seeks to generate returns from the potential mispricing of a convertible security's equity, bond, and embedded call-option features. Typically, the potential source of alpha for convertible arbitrageurs is the mispriced embedded option. Since other components of a convertible are normally priced fairly, convertible arbitrageurs hedge the risks associated with those components (i.e., convertible arbitrage managers buy the convertible bond and then hedge its equity, credit, and interest rate risks using various cash and derivative instruments).

Due diligence on a convertible arbitrage fund should first address the specific approach used by the fund:

- *What types of convertible bonds is the manager using?* Convertible bonds can be in one of three delta ranges. When the convertible bond is distressed, the strike price of the embedded option is out-of-the-money. When options are at-the-money, convertibles are in the hybrid range, while equity alternative convertible bonds have embedded options that are deep in-the-money.
- *What is the specific strategy of the fund?* Convertible arbitrage includes various substrategies, such as exploiting the mispricing of the bond, trading volatility, trading credit, and trading gamma. Each of these substrategies has different return expectations and risk profiles and requires different skill sets. In some cases, a fund manager may decide to split her portfolio between several

substrategies. The issue is whether the manager has the background, skill set, infrastructure, and supporting services to implement various convertible arbitrage substrategies.

The success of the convertible arbitrage strategy is highly dependent on the quality of the manager's pricing model. Competition makes it difficult to identify cheap convertible bonds; furthermore, not only must the manager's pricing model be able to identify the most profitable opportunities, but it must also estimate the appropriate hedge ratios for various risk components.

- *How good is the pricing and hedging model?* Sophisticated pricing models can more easily address real-world market features (e.g., time-varying interest rates and stochastic volatility) and special convertible bond features (e.g., special termination clauses and forced conversions). Convertible bond models have improved over the past several years and are still improving. As a rule, convertible arbitrageurs need to upgrade their models on a regular basis.
- *Is the same model used for pricing and hedging?* A model should compute not only the price of the convertible but all of the relevant risk and sensitivity parameters. If different models are used for hedging and pricing, it is likely to result in inconsistencies and may lead the manager to unknowingly expose his portfolio to risks that he is not prepared to manage.
- *What procedure is used to mark the portfolio?* Investors should probe the pricing policies of their hedge fund managers and determine the level of oversight exercised over portfolio pricing. A good hedge fund manager should normally use several marks from various independent brokers and have documented rules to deal with differences between the quotes. The use of discretionary marks may be unavoidable due to the lack of a viable pricing source, but they should represent a very small portion of the portfolio's value. All funds should have a documented policy regarding when and why discretionary marks instead of market quotes are used. This policy should include a requirement for approval from someone other than the portfolio manager (preferably a controller or a risk manager). Finally, the fund manager should maintain records supporting her valuation recommendations.
- *How much of the portfolio is marked to market versus marked to model?* A fund manager may decide to mark to model (e.g., in the case of illiquid instruments, in which it may be difficult to obtain a recent market quote). In such cases, there is a risk that the fund's valuation differs significantly from the potential selling price, especially if the position has to be liquidated rather quickly. A mark-to-model valuation is, by construction, less reliable than a mark-to-market valuation because it depends on the accuracy of the assumptions in the model. Furthermore, the model may not be able to account for abnormal market conditions. Recent experience of many convertible arbitrage managers has shown that even the most accurate pricing models may fail to account for the impact of market distress on prices of hard-to-value assets.

As an illustration of the importance of pricing models for convertible arbitrage, let us recall the case of Lipper Convertibles, LP, once one of the largest convertible arbitrage hedge funds. Edward J. Strafaci managed the fund until January 2002, when he and another principal left to launch their own firm. Lipper undertook a bottom-up review of the convertible bond portfolio following the departure of Mr. Strafaci. On February 20, 2002, the firm reported that it was reducing the value of its onshore fund by approximately 40%. In this specific case, it turned out that the valuation error had been intentional: The previous fund manager had knowingly and recklessly overstated the value of convertible bonds and preferred stocks held by the fund, resulting in the dissemination of materially false and misleading fund valuations and performance figures from at least 1998 until his departure. Lipper ultimately decided to liquidate the fund after being swamped with redemption requests. The Lipper Convertible Fund, which had reported approximately $722 million in partnership capital before Strafaci's resignation, reported approximately $365 million in partnership capital upon liquidation. The former fund manager was convicted, sent to prison, and fined $89 million for fraud. The SEC also initiated proceedings against the external auditor of the fund for unquestioningly relying on a valuation process that was significantly flawed. This is a classic example of what can happen when simple checks and balances are not present in the pricing process; Lipper's policy did not address exceptions, nor did it require justifications and documentation for setting valuations that differed from market consensus.

- *What is the quality of the pricing inputs?* A model is only as good as its inputs. With securities as complex as convertible bonds, it is essential to integrate information on volatility and credit spread levels into pricing models. Furthermore, some inputs may not be observable and thus need to be estimated (e.g., volatility of the equity). The quality and source of these inputs have to be carefully examined.
- *Can the manager override the model or its inputs?* Some arbitrageurs use pricing models as a support tool but take discretionary hedging positions. If so, under what conditions does this occur, how often does this happen, when was the last time, and why? Furthermore, have these discretionary positions positively impacted past performance of the fund?

In addition, there are several risk-management questions that are particularly relevant to convertible arbitrage strategy:

- *What are the risk parameters of the fund?* Risks of convertible arbitrage usually include equity risk (delta, gamma), interest rate risk (rho), volatility risk (vega), and credit risk. Most convertible arbitrageurs hedge these risks, though not necessarily completely, since they aim to take advantage of some particular market anomalies. For example, the manager may decide not to hedge the credit risk of the bond completely if she believes that the market misprices the credit risk of the sector that the issuing firm belongs to. Liquidity risk, though very important, is not generally modeled or hedged explicitly. Understanding these risk limits is essential in assessing the overall risk of the portfolio.
- *What instruments are used for hedging?* There are a variety of instruments that can be used to hedge the long position in convertible bonds, including some from the OTC market that involve counterparty risk or leaving some residual risk in the portfolio (e.g., the credit risk of a position may be hedged using a credit derivative, in which the underlying is an index rather than the issuing firm).

- *How often is a portfolio hedged?* As the market moves, arbitrage positions need to be rebalanced. There are various rebalancing strategies ranging from discretionary to systematic, such as making changes at fixed trading time intervals, making changes at fixed price intervals, or using a combined approach. It is also essential to determine if rebalancing the hedge ratio is done via program trading or manually by a trader.

- *Is the fund using leverage?* Leverage varies greatly according to the underlying trading style of the fund manager and directly influences the risk. Leverage should also be analyzed with respect to the liquidity of the underlying positions. In measuring the leverage of the fund, attention must be paid to both implicit and explicit leverage. Certain derivative products, such as options and futures, have leverage embedded in them. If leverage is measured to understand the potential volatility of the fund, then both implicit and explicit leverage should be accounted for. However, if leverage is measured to determine the risk of funding, then only explicit leverage may be looked at. While explicit leverage requires the fund to secure a source of funding, implicit leverage is automatically available whenever those derivatives are used.

- *How liquid is the portfolio?* Liquidity is a frequent concern in the convertible bond market. Many smaller bond issues tend to become less liquid once the initial flurry of postissue trading has receded. As a result, traders should have limits on the ownership of positions related to one issuer or even a given sector. Also, the fund should have limits on the size of its position relative to the total size of the issue.

- *What is the fund's ability to borrow the underlying stock?* Convertible issuers are often small to midsize companies with a small float and a very narrow ownership base. Therefore, the cost of borrowing the required shares could be quite high or the fund may be exposed to short squeezes.

- *What stress tests are run on the portfolio?* Observing the risks the manager perceives as crucial to his portfolio is usually very instructive. Typical stress tests should include variations on the shape of the yield curve, on the credit risk premium, and on the volatility of bond and equity markets.

40.2.3 Merger Arbitrage

Merger arbitrage involves profiting from the spread created between the share prices of two companies that are reorganizing. Generally, once a merger or takeover is announced, the stock of the acquiring firm declines and the stock of the target firm increases. However, the stock price of the target firm will not increase to the level of the offered price because there is always a chance that the merger may not go through. Some traditional asset managers are not prepared to manage the risks associated with failed mergers and, therefore, may sell their positions in the target firm. Merger arbitrage managers, on the other hand, specialize in managing such a risk, and would take long positions in the stock of target firms for which, in their judgment, the merger has a reasonable chance to be completed. At the same time, merger arbitrage managers do not want to remain exposed to the risks associated with fluctuations in equity markets. In a cash deal, a fund will typically buy shares of the target company on the expectation that its stock price will rise to the offered price (the equity risk may be hedged by shorting an appropriate amount of an equity index or the acquiring firm's stock). In a stock deal, the fund will purchase the stock of the target company and simultaneously short the buyer on the expectation that the two stocks will converge if the deal is successful.

Essential due diligence questions for a merger arbitrage fund should include the following:

- *Is the fund investing only in announced deals or also in potential deals?* Taking positions in announced deals is much safer but provides lower expected returns. Taking long and short positions based on potential merger activity is more risky but provides the potential for higher returns if successful. In the former case, it is essential to understand the size of positions that the manager is willing to take and whether the manager will consider certain types of mergers (e.g., cash offers and friendly takeovers). If the manager considers taking positions in potential deals, then one must further examine his skills in this area. For example, does the manager concentrate in particular sectors of the economy? Does the manager consider cross-border deals?
- *How diversified is the portfolio?* Running a diversified portfolio limits the impact of one unsuccessful merger deal falling through. On the other hand, a diversified portfolio is likely to contain positions related to deals that are not completed, which lead to losses.
- *Is the fund doing reverse mergers?* **Reverse mergers** consist of taking the inverse of the usual position (i.e., buying the acquirer and selling short the target). This trade is successful when spreads diverge because the deal fails or the market loses confidence in the completion of the deal.
- *How does the fund hedge cash deals?* Cash deal arbitrage typically involves long-only positions in the stock of the target firm. Thus, it is important to see how the fund manager hedges the long positions at the portfolio level.
- *How will the fund manager react in a scenario of reduced merger activity?* A decrease in merger activity obviously reduces the opportunity set and therefore the return. Since mergers are cyclical, this phenomenon will occur on a regular basis. Some managers will shrink the size of their fund; others will migrate toward other strategies. In the latter case, one has to determine if the manager has the skills to operate in the new area.

40.2.4 Fixed-Income Arbitrage

Fixed-income arbitrage refers to a broad set of market-neutral investment strategies followed by hedge funds. The objective is to exploit differences in valuation between various fixed income securities or derivatives. There are five major fixed income arbitrage strategies in the market (see Duarte, Longstaff, and Yu [2007]):

1. **Swap-spread arbitrage:** Historically, this has been an important strategy. For example, it was reportedly the most important source of losses for Long-Term Capital Management in 1998. To implement this strategy, an arbitrageur enters into a swap to receive a fixed coupon and to pay a floating coupon. Next, the arbitrageur takes a short position in a Treasury bond and invests the proceeds in a margin account earning the repo rate. Thus, the arbitrageur receives a net fixed coupon that is equal to the difference between what is paid on the Treasury

bond and what is received from the swap. The arbitrageur pays a net floating coupon that is equal to the difference between what is paid on the swap and what is received on the margin account. This strategy is, therefore, a bet that the fixed net cash flow will exceed the floating net cash flow.

2. **Yield-curve arbitrage:** This simple strategy takes the form of assuming both long and short positions in Treasury bonds of different maturities. For example, the arbitrageur may take a long position in a four-year duration bond and short positions in two-year and six-year duration bonds. In this case, it is perceived that the four-year duration bond is relatively cheap.

3. **Mortgage arbitrage:** This strategy involves taking a long position in mortgage pass-through securities and hedging the interest rate risk of the position using swaps or futures contracts. The major risk in pass-through securities is the prepayment risk. The manager will need to have a reliable prepayment model in order to identify profitable trades and to hedge the interest rate risk of these instruments.

4. **Volatility arbitrage:** This strategy is based on the available empirical evidence that on average, implied volatilities of both fixed-income and equity derivatives tend to overestimate realized volatilities. Thus, volatility arbitrage involves taking short positions in fixed-income derivatives and delta hedging the market risk of the position. The arbitrageur will benefit if the implied volatility is indeed higher than the realized volatility.

5. **Capital-structure arbitrage:** This strategy, which is also referred to as credit arbitrage, attempts to take advantage of mispricing between various instruments that appear on a firm's balance sheet. For example, an arbitrageur may believe that a firm's debt is relatively cheap compared to its equity. In this case, the manager would take a long position in the firm's debt and then hedge some of the position's risk by taking a short position in the equity of the same firm. Other risks may be hedged using other instruments, such as interest rate futures.

Essential due diligence questions for a fixed-income arbitrage fund should include the following:

■ *What is the investment universe of the fund?* While pure fixed-income arbitrage typically covers government and swap curves, some funds will extend it to include areas such as mortgages, inflation-linked bonds, and credit or emerging market bonds.

■ *How is leverage measured?* Measuring leverage in fixed-income securities is not trivial, and it is important to understand how the manager uses it. Since the profit margin associated with most fixed-income arbitrage trades tends to be very small, fixed-income arbitrage managers have to use significant leverage to generate reasonable returns. Some fund managers use notional positions to measure leverage, but it is not necessarily indicative of risk—for example, the same notional amount of six-month bills and 30-year bonds have different risks. Some fund managers bring all their notional exposure to one standardized quantity, for instance, five-year or 10-year equivalents. Others prefer to bucket their notional exposures along the yield curve.

■ *What is the maximum, average, and minimum leverage?* Fixed-income arbitrageurs tend to use a lot of leverage, as the expected gains of their positions are usually expressed in terms of basis points. This is particularly true for swap-spread, yield-curve, and volatility arbitrage strategies.

- *How large is the fund size in each of its underlying markets/instruments?* Fixed-income markets are large, but some specific products, such as OTC derivatives and corporate debt, are thinly traded. It is therefore essential for fund managers to ensure that they do not represent a significant portion of one contract, one maturity, or one issue.
- *What is the loss tolerance for a position?* Due to high leverage, it is essential that funds have strict exit rules on each position.

One particular aspect of fixed-income arbitrage funds is that they use instruments that require the payment of only a small fraction of their underlying value up front (e.g., futures, options, and swaps). As a result, a significant portion of the holdings that need to be managed is held in cash. This should be carefully analyzed.

- *How important are the fund's cash balances?* Cash balances of 60% or more are quite common in fixed-income arbitrage. Investors should also question any significant changes in the cash position.
- *What are the return objectives on cash balances?* What is the maturity/duration and credit quality of cash investments? As a rule, cash should not be seen as an alpha generating center. The fund should primarily focus on having immediate liquidity (in case of margin calls) and only invest in top-quality short-term instruments.
- *How well is the cash segregated?* How is the cash isolated from bankruptcy, default, and fraud? The fund manager should be prepared to explain the safeguards and procedures. Who is authorized to move cash, and what are the limits for each authorized signature? How often is a reconciliation of cash conducted? If differences are detected in reconciliation, what procedures are in place to reconcile the variance? Who signs off on differences?

40.2.5 Emerging Markets

Emerging markets hedge funds invest in equity or debt of companies in less developed countries or in the government debt of emerging market countries.

Typical questions for emerging market hedge funds include the following:

- *What is the focus of the fund?* There are numerous trading styles within the strategy, such as equity large caps versus small caps, top-down versus bottom-up, technical versus fundamental, sovereign versus corporate debt, and hard (e.g., U.S. dollar or the euro) versus local currency denominated debt.
- *What are the fund's sources of research and competitive advantages?* In particular, does the fund have proprietary research, local contacts, and privileged access to senior management?
- *What instruments does the manager use to implement the fund's strategy?* Does the fund trade local shares or American depositary receipts (ADRs; receipts for shares of a foreign company held by a U.S. bank, representing equity ownership in the company)? Does the fund invest only in publicly traded instruments, or would it consider taking positions in privately placed instruments?

- *How liquid is the portfolio?* Emerging markets may be thinly traded and tend to exhibit significant bid-ask spreads. Liquidating a portfolio can be costly and take a long time.
- *Does the fund invest in frontier markets?* **Frontier markets** are small and less accessible but investible markets that are generally considered to be at an earlier stage of economic development. They offer the potential for higher returns, but are often associated with lack of information, inadequate regulation, nontransparency, substandard reporting, market illiquidity, and the inability to transfer profit abroad in some cases.
- *How is short selling implemented?* Short selling is often difficult in emerging markets due to the lack of securities lending agreements, specific domestic rules, or even a prohibition on shorting. As a result, many hedge funds have a long bias or run imperfect hedges.
- *What is the quality of the fund's counterparties, such as brokers, banks, and custodians?* The manager may have to deal with local institutions to implement this strategy. Investors should carefully analyze the potential risks involved in dealing with institutions that are governed by different laws and in some cases could be partially or completely owned by foreign governments.
- *How is currency risk managed?* Emerging market currencies are volatile and often subject to devaluation risk or convertibility restrictions.
- *How sensitive is the fund to contagion risk?* Emerging market economies have diverse characteristics (e.g., size of country, financial markets, and foreign exchange reserves), and experienced investors differentiate between members of this heterogeneous group. However, when financial markets are in distress, contagion becomes a serious issue. **Contagion** occurs when currency or credit crises in one emerging economy quickly spill over into other emerging economies. The manager must demonstrate her knowledge of contagion risk and have policies in place to manage this risk.
- *How does the fund deal with corporate governance?* Corporate governance issues are particularly important when companies are controlled by governments and families, often the case in emerging markets. Issues such as minority shareholder protection and board quality are crucial in such cases.

40.2.6 Multistrategy Funds

Multistrategy hedge funds typically employ several strategies under a common organizational umbrella. Typical due diligence questions for multistrategy hedge funds include the following:

- *What are the fund's different strategies, and how complementary are they?* Multistrategy and multimanager funds can effectively diversify idiosyncratic risk (i.e., individual manager, strategy, region, or sector risk). However, a key determinant of this diversification is the degree of similarity between its various trading strategies, particularly in response to a common shock.
- *How is capital allocated across strategies?* Multistrategy funds are characterized by their ability to dynamically allocate capital among various strategies. Understanding the target capital allocation, changes in the target over time, and performance attribution is essential, since this is ostensibly what investors are

paying for. A fluid allocation of resources to the best performing strategies and geographies is what allows the portfolio to maximize the return for investors.

- *What are the key risks of the aggregate portfolio and what are the risk limits per strategy?* Each portfolio manager in a multistrategy fund normally has the freedom to operate within predefined risk limits (e.g., value at risk [VaR], stress tests, liquidity, and gross and net exposures). These limits should be monitored in real time by the risk-management function. Investors should understand the risk metrics employed by a multistrategy fund, including the implications and limitations of those measurements, and ascertain whether they are appropriate for the strategies and objectives of the fund.

- *How important is leverage, and how is it allocated?* Some managers leverage the overall portfolio, while others apply a different level of leverage for each strategy or even for each transaction. Investors should clearly understand how accounting and economic leverage are used in the hedge fund portfolio, based on absolute capital exposures, VaR, or similar measures.

- *What happens if one strategy blows up?* If the assets of each strategy are used to back the other strategies (so-called cross-collateralization), then the failure of one strategy can have a dramatic impact on the overall portfolio. This is exactly what happened at Amaranth, where the leverage of the massive natural gas bets was backed by the assets of the firm's other strategies, so when those gas trades went awry, the whole firm collapsed. To prevent this, some funds cautiously segregate each strategy so that if one experiences difficulties, it will not affect the others.

- *How are the various portfolio managers remunerated?* Remuneration is essential to attract and retain talented employees, but it is also used to drive the capital allocation across a multistrategy fund. For instance, there should be a clear incentive for a portfolio manager to return capital if he sees no opportunities in his space.

- *How does the fund deal with redemptions?* One unique risk in a multistrategy fund is that the most liquid positions may have to be redeemed first, resulting in a higher concentration in the least liquid positions.

- *How independent is the risk manager?* In a multistrategy fund, it is essential to have an independent risk manager whose compensation is not directly tied to portfolio performance and who reports directly to the senior management of the fund. This function should be adequately resourced and staffed by qualified personnel and be supported by appropriate risk-measurement systems with real-time feeds. Investors should also understand how various recommendations of the risk manager will be implemented by portfolio managers and who is expected to monitor compliance with those recommendations.

- *What amount of information is available on each of the subportfolios?* In a multistrategy fund, it is important to go beyond the total net performance of the fund and analyze performance and risk information on each of the substrategies.

- *How are fees charged?* Some multistrategy funds charge incentive fees at the individual book level and not at the fund level. That is, instead of applying incentive fees on the total net performance of the fund, some fund managers charge an incentive fee on each strategy that posts a gain. Multistrategy funds that charge incentive fees at the fund level, rather than at the underlying strategy level, are charging incentive fees on the net returns of the fund. The netting of incentive fees is one of the perceived values of multistrategy funds when compared to funds of funds, in which each manager receives a performance fee based on that manager's performance.

40.2.7 Distressed Securities

Distressed securities hedge funds typically take long positions in the debt of companies that are experiencing financial distress, bankruptcy, or a major reorganization. Typical questions for distressed securities hedge funds include the following:

- *Is the fund manager active or passive?* An active distressed manager will participate in the creditor committee to determine the restructuring and refinancing plans of the underlying companies. This is very labor intensive and requires extensive legal, financial, and business know-how, and a strong network of relationships. By contrast, a passive manager will simply buy debt and equity of distressed companies at a discount and hold them until they appreciate in value. An active manager must have a broad business background and must be able to demonstrate his ability to add value by being an active participant in bankruptcy and reorganization processes.
- *How senior are the fund's positions in the capital structure of the firm?* Distressed hedge funds can trade a wide range of securities, such as debtor-in-possession loans, senior secured bank debt, public high-yielding bonds, subordinated and junior debt, trade claims, nonperforming real estate loans and mortgages, letters of credit, mezzanine debt, convertible bonds, preferred stock, and common stock. The risk of the fund dramatically increases as the seniority of the positions decreases.
- *How are the positions valued?* Distressed positions are extremely difficult to value, as they are illiquid and can be marked to market only when trades occur. As a result, returns tend to exhibit low volatility and high autocorrelation. It is therefore essential that prices are validated by a third-party administrator or pricing agent.
- *What is the liquidity offered by the fund to investors?* Distressed positions are typically illiquid and require long holding periods. It is essential that the capital of the fund stays locked in during this period to avoid having to liquidate some positions at inopportune times. A distressed fund that offers generous liquidity provisions to its investors will not be able to offer attractive returns to those investors who want to be paid for bearing risks associated with illiquid assets.
- *What is the level of leverage?* Leverage on top of distressed positions can turn into a disaster if the underlying positions are not liquid or are hard to value.
- *What is the net credit exposure of the fund?* Some distressed managers may decide to hedge some of the risks associated with their long positions. These managers must communicate the fund's general policy to investors. Also, they must be prepared to discuss the fund's exposure to changes in the overall credit environment of the economy. For example, what is the impact of a widening of credit spreads on the fund's performance?

- *How diversified is the fund?* For active managers, it may be difficult to hold diversified positions. On the other hand, passive managers must hold diversified positions to reduce the risk of an unexpected development in the bankruptcy or reorganization process.
- *Does the manager use side pockets, and what is the policy with regard to the management and valuation of the side pocket?* A **side pocket** is a process in which a hedge fund separates illiquid or relatively hard to value assets from the rest of the fund's more liquid portfolio. The side pocket is normally formed by creating a new class of shares, which gives current investors a pro rata claim to the potential payoffs from the side pocket. Management must have a clear policy about when and what can be segregated into side pockets. Since assets assigned to side pockets are not valued on a regular basis, there have to be sufficient controls with regard to when assets can be moved between the regular fund and the side pockets.

Next, we present an example of due diligence applied to a hypothetical distressed securities hedge fund.[2]

John Redford, CAIA, is an alternative investment analyst at the Jennings University (JU) endowment. The endowment's board believes that the credit cycle is turning, that the default rate will pick up within the next year, and that there will be an opportunity to make investments in distressed debt. In preparation for the potential allocations that JU's board will make, John is conducting due diligence on distressed securities hedge funds. John has received the completed questionnaire for Barner Partners, LP. (See Exhibit 40.1.)

What follows is a list of pros and cons with regard to investing in the fund, highlighting and classifying any cons as either yellow or red flags.

Pro:

- The investor and fund gates match up liquidity fairly well for an active (control) distressed fund.

Cons:

- Yellow flag: The fund takes a quarterly incentive fee while marking its own portfolio in some cases, which is a conflict of interest.
- Yellow flag: The fund can move investments in and out of the side pocket at will, which is a conflict of interest.
- Yellow flag: The redemption and lockup terms seem very light for a control distressed fund.
- Red flag: Massive amounts of leverage are being used in a control distressed strategy.
- Red flag: The prime broker has the ability to mark the portfolio. Since the prime broker is the leverage counterparty for the repo and the positions are illiquid, the prime broker can effectively put the fund out of business by marking positions to the point where the fund would face a margin call, and the prime broker can liquidate the fund, leading to a total loss that could end Barner Partners.

---

[2] This example was prepared by James Gil.

EXHIBIT 40.1   AIMA/CAIA Due Diligence Questionnaire, Distressed

General Information

Fund Name	Barner Partners, LP
HQ Address	200 Stark Avenue, New York, NY 10017
Tel, Fax, E-mail	212-555-1212; 212-555-1213; info@barnerpartners.com
Fund Terms	
Subscriptions	Monthly
Redemptions	Quarterly with 30 days' notice
Lockup	Soft lockup of 4% penalty in first 6 months, 2% penalty in next 6 months, and none thereafter
Fund Gate	10% per quarter, with a 1-year cleanup provision
Investor Gate	25% per quarter; 100% can be redeemed in full, with a 5% penalty paid to the fund if the fund gate is not up.
Management Fee	2%
Incentive Fee	20% paid quarterly subject to high-water mark
Side Pocket	The manager may designate up to 20% of the fund's NAV as a side-pocket investment; the manager may move designated investments in and out of the side pocket at any time at its sole discretion.
Fund Strategy	
Is the strategy passive or active distressed?	The fund pursues an active (control) distressed strategy. It seeks to purchase senior secured bank loans of companies in or about to enter bankruptcy, chair the creditor committee, and install the Fund's management personnel as the board members of the company.
Where in the capital structure does the fund focus?	See previous answer.
How much leverage will be used?	Long market value (LMV) will initially represent 300% of NAV; as the cycle improves, LMV exposure can reach 600%. Leverage will be in the form of overnight repo from the fund's prime broker.
How are positions valued?	Positions are valued either by the fund manager or by the fund's prime broker.
How many positions does the fund have?	At its peak, the fund is expected to have between 8 and 10 positions.

These questions are illustrative of some of the key aspects that should be investigated during a due diligence process. In practice, it is essential to understand that proper due diligence needs to be tailored to the particular circumstances of each hedge fund investment.

References

2011 NACUBO-Commonfund Study of Endowments. Available at www.nacubo.org.

Ackermann, C., R. McEnally, and D. Ravenscraft. 1999. "The Performance of Hedge Funds: Risk, Return, and Incentives." *Journal of Finance* 54:833–874.

Advisory Committee on Endowment Management. 1969. *Managing Educational Endowments: Report to the Ford Foundation*. New York: Ford Foundation.

Agarwal, Vikas, and N. Naik. 2004. "Risks and Portfolio Decisions Involving Hedge Funds." *Review of Financial Studies* 17 (1): 63–98.

Ahl, Peter. 2001. "Global Macro Funds: What Lies Ahead?" *AIMA Newsletter*, April.

Ainslie, A., X. Drèze, and F. Zufryden. 2005. "Modeling Movie Life Cycles and Market Share." *Marketing Science* 24 (3): 508–517.

Ajanovic, A. 2010. "Biofuels versus Food Production: Does Biofuel Production Increase Food Prices?" *Energy*, doi:10.1016/j.energy.2010.05.019.

Akers, K., and R. Staub. 2003. "Regional Investment Allocations in a Global Timber Market." *Journal of Alternative Investments* 5 (4): 73–87.

Akey, R. P. 2005. "Commodities: A Case for Active Management." *Journal of Alternative Investments* 8 (2): 8–30.

Aldridge, I. 2009. "Systematic Funds Outperform Discretionary Funds." Working paper, ABLE Alpha Trading, Ltd.

AllianceBernstein LP. 2010. *Deflating Inflation: Redefining the Inflation-Resistant Portfolio*. New York.

Amenc, N., W. Géhin, L. Martellini, and J.-C. Meyfredi. 2007. "The Myths and Limits of Passive Hedge Fund Replication: An Attractive Concept . . . Still a Work-in-Progress." EDHEC Risk and Asset Management Research Center.

Amenc, N., W. Géhin, L. Martellini, and J.-C. Meyfredi. 2008. "Passive Hedge Fund Replication: A Critical Assessment of Existing Techniques." *Journal of Alternative Investments* 11 (2): 69–83.

Amenc, N., and L. Martellini. 2003. "Desperately Seeking Pure Style Indexes." Working paper, EDHEC Risk and Asset Management Research Center.

Amenc, N., L. Martellini, J. Meyfredi, and V. Ziemann. 2010. "Passive Hedge Fund Replication—Beyond the Linear Case." *European Financial Management* 16 (2): 191–210.

Amin, G., and H. Kat. 2002. "Hedge Fund Performance 1990–2000: Do the 'Money Machines' Really Add Value?" Working paper, City University, London.

Amin, G., and H. Kat. 2003. "Hedge Fund Performance 1990–2000: Do the 'Money Machines' Really Add Value?" *The Journal of Financial and Quantitative Analysis* 38 (2): 251–274.

Anderson, R. C. 1974. "Paintings as an Investment." *Economic Inquiry* 12 (1): 13–26.

Ang, A. 2008. "The Quant Meltdown August 2007." Case #080317, Columbia CaseWorks.

Ang, A., M. Rhodes-Kropf, and R. Zhao. 2008. "Do Funds-of-Funds Deserve Their Extra Fees?" *Journal of Investment Management* 6 (4): 34–58.

Ankrim, E., and C. Hensel. 1993. "Commodities in Asset Allocation: A Real-Asset Alternative to Real Estate." *Financial Analysts Journal* 49 (3): 20–29.

Anson, M. 1998. "Spot Returns, Roll Yield, and Diversification with Commodity Futures." *Journal of Alternative Investments* 1 (3): 16–32.

Anson, M. J. P. 2006. *Handbook of Alternative Assets.* 2nd ed. Hoboken, NJ: John Wiley & Sons.

Anson M. J. P. 2010. "Measuring a Premium for Liquidity Risk." *Journal of Private Equity* 13 (2): 6–16.

Aragon, G. 2004. "Share Restrictions and Asset Pricing: Evidence from the Hedge Fund Industry." *Journal of Financial Economics* 83:33–58.

Armesto, M. T., and W. T. Gavin. 2005. "Monetary Policy and Commodity Futures." *Federal Reserve Bank of St. Louis Review* (May): 395–405.

Arora, A., M. Ceccagnoli, and W. Cohen. 2008. "R&D and the Patent Premium." *International Journal of Industrial Organization* 26 (5): 1153–1179.

Artus, P., and J. Teïletche. 2004. "Asset Allocation and European Private Equity: A First Approach Using Aggregated Data." EVCA, Brussels.

Ashenfelter, O., and K. Graddy. 2003. "Auctions and the Price of Art." *Journal of Economic Literature* 41 (3): 763–786.

Ashenfelter, O., and K. Graddy. 2006. "Art Auctions: A Survey of Empirical Studies." In *Handbook of the Economics of Art and Culture.* Amsterdam: Elsevier.

Asness, C. S. 1997. "The Interaction of Value and Momentum Strategies." *Financial Analysts Journal* 53 (2): 29–36.

Asness, C. S., T. J. Moskowitz, and L. H. Pedersen. 2009. "Value and Momentum Everywhere." AFA 2010 Atlanta Meetings Paper. http://papers.ssrn.com/sol3/papers.cfm?abstract_id=1363476.

Avellaneda, M., and J.-H. Lee. 2009. "Statistical Arbitrage in the U.S. Equity Market." Courant Institute, New York University.

Bailey, J., T. Richards, and D. Tierney. 1990. "Benchmark Portfolios and the Manager/Plan Sponsor Relationship." In *Current Topics in Investment Management,* edited by F. J. Fabozzi and T. Dessa Fabozzi, 71–85. New York: Harper & Row.

Bailey, W., and K. C. Chan. 1993. "Macroeconomic Influences and the Variability of the Commodity Futures Basis." *Journal of Finance* 48 (2): 555–573.

Baillie, R. T., and R. P. DeGennarro. 1990. "Stock Returns and Volatility." *Journal of Financial and Quantitative Analysis* 25:203–214.

Baillie, R. T., Y.-W. Han, R. J. Myers, and J. Song. 2007. "Long Memory Models for Daily and High Frequency Commodity Futures Returns." *Journal of Futures Markets* 27 (7): 643–668.

Barber, J., and L. Zage. 2002. *Moving in Tandem?* London: Helix Associates.

Bares, P., R. Gibson, and S. Gyger. 2003. "Performance in the Hedge Fund Industry: An Analysis of Short and Long-Term Persistence." *Journal of Alternative Investments* 6 (3): 25–41.

Barlevy, G. 2007. "On the Cyclicality of Research and Development." *American Economic Review* 97 (4): 1131–1164.

Barre, M., S. Docclo, and V. Ginsburgh. 1996. "Returns of Impressionist, Modem and Contemporary European Paintings 1962–1991." *Ann. Econ. Statist.,* 143–181.

Bary, A. 2009. "Big Squeeze on Ivy League Endowments." *Barron's,* July 1.

Basel Committee on Banking Supervision. 2001. "Risk-Sensitive Approaches for Equity Exposures in the Banking Book for IRB Banks." Working paper, Basel, August.

Basuroy, S., and S. Chatterjee. 2008. "Fast and Frequent: Investigating Box Office Performance of Motion Picture Sequels." *Journal of Business Research* 61 (July): 798–803.

Basuroy, S., S. Chatterjee, and A. Ravid. 2003. "How Critical Are Critical Reviews? The Box Office Effects of Film Critics, Star Power, and Budgets." *Journal of Marketing* 67 (4): 103–117.

Bauer, M., Bilo, S., and Zimmermann, H. 2001. "Publicly Traded Private Equity: An Empirical Investigation." 2nd Draft, Working Paper No. 5/01. Universität St. Gallen, Swiss Institute of Banking and Finance, May.

Baumol, W. J. 1986. "Unnatural Value: Or Art Investment as Floating Crap Game." *American Economic Review Papers Proceedings* 76 (2): 10–14.

Beenen, J. 2005. "Commodity Investing: A Pension Fund Perspective." *Futures Industry Magazine* (September/October): 18–22.

Bekaert, G., and G. Wu. 2000. "Asymmetric Volatility and Risk in Equity Markets." *Review of Financial Studies* 13:1–42.

Berger, A. D., R. Israel, and T. J. Moskowitz. 2009. "The Case for Momentum Investing." Paper, AQR Capital Management.

Bessembinder, H. 1992. "Systematic Risk, Hedging Pressure, and Risk Premiums in Futures Markets." *Review of Financial Studies* 5 (4): 637–667.

Bessen, J. 2008. "The Value of U.S. Patents by Owner and Patent Characteristics." *Research Policy*, 37 (5): 932–945.

Bessen, J. 2009. "Estimates of Patent Rents from Firm Market Value." *Research Policy* 38 (10): 1604–1616.

Bhansali, V. 2008. "Tail Risk Management." *Journal of Portfolio Management* 34:68–75.

Bhansali, V. 2008. "Tail Risk Management: Why Investors Should Be Chasing Their Tails." *PIMCO*. December.

Bhansali, V. 2010. "Bhansali Discusses PIMCO's Approach to Tail Risk Hedging." *PIMCO*. October.

Bhansali, V. 2011. "Cash vs. Tail Risk Hedging: Which is Better?" PIMCO. August.

Bhardwaj, G., G. B. Gorton, and K. G. Rouwenhorst. 2008. "Fooling Some of the People All of the Time: The Inefficient Performance and Persistence of Commodity Trading Advisors." NBER Working Paper 14424.

Bjornson, B., and C. A. Carter. 1997. "New Evidence on Agricultural Commodity Return Performance under Time Varying Risk." *American Journal of Agricultural Economics* 79 (3): 918–930.

Black, F. 1976. "Studies of Stock Price Volatility Changes." *Proceedings of the 1976 Meeting of Business and Economics Statistics Section of the American Statistical Association* 27:399–418.

Black, F., and M. Scholes. 1973. "The Pricing of Options and Corporate Liabilities." *Journal of Political Economy* 81 (3): 637–654.

Black, K. 2004. *Managing a Hedge Fund*. New York: McGraw-Hill.

Black, K. 2006. "Improving Hedge Fund Risk Exposures by Hedging Equity Market Volatility, or How the VIX Ate My Kurtosis." *Journal of Trading* 1 (2): 6–15.

Black, K. 2009. "The Role of Institutional Investors in Rising Commodity Prices." *Journal of Investing* 18 (3): 21–26.

Black, K. 2012. "An Empirical Exploration of the CBOE Volatility Index (VIX) Futures Market as a Hedge for Equity Market and Hedge Fund Investors." *Research in Finance* 28:1–18.

Blanch, F., and S. Scheis. 2006. "Selecting a Commodity Index." Merrill Lynch Global Commodity Paper No. 4. Research Report, Merrill Lynch.

Blose, L., and V. Gondhalekar. 2008. "Gold Betas in the Fama French Context: 2006–2007." *Proceedings of 2008 Midwest Finance Association Annual Meeting*, vol. 5.

BLS, U.S. Bureau of Labor Statistics. 2010. "Number of Jobs Held, Labor Market Activity, and Earnings Growth among the Youngest Baby Boomers: Results from a Longitudinal Survey." Available at www.bls.gov/news.release/pdf/nlsoy.pdf.

Bodie, Z., A. Kane, and A. Marcus. 2010. *Investments*. 9th ed. New York: McGraw-Hill/Irwin.

Bodie, Z., and V. Rosansky. 1980. "Risk and Return in Commodity Futures." *Financial Analysts Journal* 36:27–39.

Booth, D. G., and E. F. Fama. 1992. "Diversification Returns and Asset Contributions." *Financial Analysts Journal* 48 (3): 26–32.

Brands, S., and D. Gallagher. 2003. "Portfolio Selection, Diversification and Funds-of-Funds." School of Banking and Finance, University of New South Wales, Sydney.

Brinson G. P., L. R. Hood, and G. L. Beebower. 1986. "Determinants of Portfolio Performance." *Financial Analysts Journal* 42 (4): 39–44.

Brinson G. P., B. D. Singer, and G. L. Beebower. 1991. "Determinants of Portfolio Performance II: An Update." *Financial Analysts Journal* 47 (3): 40–48.

Brown, K., L. Garlappi, and C. Tiu. 2010. "Asset Allocation and Portfolio Performance: Evidence from University Endowment Funds." *Journal of Financial Markets* 13 (2): 268–294.

Brown, S. J., T. L. Fraser, and B. Liang. 2008. "Hedge Fund Due Diligence: A Source of Alpha in a Hedge Fund Portfolio Strategy." SSRN-id 1016904 Working Paper.

Brown, S. J., W. N. Goetzmann, and R. G. Ibbotson. 1999. "Offshore Hedge Funds: Survival and Performance 1989–1995." *Journal of Business* 72 (1): 91–118.

Brown, S. J., W. N. Goetzmann, and B. Liang. 2004. "Fees-on-Fees in Funds-of-Funds." *Journal of Investment Management* 2 (4): 39–56.

Brown, S., W. Goetzmann, and J. Park. 1998. "Hedge Funds and the Asian Currency Crisis of 1997." New York University, Leonard N. Stern School Finance Department Working Paper Series 98–014.

Buelens, N., and V. Ginsburgh. 1993. "Revisiting Baumol's 'Art as Floating Crap Game'." *Europ. Econ. Rev.* 37 (7): 1351–1371.

Burghardt, G., and B. Walls. 2011. *Managed Futures for Institutional Investors: Analysis and Portfolio Construction.* Hoboken, NJ: Bloomberg Press.

Burkart, D. W. 2006. "Commodities and Real-Return Strategies in the Investment Mix." CFA Institute.

Burnside, C., M. Eichenbaum, and S. Rebelo. 2011. "Carry Trade and Momentum in Currency Markets." NBER Working Paper 16942.

Buyuksahin, B., M. Haigh, and M. Robe. 2010. "Commodities and Equities: Ever a 'Market of One'?" *Journal of Alternative Investments* 12 (3): 76–95.

CalPERS, California Public Employees' Retirement System. 2006. "Statement of Investment Policy for Opportunistic Real Estate," February 14.

Cameron, G. 1998. "Innovation and Growth: A Survey of the Empirical Evidence." Monograph. London School of Economics and Political Science.

Camp, J. 2002. *Venture Capital Due Diligence.* New York: John Wiley & Sons.

Cannon, S. E., and R. A. Cole. 2011. "How Accurate Are Commercial Appraisals? Evidence from 25 Years of NCREIF Sales Data." *Journal of Portfolio Management* 35 (5): 68–88.

Capgemini. 2011. "World Wealth Report."

Capocci, D., and G. Hubner. 2004. "Analysis of Hedge Fund Performance." *Journal of Empirical Finance* 11:55–89.

Cargill, T. F., and G. C. Rausser. 1975. "Temporal Price Behavior in Commodity Futures Markets." *Journal of Finance* 30:1043–1053.

Carhart, M. 1997. "On Persistence of Mutual Fund Performance." *Journal of Finance* 52: 57–82.

Carpenter, J. E. 2010. "Peer-Reviewed Surveys Indicate Positive Impact of Commercialized GM Crops."*Nature Biotechnology* 28 (4): 319–321.

Carter, C. 1999. "Commodity Futures Markets: A Survey." *Australian Journal of Agricultural and Resource Economics* 43 (2): 209–247.

Cashin, P., and C. J. McDermott. 2002. "The Long-Run Behavior of Commodity Prices: Small Trends and Big Variability." *IMF Staff Papers* 49:175–199.

Cashin, P., C. J. McDermott, and A. Scott. 1999. "Booms and Slumps in World Commodity Prices." IMF Working Paper 99/155.

Center for International Securities and Derivates Markets. 2006. "The Benefits of Private Equity." CISDM Research Department, Isenberg School of Management, University of Massachusetts, Amherst (May).

CFTC, Commodity Futures Trading Commission. 2008. "Staff Report on Commodity Swap Dealers & Index Traders with Commission Recommendations."

Chacko, G., C. L. Evans, H. Gunawan, and A .L. Sjoman. 2011. *The Global Economic System: How Liquidity Shocks Affect Financial Institutions and Lead to Economic Crises.* Upper Saddle River, NJ: FT Press.

Chan, L., N. Jegadeesh, and J. Lakonishok. 1996. "Momentum Strategies." *Journal of Finance* 51:1681–1713.

Chanel, O., L. Gerard-Varet, and V. Ginsburgh. 1996. "The Relevance of Hedonic Price Indices." *J. Cult. Econ.* 20 (1): 1–24.

Chen, Y., and Chang, K. 2010. "The Relationship Between a Firm's Patent Quality and its Market Value—The Case of US Pharmaceutical Industry." *Technological Forecasting & Social Change* 77:20–33.

Cheung, L., C. Howley, V. Kapoor, and A. Smith. 2003. "Rating Private Equity CFOs: Cash Flow Benchmarks." Standard & Poor's CDO Research, Special Report, January.

Chong, J., and J. Miffre. 2008. "Conditional Return Correlations between Commodity Futures and Traditional Assets." EDHEC Working Paper.

Ciccotello, C. S. 2011. "Why Financial Institutions Matter: The Case of Energy Infrastructure MLPs." *Journal of Applied Corporate Finance* 23 (3): 84–91.

Clayton, J., and G. MacKinnon. 2001. "The Time-Varying Nature of the Link between REIT, Real Estate and Financial Asset Returns." *Journal of Real Estate Portfolio Management* 7 (1): 43–54.

Congressional Budget Office (CBO). 2005. "Background Paper: R&D and Productivity Growth."

Conrad, J., and G. Kaul. 1993. "Long-Term Market Overreaction or Biases in Computed Returns?" *Journal of Finance* 48 (1): 39–63.

Cootner, P. H. 1960. "Returns to Speculators: Telser versus Keynes." *Journal of Political Economy* 68 (4): 396.

Covel, M. W. 2009. *Trend Following: Learn to Make Millions in Up or Down Markets.* Upper Saddle River, NJ: FT Press.

Cox, J. C., S. A. Ross, and M. Rubinstein. 1979. "Option Pricing: A Simplified Approach." *Journal of Financial Economics* 7:229–263.

Cremers, M., and A. Pareek. 2011. "Can Overconfidence and Biased Self-Attribution Explain the Momentum, Reversal and Share Issuance Anomalies? Evidence from Short-Term Institutional Investors." AFA 2011 Denver Meetings Paper.

Crowder, G., H. Kazemi, and T. Schneeweis. 2011. "Asset Class and Strategy Investment Tracking Based Approaches." *Journal of Alternative Investments* 13 (3): 81–101.

Cubbage, F., S. Koesbandana, P. MacDonagh, R. Rubilar, G. Balmelli, V. Morales Olmos, R. De La Torre, M. Murara, V. A. Hoeflich, H. Kotze, R. Gonzalez, O. Carrero, G. Frey, T. Adams, J. Turner, R. Lord, J. Huang, C. MacIntyre, K. McGinley, R. Abt, and R. Phillips. 2010. "Global Timber Investments, Wood Costs, Regulation and Risk." *Biomass and Bioenergy* 24 (12): 1667–1678.

Cuddington, J. T. 1992. "Long-Run Trends in Primary Commodity Prices: A Disaggregated Look at the Prebisch-Singer Hypothesis." *Journal of Development Economics* 39 (2): 207–227.

Cullen, A. 2004. "Locating Venture Capital Returns." Boston: HBS Working Knowledge.

Cumming, D., G. Fleming, and A. Schwienbacher. 2004. "Style Drift in Private Equity." Working paper, Center for International Securities and Derivatives Markets, May.

Czujack, C. 1997. "Picasso Paintings at Auction, 1963–1994." *J. Cult. Econ.* 12 (3): 229–427.

Damodaran, A. 2001. *The Dark Side of Valuation: Valuing Old Tech, New Tech, and New Economy Companies*. Upper Saddle River, NJ: Financial Times Prentice-Hall.

Daniel, K. D. 2011. "Momentum Crashes." Columbia Business School Research Paper No. 11-03.

Daniel, K., D. Hirshleifer, and A. Subrahmanyam. 1998. "Investor Psychology and Security Market Under- and Overreactions." *Journal of Finance* 53 (6): 1839–1885.

Denson, E. 2006. "Should Passive Commodities Investments Play a Role in Your Portfolio?" *Investment Viewpoints*, UBS Global Asset Management.

De Vany, A., and W. D. Walls. 1999. "Uncertainty in the Movie Industry: Does Star Power Reduce the Terror at the Box Office?" *Journal of Cultural Economics* 23 (4): 285–318.

De Vany, A., and W. D. Walls. 2002. "Does Hollywood Make Too Many R-Rated Movies? Risk, Stochastic Dominance, and the Illusion of Expectation." *Journal of Business* 75 (3): 425–451.

De Vany, A., and W. D. Walls. 2004. "Motion Picture Profit, the Stable Paretian Hypothesis, and the Curse of the Superstar." *Journal of Economic Dynamics and Control* 28:1035–1057.

Dornbusch, R. 1976. "Expectations and Exchange Rate Dynamics." *Journal of Political Economy* 84 (6): 1161–1176.

Drachman, J., and P. Little. 2010. "Enhancing Liquidity in Alternative Portfolios." Credit Suisse Asset Management.

Duarte, J., F. Longstaff, and F. Yu. 2007. "Risk and Return in Fixed Income Arbitrage: Nickels in Front of a Steamroller?" *The Review of Financial Studies* 20 (3): 769–811.

Dunsby, A., and K. Nelson. 2010. "A Brief History of Commodities Indexes—An Evolution from Passive to Active Indexes." *Journal of Indexes*: 36–39.

Dybvig, P. H. 1988. "Inefficient Dynamic Portfolio Strategies or How to Throw Away a Million Dollars in the Stock Market." *Review of Financial Studies* 1 (1): 67–88.

The Economist. 2004. "Once Burnt, Still Hopeful." November.

Edvinsson, L., and M. Malone. 1997. *Intellectual Capital*. New York: Harper Business.

Edwards, F., and J. Park. 1996. "Do Managed Futures Make Good Investments?" *Journal of Futures Markets* 16 (5): 475–517.

Eichengreen, B. J., A. Jansen, B. Chadha, L. Kodres, D. Mathieson, and S. Sharma. 1998. "Hedge Funds and Financial Market Dynamics." *IMF Occasional Papers* 166, International Monetary Fund.

Elberse, A., and J. Eliashberg. 2003. "Demand and Supply Dynamics for Sequentially Released Products in International Markets: The Case of Motion Pictures." *Marketing Science* 22 (3): 329–354.

Elder, J., and H. Jin. 2007. "Long Memory in Commodity Futures Volatility: A Wavelet Perspective." *Journal of Futures Markets* 27 (5): 411–437.

Elton, E., M. Gruber, and J. Rentzler. 1987. "Professionally Managed, Publicly Traded, Commodity Funds." *Journal of Business* 60 (2): 175–199.

Elton, E., M. Gruber, and J. Rentzler. 1989. "New Public Offerings, Information, and Investor Rationality: The Case of Publicly Offered Commodity Funds." *Journal of Business* 60 (2): 175–199.

Elton, E., M. Gruber, and J. Rentzler. 1990. "The Performance of Publicly Offered Commodity Funds." *Financial Analysts Journal* (July/August): 23–30.

Erb, C. B., and C. R. Harvey. 2006. "The Strategic and Tactical Value of Commodity Futures." *Financial Analysts Journal* 62 (2): 69–97.

Erturk, E., L. Cheung, and W. Fong. 2001. *Private Equity Fund-of-Funds: Overview and Rating Criteria*. New York: Standard & Poor's Publication.

Evans, G., and S. Honkapohja. 2001. *Learning and Expectations in Macroeconomics* (Frontiers of Economic Research). Princeton, NJ: Princeton University Press.

Fama, E. F., and K. R. French. 1987. "Commodity Futures Prices: Some Evidence on Forecast Power, Premiums, and the Theory of Storage." *Journal of Business* 60 (1): 55–73.

Fama, E. F., and K. R. French. 1988. "Business Cycles and the Behavior of Metals Prices." *Journal of Finance* 43 (5): 1075–1093.

Fama, E. F., and K. R. French. 1992. "The Cross-Section of Expected Stock Returns." *Journal of Finance* 47 (2): 427–465.

Fama, E. F., and K. R. French. 1993. "Common Risk Factors in the Return on Stocks and Bonds." *Journal of Financial Economics* 33:3–56.

Fama, E. F., and K. R. French. 1997. "Industry Costs of Equity." *Journal of Financial Economics* 43:153–193.

Fama, E. F., and K. R. French. 2007. "Dissecting Anomalies." CRSP Working Paper No. 610.

FAO, Food and Agricultural Organization. 2008. *FAO Annual Report: The State of Food and Agriculture: Biofuels: Prospects, Risks and Opportunities.* www.fao.org/publications/sofa/en/.

FAO, Food and Agricultural Organization. 2009a. *FAO Annual Report: The State of Agricultural Commodity Markets.* www.fao.org/forestry/soco/en/.

FAO, Food and Agricultural Organization. 2009b. *FAO Annual Report: The State of Food and Agriculture—Livestock in the Balance.* www.fao.org/publications/sofa/en/.

FAO, Food and Agricultural Organization. 2009c. *FAO Annual Report: The State of the World's Forests.* www.fao.org/forestry/sofo/en/.

FAO, Food and Agricultural Organization. 2009d. *FAO Statistical Yearbook 2009.* www.fao.org/economic/ess/publications-studies/statistical-yearbook/fao-statistical-yearbook-2009/it/.

Fazzari, S., J. Brown, and B. Petersen. 2009. "Financing Innovation and Growth: Cash Flows, External Equity, and the 1990s R&D Boom." *Journal of Finance* 64 (1): 151–185.

Feldman, B., and H. Till. 2006. "Backwardation and Commodity Futures Performance: Evidence from Evolving Agricultural Futures Markets." *Journal of Alternative Investments* 9 (3): 24–39.

Fisher, J. 2005. "U.S. Commercial Real Estate Indices: The NCREIF Property Index." BIS White Paper 21.

Fisher, J., D. Gatzlaff, D. Geltner, and D. Haurin. 2003. "Controlling for the Impact of Variable Liquidity in Commercial Real Estate Price Indices." *Real Estate Economics* 31:269–303.

Flag Venture Management. 2001. "The Right Level of Diversification." Flag Venture Management Special Report (1st Quarter). Venture Insights, Stamford, CT.

Flag Venture Management. 2003. "Let's Talk Terms." Flag Venture Management Special Report (4th Quarter), Stamford, CT.

Forsyth, R. 2012. "Art for Art's Sake? Or to Protect Wealth?" *Barron's*, May 1.

Fort Washington Capital Partners. 2004. "Investing in Private Equity through a Fund of Funds." White paper, Ford Washington Capital Partners, Cincinnati, OH.

Foundation Center Growth and Giving Estimates: Current Outlook. 2011 ed. New York: Foundation Center.

Frankel, J. 2006. "Commodity Prices, Monetary Policy, and Currency Regimes." NBER Working Paper C0011.

Frey, B. S., and W. W. Pommenihne. 1989. *Muses and Markets, Explorations in the Economics of the Arts.* Oxford, UK: Blackwell Publishing.

Froot, K. 1995. "Hedging Portfolios with Real Assets." *Journal of Portfolio Management* 21 (4): 60–77.

Fuertes, A., J. Miffre, and G. Rallis. 2010a. "Strategic and Tactical Roles of Enhanced-Commodity Indices." Working paper, EDHEC Risk and Asset Management Research Centre.

Fuertes, A.-M., J. Miffre, and G. Rallis. 2010b. "Tactical Allocation in Commodity Futures Markets: Combining Momentum and Term Structure Signals." *Journal of Banking and Finance* 34 (10): 2530–2548.

Fung, W., and D. A. Hsieh. 1997. "Empirical Characteristics of Dynamic Trading Strategies: The Case of Hedge Funds." *Review of Financial Studies* 10 (2): 275–302.

Fung, W., and D. A. Hsieh. 2002. "Benchmarks of Hedge Fund Performance: Information Content and Measurement Biases." *Financial Analysts Journal* 58:22–34.

Fung, W., and D. A. Hsieh. 2004. "Hedge Fund Benchmarks: A Risk Based Approach." *Financial Analysts Journal* 60:65–80.

Fung, W., and D. A. Hsieh. 2007. "Will Hedge Funds Regress Towards Index-like Products?" *Journal of Investment Management* 5 (2): 46–65.

Fung, W., D. A. Hsieh, N. Y. Naik, and T. Ramadorai. 2008. "Hedge Funds: Performance, Risk and Capital Formation." *Journal of Finance* 63 (4): 1777–1803.

Fung, W., D. Hsieh, and K. Tsatsaronis. 2000. "Do Hedge Funds Disrupt Emerging Markets?" Brookings-Wharton Papers on Financial Services: 377–421.

Gallais-Hamonno, G., and H. Nguyen-Thi-Thanh. 2007. "The Necessity to Correct Hedge Funds Returns: Empirical Evidence and Correction Method." Working Paper CEB 07-034.RS, ULB—Université Libre de Bruxelles.

GAO, U.S. Government Accountability Office. 2012. "Defined Benefit Pension Plans: Recent Developments Highlight Challenges of Hedge Fund and Private Equity Investing." GAO-12-324, February.

Gardner, B. 2003. "U.S. Commodity Policies and Land Values." In *Government Policy and Farmland Markets*, edited by C. Moss and A. Schmitz. Ames: Iowa State Press.

Geltner, D., and D. Ling. 2000. "Benchmark and Index Needs in the U.S. Private Real Estate Investment Industry: Trying to Close the Gap." RERI Study for the Pension Real Estate Association.

Geltner, D., B. D. MacGregor, and G. M. Schwann. 2003. "Appraisal Smoothing and Price Discovery in Real Estate Markets." *Urban Studies* 40:1047.

Geman, H. 2005. *Commodities and Commodity Derivatives: Modelling and Pricing for Agriculturals, Metals and Energy.* Hoboken, NJ: John Wiley & Sons.

Geman, H., and G. Martin. 2011. *Understanding Farmland as Part of a Diversified Portfolio.*

Ginsburgh, V., J. Mei, and M. Moses. 2006. "On the Computation of Price Indices." In *Handbook of Economics Art and Culture* 1, edited by V. Ginsburgh and D. Throsby. Amsterdam: Elsevier.

Goetzmann, W. N. 1993. "Accounting for Taste: Art and Financial Markets over Three Centuries." *Amer. Econ. Rev.* 83 (5): 1370–1376.

Goetzmann, W. N. 1996. "How Costly Is the Fall from Fashion? Survivorship Bias in the Painting Market." In *Economics of the Arts: Selected Essays*, ed. Ginsburgh and Pierre-Michel Menger, 71–83. Amsterdam: Elsevier.

Goodwin, B., A. Mishra, and F. N. Ortalo-Magné. 2003. "Explaining Regional Differences in the Capitalization of Policy Benefits into Agricultural Land Values." In *Government Policy and Farmland Markets*, edited by C. Moss and A. Schmitz. Ames: Iowa State Press.

Goodwin, J., and K. Ahmed. 2006. "Longitudinal Value Relevance of Earnings and Intangible Assets: Evidence from Australian Firms." *Journal of International Accounting, Auditing and Taxation* 15 (1): 72–91.

Gorton, G. B., F. Hayashi, and K. G. Rouwenhorst. 2008. "The Fundamentals of Commodity Futures Returns." Yale ICF Working Paper No. 07-08.

Gorton, G. B., and K. G. Rouwenhorst. 2006. "Facts and Fantasies about Commodities Futures." *Financial Analysts Journal* 62 (2): 47–68.

Graeser, P. 1993. "Rate of Return to Investment in American Antique Furniture." *South. Econ.* 59 (4): 817–821.

Gray, R., and D. Rutledge. 1971. "The Economics of Commodity Futures Markets: A Survey." *Review of Marketing and Agricultural Economics* 39 (4): 57–108.

Greer, R. J. 1978. "Conservative Commodities: A Key Inflation Hedge." *Journal of Portfolio Management* 4:26–29.

Greer, R. J. 2000. "The Nature of Commodity Index Returns." *Journal of Alternative Investments* 3 (1): 45–52.

Gregoriou, G. N., G. Hübner, and M. Kooli. 2010. "Performance and Persistence of Commodity Trading Advisors: Further Evidence." *Journal of Futures Markets* 30 (8): 725–752.

Gregoriou, G. N., V. Karavas, F.-S. Lhabitant, and F. Rouah. 2004. *Commodity Trading Advisors: Risk, Performance Analysis, and Selection.* Hoboken, NJ: John Wiley & Sons.

Griffoli, T. M., and A. Ranaldo. 2011. "Limits to Arbitrage during the Crisis: Funding Liquidity Constraints and Covered Interest Parity." Working paper, Ohio State University.

Gromb, D., and D. Vayanos. 2010. "Limits to Arbitrage." *Annual Review of Financial Economics* 2:251–275.

G20 Study Group on Commodities. 2011. "Report of the G20 Study Group on Commodities under the Chairmanship of Mr. Hiroshi Nakaso." November.

Haigh, M. S., J. H. Harris, J. A. Overdahl, and M. A. Robe. 2007. "Market Growth, Trader Participation and Derivative Pricing." CFTC Working Paper.

Hall, B., A. Jaffe, and M. Trajtenberg. 2005. "Market Value and Patent Citations." *RAND Journal of Economics* 36 (1): 16–38.

Hall, B., and J. Lerner. 2009. "The Financing of R&D and Innovation." NBER Working Paper 15325.

Hall, B., J. Mairesse, and P. Mohnen. 2009. "Measuring the Returns to R&D." NBER Working Paper 15622.

Halpern, J., and J. K. Liew. 2012. "Institutional-Grade Risk Management Policy: Is It Possible in Practice?" *Journal of Portfolio Management* (Spring).

Halpern, P., and R. Warsager. 1998. "The Performance of Energy and Non-Energy Based Commodity Investment Vehicles in Periods of Inflation." *Journal of Alternative Investments* 1 (1): 75–81.

Haurin, D. R. 2005. "US Commercial Real Estate Indices: Transaction-Based and Constant-Liquidity Indices." BIS Papers 21, April.

Hay, R., and J. Porter. 2006. *The Physiology of Crop Yield.* 2nd ed. Oxford: Blackwell Publishing.

Healy, T., T. Corriero, and R. Rozenov. 2005. "Timber as an Institutional Investment." *Journal of Alternative Investments* 8 (3): 60–74.

Heap, A. 2005. "China: The Engine of a Commodities Super Cycle." Research Report, Citigroup Global Markets.

HedgeBay.com. www.hedgebay.com.

Helmuth, J. W. 1981. "A Report on the Systematic Bias in Live Cattle Futures Prices." *Journal of Futures Markets* 1 (3): 347–358.

Henderson Global Investors. 2003. "The Case for Smallest Sized Private Equity Funds." Chicago, IL, Henderson Global Investors.

Hennig-Thurau, T., M. B. Houston, and T. Heitjans. 2009. "Conceptualizing and Measuring the Monetary Value of Brand Extensions: The Case of Motion Pictures." *Journal of Marketing* 73 (6): 167–183.

Hennig-Thurau, T., M. B. Houston, and G. Walsh. 2006. "The Differing Roles of Success Drivers across Sequential Channels: An Application to the Motion Picture Industry." *Journal of the Academy of Marketing Science* 34 (4): 559–575.

Hennig-Thurau, T., M. B. Houston, and G. Walsh. 2007. "Determinants of Motion Picture Box Office and Profitability: An Interrelationship Approach." *Review of Managerial Science* 1 (1): 65–92.

Hicks, J. R. 1939. *Value and Capital: An Inquiry into Some Fundamental Principles of Economic Theory.* London: Oxford University Press.

HighQuest Partners. 2010. "Private Financial Sector Investment in Farmland and Agricultural Infrastructure." OECD Food, Agriculture and Fisheries Working Paper 33, OECD Publishing.

Hill, J. M., and S. G. Teller. 2009. "Rebalancing Leveraged and Inverse Funds." Eighth Annual Guide to Exchange Traded Funds and Indexing Innovations. *Institutional Investor Journals*: 67–76.

Hong, H., and J. Stein. 1999. "A Unified Theory of Underreaction, Momentum Trading and Overreaction in Asset Markets." *Journal of Finance* 54 (6): 2143–2184.

Hosking, J. R. M. 1994. "The Four-Parameter Kappa Distribution." *IBM Journal of Research and Development* 38:251–258.

Humphreys, T. 2008. "Congress Enacts New Laws Affecting REITs." Morrison & Foerster LLP Client Alert, July 31. Available at www.mofo.com/congress-enacts-new-laws-affecting-reits-07-31-2008/ (accessed January 20, 2012).

Hurst, B., Y. H. Ooi, and L. H. Pedersen. 2010. "Understanding Managed Futures." Paper, AQR Capital Management.

Hurwicz, L. 1946. "Theory of the Firm and Investment." *Econometrica* 14 (2): 109–136.

Ibbotson, R. G., and P. D. Kaplan. 2000. "Does Asset Allocation Policy Explain 40, 90, or 100 Percent of Performance?" *Financial Analysts Journal* 56 (1): 26–33.

ICI, Investment Company Institute. 2011. *2011 Investment Company Fact Book*, 51st ed. Available at www.ici.org/pdf/2011_factbook.pdf.

Idzorek, T. 2006. "Strategic Asset Allocation and Commodities." Ibbotson Associates White Paper.

Idzorek, T., M. Barad, and S. Meier. 2007. "Global Commercial Real Estate." *The Journal of Portfolio Management*. Special Real Estate Issue, 37–53.

IEA, International Energy Agency. 2009. "IEA World Energy Outlook." www .worldenergyoutlook.org/.

Ineichen, A. M. 2002. "The Alpha in Fund of Hedge Funds: Do Fund of Hedge Funds Managers Add Value?" *Journal of Wealth Management* 5 (1): 8–25.

Ineichen, A. M. 2003. *Absolute Returns: The Risk and Opportunities of Hedge Fund Investing*. Hoboken, NJ: John Wiley & Sons.

InvestorWords.com. www.investorwords.com/1596/due diligence.html. Accessed September 2011.

Irwin, S. H., D. R. Sanders, and R. P. Merrin. 2009. "Devil or Angel? The Role of Speculation in the Recent Commodity Price Boom (and Bust)." *Journal of Agricultural and Applied Economics* 41 (2): 377–391.

Jaeger, L., P. Cittadini, and M. Jacquemai. 2002. Case Study: The SGFI Futures Index. *Journal of Alternative Investments* 5 (1): 73–80.

Jagannathan, R., A. Malakhov, and D. Novikov. 2012. "Do Hot Hands Exist among Hedge Fund Managers? An Empirical Evaluation." http://papers.ssrn.com/sol3/papers.cfm?abstract_id=686604.

Janicke, P. 2007. "Patent Litigation Remedies: Some Statistical Observations." PowerPoint presentation.

Jegadeesh, N., and S. Titman. 1993. "Returns to Buying Winners and Selling Losers: Implications for Stock Market Efficiency." *Journal of Finance* 48 (1): 65–91.

Jegadeesh, N., and S. Titman. 2011. "Momentum." *Annual Review of Financial Economics* 3 (December): 493–509.

Jensen, G. R., R. R. Johnson, and J. M. Mercer. 2002. "Tactical Asset Allocation and Commodity Futures." *Journal of Portfolio Management* 28 (4): 100–111.

Jensen, G. R., and J. M. Mercer. 2011. "Commodities as an Investment." *Research Foundation Literature Reviews* 6 (2): 1–33.

Jewell, M. 2011. "Target-Date Funds Spreading Their Investments and Risks." *San Antonio Express News*, May 21.

Jo, H. 2002. "Perspectives and Problems of Private Equity Funds-of-Funds." Leavey School of Business and Administration.

John, K., S. A. Ravid, and J. Sunder. 2002. "The Role of Termination in Employment Contracts: Theory and Evidence from Film Directors' Careers." Working paper, New York University.

Jozefowicz, J. J., J. M. Kelley, and S. M. Brewer. 2008. "New Release: An Empirical Analysis of VHS/DVD Rental Success." *Atlanta Economic Journal* 36:139–151.

Jurek, J. W. 2009. "Crash-Neutral Currency Carry Trades." Working paper, Princeton University.

Kaldor, N. 1939. "Speculation and Economic Stability." *Review of Economic Studies* 7 (1): 1–27.

Kamel, T. 2007. "Hedge Fund Replication." Iluka Hedge Fund Consulting, www.ilukacg.com.

Kaplan, S., and A. Schoar. 2005. "Private Equity Performance: Returns, Persistence, and Capital Flows." *Journal of Finance* 60 (4): 1791–1823.

Kaplan, S., and P. Strömberg. 2008. "Leveraged Buyouts and Private Equity." NBER Working Paper 14207, July.

Karavas, V., H. Kazemi, and T. Schneeweis. 2003. "Eurex Derivative Products in Alternative Investments: The Case for Hedge Funds." CISDM Working Paper. www.isenberg .umass.edu/cisdm.

Karniouchina, E., S. Carson, and W. L. Moore. 2010. "A Note on Revenue Versus Profitability as Indicators of Motion Picture Performance." Available at SSRN: http://ssrn.com/abstract=1712088 or http://dx.doi.org/10.2139/ssrn.1712088.

Kaserer, C., and C. Diller. 2004. "European Private Equity—A Cash Flow-Based Performance Analysis." EVCA, Brussels, May.

Kastens, T. 2001. "Risk and Reward: How Do Farm Returns Stack Up? Should Farm Managers Invest in the Stock Market?" Kansas State University.

Kat, H. 2002. "Managed Futures and Hedge Funds: A Match Made in Heaven." Research paper, Cass Business School, London.

Kat, H. M., and R. C. A. Oomen. 2007a. "What Every Investor Should Know about Commodities, Part I: Univariate Return Analysis." *Journal of Investment Management* 5 (1): 1–25.

Kat, H. M., and R. C. A. Oomen. 2007b. "What Every Investor Should Know about Commodities, Part II: Multivariate Return Analysis." *Journal of Investment Management* 5 (3): 1–25.

Kat, H. M., and H. P. Palaro. 2006a. "Replication and Evaluation of Fund of Hedge Funds Returns." http://papers.ssrn.com/sol3/papers.cfm?abstract_id=873465.

Kat, H. M., and H. P. Palaro. 2006b. "Who Needs Hedge Funds?" Working Paper 0027, Alternative Investment Research Centre, Cass Business School, City University, London.

Kawamoto, T., T. Kimura, K. Morishita, and M. Higashi. 2011. "What Has Caused the Surge in Global Commodity Prices and Strengthened Cross-Market Linkages?" Bank of Japan Working Paper Series, No. 11-E-3, May.

Kazemi, H., and Y. Li. 2009. "Market Timing of CTAs: An Examination of Systematic CTAs vs. Discretionary CTAs." *Journal of Futures Markets* 29 (11): 1067–1099.

Kazemi, H., T. Schneeweis, and R. Gupta. 2003. "Omega as a Performance Measure." Working paper, Isenberg School of Management, University of Massachusetts.

Kazemi, H., T. Schneeweis, and R. Spurgin. 2008. "The Benefits of Commodity Investment." Alternative Investment Analytics LLC Research Report.

Kazemi, H., T. Schneeweis, R. Spurgin, and G. Martin. 2007. "Real Assets in Institutional Portfolios: The Role of Commodities." Alternative Investment Analytics LLC Research Report.

Keating, T. 2010. "The Yale Endowment Model of Investing is Not Dead." *RIABiz*, April 20.

Keating, T. 2011. "How the Harvard and Yale Endowment Models Changed to Avoid a Repeat of 2009." *RIABiz*, February 15.

Kelly, T. 2002. "Private Equity: A Look at a Maturing Asset Class." Presentation to Chicago GSB Finance Round Table.

Kerins, F., J. Smith, and R. Smith. 2001. "New Venture Opportunity Cost of Capital and Financial Contracting." Working Paper in Economics, Claremont Graduate University.

Kestner, L. 2003. *Quantitative Trading Strategies: Harnessing the Power of Quantitative Techniques to Create a Winning Trading Program.* Boston: McGraw-Hill.

Keyfitz, R. 2004. "Currencies and Commodities: Modeling the Impact of Exchange Rates on Commodity Prices in the World Market." Development Prospect Group, World Bank.

Keynes, J. M. 1930. *A Treatise on Money.* London: Macmillan; New York: Harcourt, Brace and Co.

Khandani, A., and A. W. Lo. 2007. "What Happened to the Quants in August 2007?" *Journal of Investment Management* 5:5–54.

Khandani, A., and A. W. Lo. 2008. "What Happened to the Quants in August 2007? Evidence from Factors and Transactions Data." NBER Working Paper 14465.

Kim, D. 2012. "Is Currency Hedging Necessary for Emerging Market Investments?" *Economics Letters* 116 (1): 67–71.

King, D., and M. Young. 1994. "Why Diversification Doesn't Work." *Real Estate Review* 25, no. 2 (Summer): 6–12.

King, R. G., C. I. Plosser, J. H. Stock, and M. W. Watson. 1991. "Stochastic Trends and Economic Fluctuations." *American Economic Review* 18 (4): 819–840.

Kirwan, B., and M. Roberts. 2010. "Who Really Benefits from Agricultural Subsidies: Evidence from Field Level Data." University of Maryland.

Kochard, L. E., and C. M. Rittereiser. 2008. *Foundation and Endowment Investing: Philosophies and Strategies of Top Investors and Institutions.* Hoboken, NJ: John Wiley & Sons.

Kogelman, S. 1999. "The Importance of Asset Allocation in Managing Private Equity Commitments." Goldman Sachs Investment Research.

Kolb, R. W. 1996. "The Systematic Risk of Futures Contracts." *Journal of Futures Markets* 16 (6): 631–654.

Kosowski R., N. Y. Naik, and M. Teo. 2007. "Do Hedge Funds Deliver Alpha? A Baysian and Bootstrap Analysis." *Journal of Financial Economics* 84 (1): 229–264.

Lauritzen, S. L. 1996. *Graphical Models.* Oxford: Oxford University Press.

Lautier, D. 2005. "Term Structure Models of Commodity Prices: A Review." *Journal of Alternative Investments* 8 (1): 42–64.

Lee, C. M. C., and B. Swaminathan. 2000. "Price Momentum and Trading Volume." *Journal of Finance* 55 (5): 2017–2069.

Lerner, J. 2000. "The Future of Private Equity: Research and Hypotheses." Boston: Harvard Business School and National Bureau of Economic Research.

Lerner, J., and A. Schoar. 2004. "The Illiquidity Puzzle: Theory and Evidence from Private Equity." *Journal of Financial Economics* 72 (1): 3–40.

Lerner, J., A. Schoar, and W. Wongsunwai. 2007. "Smart Institutions, Foolish Choices? The Limited Partner Performance Puzzle." *Journal of Finance* 62 (2): 731–764.

Lerner, J., A. Schoar, and J. Wang. 2008. "Secrets of the Academy: Drivers of University Endowment Success." *Journal of Economic Perspectives* 22 (3): 207–222.

Lev, B., S. Radhakrishnan, and M. Ciftci. 2006. "The Stock Market Valuation of R&D Leaders." NYU Working Paper No. 2451/27475.

Lhabitant, F-S. 2007. "Hedge Fund Indices for Retail Investors: UCITS Eligible or Not Eligible?" *Derivatives, Use, Trading and Regulation* 12:275–289.

Lhabitant, F.-S., and M. Learned. 2003. Hedge Fund Diversification: How Much Is Enough? *Journal of Alternative Investments* 5 (3): 23–49.

Lhabitant, F.-S., and M. Learned. 2004. "Finding the Sweet Spot of Hedge Fund Diversification." *Journal of Financial Transformation* 10:31–39.

Li, H., X. Zhang, and R. Zhao. 2011. "Investing in Talents: Manager Characteristics and Hedge Fund Performances." *Journal of Financial and Quantitative Analysis* 46 (1): 59–82.

Liang, B. 2003. "On the Performance of Alternative Investments: CTA's, Hedge Funds, and Funds-of-Funds." Working paper, Case Western Reserve University.

Liew, J. 2003. "Hedge Fund Index Investing Examined." *Journal of Portfolio Management* 29 (Winter): 113–123.

Liew, J. K., F. Mainolfi, and D. Rubino. 2002. Bifurcated fund analysis model. *MFA Reporter* (November).

Liew, J., and M. Vassalou. 2000. "Can Book-to-Market, Size, and Momentum Be Risk Factors That Predict Economic Growth?" *Journal of Financial Economics* 57:221–245.

Lintner, J. 1983. "The Potential Role of Managed Commodity—Financial Futures Accounts (and/or Funds) in Portfolios of Stocks and Bonds." Paper presented at Financial Analysts Federation annual conference.

Litman, B. 1983. "Predicting the Success of Theatrical Movies: An Empirical Study." *Journal of Popular Culture* 16 (Spring): 159–175.

Litman, B. R., and H. Ahn. 1998. "Predicting Financial Success of Motion Pictures." In *The Motion Picture Mega-Industry*, edited by B. R. Litman. Boston: Allyn & Bacon.

Litman, B., and L. S. Kohl. 1989. "Predicting Financial Success of Motion Pictures: The '80s Experience." *Journal of Media Economics* 2:35–50.

Liu, Y. 2006. "Word of Mouth for Movies: Its Dynamics and Impact on Box Office Revenue." *Journal of Marketing* 70 (3): 74–89.

Ljungqvist, A., and M. Richardson. 2003. "The Cash Flow, Return and Risk Characteristics of Private Equity." Finance NBER Working Paper w9454, New York University, January.

Lo, A., and J. Hasandodzic. 2007. "Can Hedge-Fund Returns Be Replicated?: The Linear Case." *Journal of Investment Management* 5 (2):5–45.

Lo, A., and A. Khandani. 2009. "Illiquidity Premia in Asset Returns: An Empirical Analysis of Hedge Funds, Mutual Funds, and U.S. Equity Portfolios." MIT Working Paper.

Lonnstedt, L., and R. Sedjo. 2012. "Forest Ownership Changes in the United States and Switzerland." *Forest Policy and Economics* 14:19–27.

Maginn, J., D. Tuttle, D. McLeavey, and J. Pinto. 2007. *Managing Investment Portfolios: A Dynamic Process*. 3rd ed. Hoboken, NJ: John Wiley & Sons.

Malek, M. H., and S. Dobrovolsky. 2009. "Volatility Exposure of CTA Programs and Other Hedge Fund Strategies." *Journal of Alternative Investments* 11 (4): 68–89.

Mallon, B. 2012. "Managed Futures Regulation Post–MF Global Bankruptcy." *Hedge Fund Law Blog*. www.hedgefundlawblog.com/managed-futures-regulation-post-mf-global-bankruptcy.html.

Martin, G. 2005. "The Dynamics of Alpha and Pseudo-Alpha in Hedge Fund Returns: An A-Stable Approach to Risk Endogenously Determined and Observed." Preprint.

Martin, G. 2010. "The Long-Horizon Benefits of Traditional and New Real Assets in the Institutional Portfolio." *Journal of Alternative Investments* 13 (1): 6–29.

Martin, G. 2012. "Commodity Price Volatility and Farmland-Based Investment Strategies."

Masters, M. W., and A. K. White. 2008. "The Accidental Hunt Brothers: How Institutional Investors Are Driving Up Food and Energy Prices." Internet site: http://accidentalhuntbrothers.com/.

Mathonet, P.-Y., and T. Meyer. 2007. *J-Curve Exposure: Managing a Portfolio of Venture Capital and Private Equity Funds*. Chichester, UK: John Wiley & Sons Ltd.

Mathonet, P.-Y., and G. Monjanel. 2006. "Valuation Guidelines for Private Equity and Venture Capital Funds: A Survey." *Journal of Alternative Investments* 9, no. 2 (Fall): 59–70.

Maxwell, R. 2003. *To Disclose or Not to Disclose? That Is the Question*. London: AltAssets.

McCarthy, D., T. Schneeweis, and R. Spurgin. 1996. "Investment through CTAs: An Alternative Managed Futures Investment." *Journal of Derivatives* 3 (4): 36–47.

McCown, J. R., and J. R. Zimmerman. 2006. "Is Gold a Zero-Beta Asset? Analysis of the Investment Potential of Precious Metals." Working paper.

Meder, A., and R. Staub. 2007. "Linking Pension Liabilities to Assets." Society of Actuaries.

Meek, V. 2003. "Time to Deviate from the Standard?" AltAssets, London, May.

Meek, V. 2004. "Bottom of the Pile." AltAssets, London, April.

Mei, J. and M. Moses. 2001. "Art as an Investment and the Origin of the 'Master-piece Effect' Evidence from 1875–2000." Mimeo, Stern School, NYU.

Meketa Investment Group. 2010. "Timberland." Meketa Investment Group, Inc., April. www.meketagroup.com/documents/TimberlandWP_000.pdf.

Menkhoff, L., L. Sarno, and A. Schrimpf. 2011. "Currency Momentum Strategies." Available at http://papers.ssrn.com/sol3/papers.cfm?abstract_id=1809776.

Menkhoff, L., and M. P. Taylor. 2007. "The Obstinate Passion of Foreign Exchange Professionals: Technical Analysis." *Journal of Economic Literature* 45 (4): 936–972.

Merton, R. C. 1973. "Theory of Rational Option Pricing." *The Bell Journal of Economics and Management Science* 4 (1): 141–183.

Merton, R. 2006. "Allocating Shareholder Capital to Pension Plans." *Journal of Applied Corporate Finance* 18 (1): 15–24.

Meyer, T., and P.-Y. Mathonet. 2005. *Beyond the J-Curve: Managing a Portfolio of Venture Capital and Private Equity Funds*. Chichester, UK: John Wiley & Sons Ltd.

Miffre, J., and G. Rallis. 2007. "Momentum Strategies in Commodity Futures Markets." *Journal of Banking and Finance* 31 (6): 1863–1886.

Milonas, N., and S. Thomadakis. 1997. "Convenience Yields as Call Options: An Empirical Analysis." *Journal of Futures Markets* 17 (1): 1–15.

Mitchell, M., L. H. Pedersen, and T. Pulvin. 2007. "Slow Moving Capital." *American Economic Review* 97 (2): 215–220.

Mladina, P., and J. Coyle. 2010. "Yale's Endowment Returns: Manager Skill or Risk Exposure?" *Journal of Wealth Management* 13 (1): 43–50.

Moskowitz, T., and A. Vissing-Jørgensen. 2002. "The Returns to Entrepreneurial Investment: A Private Equity Premium Puzzle?" *American Economic Review* 92, no. 4 (September): 745–778.

Mou, Y. 2011. "Limits to Arbitrage and Commodity Index Investment: Front-Running the Goldman Roll." Working paper.

Mühlhofer, T. 2008. "Why Do REIT Returns Poorly Reflect Property Returns? Unrealizable Appreciation Gains Due to Trading Constraints as the Solution to the Short-Term Disparity." Conditionally accepted at *Real Estate Economics* and available at SSRN: http://ssrn.com/abstract=912807 or doi:10.2139/ssrn.912807 (accessed January 2012).

Murray, M. P. 1994. "A Drunk and Her Dog: An Illustration of Cointegration and Error Correction." *American Statistician* 48 (1): 37–39.

Naik, N. 2007. "Capacity Constraints and Hedge Fund Strategy Returns." *European Financial Management* 13 (2): 239–256.

Nakamura, L. 2009. "Intangible Assets and National Income Accounting: Measuring a Scientific Revolution." Federal Reserve Bank of Philadephia Working Paper No. 09-11.

Nash, D. 1997. "Feature: Long-Term Investing in Commodities." Morgan Stanley Dean Witter, Global Equity and Derivatives Markets, December 9, 28–29.

Neelamegham, R., and P. Chintagunta. 1999. "A Bayesian Model to Forecast New Product Performance in Domestic and International Markets." *Marketing Science* 18 (2): 115–136.

Neely, C., D. Rapach, J. Tu, and G. Zhou. 2011. "Forecasting the Equity Risk Premium: The Role of Technical Indicators." Working paper, Federal Reserve Bank of St. Louis.

New York Mercantile Exchange. 2001. *Crack Spread Handbook*. www.nymex.com/broch main.aspx.

Ngo, T. and S. R. Jory. 2008. "International Evidence on the Relationship between Trading Volume and Serial Correlation in Stock Returns." *Global Journal of Finance and Banking Issues* 2 (2): 1–13.

Okunev, J., and D. White. 2003. "Do Momentum-Based Strategies Still Work in Foreign Currency Markets?" *Journal of Financial and Quantitative Analysis* 38 (2): 425–447.

Olsen, K. 2012. "46% of Corporate Defined Benefit Pension Plans are Open." *Pensions & Investments*, January 10.

Otterlei, J., and S. Barrington. 2003. "Alternative Assets—Private Equity Fund-of-funds." Special Report, Piper Jaffray Private Capital.

Page, S., J. Simonian, and F. He. 2011. "Asset Allocation: Systemic Liquidity as a Risk Factor." *Trading* 1:19–23.

Park, C.-H., and S. H. Irwin. 2004. "The Profitability of Technical Analysis: A Review." AgMAS Project Research Report No. 2004-04, University of Illinois at Urbana-Champaign.

Park, C-H., and S. H. Irwin. 2010. "A Reality Check on Technical Trading Rule Profits in the U.S. Futures Markets." *Journal of Futures Markets* 30 (7): 633–659.

Park, P., O. Tanrikulu, and G. Wang. 2009. "Systematic Global Macro: Performance, Risk and Correlation Characteristics." Working paper, Graham Capital Management, LP.

Pearl, J. 2009. *Causality*. 2nd ed. New York: Cambridge University Press.

Pesando, J. E. 1993. "Art as an Investment. The Market for Modem Prints." *Amer. Econ. Rev.* 83 (5): 1075–89.

Pesando, J. E., and P. Shum. 1996. "Price Anomalies at Auction: Evidence from the Market for Modem Prints." In *Economics of the Arts: Selected Essays*, ed. Victor Ginsburgh and Pierre-Michel Menger, 113–134. Amsterdam: Elsevier.

Peters, C. J., J. L. Wilkins, and G. W. Fick. 2007. "Testing a Complete-Diet Model for Estimating the Land Resource Requirements of Food Consumption and Agricultural Carrying Capacity: The New York State Example." *Renewable Agriculture and Food Systems* 22 (02): 145–153.

Peterson, P. E., and R. M. Leuthold. 1982. "Using Mechanical Trading Systems to Evaluate the Weak Form Efficiency of Futures Markets." *Southern Journal of Agricultural Economics* 14 (1): 147–151.

Pindyck, R. 2001. "The Dynamics of Commodity Spot and Futures Markets: A Primer." *Energy Journal* 22 (3): 1–30.

Pindyck, R. S., and J. J. Rotemberg. 1990. "The Excess Co-Movement of Commodity Prices." *Economic Journal* 100 (403): 1173–1189.

Pirrong, C. 1994. "Squeezes, Corpses, and the Anti-Manipulation Provisions of the Commodity Exchange Act." *Regulation* 17 (4): 52–63.

Plante, M., and M. Yücel. 2011. "Did Speculation Drive Oil Prices? Market Fundamentals Suggest Otherwise." Federal Reserve Bank of Dallas *Economic Letter* 6, no. 11 (October).

Pojarliev, M., and R. Levich. 2008. "Do Professional Currency Managers Beat the Benchmark?" *Financial Analysts Journal* 64 (5): 18–32.

Pole, A. 2007. *Statistical Arbitrage: Algorithmic Trading Insights and Techniques*. Hoboken, NJ: Wiley Finance.

Preqin. 2011. *2011 Preqin Global Infrastructure Report*. New York: Preqin Ltd. Available at www.preqin.com.

Preqin. 2011. *2011 Preqin Global Private Equity Report*. New York: Preqin Ltd. Available at www.preqin.com.

Pringle, A., and T. Fernandes. 2007. "Relative-Value Trading Opportunities in Energy and Agriculture." In *Intelligent Commodity Investing: New Strategies and Practical Insights for Informed Decision Makings*, edited by H. Till and J. Eagleeye, 313–340. London: Risk Books.

Prowse, S. 1998. "The Economics of the Private Equity Market." *Economic Review*, Federal Reserve Bank of Dallas (Third Quarter): 21–34.

PSERS, Pennsylvania Public School Employees' Retirement System. 2007. "Investment Policy Statement, Objectives, and Guidelines for Closed-End Opportunistic and Value-Added Real Estate Investments." Addendum U, June 22. www.psers.state.pa.us/board/reso/reso2007.htm.

The Purple Book: DB Pensions Universe Risk Profile 2011. Pension Protection Fund and the Pensions Regulator.

Rafferty, M., and M. Funk. 2008. "Asymmetric Effects of the Business Cycle on Firm-Financed R&D." *Economics of Innovation and New Technology* 17 (5): 497–510.

Ravid, S. A. 1999. "Information, Blockbusters, and Stars: A Study of the Film Industry." *Journal of Business* 72 (4): 463–492.

Ravid, S. A. 2004. "Are They All Crazy or Just Risk Averse? Some Movie Puzzles and Possible Solutions." In *Economics of Cultural Industries*, edited by Victor Ginsburgh. Amsterdam: Elsevier.

Ravid, S. A., and S. Basuroy. 2004. "Managerial Objectives, the R-Rating Puzzle, and the Production of Violent Films." *Journal of Business* 77:155–192.

Richards, L. 2008. "Frequently-Asked Questions about SEC Examinations." SIFMA Compliance and Legal Division January General Luncheon Meeting, New York, January 17.

Robbie, K., M. Wright, and B. Chiplin. 1997. "The Monitoring of Venture Capital Firms." *Entrepreneurship Theory and Practice* 214 (June 22): 9–28.

Robinson, Brett L. 1998. "The Inefficiency Costs of Guaranteed Investment Products." *The Journal of Derivatives* 6 (1): 25–37.

Ross, M. H., and S. Zondervan. 1989. "Capital Gains and the Rate of Return on a Stradivarius." *Econ. Inquiry* 27 (3): 529–540.

Rothman, M. 2007a. "Rebalance of Large Cap Quant Portfolio." *U.S. Equity Quantitative Strategies*, Lehman Brothers Research.

Rothman, M. 2007b. "Turbulent Times in Quant Land." *U.S. Equity Quantitative Strategies*, Lehman Brothers Research.

Rothman, M. 2007c. "View from QuantLand: Where Do We Go Now?" *U.S. Equity Quantitative Strategies*, Lehman Brothers Research.

Rouvinez, C. 2006. "Top Quartile Persistence in Private Equity." *Private Equity International* (June): 76–79.

Rouwenhorst, K. G. 1998. "International Momentum Strategies." *Journal of Finance* 53 (1): 267–284.

Sadkay, R. 2009. "Liquidity Risk and the Cross-Section of Hedge-Fund Returns." Boston College Working Paper.

Safvenblad, P. 2003. "Global Macro and Managed Futures Strategies." Working paper, Stockholm School of Economics.

Sanders, D. R., and S. H. Irwin. 2010. "A Speculative Bubble in Commodity Futures Prices? Cross-Sectional Evidence." *Agricultural Economics* 41 (1): 25–32.

Sanders, D. R., and S. H. Irwin. 2012. "A Reappraisal of Investing in Commodity Futures Markets." *Applied Economic Perspectives and Policy* 34 (3). Forthcoming, perhaps Fall 2012.

Sandner, P. 2009. *The Valuation of Intangible Assets: An Exploration of Patent and Trademark Portfolios*. Wiesbaden, Germany: Gabler.

Satyanarayan, S., and P. Varangis. 1994. "An Efficient Frontier for International Portfolios and Commodity Assets." Policy Research Working Paper 1266, World Bank.

Sawhney, M. S., and J. Eliashberg. 1996. "A Parsimonious Model for Forecasting Gross Box-Office Revenues of Motion Pictures." *Marketing Science* 15 (2): 113–131.

Schaechterle, S. 2000. "Taking Away the Disadvantages." Baar-Zug, Switzerland: Partners Group.

Schneeweis, T. 2006. "The Benefits of Commodities—2006 Update." Working paper, Center for International Securities and Derivatives Markets.

Schneeweis, T. 2009. "The Benefits of Managed Futures." Benefits paper, Institute for Global Asset and Risk Management.

Schneeweis, T., V. Karavas, and R. DuBose. 2005. "Diversification in Fund of Funds Investment: How Many Hedge Fund Managers Are Enough to Represent a Strategy?" *Hedge Funds World*.

Schneeweis, T., H. Kazemi, and V. Karavas. 2003. "Fund Diversification in Fund of Funds Investment: How Many Hedge Funds Are Enough?" CISDM Working Paper.

Schneeweis, T., H. Kazemi, and R. Spurgin. 2008. "Momentum in Asset Returns: Are Commodity Returns a Special Case?" *Journal of Alternative Investments* 10 (4): 23–26.

Schneeweis, T., and R. Spurgin. 1997. "Comparison of Commodity and Managed Futures Benchmark Indices." *Journal of Derivatives* 4 (4): 33–50.

Schneeweis, T., R. Spurgin, and M. Potter. 1997. "Managed Futures and Hedge Fund Investment for Downside Equity Risk Management." *CFA Digest* (Spring): 54–56.

Schwartzman, T. 2002. "Alternative and Liquid Alternative Assets—Structuring and Oversight." Presentation to Investment Management Institute's Endowment and Foundation Forum, Atlanta, GA, Hewitt Investment Group, January.

SEI. 2011. "5th Annual Liability-Driven Investing (LDI) Poll: More Plan Sponsors Using LDI Than in Years Past." SEI Institutional Solutions, December.

Shadwick, W. F., and C. Keating. 2002. "A Universal Performance Measure." *Journal of Performance Measurement* 6 (3): 59–84.

Shearburn, J., and B. Griffiths. 2002. "Private Equity Building Blocks." *Pension Week* in association with Goldman Sachs, April.

Sheikh, A., and J. Sun. 2012. "Defending the Endowment Model: Quantifying Liquidity Risk in a Post-Credit Crisis World." *Journal of Alternative Investments* 14 (4): 9–24.

Siegel, L. 2008. "Alternatives and Liquidity: Will Spending and Capital Calls Eat Your 'Modern' Portfolio?" *Journal of Portfolio Management* 35 (1): 103–114.

Simons, K. 2000. "The Use of Value at Risk by Institutional Investors." *New England Economic Review* (November/December).

Sochay, S. 1994. "Predicting the Performance of Motion Pictures." *Journal of Media Economics* 7 (4): 1–20.

Sohn, I. 2007. "Long-Term Energy Projections: What Lessons Have We Learned?" *Energy Policy* 35 (9): 4574–4584.

Soloveichik, R. 2010. "Artistic Originals as a Capital Asset." *American Economic Review* 100 (2): 110–114.

Soloveichik, R., and D. Wasshausen. 2011. "Copyright-Protected Assets in the National Accounts." Bureau of Economic Analysis.

Sood, S., and X. Drèze. 2004. "Brand Extensions of Hedonic Goods: Movie Sequel Evaluations." *Journal of Consumer Research* 33 (3): 352–360.

Sørensen, C. 2002. "Modeling Seasonality in Agricultural Commodity Futures." *Journal of Futures Markets* 22:393–426.

Spaenjers, C. 2010. "Returns and Fundamentals in International Art Markets." *American Art*. www.hec.unil.ch/documents/seminars/ibf/430.pdf.

Spirtes, P., C. Glymour, and R. Scheines. 2001. *Causation, Prediction and Search*. 2nd ed. Cambridge, MA: MIT.

Spurgin, R. 1999. "A Benchmark for Commodity Trading Adviser Performance." *Journal of Alternative Investments* 2 (1): 11–21.

Spurgin, R., T. Schneeweis, and G. Georgiev. 2001. "Benchmarking Commodity Trading Advisor Performance with a Passive Futures-Based Index." CISDM Working Paper.

Stambaugh, R. F., J. Yu, and Y. Yuan. 2011. "The Short of It: Investor Sentiment and Anomalies." *Journal of Financial Economics* 104:288–302.

Statman, M. 2002. "How Much Diversification Is Enough?" Leavey School of Business, Santa Clara University, September.

Steers, H. 2002. "Special Rules of the Game." Frank Russell Company, AltAssets.

Stein, J. P. 1977. "The Monetary Appreciation of Painting." *J. Polito Econ.* 85 (5): 1021–1035.

Steyer, R. 2011. "48% of DC Assets in Target-Date Funds by 2020, Casey Quirk Predicts." *Pensions & Investments*, October 4.

Stoll, H. R., and R. E. Whaley. 2011. "Commodity Index Investing: Speculation or Diversification." *Journal of Alternative Investments* 14 (1): 50–60.

Stulz, R. 1996. "Rethinking Risk Management." *Journal of Applied Corporate Finance* 9 (3): 8–24.

Swensen, D. 2009. *Pioneering Portfolio Management—An Unconventional Approach to Institutional Investment.* New York: Simon & Schuster.

Szado, E. 2011. "Defining Speculation: The First Step toward a Rational Dialogue." *Journal of Alternative Investments* 14 (1): 75–82.

Takahashi, D., and A. Alexander. 2002. "Illiquid Alternative Asset Fund Modeling." *Journal of Portfolio Management* 28 (2): 90–100.

Taylor, D., and L. Coleman. 2011. "Price Determinants of Aboriginal Art, and Its Role as an Alternative Asset Class." *Journal of Banking & Finance* 35 (6): 1519–1529.

Thorp, E. O. 1962. *Beat the Dealer: A Winning Strategy for the Game of Twenty-One.* New York: Random House.

Tilburg, R., and M. V. Stichele. 2011. "Feeding the Financial Hype—How Excessive Financial Investments Impact Agricultural Derivatives Markets." SOMO Working Paper.

Till, H. 1997. "The Reasons to Invest in Commodities." Putnam Investments Working Paper.

Till, H. 2006. "Structural Sources of Return and Risk in Commodity Futures Investments." Working paper, EDHEC Risk and Asset Management Research Centre.

Till, H. 2007a. "Part I of a Long-Term Perspective on Commodity Futures Returns: Review of the Historical Literature." In *Intelligent Commodity Investing: New Strategies and Practical Insights for Informed Decision Makings*, edited by H. Till and J. Eagleeye, 39–82. London: Risk Books.

Till, H. 2007b. "Part II of a Long-Term Perspective on Commodity Futures Returns: Term Structure as the Primary Driver of Returns." In *Intelligent Commodity Investing: New Strategies and Practical Insights for Informed Decision Makings*, edited by H. Till and J. Eagleeye, 83–94. London: Risk Books.

Till, H. 2008a. "Amaranth Lessons Thus Far." *Journal of Alternative Investments* 10 (4): 82–98.

Till, H. 2008b. "Case Studies and Risk Management Lessons in Commodity Derivatives Trading." In *Risk Management in Commodity Markets: From Shipping to Agriculturals and Energy*, edited by H. Geman, 255–291. Chichester, UK: John Wiley & Sons Ltd.

Till, H. 2008c. "Long-Term Sources of Return in the Commodity Futures Markets: Evidence from the Grain Markets." *Hedge Fund Review*: 45–46.

Till, H. 2009. "Has There Been Excessive Speculation in the US Oil Futures Markets?" Working paper, EDHEC Risk and Asset Management Research Centre.

Till, H., and J. Eagleeye. 2005. "Commodities: Active Strategies for Enhanced Returns." *Journal of Wealth Management.* 42–61. Also in *The Handbook of Inflation Hedging Investments*, edited by R. Greer, 127–157. New York: McGraw-Hill.

Till, H., and J. Gunzberg. 2005. "Absolute Returns in Commodity (Natural Resources) Futures Investments." Working paper, EDHEC Risk and Asset Management Research Centre.

Towers Watson. 2011. *Global Pension Asset Study 2011.* Available at www.towerswatson.com/assets/pdf/3761/Global-Pensions-Asset-Study-2011.pdf.

Tversky, A., and D. Kahneman. 1974. "Judgment under Uncertainty: Heuristics and Biases." *Science* 185:1124–1131.

United Nations Population Division. 2008. "World Population Prospects: The 2008 Revision Population Database." http://esa.un.org/unpp/index.asp.

USDA Economic Research Service. www.ers.usda.gov/data/wheat/YBtable04.asp and www.ers.usda.gov/briefing/wheat/2012baseline.htm.

U.S. Energy Information Administration, Office of Integrated Analysis and Forecasting. 2010. "International Energy Outlook, 2010." U.S. Department of Energy, July. www.eia.gov/forecasts/ieo/index.cfm.

Vegetarian Society. 2009. "Why It's Green to Go Vegetarian." www.vegsoc.org/environment/land_use.html.

Waggle, D., and D. T. Johnson. 2009. "An Analysis of the Impact of Timberland, Farmland and Commercial Real Estate in the Asset Allocation Decisions of Institutional Investors." *Review of Financial Economics* 18 (2): 90–96.

Walls, W. D. 2006. "Screen Wars, Star Wars, and Sequels: Nonparametric Reanalysis of Movie Profitability." University of Calgary Working Paper.

Walter, I. 2003. "Strategies in Banking and Financial Service Firms: A Survey." NYU Working Paper FIN-03-050, New York, December.

Waugh, C. 2007. "Collision: Investing for the New World Commodity Order." In *Intelligent Commodity Investing: New Strategies and Practical Insights for Informed Decision Makings*, edited by H. Till and J. Eagleeye, 341–373. London: Risk Books.

Weidig, T., and, P.-Y. Mathonet. 2004. "The Risk Profiles of Private Equity." EVCA, Brussels, January.

Whitehouse, E. 2007. *Pensions Panorama: Retirement-Income Systems in 53 Countries.* Washington, DC: International Bank for Reconstruction and Development/World Bank.

Wietlisbach, U. 2002. "Private Equity Fund-of-Funds Management: A Strategic Approach." London: AltAssets, June.

Willenbrock, S. 2011. "Diversification Return, Portfolio Rebalancing, and the Commodity Return Puzzle." *Financial Analysts Journal* 67 (4): 42–49.

Williams, J., and B. Wright. 1991. *Storage and Commodity Markets.* Cambridge: Cambridge University Press.

Williamson, C. 2011. "Endowment Execs Focus on Liquidity, Volatility in Post-Crisis Market." *Pensions and Investments.* March 7.

Wood Creek Capital Management. 2008. "Intellectual Property Asset Management: Capitalizing on Innovation."

Wood Creek Capital Management. 2011. "Film Industry Overview."

Working, H. 1949. "The Theory of the Price of Storage." *American Economic Review* 39:1254–1262.

Xiong, J., T. I. Idzorek, P. Chen, and R. G. Ibbotson. 2007. "Dynamics of Fund of Hedge Funds: Flow, Size, and Performance." Working paper, Ibbotson Associates.

Zimmermann, H., M. Degosciu, H. Christophers, and S. Bilo. 2004. "The Risk and Return of Publicly Traded Private Equity." Working Paper No. 6/04, WWZ/Department of Finance, University of Basel, April.

Zulauf, C. R., H. Zhou, and M. Robert. 2006. "Updating the Estimation of the Supply of Storage." *Journal of Futures Markets* 26 (7): 657–676.

Zufryden, F. 2000. "New Film Website Promotion and Box-Office Performance." *Journal of Advertising Research* January-April:55–64.